2/94

BLOOD OF GHASTLY HORROR (Independent International, 1971) C 87 mins.

Executive producers, Samuel M. Sherman, J. P. Spohn; producer/director, Al Adamson; story, Sherman, Adamson; screenplay, Dick Poston, Chris Martino; music, Jimmy Roosa, Don McGinnis; makeup, Lee James; titles, Bob Le Bar; camera, Lewis Horvath, William Zsigmond.

John Carradine (Dr. Howard Van Ard); Kent Taylor (Dr. Elton Corey); Tommy Kirk (Lieutenant Cross); Regina Carrol (Susan Van Ard); Arne Wanda (Sergeant Grimaldi); Richard Smedley (Acro the Zombie); Joey Benson (Sergeant Frank Ward); Kirk Duncan (David Clarke); Roy Morton (Joe Corey); Tanya Marie (Vicky); Tasey Robbins (Linda Clarek); Lyle Felice (Vito); John Aimond (Nick); Barney Gelfan (Detective); Al Adamson (Gang Leader).

Here is a film which has to be screened to be believed! In a charitable mood Michael Weldon in *The Psychotronic Encyclopedia of Film* (1983) called it "an amazingly incoherent mess" and also noted, "The best scene involves ex-Disney star Tommy Kirk as a detective getting sick when he opens a gift box containing a severed head." On par with this scene is the climactic sequence where madman Kent Taylor turns Regina Carrol (the director's wife) into a spider-like old hag whose voice drops three octaves in the process.

Actually this film is a stitched together conglomerate which first saw release in 1965 by Hemisphere Pictures as PSYCHO A-GO-GO (having been produced by Victor Adamson Productions in 1963 as TWO TICKETS TO TERROR) and it was a crude gangster thriller involving a gang which heists jewels only to lose them with one of the members (Roy Morton) taking a woman (Tasey Robbins) and her small daughter (Tanya Marie) hostage. In 1969 new footage involving mad scientist John Carradine and his "Brain Component" were added, with gangster Roy Morton now a mad killer thanks to the operation. The film was then distributed as FIEND WITH THE ELECTRONIC BRAIN.

By the early 1970s still more footage was spliced in, and the feature became BLOOD OF GHASTLY HORROR. Here Roy Morton's character of Joe Corey is pictured as a catonic Vietnam war veteran who is turned into a madman by John Carradine who has put a transistor in his brain to save his life. Morton then kills Carradine and embarks on a robbery spree, but eventually is gunned down by the police after he commits several murders. The madman's father, a doctor (Kent Taylor) who practices voodoo, uses a zombie (Richard Smedley) to take revenge on those involved in his son's death and this rash of killings is investigated by two policemen (Tommy Kirk, Arne Warda). Taylor plans to turn Carradine's daughter (Regina

Advertisement for BLOOD OF GHASTLY HORROR (1971).

Carrol) into a zombie and he carries out his plan but his other zombie turns on him and they both die while Carrol drinks the antidote and returns to normal.

Released to TV as MAN WITH THE SYNTHETIC BRAIN, the movie is almost mesmeric in its inanities. Shoddily made with its choppy story relayed through flashbacks within flashbacks, the movie ranks as a choice candidate for the title of reverse classic.

THE BOOGENS (Jensen Farley Pictures, 1982) C 95 mins.

Producer, Charles E. Sellier, Jr.; director, James L. Conway; screenplay, David O'Malley, Bob Hunt; music, Bob Summers; assistant director, Leon Dudevoir; production designer, Paul Staheli; boogen designers, William Munns, Ken Horn; sound, Rod Sutton; camera, Paul Hipp; editor, Michael Spence.

Rebecca Balding (Trish Michaels); Fred McCarren (Mark Kinner); Anne-Marie Martin (Jessica Ford); Jeff Harlan (Roger Lowrie); John Crawford (Brian Deering); Med Flory (Dan Ostroff); Jon Lorimer (Blanchard); Peg Stewart (Victoria Tusker); Scott Wilkinson (Deputy Greenwalt); Marcia Reider (Martha Chapman).

THE BOOGENS is a sadly underrated, minor sci-fi-horror thriller which would have earned the blessings of producer Val Lewton in that the title monsters are hardly shown, but mostly hinted at in well-staged and eerie sequences. (E.g. the opening shot in which a woman alone in her home goes to the basement door to check on a noise only to be dragged away by something with a long whip-like tentacle.) Scenes such as this give THE BOOGENS a great deal of suspense, leading to the finale where the title creatures are shown to be fearsome indeed. Once again, we are shown the adverse effect of creatures out of sync with their surroundings because they have been thrown forward in time.

In 1912 a mine is sealed off after a disaster and nearly seven decades later a young woman, Jessica Ford (Anne-Marie Martin) and her boyfriend Roger Lowrie (Jeff Harland), come to stay in a house in the town for a weekend tryst. They have also invited the girl's friend, Trish Michaels (Rebecca Balding), and Roger's pal, Mark Kinner (Fred McCarren). The foursome get along well but their pet dog is fearful of something and people in the vicinity begin to disappear. Finally it is determined that much of the town is located over the old mine shafts which have been reopened by a mining crew and that some type of subterranean creatures from prehistoric times are invading the area. Jessica and Roger are killed by the monsters, but Trish and Mark, although cornered in the mine shafts, use fire to drive back the monsters and eventually rely on explosives to reseal the deadly creatures in the mine cavity.

At the time of its release, *Variety* claimed the film was " . . . too bland to generate much interest beyond die-hard monster pic fans." Donald C. Willis in *Horror and Science Fiction Films III* (1984) was more correct in his assessment when he wrote, "Classically discreet monster-movie saves full-view shots of its nasty centerpieces until almost the end."

THE BOWERY BOYS MEET THE MONSTERS (Allied Artists, 1954) 65 mins.

Producer, Ben Schwalb; director, Edward Bernds; screenplay, Elwood Ullman, Bernds; art director, David Milton; set decorator, Joseph Kish; wardrobe, Bert Henrickson; music supervisor, Marlin Skiles; makeup, Edward Polo; sound, Ralph Butler; visual effects, Augie Lohman; camera, Harry Neumann; editor, William Austin.

Leo Gorcey (Slip Mahoney); Huntz Hall (Horace Debussey "Sach" Jones); Bernard Gorcey (Louie Dumbrowsky); David Condon (Chuck); Bennie Bartlett (Butch); John Dehner (Dr. Derek Gravesend); Lloyd Corrigan (Anton Gravesend); Paul Wexler (Butler); Ellen Corby (Amelia Gravesend); Laura Mason (Francine Gravesend); Norman Bishop (Robot); Steve Calvert (Cosmos the Gorilla); Rudy Lee (Herbie Wilkins); Paul Bryar (Officer Martin); Pat Flaherty (Officer O'Meara); Jack Diamond (Skippy Biano).

Leo Gorcey, Huntz Hall and company, on occasion, had celluloid dealings with the supernatural, from their days as "The East Side Kids" through their numerous programmers as "The Bowery Boys." In the latter stage, they did such monster/sci-fi items as SPOOK BUSTERS (1946), MASTER MINDS (1951), and SPOOK CHASERS (1957), along with this outing which could easily have been titled "The Bowery Boys Meet the Addams Family."

Seeking an area for the local kids to play baseball, Slip Mahoney (Leo Gorcey) and Horace Debussey "Sach" Jones (Huntz Hall) visit a family which has such a vacant lot. They stumble into a bizarre household with head of the family Dr. Derek Gravesend (John Dehner) experimenting with a brain transplant for his pet gorilla; while Amelia Gravesend (Ellen Corby) keeps a huge, meat-eating plant; Francine Gravesend (Laura Mason) thinks she is a vampire; and Anton Gravesend (Lloyd Corrigan) has invented a robot called Gorog. The family utilize the boys for their own special purposes and for a time Sach is turned into a fanged monster. Eventually he returns to normal (!) and with the aid of the robot, the family is brought to justice. The boys have their baseball lot and Gorog becomes a team member.

THE BOWERY BOYS MEET THE MONSTERS contains

minor amusement, but it becomes strained once the novelty of the eccentric Gravesend family wears off.

THE BOYS FROM BROOKLYN see BELA LUGOSI MEETS A BROOKLYN GORILLA.

BRAIN OF BLOOD (Hemisphere, 1971) C 88 mins.

Executive producer, Kane W. Lynn; producers, Samuel M. Sherman, Al Adamson; associate producer, J. P. Spohn; director, Adamson; story, Sherman; screenplay, Joe Van Rodgers; titles, Bob Le Bar; camera, Louis Hurwath; editor, Spohn.

Kent Taylor (Dr. Trenton); Grant Williams (Bob Nigserian); John Bloom (Gor); Reed Hadley (Amir); Regina Carrol (Tracy); Angelo Rossitto (Dorro); Vicki Volante (Prisoner); Zandor Vorkov (Mohammed); and: Gus Peters, Bruce Kimball, Margo Hope.

Dr. Trenton (Kent Taylor) is experimenting on brain transplants with the aid of deformed giant Gor (John Bloom) and evil dwarf (Angelo Rossitto). Amir (Reed Hadley) the leader of a Middle East country, has died and his right-hand man Bob Nigserian (Grant Williams) and an associate (Zandor Vorkov) bring Amir's body to Trenton so his brain can be saved and transplanted into a new body. When his blood supply is destroyed, Trenton places Amir's brain in Gor's body but finds he cannot control his new creation. Amir's follower Tracy (Regina Carrol) arrives to inform her leader that Bob is actually the leader of a group of rebels out to take over his country. Gor is brought under control by Trenton with the use of a laser gun. Months later Amir is back in his own country talking on television with Trenton now his right-hand man, although it is the doctor who is in full control since he has now transferred Amir's brain in Bob's body.

Shown on TV as THE CREATURE'S REVENGE, this Al Adamson-Samuel M. Sherman production is a boon to lovers of bad films.

BRAIN WAVES (Motion Picture Marketing, 1983) C 81 mins.

Executive producers, Charles Aperia, Gary Gillingham, Tim Nielsen; producer, Ulli Lommel; associate producer, David DuBayl; line producer, Jochen Breitenstein; director/screenplay Lommel; additional dialogue, Buz Alexander, Suzanna Love; music, Robert O. Ragland; assistant director, Bruce Starr; art director, Stephen E. Graff; sound, Ed Christiano, John Huck; special effects, N. H. P. Inc; camera, Jon Kranhouse, Lommel; editor, Richard Brummer.

Keir Dullea (Julian Bedford); Suzanna Love (Kaylie Bedford); Vera Miles (Marian); Percy Rodrigues (Dr. Robinson); Tony Curtis

(Dr. Clavius); Paul Willson (Dr. Schroder); Ryan Seitz (Danny Bedford); Nicholas Love (Willy Meiser); Corinne Alphen (Lelia Adams); Eve Brent Ashe (Miss Simpson).

In San Francisco, a young mother, Kaylie Bedford (Suzanna Love), is in a coma suffering from severe brain trauma as a result of a car wreck. Her worried husband, Julian (Keir Dullea), agrees to let Dr. Clavius (Tony Curtis) experiment on her in a last ditch effort to return her to reality. His Clavius Process, which has not yet been tried on humans, uses electrodes to feed corrective brain wave patterns from a computer into the damaged brain areas to restore normalcy. The process is a success but Kaylie begins having flashback memories of the murder of a young woman (Corinne Alphen) and soon realizes that the dead girl's memories have become part of her thinking—and that she can reveal the murderer. The suspect (Nicholas Love), who has been cleared of the killing, realizes he may be identified by Kaylie and attempts to silence her.

This intriguing mixture of sci-fi thought transposition and murder mystery was issued on home video cassettes before making it to the big screen. It had little success in theatres and was soon relegated to cable TV movie channels. The thriller is actually well done and especially well acted. Director Ulli Lommel had previously helmed THE BOOGEY MAN (1980) and BOOGEY MAN II (1983), both starring his wife Suzanna Love. Her brother Nicholas appears as the killer in BRAIN WAVES.

THE BRIDE (Columbia, 1985) C 119 mins.

Executive producer Keith Addis; producer, Victor Drai; co-producer, Chris Kenny; associate producer, Lloyd Fonvielle; director, Franc Roddam; suggested by the novel *Frankenstein* by Mary Shelley; screenplay, Fonvielle; production designer, Michael Seymour; supervising art director, Bryan Graves; set decorator, Tessa Davies; music/music director, Maurice Jarre; music editor, Robin Clarke; costume designer, Shirley Russell; makeup, Sarah Monzani; stunt co-ordinator, Gerry Crampton; prosthetics creators, Aaron Sherman, Maralyn Sherman; sound, David John; camera, Stephen H. Burum; editor, Michael Ellis.

Sting (Baron Charles Frankenstein); Jennifer Beals (Eva); Anthony Higgins (Clerval); Clancy Brown (Viktor); David Rappaport (Rinaldo); Geraldine Page (Mrs. Baumann); Alexei Sayle (Magar); Phil Daniels (Bela); Veruschka (Countess); Quentin Crisp (Dr. Zahlus); Carey Elwes (Josef); Tim Spall (Paulus); Ken Campbell (Pedlar); Guy Rolfe (Count); Andrew De La Tour (Priest); Tony Haygarth (Tavern Keeper); Matthew Guinness, Tony Brutus (Patrons); Gary Shail, Carl Chase (Circus Hands); Bernard Padden

(Houseboy); Janine Duvitski (Serving Girl); John Sharp (Bailiff); Jack Birkett (Blind Man); Gerry Crampton (Gentleman); Fenella Fletcher (Masked Lady); Joe Kaye (Groom); Harold Coyne (Butler); Andy Barratt (Circus Ringmaster); Annie Roddam (Countess' Daughter); Sromboli, Karen Furness, John Alexander, Jacqueline Russell, Tod Cody, Laurence Temple, Gerard Naprous, Vera de Vel, Sally Oultram, Joel Baland, Miss Irta (Circus Performers).

Director Franc Roddam, best known for QUADROPHENIA (1979) and THE LORDS OF DISCIPLINE (1983), fashioned this remake of James Whale's THE BRIDE OF FRANKENSTEIN (1935) (q.v.) as a fairy tale fable rather than as a sci-fi horror study. Thus the terror aspects of the story, along with the horrific makeup, are eschewed in favor of character interaction and romance. Further, the picture takes on a feminist stance as it focuses on Frankenstein's beautiful creation and her relationship with her creator.

The storyline starts parallel with the classic 1935 feature. Dr. Frankenstein (Sting) creates a hulking male (Clancy Brown) and to compensate for his physical drawbacks and loneliness, the doctor creates a mate (Jennifer Beals) for him. The physically perfect and very beautiful creation, however, spurns her intended and in a fit of rage, the monster destroys his maker's laboratory and runs away. He meets a kindly dwarf, Rinaldo (David Rappaport), and the two join a touring circus where they become friends, with the dwarf helping his comrade find meaning to his peculiar existence. Meanwhile, Frankenstein and his female creation form a romantic entanglement which cannot be fulfilled.

While THE BRIDE is pictorially appealing, it is too literate and thus deprives the viewer of the thrills expected from a film about Frankenstein; especially to moviegoers brought up on the British Hammer Films devoted to the monster. Moreover, Sting in the title role is listless and Jennifer Beals is equally inanimate. As Jan Herman judged in the New York *Daily News,* the film is a ". . . foppish Pygmalion story full of pretentious twaddle about 'the new woman'. . . . It volleys back and forth so frequently between the two stories that it feels like the world's most expensive tennis match."

THE BRIDE OF FRANKENSTEIN (Universal, 1935) 80 mins.

Producer, Carl Laemmle, Jr.; director, James Whale; suggested by the novel *Frankenstein* by Mary Shelley; story/screenplay, John L. Balderston, William Hurlbut; art director, Charles Hall; music, Franz Waxman; makeup, Jack Pierce; electrical props, Kenneth Strickfaden; special effects, John P. Fulton; camera, John J. Mescall; editorial supervisor, Maurice Pivar; editor, Ted Kent.

Boris Karloff (Monster); Colin Clive (Dr. Henry Frankenstein);

Elsa Lanchester and Boris Karloff in THE BRIDE OF FRANKENSTEIN (1935).

Valerie Hobson (Elizabeth Frankenstein); Elsa Lanchester (The Mate/Mary Shelley); O. P. Heggie (Hermit); Ernest Thesiger (Dr. Septimus Pretorious); Dwight Frye (Karl); E. E. Clive (Burgomaster); Una O'Connor (Minnie); Ted Billings (Ludwig); Anne Darling (Shepherdess); Douglas Walton (Percy Shelley); Gavin Gordon (Lord Byron); Neil Fitzgerald (Rudy); Reginald Barlow (Hans); Mary Gordon (Hans' Wife); Gunnis Davis (Uncle Glutz); Tempe Pigott (Aunt Glutz); Lucien Prival (Albert the Butler); John Carradine, Frank Terry (Hunters); Billy Barty (Baby); Walter Brennan, Rollo Lloyd (Neighbors); Norman Ainsley (Little Archbishop); Joan Woodbury (Little Queen); Arthur S. Byron (Little King); Helen Parrish (Communion Girl); Josephine McKim (Mermaid); Kensas DeForrest (Ballerina); Ed Peil, Sr., Anders Van Haden, John George (Villagers).

Universal planned a sequel to its tremendously successful FRANKENSTEIN (1931) (q.v.) and the project went through several title changes, including RETURN OF FRANKENSTEIN and FRANKENSTEIN LIVES AGAIN! before settling on the final release title. According to James Curtis' biography of the film's director, *James Whale* (1982), "Needless to say, James Whale had no intention of making a straight sequel to FRANKENSTEIN. . . . In Whale's mind, the whole idea of a female Karloff-like monster was highly amusing. . . . THE RETURN OF FRANKENSTEIN was approached by its director as a 'hoot'." The resultant product, in fact, is really a stylish comedy, a darkly perverse and macabre one, which is more of a sendoff of the horror film genre than a straight out horror thriller. The movie's rich sets, atmospheric cinematography and old-fashioned performances make it a delight, one of the true classics of the sci-fi/horror film genre. Especially worthy of mention are Ernest Thesiger's performance as the off kilter Dr. Septimus Pretorius (a role originally conceived for Bela Lugosi who rejected it) and Una O'Connor as the addled, high-strung, screaming housemaid Minnie.

Although James Whale may have *not* planned BRIDE as a sequel to his original FRANKENSTEIN motion picture, this is exactly what resulted. The narrative opens with authoress Mary Shelley (Elsa Lanchester) relating the further adventures of the Frankensteins to husband Percy Shelley (Douglas Walton) and their friend Lord Byron (Gavin Gordon) during a terrible storm. According to Mary, the monster does *not* die in the mill fire which climaxed the initial adventure *nor* did his creator sustain permanent injury. The monster survives the fire in the lake beneath the mill and returns to kill again while Dr. Henry Frankenstein (Colin Clive) returns to his father's castle and the arms of his beautiful bride Elizabeth (Valerie Hobson). Interrupting their connubial bliss is the eerie Dr. Pretorius (Ernest Thesiger), Henry's old medical school professor, who wants him to join forces so they can create an artificial being. It seems the elderly teacher has created life, *but* in miniature, brainless form, and he requires Henry's expertise to assist in creating a life-size being. Henry refuses but Pretorius uses the monster (Boris Karloff), whom he met in the graveyard catacombs, to kidnap Elizabeth so Henry will go along with the plan. To soothe the creature, the scientists agree to create a bride for him since the monster is extremely lonely, having lost his only friend, an old blind man (O. P. Heggie) who had taught him to speak. Finally the experiment reaches its conclusion on a stormy night when the lifeless artificial being is charged with electricity from a storm and is given life. The newly-created woman (Elsa Lanchester), however, fears the monster and is attracted to her creator. This infuriates the creature and he embarks on a rampage destroying the laboratory and letting his creator escape to Elizabeth, he pulls a lever which brings down the castle walls around himself, Pretorius, and the bride.

Initially running about 90 minutes, THE BRIDE OF FRANK-

ENSTEIN was edited into a tightly running and very smooth flowing 80 minutes for its final release. One of the deleted sequences was a darkly humorous one of Pretorius relating how he was dissecting a woman who was still alive, but he found out too late to stop! The final print does include a tremendous continuity gaff. Originally Henry Frankenstein was to die in the laboratory explosion and such a sequence was shot. At the last minute it was decided to let him live and a scene of his being reunited with Elizabeth was inserted at the finale although in a long shot Henry can be seen with the laboratory collapsing around him.

THE BRIDE OF FRANKENSTEIN is a memorable cinematic excursion with many cherished moments: the stunning, eerie scene where the frightened Minnie (Una O'Connor) is confronted by the still living monster; the macabre catacomb setting where the monster tells Pretorius he hates the living but loves the dead ("You are wise in your generation," the mad scientist tells him). Top notch are the poignant scenes between the monster and his new found friend, the blind hermit, and how their friendship is destroyed by the arrival of two crass villagers (John Carradine, Walter Brennan), who immediately recognize the creature as " . . . the fiend who has been murdering half the countryside."

BRIDES OF BLOOD (Hemisphere, 1968) C 92 mins.

Executive producer, Kane W. Lynn; producer, Eddie Romero; directors, Gerardo de Leon, Romero.

John Ashley (Jim Farrell); Kent Taylor (Dr. Paul Henderson); Beverly Hills (Carla Henderson); Mario Montenegro (Stephen Powers); Eva Darren (Alma); and: Oscar Keesee, Ely Ramos, Jr., Bruno Punzalan, Andres Centenera, Pedro Navarro, Carmelita Estrella, Quiel Mendoza, Willie Tomada, Ben Sanchez, Angelita Alba.

The wonderfully atmospheric TERROR IS A MAN (1959) (see B/V) was the first "Blood Island" series entry but the first official outing was BRIDES OF BLOOD nearly a decade later, which Michael Weldon in *The Psychotronic Encyclopedia of Film* (1983) dubbed as "Terrible." That term is too strong for this sexploitation feature, shot in the Philippines, which contains captivating scenes with its eerie, living vegetation, and Kent Taylor's professional work as the scientist unravelling the island's mysteries.

Dr. Paul Henderson (Kent Taylor) and his wife Carla (Beverly Hills) arrive on a remote South Pacific island with their pilot (John Ashley) to investigate the results of nearby atomic testing on the local flora and fauna. They are guests of the island's owner (Mario Montenegro). They discover the natives, who fear a local god, sacrifice naked girls to it and they also learn that some plant life has taken on carnivorous activities. To complicate matters, Dr. Henderson is impotent, and Carla turns to their host for sexual satisfaction. She learns he has become a victim of the testing and mutates into the monster to whom the girls are sacrificed. The monster kills both the Hendersons, but the pilot destroys the mutant before leaving the isle.

Star John Ashley went on to act in, and sometimes co-produce a whole series of sequels including: MAD DOCTOR OF BLOOD ISLAND (1969), BEAST OF BLOOD (1970), BEAST OF THE YELLOW NIGHT (1971), and THE TWILIGHT PEOPLE (1972) (q.v.). Most of these entries, as well as the original, focus on the strange desire of a normal being wishing to co-habit with a man-made freak.

A.k.a.: BRIDES OF BLOOD ISLAND, BRIDES OF DEATH, GRAVE DESIRES, ISLAND OF LIVING HORROR, ORGY OF BLOOD, TERROR ON BLOOD ISLAND.

BRIDES OF BLOOD ISLAND see BRIDES OF BLOOD.

BRIDES OF DEATH see BRIDES OF BLOOD.

BUCK ROGERS IN THE 25TH CENTURY (Universal, 1979) C 89 mins.

Executive producer, Glen A. Larson; producer, Richard Caffey; supervising producer, Leslie Stevens; associate producers, Andrew Mirisch, David Phinney; director, Daniel Haller; based on the comic strip created by Philip Nolan, Richard Calkins; screenplay, Larson, Stevens; art director, Paul Peters; costumes, Jean-Pierre Dorleac; assistant directors, Phil Bowles, Jerry Sobul, Robert Villar, Judith Vogelsang; music, Stu Phillips; choreography, Miriam Nelson; camera, Frank Beascoechea; editor, John J. Dumas.

Gil Gerard (Captain William "Buck" Rogers); Pamela Hensley (Princess Ardala); Erin Gray (Lieutenant Wilma Deering); Henry Silva (Kane); Tim O'Connor (Dr. Elias Huer); Joseph Wiseman (Draco); Duke Butler, H. B. Haggerty (Tigermen); Felix Silla (Twiki); Mel Blanc (Voice of Twiki); Caroline Smith (Young Woman); John Dewey-Carter (Supervisor); Kevin Coates (Pilot); David Cadiente (Comtel Officer); Gil Serna (Technician); Larry Duran, Kenny Endoso (Guards); Eric Lawrence (Officer); Colleen Kelly (Wrather); Steve Jones, David Buchanan (Pilots); Burt Marshall (Wingman).

Twentieth century astronaut Buck Rogers (Gil Gerard) is on a mission when his deep space probe malfunctions and returns him to Earth, BUT five centuries later. It is the year 2491 and the planet is attempting to survive the aftershocks of a holocaustic war hundreds of years earlier. He is found by the alluring but totally evil Princess Ardala (Pamela Hensley) and her henchman Kane (Henry Silva), but he soon learns they are filled with dastardly plots, despite having developed scientific achievements far in advance of Buck's time. He escapes from the duo and heads for New Chicago only to be captured by Lieutenant Wilma Deering (Erin Gray), leader of the Third Force of the Earth's Directorate, and Dr. Elias Huer (Tim O'Connor), who are opposed to the princess. At first they believe Buck is a spy and they do not believe his tale about being caught in a time warp. A robot, Twiki (Felix Silla; Mel Blanc's voice) does believe him and helps him to show Wilma and Dr. Huer the truth and Buck teams with them to stop the princess and Kane from capturing Earth. With no way to return to his own time, Buck is determined to bring freedom to the 25th century.

Popular space traveler Buck Rogers first came to films in 1939 in Universal's cliffhanger BUCK ROGERS (see B/V) starring Buster Crabbe in the title role and in 1950 he became the subject of an early sci-fi TV series. This outing was originally also produced for TV in 1978 but was not telecast. Instead it was issued theatrically, especially abroad. It also served as the pilot for the new "Buck Rogers" teleseries which debuted on September 27, 1979, on NBC-TV with this feature telecast as its premiere episode. Either way it is a confused effort which is too contrived in its glitzy, but budget-conscious efforts to exploit the trendy sci-fi genre, and it suffers from a too heady infusion of "comedy." The fun of the Buster Crabbe serial is that it took itself seriously while this production did not. After 22 episodes, the series was revamped for a January 1981 re-entry, and lasted for eleven more weekly adventures, this time with Buck and his associates aboard the space craft Searcher exploring the universe in searching of the lost people of Earth.

One episode of this series is especially worth noting. In "Planet of the Slave Girls," Buster Crabbe guest-starred, reprising his famous role of Flash Gordon. This two-hour episode has since been released to TV as a feature film.

CAPRICORN ONE (Warner Bros., 1978) C 127 mins.

Producer, Paul N. Lazarus, III; associate producer, Michael Rachmil; director/screenplay, Peter Hyams; production designer, Albert Brenner; art director, David M. Haber; set decorator, Rick Simpson; costumes, Patricia Norris; music, Jerry Goldsmith; assistant directors, Irby Smith, Jack Sanders; sound, Jerry Jost; camera, Bill Butler; editor, James Mitchell.

Elliot Gould (Robert Caulfield); James Brolin (Charles Brubaker);

Brenda Vaccaro (Kay Brubaker); Sam Waterston (Peter Willis); O. J. Simpson (John Walker); Hal Holbrook (Dr. James Kelloway); David Huddleston (Hollis Peaker); David Doyle (Walter Loughlin); Denise Nicholas (Betty Walker); Robert Walden (Elliot Whittier); Lee Bryant (Sharon Willis); Alan Fudge (Capsule Communicator); Karen Black (Judy Drinkwater); Telly Savalas (Albain).

A mechanical failure forces the cancellation of the first manned flight to Mars, but NASA officials keep the scuttle a secret fearing public reaction and loss of revenues. It is decided the three astronauts, Charles Brubaker (James Brolin), Peter Willis (Sam Waterston), and John Walker (O.J. Simpson), will be taken to a remote desert locale and there a simulated Mars landing will be staged. A reporter, Robert Caufield (Elliott Gould), investigates and one of the astronauts' wives, Kay Brubaker (Brenda Vaccaro), believes something is amiss. After a spell the space men become weary of their (fake) mission and start to rebel. NASA officials decide to have them murdered, especially after the real spaceship, sent unmanned, blows up and burns upon reentry to Earth. Caufield finally realizes that the astronauts are in danger. Enlisting the services of bombastic Albain (Telly Savalas), who flies a crop duster plane, he sets out to rescue them as they flee through the desert avoiding hired assassins.

Grossing $12,000,000 at the U.S. box-office, CAPRICORN ONE is an entertaining cat-and-mouse thriller using a fake space mission as its plot crux. The gimmick has its basis in reality. When the Soviets first started sending astronauts into orbit, many skeptical sources insisted the Russian missions were staged media events. In the U.S., in the post-Watergate hysteria which engulfed Hollywood, the American government is presented as the defrauder. Hal Holbrook's NASA chief, Dr. James Kelloway, is an especially spiteful and grasping bureaucrat, a far cry from the typical government official who populated films prior to the 1970s. Elliott Gould's oafish performance as the sleazy journalist/hero aside, CAPRICORN ONE boasts solid acting from all concerned.

CAPTAIN MEPHISTO AND THE TRANSFORMATION MACHINE see MANHUNT OF MYSTERY ISLAND.

CAPTIVE WILD WOMAN (Universal, 1943) 61 mins.

Associate producer, Ben Pivar; director, Edward Dmytryk; story, Ted Fithlan, Maurice Pivar, Neil P. Varnick; screenplay, Henry Sucher, Griffin Jay; music director, Hans J. Salter; makeup, Jack Pierce; art director, John B. Goodman; camera, George Robinson; editor, Milton Carruth.

John Carradine (Dr. Sigmund Walters); Evelyn Ankers (Beth

Colman); Milburn Stone (Fred Mason); Lloyd Corrigan (John Whipple); Acquanetta (Paula Dupree); Martha MacVicar [Vicars] (Dorothy Colman); Vince Barnett (Curley Barret); Fay Helm (Miss Strand); Paul Fix (Gruen); Ray Walmer (Ringmaster); Harry Holman (Baggage Master); William Gould (Sheriff); Virginia Engel (Aerialist); Grant Withers (Doctor); Ray Corrigan (Ape).

Always seeking fresh fodder to feed the profitable horror film marketplace during the World War II years, Universal initiated a three feature series centering about a young woman who turns into a simian creature through jealousy and science gone afoul. The overall results, yet another twist on the *Frankenstein* theme, were satisfactory double-bill entries, laced with stock footage and hampered by minimal budgets. CAPTIVE WILD WOMAN was followed by JUNGLE WOMAN (1944) and JUNGLE CAPTIVE (1945) (qq.v.)

CAPTIVE WILD WOMAN has mad scientist Dr. Sigmund Walters (John Carradine) carrying out experiments involving evolution, his aim to turn a simian into a human. When an orangutan escapes from a circus, the doctor captures it and begins experimenting on the subject, using his nurse (Fay Helm) for spare parts. The result is a beautiful young woman, Paula Dupree (Acquanetta), whose looks are enhanced by plastic surgery. Paula, however, falls in love with animal trainer Fred Mason (Milburn Stone) and becomes jealous of his attentions to Beth Colman (Evelyn Ankers). Paula reverts into a killer simian and she turns on her creator, murdering him. It is Mason who shoots and kills the monster.

While the New York *Herald-Tribune* dubbed the film an "adequate thriller," contemporary writers have been far more critical. Donald C. Willis wrote in *Horror and Science Fiction Films* (1972), "Reputedly not as bad as the title might lead you to believe, actually it is. Ridiculous ideas and dialogue, many plot inconsistencies. The . . . ape makeup is all that's original." Makeup master Jack Pierce was responsible for the series' true creativity—the monster makeup. The rest of the production left much to be desired, especially with Milburn Stone wearing clothes to match footage of Clyde Beatty in THE BIG CAGE (1933).

CAPTIVE WOMEN (RKO, 1952) 65 mins.

Producers, Aubrey Wisberg, Jack Pollexfen; associate producer, Albert Zugsmith; screenplay, Wisberg, Pollexfen; production designer, Theobold Holsopple; music, Charles Koff; camera, Paul Ivano; editor, Fred R. Feitshans.

Robert Clarke (Rob); Margaret Field (Ruth); Gloria Saunders (Catherine); Ron Randell (Riddon); Stuart Randall (Gordon); Paula

Acquanetta in CAPTIVE WILD WOMAN (1943).

Dorety, Chilli Williams (Captives); Robert Bice (Bram); William Schallert (Carver); Eric Colmar (Sabron); Douglas Evans (Jason).

Around the year 3000 A.D. Manhattan and its environs is a jungle; the constantly warring factions thrown back into the stone age as a result of a nuclear holocaust. Three tribes populate the area: the Norms, who want peace; the Satan-worshipping Upriver People; and the Mutates, who have been disfigured by radiation. Riddon (Ron Randell) is the leader of the Mutates and he leads raids into the Norms' camp to carry off their women for breeding. Gordon (Stuart Randall), leader of the Upriver tribe, attacks the Norms and they and their leader Rob (Robert Clarke) are forced to run and are given sanctuary by Riddon and his people. The two tribes unite to take back Norm women kidnapped by the Upriver tribe but Mutate outcast Carver (William Schallert) allies himself with Gordon and tells him of a secret passage. It is the Hudson River Tunnel which permits the Upriver people to hit their adversaries with a surprise attack. The Norms and Mutates, however, flood the tunnel, killing Gordon and his men. By now Riddon and a Norman woman, Ruth (Margaret Field), have fallen in love and it is hoped their mating will unite the two tribes and that their offspring will be normal.

CAPTIVE WOMEN has an engrossing premise which is executed in mundane fashion. Its vision of a post-atomic Earth is one of the first for the Cold War era cinema, but its overly melodramatic plot negates the impact of an atomic aftermath. *Variety* branded the film ". . . . a dull, over-talkative piece of inept filmmaking which never catches the imagination." Phil Hardy notes in *The Film Encyclopedia: Science Fiction* (1984), "There are some interesting special effects with New York as an overgrown jungle, shooting out tentacles underneath the Hudson River, but [Stuart] Gilmore's direction is limp."

The film was made by the same producers who turned out the memorable THE MAN FROM PLANET X (1951) (see B/V) and three of that film's stars—Robert Clarke, Margaret Field, and William Schallert—appear in CAPTIVE WOMEN.

In 1957, this feature was reissued as 1000 YEARS FROM NOW.

CARAVAN OF COURAGE see EWOKS: THE BATTLE FOR ENDOR.

CARNE PER FRANKENSTEIN see FLESH FOR FRANKENSTEIN.

THE CARTER CASE (Oliver Films, 1919) fifteen chapters.

Producer, Harry Grossman; director, Donald Mackenzie; based on the character "Craig Kennedy" created by Arthur B. Reeve; screenplay, Reeve, John W. Grey.

Herbert Rawlinson (Craig Kennedy); Marguerite Marsh (Anita Carter); Ethel Gray Terry (Cleo Clark); Coit Albertson (Lester Mason); William Pike (Walter Jameson); Joseph Marba (Hugo Geist); Donald Hall (Shelby Carter); Kempton Greene (Rance Dixon); John Reinhardt (Count Von Der Witz); Gene Baker (Alma the Maid).

Chapters: 1) The Phosgene Bullet; 2) The Vacuum Room; 3) The Air Terror; 4) The Dungeon; 5) Unknown; 6) The Wireless Detective; 7) Nervagraph; 8) The Silent Shot; 9) The Camera Trap; 10) Unknown; 11) The Moonshiners; 12) The White Damp; 13) The X-Ray Detective; 14) The Ruse; 15) Unknown.

A.k.a.: THE CRAIG KENNEDY SERIAL.

THE CARTER CASE was co-scripted by Arthur B. Reeve, the writer of the "Craig Kennedy" stories which encompassed more than two dozen novels between 1911 and 1936, one of the last being *The Clutching Hand* (1934) which was turned into a serial (q.v.) two years later. Craig Kennedy was a scientific detective and America's answer to Sherlock Holmes, and he even had an intelligent assistant, Walter Jameson. THE CARTER CASE was the fourth Craig Kennedy cliffhanger, following Pathe's trilogy: THE EXPLOITS OF ELAINE (1915), THE NEW EXPLOITS OF ELAINE (1915), and THE ROMANCE OF ELAINE (1915), all starring Pearl White, with Arnold Daly as Kennedy and Creighton Hale as Jameson. Herbert Rawlinson was Craig Kennedy in THE CARTER CASE and the fifteen chapter serial was issued on the states' rights market by Oliver Films.

Craig Kennedy (Herbert Rawlinson) uses his scientific abilities to solve a crime involving an invisible, noiseless airplane and he becomes romantically involved with a young woman (Marguerite Marsh). With the usual array of scientifc gadgets associated with a Craig Kennedy adventure and such chapter titles as "The Phosgene Bullet," "The Vacuum Room," "The Air Terror," "The Wireless Detective," "The Nervagraph," and "The X-Ray Detective," the chapterplay had more than its share of vintage science fiction plot devices to tide it along.

While the Craig Kennedy character continued to maintain its literary popularity through the 1930s, he also headlined another silent serial, THE RADIO DETECTIVE (1926) with John T. Price as Kennedy. An early talkie feature, UNMASKED (1929) had Robert Warwick as the detective. The hero returned to a science-fiction format, however, in 1936, in his final celluloid chapterplay, THE CLUTCHING HAND with Jack Mulhall in the lead assignment.

LA CASA DEL TERROR see FACE OF THE SCREAMING WEREWOLF.

THE CASE OF THE MISSING BRIDES see THE CORPSE VANISHES.

CASTLE OF EVIL (United Pictures, 1966) C 81 mins.

Executive producer, Fred Jordan; producer, Earle Lyon; associate producer, Wendell Niles, Jr.; director, Francis D. Lyon; screenplay, Charles A. Wallace; art director, Paul Sylos, Jr.; music, Paul Dunlap; makeup, Bob Dawn; special effects, Roger George; sound,

John Bury; camera, Brick Marquand; supervising editor, Robert S. Eisen.

Scott Brady (Matt Granger); Virginia Mayo (Sable); David Brian (Robert Hawley); Lisa Gaye (Carol Harris); Hugh Marlowe (Dr. Corozal); Shelley Morrison (Lupe Tekal d'Esperanza); Ernest Sarracino (Tunki); William Thourlby (Electronic Man); Natividad Vacio (Machado).

At a remote island, a group arrives to hear the will of a dead scientist and these include the man's mistress, Sable (Virginia Mayo), Matt Granger (Scott Brady), Robert Hawley (David Brian), Dr. Corozar (Hugh Marlowe), and Carol Harris (Lisa Gaye). At the Caribbean island castle, the heirs find that Hawley has been killed and it develops the murder was committed by a robot created by the dead scientist in his own image. The robot is programmed to kill the heir who was responsible for disfiguring the scientist with phosphorus salts before his death. The survivors find out the robot has been reprogrammed by one of the heirs to kill off the balance of the gathering. The killer is unmasked and Granger destroys the robot with a laser gun invented by the late scientist.

Originally produced as THE HAUNTING AT CASTLE MONTEGO, this thriller is somewhat of a throwback to the murder mysteries of the 1940s; the type churned out by Monogram and Producers Releasing Corp. Overall the plot holds up and Francis D. Lyon's economical direction keeps the proceedings moving along fairly well. The film is also aided by a small, but fine cast. *Variety* tagged the product a "Rudimentary horror-cum-mystery programmer, okay for duals. Virginia Mayo excellent."

To hype the box-office draw of CASTLE OF EVIL, the producers offered a free funeral if any patrons dropped dead while watching the proceedings. Such showmanship was hardly necessary for the production had its own virtues; especially the robot killer, a ghastly looking creature with a terribly scarred face and the lack of one eye.

THE CAT FROM OUTER SPACE (Buena Vista, 1978) C 103 mins.

Producer, Ron Miller; co-producer/director, Norman Tokar; screenplay, Ted Key; music, Lalo Schifrin; art directors, John B. Mansridge, Preston Ames; assistant director, Gene Sultan; stunt coordinator, Richard Warlock; special effects, Eustace Lycett, Art Cruickshank, Danny Lee; sound, Bud Maffett; camera, Charles F. Wheeler; editor, Cotton Warburton.

Ken Berry (Frank); Sandy Duncan (Liz); Harry Morgan (General Stilton); Roddy McDowall (Stallwood); McLean Stevenson (Link);

Jesse White (Ernie); Alan Young (Wenger); Hans Conreid (Heffel); Ronnie Schell (Sergeant Duffy); James Hampton (Captain Anderson); Howard T. Platt (Colonel Woodruff); William Prince (Olympus).

Zunar 15/90 Doris 4-7 is an alien cat whose spaceship lands on Earth and is in need of immediate repair. The feline wears a collar which gives him superpowers and he contacts Frank (Ken Berry) for help in raising a large amount of gold for the necessary repairs. Also enlisted are Link (McLean Stevenson) and Liz (Sandy Duncan) who devise a scheme for the cat—now dubbed Jake—to earn the money by using telepathy in gambling. As this proceeds, the military, led by General Stilton (Harry Morgan), fears an alien invasion while the wicked Stallwood (Roddy McDowall) gets wind of the feline and attempts to steal its collar. During a big game, a veterinarian (Alan Young) accidentally puts Jake to sleep. But all ends well and the money is raised; the repairs are made; and Jake is able to rendezvous with his alien fleet.

This typically light and frothy Disney offering grossed $8,500,000 at the domestic box-office with its charming if innocuous tale of a space cat, played by sibling Abyssinians: Rumpler and Amber. The movie attempted no more than it promised, an amusing comedy with enough special effects to delight its audiences. Especially well-staged were the saucer sequences and the final aerial confrontation. Cat lovers, of course, fell for Jake, one of the more adorable aliens to come along in some time and certainly more attractive than the raft of mutants, bug-heads and other types of space creatures which seem to populate sci-fi films.

CHOSEN SURVIVORS (Columbia, 1974) C 99 mins.

Executive producer, Charles Fries; producer, Leon Benson; director, Sutton Roley; story, H. B. Cross; screenplay, Cross, Joe Reb Moffly; music, Fred Karlin; art director, Jose Rodriguez; set decorator, Ernesto Carrasco; costumes, Alfonso Rubie; vampire bat consultants/trainers, Dr. G. Clay Mitchell, William Lopez Forment; assistant director, Felipe Palomino; sound, Robert J. Litt; sound effects, Paul Laune; camera Gabriel Torres; editors, John F. Link II, Dennis Virler.

Jackie Cooper (Raymond Couzins); Alex Cord (Steven Mayes); Richard Jaeckel (Gordon Ellis); Bradford Dillman (Peter Macomber); Pedro Armendariz, Jr. (Luis Cabral); Diana Muldaur (Alana Fitzgerald); Lincoln Kilpatrick (Woody Russo); Gwen Mitchell (Carrie Draper); Barbara Babcock (Lenore Chrisman); Christina Moreno (Kristin Lerner); Nancy Rodman (Claire Farraday); Kelly Lange (Mary Louise Borden).

Filmed in Mexico, CHOSEN SURVIVORS is basically a pseu-

Bradford Dillman, Lincoln Kilpatrick, Christina Moreno, and Barbara Babcock in CHOSEN SURVIVORS (1974).

do-sci-fi/horror thriller which develops into an adventure movie. Its main premise is survival of a group of people; first from a supposed nuclear holocaust and then from the actual threat of attack from vampire bats. Despite the creative plot play, something sadly went awry and Leonard Maltin in *TV Movies and Video Guide* (1988) noted, "Dialogue and characterization [are] from grade-Z movies of the past."

Eleven individuals, including Raymond Couzins (Jackie Cooper), Alana Fitzgerald (Diane Muldaur), Peter Macomber (Bradford Dillman), Gordon Ellis (Richard Jaeckel), and Luis Cabral (Pedro Armendariz, Jr.), are sent 1700 feet underground into shelters to be spared an impending nuclear attack. Once there they find the episode is merely a drill. But trouble arises when their compound is attacked by hundreds of vampire bats from a cave connecting to their quarters. The psychological test of their reactions and survival techniques for nuclear war becomes a test of outmaneuvering the deadly bats.

CINDERELLA 2000 (Independent-International, 1977) C 95 mins.

Executive producers, Samuel M. Sherman, Dan Q. Kennis; producer/director, Al Adamson; screenplay, Bud Donnelly; music, Sparky Sugarman; art director, Eddie Garetti; sound, Corey Bailey; camera, Louis Horvath; editors, Michael Bockman, Greg Tittinger.

Catharine Erhardt (Cinderella); Eddie Caretti (Roscoe the Robot); Jay B. Larson (Fairy Godfather); Vaughn Armstrong (Tom); Erwin Fuller (Controller); Rena Harmon (Stepmother); Bhurni Cowans (Bella); Adina Ross (Irma); Olivia Michelle (Irma); Art Cacaro (Jack D. Ripper); Sherri Coyle (Jill).

"Tomorrow's Sexiest Comedy . . . Today! A Futuristic Fantasy" was the advertising slogan for this Independent-International science fiction farce which was just as silly as its title implied. Originally issued as an X-rated feature, the film was toned down to an R-rating the year after its release; but either way it was a dud. While schlock film fans may have fond memories of such Al Adamson-Sam Sherman collaborations as BLOOD OF GHASTLY HORROR (1971), BRAIN OF BLOOD (1971), DRACULA VS. FRANKENSTEIN (1971) (all q.v.), NURSE SHERRI (1977), there is little to recommend this deadly dull space take-off outside of a plethora of scantily- (or non) clad females.

Set in 2047, the fantasy tells of a world that is ruled by computers and how people are forbidden to fall in love unless the rulers give their consent. A young woman (Catharine Erhardt), however, opposes the law and finds gratification with a space man (Jay B. Larson) and the two conspire to bring an end to the existing regime.

Graced with tacky sets, men wearing rabbit masks and a fairy godfather, CINDERELLA 2000 has little relationship to the children's fable and even less to entertainment value. Also involved in this melee are various musical numbers and the unhumorous, let alone unmusical, Roscoe the Robot. The film received limited distribution, but those who did view it had unkind words, as exemplified by Michael Weldon in *The Psychotronic Encyclopedia of Film* (1983), "Al Adamson tops his previous efforts with this softcore science-fiction sex musical version of CINDERELLA. . . . The sets and makeup will bring back memories of SANTA CLAUS CONQUERS THE MARTIANS."

CISARUV PEKAR (Czechoslovensky Film, 1951) 87 mins.

Producer, Jan Werich; director, Martin Fric; screenplay, Werich, Jiri Brdecka; camera, Jan Stallich.

Jan Werich (Emperor Rudolf II/Baker); and: Marie Vasova, Natasha Gollova, Bohuslav, Zahorsky, Frantisek Filipovsky, Vaclav Tregi, Zdenek Stephanek, Jiri Plachy, Frantisek Cerny.

See: THE GOLEM (essay).

THE CLAW MONSTERS see PANTHER GIRL OF THE CONGO.

CLOSE ENCOUNTERS OF THE THIRD KIND (Columbia, 1977) C 135 mins.

Producers, Julia and Michael Phillips; director/screenplay, Steven Spielberg; music, John Williams; production designer, Joe Alves; art director, Dan Lomino; set decorator, Phil Abramson; costumes/wardrobe, Jim Linn; assistant director, Chuck Myers; stunt co-ordinator, Buddy Joe Hooker; sound, Buzz Knudson, Don MacDougall, Robert Glass, Gene Cantamesa, Steve Katz; sound effects editor, Frank Warner; special effects, Roy Arbogast, Gregory Jein, Douglas Trumbull, Matthew Yuricich, Richard Yuricich; camera, Vilmos Zsigmond, Trumbull, William A. Fraker, Douglas Slocombe, John Alonzo, Laszlo Kovacs, Richard Yuricich, Dave Stewart, Robert Hall, Don Jarel, Dennis Muren; second unit camera, Steve Poster; editor, Michael Kahn.

Richard Dreyfuss (Roy Neary); Francois Truffaut (Claude Lacombe); Teri Garr (Ronnie Nerary); Melinda Dillon (Jillian Guiler); Cary Guffey (Barry Guiler); Bob Balaban (Laughlin the Interpreter); J. Patrick McNamara (Project Leader); Warren Kemmerling (Wild Bill); Roberts Blossom (Farmer); Philip Dodds (Jean Claude); Shawn Bishop, Adrienne Campbell, Justin Dreyfuss (Neary Children); Lance Hendricksen (Robert); Merrill Connally (Team Leader); George Dicenzo (Major Benchley); Carl Weathers (M.P.); Roger Ernest (Highway Patrolman); Josef Sommers (Larry Butler).

The critics fell all over themselves praising this Stephen Spielberg-directed and written super-sci-fier which grossed over $80,000,000 at the domestic box-office. Ed Naha in *The Science Fictionary* (1980) judged it, "The Holy Grail of UFO movies." While the motion picture does sport magnificent special effects by Doug Trumbull, it is more often than not an overlong, confused, and hard-to-follow psychological drama more remembered for specific scenes, than for the film as a whole. The various UFO sequences, and reactions to the saucers are vivid, as is the big finale with the landing of the mother craft and initial contact with the aliens. The character delineations, however, soon become tiresome (although the hero's suffering wife, Teri Garr, is fine) as does the hero's (Richard Dreyfuss) deep-seated, uncerebral desire to solve his compulsion about a mountain.

UFOs are spotted over a mid-sized Indiana community and a power outage results. Repairman Roy Neary (Richard Dreyfuss) is sent to locate the source of the blackout and a UFO flies near his stalled truck. With the state police, he gives chase to it and several other space craft through the rural countryside, but the UFOs speed away. Back home Roy attempts to persuade his skeptical wife Ronnie (Teri Garr) about what he has witnessed and he begins to be haunted by a mental picture of a large mountain. The same night Roy saw the saucer, a small boy, Barry Guiler (Cary Guffey), is kidnapped by one of the UFOs, much to the grief of his mother, Jillian (Melinda Dillon). Jillian also has mental pictures of the mountain and as Ronnie rejects Roy's story, he finds himself drawn to Jillian. The two leave town together and find themselves going to Wyoming's Devil's Tower, the huge mountain of their telepathic visions. They find the area sealed off by the government due to an alleged chemical spill from a train wreck. Not believing this rationale, they

Richard Dreyfuss, Melinda Dillon, and Cary Guffey in CLOSE ENCOUNTERS OF THE THIRD KIND (1977).

climb the mountain but are captured by the army and taken to an outpost where Claude Lacombe (Francois Truffaut), a UFO expert, is leading an international team on a top secret mission. Roy and Jillian figure the scientific team is researching the UFO phenomenon and that a landing will take place at Devil's Tower. The two escape their captors and return to the mountain where they witness the arrival of UFOs and the landing of a colossal mother ship. Aliens appear from the craft as do many humans, including Barry, who is reunited with Jillian. Roy joins the members of the scientific team in boarding the craft and making contact with the aliens. He is one of those chosen to leave with the craft.

This landmark feature film was nominated for nine Academy Awards; including Spielberg as director, Melinda Dillon as best supporting actress, Michael Kahn's editing, and John Williams' original score. The movie won only two Oscars: one for Vilmos Zsigmond's cinematography and one for Frank Warner's sound effects editing. Competing against STAR WARS (q.v.), this film came in second best, since that epic won six Oscars and was nominated for Best Picture, something CLOSE ENCOUNTERS was definitely not.

In 1980 the film was reissued to theatres in a "Special Edition" which added deleted footage, mainly at the finale, showing human contact with aliens in the spacecraft. The footage was foggy and hard to follow and added little, if any, lustre to the overall production.

The main drawback to CLOSE ENCOUNTERS OF THE THIRD KIND is that it tries to be too much: the ultimate sci-fi movie in a genre where each day finds new themes and effects to outshine past efforts. As a special effects diversion, the movie is highly satisfying! As a drama of human and alien interaction, it is a dud. The cerebral approach to sci-fi may appeal to a minority, but mass audiences want ALIEN (1979) (q.v.) and STAR WARS (1977) (q.v.) in deference to gentle, fragile elfin creatures. With all its psychological overtones and puzzles, the film still tells us nothing about the makings of an alien and certainly gives no indication as to why they would want to take a dunderhead like Roy Neary with them on their return home.

THE CLUTCHING HAND (Stage And Screen, 1936) fifteen chapters.

Producer, Louis Weiss; director, Albert Herman; based on the novel by Arthur B. Reeve; screenplay, Leon D'Usseai, Dallas Fitzgerald; music, Lee Zahler; camera, James Diamond; editor, Earl Turner.

Jack Mulhall (Craig Kennedy); Marion Shilling (Verna Gironda);

Yakima Canutt (Number Eight); Reed Howes (Sullivan); Ruth Mix (Shirley McMillan); William Farnum (George Gaunt); Rex Lease (Walter Jameson); Mae Busch (Mrs. Gironda); Bryant Washburn (Denton); Robert Frazer (Dr. Paul Gironda); Gaston Glass (Louis Bouchard); Mahlon Hamilton (Montgomery); Robert Walker (Mitchell); Joseph W. Girard (Cromwell); Frank Leigh (Wickham); Charles Locher (Hobart); Franklyn Farnum (Nicky); Knute Erickson (Captain Hanson); Dick Alexander (Olaf); Milburn Morante (Marty); Henry Hall (Warden); Snub Pollard (Snub); John Elliot (Arthur J. White).

Chapters: 1) Who Is the Clutching Hand?; 2) Shadow; 3) House of Mystery; 4) The Phantom Car; 5) The Double Trap; 6) Steps of Doom; 7) The Invisible Enemy; 8) A Cry in the Night; 9) Evil Eyes; 10) A Desperate Chance; 11) The Ship of Doom; 12) Hidden Danger; 13) The Mystic Menace; 14) The Silent Spectre; 15) The Lone Hand.

The villainous character, The Clutching Hand, had appeared in the 1914 motion picture serial THE EXPLOITS OF ELAINE (see B/V) a "Craig Kennedy" mystery starring Pearl White. Arthur B. Reeve, the author of a score of "Craig Kennedy" books revived the character for his 1934 novel *The Clutching Hand* and this was adapted to the screen as a fifteen chapter economy serial by George M. Merrick and Eddy Graneman for Weiss Productions' Stage And Screen. Jack Mulhall took on the Craig Kennedy role and proved superb in the assignment, ably supported by a top notch veteran cast, including: William Farnum, Rex Lease, Mae Busch, Bryant Washburn, Robert Frazer, Gaster Glass, William Desmond, Franklyn Farnum, and Yakima Canutt. (Canutt also supervised the stunt work, particularly the well-executed fight sequences.)

The famous scientific detective Craig Kennedy (Jack Mulhall) is asked by his associate, newspaperman Walter Jameson (Rex Lease), to investigate the kidnapping of Dr. Paul Gironda (Robert Frazer) the father of Jameson's fiancee, Verna Gironda (Marion Shilling). Gironda had announced he had developed a formula for making synthetic gold prior to his disappearance. A mysterious killer called The Clutching Hand tries to get rid of Kennedy and Jameson during their investigations, but fails. Finally Kennedy calls a meeting of the International Research Foundation and discloses Dr. Gironda's formula. The doctor promptly appears demanding his property and Kennedy captures him, revealing the identity of the Clutching Hand. Craig also shows that the doctor was really only Vera's guardian and that he had devised the fake formula to cover the fact he had stolen money from the young woman and with the money from the sale of the formula, he planned to leave the country.

Writing about THE CLUTCHING HAND in *Film Fan Monthly* magazine (September, 1968), James Stringham reported the serial " . . . featured a large number of sub-plots which caused almost everyone to come under suspicion. . . . [and] they worked against the serial's effectiveness." He also commented on the " . . . wonderfully elaborate Gironda laboratory. It seemed the sort of place that *could* produce gold."

COCOON (Twentieth Century-Fox, 1985) C 117 mins.

Producers, Richard D. Zanuck, David Brown, Lili Fini Zanuck; associate producer, Robert Doudell; director, Ron Howard; story, David Saperstein; screenplay, Tom Benedek; assistant directors, Jan R. Lloyd, Hans Beimler; production designer, Jack T. Collis; conceptual artist, Ralph McQuarrie; art director, Phil Norwood; set decorator, Jim Duffy; cocoons/dolphins creator, Robert Short Productions; special alien creatures/effects, Greg Cannom; special creature consultant, Rick Baker; model supervisor, Steve Gawley; stunt co-ordinator, Ted Grossman; marine co-ordinator, Manfred Zendar; underwater consultant, Mike Nomad; music, James Horner; music arranger, Jay Gruska; song, Cruz Sembello; special dance co-ordinator, Gwen Verdon; dance consultant, Thane Cornell; alien movement choreography, Caprice Rothe; costumes, Aggie Guerard Rodgers; costume supervisor, Edward Marks; makeup, Robert Norin, Kevin Haney; sound, Richard Church, Armin Steiner; sound editors, William Hartman, Michael Corrigan, Godfrey Marks; special effects co-ordinator, Joseph Unsinn; visual effects camera, Scott Farrar; optical camera, Kenneth Smith, Donald Clark, James Lim; matte camera, Paul Huston; underwater camera, Jordan Klein; visual effects, Ken Ralston; opticals supervisor, Ed David Beery; matte painting supervisor, Chris Evans; camera, Don Peterman; editors, Michael Hill, David Hanley.

Don Ameche (Art Selwyn); Wilford Brimley (Ben Luckett); Hume Cronyn (Joe Finley); Brian Dennehy (Walter); Jack Gilford (Bernie Lefkowitz); Steve Guttenberg (Jack Bonner); Maureen Stapleton (Mary Luckett); Jessica Tandy (Alma Finley); Gwen Verdon (Bess McCarthy); Herta Ware (Rose Lefkowitz); Tahnee Welch (Kitty); Barret Oliver (David); Linda Harrison (Susan); Tyrone Power, Jr. (Pillsbury); Clint Howard (John Dexter); Charles Lampkin (Pops); Mike Nomad (Doc); Jorge Gil (Lou Pine); Jim Ritz (DMV Clerk); Charles Rainsbury (Smiley); Wendy Cooke, Pamela Prescott, Dinah Sue Rowley, Gabriella Sinclair (Aliens); Cyndi Vicino (Teller); Russ Wheeler (Doctor); Harold Bergman (Reverend); Ivy Thayer (Waitress); Fred Broderson (Dock Master); Mark Cheresnick (Salvatore); Bette Shoor (Realtor); Mark Simpson (Coast Guard,

First Class BM); Robert Slacum, Jr. (Coast Guard, Second Class BM); Rance Howard (Detective); Jean Speegle (Woman); Charles Voelker (Band Leader); Irving Krone (Jasper); Clarence Thomas, Ted Science (Policemen).

"COCOON offers the rare and deeply satisfying pleasure of watching an ensemble of old troupers play with zest, insight and consummate craft. The movie may be a piece of fluff, but they're not." (*LA Weekly*)

At a Florida retirement community, retirees Art Selwyn (Don Ameche), Ben Luckett (Wilford Brimley), and Joe Finley (Hume Cronyn), steal away to a deserted nearby estate to swim in the large indoor pool. Three aliens, Walter (Brian Dennehy), Kitty (Tahnee Welch), and Pillsbury (Tyrone Power, Jr.), arrive in the area and rent the estate. They hire Jack Bonner (Steve Guttenberg), a charter boat captain, to take them on a scuba diving outing but they return with what appears to be giant oyster shells. They hide the large shells in the estate's pool and the effects from these hidden shells cause the three retirees to become rejuvenated after swimming there. Finding themselves young again, the three men begin to shower attention on their surprised women: Mary Luckett (Maureen Stapleton), Alma Finley (Jessica Tandy), and Bess McCarthy (Gwen Verdon), Art's

Brian Dennehy, Tyrone Power, Jr., Steve Guttenberg, and Tahnee Welch in COCOON (1985).

girlfriend. When the secret of their youthfulness is revealed the inhabitants of the retirement community want to bathe in the pool; except skeptical Bernie Lefkowitz (Jack Gilford) and his wife Rose (Herta Ware). The aliens realize their mission on Earth has been jeopardized by the senior citizens and the discovery of their youth-restoring pods. When they abandon our terrain, a good many of the senior citizens agree to accompany them into the unknown.

" . . . COCOON has many familiar elements: it could be called E.T. MEETS THE OVER-THE-HILL GANG, or ON GOLDEN POD. Like last Christmas's STARMAN [q.v.], it contains a love story between an extraterrestrial (Tahnee Welch, Raquel's lithe and stunning daughter) and a young American (Steve Guttenberg), here sex is represented as a love-light that ricochets around the swimming pool. Like E.T. [q.v] and a dozen other fantasy films, it boasts gorgeous, if insubstantial special effects from George Lucas' Industrial Light & Magic studio. And there is just enough locker-room humor to keep the gross-out brigade from snoring in their seats. . . . nesting inside COCOON is a parable about life meeting death—an affecting mortality play about old people touched or affected by America's youth culture." (Richard Corliss, *Time* magazine)

COCOON received much up-front publicity from the fact that it was directed by ex-child performer Ron Howard and that veteran film star Don Ameche had a pivotal, leading role. The sentimental, optimistic production proved a tremendous financial success (grossing $75,901,168 in its first fifteen weeks at the box-office), appealing to both older and younger generations.

The critics were enthralled that this film offered so much philosophical meat to dissect. Sheila Benson (*Los Angeles Times*) decided, "The movie is about treasure. Treasure wasted: the experience of our older people. Treasure reclaimed: the fealty of a captain for his crew. New treasure: the electricity of sexual attraction. Abiding treasure: the bonds among the eight friends. And one of the greatest treasures of all: self-knowledge." "Transcending its sci-fi trappings, COCOON is a celebration of the human spirit; specifically, the determination and enthusiasm senior citizens feel for life but are hampered from fulfilling by either the infirmities of old age or the expectations of others. . . . .[T]he sci-fi structure and spaceship gadgetry is itself the protective cocoon for this wonderful and uplifting motion picture." (Duane Byrge, *The Hollywood Reporter*) "What might have been merely a maudlin film . . . is turned into genuine and genuinely spirited good humor. The scenes of the newly invigorated men splashing in the pool, commenting slyly and somewhat embarrassedly on their rejuvenated virility, are among the most memorable. In addition, the decision to shoot on location in Saint Petersburg, Florida, in an actual retirement community . . . was very wise." (Michael Sprinker, *Magill's Cinema Annual,* 1986)

Don Ameche won an Academy Award as Best Supporting Actor. A sequel, directed by Dan Petrie, based on a script by Stephen McPherson and Elizabeth Bradley, and featuring much of the original cast plus Elaine Stritch and Courtney Cox, was filmed in Florida in the spring of 1988.

COMA (United Artists, 1978) C 113 mins.

Producer, Martin Erlichman; director, Michael Crichton; based on the novel by Robin Cook; screenplay, Crichton; music, Jerry Goldsmith; production designer, Albert Brenner; set decorator, Rick Simpson; costumes/wardrobe, Eddie Marks, Yvonne Kubis; assistant directors, William McGarry, Ron Grow; sound, Bill Griffith, William McCaughey, Michael J. Kohut, Aaron Rochin; camera, Victor J. Kemper, Gerald Hirschfeld; editor, David Bretherton.

Genevieve Bujold (Dr. Susan Wheeler); Michael Douglas (Dr. Mark Bellows); Elizabeth Ashley (Mrs. Emerson); Rip Torn (Dr. George); Richard Widmark (Dr. Harris); Lois Chiles (Nancy Greenly); Harry Rhodes (Dr. Mordelind); Gary Barton (Computer Technician); Frank Downing (Kelly); Richard Doyle (Jim); Alan Haufrect (Dr. Marcus); Lance Le Gault (Vince); Michael MacRae (Chief Resident); Betty McGuire (Nurse); Tom Selleck (Murphy); Charles Siebert (Dr. Goodman); William Wintersole (Lab Technician).

Following a supposedly simple operation, Nancy Greenly (Lois Chiles) falls into a coma and dies, causing much grief to her friend, Dr. Susan Wheeler (Genevieve Bujold). Looking into the matter Susan finds several similar cases at Boston Memorial Hospital and tells her boyfriend, Dr. Mark Bellows (Michael Douglas), who can find no ready connection. Investigating the matter leads Susan to the remote Jefferson Institute where she discovers the bodies of many young people including Nancy, in suspended animation. She learns the bodies are being preserved for future transplant operations for people who will pay to retain their youth and she also learns that hospital administrators Dr. Harris (Richard Widmark) and Dr. George (Rip Torn) are behind the nightmarish scheme. Both men learn of her actions and plan to silence her with Harris performing an operation on her; but Bellows finds out the truth and stops him.

This medical sci-fi melodrama grossed a surprisingly solid $14,600,000 at the box-office, although it met with mixed critical and audience reaction to its perverted tale of physicians not only toying with the art of human creation, but playing unconscionably with human life. In *The Film Encyclopedia: Science Fiction* (1984), Phil Hardy termed it "a taut medical thriller" and added, " . . . [Director

Michael] Crichton handles the inventive, disturbing plot with panache and assurance. The film's sense of paranoia is further enhanced by Crichton's concentration on his characters in preference to the welter of medical technology on show." On the other hand, Donald C. Willis wrote in *Horror and Science Fiction Films II* (1982), "Pat medical-conspiracy material, padded out with superfluous suspense sequences. Predictable plot and character development. The two showpiece sequences—the bodies-hanging-in-bags and the coma-victims-on-wires—aren't really worth the narrative trip."

COMPUTER KILLERS see HORROR HOSPITAL.

CONDOR (Orion TV/ABC-TV, 8/10/86) C 75 mins.

Executive producer, Jerry Golod; producers, Peter Nelson, Arnold Orglini; director, Virgil W. Vogel; teleplay, Len Janson, Chuck Menville; production designer, Bill Hiney; art director, Bob Zillix; music, Ken Heller; sound, Barry Thomas; camera, Thom Neuwirth; supervising editor, Jim Gross; assistant editors, Terry Szustek, Alan Shefland.

Ray Wise (Chris Proctor); Wendy Kilbourne (Lisa Hampton), Victor Polizos (Commissioner Ward); James Avery (Cass); Cassandra Gava (Sumiko); Craig Stevens (Cyrus Hampton); Carolyn Seymour (Rachel Hawkins); Shawn Michaels (Watch Commander); Marie Roccuzzo (Manny); Catherine Battistone (Lieutenant); Barbara Beckley (Watch Controller); Diana Bellamy (Opera Singer); Gene Bicknell (Bartender); Myra Chason (Pirate Pete's Waitress); Tony Epper, Wendell Wright (Cops); Mike Freeman (Technician); Phil Forudacar (Guard).

In the 2lst century, super agent Chris Proctor (Ray Wise), an agent for Condor, is forced to take Lisa Hampton (Wendy Kilbourne) as his partner after his former teammate is murdered in Singapore. He is not happy with Lisa because she is an Android but she proves to be a worthy comrade when they are assigned to stop wicked Rachel Hawkins (Carolyn Seymour), an escaped convict, who has stolen codes which give her access to the Los Angeles police computers, thus making it easy for her to cause havoc in the city and even control police robots. At first the police chief (Victor Polizos) scoffs at the seriousness of the plot, but when Rachel uses a missile to shut down a power plant, he joins forces with the two agents who eventually stop the evil woman.

Shown as part of a science fiction telefilm double bill with NORTHSTAR (q.v.), this ABC-TV movie unsuccessfully molds the spy and sci-fi genres into a dull affair which was a pilot for an unsold series. *Variety* quipped, "Film is aptly named. . . . it's for the birds." *The Hollywood Reporter* wrote the film was " . . . another far-fetched sci-fi fizzler that expends much energy going a short distance . . . poorly plotted and never flies. This is a retro-story gussied up in the vestments of a too simplistic what-might-be."

CONGO PONGO see WHITE PONGO.

THE CORPSE VANISHES (Monogram, 1942) 64 mins.

Producers, Sam Katzman, Jack Dietz; associate producer, Barney Sarecky; director, Wallace Fox; story, Sam Robins, Gerald Schnitzer; screenplay, Harvey Gates; art director, David Milton; music, Johnny Lange and Lew Porter; camera, Art Reed; editor, Robert Golden.

Bela Lugosi (Dr. Lorenz); Luana Walters (Pat Hunter); Tristram Coffin (Dr. Foster); Elizabeth Russell (Countess Lorenz); Minerva Urecal (Eagah); Kenneth Harlan (Keenan); Vince Barnett (Sandy); Joan Barclay (Alice); Frank Moran (Angel); Angelo Rossitto (Toby); Gwen Kenyon (Peggy); George Eldridge (Mike).

THE CORPSE VANISHES was the fourth of nine thrillers Bela Lugosi made for Monogram producers Sam Katzman and Jack Dietz and it may be the best of the lot; certainly one of the most fun. Since the word "virgin" could not be used in connection with the film, the mad scientist here kidnaps new brides for his experiments with glandular liquids extracted from them. Naturally Lugosi is at his best as the mad doctor and matching his performance is Luana Waiters as the sexy, ingratiating newshound. *The Motion Picture Herald* judged the film ". . . . a gruesome offering. . . . All the accoutrements of this type of entertainment are included. . . ."

Young brides are dying suddenly at the altar and their corpses disappearing before they reach the funeral home. Reporter Pat Hunter (Luana Walters) traces the story to orchid expert, Dr. Lorenz (Bela Lugosi), who lives in a remote, spooky house with his wife, Countess Lorenz (Elizabeth Russell). Pat interviews the doctor and meets his assistant, Dr. Foster (Tristram Coffin), to whom she is attracted. Forced to stay at the Lorenz manse due to a storm, Pat witnesses the physician murdering a henchman, Angel (Frank Moran), after the latter has followed her as she investigates the passages under the house (where she finds Lorenz's laboratory and the bodies of the stolen brides). Pat sets a scheme to capture Lorenz, with the aid of Foster, but it backfires and Pat is sedated and abducted by Lorenz who plans to use her body fluids to keep his aged wife youthful. The operation fails, however, when old hag Eagah (Minerva Urecal) stabs Lorenz because he was responsible for the death of her sons, The Angel and dwarf Toby (Angelo Rossitto). The Countess, becoming a withered crone, murders Eagah, but dies of old age as Foster and the police arrive to save Pat.

The most offbeat aspect of this rich entertainment is the sight of hag Eagah with her loving sons, the moronic Angel and dwarf Toby. Then there is the scene where Lugosi beats The Angel with a whip for an infraction as Toby jumps up and down gleefully. Logical film viewers may wonder why Lorenz remains so loyal to his spouse, a real shrew.

British release title: THE CASE OF THE MISSING BRIDES.

THE CRAIG KENNEDY SERIAL see THE CARTER CASE.

THE CRAWLING HAND (Hansen Enterprises/American International, 1963) 89 mins.

Producer, Joseph F. Robertson; director, Herbert L. Strock; story, Robert Young, Joseph Granston; screenplay, William Edelson, Strock; assistant directors, Michael Messinger, Wilbur D'Arcy; sound, Earl Snyder; camera, Willard Vander Veer; editor, Strock.

Peter Breck (Steve Curan); Kent Taylor (Doc Weitzberg); Rod Lauren (Paul Lawrence); Sirry Steffen (Marta Farnstrom); Alan Hale, Jr. (Sheriff); Arline Judge (Mrs. Hotchkiss); and: Richard Arlen, Ross Elliott, Allison Hayes, Ed Wermer, Tris Coffin, Syd Saylor, G. Stanley Jones, Ashley Cowan, Jock Putnam, Beverly Lunsford, Andy Andrews.

On a space journey, an astronaut is taken over by an alien life form and begs ground control to terminate his mission. The spaceship is destroyed as it nears Earth, but one of the astronaut's hands retains life. Teenager Paul Lawrence (Rod Lauren) discovers the dismembered hand on a beach and takes it back to his boarding house where the thing comes to life and strangles his landlady (Arline Judge). Meanwhile two scientists, Steve Curan (Peter Breck) and Doc Weitzberg (Kent Taylor), search for remains of the astronaut. The sheriff (Alan Hale, Jr.) investigates the landlady's murder and Paul is cleared of the crime. However, the hand tries to kill him but fails, although the alien life form begins to control all his actions. The fingerprints on the dead woman are those of the astronaut, alerting the scientists he must still be alive. The hand attempts to force Paul to commit several killings but he finally throws the hand from him and it ends up in a dump where it is devoured by several cats.

THE CRAWLING HAND has to be one of the most embarrassingly memorable schlock sci-fi hacked-out thrillers of all time. The premise is played out so straight it borders on the hilarious. Each time Rod Lauren is possessed by the alien hand he gets black lines under his eyes. A rock group called The Rivingtons show up and sing "Papa Oom Mow Mow" a couple of times and the finale has to be one of the worst fates ever to befall a screen monster. The picture is filled with fine players—Burt Reynolds tested for the role of one of the scientists but the part went to Kent Taylor. *Fangoria* magazine (January, 1984) summed it up best when reviewing the film's home video release on Video Gems: "The movie is cliched, poorly acted, and for whatever reason, quite enjoyable."

The film was directed, co-written, and edited by Herbert L. Strock who also helmed I WAS A TEENAGE FRANKENSTEIN (1957) (q.v.).

THE CRAWLING MONSTER see THE CREEPING TERROR.

THE CRAWLING TERROR see THE CREEPING TERROR.

THE CREATION OF THE HUMANOIDS (Emerson Film Enterprises, 1962) C 75 mins.

Producers, Wesley Barry, Edward J. Kay; director, Barry; based on ideas in the novel *The Humanoids* by Jack Williamson; screenplay, Jay Simms; art director, Ted Rich; makeup, Jack Pierce; camera, Hal Mohr; editor, Leonard W. Herman.

Don Megowan (Cragis); Don Doolittle (Dr. Raven); Erika Elliott (Maxine); Frances McCann (Esme); David Cross (Pax); Richard Vath (Mark); Malcolm Smith (Court); George Milan (Acto); Dudley Manlove (Logan); Reid Hammond (Hart); Gil Frye (Orus); Pat Bradley (Moffitt); William Hunter (Ward); Paul Sheriff (Cop); Alton Tabor (Volunteer).

This minor, but fairly well-produced, sci-fier has a narrow cult following as noted by *Castle of Frankenstein* magazine (No. 8, 1966), "This 'futuristic Frankenstein' film achieved certain underground fame after leading pop film-art experimentalist Andy Warhol called it one of the year's best movies." On the other hand, Donald C. Willis in *Horror and Science Fiction Films* (1972) labeled it, "Pretty silly." Michael Weldon in *The Psychotronic Encyclopedia of Film* (1983) judged it "An incredible little film" and added, it was "Filmed on minimal sets as if it were a play. . . ."

Set in the 23rd century following the last war, the human race is surviving by using robots (purple/green in color) to accomplish all the work. The Earthlings, thanks to atomic fallout, are barely able to reproduce themselves and the robots are used to rebuild cities. Scientist Dr. Raven (Don Doolittle) tries to humanize the robots by giving them blood transfusions from humans and as a result, Maxine (Erika Elliott), the lover of security officer Cragis (Don Megowan), becomes enamoured with one of the creations. Cragis, who distrusts the robots, tries to stop Raven only to learn that he, Cragis, too is a humanoid.

THE CREATION OF THE HUMANOIDS was produced by Edward J. Kay, best remembered for his music scores at Monogram Pictures in the 1940s, and former child star Wesley Barry, who also directed. The makeup was by Jack P. Pierce, who created the famous monster makeups (Frankenstein's monster, The Wolfman, the Mummy, etc.) at Universal in the 1930s and 1940s. In a supporting role was Dudley Manlove, the florid radio performer best noted for his outlandish appearance as the alien invader in PLAN 9 FROM OUTER SPACE (1959) (see B/V).

CREATURE (Cardinal Entertainment/Trans World Entertainment, 1985) C 100 mins.

Executive producers, Moshe Diamoant, Ronnie Hadar; producers, William Dunn, Jr., William Malone; director, Malone; associate producer, Don Stern; screenplay, Malone, Alan Reed; music/music directors, Thomas Chase, Steve Rucker; assistant directors, Gordon Boos, Steven Wolfe, Matt Hinkley, Ned McCloud; visual effects, L. A. Effects Group; animator creator, Robert Alvarez; special designs, Robert Skotak; set decorators, Bernard Munoz, Steve Caldwell, Dan Smith, Debra Deliso; scenic decorators, Jay Burkhart, Joe Braus; special effects weapons creator, Robert Short Productions; technical adviser, Robert Short; special props creator, David Nelson; Titan Find creature creator, Michael McCraken; sound, Steve Nelson, Trevor Black, Sheridan Wolf Eldridge; special sound effects, Jamie Ledner; camera, Harry Mathias; effects camera, George Dodge; editor, Betty Cohen.

Stan Ivar (Captain Mike Davidson); Wendy Schaal (Beth Sladen); Lyman Ward (David Perkins); Robert Jaffe (John Pennel); Diane Salinger (Melanie Bryce); Annette McCarthy (Dr. Wendy H. Oliver); Marie Laurin (Susan Delambre); Klaus Kinski (Hans Rudy Hofner); John Stinson, Jim McKeny (Astronauts); Buckley Norris, Michael Griswold (Concord Technicians); David Moses (Mission Co-ordinator); Earl Dugan, Thomas C. James (Technicians); Eileen Seeley (Voice Over Loud Speaker in Concord); Ashit Shah, Bud Walker (Dead Germans).

On Saturn's moon Titan, a space team is destroyed mysteriously and another group of astronauts, headed by Mike Davidson (Stan Ivar), the ship's captain, and David Perkins (Lyman Ward), an executive for the company who has bankrolled the expedition, go to study the situation. Aboard, among others, are scientist Dr. Wendy Oliver (Annette McCarthy), and security officer Melanie Bryce

(Diane Salinger). Their ship is damaged badly when they crash land on Titan and they discover a rival West German company has beaten them to the moon. All of the crew, however, prove to be dead except for Hans Rudy Hofner (Klaus Kinski), captain of the vessel. He alerts them the sphere is controlled by a monstrous creature which kills its victims and then animates them to kill others. Hofner has rigged a bomb to destroy the creature but it gets him first. The thing also murders astronaut Susan Delambra (Marie Laurin) whose dead body lures another astronaut, John Pennel (Robert Jaffe) to his demise. The latter's corpse then chases Melanie, who runs away. Only Davidson, Perkins and astronaut Beth Sladen (Wendy Schall) remain on the ship which is invaded by the alien. They plan to use Hofner's bomb to kill the creature but their trap fails and Perkins is killed, although the monster is trapped by the bomb which fails to explode. Melanie returns, having escaped death on the moon, and shoots a bullet which causes the bomb to explode, finally killing the alien. The survivors return home on the German vessel.

With elements of ALIEN and the remake of THE THING (qq.v.), CREATURE was initially issued as THE TITAN FIND. *Variety* suggested, "Playing it for laughs could have helped but production opts for a serious tone unlikely to please fans of the genre. . . . Unfortunately, effects are basically routine with few thrills and chills to be found." Tom Milne in the British *Monthly Film Bulletin* noted, " . . . the set of cardboard characters is being clumsily shuffled through a routine made no less dreary by knowing allusions to THE THING." He also complained that William Malone's " . . . direction owes more to schlock tactics than to style."

THE CREATURE WASN'T NICE (Creature Films, 1981) C 88 mins.

Executive producers, Albert Schwartz, Elyse England; producer, Mark Haggard; associate producers, Alain Silver, Patrick Regan; director/screenplay, Bruce Kimmel; production designer, Lee Cole; assistant director, Regan; makeup, Hud Bannon; costumes, Katherine Dover; music, David Spear; visual effects, William J. Hedge, Bob Greenberg, Anthony Doublin, Thomas H. Payne; miniatures, Jene Omens, Carl Bostrom, Will Guest; sound, James Mountain; camera, Denny Lavi; editor, David Blangsted.

Cindy Williams (McHugh); Bruce Kimmel (John); Leslie Nielsen (Jameson); Gerrit Graham (Rodzinski); Patrick Macnee (Stark); Ron Kurowski (Creature).

Also called SPACESHIP, this sci-fi spoof was written and directed by Bruce Kimmel, who also co-starred as well as co-writing the film's songs. A blatant poke in the ribs at ALIEN (1977) (q.v.)

and its ilk, the film was just not funny and hardly amusing. Its mugging style of comedy did not work and it sadly wasted one of Hollywood's finest talents, Cindy Williams, who appears to have had more success on the small screen than in theatrical releases.

In the year 2012 the crew of a spaceship finds a new planet and names it Stark, after the scientist (Patrick Macnee) on board. Exploring the planet they find a deserted city and a life form which they bring aboard. Stark hooks the creature (Ron Kurowski) to a communications computer to determine its intelligence level and the thing sings "I Want to Eat Your Face." The crew members, including the captain (Leslie Nielsen) and his co-pilot (Gerritt Graham), and astronauts McHugh (Cindy Williams) and John (Bruce Kimmel), realize the creature is out to destroy them. Stark, however, wants to protect the alien life form from them but it kills him and the captain and co-pilot before McHugh tricks it out of the craft and into endless space.

Variety pegged the film as " . . . a likably silly sendup of outer-space horror pics . . . but misses too many times for breakaway success." In *Horror and Science Fiction Films III* (1984), Donald C. Willis labels it "ALIEN with laughs" and kindly judges it "A generally deft, charming minor-league comedy." Overall, the movie is a dud.

CREATURE WITH THE ATOM BRAIN (Columbia, 1955) C 69 mins.

Producer, Sam Katzman; director, Edward L. Cahn; story/screenplay, Curt Siodmak; music director, Mischa Bakaleinikoff; art director, Paul Palmentola; camera, Fred Jackman, Jr.; editor, Aaron Stell.

Richard Denning (Dr. Chet Walker); Angela Stevens (Joyce Walker); S. John Launer (Captain Dave Harris); Michael Granger (Frank Buchanan); Gregory Gaye (Professor Steigg); Linda Bennett (Penny Walker); Tristram Coffin (District Attorney MacGraw); Harry Lauter, Larry Blake (Reporters); Charles Evans (Chief Camden); Pierre Watkin (Mayor Bremer); Lane Chandler (General Saunders); Nelson Leigh (Dr. Kenneth Norton); Don C. Harvey (Lester Banning); Paul Hoffman (Dunn); Edward Coch (Jason Franchot); and: Karl Davis.

Police doctor Chet Walker (Richard Denning) investigates the murder of a gambling house boss by a man (Karl Davis) with apparent superstrength. He learns the killer is powered by atomic energy. It seems that exiled crime boss Frank Buchanan (Michael Granger) has returned to the United States and is bankrolling Professor Steigg (Gregory Gaye) in his experiments with atomic-controlled zombies which he creates by removing the victim's brain and replacing it with a radio device. Buchanan uses the atomic zombies to eliminate those responsible for his deportation and he starts destroying the city, much to the chagrin of the district attorney (Tristram Coffin) and the mayor (Pierre Watkin). Chet realizes the situation and puts the last proposed victims in jail, but Buchanan operates on Chet's partner, Captain Dave Harris (S. John Launer) and he commits the murders. The police corner Buchanan in his laboratory and once the zombies are thwarted, Buchanan is killed.

In the book *Incredibly Strange Films* (1986), Jim Morton evaluates the film as " . . . a classic example of fifties science fiction. Unforgettable is the scene in which the police battle to the death with zombies in front of the scientist's house. The 'creatures' in the film wear business suits and ties, and aside from the stitches in their foreheads, appear quite normal. Yet their mundane appearances make the monsters all the more frightening."

This film was veteran director Edward L. Cahn's first venture into the sci-fi-horror field after nearly a quarter of a century as a director. This production was quickly followed by numerous other genre outings such as THE SHE CREATURE (1956) (q.v.), ZOMBIES OF MORA-TAU (1957), VOODOO WOMAN (1957) (q.v.), INVASION OF THE SAUCER MEN (1957) (see B/V), CURSE OF THE FACELESS MAN (1958), IT! THE TERROR FROM BEYOND SPACE (1958) (see B/V) which inspired ALIEN (q.v.); THE FOUR SKULLS OF JONATHAN DRAKE (1959), INVISIBLE INVADERS (1959) (see B/V), which inspired NIGHT OF THE LIVING DEAD (see B/V); and BEAUTY AND THE BEAST (1963).

THE CREATURE'S REVENGE see BRAIN OF BLOOD.

THE CREEPING TERROR (Metropolitan International Pictures, 1964) 75 mins.

Producer, William Alland; director, John Sherwood; screenplay, Arthur Ross; sets, Clifford Stone, John Lackey; camera, Maury Gertsman; editor, Argyle Nelson, Jr.

With: Vic Savage [Argyle Nelson, Jr.], Shannon O'Neil, William Thourlby, Norman Boone, John Caresio, Buddy Mize, Robin James, Lewis Lawson, Ray Wickman, Connie Valdie, Rita Tubin, Kelly Adams, Karl Goldenberg, Jack King, Mary Price, Mary Field, Al Lewis, Ken Savage, Myra Lee, Jerre Kopp, Louise Lawson.

A.k.a.: THE CRAWLING MONSTER.

A flying saucer crash lands in the desert and the Army and scientists converge on the craft to gain information on the ship and its occupants. One of two creatures in the craft escapes and heads for Lake Tahoe where the large furry, snake-like thing devours several people, including a chorus girl, the patrons of a drive-in movie, and teenagers at a rock 'n roll beach party. The Army corners the creature and kills it with a bazooka. One of the scientists returns to the spacecraft and destroys the remaining monster with a flame thrower. Meanwhile the creatures' victims have been analyzed by the invaders and their knowledge has been transmitted to the aliens' home planet.

Shot on location in Lake Tahoe, sans a soundtrack, this unbelievably bad sci-fier was also known as THE CRAWLING TERROR. Since no dialogue was recorded, the entire movie uses a narrative voiceover. *Fangoria* magazine (December, 1983) pointed out some of the feature's almost endless deficiencies in its evaluation of the video cassette edition: " . . . there is a monumental monster that no one can forget (a bunch of guys huddled under a carpet) and a gut-wrenching finale in which a soldier pulls the pin out of [a] grenade and hangs onto it for 27 seconds before tossing it at the creature. The movie does, however, suggest the possibility that there is a limit to how bad a movie can be and still remain within the realm of unintentional entertainment." Michael Weldon wrote in *The Psychotronic Encyclopedia of Film* (1983), "The feet of people playing the alien are visible." He added, "The story of two hairy monsters resembling giant erect penises with suction mouths at the base is undoubtedly one of the top five worst movies of all time."

Producer/director/co-editor Argyle (Art) Nelson, Jr. also played the lead role in the film billed as Vic Savage. It boggles the mind to think that he soon became co-editor of George Stevens' Biblical spectacle, THE GREATEST STORY EVERY TOLD (1965).

CREEPSHOW (Warner Bros., 1982) C 129 mins.

Executive producer, Salah Hassanein; producer, Richard Rubinstein; director, George Romero; screenplay, Stephen King; production designer, Cletus Anderson; music, John Harrison; costumes, Barbara Anderson; special makeup effects, Tom Savini; camera, Michael Gornick; editors, Pat Buba, Paul Hirsch, Michael Spolan, Romero.

Hal Holbrook (Henry Northrop); Adrienne Barbeau (Wilma Northrop); Fritz Weaver (Dexter Stanley); Leslie Nielsen (Richard Vickers); Carrie Nye (Sylvia Grantham); E. G. Marshall (Upton Pratt); Viveca Lindfors (Aunt Bedelia); Stephen King (Jordy Verrill); Ed Harris (Hank); Ted Danson (Harry); Robert Harper (Charlie); Jon Lormer (Nute); Joe King (Billy); Ted Atkins (Stan).

The screen collaboration of director George Romero (NIGHT OF THE LIVING DEAD (1968) (see B/V) and writer Stephen King, resulted in this episodic horror/sci-fi feature film which utilized comic book stories and the comics themselves to bridge the quintet of tales unfolded herein. The production is well executed but the mini-scenarios are weak, although the strong cast (save for King's performance) holds the narrative together.

"Father's Day," the opening sequence is difficult to follow, telling of a hated father returning from the grave. The next episode, "The Lonesome Death of Jordy Verrill" is downright awful, thanks to author Stephen King's amateurish theatricals as the segment's sole performer. He appears as a dullard hillbilly who decides to market a meteorite which falls on his wreck of a farm, only to have its effects turn him into a plant-like creature. Much better is "Something to Tide You Over" in which wealthy husband Richard Vickers (Leslie Nielsen) causes the watery death of his wife and her lover, only to have them haunt him into a similar fate. The film's best sequence and the one that brings this movie into the sci-fi genre is "The Crate" in which a professor (Fritz Weaver) unleashes a horrible monster which has been brought back from an Arctic expedition. The film closes with the disgusting "They're Creeping Up on You," in which a reclusive and cleanliness-phobic millionaire (E. G. Marshall) is attacked by thousands of bugs.

The best element of CREEPSHOW is the fact the film does not take itself seriously. *Variety* noted the presence of " . . . animated ads for jokes and body-building books commonly found in old comic books. There's a real sense of fun in Romero and King's playful approach."

The film, which did respectably well at the box-office spawned a sequel, CREEPSHOW II (1986).

THE CRIMSON GHOST (Republic, 1946) twelve chapters.

Associate producer, Ronald Davidson; directors, William Witney, Fred C. Brannon; screenplay, Albert De Mond, Basil Dickey, Jesse Duffy, Sol Shor; music, Mort Glickman; special effects, Howard Lydecker, Theodore Lydecker; camera, Bud Thackery; editors, Harold R. Minter, Cliff Bell.

Charles Quigley (Duncan Richards); Linda Stirling (Diana Farnsworth); Clayton Moore (Ashe); I. Stanford Jolley (Blackton); Kenne Duncan (Professor Chambers); Forrest Taylor (Van Wyck); Emmett Vogan (Anderson); Sam Flint (Maxwell); Joe Forte (Professor Parker); Stanley Price (Fator); Wheaton Chambers (Wilson); Tom Steele (Stricker); Dale Van Sickel (Harte); Rex Lease (Bain); Fred Graham (Zane); Bud Wolfe (Gross); Joe Yrigoyen (Henchman).

Viveca Lindfors in CREEPSHOW (1982).

Chapters: 1) Atomic Peril; 2) Thunderbolt; 3) The Fatal Sacrifice; 4) The Laughing Skull; 5) Flaming Death; 6) Mystery of the Mountain; 7) Electrocution; 8) The Slave Collar; 9) Blazing Fury; 10) The Trap that Failed; 11) Double Murder; 12) The Invisible Trail.

The Cyclotrode is a counter-weapon invented by internationally known physicist Professor Chambers (Kenne Duncan) to counteract atomic bombs by cutting off electrical power in the vicinity of powerful rays. Later two henchmen (Clayton Moore, Joe Yrigoyen) of the masked Crimson Ghost attempt to steal the device and Chambers destroys it. Just as he is about to be kidnapped by the henchmen, Chambers is saved by criminologist Duncan Richards (Charles Quigley) whom he tells that he has another counter-weapon hidden away. Professor Parker (Joe Forte) and secretary Diana Farnsworth (Linda Stirling) try to help Chambers but he is again kidnapped and Diana alerts Duncan. He locates Chambers, the Crimson Ghost, and the remaining henchman (Moore) at the vault which contains the second device, but the crooks escape with Chambers and Duncan pursuing. The Crimson Ghost unleashes a

Charles Quigley and Linda Stirling in the serial THE CRIMSON GHOST (1946).

ray which causes Duncan's car to crack up. He escapes injury and saves Chambers. The Crimson Ghost is unmasked as one of the doctor's supposed allies.

This fun serial, with the title villain clad in a black robe and hood and wearing a skull mask, cast usual serial villain Kenne Duncan in the role of the good guy professor. The producers went to great lengths to keep the culprit's true identity a secret till the final moments of the last chapter. Beneath the robes and mask The Crimson Ghost was played by Bud Geary, but when he spoke his voice was dubbed by I. Stanford Jolley, who briefly played another character in the cliffhanger. *Neither* of these actors, however, proved to be playing the part at the final denouement. It is interesting to note that the atomic age had become a part of the serial format by this time with the crux of the chapterplay being a device to neutralize the much feared atomic bomb.

In 1966 this serial was issued to TV in a 100-minute feature version called CYCLOTRODE X.

CRITTERS (New Line Cinema, 1986) C 86 mins.

Executive producer, Robert Shaye; producer, Rupert Harvey; associate producer, Sara Risher; director, Stephen Herek; screenplay, Herek, Dominic Muir; additional material, Don Opper; assistant directors, Leon Dudevoir, Perry Husman, Whitney Hunter, George Parra, Bob Esposito, Matia Karrell, Linda Grame; second unit directors, George Perkins, Matia Karrell; production designer, Gregg Fonseca; art directors, Philip Foreman, Isabel Madden; set decorator, Anne Huntley; Critters designer/supervisors, Charlie Chiodo, Steve Chiodo; music, David Newman; songs: Terrence Mann, Richie Vetter, and Dodie Pettit; Vetter and Pettit; Brian Drucks and Lee Howard; Che Zuro; costume designer supervisor, Hilary Wright; makeup, Kat Estocin; transformation/Zanti makeup, Christopher Biggs; stunt co-ordinator, Mike Cassidy; sound, Donald Summer, Robert S. Willis; camera, Tim Shuhrstedt; additional camera, Russ Carpenter; second unit camera, Chris Tufty; miniature effects camera, John Huneck, Ivan Craig; editor, Larry Bock.

Dee Wallace Stone (Helen Brown); M. Emmet Walsh (Harv); Billy Green Bush (Jay Brown); Scott Grimes (Brad Brown); Nadine Van Der Velde (April Brown); Don Opper (Charlie McFadden); Billy Zane (Steve Elliot); Ethan Phillips (Jeff Barnes); Terrence Mann (Jonny Steele); Jeremy Lawrence (Reverend Miller); Lin Shaye (Sally); Michael Lee Gogin (Warden Zanti); Art Frankel (Ed); Douglas Koth (First and Second Bowler); Montrose Hagins (Organist/Second Woman); Roger Hampton (Jake); Chuck Lindsley, David Stenstrom (Pool Player); Adele Malis-Morey (Woman).

Following the success of ANDROID (1982) (q.v.), several of the creative talents who worked on that project, including producer Rupert Harvey, director Stephen Harek, scripter Dominic Muir, and co-scripter/actor Don Opper, turned out this serious sci-fi outing, which starred Dee Wallace Stone, who as Dee Wallace had headlined such horror features as THE HOWLING (1981) and CUJO (1983). This production emerged more of a Western in an updated sci-fi guise, with the aliens taking over the role of Indians who attack an isolated farm family. Steve Jenkins assessed in the British *Monthly Film Bulletin* that the feature " . . . disappointingly lacks the 'subversive' edge which characterized the best of New World. . . . The result is a film which is likeable but quite unremarkable." *Variety* registered, "Critters resemble oversize hairballs and roll like tumbleweeds when prodded into action, the perfect menace for this irritatingly insipid and lightweight film which unfolds with plodding predictability and leaves few cliches unturned. . . . .The final result is neither scary nor humorous and the only real feeling a viewer leaves with is the hope that the sequel intimated in the final frames never gets made." Charles Ryweck of *The Hollywood Reporter* added, "In approaching CRITTERS, audiences will have to suspend belief—in one jolly sequence the critters talk among themselves and subtitles appear on the screen."

Murderous Krites, small aliens, manage to escape from a maximum security astroid and come to Earth (to Grovers Bend, Kansas), being chased by two alien bounty hunters who have the ability to take on the guise of Earthlings. The Krites kill a cow as a local drunk (Don Opper) tells the sheriff (M. Emmet Walsh) he has received messages from them. Young April Brown (Nadine Van Der Velde) is sexually attracted to her boyfriend Steve Elliot (Billy Zane), much to the chagrin of her parents Jay and Helen (Billy Green Bush, Dee Wallace Stone), while her younger brother Brad (Scott Grimes) makes the usual nuisance of himself. The aliens kill a policeman (Ethan Phillips) and then attack the Brown farm as the bounty hunters tear up a nearby town searching for the Krites. Tiring from the attack, Jay sends Brad to town for help and he meets the bounty hunters and brings them back to the farm where a battle takes place with the aliens destroyed along with the farm. When the bounty hunters depart, they restore the farm. The Krites, apparently, have taken sanctuary in unhatched chicken eggs.

CRITTERS grossed $10,936,572 in its first ten weeks at the domestic box-office. In 1988 CRITTERS II was produced, directed by Mick Garris for New Line Cinema.

THE CURSE OF FRANKENSTEIN (Warner Bros., 1957) C 83 mins.

Executive producer, Michael Carreras; producer, Anthony Hinds; director, Terence Fisher; based on the novel *Frankenstein* by Mary Shelley; screenplay, Jimmy Sangster; art director, Ted Marshall; music, James Bernard; makeup, Phil Leakey, Roy Ashton; camera, Jack Asher; editor, James Needs.

Peter Cushing (Baron Victor Frankenstein): Christopher Lee (The Creature); Hazel Court (Elizabeth); Robert Urquhart (Paul Krempe); Valerie Gaunt (Justine); Noel Hood (Aunt Sophia); Marjorie Hume (Mother); Melvyn Hayes (The Young Victor); Sally Walsh (The Young Elizabeth); Paul Hardtmuth (Professor Bernstein); Fred Johnson (Grandfather); Claude Kingston (Small Boy); Henry Cained (Schoolmaster); Michael Mulcaster (Werner); Patrick Troughton (Kurt); Joseph Behrman (Fritzi); Hugh Dempster (Burgomaster); Anne Blake (Burgomaster's Wife); Raymond Bullett (Father Felix); Alex Gallier, Eugene Leahy (Priests); Ernest Jay (Undertaker); J. Trevor Davis (Uncle); Bartlett Mullins (Tramp).

In the mid-1950s, Hammer Films of England began producing sci-fi and horror films in great abundance. One of its projects was a remake of FRANKENSTEIN (1931) (see B/V) which was closer than the 1932 Universal film (q.v.) to Mary Shelley's novel, although it too varied the plot. Made on a $350,000 budget, the production grossed over $8,000,000 worldwide and set the studio on a course which resulted in a half dozen more "Frankenstein" features, plus scores of other horror/sci-fi/fantasy movies. Shot in color, this movie caused a stir for its graphic (very mild by today's standards) gore effects and the London *Observer* critic labeled it ". . . . among the half-dozen most repulsive films I have ever encountered."

Baron Victor Frankenstein (Peter Cushing) is awaiting execution and he tells his story to a priest. He had been experimenting with the revival of the dead with his teacher Paul Krempe (Robert Urquhart) and together they created an artificial man. Victor murdered a famous scientist for his brain which was then accidentally damaged by Krempe. Krempe, now fearing for Victor's fiancee Elizabeth (Hazel Court), refuses to help give the creature life and Victor's experiment fails. But that night a lightning bolt animates the being and brings him (Christopher Lee) to life. The Creature turns on Frankenstein and then kills an old man, forcing his creator to shoot him. Victor revives the Creature and has it eliminate a servant girl (Valerie Gaunt) who was pregnant with the Baron's child. When Krempe finds out the Creature is living, he informs the police. The Creature escapes and abducts Elizabeth. The Baron fires at it, but instead kills his fiancee and as the creation attacks him he incinerates

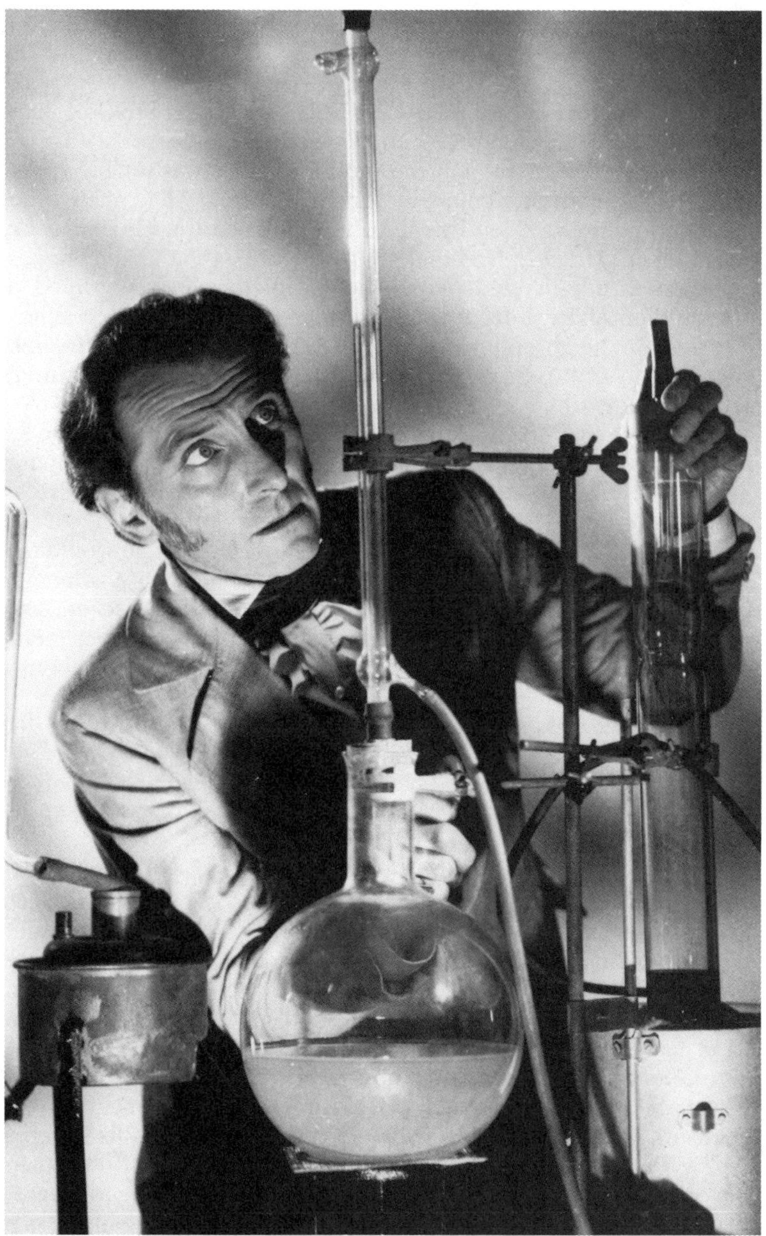

Peter Cushing in THE CURSE OF FRANKENSTEIN (1957).

it with the fire from a lamp. Krempe later visits Victor in prison, but will not admit the Creature ever existed. The Baron is sent to the Guillotine.

THE CURSE OF FRANKENSTEIN made genre stars of Peter Cushing and Christopher Lee and helped revive horror/sci-fi films in the late 1950s. Although the motion picture was unable to use Universal's copyrighted makeup for the monster, it had many other pluses going for it. Allen Eyles, Robert Adkinson and Nicholas Fry noted in *The House of Horror* (1973), " . . . it had the novelty appeal of being a fully-fledged *British* horror picture; it was filmed in colour, then a fairly infrequent addition to this kind of film, but most effective in heightening the impact of bleeding parts and fiery violence; it took its subject seriously, helped by Peter Cushing's sensitive performance as the Baron, and restored dignity to a monster that, in Universal's hands, had degenerated into a stooge for Abbott and Costello; and, finally, it was made with care, if not perhaps inspiration, and its sets, music and photography were all excellent."

As every new retelling of Mary Shelley's classic tale would (re) demonstrate, audiences never tire of witnessing man challenging nature's ability to create human life. As civilization's technology advances, the gap between the probability of such experiments coming true and the actuality of it really happening in life becomes less.

Note: Extracts from this feature appear in LOLITA, the 1962 film starring James Mason, Shelley Winters, and Sue Lyons.

CURSE OF THE SWAMP CREATURE (Azalea/American International TV, 1966) C 80 mins.

Producer/director, Larry Buchanan; screenplay, Tony Huston; art director, Jim Sullivan; camera, Ralph K. Johnson; editor, Buchanan.

John Agar (Barry Rogers); Francine York (Doctor's Wife); and: Shirley McLine, Bill Thurman, Jeff Alexander, Cal Duggan, Charles McLine, Bill McGee, Rodger Ready, Ted Mitchell, Tony Houston, Annabelle Weenick, J. V. Lee, Gayle Johnson, Michael Tolden, Pat Cranshaw, Naomi Lee.

Geologist Barry Rogers (John Agar), with two associates (Jeff Alexander, Cal Duggan) and a beautiful woman (Francine York) head into deadly Bayou swamp country seeking oil deposits. Deep in the swampland they find a compound where a doctor (Bill Thurman) is working on secret experiments. They learn he is trying to create a being; half human, half alligator. The local natives burn a likeness of the doctor, fearing the creatures he has created. The physician takes the visitors prisoner and experiments on his wife (Shirley McLine) turning her into a swamp creature who is eaten by alligators when she falls into a reptile pit. The situation turns when the doctor becomes a swamp monster himself; he too is devoured by the creatures upon whom he experimented.

A very loose remake of VOODOO WOMAN (1957) (q.v.), CURSE OF THE SWAMP CREATURE is one of a series of remakes producer/director Larry Buchanan churned out for American International Television in the 1960s on a $20,000 per film budget; shooting in 16mm and tepid color. The monster mask—a bald, latex rubber creation with ping pong balls for eyes—also showed up in Buchanan's CREATURE OF DESTRUCTION (1967) and IT'S ALIVE (1968) (q.v.). The film is a bit more colorful and less stilted than the other AIP-TV remakes because of its eerie swampland atmosphere, but production, acting, and scenario are just as crazily inane as in the other entries. In *The Psychotronic Encyclopedia of Film* (1983), Michael Weldon tagged it, "An all-time favorite of American insomniacs."

CYCLOTRODE X see THE CRIMSON GHOST.

THE DARK CRYSTAL (Universal, 1982) C 97 mins.

Executive producer, David Lazer; associate producer, Bruce Sharman; producers, Jim Henson, Gary Kurtz; directors, Henson, Frank Oz; story, Henson; screenplay, David Odell; conceptual designer, Brian Froud; production designer, Harry Lange; art director, Charles Bishop; choreography/mime, Jean Pierre Amiel; assistant director, Dusty Symonds; camera, Oswald Morris; editor, Ralph Kemplen.

Character Performers: Jim Henson (Jen); Kathryn Mullen (Kira); Frank Oz (Aughra); Dave Golez (Fizzgig); Frank Oz (Chamberlain); Dave Goelz (General); Jim Henson (High Priest); Steve Whitmire (Scientist); Louise Gold (Gourmand); Brian Huehl (Ornamentalist); Bob Payne (Historian); Mike Quinn (Slave Master); Tim Rose (Treasurer); Brian Muehl (Urzah/Dying Master); Jean Pierre Amiel (Weaver); Hugh Spight (Cook); Robbie Barnett (Numerologist); Swee Lim (Hunter); Simon Williamson (Chanter); Hus Lefvant (Scribe); Toby Philpott (Alchemist); Dave Greenaway, Richard Slaughter (Healer).

Character Voices: Stephen Garlick (Jen); Lisa Maxwell (Kira); Billie Whitelaw (Aughra); Percy Edwards (Fizzgig); Barry Dennen (Chamberlain); Michael Kilgarriff (General); Jerry Nelson (High Priest/Dying Emperor); Steve Whitmire (Scientist); Thick Wilson (Gourmand); Brian Muehl (Ornamentalist); John Baddeley (Historian); David Buck (Slave Master); Charles Collingwood (Treasurer);

Brian Muehl (Dying Master); Sean Barrett (Urzah); Joseph O'Conor (Urskeks/Narrator).

Issued for the moppet Yuletide trade in 1982, THE DARK CRYSTAL was made by the creators of "The Muppets," Jim Henson and Frank Oz. Here they have established a nether world inhabited by seemingly endless variations of wee creatures and monsters; a good versus evil moral tale for the younger set. *Variety* termed the feature, " . . . a dazzling technological and artistic achievement."

On another world, the good and evil of a planet will become one after a thousand years because the Dark Crystal has lost a shard. The planet is ruled by the evil Skeksis, who use the monstrous Garthims to maintain their control. The good inhabitants are the Gelflings and there are very few of them surviving. Two of them, Jen and Kira, fall in love and decide to stop the Skeksis by finding the missing shard and replacing it in the Dark Crystal, thus avoiding doomsday. The young Gelflings are assisted by the Mystics, whose leader picked Jen for the mission, and Aughra, the old hag keeper of an oracle who does not like the Gelflings but does what is required when she is needed. The Gelflings fight all kinds of obstacles and creatures, before returning the shard to the Crystal. The Skeksis are defeated.

Variety further commented, "The creation of a small world of memorable characters is the main contribution of Henson and Oz. In addition, the actually sketchy tale and the balance between fearsome and gruesome-monsters and adorable, usually tiny innocents, is exceptionally well handled. With the two gelflings providing the romance, plus tension and terror from the unbelievably ugly Skeksis (whose soldiers resemble giant cockroaches), there's need for considerable humor and it is generously provided."

"THE DARK CRYSTAL is, by all odds, the most densely-and-delightfully-populated other-universe of creatures since Starevitch's THE MAGIC CLOCK (1926). . . . It is, in effect, an unending roll call of unearthly Muppets, and, as such, constitutes one of the more imaginative deployments of men-(and hands)-in-suits creations in fantasy films." (Donald C. Willis, *Horror and Science Fiction Films III* [1984]).

DARK STAR (Jack H. Harris Enterprises, 1974) C 83 mins.

Executive producer, Jack H. Harris; producer/director/ screenplay, John Carpenter, Dan O'Bannon; assistant director, J. Stein Kaplan; production designer, O'Bannon; special effects, Bob Greenberg; camera, Douglas Knapp; editor, O'Bannon.

Brian Narelle (Doolittle); Andreijah Pahich (Talby); Carl Kuniholm (Boiler); Dan O'Bannon (Sergeant Pinback); Cookie Knapp (Voice of Computer); Joe Sanders (Commander Powell).

For twenty years the crew of the ship *Dark Star* has roamed the universe in search of unstable stars to destroy so that earthlings of the 21st century may safely colonize other planets. The crew, Doolittle (Brian Narelle), Sergeant Pinback (Dan O'Bannon); Boiler (Carl Kuniholm), and Talby (Andreijah Pahich), have long been burned out on their mission and can barely cope with one another and their shipboard life. The craft itself, is fallng apart, and one of its Thermostellar bombs, which has a high intelligence of its own, is itching to explode, even if it destroys the craft. The ship's computer (voice of Cookie Knapp) is of no help and the crew becomes endangered when the craft's pet alien, a large protoplasm ball, threatens Pinback. At a loss as to what to do, the crew summons aid from their dead commanding officer Powell (Joe Sanders), who has been kept frozen so he might return to them in time of need. It is the bomb, however, which convinces the crew that by exploding it will make their dreams, and its, come true.

John Carpenter and Dan O'Bannon made DARK STAR as a 40 minute student film project in the early 1970s and distributor Jack H. Harris provided the funds to add footage and Bob Greenberg's excellent special effects for theatrical release. The tongue-in-cheek satire of 2001: A SPACE ODYSSEY (see: B/V) and the "Star Trek" teleseries won immediate critical approval and launched the motion picture careers of Carpenter (THE THING, q.v.) and O'Bannon (ALIEN, q.v.). *Fangoria* magazine (October, 1983) wrote of the VCI video cassette release of the feature, "The movie is an amusing offbeat spoof of space movies that gets good mileage out of an endearingly amateurish cast . . . and surprisingly good, low-budget effects. The film's sense of humor is truly unique, and every once in a while it scores a real bull's eye. . . ."

Like most cult films, DARK STAR is either adored or disliked by viewers. While its wry humor is refreshing, its characters are NOT very likeable and more often than not the film's pacing drags.

D.A.R.Y.L. (Paramount, 1985) C 100 mins.

Producer, John Heyman; co-producers, Burtt Harris, Gabrielle Kelly; director, Simon Wincer; screenplay, David Ambrose, Allan Scott, Jeffrey Ellis; music, Marvin Hamlisch; camera, Frank Watts; editor, Adrian Carr.

Mary Beth Hurt (Joyce Richardson); Michael McKean (Andy Richardson); Kathryn Walker (Ellen Lamb); Colleen Camp (Elaine); Josef Sommer (Dr. Jeffrey Stewart); Barret Oliver (D.A.R.Y.L.); Daniel Bryan Corkill (Turtle); Steve Ryan (Howie Fox); Amy Linker (Sherie).

A ten year old boy, Daryl (Barret Oliver) is left stranded in the Florida woods when his driver disappears. A welfare officer, Howie Fox (Steve Ryan), finds the boy and arranges for him to stay with foster parents Andy (Michael McKean) and Joyce (Mary Beth Hurt) Richardson. Daryl becomes pals with Fox's son Turtle (Danny Corkill) and proves to be a very highly intelligent child. Two government scientists, Ellen Lamb (Kathryn Walker) and Dr. Jeffrey Stewart (Josef Sommer), pretend to be his parents. Dr. Stewart examines the boy and reports back to the military who have actually developed the youngster as D.A.R.Y.L., (an acronym which stands for Data Analyzing Robot Youth Lifeform), an experimental robot. The military brass decide to destroy Daryl but Dr. Stewart fakes his death and the two escape from the base, although the doctor is killed by police at a roadblock. Daryl steals a supersonic jet and flies to the Richardsons' home and bails out just as the plane is shot down by the army. He falls into a lake and is pronounced dead at a nearby hospital. Ellen, however, reactivates the boy's computer brain and he is reunited with the Richardsons.

D.A.R.Y.L. attempts to unite the elements of the family unit with futuristic robot clone experiments, with only fair creative and mild box-office results. The film is at its best when the boy/robot is proving himself to be superior mentally and physically to his peers and the scene where he intentionally throws a championship baseball game to make pal Turtle the local hero, is especially well-executed. Overall, though, the motion picture is a too predictable thriller lacking a strong enough plot or engrossing situations.

In the British *Monthly Film Bulletin,* Adrian Wooton noted, ". . . the two halves of D.A.R.Y.L.'s plot—family comedy and high-tech thriller—never completely gel. . . . The plot is led into greater and greater absurdities, with a happy ending that would have most children shaking their heads in disbelief, never mind those unfortunate adults dragged along for the evening."

DAUGHTER OF DR. JEKYLL (Allied Artists, 1957) 71 mins.

Producer, Jack Pollexfen; director, Edgar G. Ulmer; suggested by the novel *The Strange Case of Dr. Jekyll and Mr. Hyde* by Robert Louis Stevenson; screenplay, Pollexfen; art director, Theobold Holsopple; music supervisor, Melvyn Leonard; camera, John F. Warren; editor, Holbrook N. Todd.

John Agar (George Hastings); Gloria Talbott (Janet Smith); Arthur Shields (Dr. Lomas); John Dierkes (Jacob); Martha Wentworth (Mrs. Merchant); Mollie McCart (Maggie).

See: DR. JEKYLL AND MR. HYDE (essay).

DAWN OF THE DEAD (United Film Distributing, 1979) C 125 mins.

Presenters, Herbert Steinmann, Billy Baxter; producer, Richard Rubinstein; director/screenplay, George Romero; script consultant, Dario Argento; costumes, Josie Caruso; assistant director, Christine Forrest; makeup/special effects, Tom Savini; sound, Tony Buba; camera, Michael Gornick; editors, Romero, Kenneth Davidow.

David Emge (Stephen); Ken Foree (Peter); Scott Reiniger (Roger); Gaylen Ross (Francine).

The amateurish gore-fest NIGHT OF THE LIVING DEAD (1968) (see B/V) became a cult classic and bestowed cult status on its director, George Romero. Based in Pittsburgh, Romero continued to churn out a number of feature films; some technically proficient, which cemented his professional status. Since he had planned a "Living Dead" trilogy, his followers long awaited the second installment in the series, DAWN OF THE DEAD, which was issued in 1979. Unlike the original feature, this picture was shot in color and contains a good dollop of dark humor. The gore-choked film's main highlight is Tam Savini's makeup and special effects.

The flesh-devouring zombies who prey on humans have returned. Radiation fallout is to blame for their existence and the only way to eradicate them is a bullet in the head. Two former National Guardsmen, Roger (Scott Reiniger) and Peter (Ken Foree), team with television technician Francine (Gaylen Ross) and her boyfriend Stephen (David Emge) in escaping from the zombies. They fly a helicopter, first into a ghetto area and then take refuge in a shopping mall. There they fortify the place, killing any attacking zombies, and become happy with their new-found largess in the large shopping arena. A gang of bikers, however, invade the premises, and the zombies follow with the bikers joyfully picking them off before being overcome by them. Stephen and Roger are killed, but Peter and Francine escape.

In his essay on George Romero in *Incredibly Strange Films* (1986), Mark Spainhower wrote, "The most visually luxurious of Romero's films, DAWN expands the investigation of territoriality to unexpectedly satiric extremes by confining the action within a suburban shopping mall. . . . The gore is even more explicit than in NIGHT (thanks to Savini), yet somehow absurd—this movie has some of the funniest gore around."

The third installment, DAY OF THE DEAD would appear in 1985.

THE DAY AFTER (ABC-TV, 11/20/83) C 135 mins.

Producer, Robert A. Papazian; associate producer, Stephanie Austin; director, Nicholas Meyer; teleplay, Edward Hume; music, David Raksin; production designer, Peter M. Wooley; camera, Gayne Rescher; editors, Robert Florio, William Paul Dornisch.

Jason Robards (Dr. Russell Oakes); JoBeth Williams (Nancy Bauer); Steve Guttenberg (Stephen Klein); John Cullum (Jim Dahlberg); John Lithgow (Joe Huxley); Bibi Besch (Eve Dahlberg); Lori Lethin (Denis Dahlberg); Amy Madigan (Alison Ransom); Jeff East (Bruce Gallatin); Georgann Johnson (Helen Oakes); William Allen Young (Airman McCoy); Calvin Jung (Dr. Sam Hachiya); Lin McCarthy (Dr. Austin); Dennis Lipscomb (Reverend Walker); Clayton Day (Dennis Hendry); Doug Scott (Danny Dahlberg); Ellen Anthony (Jolene Dahlberg); Kyle Aletter (Marilyn Oakes); Alston Ahearn (Cynthia); William Allyn (Professor); Antonie Becker (Ellen Hendry); Pamela Brown (Nurse); Jonathan Estrin (Julian French); Stephen Furst (Aldo); Arliss Howard (Tom Cooper); Rosanna Huffman (Dr. Wallenberg); Barbara Iley (Cleo Mackey); Madison Mason (TV Host); Bob Meister (Cody); Vahan Moosekian (Mack); George Petrie (Dr. Landowska); Glenn Robards, Tom Spratley (Barbers); Stan Wilson (Vinnie Conrad).

Shown on ABC-TV on its "ABC THEATRE," this made-for-television film was issued theatrically abroad and also to the home video market. It received a great deal of hoopla prior to its airing because of its grim subject matter of a nuclear holocaust; so much so that even the White House wanted to respond to it. A post-telecast program, "Viewpoint," showed various viewpoints on nuclear war, including the government's reaction to the production. *Variety* noted, "To watch THE DAY AFTER is a thoughtful experience, maybe even terrifying."

Relations between the U.S. and the Soviet Union are so strained that the merest incident can spark the release of nuclear missiles by each side. The narrative focuses on Lawrence, Kansas (site of America's missile arsenal) and on two families in particular. In one situation, a college professor (Jason Robards) is adjusting to his daughter's (Kyle Aletter) moving to Boston, while in the other, a farmer (John Cullum) and his family struggle to survive the initial falling of missiles near their farm; the blast having destroyed the nearby town. Following the nuclear attacks, there are survivors, but many are deathly sick from radioactive fallout and the human race faces a gloomy future at best.

Adding to the fuel of this controversial project is the no-holds-barred manner in which actual nuclear destruction is depicted. There is no poetic romanticized vision of the holocaust (as in Stanley Kramer's ON THE BEACH, 1959, see B/V) but a picturization of death via incineration for a great many.

The highly-regarded project received twelve Emmy Award nominations; including: Outstanding Drama Special; Best Direction, Best Teleplay, Best Cinematography, Best Art Direction/Set

Decoration, and Best Supporting Actor (John Lithgow). THE DAY AFTER won an Emmy for Best Special Visual Effects.

DAY OF THE DEAD (United Film Distribution, 1985) C 102 mins.

Executive producer, Salah M. Hassanein; producer, Richard P. Rubinstein; co-producer, David Ball; associate producer, Ed Lammi; director/screenplay, George A. Romero; assistant directors, John Harrison, Katarina Wittich, Annie Loeffler; production designer, Cletus Anderson; art director, Bruce Miller; set decorator, Jan Pascale; costumes, Barbara Anderson; stunt co-ordinator, Taso N. Stavrakis; music, John Harrison; makeup, Bonnie Priore, Jeanne Josefszyk, Natalka Voslakov; special makeup effects, Tom Savini; special effects, Steve Kirshoff, Mark Mann; camera, Michael Gornick; editor, Pasquale Buba.

Lori Cardille (Sarah); Terry Alexander (John); Joseph Pilato (Captain Rhodes); Jarlath Conroy (McDermott); Antone DiLeo (Miguel); Gary Howard Klar (Steele); Ralph Marrero (Rickles); John Amplas (Fisher); Richard Liberty (Dr. Logan); Howard Sherman (Bub); Don Brockett, William Cameron, Deborah Carter, Winnie Flynn, Debra Gordon, Jeff Hogan, Barbara Holmes, David Kindlon, Bruce Kirkpatrick, William Andrew Laczko, Susan Martinelli, Kim Maxwell, Barbara Russell, Gene A. Saraceni, John Schwartz, Mark Tierno, Michael Trcic, John Vulich (Zombies); and: Philip G. Kellams, Taso N. Stavrakis, Gregory Nicotero.

The third and final entry in the "Living Dead" trilogy came in 1985, with DAY OF THE DEAD reverting to the downbeat, depressing ambiance of the initial feature. In Florida a few human survivors of the zombie plague have taken refuge in a massive underground military complex. The survivors have split into two groups with Captain Rhodes (Joseph Pilato) leading military followers who favor the continued obliteration of the living dead with bullets. Rhodes' position is not tenable since the zombies now massively outnumber the humans. A female scientist (Lori Cardille), however, heading another contingent, wants to attempt co-existence with the zombies and an older scientist, Dr. Logan (Richard Liberty) prefers experimenting on the zombies to tame them into domestication. One of the soldiers, Miguel (Antone DiLeo), who is Sarah's boyfriend, just want to survive and leave all conflict behind. Eventually through his researching, Dr. Logan "tames" one of the zombies whom he calls Bub (Howard Sherman) and teaches him pacification with humans. A confrontation with Rhodes leaves Miguel near death and he lets the zombies into the complex, while Rhodes kills Dr. Logan for allowing Bub to feed on their dead comrades. In the invasion, Rhodes is devoured, while Sarah and a few others escape by helicopter to a remote island, uninfested by zombies.

Kim Newman points out in the British *Monthly Film Bulletin,* " . . . DAY OF THE DEAD is not necessarily the final chapter. . . . the game plan was for NIGHT to deal with the beginnings of the holocaust, DAWN to follow the complete breakdown of society, and DAY to depict a future world where living and dead have come to terms, and trained zombies fight wars on behalf of human masters who live in walled city states. . . . [T]o avoid the stigma of an 'X' rating, Romero had to abandon his elaborate original script for DAY OF THE DEAD as economically unfeasible. Instead, he has backtracked in the history of the zombie apocalypse to the point when—following hints dropped in DAWN—it is generally acknowledged that the living dead retain some species of conscious thought, and science in the shape of the Frankensteinian Dr. Logan is pioneering the domestication of the zombies hordes."

There were many reviewers who noted that DAY OF THE DEAD had a healthy similarity to Richard Matheson's novel *I Am Legend* (1954) (which itself inspired two science fiction films) and that although the film's working title of ZOMBIES IN THE WHITE HOUSE was abandoned, the movie still pokes strong satirical barbs at the political and military situation in the United States.

Not to disappoint fans or to lessen the box-office, this issue of the DEAD story contains the usual doses of blood and gore as the flesh-eating zombies prowl again.

See: DAWN OF THE DEAD.

THE DAY TIME ENDED (Compass International/Manson International, 1980) C 79 mins.

Executive producer, Charles Band; producers, Wayne Schmidt, Steve Niell; director, John "Bud" Cardos; screenplay, Schmidt, J. Larry Carroll, David Schmoeller; music, Richard Band; assistant director, Bob Shug; art director, Rusty Rosene; models design, Lain Liska; models execution, Greg Jein; special visual effects, Paul W. Gentry, David Allen, Randy Cook; "City of Light" visual effects, Jim Danforth; stop motion animation, Lyle Conway; animation effects supervisor, Pete Kuran; camera, John A. Morrill; editor, Ted Nicolaou.

Jim Davis (Grant Williams); Christopher Mitchum (Richard); Dorothy Malone (Anna Williams); Marcy Lafferty (Beth Williams); Scott Kolden (Steve Williams); Natasha Ryan (Jenny Williams); and: Roberto Contreras.

Originally filmed as TIME WARP, this story tells of a typical American family, Grant Williams (Jim Davis) and his wife Anna (Dorothy Malone) and their children Richard (Chris Mitchum),

Beth (Marcy Lafferty), and Jenny (Natasha Ryan), moving into a new home in the country only to find it has been vandalized. Suddenly they are in a time warp with the house shifting to another planet where an alien creature attempts to protect them from two malevolent ones. The alien also warns them the Earth is about to be destroyed.

Highlighted by David Allan's special effects, THE DAY TIME ENDED is a hard-to-follow sci-fier which some sources claim was never really completed. This could explain the variances in plot activities ranging from aliens to dinosaurs to a city of light and crystal. Even the cast, although a good one, appears to be amazed by the plot continuity.

Director John "Bud" Cardos previously helmed the fine KINGDOM OF THE SPIDERS (1977) (q.v.) and THE DARK (1979) in the genre, but this proved to be his least effort. Phil Hardy reports in *The Film Encyclopedia: Science Fiction* (1984), "The references to Steven Spielberg, back to CLOSE ENCOUNTERS OF THE THIRD KIND (1977) and forward to E.T. and POLTERGEIST (both 1982) abound, but the special effects . . . are so crudely animated as to destroy any belief in the plot. The result is a film with no sense of wonder at all." It should be noted the film's subplot of having an alien playmate for one of the children does, in fact, predate E.T. (1982) (q.v.).

DEMONS OF THE SWAMP see ATTACK OF THE GIANT LEECHES.

DESTROY ALL MONSTERS (American International, 1969) C 88 mins.

Executive producer, Tomoyuki Tanaka; director, Ishiro Honda; screenplay, Kaoru Mabuchi, Honda; art director, Takeo Kita; music, Akira Ifukube; assistant director, Seiji Tani; sound, Shoichi Yoshizawa, Hisashi Shimonaga; special effects, Eiji Tsuburaya, Sadamasa Arikawa; camera, Taiichi Kankura; editor, Ryohei Fujii.

Akira Kubo (Captain Katsuo Yamabe); Jun Tazaki (Dr. Yoshido); Yoshio Tsuchiya (Dr. Otani); Kyoko Ai (Queen of the Kilaaks); Yukiko Kobayashi (Kyoko); Kenji Sawara (Nishikawa); Andrew Hughes (Dr. Stevenson); and: Nadao Kirino, Susumu Kurobe, Hisaya Ito, Yoshifumi Tajima, Naoya Kusakawa, Ikio Sawamura, Wataru Omura, Kazuo Suzuki, Yutaka Sada.

"GODZILLA attacks New York! RODAN devastates Moscow! MANDA obliterates London! and MOTHRA smashes Peking!" read the poster blurb when AIP issued DESTROY ALL MONSTERS in the U.S. Made by Toho in 1968 as KAIJU

SOSHINGEKI [Attack of the Marching Monsters] by perennial Japanese monster movie director Ishiro Honda, the film, with its futuristic, science fiction overtones, is an all-star monster party, not only featuring the above prehistoric creatures but also Minya, Spiega, Baragon, Angurus, Varan, and the three-headed flying alien dragon Ghidrah. Footage from other past Toho productions (THE WARS OF THE GARGANTUAS, FRANKENSTEIN CONQUERS THE WORLD; GHIDRAH, THE THREE-HEADED MONSTER!; RODAN) was interpolated to save money. DESTROY ALL MONSTERS is the biggest and most enjoyable celluloid monster rally of all time.

By the year 1999 the various monsters which terrorized Japan have been isolated on Ogasaware, a Japanese island where they are kept under scientific observation. A gas destroys the island's electronic barriers and the monsters leave, attacking the world's capitols. When it is determined that alien forces are responsible for the trouble, Moon Rocket SY-3 commander, Captain Yamabe (Akira Kubo), is ordered to the island to investigate. There he meets a female alien who informs him she is from the planet Kilaak, whose inhabitants will conquer the Earth and are controlling the monsters to do so. Later it is proved the aliens are building a base under Tokyo and Yamabe destroys their Moon base and they turn to stone. To save themselves, the remaining aliens summon Ghidrah, the three-headed flying dragon, and he does battle with Godzilla and the other monsters who are now under Earth's control. Ghidrah is overwhelmed, Moon Rocket SY-3 destroys the alien's craft, and Godzilla demolishes the Kilaak headquarters. The monsters return to their island paradise.

THE DEVIL AND DR. FRANKENSTEIN see FLESH FOR FRANKENSTEIN.

THE DEVIL COMMANDS (Columbia, 1941) 66 mins.

Producer, Wallace MacDonald; director, Edward Dmytryk; based on the novel *The Edge of Running Water* by William Sloane; screenplay, Robert D. Andrews, Milton Gunzburg; music director, Morris W. Stoloff; sound effects, Phil Faulkner; camera, Allen G. Siegler; editor, Al Clark.

Boris Karloff (Dr. Julian Blair); Richard Fiske (Dr. Richard Sayles); Amanda Duff (Anne Blair); Anne Revere (Mrs. Walters); Dorothy Adams (Mrs. Marcy); Walter Baldwin (Seth Marcy); Shirley Warde (Helen Blair); Kenneth MacDonald (Sheriff Willis); Ralph Penney (Karl).

The colleagues of Dr. Julian Blair (Boris Karloff) scoff at his theories about communicating with the dead through electrical brain waves. He creates a machine to record these brain waves from beyond the grave and tries to put them into practice when his wife Helen (Shirley Warde) is killed in an auto accident. Using a medium, Mrs. Walters (Anne Revere), who can withstand huge amounts of electricity, he seeks to communicate with his wife. During one experiment, a servant (Ralph Penney) is injured and becomes a deaf-mute and later a maid is frightened to death. Blair's daughter, Anne (Amanda Duff), comes to his remote home and begs him to stop his experiments but when Mrs. Walters dies from too much voltage he forces Anne to replace her. Finally the locals rebel against Blair's experiments and grave-robbing and surround his home. Anne's fiancé Dr. Richard Sayles (Richard Fiske) is able to get her out before Blair's laboratory equipment explodes, killing him and destroying the house.

THE DEVIL COMMANDS is an exciting and horrific film, coming near the end of a series of such thrillers in which star Boris Karloff played mad scientists in outings like NIGHT KEY (1937), THE MAN THEY COULD NOT HANG (1939) (q.v.),BLACK FRIDAY (1940) (see B/V), THE MAN WITH NINE LIVES (1940), BEFORE I HANG (1940) (q.v.), and THE APE (1940) (q.v.). Of course Karloff was perfectly at home in the role of the scientist, a part he played with equal shares of pathos and madness. *The Motion Picture Herald* judged the film "somewhat slow" but "contains the necessary continuity to make it an interesting melodrama of horror and suspense." When issued in Great Britain the censors cut it considerably, making the finale incomprehensible when the scene where Karloff contacts his dead wife was removed. Still, the *Kinematograph Weekly* evaluated it a "spectacular thriller" and added, "Whatever the mood, the film is good Karloff and that is good enough to promote excitement and win the approbation of the masses."

THE DEVIL DOLL (Metro-Goldwyn-Mayer, 1936) 70 mins.

Producer, Edward J. Mannix; director, Tod Browning; based on the novel *Burn, Witch, Burn!* by Abraham P. Merritt and the story "The Witch of Timbuctoo" by Browning; adaptor, Browning; screenplay, Garrett Fort, Guy Endore, Erich von Stroheim; art director, Cedric Gibbons; music, Franz Waxman; camera, Leonard Smith; editor, Frederick Y. Smith.

Lionel Barrymore (Paul Levond/Madame Mandelip); Maureen O'Sullivan (Lorraine); Frank Lawton (Toto); Robert Greig (Couvet); Lucy Beaumont (Mme. Lavond); Henry B. Walthall (Marcel); Grace Ford (Lachna); Pedro de Cordoba (Metin); Arthur Hohl (Radin);

Rafaela Ottiano (Malita); Juanita Quigley (Marquierte); Claire du Brey (Mme. Coulvet); Rollo Lloyd (Detective); E. Allyn Warren (Commissioner).

Prisoners Paul Lavond (Lionel Barrymore) and Marcel (Henry B. Walthall) escape from Devil's Island and return to the latter's home where his wife Malita (Rafaela Ottiano) has been continuing his experiments with shrinking people into small dolls. Marcel dies and Lavond and Malita move to Paris where Lavond masquerades as an old woman, Madame Mandelip, while planting the small dolls in the homes of the crooked bankers responsible for the swindle which sent him to prison. When the dolls are in place he orders the dolls to come to life and kill the men. Lavond also finds his pretty daughter Lorraine (Maureen O'Sullivan) who is in love with a young man, Toto (Frank Lawton). Eventually the crazed Malita turns on Lavond and their doll shop, which is a front for the laboratory used to make the "dolls," goes up in flames and Malita is killed. Lavond, however, survives and sees to it that his daughter has a life of happiness.

THE DEVIL DOLL was directed by Tod Browning, famous for his 1920s thrillers with Lon Chaney, as well as such talkie chillers as DRACULA (1931), FREAKS (1932), and THE MARK OF THE VAMPIRE (1935). The character played by Lionel Barrymore in THE DEVIL DOLL is very reminiscent of the one done by Lon Chaney in his two versions of THE UNHOLY THREE (1925, 1930); Browning helmed the 1925 edition. The most engrossing aspect of THE DEVIL DOLL was the scientific sets used to create the miniature humans and the effects employed to animate them. Franz Waxman's eerie score was also a creative plus. Syndicated columnist Louella Parsons wrote, "Eerie and creepy, [it] will intrigue any audience with its sheer novelty." Barrymore repeated the lead assignment on Parsons' radio show, "Hollywood Hotel," to promote the production.

THE DEVIL DOLL's premise of miniaturized people was used more than two decades later by producer/director Bert I. Gordon in ATTACK OF THE PUPPET PEOPLE (1958) (see B/V), but it was a bland affair compared to this highly competent thriller.

THE DIABOLICAL DR. Z (U.S. Films, 1967) 86 mins.

Producers, Serge Silberman, Michel Safra; director, Henri Baum [Jesus Franco]; story, David Kuhne [Franco] screenplay, Jess Franco [Franco], Jean-Claude Carriere; art director, Antonio Cortes; music, Daniel White; assistant director, Robert Demolliere; sound, Louis Hochet; camera, Clemente Manzano; editor, Jean Feyte.

Mabel Karr (Irma); Fernando Montes (Philip); Estella Blain (Nadia); Antonio J. Escribano (Dr. Von Zimmer); Howard Vernon

(Vikass); Guy Mairesse (Bergen); and: Marcelo Arroita, Lucia Prado, Ana Castor, Alberto Dalbes, Jose Maria Prada.

"Nothing Ever Stripped Your Nerves Screamingly Raw Like THE DIABOLICAL DR. Z. . . . SEE! The Evil Dr. Z and His Brain Machine! SEE! The Evil Dr. Z Turn Humans Into Demons! SEE! All New Terror That Grips You with The Exotic Dance of Death!" read the poster blurb for this Spanish-French co-production issued in the United States by U.S. Films. The motion picture actually provides little promised by its advertising and was a hard-to-fathom sci-fi effort made even more incoherent in its dubbed English language version. For the record, director, Henri Baum, co-scripter Jess Franco and book author David Kuhne are all the same person—the high prolific but near-hack Spanish director Jesus Franco.

After working three decades on a device, which, when inserted in the brain, will control a person's will, Dr. Von Zimmer (Antonio J. Escribano) dies after being ridiculed by the authorities. His daughter, Irma (Mabel Karr), also a doctor, vows revenge. She changes her looks via cosmetic surgery after murdering a young woman and taking her identity. She is assisted by Bergen (Guy Mairesse), an escaped convict upon whom her father had experimented before his death. Irma meets beautiful Nadia (Estella Blain), a dancer, and decides to use her to kill the three scientists most responsible for her father's death. Irma kidnaps Nadia and operates on her, implanting the mind-controlling device in her brain. The latter murders the first victim, Vikass (Howard Vernon). Irma and Bergen kill the second scientist. The third scientist, despite being watchful, is eventually killed too. In a showdown with the police, Irma is killed and Philip, a young doctor in love with Nadia, tells her he will do all he can to return her to normalcy.

DR. BLACK, MR. HYDE (Dimension Pictures, 1976) C 87 mins.

Producer, Charles Walker; director, William Crain; suggested by the novel *The Strange Case of Dr. Jekyll and Mr. Hyde* by Robert Louis Stevenson; screenplay, Larry LeBron; music, Johnn Pate; camera, Tak Fujimoto; editor, Jack Horger.

Bernie Casey (Dr. Pride/Hyde); Rosalind Cash (Dr. Billie Worth); Marie O'Henry (Linda); Ji-Tu Cumbuka (Lieutenant Jackson); Milt Kogan (Lieutenant O'Connor); Stu Gilliam (Silky).

A.k.a. THE WATTS MONSTER.

See: DR. JEKYLL AND MR. HYDE (essay).

DR. HECKYL AND MR. HYPE see DR. JEKYLL AND MR. HYDE (essay).

DR. JEKYLL AND MISS OSBOURNE see DR. JEKYLL AND MR. HYDE (essay).

DR. JEKYLL AND MR. HYDE (Selig Polyscope, 1908) 1,035 feet.
Producer, Colonel William Selig; based on the novel *The Strange Case of Dr. Jekyll and Mr. Hyde* by Robert Louis Stevenson.
A.k.a. THE MODERN DR. JEKYLL.

DR. JEKYLL AND MR. HYDE (Thanhouser, 1912) 1 reel.
Producer, Edwin Thanhouser, director, Lucius Henderson; based on the novel *The Strange Case of Dr. Jekyll and Mr. Hyde* by Robert Louis Stevenson.
James Cruze (Dr. Jekyll), Marguerite Snow (Minister's Daughter); Harry Benham (Mr. Hyde).

DR. JEKYLL AND MR. HYDE (Universal, 1913) 2 reels.
Producer, Carl Laemmle; director, King Baggot; based on the novel *The Strange Case of Dr. Jekyll and Mr. Hyde* by Robert Louis Stevenson.
King Baggot (Dr. Jekyll/Mr. Hyde); Jane Gail (Alice); Matt Snyder (Alice's Father); Howard Crampton (Dr. Lanyon); William Sorrell (Utterson).

DR. JEKYLL AND MR. HYDE (Paramount, 1920) 6,355 feet.
Producer, Adolph Zukor; director, John S. Robertson; based on the novel *The Strange Case of Dr. Jekyll and Mr. Hyde* by Robert Louis Stevenson; screenplay, Clara S. Beranger; camera, Ray Overbough.
John Barrymore (Dr. Henry Jekyll/Edward Hyde); Nita Naldi (Gina); Brandon Hurst (Sir George Carew); Louis Wolheim (Cabaret Manager); Charles Lane (Dr. Richard Lanyon); George Stevens (Poole); Martha Mansfield (Millicent Carew); J. Malcolm Dunn (John Utterson); Cecil Clovelly (Edward Enfield).

DR. JEKYLL AND MR. HYDE (Paramount, 1932) 98 mins.
Producer/director, Rouben Mamoulian; based on the novel *The Strange Case of Dr. Jekyll and Mr. Hyde* by Robert Louis Stevenson; screenplay, Samuel Hoffenstein, Percy Heath; art director, Hans Drier; makeup, Wally Westmore; camera, Karl Struss; editor, William Shea.
Fredric March (Dr. Henry Jekyll/Mr. Hyde); Miriam Hopkins (Ivy Pearson); Rose Hobart (Muriel Carew); Holmes Herbert (Dr. Lanyon); Edgar Norton (Poole); Halliwell Hobbes (Brigadier General Carew); Arnold Lucy (Utterson); Tempe Pigott (Mrs. Hawkins);

Colonel McDonnell (Hobson); Eric Wilton (Briggs); Douglas Walton (Student); John Rogers (Waiter); Murdock MacQuarrie (Doctor); Major Sam Harris (Dance Extra).

DR. JEKYLL AND MR. HYDE (Metro-Goldwyn-Mayer, 1941) 127 mins.

Producer/director, Victor Fleming; based on the novel *The Strange Case of Dr. Jekyll and Mr. Hyde* by Robert Louis Stevenson; screenplay, John Lee Mahin; art directors, Cedric Gibbons, Daniel B. Cathcart; set decorator, Edwin B. Willis; music, Franz Waxman; men's wardrobe; Gile Steele; women's gowns, Adrian; makeup, Jack Dawn; montages, Peter Ballbusch; special effects, Warren Newcombe; camera, Joseph Ruttenberg; editor, Howard F. Kress.

Spencer Tracy (Dr. Henry Jekyll/Mr. Hyde); Ingrid Bergman (Ivy Peterson); Lana Turner (Beatrix Emery); Donald Crisp (Sir Charles Emery); Barton MacLane (Sam Higgins); C. Aubrey Smith (Bishop); Peter Godfrey (Poole); Sara Allgood (Mrs. Higgins); Frederic Worlock (Dr. Heath); William Tannen (Interne Fenwick); Frances Robinson (Marcia); Denis Green (Freddie); Billy Bevan (Mr. Weller); Forrester Harvey (Old Prouty); Lumsden Hare (Colonel Weymouth); Lawrence Grant (Dr. Courtland); John Barclay (Constable); Doris Lloyd (Mrs. Marley); Gwen Gaze (Mrs. French); Hillary Brooke (Mrs. Arnold); Mary Field (Wife); Aubrey Mather (Inspector).

DR. JEKYLL AND SISTER HYDE (American International, 1972) C 97 mins.

Producers, Albert Fennell, Brian Clemens; director, Roy Ward Baker; suggested by the novel *The Strange Case of Dr. Jekyll and Mr. Hyde* by Robert Louis Stevenson; screenplay, Clemens; production designer, Robert Jones; makeup, John Wilcox; music, David Whittaker; music director, Philip Martell; song, Brian Clemens; camera, Norman Warwick; editor, James Needs.

Ralph Bates (Dr. Jekyll); Martine Beswick (Sister Hyde); Gerald Sim (Professor Robertson); Lewis Flander (Howard); Dorothy Alison (Mrs. Spencer); Neil Wilson (Older Policeman); Ivor Dean (Burke); Paul Whitsun-Jones (Sergeant Danvers); Philip Madoc (Byker); Tony Calvin (Hare); Susan Brodrick (Susan); Dan Meaden (Town Crier); Virginia Wetherell (Betsy); Geoffrey Kenion (Policeman); Irene Bradshaw (Yvonne); Anna Brett (Julie); Jackie Poole (Margie); Rosemary Lord (Marie); Petula Portell (Petra); Pat Brackenbury (Helen); Liz Romanoff (Emma); Will Stampe (Mine Host); Roy Evans (Knife Grinder); Derek Steen, John Lyons (Sailors); Jeanette Wild (Jill); Bobby Parr (Young Apprentice); Julia Wright (Street Singer).

Robert Louis Stevenson first published his classic novel *The Strange Case of Dr. Jekyll and Mr. Hyde* in 1886 and almost immediately it was adapted to the stage with Richard Mansfield famous in the dual role. Although Stevenson wrote the novel as a mystery story, it has many levels, including a Freudian psychological one in its delineation of the good and evil sides of personality. In films, the horror aspects, specifically the transformation from the good Jekyll to the evil Hyde, and the latter's horrific appearance, have been emphasized but it must be remembered the crux of the whole premise is science fiction, since it is through science that Dr. Jekyll develops the formula which converts him into the sinister, murderous, lustful Hyde. And, of course, without Mary Shelley's pioneering piece of fiction, *Frankenstein,* Stevenson may never have been inspired to create his masterpiece.

Dr. Jekyll and Mr. Hyde is one of the most filmed fictional works of all time. Supposedly a motion picture version was first produced in 1897 but the first proven filming came in 1908 by Selig in a silent one reel version also known as THE MODERN DR. JEKYLL. A version in Denmark DEN SKAEBNESVANGRE OPFINDELSE (1910) and Britain, THE QUALITY OF MAN (1910) followed but the best known early screen edition was the 1912 Thanhouser production with James Cruze playing Jekyll and Harry Benham as Hyde. Matinee idol King Baggott did the dual role the next year for Universal and 1913 also saw the first color version from the Kinemacolor Company and Albert Basserman played Jekyll/Hyde in a version for Vitascope. In 1920 German director F. W. Murnau made DER JANUSKOPT [Janus-Faced] with Conrad Veidt as Jekyll/Hyde, here as Dr. Warren and Mr. O'Connor since it was an *unauthorized* adaptation of the Stevenson work. Instead of a drug, Warren is turned into O'Connor because of his obsession with the two-faced god Janus. Bela Lugosi was cast as Warren's butler. Since the early teens the Stevenson novel has also been used for various comedy outings and the year 1920 had Hank Mann in one of these, DR. JEKYLL AND MR. HYDE, for Arrow. That year also saw a feature version of the story with Sheldon Lewis as Jekyll/Hyde in a sub-par production for producer Louis B. Mayer's Pioneer Films. Lewis also became the first sound Jekyll/Hyde when he recreated the role in the 1929 short subject, DR. JEKYLL AND MR. HYDE.

The year 1920 also saw the most exciting silent film version of the Stevenson novel, Paramount's DR. JEKYLL AND MR. HYDE starring the illustrious stage star, John Barrymore. Directed by John S. Robertson, the film was adapted by Clara S. Beranger who

Spencer Tracy and Ingrid Bergman in DR. JEKYLL AND MR. HYDE (1941).

Ralph Bates in DR. JEKYLL AND SISTER HYDE (1972).

interpolated ideas from Oscar Wilde's book *The Picture of Dorian Gray* (1891), including the character of evil Lord Henry, here as Sir George Carew. The plot has Carew (Brandon Hurst) suggesting to kindly Dr. Jekyll (John Barrymore) that man might enjoy living a double life as his baser self. Jekyll, who maintains a clinic for the indigent, is in love with Carew's virginal daughter Millicent (Martha Mansfield). In his laboratory, Jekyll develops a formula which he takes and which turns him into the evil, spider-like Hyde. The latter haunts Limehouse and takes up with dancer Miss Gina (Nita Naldi), who becomes his mistress. Carew finally realizes Jekyll's secret and as Hyde he kills Carew and tries to rape Millicent. The drug, however, has become a poison to him and he dies, transforming at death back into a peaceful Jekyll.

The most notable sequence in the silent production is Barrymore's transformation from Jekyll to Hyde, one which many claimed was done *without* makeup or trick photography. Actually both of these techniques were used, but most of the transformation occurs through Barrymore's capacity for distorting his face and body and quick transitional cuts as makeup changes are applied. His Hyde is horrific without being monstrous and Barrymore, who had an affinity for the bizarre in his own art work, relished the part. Almost equally impressive is Nita Naldi as the voluptuous prostitute whose life is drained from her due to her physical contacts with Hyde. Joe Franklin in *Classics of the Silent Screen* (1959), chose this film as one of the fifty great American silent motion pictures and commented, "A fine Grand Guignol thriller in its day, it remains a powerful and effective film even now, despite several ambitious later versions . . ." He also noted how Barrymore possessed ". . . . the astounding zest with which he throws himself into the more gruesome moments."

Perhaps the most enduring screen adaptation of the Stevenson work is the 1932 Paramount feature, DR. JEKYLL AND MR. HYDE, for which Fredric March won an Academy Award as Best Actor. Equally notable was Miriam Hopkins as the whore Ivy Pearson. The story has the usually kindly Dr. Henry Jekyll (Fredric March) wanting to wed lovely Muriel Carew (Rose Hobart), but her stuffy military father (Halliwell Hobbes) refuses to allow an early marriage. Frustrated, Jekyll drinks a formula he has developed and he becomes the ugly and base Mr. Hyde (Fredric March) who roams Soho and seeks out prostitute Ivy (Miriam Hopkins), who once sexually attracted Jekyll. Ivy becomes Hyde's mistress but he is brutal to her. With each intake of the drug, Hyde begins increasingly to take over Jekyll's life and, as Hyde, he murders Ivy when Jekyll becomes engaged to Muriel. Needing chemicals from Dr. Lanyon (Holmes Herbert) for his formula, Hyde promises to break off the engagement to Muriel, but ends up killing her father when he tries to stop Hyde from molesting his daughter. Lanyon identifies Hyde as the killer and Jekyll becomes his evil alter-ego and is gunned down by the police.

In *Classic Movie Monsters* (1978), Donald F. Glut noted that director Rouben ". . . . Mamoulian was known as an experimentalist and would introduce such ideas in DR. JEKYLL AND MR. HYDE as voice-over dialogue to reveal a character's thoughts, dissolves with one scene directly relating to the next, and diagonal split screens with the character in one shot indirectly interacting with the character in the other shot." Mamoulian patterned the Mr. Hyde makeup after that of a Neanderthal man but would never reveal just how the transformation was accomplished on film. Glut, however, says " . . . the mechanics can be deduced by anyone with a basic knowledge of film lighting and the use of filters."

The 1932 feature was reissued in 1967, with some footage deleted, and issued on a triple bill by MGM with its MARK OF THE VAMPIRE (1935) and FREAKS (1932). In 1950 Fredric March recreated Jekyll/Hyde on CBS radio's "Theatre Guild on the Air."

The 1967 reissue by MGM of a 1932 Paramount film was due to the fact that decades before MGM had purchased the Fredric March version from Paramount to keep it off the market so that it could make a new version to star Robert Donat. That actor, however, was replaced by Spencer Tracy, who was hardly suited for either Jekyll or Hyde. The plot of the 1941 MGM version, directed by Victor Fleming, remained close to the Paramount feature although here the horrific is eschewed in deference to Freudian psychology. Legend has it that Ingrid Bergman, cast as the fiancee and Lana Turner, set to appear as the immoral Ivy, conspired to switch roles, to each other's advantage (although Bergman appears to have won the better of the deal.) The film's penchant for the psychological even includes a ridiculous scene in which Jekyll dreams he beats two horses who become Ivy and Beatrix, the latter the new character name given to the fiancee. Still the movie was good box-office, due mainly to Tracy's fine acting as Jekyll/Hyde (he avoided using any horrific makeup) and the two female leads.

Although Jekyll/Hyde had no offspring in the Stevenson novel, the 1950s screenwise saw both the emergence of a son and daughter. In 1951 Columbia issued THE SON OF DR. JEKYLL with Louis Hayward in the title role, shown here as Hyde's illegitimate son. The film begins with Jekyll/Hyde's death and with Jekyll/Hyde's pals Dr. Curtis Lanyon (Alexander Knox) and lawyer John Utterson (Lester Matthews) taking his infant son and raising him as Edward Jekyll (Louis Hayward). He attends medical school but is dismissed for his bizarre theories and Lanyon tells him the true story of his background. Deciding to prove his father was not a monster, young Jekyll decides to delay his marriage to pretty Lynn (Jody Lawrence) and restore his father's laboratory to concoct the same drug he used. However,Lanyon secretly adds another ingredient to that drug. Edward swallows it but fails to exonerate his father and is blamed when a series of murders take place. When he is put in Lanyon's sanitarium he learns it is Lanyon who is behind the homicides, and in a final confrontation between the two, Edward escapes while an unruly crowd forces Lanyon to his death in his burning laboratory.

THE SON OF DR. JEKYLL was pale indeed compared to the 1920, 1932, and 1941 features but worse came with ABBOTT AND COSTELLO MEET DR. JEKYLL AND MR. HYDE (1953) (q.v.) and 1957's DAUGHTER OF DR. JEKYLL. Edgar G. Ulmer directed the latter, an outlandish hackneyed version of the story about Janet Smith (Gloria Talbott) and her fiancee George Hastings (John Agar) coming to England to claim her father's inheritance and being told by her guardian, Dr. Lomas (Arthur Shields) that it was rumored her father was a werewolf known as Hyde. When a number of werewolf killings plague the locale, Janet believes she is to blame and is at the point of suicide when George finds out that Lomas has been hypnotizing her and that he is really the werewolf and was to blame for her father's unnecessary demise. Alerting the villagers, George leads the chase against Lomas who is cornered in a cave and killed when a stake is driven through his heart. Only Gloria Talbott's appearance in the film gives it any interest. When the movie was issued to TV in the early 1960s, its 7l-minute running time was augmented by footage from another Allied Artists clinker, FRANKENSTEIN 1970 (q.v.).

Hammer Films churned out a version of the narrative in 1960 called THE TWO FACES OF DR. JEKYLL, which was issued in the U.S. as HOUSE OF FRIGHT. Here Dr. Henry Jekyll (Paul Massie) becomes the handsome Mr. Hyde only to find out his wife Kitty (Dawn Addams) is having an affair with his friend, gambler Paul Allen (Christopher Lee). As Hyde becomes dominant over Jekyll, he brings about the demise of Kitty and Paul as well as another girl, Maria (Norma Maria), before finally realizing that to rid himself of Hyde forever, he must kill himself. The film was intriguing in that it presented Hyde as debonair in contrast to the bearded, staid Jekyll, but despite rich production trimmings, the feature was not overly entertaining. This film was produced in England but its foreign roots were predated by Italy's 1951 production IL DOTTOR JEKYLL with Mario Scoffi, and followed by the Mexican film, PACTO DIABOLICO [Diabolical Pact] (1968) starring John Carradine as an aged Dr. Jekyll who is transformed by his newly developed formula taken from young girls' body fluid into the youthful and lustful Hyde (Miguel Alvarez).

French television filmed a version of the story in 1959 as LE TESTAMENT DU DR. CORDELIER [The Testament of Dr. Cordelier] with Jean-Louis Barrault as Dr. Cordelier who becomes the evil Monsieur Opale, under the direction of Jean Renoir. Another TV version was done in Canada in 1967 as THE STRANGE CASE OF DR. JEKYLL AND MR. HYDE starring Jack Palance. It was telecast as an ABC-TV movie-for-television and Palance proved more than satisfactory in the dual role, although the production itself was vapid. More astounding was the fact that Kirk Douglas was Jekyll/Hyde in the 1973 NBC-TV presentation DR. JEKYLL AND MR. HYDE, which was turned into a musical!

The year 1971, on the big screen, saw two rather interesting adaptations of the Stevenson story, but both variations went awry. I, MONSTER was an Amicus production which was begun in 3-D and then filmed in normal dimension. It retold the familiar story with Jekyll/Hyde becoming Dr. Charles Marlowe, a Freudian psychologist, and his alter-ego Edward Blake; both played by Christopher Lee (who had been the gambler in THE TWO FACES OF DR. JEKYLL in 1960). Peter Cushing co-starred as Marlowe's associate, Utterson, who tries to keep his associate on the straight and narrow, but fails. Unfortunately both fine actors were unable to keep this feature from being mundane. This production received only minor showings when distributed in the United States in 1973 by Cannon Films.

More engrossing, plotwise, but not much more successful, was Hammer Films' DR. JEKYLL AND SISTER HYDE. This outing has Dr. Jekyll (Ralph Bates) experimenting with flies in developing a life-prolonging formula. He is successful but finds the drug transforms its taker into a female. Needing bodies for his experiments he hires graverobbers Burke (Ivor Dean) and Hare (Tony Calvin) to aid him, but a mob kills Burke and blinds Hare. Forced to work alone, Jekyll goes to London's Whitechapel district where he becomes known as Jack the Ripper for his grizzly murdering of local whores. When the law falls on his trail he takes his own formula and turns into the beautiful Sister Hyde (Martine Beswick). Sister falls in love with Howard (Lewis Fianer) whose sibling Susan (Susan Brodrick) is loved by Jekyll. The latter decides to get rid of Sister forever, but has to commit another murder and the blind Hare turns him in. A mob chases the villain to a rooftop and becoming Sister he falls to the street below, a hideous combination of man and woman. In its advertising, the producers exclaimed, "WARNING! The sexual Transformation of a Man Into A Woman Will Actually Take Place Before Your Very Eyes!" but the actual scene was tame indeed.

Another 1971 release came from Spain and was called DOCTOR JEKYLL Y EL HOMBRE LOBO [Dr. Jekyll and the Werewolf] and it starred Paul Naschy in his recurring character of wolfman Waldemar Daninsky. Here he saves a young woman (Shirley Corrigan) from muggers only to find out she is the fiancee of the grandson of Dr. Jekyll/Mr. Hyde. The young scientist (Jack Taylor) has developed a new formula which he tries on Daninsky and it cures him of lycanthropy, but the jealous girl increases the injected dose and Daninsky becomes a super-evil Mr. Hyde. In the steps of BLACULA (1972), BLACKENSTEIN (1973) (q.v.), and SCREAM, BLACULA, SCREAM (1973), came the horror black exploitation thriller DR. BLACK, MR. HYDE in 1975. (It was also known as THE WATTS MONSTER.) In this entry, kindly Dr. Henry Pride (Bernie Casey) is experimenting with a serum which turns laboratory animals white and he takes it and becomes an ashen-colored zombie, who murders hookers. Eventually he is cornered at the top of the Watts Tower and shot by the police.

Other recent offshoots of the Stevenson literary classic have included the dark comedy, DR. HECKYL AND MR. HYPE (1980), written and directed by Charles B. Griffith, about an ugly podiatrist (Oliver Reed) who takes poison to kill himself and turns into a debonair killer. From France came DR. JEKYLL AND MISS OSBOURNE (1981) with Udo Kier as Jekyll and issued in its homeland as DR. KEULL ET LES FEMMES. In 1982 James Mathers starred in DR. JEKYLL'S DUNGEON OF DEATH, directed by James Woods. In mid-1988 a new Broadway musical of the JEKYLL AND HYDE tale was scheduled for production, with adaptation by Steve Cuden and the score by Cuden and composer Frank Wildhorn. Also scheduled for 1988 theatrical release was yet another rendition of Stevenson's classic tale, this time starring Anthony Perkins in the dual roles.

And not to be forgotten is Jerry Lewis' interpretation of the Stevenson tale in THE NUTTY PROFESSOR (1963).

DR. JEKYLL'S DUNGEON OF DEATH see DR. JEKYLL AND MR. HYDE (essay).

DR. KEULL ET LES FEMMES see DR. JEKYLL AND MR. HYDE (essay).

DR. RENAULT'S SECRET (Twentieth Century-Fox, 1942) 58 mins.

Producer, Sol M. Wurtzel; director, Harry Lachman; screenplay, William Bruckner, Robert F. Metzler; art directors, Richard Day, Nathan Juran; music, David Raksin; music director, Emil Newman; camera, Virgil Miller; editor, Fred Allen.

J. Carrol Naish (Mr. Noel); John Shepperd [Shepperd Strudwick] (Dr. Larry Forbes); Lynne Roberts (Madeline Renault); George Zucco (Dr. Renault); Bert Roach (Proprietor); Eugene Borden (Coroner); Jack Norton (Austin).

Almost forgotten today, DR. RENAULT'S SECRET is a pleasant, minor horror/sci-fi item from Twentieth Century-Fox; a production greatly enhanced by J. Carrol Naish's performance as the hapless man who finds out he was generated from an ape by a scientist (George Zucco). Zucco, too, is sturdy as the cold, calculating madman. While the film has many of the trappings of a poverty row thriller of the period, its combination of players, director and good production values, make it a memorable experience. Particularly poignant is the scene in which Naish finds a series of photographs showing him his heritage as he is pictured in the various stages of change from ape to human.

Mr. Noel (J. Carrol Naish) is the servant of scientist Dr. Renault (George Zucco). Noel cannot recollect his past and is a patient of the doctor. He is attracted to pretty Madeline (Lynne Roberts) who loves Forbes (John Sheppard [Sheppard Strudwick]) and the doctor forbids him to have anything to do with her. Noel stumbles accidentally across the doctor's notes and finds photographs of himself showing how he was changed from a gorilla to a human. This angers him and he turns on the doctor and kills him, but Noel too dies in the fracas.

George Zucco was a suave, wonderful British actor who almost made a screen career playing sinister, mad doctors experimenting with human brains. In CHARLIE CHAN IN HONOLULU (1938) he was a scientist who carries a brain aboard a boat cruise, while in THE MONSTER AND THE GIRL (1941) he places a human brain inside the head of a gorilla. He also conducts weird experiments as the insane scientist in items such as THE MAD GHOUL (1943) and DEAD MEN WALK (1943). In VOODOO MAN (1944) (q.v.) he moonlights as a gas station attendant (!) and then there is THE FLYING SERPENT (1946).

DOCTOR X (First National, 1932) C 77 mins.

Director, Michael Curtiz; based on the play by Howard W. Comstock, Allen C. Miller; screenplay, Robert Tasker; Earl Baldwin; art director, Anton Grot; camera, Richard Tower, Ray Rennahan; editor, George Amy.

Lionel Atwill (Dr. Xavier); Lee Tracy (Lee); Fay Wray (Joan Xavier); Preston Foster (Dr. Wells); Arthur Edmund Carewe (Dr. Rowitz); John Wray (Dr. Haines); Harry Beresford (Dr. Duke); George Rosener (Otto Xavier); Leila Bennett (Mamie the Housekeeper); Robert Warwick (Police Commissioner Stevens); Willard Robertson (O'Halloran); Thomas Jackson (Editor); Harry Holman (Policeman); Tom Dugan (Sheriff); Mae Busch (The Madame).

A series of horrible "mood murders," taking place only during the full moon, plagues a city. The killer is a fiend who strangles his victims and then cannibalizes them. The police believe the madman is part of a scientific academy headed by Dr. Xavier (Lionel Atwill). He and his associate, the one-armed Dr. Wells (Preston Foster), agree to aid Commissioner Stevens (Robert Warwick), Inspector O'Halloran (Willard Robertson) and newsman Lee Taylor (Lee Tracy) in solving the case. The police set a trap to catch the lunatic but he abducts Xavier's beautiful daughter Joan (Fay Wray), who narrowly escapes his clutches. Finally it is discovered the killer has developed a formula for artificial skin by which he makes a new face and arm. The police and Lee corner the killer in his laboratory and Lee throws a kerosene lamp at him and he goes up in flames.

When DR. X was issued theatrically late in the summer of 1932 the *New York Times* judged that it "Almost makes FRANKENSTEIN seem tame and friendly" and added it was a " . . . parcel of thrills streaked with fun." The movie was made in two-color Technicolor and was thought to be lost for years, but resurfaced in the 1970s. William K. Everson reappraised the production in his book *Classics of the Horror Film* (1974), "It remains one of the most enjoyable thrillers of its period, and if it doesn't have quite the Gothic style or the comic subtlety of James Whale's films, it nevertheless has the slickness, pace, and recognizable visual style (with it stress on shadows and sharp, angular images) that distinguished all of Michael Curtiz' work." He added, ". . . . DR. X is a grand chiller of the old school, replete with clutching hands, a weird laboratory, a hooded killer, gas jets, secret panels, a wonderful group of suspects. . . ." Carlos Clarens noted in *An Illustrated History of the Horror Film* (1967), "Throughout the movie runs a salutary vein of wise-cracking humor that very deftly places the horror element in modern Manhattan of the thirties, even though a good deal of the action takes place in the usual Teutonic old house perched on top of a Long Island cliff."

DOOM OF DRACULA see HOUSE OF FRANKENSTEIN.

DRACULA VS. FRANKENSTEIN (Independent International, 1971) C 90 mins.

Executive producer, Mardi Rustam; producers, Al Adamson, John Van Horne; director, Adamson; based on characters created by Mary Shelley and Bram Stoker; screenplay, William Pugsley, Samuel M. Sherman; art director, Ray Markham; art design, Gray Morrow; music, William Lava; special makeup design, George Barr; titles/visual effects, Bob Le Bar; special effects, Ken Strickfaden; camera, Gary Graver, Paul Glickman; editor, Erwin Cadden.

J. Carrol Naish (Dr. Dureau/Dr. Frankenstein); Lon Chaney (Groton); Anthony Eisley (Mike); Jim Davis (Sergeant Martin); Regina Carrol (Judith); Russ Tamblyn (Rico); Angelo Rossitto (Grazbo); Zandor Vorkov (Dracula); John Bloom (The Monster); Shelly Weiss (The Creature); Greydon Clark (Strange); Anne Morrell (Samantha); William Bonner, Bruce Kimball (Bikers); Maria Lease (Joan); Forrest J. Ackerman (Dr. Beaumont); Albert Cole, Irv Saunders (Policemen); Gary Kent (Beach Boy); Connie Nelson (Beach Girl); Lu Dorn (Hippie Girl).

"Love Tramps Seduced by Creatures from the Grave!" and "Yesterday They Were Cold and Dead—Today—They're Hot and Bothered" proclaimed the ad blurbs for DRACULA VS. FRANKENSTEIN which was the final release title for this exploitation horror/sci-fi thriller. The movie's background is more diverse than its plot. Filming commenced in 1969 as THE BLOOD SEEKERS, a horror thriller starring J. Carrol Naish and Lon Chaney. New footage interpolating the characters of Count Dracula and Frankenstein's monster were added the next year and it got some distribution as BLOOD OF FRANKENSTEIN and SATAN'S BLOOD FREAKS. The climactic battle sequence between the two creatures was filmed and tacked on the end for the more commercially titled DRACULA VS. FRANKENSTEIN.

At a sleazy California seaside resort, wheelchair-ridden Dr. Dureau (J. Carrol Naish) runs a chamber of horrors aided by dimwitted giant Groton (Lon Chaney) and dwarf Grazbo (Angelo Rossitto). The exhibit is a front for the scientist who is really Dr. Frankenstein; he is experimenting on a rejuvenation serum concocted from the blood of recently decapitated young girls axed to death by Groton and placed in a state of suspended animation by the doctor. Meanwhile Count Dracula (Zandor Vorkov) digs up the long-buried Frankenstein monster (John Bloom) and orders Dureau to develop a serum to permit him access to daylight. A nightclub singer Judith (Regina Carrol) contacts police Sergeant Martin (Jim Davis) about her missing sister, a victim of Groton's axe. With the aid of aging hippie Mike (Anthony Eisley) and his friends Strange (Greydon

John Bloom and Regina Carrol in DRACULA VS. FRANKENSTEIN (1971).

Clark) and Samantha (Anne Morrell), Judith traces her sister to Dureau's chamber of horrors. In seeking the girl, the group causes the death of the doctor and Grazbo and revengeful Groton abducts Judith, but is shot by Martin. Dracula and the monster kidnap Judith and when Mike attempts to rescue her, he is killed by Dracula's magic ring. The two monsters take the young woman to an old church where Dracula prepares to make her his bride, but is stopped by the monster who has developed a craving for Judith. The two creatures engage in a hideous battle outside the church with Dracula tearing the monster to pieces before being destroyed himself by the rays of the rising sun.

Critical comment for this film has been almost totally negative. In *The Psychotronic Encyclopedia of Film* (1983), Michael Weldon observes, "Al Adamson's most famous celluloid atrocity is an embarrassing mixture of old actors and ideas with modern exploitation devices." Ed Naha in *The Science Fictionary* (1980) opined, "Home-movie time . . . resembles that last super-8mm film your great-aunt Tessie took at Marineland in Florida." In *The Dracula Book* (1975), Donald F. Glut noted, " . . . the film itself was shoddy from every artistic and technical standpoint and maintains the distinction of being one of the very worst of the 'straight' Dracula/Frankenstein films ever made." For the viewer, however, Richard Meyers in *For One Week Only* (1983) may have been more on the mark when he stated, "The film is a camp-lover's delight."

About the same time this film was issued, the title DRACULA VS. FRANKENSTEIN was used for the British release of EL HOMBRE QUE VINO DE UMMO; shown in the United States only on TV as ASSIGNMENT TERROR (see B/V).

DREAMSCAPE (Twentieth Century-Fox, 1984) C 95 mins.

Executive producers, Stanley R. Zupnik, Tom Curtis; producer, Bruce Cohn Curtis; co-producer, Jerry Tokofsky; director, Joe Ruben; screenplay, David Loughery, Chuck Russell, Ruben; assistant directors, Michael Daves, Thomas Lofaro, Bob Doherty, Jerry Ketcham; art director, Jeff Staggs; costumes, Linda M. Bass; chief animator,Edward Manning; music, Maurice Jarre; optical/special effects, Craig Reardon, Peter Kuran, Richard Taylor; camera, Brian Tufano; special camera, Kevin Kutchaver; editor, Richard Halsey.

Dennis Quaid (Alex Garner); Max Von Sydow (Dr. Paul Novotny); Christopher Plummer (Robert Blair); Eddie Albert (The President); Kate Capshaw (Dr. Jane de Vries); David Patrick Kelly (Tommy Ray Glatman); George Wendt (Charlie); Larry Gelman (Webber); Larry Cedar (Snakeman); Cory Yothers (Buddy); Redmond Gleeson (Snead); Peter Jason (Babcock); Chris Mulkey (Finch); Jana Taylor (Mrs. Webber); Madison Mason (Fred); Kendall Carly Browne (Mrs. Matusik); Kate Charleson (President's Daughter); Eric Gold (Tommy's Father); Virginia Kiser (President's Wife); Carl Strano (Edward); Brian Libby (McClaren); Bob Terhune (Dobbs); Fred M. Waugh (Hardy); Timothy Blake (Mrs. Blair); Carey Fox, Marii Mak, Claudia Lowe (Tech Aides); Anna Chavez (Newswoman); Ben Kronen (Conductor); John Malone (Trolley Conductor); Mindi Iden (Waitress); Betty Kean (Grandma); Trent Dolan (Guard); Andrew Boyer (Webber's Brother); George Caldwell (Buddy's Father); Ernest Harada (Gardener); Tina Greenberg (Nurse); Alan Buchdahl (Announcer).

This film is another Hollywoodian vision of political right-wingers gone amuck in a let's-assassinate-the-president plot. This time the motivating force behind the assassination is to prevent the President's arms reduction negotiations with the Soviets.

College professor Dr. Paul Novotny (Max Von Sydow) has established a project at his Los Angeles college in which he practices "dreamlinking," the use of one person's dreams to receive the thoughts of another individual. He has used Tommy Ray Glatman (David Patrick Kelly) in his experiments, but finds a more useful tool in Alex Garland (Dennis Quaid), who has super-mental powers which he has used thus far only on making horse racing bets and seducing nubile young women. Novotny enlists Garland's aid in his project and, while there, the young man meets the doctor's assistant, Dr. Jane de Vries (Kate Capshaw), whom Garland learns from entering *her* dreams is sexually attracted to him. Meanwhile government agent Robert Blair (Christopher Plummer) has been surveilling Novotny's experiments and decides to use the jealous Glatman to kill the U.S. president (Eddie Albert) in order to stop his upcoming nuclear arms treaty with Russia. Garland learns of the scheme and he and Glatman are projected into the president's dreams where they duel to the finish.

Variety summed up this mildly received production as " . . . a run of the mill sci-fi thriller that wastes some good performances in an intriguing but tediously executed storyline."

DUNE (Universal, 1984) C 140 mins.

Producer, Rafacila De Laurentiis; associate producer, Jose Lopez Rodero; director, David Lynch; based on the novel by Frank Herbert; screenplay, Lynch; music, Toto; adaptor/additional music, Marty Paich; "Prophecy" theme by Brian Eno—composed by Brian Eno, Daniel Lanois, Roger Eno; production designer, Anthony Masters; supervising art director, Pierluigi Basile; art director, Benjamin Fernandez; set decorator, Giorgio Desideri; costume designer, Bob Ringwood; creative makeup, Gianetto DeRossi; model unit supervisor, Brian Smithies; assistant director, Rodero; sound, designer, Alan Splet; sound, Nelson Stoll; special visual effects, Barry Nolan; additional special visual effects, Albert J. Whitlock; camera, Freddie Francis; editor, Antony Gibbs.

Francesca Annis (Lady Jessica); Leonardo Cimino (The Baron's Doctor); Brad Dourif (Piter De Vries); Jose Ferrer (Padishah Emperor Shaddam IV); Linda Hunt (Shadout Mapes); Freddie Jones (Thufir Hawat); Richard Jordan (Duncan Idaho); Kyle MacLachlan (Paul Atreides); Virginia Madsen (Princess Irulan); Silvana Mangano (Reverend Mother Ramallo); Everett McGill (Stilgar); Kenneth McMillan (Baron Vladimir Harkonnen); Jack Nance (Nefud); Sian Phillips (Reverend Mother Gaius Helen Mohiam); Jurgen Prochnow (Duke Leto Atreides); Paul Smith (The Beast Rabban); Patrick Stewart (Gurney Halleck); Sting (Feyd Rautha); Dean Stockwell (Dr. Wellington Yueh); Max Von Sydow (Dr. Kynes); Alicia Roanne Witt (Alia); Sean Young (Chani).

Directed and written by David Lynch, who had helmed the cult favorites ERASERHEAD (1978) and THE ELEPHANT MAN

(1980), DUNE was based on Frank Herbert's 1965 best seller,* a detailed sci-fi adventure, which itself had obtained cult status.

" . . . DUNE, with its evocative and densely detailed vision of a desert planet where mammoth worms capable of swallowing whole express trains burrow through the sand, is one of the year's most peculiar films. It's cold, strange and remote. It's lit in such dark tones that, watching it, we often seem to be wandering through some vast, echoing mausoleum. It unfolds at a measured, lugubrious, almost maddening pace. And Herbert's byzantine plot is ruthlessly condensed and shoe-horned into a 140-minute running time that seems barely adequate." (Michael Wilmington, *Los Angeles Times*)

In the year 10,991, the universe is under the domination of a feudal lord Baron Vladimir Harkonnen (Kenneth McMillan) and his minions, who have the blessing of Emperor Shaddam IV (Jose Ferrer); the latter not knowing the devious Baron plans to eliminate him. Young idealistic Paul Atreides (Kyle MacLachlan) travels with his royal consort mother (Francesca Annis) and father (Jurgen Prochnow) to Arrakis, a desert planet known as Dune, where a powerful substance (melange—which extends life, allows travel in time and space, etc.) is mined from the underground; but often the miners are eaten by huge worms. While on the arid planet, the Baron and his followers conquer the planet and Atreides and his mother escape into the desert frontier where Paul vows revenge. Possessed of mystical powers of combat and a prophecy of preordained greatness, he trains the Fremen to aid him and makes allies of the sandworms. The Baron's forces are vanquished and in a hand-to-hand combat with the Baron's nephew, Feyd Rautha (Sting), Paul is victorious. He is now in full control of the planet, the valuable spice, and the universe itself.

An ambitious failure both commercially and artistically, there were many who analyzed the complex reasons for its misfire. Philip Strick (British *Monthly Film Bulletin*) analyzed, "Herbert's *Dune,* while well-embroidered with pageantry, offers much of its substance in the wholly non-visual form of two-level communication from the characters, their thoughts as open to the reader as their words. Through this sub-text of signals, memories, and hints of possible futures, the extraordinary insights that enable Paul to understand the implications of his mother's behaviour and the consequences of his own decisions make him, for all his powers, a relatively human and sympathetic guide. The device is an interesting

*To date there are six books in the Dune series: *Dune* (1965), *Dune Mesiah* (1975), *Children of Dune* (1976), *God Emperor of Dune* (1981), *Heritage of Dune* (1983), and *Chapter House: Dune* (1985).

failure on film, particularly in stereo when off-screen sounds are plentiful; . . . Lynch's talent is honourably confirmed as a portrayer of remarkable horrors (the wild excesses of Baron Vladimir are a triumph of depravity), but among the intricate quicksands of DUNE, an oasis or two of simple story-telling would have provided welcome nourishment."

Variety reasoned, " . . . the viewer strains to keep track and is offered only the promise of a strong narrative in which to become involved. . . . [H]e has overloaded the film with so many elements that many of them ultimately get lost in the shuffle." In fact, filmgoers were given a two-sided sheet* of *Dune* terminology as they entered the movie; yet another indication that this film was unable to stand on its own, a sure sign that it would fail with the masses.

LA Reader opined, "The actors intone their dialogue in the measured, characterless style that Hollywood deems appropriate for both period and futuristic films, and the potentially kinetic story is little more than a dead weight in the film's center. . . . the director's style seems to consist of things to look at rather than a way of looking."

One of the many lopsided aspects of DUNE is that the villains are far more engaging than the bland, pontificating "heroes"; especially the charismatic Sting as Feyd Rautha. "And, as the arch-heavy Baron Harkonnen, Kenneth McMillan—bulbously fat, his face a rotting mass of diseased eruptions, his eyes darting with outrageous lewdness, his entire body encased in an outlandish flying suit as he commits act after act of unrestrained degeneracy and vileness—all but blows every other actor off the screen. (It's here, in fact, that Lynch's imagination seems more unfettered, where his black, weird, incandescent humor bubbles over.)" (Wilmington, *Los Angeles Times*).

EARTH VS. THE SPIDER (American International, 1958) 73 mins.

Producer/director/story, Bert I. Gordon; screenplay, Laszlo Goring, George Worthing Yates; set designer, Walter Keller; music,

*Some examples illustrate the complexities of Frank Herbert's elaborate vision of the future world:

"BOIE: a technique originated by the Bene Gesserit which permits an adept to control others merely by selected tone shadings of the voice.

MELANGE (May-lahnj): the 'spice of spices,' the crop for which Arrakis is the unique source. The spice, noted for its geriatric qualities, is of greatest importance in empowering the Guild Navigators with the ability to 'fold space,' thus uniting the Universe under the Emperor.

WATER OF LIFE: the liquid exhalation of a sandworm produced at the moment of its death from drowning, which is changed by a Fremen Reverend Mother to become the narcotic which increases awareness. Since it is, before changing, a poison, only those worthy of becoming Reverend Mothers among the Fremen survive it."

Albert Glasser; makeup, Allen Snyder; special effects, Bert I. Gordon, Flora Gordon; camera, Jack Marta; editor, Ronald Sinclair.

Ed Kemmer (Mr. Kingman); June Kennedy (Carol Flynn); Gene Persson (Mike Simpson); Gene Roth (Sheriff Cagle); Hal Torey (Mr Simpson); Sally Fraser (Helen Kingman); June Jocelyn (Mrs. Flynn); Mickey Finn (Mr. Haskel); Troy Patterson (Joe); Hank Patterson (Hugo the Janitor); Skip Young (Sam); Howard Wright (Jake); Bill Giorgio (Deputy Sheriff Sanders); Jack Kosslyn (Mr. Frasher); Bob Garnet (Pest Control Man); Shirley Falls (Switchboard Operator); Bob Tetrick (Deputy Sheriff Dave); Nancy Kilgas (Dancer); George Stanley (Man in Cavern); David Tomack (Line Foreman); Merritt Stone (Mr. Flynn).

The father of teenager Carol Flynn (June Kennedy) is missing and she and her boyfriend Mike Simpson (Gene Persson) set out to locate him. They find his truck abandoned near a cave and once inside the black hole stumble upon a huge web and a giant spider. They make a hasty retreat and go to the local sheriff (Gene Roth), but he doesn't believe their story so they go to their science teacher Mr. Kingman (Ed Kemmer) who does after examining the piece of web they retrieved from the cave. He convinces the lawman and they all troop to the cave and find Carol's father's shriveled body as well as the spider and its web. The lawman orders the beast sprayed with DDT. This act apparently kills it. Kingman has the spider hauled to town and placed in the school gym for inspection by visiting scientists. That evening Carol and Mike return to the cave to retrieve a locket she dropped there. Sam (Skip Young) and other teenagers start a rock 'n roll party in the gym which reawakens the spider who kills the janitor (Hank Paterson) and embarks on a rampage in the town. The beast returns to its lair and the sheriff dynamites the cave entrance but soon discovers that teenagers are trapped inside with the spider. Kingman opens a hole above the cave and sends down an electrical arc which Mike connects and they electrocute the giant insect which falls to the cave floor and is impaled on a huge stalagmite.

Radiation is again hinted at in the narrative as the cause of this mutant, one of several such monsters to plague late 1950s' big screen. This one, however, is minor indeed thanks to producer/director/scripter Bert I. Gordon's tepid special effects; yet it may be his best monster film. *Variety* tagged it a "good exploitationer." One scene which has many levels of humor is the sequence in which the supposedly dead spider is reactivated by the rock 'n roll party. This huge insect was the first of several screen monsters to be agitated by rock 'n roll music!

A.k.a.: THE SPIDER.

ELIMINATORS (Empire, 1986) C 96 mins.

Producer, Charles Band; associate producer, Debra Dion; director, Peter Manoogian; screenplay, Paul De Meo, Danny Bison; production designer, Philip Foreman; art director, Gumersindo Andres Lopez; stunt co-ordinator, Jose Luis Chinchilla; costume designer, Jill Ohanneson; assistant director, Betsy Magruder; sound, Antonio Bloch Rodriguez; special effects chief, Juan Ramon Molina; special effects makeup, John Buechler; camera, Mac Ahlberg; editor, Andy Horvitch.

Andrew Prine (Harry Fontana); Denise Crosby (Nora Hunter); Patrick Reynolds (Mandroid); Conan Lee (Kuji); Roy Dotrice (Dr. Abbott Reeves): Peter Schrum (Ray); Peggy Mannix (Bajou Betty); Fausto Bara (Luis); Tad Horino (Takada); Luis Lorenzo (Maurice).

A man nearly dies in a plane crash but he is saved by a mad scientist, Dr. Abbott Reeves (Roy Dotrice), who turns him into Mandroid (Patrick Reynolds), half-man, half-machine, equipped with futuristic weapons. Mandroid, however, is unhappy with his status and seeks revenge against Reeves and joins forces with jungle boat owner Harry Fontana (Andrew Prine), pretty Nora Hunter (Denise Crosby), martial arts expert Kuji (Conan Lee), and S.P.O.T., a small flying robot. The group heads up river after Reeves but find themselves opposed by masculine river ruler Bayou Betty (Peggy Mannix) and her gang, a tribe of stone age natives and Reeves' hired killers.

Although ELIMINATORS was set in Mexico, it was filmed in Spain with location shooting in Los Angeles. *Variety* assessed, "ELIMINATORS is a good-natured but undisguisedly cheap entry in the ever-expanding half-man, half-robot genre. Ample amount of action will probably keep undiscriminating fans happy through the tiresomely predictable revenge plot. . . ."

THE EMPEROR AND THE GOLEM see THE GOLEM (essay).

THE EMPEROR'S BAKER see THE GOLEM (essay).

EMPIRE OF THE ANTS (American International, 1977) C 89 mins.

Executive producer, Samuel Z. Arkoff; producer/director, Bert I. Gordon; based on the story by H. G. Wells; screen story, Gordon; screenplay, Jack Turley; production designer, Charles Rosen; set decorator, Anthony C. Montenaro; costumes/wardrobe, Joanne Haas; assistant directors, David McGiffert, Mel Efros; stunt co-ordinator, Buddy Joe Hooker; camera, Reginald Morris; editor, Michael Luciano.

Joan Collins, Robert Pine (2nd from right), and Robert Lansing (right) in EMPIRE OF THE ANTS (1977).

Joan Collins (Marilyn Fryster); Robert Lansing (Dan Stokely); John David Carson (Joe Morrison); Albert Salmi (Sheriff Kincade); Jacqueline Scott (Margaret Ellis); Pamela Shoop (Coreen B. Gradford); Robert Pine (Larry Graham); Edward Power (Charlie Pearson); Brooke Palance (Christine Graham); Tom Fadden (Sam Russell); Irene Tedrow (Velma Thompson); Harry Holcombe (Harry Thompson); Jack Kosslyn (Thomas Lawson); Ilse Earl (Mary Lawson); Janie Gavin (Ginny); Norman Franklin (Anson Parker); Florence McGee (Phoebe Russell).

It was like old home week with producer/director Bert I. Gordon returning to American International Pictures after nearly two decades and making a movie about giant ants. Although the budget was bigger, Gordon still used real ants superimposed over already shot footage to create his monsters; a gimmick he used back in the glorious 1950s with his sub-par outings like KING DINOSAUR (1955) (see B/V), BEGINNING OF THE END (1957) (see B/V), EARTH VS. THE SPIDER (1958) (q.v.) and his trilogy of "Cyclops" movies: THE CYCLOPS (1957), THE AMAZING COLOSSAL MAN (1957), and WAR OF THE COLOSSAL BEAST

(1958) (see B/V). Somehow though, the charm of those dual billers was missing from EMPIRE OF THE ANTS which proved to be "Terrible science fiction . . . [with] lots of boredom. . . ." (Michael Weldon, *The Psychotronic Encyclopedia of Film,* 1983)

Attempting to retrieve her fortunes, Marilyn Fryster (Joan Collins) tries to interest wealthy clients in a housing development on a remote Florida island, intending to swindle them and abscond with the funds. Problems develop, however, since radiation contamination on the isle has turned ants into gigantic predators. While touring the isle, Marilyn, boat captain Dan Stokely (Robert Lansing) and the rest of the party are attacked by the ants and become marooned in the swamps, trying to save themselves. They finally learn the queen ant has her headquarters in a sugar refinery and is using gas to make slaves out of humans to provide the nourishment needed for the giant insects. Skokely and some of the remaining guests defeat the ants, but in the fracas Marilyn is also killed.

In *The Film Encyclopedia: Science Fiction* (1984), Phil Hardy tagged the undernourished feature " . . . a charmless, silly film" allegedly based on a story (written in 1905) by H. G. Wells. The film was sometimes issued on a double bill with Gordon's second adaptation of another Wells' work, THE FOOD OF THE GODS (1976) (q.v.).

THE EMPIRE STRIKES BACK (Twentieth Century-Fox, 1980) C 124 mins.

Executive producer, George Lucas; producer, Gary Kurtz; associate producer, Robert Watts, James Bloom; director, Irvin Kershner; story, Lucas; screenplay, Leigh Brackett, Lawrence Kasdan; art directors, Leslie Dilley, Harry Lange, Alan Tomkins; set decorator, Michael Ford; makeup/creature design, Stuart Freeborn; costumes, John Mollo; design consultant, Ralph McQuarrie; music, John Williams; studio second unit directors, Harley Cokliss, John Barry; location second unit director, Peter MacDonald; assistant directors, David Tomblin, Dominic Fulford, Bill Westley, Ola Solum; mechanical effects supervisor, Nick Allder; sound design, Ben Burtt; sound, Peter Sutton, Steve Maslow, Bill Varney, Greg Landaker; special visual effects, Brian Johnson, Richard Edlund; effects camera, Dennis Muren; optical camera, Bruce Nicholson; stop motion animators, Jon Berg, Phil Tippet; matte painting, Harrison Ellenshaw; model maker, Lorne Peterson; animator/rotoscope, Peter Kuran; camera, Peter Suschitzy; editor, Paul Hirsch; visual effects editor, Conrad Buff.

Mark Hamill (Luke Skywalker); Harrison Ford (Han Solo);

Carrie Fisher (Princess Leia Organa); David Prowse (Darth Vader); Anthony Daniels (C3PO); Peter Mayhew (Chewbacca); Kenny Baker (R2-D2); Frank Oz (Yoda); Billy Dee Williams (Lando Calrissian); Alec Guinness (Ben Kenobi); Jeremy Bullock (Bobo Fett); Jack Purvis (Chief Ugnaught); Des Webb (Snow Creature); Kathryn Mullen (Performing Assistant for Yoda); Clive Revill (Voice of Emperor); *Imperial Forces:* Kenneth Colley (Admiral Piett); Julian Glover (General Veers); Michael Sheard (Admiral Ozzel); Michael Culver (Captain Needa); John Dicks, Milton Johns, Mark Jones, Oliver Maguire, Robin Scoby (Officers); *Rebel Forces:* Bruce Boa (General Rieekan); Christopher Malcolm (Zev); Dennis Lawson (Wedge); Richard Oldfield (Hobbie); John Morton (Dak); Ian Liston (Janson); John Ratzenberger (Major Derlin); Jack McKenzie (Deck Lieutenant); Jerry Harte (Head Controller); Norman Chancer, Norwich Duff, Ray Hassett, Brigitte Kahn, Burnell Tucker (Officers); James Earl Jones (Voice of Darth Vader).

Producer George Lucas announced that a dozen films would be made in his STAR WARS (1977) (q.v.) film saga and the second feature was THE EMPIRE STRIKES BACK which scripter Leigh Brackett based on a concept by Lucas; it was completed by Lawrence Kasdan following Brackett's death and was novelized by Donald F. Glut, the author of several film reference texts. THE EMPIRE STRIKES BACK grossed over $140,000,000 at the box-office and was followed by THE RETURN OF THE JEDI (q.v.) three years later.

On the ice-covered planet of Hoth, Empire forces led by Darth Vader (David Prowse; voice of James Earl Jones) discover the headquarters of the Rebel forces guided by Princess Leia Organa (Carrie Fisher). In an intense battle the Rebels are nearly destroyed and the Princess escapes with Han Solo (Harrison Ford) in his ship the *Millennium Falcon* along with his co-pilot, Chewbacca (Peter Mayhew), a Wookie, and robot C-3PO (Anthony Daniels). Luke Skywalker (Mark Hamill) and another robot, R2-D2 (Kenny Baker), get away in a smaller craft and the spirit of Jedi Knight Ben Kenobi (Alec Guinness) tells Luke to go to the Bog planet and learn the ways of "The Force" from Yoda (Frank Oz), a Jedi Master. Han Solo lands his ship at the Cloud City of Bespin ruled by none-too-honest pal Lando Calrissian (Billy Dee Williams), but he has been captured by Darth Vader while Boba Fett (Jeremy Bullock), a bounty hunter, is after Solo, whom he captures. Learning this, Luke abandons his instructions and goes to the city where Vader forces him into a duel with light sabres and young Luke not only loses a hand, but finds out Vader is his father. Luke jumps from the city and is saved by Calrissian who has taken Solo's ship and the rebels aboard

Yoda (Frank Oz) in THE EMPIRE STRIKES BACK (1980).

and he saves Luke and they take him to a medical center for treatment; Solo has been frozen by Fett. When he is better, Luke returns to the Bog planet for his final instructions and his hand is regenerated. He joins with Leia, Calrissian and the others to free Solo and defeat the evil Empire.

THE EMPIRE STRIKES BACK starts out in good form with a zinging battle between the forces of good and evil on the ice covered planet of Hoth. Unfortunately this is the real highlight of the feature which quickly becomes a springboard for a cornucopia of special effects and various monsters and for the unappealing Jedi Master character of Yoda. "The first half of the movie contains most of the monsters and is livelier than the Luke-learns-more-and-more (more even than he cares to) second half, in which he begins to seem like, simply, a space in the screen which was reserved for some never-finished special effects." (Donald C. Willis, *Horror and Science Fiction Films II,* 1982.)

In *The Film Encyclopedia: Science Fiction* (1984), Phil Hardy calls it "the least interesting of the films" in the trilogy and adds, "Its $32 million budget and Oscar-wining special effects testify to its technical polish but the characters are never developed beyond the cardboard cut-outs of STAR WARS. In the manner of the James Bond films, it falls into the trap of committing itself to the spectacular at the expense of the personal. Even though Kasdan's and Brackett's screenplay spends more of its time on the individual adventures of Hamill, Ford and Fisher, they remain stereotypes." In the latter vein, only the romance between Solo and Leia holds any interest.

Nominated for such Academy Awards as Art Direction/Set Direction, Sound, and Best Original Score, THE EMPIRE STRIKES BACK won Oscars for Sound, and a Special Achievement Award for Visual Effects.

ENDANGERED SPECIES (Metro-Goldwyn-Mayer/United Artists, 1982) C 97 mins.

Executive producer, Zalman King; producer, Carolyn Pfeiffer; director, Alan Rudolph; story, Judson Klinger, Richard Woods; screenplay, Rudolph, John Binder; production designer, Trevor Williams; set decorator, R. Chris Westlund; music, Gary Wright; assistant director, James Ragan; camera, Paul Lohhmann; editor, Tom Walls.

Robert Urich (Ruben Castle); JoBeth Williams (Harriet Purdue); Paul Dooley (Joe Hiatt); Hoyt Axton (Ben Morgan); Peter Coyote (Steele); Marin Kanter (Mackenzie Castle); Gailard Sartain (Mayor); Dan Hedaya (Peck); Harry Carey, Jr. (Dr. Emmer); John Considine (Burnside); Margery Bond (Judy); Joseph G. Medalis (Lawyer); Patrick Houser (Chester); Alvin Crow (Deputy Wayne); Ned Dowd (Deputy Bobby); Kent Rizley (Deputy Ray); Heather Menzies (Susan); Michelle Davison (Mrs. Haskins); Henry G. Sanders (Dr. Ross); Vernon Weddle (Varney).

Trying to recover from alcoholism, former New York city detective Ruben Castle (Robert Urich) arrives in rural Buffalo, Wyoming, with teenage daughter Mackenzie (Marin Kanter) to visit one-time big city newspaperman Joe Hiatt (Paul Dooley), who now operates the community's small journal. Cattle in the area have been dying mysteriously and sheriff Harriet Purdue (JoBeth Williams) enlists Castle's aid with the case and the two become involved romantically. More and more cattle disappear and are found mutilated. Sinister businessman Ben Morgan (Hoyt Axton) dies tragically and several citizens are subject suddenly to mysterious bleeding spells. Eventually Castle and Harriet trace the activities to a local abandoned Air Force missile site where the government is apparently developing germ warfare to be used against the Soviets.

While the early portion of this film leans towards Flying Saucers as the ultimate cause of all the cattle problems, the movie soon develops into a mystery which changes over to an internal espionage caper. Here the government proves to be the culprit, toying with the balance of nature through germ warfare. It is a plot ploy hinted at in the beginning of ENDANGERED SPECIES when the audience is informed that chemical and germ warfare testing in the area has been banned since 1969. With all its shrouded subplots, the feature never

Robert Urich in ENDANGERED SPECIES (1982).

comes together into a homogeneous whole. "The real reasons for the mutilations are never explained in detail nor are the people behind it. Thus it's difficult not to feel cheated when the entire affair is over." (*Variety*)

In *Horror and Science Fiction Films III* (1984), Donald C. Willis felt, "ENDANGERED SPECIES is more or less an unofficial updating of William Cameron Menzies' THE WHIP HAND (1951). This time, however, the experimenters are working *against* not *for* the U.S.S.R. And the villains, naturally, are now on the right rather than on the left. The paranoia is the same—only the affiliations have changed."

ENEMY MINE (Twentieth Century-Fox, 1985) C 108 mins.

Executive producer, Stanley O'Toole; producer, Stephen Friedman; director, Wolfgang Petersen; story, Barry Longyear; screenplay, Edward Khmara; music/music director, Maurice Jarre; music editor, Bob Hathaway; stunt co-ordinator, Martin Grace; production designer, Rolf Zehetbauer; costumes, Monika Bauert; assistant directors, Bert Blatt, Gerd Huber, Robert Hottarek; second unit director, Hannes Nikel; aliens creator/designer, Chris Walas; special creature effects, Chris Walas, Carol Walas; sound supervisors, Milan Bor, Christian Schubert; visual effects, Don Dow; special effects supervisor, Bob MacDonald, Jr.; camera, Tony Imi; second unit camera, Heinz Holscher; optical camera supervisor, Bruce Nicholson; matte camera supervisors, Chris Evans, Craig Barron; editor, Hannes Nikel; visual effects editors, Christiane Jahn, Bill Kimberlin.

Dennis Quaid (Willis Davidge); Louis Gossett, Jr. (Jeriba Shigan, the Drac); Brion James (Stubbs); Richard Marcus (Arnold); Carolyn McCormick (Morse); Bumper Robinson (Zammis); Jim Mapp (Old Drac); Lance Kerwin (Wooster); Scott Kraft (Jonathan); Lou Michaels (Wilson); Andy Geer (Bates); Henry Stolow (Cates); Herb Andress (Hoffer); Danmar (Wise Guy); Mandy Hausenberger (Medic); Emily Woods (Simpson); Barry Stokes (Huck); Tony Moore, Kevin Taylor, Cheyenne Jade (Upfront Dracs); Colin Gilder (Dhavo); Charley Huber (Kranzer); Ulrich Gunther (Daggett); Frank Henson (Lump); Jazzer Jeys (Scarbreath); Doug Robinson (Walker); Mark McBride (Hensler); Balog Meynert (Mills).

ENEMY MINE appears to be the HEAVEN'S GATE (1980) of the sci-fi genre, an ultra costly, production-plagued feature which ended up a box-office bust. Originally budgeted at $17,000,000, the film eventually cost between $40 and $50 million (including marketing expenses), yet earned only slightly over $2,000,000 during the traditionally big grossing Christmas week and thereafter brought in a total of $11,746,281 in its first six weeks at the domestic box-office. It was estimated by industry savants that the film would have to gross at least $100,000,000 from filmgoers *just to break even.* (It never did!) After production approval in 1983, filming on the elaborate project began in the spring of 1984 by director Richard Longcraine in Iceland and Budapest. However, after $9,000,000 was spent, production control at the studio, Twentieth Century-Fox, changed and a new director, Wolfgang Peterson, was hired. Old footage was deemed unusable, locations were changed, and other exorbitant add-ons occurred before the motion picture was completed more than a year after it began. As one industry-ite quipped in the post-opening analysis of the ultra-expensive ENEMY MINE, "The amazing thing about this movie is that no one seems fazed by it all. I guess $40 million just doesn't mean what it used to."

Set in the 21st Century, ENEMY MINE relates the account of Earth fighter pilot Willis Davidge (Dennis Quaid) being shot down over the desolate planet Fyrine IV with an enemy, Jeriba Shigan (Louis Gossett, Jr.). The latter is a Drac, a lizard-like being from the

Louis Gossett, Jr. and Dennis Quaid in ENEMY MINE (1985).

planet Dracon, which is warring with Earth. At first the lone survivors are enemies, but both realize the necessity to survive in a hostile environment. They overcome language and cultural barriers and eventually (with long stumbling lags in the narrative) join forces and become friends as they combat flesh-eating metal creatures, meteor barrages, and Scavengers (renegade Earthmen who are crude, murderous space miners). Along the way, the Drac gives birth to a child, whom Davidge names Zammis (Bumper Robinson) and whom he promises his dying friend he will one day return to Dracon. Later Zammis is captured by the Scavengers and Davidge left for dead. He is saved by an Earth craft and once recovered, goes in search of Zammis, now a prisoner in the mines controlled by the Scavengers. After the Scavengers are overcome, he returns Zammis to Dracon and signs a peace treaty between the two opposing planets.

The production's most striking features are Louis Gossett, Jr.'s sensitive creation of the alien Drac and the hostile planet's impressive visuals, filmed by Bavaria Studios and shot on the island of Lanzarote on the West coast of Africa.

Critical reaction to ENEMY MINE was decidedly mixed. Janet Maslin (*New York Times*) slammed it as " . . . a costly, awful-looking science-fiction epic with one of the weirdest story lines ever to hit the screen." And the critic added as a final insult, that ENEMY MINE was "this year's DUNE". *Daily Variety* reported, "ENEMY MINE is proof once again that there are no new stories in Hollywood. . . . [It] is neither nonstop action for the teen audience or thoughtful relationship fare for the older crowd. It's a bit of both." Duane Byrge (*The Hollywood Reporter*) decided, "It seems a film likely to disappoint its target audience, and one that will not attract those who might appreciate it."

When the film debuted in England in the summer of 1986 fifteen minutes had been trimmed from the running time. By now, memory of the daily woes of filming the superexpensive production had dimmed, and reviewers focused more on the quality of the completed film itself. Julian Petley (British *Monthly Film Bulletin*) championed, "Right from the opening dogfight, ENEMY MINE is nothing if not thoroughly spectacular. . . . what distinguishes ENEMY MINE from space operas like STAR WARS [q.v.] is its successful marriage of the small and the large scale, the personal and the spectacular. The device of setting down two sworn enemies in conditions in which they cannot escape from each other, indeed in which they need each other is, of course, a familiar one. . . . But a combination of sensitive acting, direction and writing . . . endows the situation with a certain freshness and vitality."

ESCAPE FROM NEW YORK (Avco Embassy, 1981) C 99 mins.

Producers, Larry Franco, Debra Hill; associate producer, Barry Bernardi; director, John Carpenter; screenplay, Carpenter, Nick Castle; music, Carpenter in association with Alan Howarth; production designer, Joe Alves; set decorator, Cloudia; costume designer, Stephen Loomis; assistant director, Franco; sound, Tommy Causey; camera, Dean Cundey; editor, Todd Ramsay.

Kurt Russell (Snake Plissken); Lee Van Cleef (Bob Hauk); Ernest Borgnine (Cabbie); Donald Pleasence (President of the United States); Isaac Hayes (Duke of New York); Season Hubley (Girl in Chock Full O'Nuts Restaurant); Harry Dean Stanton (Brain); Adrienne Barbeau (Maggie); Tom Atkins (Rehme); Charles Cyphers (Secretary of State); Ox Baker (Slag); Frank Doubleday (Romero); Joe Unger (Taylor).

Futuristic films almost always deal with an Earth which has degenerated and where the denizens are an evil lot who exist in squalor without much hope of redemption. Only a very few sci-fi films, such as JUST IMAGINE (1930) (see B/V), have depicted a bright future world without the need of the intervention of a (super)hero of some type to turn things around. ESCAPE FROM NEW YORK is one of those nilhilistic features where the Earth of the near future is not only short on females but also, apparently, short of soap.

In 1997 New York City has become a maximum security prison where the inmates have divided into two groups, one living above ground and ruled by the Duke of New York (Isaac Hayes) and another which has taken to living in the sewers and apparently has reverted to cannibalism. The plane carrying the president (Donald Pleasence) of the United States is forced to land in this hellhole and he is captured by the Duke and his minions. Rescue Operations Officer Hauk (Lee Van Cleef) assigns notorious criminal Snake Plissken (Kurt Russell) to bring in the chief executive and in return be set free. He is dropped into the city/prison and there meets Cabbie (Ernest Borgnine) who aids him in getting around the devastated metropolis. He becomes allied with Brain (Harry Dean Stanton) and his mistress Maggie (Adrienne Barbeau), but they turn on him and he is captured by Duke and placed in a gladiatorial combat with massive Slag (Ox Baker) whom he defeats. Finally Snake brings about the supposed release of the President only to find that he is to be a pawn in the proceedings. He takes measures to protect himself and escapes from the Gotham jail.

Director John Carpenter built a solid reputation with horror films such as HALLOWEEN (1974) and THE FOG (1980), but since then his features have failed to substantiate the optimism for future success. ESCAPE FROM NEW YORK, a totally bleak movie, is hardly one of his best. Although *Variety* acknowledged that the feature was "a solidly satisfying actioner" it was more on the mark when complaining about the film's " . . . letdown at the flip, too-cynical ending, which tries to have it both ways in satisfying demands for victory over the baddies and retaining moral superiority of Russell over the establishment."

Because ESCAPE FROM NEW YORK grossed $10,900,000 in domestic box-office rentals, Carpenter in recent years has stated an interest in producing a "sequel" to this adventure.

ESCAPE TO WITCH MOUNTAIN (Buena Vista, 1975) C 97 mins.

Executive producer, Ron Miller; producer, Jerome Courtland; director, John Hough; based on the book by Alexander Key; screenplay, Robert Malcolm Young; music, Johnny Mandel; art directors, John B. Mansbridge, Al Roelofs; assistant directors, Fred Brost, Jerry Ballew; costumes, Chuck Keehne; sound, Herb Taylor, Frank Regula; special effects, Art Cruickshank, Danny Lee; camera, Frank Phillips; editor, Robert Stafford.

Eddie Albert (Jason); Ray Milland (Aristotle Bolt); Donald Pleasence (Deranian); Kim Richards (Tia); Ike Eisenmann (Tony); Walter Barnes (Sheriff Purdy); Reta Shaw (Mrs. Grindley); Denver Pyle (Uncle Bene); Alfred Ryder (Astrologer); Lawrence Montaigne (Ubermann); Terry Wilson (Biff Jenkins); George Chandler (Grocer); Dermott Downs (Truck); Shepherd Sanders (Guru); Don Brodie (Gasoline Attendant); Paul Sorenson (Sergeant Foss); Alfred Rossi (Policeman); Tiger Joe Marsh (Lorko); Harry Holcombe (Captain Malone); Sam Edwards (Mate); Dan Seymour (Psychic); Eugene Daniels (Cort); Al Dunlap (Deputy); Rex Holman, Tony Giorgio (Hunters).

Producer Jerome Courtland and director John Hough turned out two successful theatrical films in Walt Disney's "Witch Mountain" series, with a later TV pilot coming along but not establishing itself as a video series. The basic appeal of the two movies was in its two lead players, youngsters Kim Richards and Ike Eisenmann, and when they outgrew their roles of alien children with telepathic powers, the property fizzled. The initial film grossed $9,500,000 when released, paving the way for its less successful sequel (which grossed $7,398,000), and the eventual telefeature.

ESCAPE TO WITCH MOUNTAIN has orphaned youngsters

Tia (Kim Richards) and Tony (Ike Eisenmann), sister and brother, being outcasts at their orphanage home with both youngsters having psycho-kinetic powers. Tia has memories of previous experiences but neither can recall the past. Disgusted with their peers, they flee the orphanage and are picked up by a friendly man (Eddie Albert) who is traveling cross country in his camper. The children's powers, however, are seen by others and an evil millionaire (Ray Milland) has them kidnapped so he and his henchman (Donald Pleasence) can use them for their own gains. Their friend, however, comes to their rescue and in a chase with the bad guys, the children cause the camper to fly through the sky. It is revealed the children are from another galaxy and their friend leads them to a reunion with their own kind at their compound on Witch Mountain.

RETURN FROM WITCH MOUNTAIN finds Tony (Ike Eisenmann) kidnapped by mad scientist Dr. Victor Gannon (Christopher Lee) and his cohort, Letha (Bette Davis). Gannon has invented a means to control the human mind and he wants to use Tony's power to control the world, while Letha wants all its gold. Tia searches for her brother and is accosted by a group of tough urchins (Christian Juttner, Brad Savage, Poindexter, Jeffrey Jacquet) who quickly get on her side after Tia demonstrates her mental prowess. Together they ferret out where Tony has been taken and Tia does battle with Gannon in a war of psychic powers and thwarts the villains' evil machinations.

RETURN FROM WITCH MOUNTAIN is nowhere as good as its predecessor. The film's main weakness is the bland villainy of Bette Davis and Christopher Lee, neither of whom has a substantial acting assignment.

Early in 1982 Disney Productions revived the "Witch Mountain" theme with the one-hour TV pilot BEYOND WITCH MOUNTAIN starring Tracey Gold and Andy Freeman as the psychic kids. This outing was a reversing of the initial theatrical feature with the two youngsters joining forces with their alien uncle (Noah Beery) and leaving their Witch Mountain home to find a peer who has disappeared. They meet an old friend (Eddie Albert—repeating his role from the first film) following their uncle's untimely death. A grasping millionaire (Efrem Zimbalist, Jr.) finds out about the children being away from their stronghold and assigns his henchmen (J. D. Cannon, James Luisi) to kidnap them. The duo capture Albert and the children come to his rescue and defeat their adversary.

Variety reported, "The gimmick is that the kids' powers enable them to outwit adults as well as talk to animals (and to each other without being heard)—all tricks guaranteed to please the urchins in the audience. Trick photography and the usual Disney magic with animals worked well in the pilot, but the drawback was there was little to engage adult audiences."

E.T., THE EXTRA-TERRESTRIAL (Universal, 1982) C 120 mins.

Producers, Steven Spielberg, Kathleen Kennedy; associate producer, Melissa Mathison; director, Spielberg; screenplay, Mathison; production designer, James D. Bissell; set decorator, Jackie Carr; music, John Williams; assistant directors, Katy Emde, Daniel Attias; second unit director, Glenn Randall; costumes, Deborah Scott; sound, Gene Cantamessa; E. T. creator, Carlo Rambaldi; special visual effects supervisor, Dennis Muren; camera, Allen Daviau; editor, Carol Littleton; sound editor, Charles L. Campbell.

Dee Wallace (Mary); Henry Thomas (Elliott); Peter Coyote (Keys); Robert MacNaughton (Michael); Drew Barrymore (Gertie); K. C. Martel (Greg); Sean Frye (Steve); Tom Howell (Tyler); Erika Eleniak (Pretty Girl); David O'Dell (Schoolboy); Richard Swingler (Science Teacher); Frank Toth (Policeman); Robert Barton (Ultra Sound Man); Michael Darrell (Van Man); Milt Kogan (Doctor).

Grossing well over $200,000,000 at the domestic box-office (which does not include merchandise licensing nor the video cassette version of the film), E.T. is the biggest moneymaking motion picture within the sci-fi genre, outdistancing even the STAR WARS (q.v.) trilogy, which were much more expensive to produce. Actually E.T. was a moderately budgeted, non-star name film, which caught the public's fancy and became a money-making sensation. The tender camaraderie between the alien (created by Carlo Rambaldi) and its three moppet protectors made this optimistic film extremely appealing to family audiences, tired of violent R-rated fare and far-out special effects.

An alien spaceship makes a hasty departure when the armed services close in on it and one of its occupants, a small intelligent creature, is left stranded in a California suburb. He is discovered by young Elliott (Henry Thomas) who decides to protect the alien and he teaches him English and they become close pals. Henry permits his older brother Michael (Robert MacNaughton) and little sister Gertie (Drew Barrymore) to know about the creature and the three keep him a secret from their mother, Mary (Dee Wallace) for the time being. The authorities, advised by a scientist Keys (Peter Coyote) and his team, find out about E.T. who has become very ill from the Earth's polluting atmosphere, hovering near death and then seemingly expires. Elliott, who has the same death-inducing symptoms as E.T. almost dies but makes a recovery. Then E.T. has a magical transformation back to health. Thereafter, the three children kidnap E.T. and take him to the forest site where another spacecraft lands, picks him up, and the tearful E.T. returns to his heavenly home.

Variety endorsed this optimistic fantasy sci-fi feature as " . . . the best Disney film Disney never made. Captivating, endearingly optimistic and magical times. . . . [it] is certain to capture the imagination of the world's youth. . . ." Phil Hardy in *The Film Encyclopedia: Science Fiction* (1984) observed, "The film's major achievements are in the simplicity and directness of its vision and Spielberg's ability to both articulate that vision and transfer to the audience/screen relationship the E.T./Elliott empathy. . . ."

Judith M. Kass, in analyzing this blockbuster for *Magill's Cinema Annual* (1983), noted, "The film captures the whole gamut of childhood experience: fear of losing one's parents, homesickness, instinctive identification with the unprotected, and the unique relationship children have with their pets." She also enthuses, "The most wondrous effect. . . . is the extraterrestrial himself. . . . E.T. looks like a Naugahyde elf. He has a bulbous head, huge eyes, an extendable neck, a pear-shaped body with a stomach that grazes the ground, and webbed feet. He has a heart that glows when he is in touch with his own kind, and with Elliott, and a glowing index finger that heals all wounds. He is magic, . . ."

E.T. was nominated for Academy Awards in many categories (including Best Picture, Best Direction, Best Screenplay, etc.) and won four Oscars: Best Score (John Williams), Best Visual Effects, Best Sound Effects Editing, and Best Sound. There were theorists who insisted that the super overmerchandizing of the film caused a counter-feeling in the film industry, which turned off many insiders from voting additional awards to this spectacular consumer-appealing film.

Three items within E.T. became film legend: the image of the children on their bikes pedalling through the air on their rescue mission; E.T.'s extreme fondness for Reese's Pieces candy; and the catch phrase of the year, "E.T. Phone home!"

THE EVIL OF FRANKENSTEIN (Universal, 1964) C 86 mins.

Producer, Anthony Hinds; director, Freddie Francis; based on characters created by Mary Shelley in the novel *Frankenstein;* story/screenplay, John Elder [Hinds]; art director, Don Mingaye; music, Don Banks; music supervisor, Philip Martell; music director, John Hollingsworth; assistant directors, Bill Cartlidge, Hugh Harlow; makeup, Roy Ashton; sound, Ken Rawkins; special effects, Les Bowie; camera, John Wilcox; supervising editor, James Needs; sound editor, Roy Hyde.

Peter Cushing (Baron Frankenstein); Peter Woodthorpe (Professor Zoltan); Duncan Lamont (Chief of Police); Sandor Eles (Hans); Katy Wild (Beggar Girl); David Hutcheson (Burgomaster); James Maxwell (Priest); Howard Goorney (Drunk); Kiwi Kingston (The Creature); Caron Gardner (Burgomaster's Wife); Tony Arpino (Bodysnatcher); Timothy Bateson (Hypnotized Man); Alister Williamson (Landlord); Frank Forsyth (Manservant); Kenneth Cove (Cure); Michele Scott (Little Girl); Anthony Blackshaw (Burly Constable); David Conville (Young Constable); Derek Martin, Robert Flynn, Anthony Poole, James Garfield (Roustabouts).

Peter Cushing played Baron Frankenstein for yet the third time in this Hammer Films production, six years after THE REVENGE OF FRANKENSTEIN (q.v.) in 1958, which had been preceded by the initial feature in the series, THE CURSE OF FRANKENSTEIN (1957) (q.v.). This entry retells the tale and is not directly related plotwise to its celluloid predecessors.

Baron Frankenstein (Peter Cushing) and his assistant Hans (Sandor Eles) return to the Baron's castle/laboratory after many years absence and find it looted. A long time before the Baron had created an artificial man who became a monster and was driven off a cliff to its death by angry villagers, forcing the Baron to leave the vicinity. After a confrontation with the local Burgomaster (David Hutcheson), the duo take refuge with hypnotist The Great Zoltan (Peter Woodthorpe) and later they hide in a cave where they find Rena (Katy Wild), a young mute beggar, and buried there in the ice is Frankenstein's monster (Kiwi Kingston). Back at the laboratory, Frankenstein revives the creature but it will only respond to the will of Zoltan who uses it to murder several locals, including the Burgomaster, who had run him out of town as a fake. When Frankenstein learns of this, he orders Zoltan to leave and the hypnotist orders the monster to kill his creator. But in a battle of wills, Frankenstein overcomes Zoltan who is eliminated by the creature. Drinking a mixture of chloroform and whiskey, the monster embarks on a rampage and wrecks the castle which starts a fire. It is destroyed as well as his creator.

A dull feature, EVIL OF FRANKENSTEIN at least presents a monster which "resembles" the one made famous by Boris Karloff years before. The reason for this was that Universal issued the film in the U.S. and Hammer, therefore, had access to Jack Pierce's makeup designs for the monster. Donald F. Glut in *The Frankenstein Legend* (1973) chided that the makeup so used was "anything but convincing" adding, "The image . . . aroused many giggles from young members of the audience who could have done better."

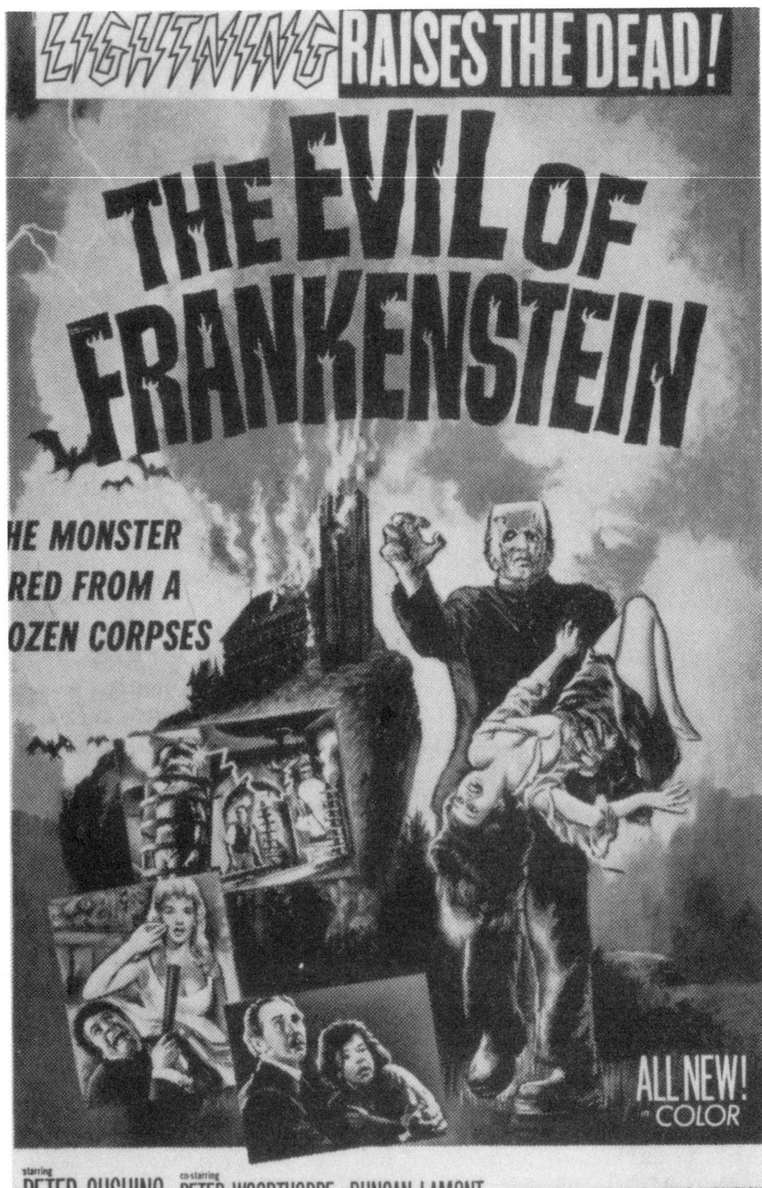

Advertisement for THE EVIL OF FRANKENSTEIN (1964).

EVILS OF THE NIGHT (Shapiro Entertainment, 1985) C 98 mins.

Executive producer, Mohammed Rustam; producer, Mardi Rustam; associate producers, John Kasha, Jim Talmadge; director, Mardi Rustam; screenplay, Mardi Rustam, Phillip D. Connors; music, Robert O. Ragland; songs, Rod Burton, Richard Bellis; assistant directors, Richard Kanter, William Nettles; sound, Gerald Wolfe; camera, Don Stern; editor, Henri Charr.

Neville Brand (Kurt); Aldo Ray (Fred); Tina Louise (Cora); John Carradine (Dr. Kozmar); Julie Newmar (Dr. Zarma); Karrie Emerson (Nancy); Bridget Holloman (Heather); G. T. Taylor (Connie); David Hawk (Brian); Keith Fisher (Ron); Tony O'Dell (Billy); Kelly Parsons (Laura Lee); and: Scott Hunter, Lonnie J. Karlyle, Susan Pastor, Kimberly Bleier, Kari Thompson, Diana Payne, Walter Zeri, Keith Johnson, Erika Marr.

Fans of low-grade, junk entertainment should be very pleased with EVILS OF THE NIGHT, one of those rarely seen, almost no-budget sensational ripoffs which is loaded with "names" (Neville Brand, Aldo Ray, John Carradine, Tina Louise, Julie Newmar) from the past, in a plot involving sexually agitated teenagers (and plenty of bare flesh), a mad scientist and his henchmen, a formula requiring blood, and two comely aliens. Created by the team of Mardi Rustam and Mohammed Rustam, who have been associated with such bottom-of-the-barrel cinema as DRACULA VS. FRANKENSTEIN (1971) (q.v.) and THE FEMALE BUNCH (1971), *Variety* judged this paltry thriller, "Strictly formula stuff, with weak dialog and almost no suspense, this will have to play off fast to undiscriminating audiences to make a buck."

A group of teenagers go on a campout near a beautiful lake, intending a fun-filled time of partying and sex. They soon realize, however, they are being stalked and that a scientist (John Carradine) is headquartered nearby. He is working on a formula which demands the blood of young people and he hires none-too-bright mechanics Kurt (Neville Brand) and Fred (Aldo Ray) to abduct comely young ladies for his special needs. Added to this is the lakeside invasion by two aliens (Tina Louise, Julie Newmar).

Although concocted in 1983, this feature was not issued until 1985.

THE EWOK ADVENTURES (ABC-TV, 11/24/84) C 97 mins.

Executive producer, George Lucas; producer, Thomas G. Smith; associate producer, Patricia Rose Duignan; director, John Korty; story, Lucas; screenplay, Bob Carrau; production designer, Joe Johnston; art director, Harley Jessup; assistant directors, Toby Lovallo, John Syrjamaki; music, Peter Bernstein; "Wicket's Theme" adapted from John Williams; orchestrator, Christopher Palmer; music editor, Kathy Durning; costume designers, Cathleen Edwards, Michael Becker; makeup, Yvonne Curry; Ewok co-ordinator, Kirk Thatcher; Ewok choreography, Wendy Rogers; Ewok language, Mari Mine-Rutka; stunt co-ordinator, Mike Cassidy; sound effects editors, Victor Livingston, Rob Fruchtman; sound designer, Randy Thom; visual effects supervisor, Michael Pangrazio; camera, Korty; second unit camera, Isidore Mankofsky; matte camera, David Fincher, Wade Childress, Paul Huston; supervising sound editor (dialogue), Suzanne Fox.

Burl Ives (Narrator); Eric Walker (Mace); Warwick Davis (Wicket); Fionnula Flanagan (Catarine); Guy Boyd (Jeremitt); Aubree Miller (Cindel); Dan Frishman (Deej); Debbie Carrington (Weechee); Tony Cox (Widdle); Kevin Thompson (Chukha-Trok); Margarita Fernandez (Kaink); Pam Grizz (Shodu); Bobby Bell (Logray); *Ewok Voices:* Daryl Henriquez (Wicket); Sydney Walker (Deej); Nancy Carlin (Shodu); Jim Cranna (Widdle); Hal Rayle (Weechee); Robert Elross (Logray); Pat Franklin (Kaink); Michael Pritchad (Chukla-Trok).

EWOKS: THE BATTLE FOR ENDOR (ABC-TV, 12/24/85) C 97 mins.

Executive producer, George Lucas; producer, Thomas G. Smith; directors, Jim Wheat, Ken Wheat; story, Lucas; teleplay, the Wheats; production designers, Joe Johnston, Harlen Jessup; art director, William George; music, Peter Bernstein; sound, Agamemmon Andrianos; camera, Isadore Mankofsky; editor, Eric Jenkins.

Wilfrid Brimley (Noa); Warwick Davis (Wicket); Aubree Miller (Cindel); Sian Phillips (Charal); Carel Struycken (Terak); Daniel Frishman (Deej); Tony Cox (Widdle); Niki Botherlo (Teek); Eric Walker (Mace); Pam Grizz (Shodu); and: Marianne Horine, Daniel Frishman, Roger Johnson, Johnny Weissmuller, Jr., Michael Pritchard.

The furry creatures called Ewoks, from RETURN OF THE JEDI (1983) (q.v.), sufficiently captured the public's imagination for executive producer George Lucas to turn out two rather expensively-mounted telefeatures based on their adventures with human youngsters. Initially telecast as an "ABC Sunday Night Movie Special," THE EWOK ADVENTURE was Lucas' first telefilm and *Variety* judged it ". . . a delight, imaginatively put together with more than enough originality. . . . an evergreen event for the whole family."

Two youngsters, teenager Mace (Eric Walker) and his little sister Cindel (Aubree Miller), find their spaceship crashing on the planet Endor with their parents being captured by an evil giant,

Jason Presson in EXPLORERS (1985).

Gorak, who plans to fatten them up for a dinner feast. The youngsters, however, try to rescue their parents and are aided by the furry Ewoks. Along the way they must battle a variety of monsters before accomplishing their mission.

Less enthusiastic about the Ewoks was Philip Strick (British *Monthly Film Bulletin*) when the telefeature was released theatrically in England as CARAVAN OF COURAGE. "Sadly, however, closer acquaintance with the Ewok personality reveals only its limitations: a fixed, unblinking mask set in a rictus of amiability and accompanied by an unintelligble, vaguely Oriental murmur, the creature has neither the limpid appeal of an E.T. nor the demonic glee of a Gremlin. And since Lucas appears to have scribbled the menu for this between-meals confection on the back of a bus ticket, little is required of the Ewok community. . . ."

Albeit the American telefilm was diverting enough to spawn a sequel (not to mention additional Ewok toy merchandizing), EWOKS: THE BATTLE FOR ENDOR, the next year in which little Cindel (Aubree Miller) must find a wicked witch to alleviate a curse and is aided in the task by an old hermit (Wilford Brimley) and her Ewok pals.

Regarding the merits of this ABC-TV production, *Variety* was of two minds: "There are lavish production values, superb special effects, clashes of near-epic proportions and, best of all, imagination-run-rampant at every turn. . . . The biggest blunder of the film is the decision to kill off the family of lead character Cindel. . . . It's distressing on sheer emotional grounds, but also because the plot device is annoyingly reminiscent of what happened to Luke Skywalker's foster parents in STAR WARS. . . . And on purely commercial terms, the move may also prove to be a disaster. The first EWOK film, . . . featured the daring rescue of Cindel's family. But what kind of aftermarket exists for a film about rescuing people who've already been killed off in a sequel?"

EXPLORERS (Paramount, 1985) C 110 mins.

Executive producer, Michael Finnell; producers, Edward S. Feldman, David Bombyk; associate producer, Tom Jacobson; director, Joe Dante; screenplay, Eric Luke; production designer, Robert F. Boyle; music, Jerry Goldsmith; assistant directors, Pat Kehoe, Carol Green; costumes, Rosanna Norton; special makeup effects, Rob Bottin; visual effects, Industrial Light & Magic; camera, John Hora; editor, Tina Hirsch.

Ethan Hawke (Ben Crandall); River Phoenix (Wolfgang Muller); Jason Presson (Darren Woods); Amanda Peterson (Lori Swenson); Dick Miller (Charlie Drake); Robert Picado (Wak/Starkiller); Leslie Rickert (Neek); James Cromwell (Mr. Muller); Dana Ivey (Mrs Muller); Bobby Fite (Steve Jackson); Meshach Taylor (Gordon Miller); and: Bradley Gregg, George Olden, Chance Schwass, Brooke Bundy, Tricia Bartholome, Eric Luke, Taliesin Jaffe, Karen Mayo-Chandler, Robert F. Boyle, John P. Navin, Jr., Mary Hillstead, Simone Blue, Christa Denton, Angela Lee, Deborah A. Paddock, Elaine Pagnozzi; *voices:* Frank Welker, Fred Newman, Joanie Gerber, Belinda Balaski, Roger Behr, Roger Peltz, Neil Ross, Marilyn Schreffler, Bill Ratner, Jane Kean, Robert Holt, Jay Stewart.

Two youngsters, Ben Crandall (Ethan Hawke) and Wolfgang Muller (River Phoenix), tired of school and local bullies and in love with science fiction, decide to build a spacecraft. They are abetted by local misfit Darren Woods (Jason Presson). Using assorted scraps, junk, and a used television set, the boys find a discarded Tilt-A-Whirl and use it as the craft's body. Surprisingly they get it spaceborne and maneuver it over a drive-in theatre before heading into space where they are gobbled up by a huge spaceship. Hurled through a maze of tunnels, they meet a green monster (Robert Picardo) who spouts dialogue and songs from movies and television. The boys realize the aliens have learned all about Earthlings from space signals and they also discover the aliens will not land on Earth because sci-fi films have pictured them as so villainous. With a better understanding between both humans and aliens, the youths are returned home.

Director Joe Dante, a long-time horror and science fiction movie buff, who directed such fare as HOLLYWOOD BOULEVARD (1976) and THE HOWLING (1981), helmed this film in a loving, tongue-in-cheek manner as noted by *Daily Variety.* "To those who have followed Joe Dante's career, it will be clear that this is a very personal film for the director. EXPLORERS not only stands as an extension of the central idea of his 'It's a Good Live' episode from TWILIGHT ZONE—THE MOVIE, but as a $20,000,000-plus variation on his first (codirected) picture, the film-buff-crazed HOLLYWOOD BOULEVARD."

While the feature contains many inside jokes for genre film enthusiasts, it is still a bit unnerving to have a movie go from a tale of three carefree youngsters catapulting themselves into space in a homemade craft, to the sudden change of them meeting a green creature who sings the theme from "Mr. Ed" and imitates Little Richard. Another problem with the bizarre film was noted by Duane Byrge (*The Hollywood Reporter*), "While the film's creators have quite understandably downplayed the hardware elements in their human-centered story, film's visual look is nevertheless a disappointment."

For its cable television and video cassette release, Dante made alterations in the feature which eliminated approximately three minutes of running time.

THE FACE AT THE WINDOW (Eros, 1939) 65 mins.

Producer/director, John King; based on the play by F. Brooke Warren; screenplay, A. R. Rawlinson, Randall Faye; music, Jack Beaver; art director, Philip Bawcomber; camera, Hone Glendinning; editor, Jack Harris.

Tod Slaughter (Chevalier del Gardo); Marjorie Taylor (Cecile Brisson); John Warwick (Lucien Cortier); Leonard Henry (Gaston); Aubrey Mallalieu (de Brisson); Robert Adair (Inspector Guffert); Wallace Evennett (Professor le Blanc); Kay Lewis (Babette); Margaret Yarde (Le Pinan); Harry Terry (The Face); and: Billy Shine.

Tod Slaughter made his film debut at the age of fifty in 1935 in MARIA MARTEN; OR, THE MURDER IN THE RED BARN and quickly became Britain's equivalent to Bela Lugosi and Boris Karloff in a series of full-blown, melodramatic features which were highlighted by his florid acting and lecherous, murderous motives in the plotlines. THE FACE AT THE WINDOW is considered one of the best of his vehicles and it has touches of sci-fi in that a scientist employs electricity to revitalize the brains of recently deceased corpses to capture their final thoughts. In addition the film features a deformed madman and the usual portions of gleeful oncamera killings by the star.

In 1880 Paris The Wolf is committing a rash of murders. Banker de Brisson (Aubrey Mallalieu) is robbed and his only hope of financial recovery is to obtain the fortunes of Chevalier del Gardo (Tod Slaughter) who promises to oblige in return for the banker's pretty daughter Cecile (Marjorie Taylor) who loves clerk Lucien Cortier (John Warwick). When Cecile spurns him, Chevalier has Lucien framed for the murder and when the banker finds out he dies after seeing a hideous face at the window. Chevalier accuses Lucien of the crime and they agree to a duel, but del Gardo has his underworld minions kidnap Lucien and throw him in the Seine. He escapes and goes to the Blind Rat tavern in disguise. There, Chevalier, who has lured Cecile to the same destination, spots him. Lucien rescues Cecile and escapes. Lucien plans to trap Chevalier by using the experiments of his friend Professor le Blanc (Wallace Evennett) who plans to use electricity to extract the killer's identity from the brain of de Brisson. Chevalier, however, who is The Wolf, kills the scientist. Nevertheless, Lucien conducts the experiments himself after the arrival of the police and Cecile. Chevalier is revealed as the killer. He escapes to his home to kill his deformed brother (Harry Terry), the face he has used in his crimes, but the brother turns on him and they both drown in the Seine.

FACE OF THE SCREAMING WEREWOLF (Associated Distributors, 1965) 60 mins.

Producer/director (English language version), Jerry Warren; director (Spanish language version), Gilbert Solar; screenplay, Solar, Fernando de Fuentes; adaptors, Solar, Juan Garcia; art director, Jorge Fernandez; music, Luis Hernandez Breton; sound, Jose de Perez; camera, Raul Martinez Solares; editor, Carlos Savage.

Lon Chaney (The Mummy/The Werewolf); German 'Tin Tan' Valdes (Casamiro the Janitor); Raymond Gaylord (Scientist); Yolanda Varela (Paquita); and: D. W. Barron, Yerye Beirute, Agustin Fernandez, Consuelo Guerrero de Luna, Oscar Ortiz de Pinedo.

This pasted together sci-fi/horror thriller was created in Mexico by Diana Films in 1959 as LA CASA DEL TERROR [The House of Terror], a comedy/horror film headlining German Valdes, known as Tin Tan, and America's horror king of the 1940s, Lon Chaney, who had a big following in Mexico. When the film was released in the United States in 1965 (after scattered initial showings in Mexican-language theatres) it lost about twenty minutes of

Advertisement for FACE OF THE SCREAMING WEREWOLF (1965).

running time and "new" producer/director Jerry Warren added footage from another Mexican feature, LA MOMIA [The Mummy] (1957) to pad the proceedings. Issued on a dual bill with another Warren release, CURSE OF THE STONE HAND, the butchered version called FACE OF THE SCREAMING WEREWOLF was nearly incomprehensible.

A mad scientist (Raymond Gaylord) is working in Mexico City where he revives dead bodies with blood extracted from office janitor Casamiro (Tin Tan). When the police put a guard on the cemetery, the mad doctor and his assistants steal an Egyptian mummy which is on exhibit at the museum. Legend has it the mummy was once a werewolf. The serum created from Casamiro's blood does not revive the mummy but when lightning from a thunderstorm strikes the laboratory equipment, the jolt brings the mummy (Lon Chaney) back to life. The full moon shines and the mummy is transformed into a werewolf, but is finally caged by the scientist and his assistants. When one of the helpers is killed by the beast, his brain is transplanted into the creature. The latter escapes and abducts Paquita (Yolanda Varela), Casamiro's girlfriend. He follows them as the creature carries the girl to the top of the skyscraper. There the werewolf sets the girl down and accidentally falls over the ledge to his death on the street below.

For the U.S. release, most of Tin Tan's "comedy" footage was deleted in favor of making this a straight horror/sci-fi thriller.

FIEND WITH THE ELECTRONIC BRAIN see BLOOD OF GHASTLY HORROR.

FIEND WITHOUT A FACE (Metro-Goldwyn-Mayer, 1958) 74 mins.

Producers, John Croydon, Richard Gordon; director, Arthur Crabtree; story, Amelia Reynolds Long; screenplay, Herbert J. Leder; music, Buxton Orr; camera, Lionel Banes; editor, R. Q. McNaugh.

Marshall Thompson (Jeff Cummings); Terence Kilburn (Captain Chester); Michael Balfour (Sergeant Kasper); Gil Winfield (Dr. Warren); Shane Cordell (Nurse); Stanley Maxted (Colonel Butler); James Dyrenforth (Mayor Hawkins); Kim Parker (Barbara); Kerrigan Prescott (Atomic Engineer); Kynaston Reeves (Professor Walgate); Peter Madden (Dr. Bradley); R. Meadows White (Ben Adams); Lala Lloyd (Amelia Adams); Robert MacKenzie (Gibbons); Launce Maraschal (Melville).

This John Croydon and Richard Gordon production is one of the most underrated sci-fi fright films of the 1950s. It is well-structured and very exciting, with some of the most frightening monsters ever to populate a genre outing. Fortunately the film has taken on a cult following in recent years and thanks to the video marketplace has become one of the most recognizable of 1950s science fiction thrillers.

Although filmed in Great Britain, the feature is set along the U.S.-Canadian border where the American Air Force is testing atomic powered-boosted radar. Several people are found dead nearby with their brains removed from their bodies, and the Air Force is blamed. Major Jeff Cummings (Marshall Thompson) is assigned to solve the case. It develops a retired professor (Kynaston Reeves) has been using energy from the Air Force's "Operation Dewdrop" project in his mind transfer experiments and as a result his own evil thoughts have created brain-like creatures which live by devouring human brains. Cummings, Barbara Grisselle (Kim Parker) and several others are trapped in a house and besieged by these creatures which are killed with bullets.

Donald C. Willis wrote in *Horror and Science Fiction Films* (1972), "The action begins (finally) when the fiends become visible. Their method of moving and killing makes them one of the most fascinating of the late-'50s myriad monsters." Ed Naha comments in *The Science Fictionary* (1980), "Better-than-average special effects liven up this thriller a bit." Michael Weldon opined in *The Psychotronic Encyclopedia of Film* (1983), "The scenes of these partially animated creatures choking their screaming victims with their cords while sucking their brains out are the most nightmarish and shocking you'll ever see. Real breathtaking stuff!" *Fangoria* magazine (May, 1985) determined that the film is " . . . one of the classics of low-budget sci-fi/horror from the 50's" and added, "The climactic sequence of the heroes blasting away with .45s at the flying brains is a slam-bang, gory finale to be cherished by horror fans everywhere."

FIGHTING DEVIL DOGS (Republic, 1938) twelve chapters.

Associate producer, Robert Beche; directors, William Witney, John English; screenplay, Barry Shipman, Franklyn Adreon, Ronald Davidson, Sol Shor; music director, Alberto Colombo; camera, William Nobles; editors, Helene Turner, Edward Todd.

Lee Powell (Lieutenant Tom Grayson); Herman Brix [Bruce Bennett] (Frank Corby); Eleanor Stewart (Janet); Montagu Love (General White); Hugh Sothern (Warfield); Sam Flint (Colonel Grayson); "?" (The Lightning); Perry Ivins (Crenshaw); Forrest Taylor (Benson); John Picorri (Gould); Carleton Young (Johnson); John Davidson (Lin Wing); Henry Otho (Sam Hedges); Reed Howes (Parker); Tom London (Wilson); Edmund Cobb (Ellis); Alan Gregg (Macro); Allan Mathews (Todd).

Chapters: 1) The Lightning Strikes; 2) The Mill of Disaster; 3) The Silent Witness; 4) Cargo of Mystery; 5) Undersea Bandits; 6) The Torpedo of Doom; 7) The Phantom Killer; 8) Tides of Trickery; 9) Attack from the Skies; 10) In the Camp of the Enemy; 11) The Baited Trap; 12) Killer at Bay.

Marines Tom Grayson (Lee Powell) and Frank Corby (Herman Brix [Bruce Bennett]) lead a platoon fighting bandits on a tropical island protected by the United States. A death ray wipes out the entire group except for Grayson and Corby and when no one believes their "incredible" tale, they are sent home for courtmartial. However, they are proven innocent when the death weapon is later used to destroy a freighter. In actuality, a master criminal known only as "The Lightning" has developed the weapon and several scientists are organized to find a defense against it. They include Tom's father, Colonel Grayson (Sam Flint), manufacturer Warfield (Hugh Sothern), his daughter Janet (Eleanore Stewart), and electrical inventor Crenshaw (Perry Ivins). Tom finds the Lightning's headquarters but he escapes, having killed Tom's dad by electrifying his laboratory. The villain also uses the *Wing*, his new superplane.

Tom decides one of the scientists must be the culprit and brings the group together announcing he knows the Lightning's identity. Just as he is about to name the madman, a shot is fired by Warfield who tries to escape in his plane. However, he is killed by a ray gun developed by Crenshaw.

FIGHTING DEVIL DOGS is a fast-paced action cliffhanger from the master serial team of directors William Witney and John English. Its sci-fi subplot adds to the proceedings with the gadgetry of the lightning ray and the superplane. The weapon had been employed previously in two other serials THE FIGHTING MARINES (*infra*) and DICK TRACY (1936) (see B/V). This chapterplay proved to be popular and was reissued in a feature version in 1943. In 1966 a 100 minute feature was culled from the chapters and issued to television as TORPEDO OF DOOM.

THE FIGHTING MARINES (Mascot, 1935) twelve chapters.

Executive producer, Nat Levine; supervisor, Barney Sarecky; directors, B. Reeves Eason, Joseph Kane; story, Wallace MacDonald, Maurice Geraghty, Ray Trampe; screenplay, Sarecky, Sherman Lowe; special effects, Howard Lydecker, Jr.; camera, William Nobles; editor, Dick Fantl.

Grant Withers (Corporal Lawrence); Adrian Morris (Sergeant McGowan); Ann Rutherford (Frances Schiller); Robert Warwick (Colonel Bennett); George Lewis (Bill Schiller); Pat O'Malley (Captain Grayson); Victor Potel (Native Chief); Jason Robards (Kota); Donald Reed (Pedro); Lieutenant Franklyn Adreon (Captain Homes); Richard Alexander (Ivan); Frank Reicher (Steinbeck).

Chapters: 1) Human Targets; 2) Isle of Missing Men; 3) The Savage Horde; 4) The Mark of the Tiger Shark; 5) The Gauntlet of Grief; 6) Robbers' Roost; 7) Jungle Terrors; 8) Siege of Halfway Island; 9) Death from the Sky; 10) Wheels of Destruction; 11) Behind the Mask; 12) Two Against the Horde.

The Marines, under Colonel Bennett (Robert Warwick), attempt to establish a landing field on Halfway Island, but they are being sabotaged. The leader of this counter-operation is the mysterious Tiger Shark, who with his minions, has taken millions in pirated booty and developed a radio gravity gun to combat his personal enemies. Corporal Lawrence (Grant Withers) and Sergeant McGowan (Adrian Morris) are ordered to find the Tiger Shark and they trace him to a deserted warehouse which is his base of operations, but he eludes them. Later the Tiger Shark uses his ray gun to destroy an aircraft carrying Lawrence and McGowan, but they parachute to safety. In a shootout as the Tiger Shark tries to leave the isle, a bullet hits a bottle of nitroglycerin, blowing up the cave hideout and the Tiger Shark with it.

THE FIGHTING MARINES was Mascot Pictures' final serial before it became absorbed into the Republic Pictures conglomerate. The cliffhanger's sci-fi aspects are centered around the mad villain and his invention, the futuristic ray gun. The special effects, by uncredited Howard Lydecker, Jr., are the highlight of the chapterplay whose weakness is its scenario. As Jon Tuska noted in *The Vanishing Legion* (1982), ". . . . the plot was exceedingly thin, as if everyone working on the chapterplay realized that it was being made only to fulfill existing contracts with exhibitors."

THE FINAL PROGRAMME see THE LAST DAYS OF MAN ON EARTH.

FLASH GORDON (Universal, 1980) C 100 mins.

Executive producer, Bernard Williams; producer, Dino De Laurentiis; director, Mike Hodges; based on comic strip characters created by Alex Raymond; adaptor, Michael Allin; screenplay, Lorenzo Semple, Jr.; production designer/set designer/costumes, Danilo Donati; supervising art director, Frank Van Der Veer; music, Howard Blake, Queen; assistant director, Brian Cook; second unit director, William Kronick; sound, Ivan Sharrock, Gerry Humphreys; special effects consultant, Glen Robinson; art director (models); Norman Dorme; special effects (models/skies), Richard Conway; co-ordinator of action/movement, Bill Hobbs; Zarkov brain-drain sequence director, Denis Postel; special effects (flying), Derek Botell; matte paintings, Lou Lichtenfield, Bob Scifo; camera, Gil Taylor; additional camera, Harry Waxman; editor, Malcolm Cooke.

Sam J. Jones (Flash Gordon); Melody Anderson (Dale Arden); Topol (Dr. Hans Zarkov); Max Von Sydow (Emperor Ming); Ornella Muti (Princess Aura); Timothy Dalton (Prince Barin); Brian Blessed (Prince Vultan); Peter Wyngarde (Klytus); Mariangela Melato (Kala); John Osborne (Arborian Priest); Richard O'Brien (Fico); John Hallam (Luro); Philip Stone (Zogi the High Priest); Suzanne Danielle (Servant); William Hootkins (Munson); Bobbie Brown (Hedonia); Ted Carroll (Biro); Adrienne Kronenberg (Vultan's Daughter); Robbie Coltrane (Man); Peter Duncan (Treeman); Tessa and Venetia Spicer (Hawkwomen); Leon Greene (Colonel); George Harris (Prince of Ardentia); Doretta Dunkley (Queen of Frigia); Sally Nicholson (Queen of Azuria).

The 1980 remake of FLASH GORDON is a disappointing rendition whose exciting visuals do NOT compensate for either its bland plot or the colorless interpretation of the Alex Raymond comic strip characters. The film is unable to muster any of the charm of the Universal serials starring enthusiastic, rambunctious Buster Crabbe (see B/V). Despite $16,000,000 in domestic box-office receipts (it cost $20,000,000 to make!), the movie, like the previous year's BUCK ROGERS IN THE 25TH CENTURY (q.v.), failed to live up to its illustrious celluloid predecessor. The main appeal of this feature is its myriad of strange creatures and futuristic weapons plus the colorful and exotic ambiance of the planet Mongo. The heavy-handed, tongue-in-cheek approach, however, doomed the film to being nothing more than a minor camp takeoff of characters who must take themselves seriously to be enjoyed. Even the undernourished sexploitation feature FLESH GORDON (1973) (see B/V) is far more fun.

Flash Gordon (Sam J. Jones), Dale Arden (Melody Anderson), and Dr. Zarkov (Topol), hasten to the outlaw planet Mongo to investigate it. There they find Mongo under the rule of the evil Ming the Merciless (Max Von Sydow). Ming, through various tests, has determined humans are too dangerous to continue to exist and he plans to send the moon crashing into the Earth to destroy it. Flash and his pals must (and do) stop him.

Phil Hardy observed in *The Film Encyclopedia: Science Fiction* (1984), " . . . it has none of the mythological appeal of Frederick Stephani's chapterplay which drew out the perversity of Alex Raymond's original comic strip both in the interactions of the various paired characters and in the elaborate decor of Mongo and its environs. In its place [director Michael] Hodges put a knowingness and literalness that works completely against the sense of pulp poetry so essential if we are to believe in Flash, Dale Arden and Zarkov."

THE FLESH EATERS (Cinema Distributors of America, 1964) 92 mins.

Producers, Jack Curtis, Terry Curtis, Arnold Drake; director, Jack Curtis; screenplay, Arnold Drake; music, Julian Stein; technical consultant, Evan J. Aivton; sound effects, Ray Benson; camera, Carson Davidson; editor, Radley Metzger, Frank Forest.

Martin Kosleck (Peter Bartell); Rita Morley (Laura Winters); Byron Sanders (Grant Murdock); Ray Tudor (Omar); Barbara Wilkin (Jan Letterman).

Filmed in 1961 in New York City and its environs, this cheaply-produced poverty row outing did not gain theatrical release for several years. When it did those few who saw it were offered "Instant Blood" packets to protect them from the title creatures. What moviegoers *should have* been protected from was this poorly photo-

Martin Kosleck, Barbara Wilkin, Rita Morley, and Byron Sanders in THE FLESH EATERS (1961).

graphed, inane effort. The title monsters were created by scratching the film, although gore hounds may appreciate the after effects of the monsters' attack on their victims.

Drunken movie star Laura Winters (Rita Morley), traveling with her secretary, Jan Letterman (Barbara Wilkin), hires seaplane pilot Grant Murdock (Byron Sanders) to fly her to her destination. A storm, however, forces them to land on an island where Peter Bartell (Martin Kosleck), a marine biologist is headquartered. They find a skeleton on the shore and are soon under attack by scads of flesh-devouring small sea creatures. At first Bartell denies knowing anything about the situation, but later admits he is trying to control them by using electrical charges to increase their size. When Bartell attempts to force Murdock, at gunpoint, to aid him in his mad scheme to electrify the ocean, Laura tries to stop him and is killed. Meanwhile, another shipwrecked person, beatnik Omar (Ray Tudor), ends being fed to the fish. Bartell is now able to combine the tiny flesh eaters into a huge monster which devours him, but is killed when Grant injects it with Laura's blood. Grant and Jan leave the cursed island.

FLESH FEAST (Viking International, 1970) C 72 mins.

Producers, Veronica Lake, Brad F. Grinter; director, Grinter; screenplay, Grinter, Thomas Casey; makeup, Doug Hobart; production designer, Harry Kerwin; camera, Casey, Andy Romanoff.

Veronica Lake (Dr. Elaine Frederick); Phil Philbin (Ed Casey); Heather Hughes (Kristine); and: Martha Mischon, Yanka Mann, Dian Wilhite, Chris Martell.

Released from a mental institution, Dr. Elaine Frederick (Veronica Lake) moves to Miami and sets up her laboratory headquarters in the basement of a mansion and perfects her youth restoration process which utilizes flesh-eating maggots. As a front she rents room in the house to student nurses. A newspaper reporter has recently been murdered while following a story and his editor, Ed Casey (Phil Philbin), traces the connection to the doctor. He hires detective Kristine (Heather Hughes) who poses as a nurse and rents a room from Dr. Frederick. Soon she is the doctor's assistant. She and Casey learn the leader of a worldwide revolutionary movement is coming to the house for treatment. The revolutionaries take over the house and Dr. Frederick learns their commander is really Adolf Hitler who was responsible for her mother's death. The doctor turns the flesh-eating maggots on Hitler and he dies a violent death.

One-time Paramount glamour star Veronica Lake (of the peek-a-boo hair fame) was down on her professional luck in Miami, Florida when producer/director Brad F. Grinter asked her to star in and co-produce this low-grade thriller. Lake does sufficiently well as the mad scientist (in a role originally written for a male), but the lame production values negate her appearance. Although the motion picture received full distribution it did little to enhance the star's comeback hopes.

FLESH FOR FRANKENSTEIN (CFDC, 1974) C 95 mins.

Presenter, Andy Warhol; executive producers, Carlo Ponti, Jean Yanne, Jean-Pierre Rassam; producer, Andrew Braunsberg; director, Paul Morrissey; based on characters created by Mary Shelley; screenplay, Morrissey; music, Carlo Gizzi; camera, Luigi Kueveillier; editor, Ted Johnson.

Joe Dallesandro (Nicholas); Udo Kier (Baron Frankenstein); Monique Van Vooren (Katrin); Arno Juerging (Otto); Srodjan Zelenovik (Man Monster); Dalila Di Lazzaro (Girl Monster).

Produced abroad amidst much fanfare by pop culturist Andy Warhol, this blood-and-guts version of *Frankenstein* has a multitude of alternate release titles: CARNE PER FRANKENSTEIN [Flesh for Frankenstein], ANDY WARHOL'S FRANKENSTEIN, WARHOL'S FRANKENSTEIN, FRANKENSTEIN EXPERI-

Advertisement for FLESH FOR FRANKENSTEIN (1974) (a.k.a. ANDY WARHOL'S FRANKENSTEIN).

MENT, and THE DEVIL AND DR. FRANKENSTEIN, to name a few. It was filmed in 3-D and was a companion piece to BLOOD FOR DRACULA (1974), which featured much of the same production team. Grossing $5,000,000, it was one of those productions a filmgoer either loathed or loved, depending on one's penchant for gore and sex.

Deranged scientist Baron Frankenstein (Udo Kier), with the aid of his equally unbalanced assistant, Otto (Arno Juerging), plots to create a master Serbian race of zombies but falls in love with his beautiful female creation (Dalia Di Lazzaro). Meanwhile his wife (Monique Van Vooren), who is also his sister, seduces a field hand (Joe Dallesandro). The Baron decides to make a male (Srojan Zelenovik) to mate with his artificial woman and he kills a farmer and plants his head on a body he has created. The Baron's wife eventually seduces the monster while the Baron is eliminated by his creation in a bloody finale.

Ed Naha noted in *The Science Fictionary* (1980), that the feature was termed "a put-on by some and a sham by others" and he labeled it a "gory little piece of fluff." Phil Hardy in *The Film Encyclopedia: Science Fiction* (1984) wrote of this 3-Dimensional pastiche, "The result is an ugly looking would-be Jacobean tragedy in which the corpses pile up in a suitable enough fashion but to little purpose." On the other hand, Michael Weldon decided in *The Psychotronic Encyclopedia of Film* (1983), "It's a comedy-gore-sex-horror movie that delivers . . . totally sick and disgustingly wonderful."

The feature was reissued theatrically in 1982.

THE FLY (Twentieth Century-Fox, 1986) C 100 mins.

Producer, Stuart Cornfeld; co-producer, Marc-Ami Boyman, Kip Ohman; director, David Cronenberg; based on the short story by George Langelaan; screenplay, Charles Edward Pogue, Cronenberg; assistant directors, John Board, Kim Winther, Patricia Rozema, Thomas P. Quinn; production designer, Carol Spier; visual consultant, Harold Michaelson; art director, Rolf Harvey; set designer, James McAteer, Kirk Cheney; set decorator, Elinor Rose Galbraith; The Fly creator/designer, Chris Walas, Inc.; music, Howard Shore; orchestrator, Homer Dennison; music editor, Jim Weidman; costume designer, Denis Cronenberg; makeup, Shonagh Jabour; stunt co-ordinator, Dwayne McLean; sound, Bryan Day, Michael Lacroix, Keith Grant; sound effects editor, Jane Tattersall; sound editors, David Evans, Wayne Griffin, Richard Cadger; computer/video effects supervisor, Lee Wilson; camera, Mark Irwin; additional camera, Robin Miller; editor, Ronald Sanders.

Jeff Goldblum (Seth Brundle); Geena Davis (Veronica Quaife);

Jeff Goldblum in THE FLY (1986).

John Getz (Stathis Borans); Joy Boushel (Tawny); Les Carlson (Dr. Cheevers); George Chuvalo (Marky); Michael Copeman (Man in Bar); David Cronenberg (Gynecologist); Carol Lazare (Nurse); Shawn Hewitt (Clerk).

Exceptional scientist Seth Brundle (Jeff Goldblum) is secretly working on a matter transmitter and unsuccessfully transports a baboon, who comes back inside out. Still he feels he will perfect the machinery and tells this to pretty journalist Veronica Quaife (Geena Davis) who wants to report his amazing discovery to the world via a scientific journal run by her ex-lover Stathis Borans (John Getz). Seth and Geena become lovers but jealous Stathis enters the scene and in a drunken mood, the scientist puts himself through the matter transmitter. He doesn't realize a fly has joined him in the module. Emerging from the experiment, Seth finds himself full of energy, with a terrific appetite for sex and sweets. Eventually, however, he begins to note physical changes and realizes he is developing the characteristics of a fly ("no compassion, no compromise") as parts of his body begin to fall away, only to be replaced by those of a fly.

As one might anticipate, director David Cronenberg's loose remake of the well-regarded 1958 feature (see B/V) is hardly for the weak of stomach. R-rated because of its extremely graphic scenes (the baboon turned inside out, a monster getting sick, an abortion, etc.), the film is directed to blood-and-guts voyeurs, all part of Cronenberg's following. The film, however, does have a tender romance between the "hero" and heroine and the roles are acceptably played by Goldblum and Davis, with the former expressing dark humor about his tragic plight. (As Dennis Fischer notes in *The Hollywood Reporter,* "Though Brundle slowly loses his humanity, he doesn't lose his sense of humor and the absurd, referring to himself as 'Brundle-Fly,' making a video demonstrating how his eating techniques now resemble a fly's, and setting up a museum of lost body parts in his medicine chest.")

Daily Variety cited its reservations, "[It] lacks a vision which would give . . . [it] weight and import. Instead they [the scenes] tend to rise and then fall with a thud until the next one comes along. . . . Cronenberg's version centers on a slow disintegration with little energy spent on trying to undo the deed. Consequently, the sympathy from the early going is squandered on sensationalism later on. . . . THE FLY is too trapped by its desire to shock to be truly affecting."

On the other hand, Patrick Goldstein (*Los Angeles Times*) was enthralled with the film which for him " . . . unfolds with such eerie grandeur that it will leave you stoked with a creepy high for hours after you've left the theater. . . . He's spun a tale that peeks into the darkest corners of our wildest dreams."

The film grossed $34,861,294 in its first nine weeks at the domestic box-office and won an Academy Award for its artful makeup. It led to THE FLY II (1989) with Eric Stoltz.

THE FOOD OF THE GODS (American International, 1976) C 88 mins.

Executive producer, Samuel Z. Arkoff; producer/director, Bert I. Gordon; based in part on the novel by H. G. Wells; screenplay, Gordon; art director, Graeme Murray; set decorator, John Stark; assistant director, Flora Gordon; sound, George Mulholland; camera, Reginald Morris; editor, Corky Ehlers.

Marjoe Gortner (Morgan); Pamela Franklin (Lorna); Ralph Meeker (Bensington): Ida Lupino (Mrs. Skinner); John Cypher (Brian Oster); Belina Balaski (Rita); Tom Stovall (Tom); John McLiam (Mr. Skinner); Chuck Courtney (Robert Davis).

Producer/director Bert I. Gordon twice picturized H. G. Wells' novel *Food of the Gods* (1924); first in 1964 with the inane VILLAGE OF THE GIANTS (q.v.) and this version a dozen years later. With a bigger budget and better special effects (some of the monsters were constructed by talented Rick Baker), the new edition is definitely the superior of the two. Nevertheless, it is still a mundane thriller about science gone awry.

On an isolated isle, a mysterious substance seeps through the ground and a local farmer (John McLiam) feeds it to his chickens and they become giants. Corrupt businessman Bensington (Ralph Meeker) learns of this discovery and he tries to isolate the substance by bringing a number of scientists and investors to the isle, unaware the ingredient has also turned insects and rats into giants. Ex-football hero Morgan (Marjoe Gortner) and his buddy Brian Oster (John Cypher) vacation on the island and they aid bacteriologist Lorna Scott (Pamela Franklin) in trying to destroy the menace. Both the farmer and his wife (Ida Lupino) are destroyed by the giant creatures as huge rats devour Bensington. Morgan uses the island's water supply to drown the creatures.

Filmed at Bowne Island, near Vancouver, British Columbia, this Samuel Z. Arkoff presentation contains special effects "which range from impressive to poor" (*Boxoffice* magazine). Better than the average Bert I. Gordon sci-fi feature, the movie's "dialogue and script are laughable as usual" (Michael Weldon, *The Psychotronic Encyclopedia of Film* [1983]), while Ed Naha in *The Science Fictionary* (1980), judged it a "Fairly juvenile adaptation of the H. G. Wells novel . . . ." The film used only a portion of the Wells work, thus leaving the path clear for a sequel—which mercifully did not appear.

FORBIDDEN WORLD (New World, 1982) C 84 mins.

Producer, Roger Corman; co-producer, Mary Ann Fisher; director, Allan Holzman; story, Jim Wynorski, R. J. Robertson; screenplay, Tim Curnen; music, Susan Justin; production designers, Chris Horner, Robert Skotak; art directors, Joe Garrity, Wayne Springfield; set decorator, Chuck Seaton; special makeup effects, J. C. Buechler, Don Olivera; assistant director, Mark Allan; second unit director, Aaron Lipstadt; sound, Mark Ulano; camera, Tim Suhrstedt; editor, Holzman.

Jesse Vint (Mike Colby); June Chadwick (Dr. Barbara Glaser); Dawn Dunlap (Tracy Baxter); Linden Chiles (Dr. Gordon Hauser); Fox Harris (Dr. Cal Tinburgen); Raymond Oliver (Brian Beale); Scott Paulin (Earl Richards); Michael Bowen (Jimmy Swift).

This is another hastily-assembled entry from producer Roger Corman's New World Pictures which utilized sets from GALAXY OF TERROR (1981), which in turn used left-over interiors from BATTLE BEYOND THE STARS (1980) (q.v.) whose space scenes turn up here also. In *The Psychotronic Encyclopedia of Film* (1983), Michael Weldon quipped, "A pretty sick quickie for the legions of undiscriminating science-fiction/gore fans." Like most Corman low-budget entries, the film has an underlying sense of macabre humor and for its R-rating, some gory sex scenes. Allegedly to avoid an X-rating, the filmmakers deleted a scene in which a young woman is raped by an alien monster.

On a faraway planet, research scientists have implanted an altered cell into a woman and she gives birth to a creature which matures into a spider-like monster which devours all the laboratory animals as well as a lab assistant. Mike Colby (Jesse Vint), a high-paid hit man, is called to the planet to put the beast under control, but as it continues to grow, the very intelligent monster attacks nude Tracy Baxter (Dawn Dunlap) and devours a doctor (Linden Chiles). When another doctor (June Chadwick) attempts to communicate with the alien being via computer, to which the monster has attached itself, the thing responds by raping her with a tentacle which it proceeds to run through her neck. It is now clear the monster will take control. However, yet another doctor (Fox Harris), dying of liver cancer, forces Colby to remove the cancerous growth and feed it to the creature, thus bringing about its quick demise.

Variety noted, "If nothing else, Roger Corman & Co. can be credited in FORBIDDEN WORLD with creating the first screen monster to die of cancer. Unfortunately, that's about the only novel twist in this mini-budget sci-fi horror show which, if you've seen ALIEN, is thoroughly predictable from start to finish."

FRANKENSTEIN (Universal, 1931) 71 mins.

Producer, Carl Laemmle, Jr.; director, James Whale; based on the play by Peggy Webling from the novel by Mary Shelley; adaptors, Robert Florey, John L. Balderston; screenplay, Garrett Fort, Florey, Francis Edward Faragoh; art director, Charles D. Hall; set decorator, Herman Rosse; makeup, Jack Pierce; music, David Brockman; special electrical effects, Kenneth Strickfaden; special effects, John P. Fulton; camera, Arthur Edeson; editor, Clarence Kolster.

Colin Clive (Dr. Henry Frankenstein); Mae Clarke (Elizabeth); John Boles (Victor Moritz); Boris Karloff (The Monster); Frederick Kerr (Baron Frankenstein); Edward Van Sloan (Dr. Waldman); Dwight Frye (Fritz); Lionel Belmore (The Burgomaster); Marilyn Harris (Little Maria); Michael Mark (Peasant Father); Arletta Duncan, Pauline Moore (Bridesmaids); Francis Ford (Wounded Villager on the Hill/Extra at Lecture)

The granddaddy of all horror films is no doubt the first talking version of FRANKENSTEIN, the 1931 Universal production, so grandly Gothic and horrific. While the film is considered most often a straight horror picture, it should be remembered that science fiction plays a great part in it, for the monster is created by a mixture of science and nature, precipitating the horrors which were to follow. Conceived on a budget slightly under $300,000 (some $30,000 over its scheduled cost), the film, issued for the 1931 Christmas holiday trade, grossed over $5,000,000 in its initial release and made many more millions in its various reissues, including a most successful mid-1930s pairing with DRACULA (1931) starring Bela Lugosi.

The property had originally been purchased to star Lon Chaney, "The Man of a Thousand Faces," but he died in 1930 after making only one talkie, THE UNHOLY THREE (1930). The project was then handed to director Robert Florey who intended to film it with Bela Lugosi as the monster. Lugosi was unhappy with a non-speaking role and the heavy makeup required for the characterization and he and Florey were instead teamed for MURDERS IN THE RUE MORGUE (1932). Britisher James Whale took over as director of FRANKENSTEIN and his sense of the Gothic plus underlying gallows humor gave the production the needed flavor and edge for its mass appeal. This was emphasized by Jack Pierce's masterful makeup for the monster, the casting of Boris Karloff as the creation and fine work by Colin Clive as Dr. Frankenstein, Mae Clarke as his fiancee, Edward Van Sloan as his mentor, and especially Dwight Frye as his demented, hunchback assistant. Although all these roles have since become stereotyped in screen legend, the film and these characters remain excitingly fresh with each new viewing.

FRANKENSTEIN opens with a real punch with the eerie burial scene and the arrival of Frankenstein (Colin Clive) and Fritz (Dwight Frye) to cut down the hanged corpse so the cadaver may be used by the scientist in his experiments with creating life. Housed in a remote old mill, Frankenstein has fashioned a body of a man from parts from the living and he plans to give it life via formulas he has created and the added spark from electricity. Worried about his state of mind, Frankenstein's fiancee, Elizabeth (Mae Clarke) and his best friend, Victor Moritz (John Boles), go to his medical school professor, Dr. Waldman (Edward Van Sloan), for advice. The three trek to the old mill on a stormy night to see Frankenstein and are forced to watch him instill the creature (Boris Karloff) he has created with life. The hideously ugly giant, whose head contains a criminal brain stolen from Waldman's medical school, reacts violently and the sadistic Fritz beats it. The creature murders Fritz, and Frankenstein, now at his wits end, decides to destroy the thing by decapitation. Waldman agrees to perform the operation on Frankenstein's wedding day, but the monster awakens and kills Waldman. The creature terrorizes the countryside, accidentally drowning a small girl. The monster breaks into Frankenstein's home and abducts Elizabeth with the angry villagers and the Baron on their trail. Frankenstein confronts his monster in an old windmill and it lets Elizabeth go before carrying his creator to the mill top. The villagers set fire to the structure as the angry creature throws Frankenstein down to them. The fire consumes the monster and the mill, but Frankenstein is only slightly injured. He and Elizabeth marry.

FRANKENSTEIN was strong stuff for 1931, and it caused a sensation. John P. Fulton's special effects and Charles D. Hall's art direction played a major part in the film's appeal as did Kenneth Strickfaden's special electrical effects. The machinery that Strickfaden concocted for the laboratory scenes were used and reused and even today remain the epitome of the equipment for a mad scientist's lab—he even used them for YOUNG FRANKENSTEIN (1974) (q.v.).

One scene in the original print was deleted before general release—that of the monster accidentally drowning its new playmate, the young girl. In 1987 MCA Home Video issued a restored version of the classic, including this sequence, on videocassette and laser disc.

FRANKENSTEIN AND THE MONSTER FROM HELL (Paramount, 1974) C 93 mins.

Producer, Roy Skeggs; director, Terence Fisher; based on characters created by Mary Shelley; screenplay, John Elder [Anthony Hinds]; music, James Bernard; art director, Scott Macgregor; assistant director, Derek Whitehurst; sound, Maurice Askew, Les Hammond; camera, Brian Probyn; editor, James Needs.

Peter Cushing (Baron Frankenstein); Shane Briant (Dr. Simon Helder); Madeline Smith (Sarah); David Prowse (The Monster); John Stratton (Klaus the Asylum Keeper); Charles Lloyd-Pack (Professor Durendel); Bernard Lee (Tarmud); Sydney Bromley (Muller); Patrick Troughton (Body Snatcher); Janet Hargreaves (Chatter); Philip Voss (Ernst).

Young Dr. Simon Helder (Shane Briant) works to create life as did his idol, the late Dr. Victor Frankenstein. However, he is arrested and tried for sorcery and sent to Carlsbad's Criminal Lunatic Asylum where he is badly mistreated until the prison physician, Dr. Victor (Peter Cushing), comes to his defense. He learns the doctor is actually Dr. Frankenstein who really runs the asylum since he has information on those officials in charge. Frankenstein is aided in his chores by a young mute girl, Sarah (Madeline Smith), known as "The Angel." Frankenstein asks Helder's help since his hands have been burned and he cannot perform surgery. Helder discovers Frankenstein has created a new being from the body of a monstrous inmate and the creation is a grotesque giant with the brain of a professor whom Frankenstein caused to commit suicide. The creature (David Prowse) cares for The Angel since in his former life he saved her from an attack by her father, the asylum director, Klaus (John Stratton). When the creature proves to be dangerous, Frankenstein plans to mate him with The Angel to produce a calmer offspring. Before this happens, the creature goes berserk and attacks Frankenstein. But the girl, whose voice returns, saves the doctor as the creature escapes and kills Klaus. As the warders search for the creature, the inmates are turned loose and when the creature approaches Angel for help, the inmates think he is hurting her and they tear him to pieces. Recovering from his wounds, Dr. Frankenstein plans another artificial creation.

FRANKENSTEIN AND THE MONSTER FROM HELL was Peter Cushing's sixth appearance as Dr. Frankenstein for Hammer Films and the feature is a cut above most of the series entries. Finely directed by Terence Fisher, the film was horrific enough to please genre audiences who also appreciated Peter Cushing's return to the role that brought him horror film stardom in 1956 in THE CURSE OF FRANKENSTEIN (q.v.). David Prowse (later Darth Vader in the STAR WARS [q.v.] series) made a most grotesque, but not overly appealing, monster. Like most horror efforts of the 1970s, the movie had its share of multi-color gore, mostly on the medical side.

Eric Hoffman wrote in *Monsters of the Movies* magazine (Number 5, 1975), "The screenplay, by long-time Hammer producer Anthony Hinds (under his pseudonym of John Elder) is a bit on the slow side, lapsing at times into periods of talk that could possibly have been shortened or even done away with. Besides limiting the film's range of setting, the screenplay also causes the character of Baron Frankenstein to suffer a slight lapse, making him just a bit more ruthless than we've possibly seen him. In total, it's about 80 percent effective in final execution."

FRANKENSTEIN CREATED WOMAN (Twentieth Century-Fox, 1966) C 92 mins.

Producer, Anthony Nelson Keys; director, Terence Fisher; based on characters created by Mary Shelley; screenplay, John Elder [Anthony Hinds]; production designer, Bernard Robinson; art director, Don Mingaye; music, James Bernard; music supervisor, Philip Martell; assistant director, Douglas Hermes; makeup, George Partleton; sound, Ken Rawkins; special effects, Les Bowie; camera,

Arthur Grant; supervising editors, James Needs, Spencer Reeve; sound editor, Roy Hyde.

Peter Cushing (Baron Frankenstein); Susan Denberg (Christina) Thorley Walters (Dr. Hertz); Robert Morris (Hans); Duncan Lamont (Prisoner); Peter Blythe (Anton); Barry Warren (Karl); Derek Fowlds (Johann); Alan MacNaughtan (Kleve); Peter Madden (Chief of Police); Philip Ray (Mayor); Ivan Beavis (Landlord); Colin Jeavons (Priest); Bartlett Mullins (Bystander); Alec Mango (Spokesman); Stuart Middleton (Hans as a Boy); John Maxim (Police Sergeant); Kevin Flood (Jailer).

Dr. Frankenstein (Peter Cushing) is revived by electricity and he and his assistant Dr. Hertz (Thorley Walters) continue his experiments in creating life. The doctor is convinced that a human soul is required to sustain artificial life successfully. Frankenstein rescues a young lass from drowning and turns her into the beautiful Christina (Susan Denberg) and, in turn, is able to infuse her dead boyfriend's soul into her body. The doctor is justly proud of his finest creation but problems arise when the soul of the dead man, sent to the gallows for a crime he did not commit, takes over the girl's mental processes and she starts killing those who falsely accused him. The locals become angered by the killings and turn on Frankenstein and Christina. The girl, who has murdered the three men responsible for her lover's death, jumps off a cliff to her death while Frankenstein escapes.

FRANKENSTEIN CREATED WOMAN was the fourth Hammer production to star Peter Cushing as Dr. Frankenstein and it was far superior to its predecessor, THE EVIL OF FRANKENSTEIN (1963) (q.v.).

FRANKENSTEIN MEETS THE SPACE MONSTER (Allied Artists, 1965) 78 mins.

Executive producer, Alan V. Iselin; producer, Robert McCarthy; director, Robert Gaffney; suggested by characters created by Mary Shelley; story, George Garrett, John Rodenbeck, R. H. W. Dillard; screenplay, George Garrett; camera, Saul Midwall; editor, Laverne Keating.

James Karen (Dr. Adam Steele); David Kernan (General Bowers); Nancy Marshall (Karen Grant); Marilyn Hanold (Princess Marcuzan); Lou Cutell (Nadir); Robert Reilly (Colonel Frank Saunders/Frankenstein).

A "Frankenstein" film in name only, this schlock masterpiece is so out of kilter that it provides almost endless amusement for fans of non-mainstream sci-fi features. Where else could one find such pleasures as: an android astronaut who has his face disfigured and goes mad; a sexy female alien leader and her fussy bald dwarf associate who kidnap young girls from a pool party to breed on their planet; a horrific monster with three claws on each hand and bulging eyes; and a soundtrack with a rock group belting out "That The Way It's Got To Be"? Who could ask for more?

Scientists Dr. Adam Steele (James Karen) and Karen Grant (Nancy Marshall) develop a spacecraft manned by android Colonel Frank Saunders (Robert Reilly). The craft is shot down by an alien saucer and Saunders parachutes to safety in Puerto Rico where the outer space craft also lands. The aliens, led by beautiful Princess Marcuzan (Marilyn Hanold), and assisted by dwarf Nadir (Lou Cutell), have come to Earth for young females to bring back to their war-scarred planet for repopulation purposes. On the craft with them is a giant monster called Mull. The aliens use a laser gun on Frank, disfiguring his face and short circuiting his brain, causing him to go mad. The two scientists try to locate Frank while the aliens steal young girls and imprison them on their ship. Frank is found and repaired. He later sets the girls free and plants a bomb on the craft. Just as Mull is about to destroy him, Frank detonates the explosives and all aboard the spaceship are blown up.

Michael Weldon in *The Psychotronic Encyclopedia of Film* (1983) enthused, "Don't miss. It's the worst." Donald F. Glut commented in *The Frankenstein Legend* (1973), "Much of the film consisted of newsreel footage of astronauts, rockets, and the army. The rest of the film was a travesty of the name of Frankenstein."

FRANKENSTEIN MEETS THE WOLFMAN (Universal, 1943) 74 mins.

Producer, George Waggner; director, Roy William Neill; suggested by characters in the novel *Frankenstein* by Mary Shelley; screenplay, Curt Siodmak; art directors, John B. Goodman, Martin Obzina; set decorators, Russel A. Gausman, E. R. Robinson; make-up, Jack Pierce; music director, Hans J. Salter; assistant director, Melville Shyer; gowns, Vera West; sound, Bernard B. Brown; special effects, John P. Fulton; camera, George Robinson; editor, Edward Curtiss.

Lon Chaney (The Wolfman/Lawrence Talbot); Ilona Massey (Baroness Elsa Frankenstein); Patric Knowles (Dr. Mannering); Lionel Atwill (Mayor); Bela Lugosi (Monster); Maria Ouspenskaya (Maleva); Dennis Hoey (Inspector Owen); Don Barclay (Franzec); Rex Evans (Vazec); Dwight Frye (Rudi); Harry Stubbs (Bruno); Adia Kuynetzoff, Beatrice Roberts (Villagers); Doris Lloyd (Nurse); Martha Vickers (Young Girl); Eddie Parker (Stuntman); Jeff Corey, Torben Meyer (Grave Robbers).

Assuming two monsters for the price of one was what was needed to beef up the "Frankenstein" series during World War II,

Lon Chaney and Ilona Massey in FRANKENSTEIN MEETS THE WOLFMAN (1943).

Universal combined Frankenstein and the Wolfman into one package, deftly picking up the plots from THE WOLFMAN (1941) and THE GHOST OF FRANKENSTEIN (1942) (q.v.) into a chiller which stands on its own as a fast-paced, actionful and exceedingly entertaining motion picture. Since Lon Chaney had played both monsters in the preceding films, and he could only play one here, he was recast as The Wolfman, while Bela Lugosi, who had rejected the assignment a dozen years earlier, was now cast as Frankenstein's monster. "The producers have spent time and money on the production and have gone to considerable trouble to give it the proper atmospheric touches that seem to delight the horror addicts," Kate Cameron wrote in the *New York Daily News.*

Actually it is surprising that FRANKENSTEIN MEETS THE WOLFMAN is as good as it is, considering the tampering that went on following its filming. In THE GHOST OF FRANKENSTEIN (q.v.), the monster had talked at the finale since the brain of broken-necked Ygor had been placed in his skull. Bela Lugosi played Ygor to perfection so it was logical he would speak as the monster in this production and that is what was filmed. For some unknown reason, his dialogue scenes were cut although in several sequences his lips can be seen moving. Also Lugosi was too old for any strenuous scenes and he was doubled by Eddie Parker and the producers were careless in showing too many closeups of Parker as the monster, whose face was fuller than that of Lugosi's. Finally Lugosi has often been lambasted by critics for his portrayal of the monster as a weak, lumbering creature, lacking the strength of the Karloff and Chaney, and later Glenn Strange, interpretations. In reality, Lugosi played the part well since the monster is supposed to be weakened by age but the explanation for this in the film seems to be missing. There is a powerful scene near the finale when the monster has been infused with life and Lugosi turns to mad scientist Patric Knowles and smiles a malevolent smile. In this one facial feature Lugosi brilliantly manages to convey the horrible truth that the monster is strong again and at his full physical potential.

Graverobbers pillage the burial place of Lawrence Talbot (Lon Chaney) and the full moon revives his corpse and he becomes a werewolf again. Wanting to be dead forever, Talbot searches out old gypsy Maleva (Maria Ouspenskaya), whose son Bela had bitten Talbot, making him a lycanthrope. She feels responsibility for him and escorts him to Dr. Frankenstein but upon arrival in the village of Vasaria they find the doctor is dead and his castle/laboratory in ruins. Following the murder of a young girl (Martha Vickers), Talbot flees to the ruins where he digs up the body of Frankenstein's monster (Bela Lugosi) out of its icy grave. The revived, but weak, creature, shows Talbot the location of Frankenstein's diaries, but they are useless. Hoping the late doctor's daughter, Elsa (Ilona Massey), will have the journals he needs, Talbot contacts her and she arrives at festival time, but does not know of their location. The monster comes to the village and is whisked away in a wagon by Talbot. Dr. Mannering (Patric Knowles), who once tried to treat Talbot, follows him to Vasaria and agrees to help him and the monster by draining off their life sources. The villagers become angry by the renewed activity at Frankenstein's castle, but the mayor (Lionel Atwill) tries to calm them. Mannering becomes obsessed with seeing the monster at its full power and gives it the electricity it requires before coming to its senses. It is too late as the monster breaks free and begins wrecking the laboratory but at the same time the moon becomes full and Talbot turns into a werewolf and he and the monster do battle while Mannering and Elsa escape. One of the villagers (Rex Evans) dynamites the old dam above the castle and the avalanche of water drowns the two battling creatures.

Naturally the box-office success of this installment brought back the two monsters, along with Count Dracula for two cinematic followups: HOUSE OF FRANKENSTEIN (1944) and HOUSE OF DRACULA (1945) (qq.v.)

FRANKENSTEIN MUST BE DESTROYED (Warner Bros., 1970) C 97 mins.

Producer, Anthony Nelson Keys; director, Terence Fisher; based on characters created by Mary Shelley in the novel *Frankenstein;* story, Keys, Bert Batt; screenplay, Batt; art director, Bernard Robinson; music, James Bernard; music director, Philip Martell; assistant director, Batt; wardrobe supervisor, Rosemary Burrows; make-up, Eddie Knight; sound, Tony Lumkin; camera, Arthur Grant; supervising film editor, James Needs; editor, Gordon Hales; sound editor, Don Ranasinghe.

Peter Cushing (Baron Frankenstein); Simon Ward (Dr. Karl Holst); Veronica Carlson (Anna Spengler); Thorley Walters (Inspector Frisch); Freddie Jones (Dr. Richter); Maxine Audley (Ella Brandt); Geoffrey Bayldon (Police Doctor); George Pravda (Dr. George Brandt); Colette O'Neil (Madwoman); Harold Goodwin (Burglar); Frank Middlemas (Guest); George Belbin, Norman Shelley, Michael Gover (Anna's Lodgers); Peter Copley (Principal); Jim Collier (Dr. Heidecke); Alan Surtees, Windsor Davies (Police Sergeants).

This was the fifth Hammer Films feature starring Peter Cushing as Dr. Frankenstein and by now the lunatic scientist was depicted as being as evil as his creation. " . . . [the] complicated plot was more than usually interesting and Terence Fisher's direction gave it lively treatment," wrote Allen Eyles, Robert Adkinson and Nicholas Fry in *The House of Horror* (1973), a history of Hammer Films. Michael Weldon commented in his *The Psychotronic Encyclopedia of Film* (1983), "A scene with a buried body bursting through the soil because of a broken water pipe is memorable, but some of the [tame] gore effects get a little silly, especially when the doctors use a drill and a saw to remove a brain."

A series of brutal murders plague a European city and it develops the fiend is Dr. Frankenstein (Peter Cushing) who needs body parts for his brain transplant experiments. He sets up his laboratory in a house owned by Anna Spengler (Veronica Carlson) who deals in stolen drugs along with her lover, Dr. Karl Hoist (Simon Ward), the latter stealing them from the asylum where he is employed. Frankenstein blackmails the two into assisting him with his work and they kidnap an asylum inmate, Dr. Frederick Brandt (George Pravda), but he is killed in the attempt. At the laboratory,

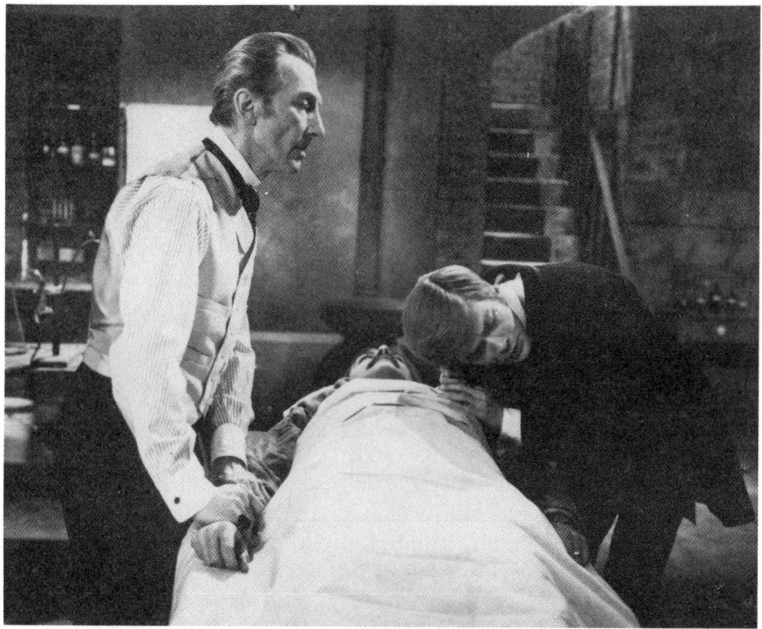

Peter Cushing and Simon Ward in FRANKENSTEIN MUST BE DESTROYED (1970).

the scientist salvages Brandt's brain and transplants it into the head of a giant (Freddie Jones). When he revives, the creature realizes what has happened and Anna stabs him. He escapes and goes to his home where Brandt's wife (Maxine Audley) is terrified of him. The creature then only wants to kill Frankenstein for what he has done. The doctor, however, murders Anna because he believes she has set it free. The monster burns the house, but the doctor escapes with Brandt's notes only to be cornered by his creation and carried into the burning house to die.

FRANKENSTEIN—1970 (Allied Artists, 1958) 83 mins.

Producer, Aubrey Schenck; director, Howard W. Koch; based on characters created by Mary Shelley; story, Schenck, Charles A. Moses; screenplay, Richard Landau, George Worthing Yates; production designer, Jack T. Collis; makeup, Gordon Bau; music, Paul A. Dunlap; camera, Carl E. Guthrie; editor, John A. Bushelman.

Boris Karloff (Baron Victor von Frankenstein); Tom Duggan (Mike Shaw); Jana Lund (Carolyn Hayes); Donald Barry (Douglas

Row); Charlotte Austin (Judy Stevens); Irwin Berke (Inspector Raab); Rudolph Anders (Wilhelm Gottfried); John Dennis (Morgan Haley); Norbert Schiller (Shuter); Mike Lane (Hans/The Creature).

Boris Karloff returned to the "Frankenstein" series in this weak Allied Artists feature, but this time he was Baron Victor von Frankenstein, a descendant of the notorious scientist, and the resultant film was hardly one of his best. Outside of an extremely well-executed opening sequence, which proved to be a scene for a TV show shot at Castle Frankenstein, the production lacks entertainment appeal. Most notable of all, Karloff's performance is sub-par. Only ex-cowboy star Don "Red" Barry, as a smart-mouthed film director, and lovely leading ladies Charlotte Austin and Jana Lund give the proceedings spice.

Set in 1970, the film has a reluctant Baron von Frankenstein (Boris Karloff), who has been disfigured by the Nazis, permitting a TV crew to film the story of his ancestor and his infamous creation at the family mansion. Actually the monster still lives in a laboratory beneath the castle and the Baron gives it a new brain when his servant (Norbert Schiller) accidentally finds out about his employer's bizarre experiments. Eyes for the creature (Mike Lane) are provided by another acquaintance (Rudolph Anders) and the Baron plans to take revenge on the obnoxious director (Don Barry) and his cast/crew. When the police learn of the murders, the Baron intends to destroy his incriminating handiwork. However, the creature turns on his maker and both die in a laboratory explosion.

Indulgent contemporary reviewers seem to appreciate FRANKENSTEIN 1970. *Variety* judged it a "Well-made entry in the horror class." and the British *Kinematograph Weekly* acknowledged, "It follows the pattern of previous Frankenstein films inasmuch as the central character seeks the eyes, brains and limbs of the living, but the introduction of the television unit gives the shenanigans zip. . . ." However, Donald C. Willis was much more to the mark in his terse review of the film in *Horror and Science Fiction Films* (1972), "Dismal."

It should be noted that the monster appears in this film in two different guises. First in the opening film-within-a-fight sequence and later as a bandaged giant, both times played by Mike Lane, an actor/wrestler best known for his role as the Primo Carnera-like boxer in THE HARDER THEY FALL (1956). Lane also played the monster on NBC-TV's "Matinee Theatre" on February 5, 1957.

FRANKENSTEIN: THE TRUE STORY (Universal/NBC-TV 11/30-12/1/73) C 200 mins.

Producer, Hunt Stromberg, Jr.; associate producer, Ian Smith; director, Jack Smight; based on the novel by Mary Shelley; teleplay,

Christopher Isherwood, Don Bachardy; music, Gil Melle; art directors, Fred Carter, Wilfred J. Shingleton; camera, Arthur Ibbetson; editor, Richard Marden.

James Mason (Dr. Polidori); Leonard Whiting (Dr. Victor Frankenstein); David McCallum (Henri Clerval); Jane Seymour (Agatha/Prima); Nicola Pagett (Elizabeth Fanschawe); Michael Sarrazin (Adam, the Creature); Michael Wilding (Sir Richard Fanschawe); Clarissa Kaye (Lady Fanschawe); Agnes Moorehead (Mrs. Blair); Margaret Leighton (Francoise DuVal); Ralph Richardson (Mr. Lacy); John Gielgud (Chief Constable); Tom Baker (Sea Captain); Dallas Adams (Felix); Julian Barnes (Young Man); Arnold Diamond (Passenger in Coach)

The famous Mary Shelley novel was never filmed exactly as she wrote it, so in 1973 NBC-TV presented an elaborate, four hour, two-part telefeature purporting to present "The True Story." What it related was a mixture of the novel along with plot ploys borrowed from several of the films, resulting in "a thinking man's horror movie" (Leonard Maltin, *TV Movies and Video Guide,* 1987). Perhaps the most engaging aspect of the production was the fact the artificial man was created as perfect and as time passes, he degenerates physically into a monster.

Dr. Victor Frankenstein (Leonard Whiting) perceives no hope for the human race and its brutality. So, with associate Dr. Henry Clerval (David McCallum), he seeks to create a perfect man, called Adam (Michael Sarrazin). His creation proves to be a handsome, urbane man with an eye for the ladies, although he has fits of rage. Older scientist Dr. Polidori (James Mason) finds out about Frankenstein's artificial man and insists they work together to create a mate for him. The head of the creature's girlfriend, a farm girl (Jane Seymour), is used to create the perfect woman, Prima (Jane Seymour). The monster, by now, however, has begun to degenerate and Frankenstein and his colleagues have no cure. The night Prima is introduced into society, the monster raids the party and kills Prima by decapitation. Frankenstein gives chase to his creation and finds him aboard a ship where he learns that he has also killed his creator's wife (Nicola Pagett). In the Arctic the monster realizes he is doomed and he causes an avalanche, destroying both himself and his haunted creator.

The telefilm was re-edited into a two hour movie which was distributed in Europe and then syndicated to American television. In *Movies Made for Television* (1987), Alvin H. Marill judged the original, "A literate retelling of Mary Shelley's Gothic horror classic with the accent here on character instead of terror, establishing an offbeat relationship between the doctor and his creature."

FRANKENSTEIN'S BLOODY TERROR see FURY OF THE WOLFMAN.

FRANKENSTEIN'S DAUGHTER (Astor, 1957) 85 mins.

Producer, Marc Frederic; director, Richard Cunha; suggested by characters created by Mary Shelley; screenplay, H. E. Barrie; makeup, Harry Thomas; music, Nicholas Carras; special effects, Ira Anderson; camera, Meredith Nicholson; editor, Everett Dodd.

John Ashley (Johnny Bruder); Sandra Knight (Trudy Morton); Donald Murphy (Dr. Oliver Frank/Dr. Frankenstein); Sally Todd (Suzie Lawler); Harold Lloyd, Jr. (Don); Felix Locher (Carter Morton); Wolfe Barzell (Elsu); John Zaremba (Lieutenant Boyle); Robert Dix (Detective Dillon); Voltaire Perkins (Mr. Rockwell); Bill Coontz, George Barrows (Warehouse Employees); Charlotte Portney (Woman); Page Cavanaugh Trio (Themselves); Harry Wilson (The Monster).

A.k.a. SHE MONSTER OF THE NIGHT (in 8mm release).

One of the great stories involving sci-fi films concerns this

Harry Wilson, John Ashley, Sandra Knight, and Donald Murphy in FRANKENSTEIN'S DAUGHTER (1957).

poverty row "classic." Makeup man Harry Thomas created a hideous face for actor Harry Wilson portraying Frankenstein's monster, not knowing the creature was to be female. Thomas then did the only thing he could think of to show gender; he added a huge layer of dark red lipstick. Donald F. Glut describes the title abortion in *The Frankenstein Legend* (1973), "The left half of the face was a mass of twisted tissue. An open, stitched wound ran down the center of the forehead to the tip of the nose. Enormous metal rods protruded from the neck. The back and sides of the head were enclosed in bandages." He judged the film " . . . Astor Pictures' contribution to the list of worst horror films of all time."

Insane scientist Dr. Oliver Frank (Donald Murphy) stays with older scientist Carter Morton (Felix Locher) and his comely teenage niece Trudy (Sandra Knight), who dates classmate Johnny Bruder (John Ashley). Frank is really Dr. Frankenstein, the grandson of the infamous creator of a monster. Oliver too works at creating human life, but his male creations will not obey him, so he decides to create a woman. When Suzie Lawler (Sally Todd) refuses his advances, Oliver runs over her with his car and uses her head on the body he has already created, developing a monster (Harry Wilson). The creation escapes and kills a mechanic and returns home for more energy. Frank also injects Trudy with a formula which transforms her into a buck-toothed monster for brief periods. Finally Trudy and Johnny confront Frank about the monster and he orders it to kill Johnny so he can have Trudy. Johnny throws acid at the monster but hits and kills Frank, while the monster brushes against a Bunsen burner and catches fire. It dies as the teenagers escape the inferno.

The most unintentionally funny scene in the film is where Frank, Morton, Trudy, and Johnny are talking and there is a knock at the door. Trudy opens it, and there stands the monster, home from a killing spree. Apparently the creature had etiquette enough to knock rather than break down the door. Also not to be overlooked is the rock 'n roll music, performed by Harold Lloyd, Jr.

FRANKENSTEIN'S EXPERIMENT see FLESH FOR FRANKENSTEIN.

FRANKENSTEIN'S GREAT AUNT TILLIE (Tillie-Filmier, 1985) C 93 mins.

Director, Myron J. Gold; suggested by characters created by Mary Shelley; screenplay, Gold; music, Ronald Stein; sets, Teresa Pecanins; sound, Victor Rojo; camera, Miguel Garzon; editor, John Horger.

Donald Pleasence (Victor Frankenstein/Baron Frankenstein);

Yvonne Furneaux (Aunt Matilda "Tillie" Frankenstein); June Wilkinson (Randy Woonsock); Rod Colbin (Niederhangen); Garnet Smith (Schnitt); Zsa Zsa Gabor (Herself).

Filmed in Mexico, but entirely in English, this horror comedy was unjustly overlooked when released and appears to be one of those films awaiting re-discovery from cult movie followers. With its looney script, larger-than-life portrayals and horror movie trappings, the film is an amusing, often funny spoof on 1930s Gothic horror thrillers. *Variety* reported, "[Director/writer Myron J.] Gold's terse script brims with pans, asides, throwaway lines, anachronisms and verbal jibes, interspersed with slapstick gags on the Keystone Cops level."

At the turn-of-the-century, the area around Castle Frankenstein is awakening from the Dark Ages (the local women have discovered underwear!) and the town's corrupt politicos plan to take over the abandoned castle for overdue taxes. Victor Frankenstein (Donald Pleasence) returns with his lover Randy (June Wilkinson) and his aged aunty, the 109-year old Matilda (Yvonne Furneaux), who has kept youthful via a rejuvenating body cream. Since the late Baron Frankenstein's fortune is rumored hidden in the castle, Victor is determined to find it, while Aunt Tillie enters the Trans-Balkan Road Race. Although he does not locate the treasure, Victor does uncover the Frankenstein monster and he and Randy and Aunt Tillie revive it, setting the creatures on the locals out to grab the estate.

FROGS (American International, 1972) C 90 mins.

Producers, George Edwards, Peter Thomas; director, George McCowan; story, Robert Hutchison; screenplay, Hutchison, Robert Blees; music, Les Baxter; sound, John Speak; camera, Mario Tosi; editor, Fred R. Feitshans.

Ray Milland (Jason Crockett); Sam Elliott (Pickett Smith); Joan Van Ark (Karen); Adam Roarke (Clint); Judy Pace (Bella); Lynn Borden (Jenny); Mae Mercer (Maybelle); David Gilliam (Michael); Nicholas Cortland (Kenneth); George Skaff (Stuart); Lance Taylor, Sr. (Charles); Holly Irving (Iris); Dale Willingham (Tina); Hal Hodges (Hay); Carolyn Fitzsimmons (Lady in Car); Robert Sanders (Young Boy in Car).

For years wealthy Jason Crockett (Ray Milland) has abused ecology to make money. Now wheelchair-ridden, he lives on a remote Southern island with his family, which includes: Karen (Joan Van Ark), Jenny (Lynn Borden), sister Iris (Holly Irving), and son Clint (Adam Roarke). Suddenly the isle is overridden with reptile and insect life and Jenny is devoured by huge snapping turtles and

Nicholas Cortland and Judy Pace in FROGS (1972).

Iris dies in quicksand while after a butterfly. When a house guest (David Gilliam) is poisoned by hordes of spiders, Jason and the others realize they are at war with nature. The predators cut off communication to the mainland and another guest, photographer Pickett Smith (Sam Elliott), and Karen, manage to escape. But Jason, who decides to stay and defend his property, dies.

FROGS, which was filmed at Eden State Park in Florida, is a nature gone awry sci-fi feature. Instead of atomic power being the culprit, it is ecology and its unbalance (caused by man) which prompts the revolt of reptiles and insects. Naturally the main emphasis is on the wild life and NOT the human characters (although Ray Milland presents a fine portrayal of the self-centered patriarch). The film abounds with scenes of oozing, crawling, flying things doing harm to humans. The graphic visuals were sufficient for the film to do well at the box-office.

THE FURY (Twentieth Century-Fox, 1978) C 117 mins.

Executive producer, Ron Preissman; producer, Frank Yablans; director, Brian De Palma; based on the novel by John Farris;

screenplay, Farris; music, John Williams; production designer, Bill Malley; art director, Richard Lawrence; set decorator, Audrey Blasdel-Goddard; costumes/wardrobe, Theoni V. Aldridge, Seth Banks, Margo Baxley; assistant director, Donald E. Heitzer; stunt co-ordinator, Mickey Gilbert; sound, Richard Vorisek, Hal Etherington; special effects, A. D. Flowers; camera, Richard H. Kline; editor, Paul Hirsch.

Kirk Douglas (Peter Sandza); John Cassavetes (Childress); Carrie Snodgress (Hester); Charles Durning (Dr. McKeever); Amy Irving (Gillian); Fiona Lewis (Susan Charles); Andrew Stevens (Robin Sandza); Carol Rossen (Dr. Lindstrom); Rutanya Alda (Kristen); Joyce Easton (Mrs. Bellaver); William Finley (Raymond Dunwoodie); Jane Lambert (Vivian Nuckells); Dennis Franz, Michael O'Dwyer (Kidnapped Cops); Mickey Gilbert (CIA Agent); Frank Yablans (Goon on Radio); Felix Shuman (Dr. Ives); Rutanya Alda (Kristen); Bernie Kirby (Nuckles); J. Patrick McNamara (Robertson).

Along with the ability to create life, the capacity to control the mind for "super" human purposes has long been a favorite subject of sci-fi films.

Businessman Peter Sandza (Kirk Douglas) vows to find his son Robin (Andrew Stevens) when the young man is kidnapped. He learns the abductor is Childress (John Cassavetes), a scientist working on a top secret government program. Gillian (Amy Irving), a young woman with great mental powers, aids Peter in the search as does his friend Hester (Carrie Snodgress), but she is killed in an aborted attempt on Sanza's life. Peter and Gillian find Robin at a remote home which is being used as a laboratory by the program group who are attempting to utilize telekinetics to create a platoon of young adults as a brain trust for mental weaponry. The operation is run by Childress and Susan Charles (Fiona Lewis). Robin—due to the experimentations—is now almost a maniac. Robin turns on Susan and kills her and is himself eliminated. Peter gives up his life in trying to halt the project. Childress plots to use Gillian for his work, but she turns on him and he explodes into pieces.

THE FURY is best remembered for its finale when the character of Childress literally explodes before viewers' eyes. However, much of the narrative before this is tedious. The revenge plot is unexceptional, the acting erratic, and Brian De Palma's direction too static. With its limp storyline, the film too often must rely on shock sequences to survive and they are too few and far between (i.e. Carrie Snodgress' head smashing through a windshield in a car crash, Arabs being hurled off a merry-go-round and through a wall to their death, etc.)

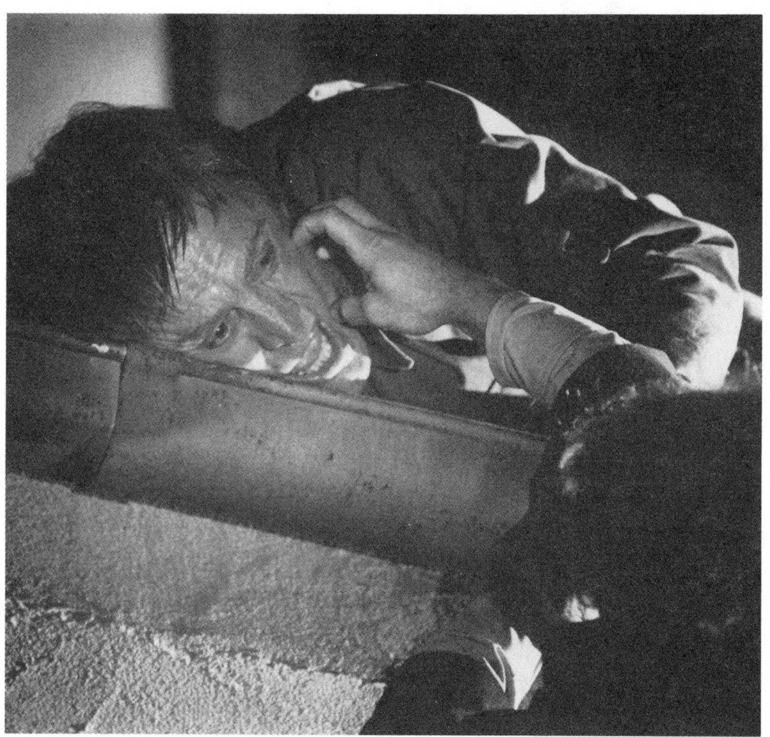

Kirk Douglas and Andrew Stevens in THE FURY (1978).

THE FURY OF THE WOLF MAN (Avco-Embassy, 1970) C 80 mins.

Director, Jose Maria Zabalza; screenplay, Jacinto Molina [Paul Naschy].

Paul Naschy (Waldemar Daninsky); Perla Cristal (Dr. Illona Helman); Veronica Lujan (Mrs. Daninsky); Michael Reviere (Doctor).

Spanish horror film star Paul Naschy (real name: Jacinto Molina) has headlined more than a score of genre outings and his most famous role is that of werewolf Waldemar Danisky, the Spanish counterpart of Lon Chaney's Lawrence Talbott from the Universal horror films of the 1940s. Naschy has performed the role in several films, including LA FURIA DEL HOMBRE LOBO (issued in a butchered version in the United States by Avco-Embassy as FURY OF THE WOLFMAN), written under his real name. Naschy has a penchant for the plots of the Universal horrors and this one borrows not only from THE WEREWOLF OF LONDON (1935), but also from many of the 1940s mad scientist thrillers.

On an expedition to Tibet, Polish surgeon Waldemar Daninsky (Paul Naschy) is attacked and bitten by a strange beast. Recovering, he is given a small box by a holy man and warned he may be cursed. Back home he finds his wife (Veornica Lujan) distant and he goes to his ex-lover, scientist Dr. Illona Helman (Perla Cristal) for help. Jealous of losing Waldemar, the woman realizes he has the sign of the beast and will become a werewolf, and she manipulates the wife into having an affair with another doctor (Michael Reviere) and then causing Waldemar, as a werewolf, to murder them. All three appear to die in a car crash but the scientist takes their bodies to a remote castle and revives them, planning to use the werewolf to commit a series of crimes, that include turning his own revived spouse into a werewolf.

FURY OF THE WOLFMAN has all the necessary horror trimmings and Perla Cristal is a delightful insane experimenter, using science to her own deranged ends to generate evil and, of course, paying the consequences at the finale.

When distributed in the U.S., scenes from the first Danisky feature, LA MARCA DEL HOMBRE LOBO [The Mark of the Wolfman] (1968)—issued in the U.S. as FRANKENSTEIN'S BLOODY TERROR—were interpolated.

FUTUREWORLD (American International, 1976) C 107 mins.

Executive producer, Samuel Z. Arkoff; producers, Paul Lazarus III, James T. Aubrey, Jr.; director, Richard T. Heffron; screenplay, Mayo Simon, George Schenck; music, Fred Karlin; art director, Trevor Williams; set decorator, Dennis Peoples, Marvin March;

assistant director, Robert Koster; sound, Charlie Knight; visual effects supervisor, Brent Sellstrom; camera, Howard, Schwartz, Gene Polito; second unit camera, Robert Jessup; editor, James Mitchell.

Peter Fonda (Chuck Browning); Blythe Danner (Tracy Ballard); Arthur Hill (Duffy); Yul Brynner (Gunslinger); Jim Antonio (Game Show Winner); John Ryan (Dr. Schneider); Stuart Margolin (Harry).

In 1985, over a decade after the disaster at the Delos amusement center, the resort is set to reopen. For publicity, and to ease everyone's fears about the terrible slaughter that took place there when the robots went out of control, the manager, Duffy (Arthur Hill), permits the IMC Communications Network to have exclusive coverage of the reopening and the elaborate preparations for it. IMC dispatches ace reporters Chuck Browning (Peter Fonda), who broke the original story, and Tracy Ballard (Blythe Danner), to the Center. Once there they find many world leaders are also present. Chuck and Tracy tour the facilities and enlist the aid of Harry (Stuart Margolin), a maintenance technician, and find that the owners are making robot duplicates of the global chieftains. The plan is to replace them with their creations in a bid for world dominance. The reporters attempt to escape and find their own robot duplicates waiting for them and that Duffy, too, is a robot. Eventually they are

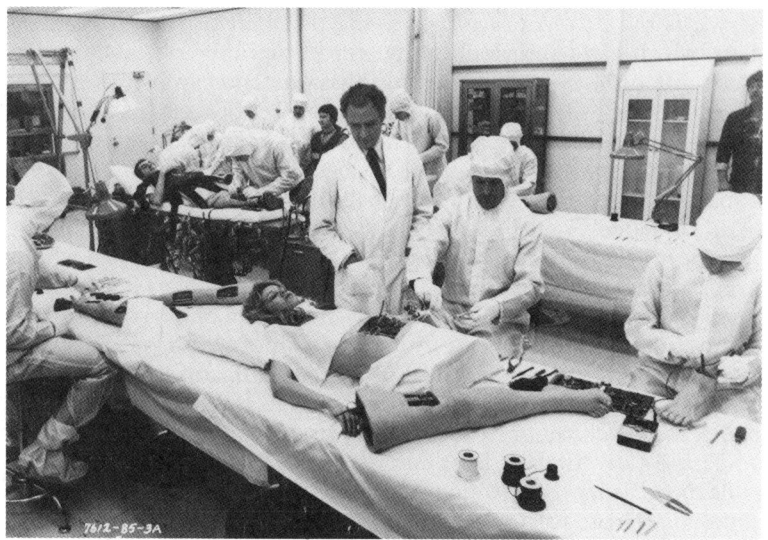

The robot assembly line in FUTUREWORLD (1976).

able to overcome the androids and make it to the outside world to report their scoop.

This "thoroughly delightful sequel to WESTWORLD [1973, see B/V]" (Ed Naha, *The Science Fictionary,* 1980) grossed $4,000,000 at the domestic box-office and is a bit lighter in concept (e.g. the card-playing robot technician) than its innovative predecessor, but also not as entertaining. While the initial film was more of a Western set in the anything's-possible future, this production opts for more conventionally sinister ploys, such as the robots turning on their creators for world control, and it failed to click. To be appreciated, though, is the guest appearance by Yul Brynner, briefly recreating his gunslinger robot from the original.

GALAXINA (Crown International, 1980) C 95 mins.

Producers, Marilyn J. Tenser;, George E. Mather; associate producer/director/screenplay, William Sachs; production designer, Tom Turliey; special camera effects supervisor, Chuck Colwell; camera, Dean Cundy; editor, Larry Bock.

Stephen Macht (Thor); Dorothy R. Stratten (Galaxina); James David Hinton (Buzz); Avery Schreiber (Captain Butt); Ronald Knight (Ordric); Lionel Smith (Maurice); Tad Horino (Sam Wo); Herp Kaplowitz (Rock Eater/Kitty/Ugly Alien Woman); Nancy McCauley (Elexia); Fred S. Scott (Commander); George E. Mather (Horn Man).

It is the 21st century. Following the theft of the "Blue Star" gem, which can control all the power in the universe, a spaceship blasts off on a two-decades-long mission to recapture the jewel from the thief, Ordric (Ronald Knight), a robot-lizard. The rescue craft is commanded by Captain Butt (Avery Schreiber) and the crew includes: Sergeant Thor (Stephen Macht), Buzz (James David Hinton), a space cowboy; Sam Wo (Tad Horino), an aged Oriental engineer; Maurice (Lionel Smith), a flying black engineer; and Galaxina (Dorothy R. Stratten), a beautiful blonde robot who cannot speak and who is programmed to shock anyone electrically who touches her. During the trek, the captain eats an alien egg and a small being comes out of his mouth and hides on the ship. After an orgy at a space station brothel, the crew is placed in suspended animation for the trip's duration, but the alien thinks the captain is its mother, and opens his compression chamber. As a result, after the two decades voyage when the crew awakes, Butt emerges an old man. Thor, who loves Galaxina, is surprised to find her talking and no longer electrically shocking. The spaceship crashes on Ordric's planet and it is Galaxina who hunts for the precious stone, fighting cannibal aliens in a Western ghost town and being captured by a gang of bikers. Thor and Buzz set out to rescue Galaxina, but end up being captured by one of Ordric's robots. The little alien, who has adopted the captain as its mother, stops the villains, but in the end Ordric swallows the gem.

GALAXINA, which grossed a little over $4,000,000 at the box-office, is best remembered as the only starring feature of Dorothy Stratten, the model and *Playboy* magazine playmate who was murdered by her estranged husband shortly before the film's release. Her striking good looks are the movie's saving grace. While the film pays hommage to other genre efforts, including ALIEN (1979) (q.v.) and WESTWORLD (1973) (see B/V), its lack of structural excitement and its convoluted comedy make it tough going.

GALAXY OF TERROR (New World, 1981) C 80 mins.

Producers, Roger Corman, Marc Siegler; director, B. D. Clark; screenplay, Siegler, Clark; music, Barry Schrader; production designers, Jim Cameron, Bob Skotak; art directors, Alex Hajdu, Steve Graziani; costumes, Timaree McCormick; assistant director, Pete Manoogian; second unit director, Cameron; sound, Ken Beauchane; special effects supervisor, Tom Campbell; camera, Jacques Haitkin; editors, Robert J. Kizer, Larry Boch, Barry Zetlin.

Edward Albert (Cabren); Erin Moran (Alluma); Ray Walston (Kore); Bernard Behrens (Livar); Zalman King (Baelon); Robert Englund (Ranger); Taaffe O'Connell (Damelia); Sid Haig (Quuhod); Grace Zabriskle (Captain Trantor); Jack Blessing (Cos); Mary Ellen O'Neill (Mitre).

Made on the leftover sets of BATTLE BEYOND THE STARS (1980) (q.v.), with unused footage from that feature incorporated as well, this New World cut-and-paste film was also issued as MINDWARP: AN INFINITY OF TERROR and PLANET OF HORROR. *Variety* reviewed, "As long as GALAXY OF TERROR sticks to stuff like rocket ships making rough landings on hostile terrain or monsters devouring space explorers, it nicely passes muster. But when all the exposition about cosmic mind games is laid out toward the end, pic comes crashing down like an early Vanguard missile."

In the future, The Master sends a group of astronauts, including Cabren (Edward Albert), Alluma (Erin Moran), and Kore (Ray Walston), to a distant planet to bring back a stranded spaceship. They find the planet to be a dark and forbidding world with boggy terrain. The astronauts, however, begin to disappear one by one and one of their number (Sid Haig) cuts off his arm after a metal object works its way under his skin. The group realize that an alien life form is trying to destroy them and Damelia (Taaffe O'Connell) is violently raped and murdered by the alien in the form of a giant worm. Dabren burns the girl's corpse, but his lover Alluma is blown to pieces by the alien who is shown to be one of the crew. Eventually the intruder is destroyed and the astronauts plan to return home.

Running a brief 80 minutes, GALAXY OF TERROR harkens back to the type of shoestring celluloid fare producer Roger Corman made his reputation with in the 1950s and early 1960s. The film is obviously low budget and its dark, bleak exteriors help to disguise the lack of funds for more elaborate sets. Overall the film's mood is dour and the villain's ability to take on various guises is borrowed from the original story for THE THING (q.v.) which was remade the following year.

THE GHOST see THE HORRIBLE DR. HICHCOCK.

THE GHOST OF FRANKENSTEIN (Universal, 1942) 68 mins.

Associate producer, George Waggner; director, Erle C. Kenton; based on characters created by Mary Shelley; story, Eric Taylor; screenplay, Scott Darling; assistant director, Charles S. Gould; art director, Jack Otterson; makeup, Jack P. Pierce; music director, Hans J. Salter; camera, Milton Krasner, Woody Bredell; editor, Ted J. Kent.

Lon Chaney (The Monster); Sir Cedric Hardwicke (Baron Ludwig Frankenstein); Ralph Bellamy (Erik); Lionel Atwill (Dr. Bohmer); Bela Lugosi (Ygor); Evelyn Ankers (Elsa); Janet Ann Gallow (Cloestine); Barton Yarborough (Dr. Kettering); Doris Lloyd (Martha); Leyland Hodgson (Chief Constable); Olaf Hytten (Russman); Holmes Herbert (Magistrate); Eddie Parker (Stunts); Dwight Frye, Harry Cording (Villagers); Michael Mark (Mayor's Assistant); and: Lionel Belmore, Dick Alexander, George Eldridge, Ernie Stanton, Brandon Hurst.

Boris Karloff wisely abandoned the screen role of the Frankenstein monster following SON OF FRANKENSTEIN (1939) (q.v.) and when Universal determined to make THE GHOST OF FRANKENSTEIN in 1942 it cast Lon Chaney, fresh from his success in MAN MADE MONSTER (1941) (see B/V) and THE WOLFMAN (1941), as the murderous, artificial man. His interpretation of the monster lacks the pathos of Karloff, and replaces it with a creature of superhuman strength and size. Thankfully, Bela Lugosi repeats his captivating assignment as Ygor from SON and aids the proceedings immensely as does Lionel Atwill as the traitorous Dr. Bohmer. While not as substantial as its three highly-regarded predecessors,

Lon Chaney and Elaine Morey on the set of THE GHOST OF FRANKENSTEIN (1942).

THE GHOST OF FRANKENSTEIN is nonetheless an imaginative offering.

The villagers of Frankenstein are disconcerted because broken-necked Ygor (Bela Lugosi) is still alive. They hasten to Castle Frankenstein and blow it up and in doing so resurrect the Frankenstein monster (Lon Chaney) who has been buried in solidified sulphur. Ygor leads the creature away and in a graveyard the monster is struck by a bolt of lightning which provides it with renewed strength. He and Ygor go to Vasaria to see Dr. Ludwig Frankenstein (Cedric Hardwicke), the second son of the monster's creator, who operates a mental hospital. The creature tries to make friends with a small girl (Janet Ann Gallow), but is arrested and placed in Frankenstein's custody. Ygor blackmails the doctor into helping him, but when the creature kills his assistant (Barton Yarborough) and bothers his daughter Elsa (Evelyn Ankers), Ludwig gasses the monster. He plans to dissect it with the aid of jealous associate Dr. Bohmer (Lionel Atwill), but the spectre of his father tells him to give it full power by replacing its criminal brain with one from a law-abiding person. Ludwig decides to give it the killed assistant's brain, but Ygor intercedes with Bohmer to have his brain placed inside the monster's head. This is done and when he awakens, the monster has new powers, Ygor's voice, and exceedingly devilish plans. By now the distraught locals storm the castle and Elsa escapes with her fiancee Erik (Ralph Bellamy). The monster, however, goes blind, and in a rage kills Bohmer and starts a fire which consumes him and Ludwig.

This successful feature would be followed by a direct sequel, FRANKENSTEIN MEETS THE WOLFMAN (1943) (q.v.) and the finale fire sequence would be used—for economy reasons—to conclude Universal's HOUSE OF DRACULA (1945) (q.v.), the last of the motion picture series.

GHOST PATROL (Puritan, 1936) 58 mins.

Producers, Sig Neufeld, Leslie Simmonds; director, Sam Newfield; story, Joseph O'Donnell; adaptor, Wyndham Gitten; special electrical effects, Kenneth Strickfaden; camera, John Greenhaigh; editor, Jack English.

Tim McCoy (Tim Caverly); Claudia Dell (Natalie Brent); Walter Miller (Dawson); Wheeler Oakman (Kincaid); Jim Burtis (Henry); Dick Curtis (Charlie); Lloyd Ingraham (Professor Brent); Jack Casey (Mac); Slim Whitaker (Frank); Artie Ortego (Ramon); Art Dillard (Shorty); Fargo Bussey (Bill).

The Federal Bureau of Investigation sends agent and former cowboy Tim Caverly (Tim McCoy) to solve the mysterious crashes of two mail planes whose cargo have been stolen. He uncovers a gang hiding in a desert ghost town which was once a booming gold mining community. Pretending to be an outlaw, Tim befriends the gang and learns the airplanes were destroyed by a death ray invented by Professor Brent (Lloyd Ingraham) who is being held a prisoner at the outpost, along with his daughter Natalie (Claudia Dell), by bandit leaders Dawson (Walter Miller) and Kincaid (Wheeler Oakman). When the gang intends to shoot down another plane for its cargo, Tim prevents them, rescues the professor and his daughter, and rounds up the gang members.

"The action is well staged (in view of the fast production schedule) in California desert settings, with dialogue kept to a minimum and with plenty of emphasis on adventure and gunplay." wrote George E. Turner and Michael H. Price in *Forgotten Horrors* (1979). The movie was shot in a week as part of Tim McCoy's eight picture Western deal with producers Sigmund Neufeld and Leslie Simmonde and it was directed competently by Neufeld's brother, the prolific Sam Newfield. Perhaps the most interesting aspect of the film is its use of Kenneth Strickfaden's electrical effects which had become famous via his work on the FRANKENSTEIN (q.v.) series at Universal.

Four years later, the same plot would be revamped for SKY BANDITS (q.v.), an entry in Monogram's "Renfrew of the Royal Mounted" series.

THE GIANT GILA MONSTER (McLendon Radio Pictures, 1959) 74 mins.

Executive producer, Gordon McLendon; producer, Ken Curtis; director, Ray Kellogg; screenplay, Ray Simms; music, Jack Marshall; sound effects, Milton Citron, James Richard; camera, Wilfred Cline; editor, Aaron Stell.

Don Sullivan (Chance Winstead); Lisa Simone (Lisa); Shug Fisher (Mr. Harris); Jerry Cortwright (Bob); Beverly Thurman (Gay); Don Flourney (Gordy); Clarke Browne (Chucky); Pat Simmons (Sherry); Pat Reeves (Rick); Anne Sonka (Whila); Fred Graham (Sheriff); Bob Thompson (Wheeler); Cecil Hunt (Compton); Ken Knox (Steamroller Smith); Yolanda Salas (Liz Humphries); Howard Ware (Ed Humphries); Stormey Meadows (Agatha Humphries); Janice Stone (Missy Winstead).

THE GIANT GILA MONSTER was released on a double bill with KILLER SHREWS (q.v.) with both productions made by Houston, Texas, radio station owner Gordon McLendon, directed by Ray Kellogg and written by Ray Simms. Even the Sons of the Pioneers have partial involvement, as Shug Fisher is in this feature and Ken Curtis (who produced this film) is one of the KILLER

SHREWS co-stars. The minor highlight of this entry is the use of a real gila monster to move about miniature sets and to be seen in blowup closeup shots. Don Sullivan appears as a ukulele playing rock 'n roll singer performing some of his self-penned ditties. The movie was shot on location in Texas.

A teenage couple disappear one night after being attacked by a giant gila monster and the sheriff (Fred Graham) attempts to locate them. He goes to rock 'n roll singer/teenager Chance Winstead (Don Sullivan), whose late father was an oil rigger, for aid. Chance and his girl Lisa (Lisa Simone) agree to help and while searching, Chance helps a stranded motorist (Ken Knox) who turns out to be a disc jockey who offers to get Chance on the air with his songs. Hot-rodder Chance is the sole support for his mother and crippled little sister Missy (Janice Stone) and needs the money. Eventually Chance has the opportunity to destroy the monster with the help of explosives.

THE GIANT LEECHES see ATTACK OF THE GIANT LEECHES.

THE GIANT SPIDER INVASION (Group I, 1975) C 82 mins.

Executive producer, William W. Gillette, Jr.; producers, Richard L. Huff, Bill Rebane; director, Rebane; screenplay, Huff, Robert Easton; special effects, Richard Albain, Robert Millay, camera, Jack Willoughby.

Steve Brodie (Dr. J. R. Vance); Barbara Hale (Dr. Jenney Langer); Leslie Parrish (Ev); Robert Easton (Dan Kester); Alan Hale (Sheriff); Dianne Lee Hart (Terri); Bill Williams (Dutch); Christiane Schmidtmer (Helga); and Kevin Brodie.

Midwestern rancher Dan Kester (Robert Easton) finds what he thinks are diamonds, but what prove to be the eggs of a spider which were filled with radiation as a result of a gamma ray shower. When spiders of all sizes begin prowling the outlying territory and invade a small town, investigators J. R. Vance (Steve Brodie) and Dr. Jenney Langer (Barbara Hale) arrive but Kester refuses to divulge the location of the spider eggs. When he goes to retrieve them, Kester is devoured by a giant queen spider whose helpers then attack the locals before the investigators, now in love, repel them.

With its stars (Steve Brodie, Barbara Hale, Bill Williams, Alan Hale, Jr.) and plot, this film filmed in Wisconsin is a throwback to the 1950s and indeed it was aimed for the then dying drive-in trade. Co-written by Robert Easton who plays the rancher, the film has many similarities to the much superior TARANTULA (1955) (see B/V). Michael Weldon (*The Psychotronic Encyclopedia of Film*) (1983) added, "There hasn't been a movie with special effects so bad since THE

GIANT CLAW." Regarding the spiders he noted, "The big ones are stripped-down Volkswagens with legs and eyes added. Lots of laughs. . . ."

GOBOTS: BATTLE OF THE ROCKLORDS (Entertainment, 1986) C 74 mins.

Executive producers, William Hanna, Joseph Barbera, Stephen G. Shank; co-executive producer, Joe Taritero; producers, Kay Wright, Patrick S. Feely; co-producer, Raymond E. McDonald; associate producers, Lynn Hoag, Mark W. Ludke; directors, Ray Patterson, Don Lusk, Alan Zaslove; story consultant, Kelly Ward; screenplay, Jeff Segal; animation supervising director, Paul Sabella; animation supervisor, Janine Dawson; music director, Hoyt Curtin; music editors, Cecil Broughton, Terry Moore, Daniel McLean, Joe Sandusky; sound, Gordon Hunt; sound editors, Alvy Dorman, Phil Flad; supervising editor, Larry C. Cowan.

Voices of: Margot Kidder (Solitaire); Roddy McDowall (Nuggit); Michael Nouri (Boulder); Telly Savalas (Magmar); Ike Eisenmann (Nick); Bernard Erhard (Cy-Kill); Marilyn Lightstone (Crasher); Morgan Paul (Matt); Lou Richards (Leader-I); Leslie Speights (A. J.); Frank Welker (Scooter/Zeemon/Rest-Q/Pulver-Eye/Sticks/Narliphant); Michael Bell (Slime Stone/Granite/Narligator); Foster Brooks (Stone Heart/Fossil Lord); Arthur Burghardt (Turbo/Cop-Tur/Talc); Ken Campbell (Vanguard); Philip Lewis Clarke (Herr Fiend/Crack-pot/Tork); Peter Cullen (Pincher/Tombstone/Stone); Dick Gautier (Brimstone/Klaws/Rock Narlie); Darryl Hickman (Marbles/Hornet); B. J. Ward (Small Foot); Kelly Ward (Fitor); Kirby Ward (Heat Seeker).

The planet Quartex, which is dominated by living rocks, is being menaced by rock lord Magmar who seeks all the planet's power sceptres to transform into one weapon to conquer the universe. Quartex's Gem queen, Solitaire, accompanies her friend Nuggit to the planet Gobotron to beg the aid of the giant robots called GoBots, who can transform into many other forms, in opposing Magmar. Rebel GoBots led by Cy-Kill attack Solitaire and steal her power scepter and kidnap her along with GoBot Small Foot and two human children, Nick and A.J. Cy-Kill goes to Quartex and allies himself with Magmar. Three GoBots, Lader-1, Turbo and Scotter, along with Nuggit and human Matt land on Quartex and are aided by rock lord Boulder who is opposed to Magmar and Cy-Kill. Magmar is able to complete his ultimate weapon but the Go-Bots rescue the captives and Cy-Kill and Magmar fight one another as the GoBots oppose the rebels and defeat them.

Adapted from the popular children's teleseries, "GoBots," this animated feature is technically enjoyable, but has a mundane plot. Before long, the moviegoer is weary of seeing GoBots transform into other objects such as race cars and fighter jets. Although a number of well-known performers provide the voices of the animated characters, they cannot breathe sufficient life into them.

GODZILLA 1985 (New World, 1985) C 91 mins.

Producers, Tomoyuki Tanaka, Anthony Randel; associate producers, Fumio Tanaka, Andrea Stern; directors, Kohji Hashimoto, R. J. Kizer; story, Tanaka; screenplay, Schuichi Nagahara, Lisa Tomei; production designer, Akira Sakuragi; music, Reijiro Koroku; assistant director, Takao Ohgawara; special effects, Teryuoshi Nakano; camera, Kazutami Hara; editors, Yoshimati Kuroiwa, Michael Spence.

Raymond Burr (Steve Martin); Keiju Kobayashi (Prime Minister Mitamura); Ken Tanaka (Goro Maki); Yasuko Sawaguchi (Naoko Okumura); Shin Takuma (Hiroshi Okumura); Eitaro Ozawa (Kanzaki); Taketoshi Naito (Takegami); Nobuo Kaneko (Isomura); Takeshi Katoh (Kasaoka); Mizuho Suzuki (Kanzaki); Junkichi Orimoto (Mohri); Shinsuke Mikimoto (Kakurai); Mikita Mori (Ohkochi); Yoshifumi Tajime (Hidaka); Kiyoshi Tamamoto (Kajita); Hiroshi Koizumi (Minami); Junio Murai (Henmi); Kei Sato (Gondo); Takenori Emoto (Kitagawa); Shinpei Hayashiya (Kamijo); Yosuke Natsuki (Hayashida); and: Takeo Morimoto, Koji Ishizaka, Tetsyua Takeda.

Poster blurbs for this Japanese remake of GODZILLA, KING OF THE MONSTERS (1956) (see B/V) announced, "The Legend Is Reborn . . . Your Favorite Fire Breathing Monster . . . Like You've Never Seen Him Before." Laudatory reviews emblazoned the advertising materials: "The best Godzilla in 30 years . . . Hysterical Fun" insisted Joel Siegel on TV's "Good Morning, America," while Peter Stack in the *San Francisco Chronicle* opined, "Godzilla makes Rambo, Eastwood, Bronson and Schwarzenegger look like mere swizzle sticks . . . a camp treat." The film attempts to retell the 1956 version but with a new angle and updated special effects techniques. Like the original, this Japanese production inserts footage of Raymond Burr, now playing an expert on Godzilla (thanks to his experiences when the monster decimated Tokyo years before).

A Soviet submarine is destroyed and the Americans are blamed. Nuclear war almost breaks out, until it is determined that prehistoric fire-breathing monster Godzilla has re-emerged from the ocean and is causing the destruction. Leaders from nations around the world converge to decide what to do about Godzilla, but the Japanese Prime Minster (Keiju Kbayashi) refuses to permit nuclear weapons to be used to destroy the reptile, for fear of radiative side effects. American Steve Martin (Raymond Burr), a former newspaperman who covered the story in Tokyo when Godzilla first emerged and destroyed the city, is called in as an expert on the creature. Meanwhile, Godzilla wrecks havoc and even ultra-modern weapons cannot stop him.

Vincent Canby wrote in the *New York Times,* "Though special effects experts in Japan and around the world have vastly improved their craft in the last thirty years, you wouldn't know it from this film. Godzilla, who is supposed to be about 240 feet tall, still looks like a wind-up toy, one that moves like an arthritic toddler with a fondness for walking through teeny-tiny skyscrapers instead of mud puddles."

Original Japanese release title: GOJIRA.

GOJIRA see GODZILLA 1985.

GOLD (L'OR) (UFA, 1934) 120 mins.

Producer, Alfred Zeisler; Director, Karl Hartl; screenplay, Rolf E. Vanloo; sets, Otto Hunte; music, Hans-Otto Borgmann; camera, Gunther Rittau, Otto Baecker, Werner Bohne.

Hans Albers (Holk); Michael Bohnen (Wills); Brigitte Helm (Florence Wills); Ernst Karchow (Scientist); Friedrich Kayssler (Achenbach); and: Eberhard Leithoff, Lien Deyers, Rudolf Platte.

French language version: Director: Serge de Poligny; screenplay, Jacques Thierry; sets, Otto Hunte.

Pierre Blanchar (Francois Berthier); Brigitte Helm (Florence Wills); Lien Noro (Patient); Jacques Dumnesil (Malesoot); Roger Karl (John Wills); Louis Gauthier (Lefevre); Rosine Derean (Helene); Marc Valbel (Harns); Henri Bosc (Guerin); Robert Goupil (Journalist).

Alchemy centering around the artificial creation of gold has been a popular subject since ancient times and several films like THE GOLEM and THE CLUTCHING HAND (1936) (qq.v.) have used it for a subplot. This German feature, however, deals with the changing of lead into gold. Popular German actress Brigitte Helm, who starred in METROPOLIS (1926) (see B/V) headlined this feature as well as a separately made French language version which followed the same plotline. Legend has it the reactor constructed for this film, which was designed by Otto Hunte, so impressed the Allies, that after World War II they had it examined to determine if the Germans actually possessed atomic energy secrets!

Scientist Achenbach (Friedrich Kayssler) and his associate Holk (Hans Albers) are perfecting their atomic reactor which will transmute lead into gold. They work in an underwater laboratory and eventually achieve their goal. News leaks out and a Scottish businessman (Michael Bohnen), who has corralled the world's lead supply, makes them a huge offer for the device and they accept. Another scientist (Ernst Karchow) implores them to abandon the idea because it will eventually wreck the world's economy which is based on gold. Following the successful demonstration of their invention, the two scientists destroy it rather than have it destroy the world's money system.

John Baxter wrote in *Science Fiction in the Cinema* (1970) "[Gunther] Rittau's process photography and [Otto] Hunte's set make much of the climax with the huge machine flashing lightning from enormous condensers . . . Aside from these scenes, GOLD is largely routine, although in cost and shooting time it far exceeded METROPOLIS."

Scenes from GOLD were used for the final reel of THE MAGNETIC MONSTERS (1953) (see B/V).

DER GOLEM [THE GOLEM] (Bioscop, 1915) 55 mins.

Directors, Paul Wegener, Henrik Galeen; based on the novel by Gustav Meyrink; screenplay, Galeen; art director, Robert A. Dietrich; costumes, R. Gliese; camera, Guido Seeber.

Paul Wegener (Golem); Albert Steinruck (Rabbi Loew); and: Ernst Deutsch, Henrik Galeen, Lydia Salmanova.

Released in the U.S. in 1917 as THE MONSTER OF FATE.

DER GOLEM, WIE ERIN DIE WELT KAM [The Golem, How He Came Into the World] (UFA, 1920) 84 mins.

Directors, Paul Wegener, Carl Boese; directorial supervisor, Ernst Lubitsch; based on the novel by Gustav Meyrink; screenplay, Wegener, Henrik Galeen; art director, Hans Polzig; costumes, Rochus Gliese; camera, Karl Freund, Guido Seeber; assistant camera, Edgar G. Ulmer.

Paul Wegener (Golem); Albert Steinrueck (Rabbi Loew); Ernst Deutsch (Famulus); Lyda Salmanova (Miriam); Hanns Sturm (Rabbi Jehuda); Greta Schroder (Rose Girl); Loni Nest (The Child); Lothar Muthel (Florian); Otto Gebuhr (Emperor Luhois); Max Kronert (Tempildiener); and: Dora Paetzold, Ferdinand von Alten, Henrik Galeen.

Released in the U.S. in 1921 by Paramount as THE GOLEM.

LE GOLEM (THE GOLEM: THE LEGEND OF PRAGUE) (French, 1937) 95 mins.

Producer, Charles Philipp; director, Julien Duvivier; based on the play by Jan Werich, Jiri Voskovec; screenplay, Duvivier, Andre-Paul Antoine; art director, A. Andrejev, S. Kopecky; music, Joseph

Kumok; sound, Polednik; camera, Vaclav Vich, Jan Stallich; English titles (U.S. release), Martin J. Lewis.

Harry Baur (Emperor Rudolf); Roger Karl (Chancellor Lang); Ferdinand Hart (The Golem) Charles Dorat (Rabbi Jacob); Aimos (Toussaint); Roger Duchesne (Trignac); Gaston Jacquet (Police Chief); Germaine Aussey (Countess Strada); Jenny Holt (Rachel); Tanja Doll (Mme. Benoit).

British release title: THE MAN OF STONE.

Released in the U.S. in 1937 at 91 minutes.

LE GOLEM (ORTF, 1966) 80 mins.

Producer, L. Bureau; director, Jean Kerchbron; based on the novel by Gustav Meyrink; screenplay, Louis Pauwels, Kerchbron; art directors, J. Gourmelin, A. Negre; makeup, R. Simon; music, Jean Wiener; camera, Albert Schimel; editors, G. Fourmond, M. Gourot.

Andre Reybaz (The Golem); and: Pierre Tabard, Michael Etchevery, Marika Green, Francois Vibert, Douking, Robert Etchevery, Magali Noel.

GOLEM [THE GOLEM] (Film Polski/PFU, 1979) C 92 mins.

Director, Piotr Szulkin; based on the novel by Gustav Meyrink; screenplay, Szulkin, Tadeusz Sobo; sets, Zbrgniew Warpechowski, Janusz Walsow; camera, Zygmunt Samosiuk.

Marek Walczewski (Pernat); Mariusz Dmochowski (Dr. Holtrum); Wieslaw Drzewica (Miriam's Father); Krzysztof Majchrzak (Student); Joanna Zolkowska (Miriam); and: Krystyna Janda, Henryk Bak, Jan Nowick, Wojciech Pszoniak.

The Golem, the soulless man of clay from Jewish legend, has been transferred to the screen several times and has been used for box-office draw in other features, although the creature is hardly as famous to moviegoers as Dracula or Frankenstein's monster. Popular German actor Paul Wegener played the Golem on the screen in the silent days and his performance is considered the definitive one. Of course, the story is quite similar to *Frankenstein* although here the monster is created by alchemy rather than electricity (at least that's how Frankenstein's fiend was created on film; Mary Shelley is vague about the creation in her novel).

Paul Wegener and Henrik Galeen first adapted the old Jewish folk lore tale to the screen in 1915, and also co-directed it, as DER GOLEM [The Golem] and it was issued in the United States as THE MONSTER OF FATE. The story has workmen digging in an old synagogue and finding a strange statue of a huge man which they sell to an antique dealer. In an old book the dealer learns the statue is really an artificial man, The Golem (Paul Wegener), and the dealer uses a magic formula to bring it to life. Thereafter the creature is his servant. But the latter falls in love with the man's daughter (Lyda Salmonova) and this causes the Golem to have a soul. The young woman, however, is afraid of the creature and runs from him. This leads the Golem to embark on a rampage, destroying the town. Finally he climbs to the top of a tower and falls off; shattering to pieces on the street below.

The silent movie was very successful, but the intervention of World War I prevented Wegener and Galeen from producing a followup feature, although in 1916 a Danish company produced a version of THE GOLEM. Finally in 1920 Wegener and Galeen reteamed again for DER GOLEM, WIE ER IN DIE WELT KAN, released in America as THE GOLEM. Wegener co-directed with Carl Boese and the movie was photographed by Karl Freund, who was assisted by Edgar G. Ulmer. Freund later photographed Fritz Lang's classic METROPOLIS (1926) (see B/V) and directed THE MUMMY (1932) and MAD LOVE (1935) (q.v.).

The 1920 THE GOLEM has a storyline which predates the 1915 version. Set in Prague in the 15th century, the narrative has the emperor issuing an edict against the Jews for practicing black magic. To defend his people, Rabbi Loew (Albert Steinrueck), with assistant Famulus (Ernst Deutsch), digs up the body of the Golem (Paul Wegener), which was buried in an old crypt. He tells Famulus that the creature was made by a magician in Thessaly and that he is given life by a magic amulet. Loew brings the creature to life, but his daughter Miriam (Lyda Salmanova) fears it. Loew takes the Golem to the emperor and the creature shows its strength and the emperor agrees to pardon the city's Jewish population. When Loew attempts to remove the amulet from the creature it turns on him but he finally immobilizes it. When the Rabbi later finds his daughter with Florian, the emperor's messenger, he awakens the Golem to save her, but the creature kidnaps the girl and burns the house where Famulus tries to protect her. The house is destroyed and Florian dies in the fire. The Golem leaves the girl and goes to the city's ghetto gate and breaks through it. Everyone flees excepts a small girl who offers the creature an apple. When he picks her up, her hand brushes across his chest, removing the amulet and bringing about the creature's demise.

Like many post-war German films, THE GOLEM was highly artistic with its expressionistic sets. In *From Caligari to Hitler* (1947), Siegfried Kracauer described the ghetto sets as " . . . a dream-like maze of crooked streets and stooped houses" and he also commented on the scene where the Rabbi uses the Golem's fearsome strength to liberate his people. "Here reason avails itself of brute force as a tool to liberate the oppressed. But instead of following up this motif, the film concentrates upon the Golem's emancipation, from his master, and becomes increasingly entangled in half-truths."

In the interim between his two productions of DER GOLEM, Paul Wegener also played the title role in an obscure Bioscop production, DER GOLEM UND DIE TANZERIN [The Golem and The Dancing Girl]. In 1921 DER GOLEMS LETZTES ABENTEUER [The Golem's Last Adventure] was made in Austria, and the first sound version of the legend was produced in 1935 as a French-Czech co-production called THE GOLEM, issued in the United States as THE LEGEND OF PRAGUE. Taken from Gustav Meyrink's 1915 novel, this version had The Golem (Ferdinand Hart) controlled by Rabbi Jakob (Charles Dorat), the successor to Rabbi Loew and related how Rudolf II (Harry Baur) wanted to destroy the powerful creature. When his mistress (Germaine Aussey) finds Rudolf with two other women, she gives the creature access to his castle and the Golem destroys it. Filmed in Prague, the movie contains a most intriguing performance by Ferdinand Hart as the fearsome creature. Scenes from this production would appear in the 1943 compilation film, DR. TERROR'S HOUSE OF HORRORS.

In 1951 the Golem returned to the screen in Czechoslovakia, but this time in a political satire called CISARUV PEKAR which had numerous alternate titles including THE EMPEROR AND THE GOLEM, THE EMPEROR'S BAKER, THE GOLEM AND THE EMPEROR'S BAKER, and THE RETURN OF THE GOLEM. The story, again set in 1600 Prague, has Rudolf II (Jan Werich) letting the populace starve while he uses the country's treasury to find ways to create gold and resurrecting the Golem for his own means. A baker (Jan Werich) finds the creature and dislodges the emperor and uses the Golem to make bread to feed the people. The title creature here resembled a huge glob of walking clay.

The French produced another version of the folk tale in 1966 for television called LE GOLEM and it received theatrical release as MASK OF THE GOLEM. Two years later the legend turned up in an altered form as a framing story, "Fabricius," in the three part Czech film PRADZSKE NOCI [Prague Nights], also known as THE NIGHTS OF PRAGUE. Here Rudolph II has a Rabbi (Jan Klusak) create a Golem but Rabbi Loew causes him to be seduced by a a young woman (Jana Brezkova) who destroys the Golem by wiping its magic formula from its forehead, and as it crumbles the creature suffocates its creator. The girl, however, herself is a Golem made by Loew. A 1971 French horror motion picture, LA GOULVE, used the alternate title of THE GOLEM'S DAUGHTER.

Poland, where the legend began, produced the screen's most recent Golem feature and it turned out to be a futuristic tale called GOLEM, issued in 1979. Set after the "final" war, the human race is mentally controlled by doctors in a robot-like society. Pernat (Marek Walczewski), however, is different and he is alienated from society. A doctor (Mariusz Dmochowski) creates an artificial being and Pernat becomes involved with it. Phil Hardy notes in *The Film Encyclopedia: Science Fiction* (1984), "Shot mostly in sepia, the film's main target appears to be the notion that forms of mass communication mold reality and programme people into a life of ordinary madness. Echoes of Khafa reverberate, strengthened by elements of the extremely vital though disturbing tradition of Polish surrealism."

THE GOLEM AND THE EMPEROR'S BAKER see THE GOLEM (essay).

THE GOLEM'S DAUGHTER see THE GOLEM (essay).

LA GOULVE see THE GOLEM (essay).

GRAVE DESIRES see BRIDES OF BLOOD.

H.G. WELLS' THE SHAPE OF THINGS TO COME see THE SHAPE OF THINGS TO COME.

HAND OF DEATH (Twentieth Century-Fox, 1962) 60 mins.

Producer, Eugene Ling; director, Gene Nelson; screenplay, Ling; set decorator, Harry Reif; music/music director, Sonny Burke; assistant director, Willard Kirkham; wardrobe, John Intlekofer; makeup, Bob Mark; sound, Vic Appel; camera, Floyd Crosby; supervising editor, Jodie Copelan; editor, Carl Pierson; supervising sound editor, Jack Cornall.

John Agar (Dr. Alex Marsh); Paula Raymond (Carol Wilson); Steve Dunne (Tom Holland); Roy Gordon (Dr. Ramsey); John Alonzo (Carlos); and: Jack Younger, Joe Besser, Butch Patrick, Norman Burton, Fred Krone, Kevin Enright, Jack Donner, Chuck Niles, Ruth Terry, Bob Whitney.

Working in his desert laboratory, Dr. Alex Marsh (John Agar) develops a paralyzing gas which can also make the mind susceptible to suggestion. Realizing this may be a way to end war, Alex takes his

Advertisement for HAND OF DEATH (1962).

find to the head of the research project, Dr. Ramsey (Roy Gordon), who reluctantly gives the go-ahead. Back at his laboratory, Alex mixes chemicals and has an accident and becomes ill. When his assistant (John Alonzo) returns, Alex touches him and the man dies. Alex realizes his touch is fatal but that he has an immunity. On his way to Los Angeles to seek aid from Ramsey two others die. Ramsey agrees to find an antidote and is assisted by Alex's fiancee, Carol (Paula Raymond), and scientist Tom Holland (Steve Dunne). By now, however, Alex's skin has become bloated and reptile-like. Ramsey insists on turning Alex over to the law and he kills him, escaping to Malibu Beach where Carol is staying. Alex begs Carol to help him, but she realizes he is insane. The police close in and Alex dies by drowning as he seeks to escape.

Directed by actor Gene Nelson on a small budget, HAND OF DEATH is a minor science-gone-awry effort whose poster blurb enthused, "No one dared come too close!" The big selling point of the film was star John Agar's monster makeup (by Bob Mark) which Michael Weldon in *The Psychotronic Encyclopedia of Film* (1983) judged it "a unique creation."

HANDS OF A STRANGER (Allied Artists, 1962) 95 mins.

Producers, Newton Arnold,, Michael duPont; director/story/screenplay, Arnold; music, Richard LaSalle; camera, Henry Cronjager; editor, Bert Honey.

Paul Lukather (Dr. Gil Harding); Joan Harvey (Dina Paris); James Stapleton (Vernon Paris); Ted Otis (Dr. Russ Compton); Michael duPont (Dr. Ken Fry); Larry Haddon (Police Lieutenant Syms); Michael Rye (George Britton); Elaine Martone (Eileen Hunter); George Sawaya (Cab Driver); Barry Gordon (Skeet); David Kramer (Carnival Barker); Sally Kellerman (Sue); Irish McCalla (Holly).

HANDS OF A STRANGLER (Continental Distributing, 1964) 87 mins.

English language version: Producers, Steve Pallos, Donald Taylor; director, Edmond T. Greville; based on the novel *Les Mains d'Orlac* by Maurice Renard; screenplay, John Baines, Edmond T. Greville; dialog, Donald Taylor; art director, John Blezard; music, Claude Bolling; concert music director, Ilona Kabos; choreography, Hasel Gee; assistant directors, Basil Rabin, Timothy Buriill, Henry Emery; costumes, Yvonne Richards; makeup, Stuart Greeborn; camera, Desmond Dickinson; editor, Oswald Hafenrichter.

French language version: Dialog, Max Montagu; art director,

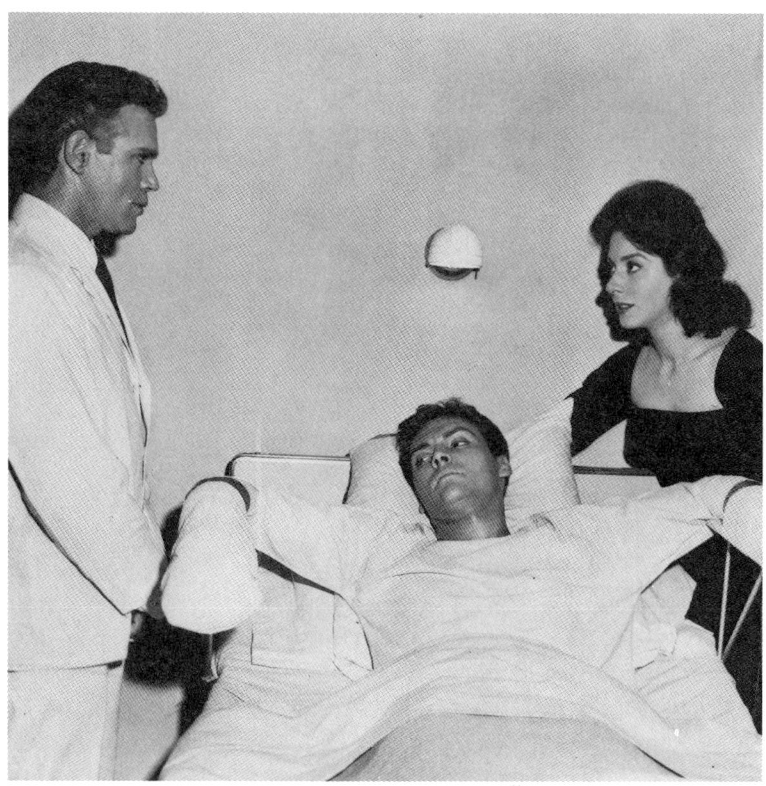

Paul Lukather, James Stapleton and Joan Harvey in HANDS OF A STRANGER (1962).

Eugene Pierac; assistant director, Jacques Corbel; sound, Robert Biart; camera, Jacques Lemare; editor, Jean Ravel.

Mel Ferrer (Steven Orlac); Christopher Lee (Neron); Dany Carrel (Li-Lang); Felix Aylmer (Dr. Cochrane); Basil Sydney (Siedelman); Lucile Saint-Simon (Louise Cochrane); Donald Wolfit (Professor Volcheff—English language version); Antoine Balpetre (Professor Volcheff—French language version); Anita Sharp Bolster (Volcheff's Assistant); Mireille Perrey (Madame Aliberti); Donald Pleasence (Coates); Campbell Singer (Inspector Henderson); Peter Reynolds (Felix); Yanilou (Emilie); Edouard Hemme (Ange); Manning Wilson (Jagger); Arnold Diamond (Dresser); David Peel (Pilot); Walter Randall (Waiter); and: Franca Bel.

Opened in Paris in April, 1961 as LES MAINS D'ORLAC at a

105 minute running time. It debuted in England in April, 1962 at 95 minutes, under the title of THE HANDS OF ORLAC.

U.S. TV title: HANDS OF ORLAC.

THE HANDS OF ORLAC (Awyon Films, 1928) 80 mins.

Director, Dr. Robert Wiene; based on the novel *Les Mains d'Orlac* by Maurice Renard; screenplay, Louis Nerz; art director, S. Wessely; camera, Guenther Krampf, Hans Androschin; editor.

Conrad Veidt (Stephen Orlac), and: Fritz Kortner, Carmen Cartellieri, Alexandra [Vera] Sorina, Paul Askonas, Fritz Strassny.

Originally released in Austria in 1925 as ORLACS HANDE.

Maurice Renard's 1920 novel *Les Mains d'Orlac* has been the basis for a quartet of films and while the plots deal basically with horror, the theme of the grafting of limbs—in this case hands—gives it a sci-fi bent; especially in the concept of the first two screen versions.

The first movie version of the novel appeared in 1925 with ORLACS HANDE, directed in Austria by Robert Weine who had done the expressionistic classic THE CABINET OF DR. CALIGARI, a half-dozen years earlier. Conrad Veidt, who had played the somnambulist in that film, took over the title role in this outing. Here he was cast as pianist Stephen Orlac who loses his hands in a train accident. New hands are grafted onto his arms but he finds out they belonged to a strangler and when several such killings occur, he is blackmailed by a mysterious man (Fritz Kortner). Eventually Orlac learns the ordeal is an attempt to drive him insane. Carlos Clarens wrote in *An Illustrated History of the Horror Film* (1967), "The film has little of Wiene's CALIGARI in it but shares the director's obsession with the explaining of the supernatural . . . Veidt . . . gave a powerful, hallucinated performance."

For the first sound version of the Renard novel, Metro-Goldwyn-Mayer produced MAD LOVE (1935), a lavish film directed by Karl Freund who had photographed THE GOLEM (1920) (q.v.) and DRACULA (1931) and had directed THE MUMMY (1932). It was adapted by Guy Endore, the author of *The Werewolf of Paris,* and was co-scripted by John J. Balderson, who had co-written the stage version of Bram Stoker's *Dracula.* Further the feature enhanced Peter Lorre's "Boogie Man" image and co-starred Colin Clive as Orlac, solidifying his macabre film stardom along with having played Dr. Frankenstein in *Frankenstein* (1931) and THE BRIDE OF FRANKENSTEIN (1935) (qq.v.). Although it is considered a genre classic, MAD LOVE is rarely screened today and at the time of its release, it was even lost in the shuffle of contemporary popular horror films.

The narrative of MAD LOVE follows the original closely with pianist Stephen Orlac (Colin Clive) losing his hands in a train crash. His wife Yvonne (Frances Drake), who has spurned the lustful Dr. Gogol (Peter Lorre), begs the surgeon to help her husband and he transplants the hands of a recently-executed knife thrower (Edward Brophy) onto Orlac's limbs. The operation is successful but Gogol convinces Orlac that he is now a mad killer who caused the deaths of several people murdered by thrown knives. Orlac is haunted by the spectre of a man with steel hands claiming Gogol has brought him back to life. Gogol kidnaps Yvonne but Stephen, who has acquired knife-throwing skills, saves her with his new found ability and learns the truth about the mad surgeon. It was he who masqueraded as the supposedly dead killer.

Most of the critical notice in MAD LOVE went to Peter Lorre as the insane Dr. Gogol. The *New York Herald-Tribune* called him a "one-man chamber of horrors" while the *New York Times* noted, " . . . with his gift for supplementing a remarkable physical appearance with his acute perception of the mechanics of insanity, cut deeply into the darkness of the morbid brain. . . ."

In 1960 French and English language versions of the story were filmed as LES MAINS D'ORLAC and issued in Great Britain in 1962 as THE HANDS OF ORLAC. The film was shown in the U.S. in 1964 as HANDS OF A STRANGLER but reverted to the British title when shown on television. This new edition of the thriller stayed true to the Renard novel, but updated the story to have pianist Steven Orlac (Mel Ferrer) badly burned in a plane crash with his rich fiancee Louise (Lucile Saint Simon) asking noted surgeon, Professor Volchett (Donald Wolfit), to perform plastic surgery. Recovering, Orlac reads that a convicted strangler was executed the night of his operation and he becomes convinced his hands belonged to the dead man. Orlac becomes so obsessed with the idea that he nearly strangles an old gardener and fearful he will hurt Louise, he flees to Marseilles. At a cheap boarding house he meets sleazy magician Neron (Christopher Lee) who becomes aware of Orlac's phobia and plans to blackmail him by using his comely assistant, Li Lang (Dany Carrel). The girl, however, turns on Neron and he murders her during their stage-knife act and is apprehended by Orlac, who turns him over to the police because he has learned of the innocence of the executed man.

A fourth screen adaptation of the novel appeared in 1962 with the U.S. production of HANDS OF A STRANGER. This low budget item told of a concert pianist Vernon Paris (James Stapleton) losing his hands in an accident but having new ones grafted onto his arms by a famous surgeon, Dr. Gil Harding (Paul Lukather). Paris learns, however, that the hands belonged to a murderer and that they can control him, forcing him to kill. The pianist goes insane and after committing several murders is hunted and killed by the law. This downbeat version was highlighted by a sound performance by Paul Lukather as the well-meaning surgeon.

HANGAR 18 (Schick Sunn Classic Pictures, 1980) C 93 mins.

Producer, Charles E. Sellier, Jr.; associate producer, Bill Cornford; assistant producer, Carole Fontana; director, James L. Conway; story, Tom Chapman, Conway; screenplay, Steven Thornley; music, John Cacvavas; assistant directors, Henning Schellerup, Leon Dudevoir; costumes, Julie Staheli; art director, Chip Radaelli; special effects, Harry Woodman; optical effects supervisor, John Forrest; camera, Paul Hipp; editor, Michael Spence.

Darren McGavin (Harry Forbes); Robert Vaughn (Gordon Cain); Gary Collins (Steve Bancroft); James Hampton (Lew Price); Philip Abbott (Frank); Pamela Bellwood (Sarah); Tom Hallick (Phil); Steven Keats (Paul); William Schallert (Mills); Cliff Osmond (Sheriff); Andrew Block (Neal); Stuart Pankin (Sam); Betty Ann Carr (Flo); and: H. M. Wynant, Bill Zuckert, Jesse Bennett, Robert Bristol, Ed E. Carroll, J. R. Clark, Craig Clyde, John William Galt, Anne Galvan, Ken Hapner, Michael Irving, Bruce Katzman, Peter Linkakis, Debra MacFarlane, Chet Norris, H. E. D. Redford, Max Robinson, Ocie Robinson, Michael Ruud.

Schick Sunn Classics had made ample profits with speculative features such as IN SEARCH OF NOAH'S ARK (1976) (q.v.) which were distributed to great success, especially in non-metropolitan areas. For years tabloids had been featuring stories, some with photographs, of how the government had been covering up a crashed UFO and its alien inhabitants. This situation was used by Sunn for one of its first general releases, HANGAR 18, which refers to the Air Force hangar where the crashed UFO was allegedly secreted. The movie, which took a possibly true situation and made a ficitonal movie about it, grossed nearly $6,000,000 at the box-office, despite critical lambasting.

Space shuttle commanders Steve Bancroft (Gary Collins) and Lew Price (James Hampton) have a near fatal crash with a UFO. Following the spaceship's crash landing in Texas, government officials board the craft and find dead aliens. The ship and corpses are taken to a remote Air Force hangar for examination while the two astronauts are given official blame for the loss of the spaceshuttle by corrupt government bureacrat Gordon Cain (Robert Vaughn). NASA's Harry Forbes (Darren McGavin) believes the astronauts are not to blame and he finds alien plans to invade the planet. The government covers up the entire affair by exploding the craft and the dead aliens, upon orders from the White House.

THE HAUNTING AT CASTLE MONTEGO see CASTLE OF EVIL.

HEARTBEEPS (Universal, 1981) C 79 mins.

Executive producer, Douglas Green; producer, Michael Phillips; director, Allan Arkush; screenplay, John Hill; production designer, John W. Corso; makeup effects, Stan Winston; assistant

Andy Kaufman and Bernadette Peters in HEARTBEEPS (1981).

director, Don Zepfel; costumes, Madeline Grancto; music, John Williams; sound, Jim R. Alexander; visual effects, Albert Whitlock; camera, Charles Rosher, Jr.; editor, Tina Hirsch.

Andy Kaufman (Val); Bernadette Peters (Aqua); Randy Quaid (Charlie); Kenneth McMillan (Max); Melanie Mayron (Susan); Christopher Guest (Calvin); Jack Carter (Catskill's Voice); Dick Miller (Walter Paisley).

Issued for the Christmas trade in 1981, HEARTBEEPS proved to be one of the movie duds of the year. Costing some $10,000,000, the dull production ran less than eighty minutes and its account of a love affair between two highly intelligent robots was pointless. Moreover, leading lady Bernadette Peters seemed almost lifeless as one of the robots while top-billed Andy Kaufman unconvincingly carried out his role as the love struck automan. Despite the film's abbreviated length, *Variety* correctly decided, "Unfortunately, each moment passes like hours waiting for this slumgullion to slide by."

In 1995 a company manufactures companion robots and two in the series, Val (Andy Kaufman) and Aqua (Bernadette Peters), fall into love. They decide to escape from their overseers (Randy Quaid, Kenneth McMillan) and head into the woods accompanied by Catskill (voice of Jack Carter), a robot who spouts an endless series of one-liners. The manufacturers turn a vicious crimebuster robot after the fugitives to recapture them. However, the trio meet junkyard owner Susan (Melanie Mayron) and Calvin (Christopher Guest) and they provide them sanctuary. As a result the lovers fashion an offspring, Phil, and live happily ever after.

Apparently the character of the crimebuster robot was added to give melodrama to the film after disastrous preview showings. The nasty robot, however, adds little to the lackluster proceedings. For genre fans, Dick Miller has a bit as a factory worker named Walter Paisley, the same character which brought him cult fame in Roger Corman's A BUCKET OF BLOOD (1959).

THE HEAVENS CALL see BATTLE BEYOND THE SUN.

HOLD ONTO YOUR DREAMS see UFORIA.

HOMUNCULUS [Die Rache des Homunkulus] (Deutsche Bioscop, 1916) 6 chapters.

Director, Otto Rippert; based on the novel by Robert Reinert; screenplay, Rippert, Robert Neuss; art director, Robert A. Dietrich camera, Carl Hoffman.

Olaf Foenss (Homunculus); Friedrich Kuehne (Professor

Hansen); and: Ernst Ludwig, Albert Paul, Lore Rueckert, Max Ruhbeck, Lia Borre, Ernst Benzinger, Margerete Ferida, Ilse Lersen.

Chapters: 1) Homunculus; 2) Das Geheimnisvolle Buch; 3) Die Liebestragoedie des Homunculus; 4) Die Rache des Homunculus; 5) Die Vernichtung der Menschheit; 6) Das Ende des Homunculus.

An artificial man, Homunculus (Olaf Foenss), is created by scientist Professor Hansen (Friedrich Kuehne) and he proves to be a perfect being except that he has no soul. Out in the world he is rejected by the human race and goes from nation to nation until he takes over a country and foments a revolution. He plans to conquer the world. Meanwhile the scientist searches for him in hopes of undoing the wrong he has committed. Homunculus is later struck and killed by lightning.

The serial HOMUNCULUS was made by the German Deutsch Bioscop company during World War I and was issued in six different parts, with over 400 minutes in running time. It is said to have been so popular, it affected Berlin fashion. In 1920 it was released in a three-part 275 minute condensed version: 1) Der Kuenstliche Mensch; 2) Die Vernichtung der Menschheit; 3) Ein Titanenkampf.

John Baxter wrote in *Science Fiction in the Cinema* (1970), "HOMUNCULUS seems a primer of almost every sf film element. The experimental ergo dangerous ergo evil formation of the 'mad scientist' stereotype is apparent in [Otto] Ripert's drawing of Professor Hansen, the creature's inventor, and the progression from Homunculus to more modern creatures is equally clear. Additionally, however, we can see the curious and again illogical imputation of superior physical strength to the manufactured creature, as if pure reason implied a natural mental and physical tyranny. Finally there is the divine destruction of the godless man, the obligatory blast of heat and light that destroys him with the element that created him. Countless deaths by fire, lightning, electricity and other similar causes can be traced directly to the climax of HOMUNCULUS."

THE HORRIBLE DR. HICHCOCK (Sigma III, 1964) C 76 mins.

Producers, Louis Mann, Luigi Carpentieri, Ermanno Donati; director, Robert Hampton [Riccardo Freda]; screenplay, Julyan Perry [Ernesto Gastaldi]; art director, Frank Smokecocks [Franco Fumagalli]; set decorator, Joseph Goodman; costumes, Inoa Starly; music, Roman Vlad; assistant director, John M. Farquahar; sound, Jackson MacGregor; camera, Donald Green [Raffaele Masciocchi]; editor, Donna Christie [Ornella Micheli].

Robert Flemyng (Dr. Bernard Hichcock); Barbara Steele (Cynthia); Teresa Fitzgerald (Margaret Hichcock); Harriet White (Martha); Montgomery Glenn (Dr. Kurt Lowe); Neil Robinson, Spencer Williams (Hospital Assistants); Howard Nelson Rubien (Laboratory Specialist); and: Al Christianson, Evar Simpson, Nat Harley.

Scientist Dr. Bernard Hichcock (Robert Flemyng) blames himself for the death of his wife Margaret (Teresa Fitzgerald) and leaves his home after burying her there. A dozen years later he returns with a new bride, Cynthia (Barbara Steele), but strange things happen. A veiled woman is seem moving along the mansion grounds at night, shrieks are heard and a skull is found in Cynthia's

Barbara Steele and Robert Flemyng in THE HORRIBLE DR. HICHCOCK (1964).

bed. Hichcock finds the veiled figure is actually Margaret, withered and mad from his having buried her alive. He plots to murder Cynthia and drain her blood to transfuse it to Margaret to restore her youth. Cynthia becomes suspicious, however, and goes to Dr. Kurt Lowe (Montgomery Glenn), Hichcock's assistant, for help, and when her husband tries to carry out his plan, Lowe comes to Cynthia's rescue. A fire breaks out during the fight between the two men and Cynthia and Lowe escape, but Hichcock and Margaret are consumed in the blaze.

Filmed in Rome in 1962 as L'ORRIBLE SEGRETO DEL DR. HICHCOCK [The Horrible Secret of Dr. Hichcock] by director Riccardo Freda (billed in the U.S. as Robert Hampton), this thriller is best known as one of the horror films cult actress Barbara Steele made in Europe in the 1960s. Its sci-fi aspects come from its 1885 English settings in which the doctor transfuses blood to restore youth. With its aura of ghostly happenings, necromancy, sexual deviation and premature burial, the film proved quite successful abroad and resulted in a sequel, LO SPETTRO DE DR. HICHCOCK [The Spectre of Dr. Hichcock] (1963), also helmed and written by Riccardo Freda. It was issued in the U.S. in 1965 by Magna as THE GHOST and in Britain as THE SPECTRE. This outing, also starring Barbara Steele, was a pure horror film.

THE HORRIBLE SECRET OF DR. HICHCOCK see THE HORRIBLE DR. HICHCOCK

HORROR EXPRESS (Scotia International, 1972) C 88 mins.

Producer, Bernard Gordon; director, Eugenio [Gene] Martin; story/screenplay, Arnaud d'Usseau, Julian Halevy; art director, Ramiro Gomez; music, John Cavacas; camera, Teodor Escamila; editor, Robert Dearberg.

Christopher Lee (Sir Alexander Caxton); Peter Cushing (Dr. Wells); Telly Savalas (Captain Kazan); Albert de Mendoza (Inspector Mirov); Silvia Tortosa (Irina Petrovski); Helga Line (Natasha); Jorge Rigaud (Count Petrovski); Alice Reinhart (Miss Jones).

HORROR EXPRESS, filmed in Spain late in 1971 as PANICO EN EL TRANSIBERIANO, is a most interesting motion picture which takes the motif of murder-on-a-train and successfully transfers it to the sci-fi genre. Set just after the turn of the century on the Trans-Siberian Express, the movie is lushly photographed by Teodor Escamila, and art director Ramiro Gomez beautifully captures the flavor of the period in the settings. With its captivating plot, the film sustains suspense, despite the detriment of Telly Savalas's overwrought hamming as a Czarist official. The London *Evening*

Standard reported the film " . . . has far more style and much, much more speed than home-grown horrors. . . ."

British anthropologist Sir Alexander Saxton (Christopher Lee) discovers a sub-human preserved in a remote Chinese province in 1905 and takes the specimen aboard the Trans-Siberian Express on his return to England. On the train is an old rival, Dr. Wells (Peter Cushing), who wants to find out what Saxton has in his huge crate and he bribes a baggage clerk who is later found drained of life, and the fossil is missing. A spy (Helga Line) is later murdered and the two scientists discover the victims appear to have their memories erased by their killer. When the creature attacks Wells, Police Inspector Mirov (Albert de Mendoza) kills it, but an autopsy on the fossil shows its eyes retain pictures from the past, such as prehistoric creatures and the Earth as seen from outer space. The scientists deduce the creature was actually controlled by an alien who can take over the minds and bodies of others. Brutal Tartar officer Kazan (Telly Savalas) boards the train with his men and kills Mirov, whom the alien has taken over, and its presence is then passed into a priest who kills all the soldiers, and then attacks Count Petrovski (Jorge Rigaud) and his wife, Irina (Silvia Tortoa). However, Saxton saves her. The alien reanimates all its victims, but Saxton wires ahead and orders the train derailed at the next stop. With all the remaining living passengers in the baggage car, Saxton and Wells detach it from the train. The cars carrying the alien and the zombies plunge over a cliff and explode.

The film was successful theatrically thanks to the reteaming of popular British horror film greats Peter Cushing and Christopher Lee.

HORROR HOSPITAL (Balch Films, 1973) C 91 mins.

Producer, Richard Gordon; associate producer, Ray Corbett; director, Antony Balch; screenplay, Balch, Alan Watson; art director, David Bill; music, De Wolfe; camera, David McDonald; editor, Robert Dearberg.

Michael Gough (Dr. Storm); Robin Askwith (Jason Jones); Vanessa Shaw (Judy Peters); Ellen Pollock (Aunt Harris); Skip Martin (Frederick); Dennis Price (Pollack); Kurt Christian (Abraham Warren); Kenneth Benda (Carter); Barbara Wendy (Millie); George Herbert (Assistant).

Rock singer Jason Jones (Robin Askwith) goes to Dr. Storm's (Michael Gough) health clinic for a rest where his assistant Aunt Harris (Ellen Pollock) is also staying. There Jason falls in love with Judy Peters (Vanessa Shaw) who has come to visit Harris, her only relative. Strange things occur at the hospital and it is rumored a hideous fiend stalks the grounds. Jason notices that several of the young people who have come to the clinic for treatment now have scarred foreheads and that the facility is patrolled by black leather-wearing bikers. Finally Jason and Judy, along with another patient Millie (Barbara Wendy) and her boyfriend Abraham Warren (Kurt Christian), discover Storm is carrying out experiments which turn the young people into zombies via surgery and he controls them through a computer. When they learn Judy and Millie are scheduled for such experimentation, the quartet try to escape but they are stopped by the bikers. The rampaging fiend kills Aunt Harris and the four attempt to kill the guards and get away, but the monster kills Judy before Jason reveals it to be Storm, who wears a flesh-like mask of his own creation. Jason, Judy and Abraham put an end to Storm and his horrors.

"Black Gloves of Evil Silence The Screams of Horror!" read the poster copy for this Richard Gordon production; also known as COMPUTER KILLERS in the U.S. Outside of Michael Gough's rich, hammy acting as Storm, and Dennis Price's amusing cameo as a highly effeminate travel agent, the film has little to offer.

THE HORROR OF FRANKENSTEIN (American-Continental, 1971) C 95 mins.

Producer/director, Jimmy Sangster; based on characters created by Mary Shelley; screenplay, Sangster, Jeremy Burnham; art director, Scott MacGregor; makeup, Tom Smith; music, Malcolm Williamson; assistant director, Derek Whitehurst; sound, Terry Poulton; camera, Moray Grant; editor, Chris Barnes.

Ralph Bates (Dr. Victor Frankenstein); Kate O'Mara (Alys); Graham James (Wilhelm); Veronica Carlson (Elizabeth); Bernard Archard (Professor); Dennis Price (Grave Robber); Joan Rice (Grave Robber's Wife); David Prowse (The Monster); and: Jon Finch.

In 1970 Hammer Films decided to infuse new life in its rapidly deteriorating "Frankenstein" series by adding humor to the proceedings and bringing in a new Dr. Frankenstein, Ralph Bates. The company remade CURSE OF FRANKENSTEIN (1957) (q.v.), the initial entry, but the new version proved unsatisfactory commercially. Peter Cushing, the Frankenstein in the other episodes of the Hammer series, was thankfully soon back in his final (to date) entry, FRANKENSTEIN AND THE MONSTER FROM HELL (1973) (q.v.).

Baron Victor Frankenstein (Ralph Bates) wants to follow in his father's path and create human life. He begins by bringing a dead tortoise back to life. He returns to the family castle near Ingoldstadt and sets up his laboratory, enlisting the aid of a grave robber (Dennis

Price) whose wife (Joan Rice) does all the work. To provide a brain for his creation, the doctor eliminates a noted professor (Bernard Archer) whose daughter Elizabeth (Veronica Carlson) has been Frankenstein's sweetheart since childhood. Hounded by creditors and nowhere to go, the doctor makes the girl his cook. When the creature (David Prowse) finally is brought to life he proves to be very unfriendly, probably because the brain placed in his cranium had been dropped prior to the transplant. Frankenstein follows his rampaging creation and captures him and uses him to kill the graverobber and his wife. The creature becomes lustful for Elizabeth but the police arrive on the scene. Frankenstein hides the monster in a large laboratory container. While the law interrogates the doctor, a small girl comes into the lab and accidentally brushes against a lever which drops the monster into an acid vat, disintegrating him.

Allen Eyles, Robert Adkinson and Nicholas Fry wrote in *The House of Horror* (1973), "The plot essentially recapitulated the first FRANKENSTEIN film but was embroidered with some macabre touches of sick humor, with the monster being an unsympathetic thug, compared to the creature of latent sensitivity portrayed by Karloff in the real original of the series." Also annoying was Ralph Bates' (mis)interpretation of Dr. Frankenstein, shown here more as a naughty child than a man of science.

THE HORROR OF TERROR see FACE OF THE SCREAMING WEREWOLF.

HORROR PLANET (Almi Films, 1982) C 86 mins.

Presenter, Sir Run Run Shaw; executive producer, Peter Schlesinger; producers, Richard Gordon, David Speechley; director, Norman J. Warren; screenplay, Nick Maley, Gloria Maley; music, John Scott; production designer, Hayden Pearce; assistant director, Gary White; stunt co-ordinator, Peter Brayham; special effects makeup Nick Maley; sound, Simon Okin; special effects, Oxford Scientific Films, Camera Effects; camera, John Metcalfe; editor, Peter Boyle.

Judy Geeson (Sandy); Robin Clarke (Mark); Jennifer Ashley (Holly); Stephanie Beacham (Kate); Stephen Grives (Gary); Barry Houghton (Karl); Rosalind Lloyd (Gail); Victoria Tennant (Barbara); Trevor Thomas (Mitcdh); Heather Wright (Sharon); David Baxt (Ricky); Dominic Jephcott (Dean); John Segal (Jeff); Kevin O'Shea (Corin).

Roger Corman films such as HUMANOIDS FROM THE DEEP (1980) and GALAXY OF TERROR (1981) (q.v.) revelled in the plot ploy of having comely Earth women sexually molested by monsters and aliens. HORROR PLANET, issued in its homeland of Great Britain as INSEMINOID in 1981 and censored here to avoid an X-rating, carried on this rape motif. Not only is Judy Geeson defiled by an alien creature, it impregnates her and she spends the entire film attempting to protect this procreation from her comrades who would abort the unholy alliance.

A group of astronauts, including Sandy (Judy Geeson), Mark (Robin Clarke), Holly (Jennifer Ashley) and Kate (Stephanie Beacham) set out to explore the underworld of a newly-discovered planet which orbits around two identical suns. After a crew member dies from touching mysterious crystals, Sandy is attacked by a monstrous creature which rapes and impregnates her. After the event, Sandy loses her sanity and becomes convinced that the only way to save her offspring is to kill her fellow crew members. She begins her task, aided by the fact that the rape and the absorption of the monster's body fluids has made it possible for her to exist without oxygen in the planet's atmosphere. Sandy murders all except Mark and then gives birth to twins, neither of whom carry any of her characteristics. The finale has Mark trying to save himself and getting rid of the offspring.

HORROR PLANET is a very claustrophobic film with its entire action set within the confines of the spaceship and the catacombs beneath the planet. Much of the action, especially the chase sequences, occur in tepid lighting. The movie has heavy sexual overtones, not only because of the impregnation of Sandy, but due to its alluring female crew members, all of whom meet unfortunate fates. Even in its abridged form, HORROR PLANET is full of gore and nudity, two seemingly requisite ingredients to appeal to a 1980s mass audience.

THE HOUGHLAND MURDER CASE see MURDER BY TELEVISION.

HOUSE OF DRACULA (Universal, 1945) 67 mins.

Executive producer, Joseph Gershenson; producer, Paul Malvern; director, Erle C. Kenton; based on characters created by Mary Shelley and Bram Stoker; story, George Bricker, Dwight V. Babcock; screenplay, Edward T. Lowe; art directors, John B. Goodman, Martin Obzina; makeup, Jack Pierce; music director, Hans J. Salter; music, Edgar Fairchild; special camera effects, John P. Fulton; camera, George Robinson; editor, Russell Schoengarth, John P. Fulton.

Lon Chaney (Lawrence Talbot); John Carradine (Count Dracula); Martha O'Driscoll (Miliza Morrell); Lionel Atwill (Inspector Holtz);

Jane Adams (Nina); Onslow Stevens (Dr. Edelmann); Ludwig Stossel (Ziegfried); Glenn Strange (The Monster); Skelton Knaggs (Steinmuhl); Joseph E. Bernard (Brahms); Dick Dickinson, Harry Lamont (Villagers); Fred de Cordova, Carey Harrison (Gendarmes); Gregory Muradian (Johannes); Beatrice Gray (Mother).

With World War II winding down, horror films were losing their audience pull and Universal was stocking more and more monsters into *each* feature for box-office receipts. FRANKENSTEIN MEETS THE WOLFMAN (1943) and HOUSE OF FRANKENSTEIN (1944) (*infra*) had done the trick, but by the time HOUSE OF DRACULA came along in 1945, it was made on a smaller budget with its finale lifted intact from GHOST OF FRANKENSTEIN (1942) (q.v.). *The New York Herald-Tribune* noted the feature was "substituting quantity for imagination." Still producer Paul Malvern and director Erle C. Kenton, who had teamed for THE HOUSE OF FRANKENSTEIN, churned out an entertaining minor thriller which was a satisfactory finale to the "Frankenstein" series—not counting the comedy/parody ABBOTT AND COSTELLO MEET FRANKENSTEIN (q.v.), three years later.

In the village of Vasaria kindly Dr. Edelmann (Onslow Stevens) is experimenting on molds to soften bones to help his pretty but hunchbacked assistant, Nina (Jane Adams). He is visited by Count Dracula (John Carradine) who asks Edelmann's help in lifting his vampiristic curse and the doctor agrees. That night Edelmann is also visited by Lawrence Talbot (Lon Chaney) but cannot meet with him. Later Inspector Holtz (Lionel Atwill) has Edelmann come to the jail where, behind bars, Talbot transforms into a werewolf. Edelmann believes his new mold will help both Dracula and Talbot but he must produce more of it to aid them and Nina. Talbot, however, tries to commit suicide by jumping off a cliff and Edelmann finds him in a cave. There they uncover the Frankenstein monster (Glenn Strange) preserved in hardened quicksand. Dracula, meanwhile, is attracted to local beauty Miliza Morrell (Martha O'Driscoll) who in turn loves Talbot. During a blood transfusion Dracula places some of his blood in Edelmann's arm and later the doctor tries to stop him from attacking Miliza. At dawn, Dracula returns to his coffin but Edelmann opens it and lets the sunlight destroy the vampire. Contaminated by Dracula's blood, Edelmann has periods in which he is a madman and he kills his brother (Ludwig Stossel), but while sane he operates on Talbot and cures him of lyncanthropy. Edelmann reactivates the monster and when Nina tries to stop him, he murders her. The villagers descend on his laboratory and in the foray the monster, now at its full power, goes berserk while Edelmann murders Holtz. Talbot shoots the scientist and the monster turns on him and Miliza.

They push a cabinet filled with chemicals on the creature and set him afire. As the monster dies in the blaze, Talbot and Miliza leave the chamber of horrors for a life of happiness.

Variety judged the film " . . . Universal's horror special for the year and [it] upholds traditions of company's past offerings in this field. In point of eerie effects, fantastic characters and a plot in keeping with the mood early established, DRACULA has been well turned out by Paul Malvern, on production end, and Erle C. Kenton directing . . . picture as a whole shall please horror addicts."

The most unique (and satisfying) aspect of HOUSE OF DRACULA was witnessing Lawrence Talbot's hard-won freedom from his werewolf curse—for the time being at least; he was back in the role in ABBOTT AND COSTELLO MEET FRANKENSTEIN (1948) (q.v.) (as was Glenn Strange as the monster).

HOUSE OF FRANKENSTEIN (Universal, 1944) 71 mins.

Producer, Paul Malvern; director, Erle C. Kenton; based on characters created by Mary Shelley and Bram Stoker; story, Curt Siodmak; screenplay, Edward T. Lowe; art directors, John B. Goodman, Martin Obzina; makeup, Jack Pierce; music director, Hans J. Salter; special camera effects, John Fulton; camera, George Robinson; editor, Phillip Cahn.

Boris Karloff (Dr. Niemann); Lon Chaney (Lawrence Talbot); J. Carrol Naish (Daniel); John Carradine (Count Dracula); Anne Gwynne (Rita); Peter Coe (Carl Hussman); Lionel Atwill (Inspector Arnz); George Zucco (Professor Bruno Lampini); Elena Verdugo (Ilonka); Sig Rumann (Hussman); William Edmunds (Fejos); Charles Miller (Toberman); Philip Van Zandt (Muller); Julius Tannen (Hertz); Hans Herbert (Meler); Dick Dickinson (Born); George Lynn (Gerlach); Michael Mark (Strauss); Olaf Hytten (Hoffman); Frank Reicher (Ullman); Brandon Hurst (Dr. Geissler); Glenn Strange (The Monster); and: Gino Corrado, Charles Miller, Joe Kirk.

Following the successful teaming of the Universal monsters in FRANKENSTEIN MEETS THE WOLFMAN (1943) (q.v.), HOUSE OF FRANKENSTEIN emerged late the next year, not only reuniting these creatures but adding Count Dracula, a mad scientist and his hunchback assistant! The result was a satisfying continuation of the series which *Variety* dubbed a "chiller-diller meller." Besides retaining the Gothic horror flavor of the series, this movie also offered patrons five genre stars: Boris Karloff, Lon Chaney, John Carradine, J. Carrol Naish and George Zucco.

Lightning strikes the prison near Neustadt and inmates Dr.

Boris Karloff and John Carradine in HOUSE OF FRANKENSTEIN (1944).

Niemann (Boris Karloff) and hunchback Daniel (J. Carrol Naish) escape and take refuge with Dr. Lampini's (George Zucco) traveling horror show, which features Count Dracula's skeleton. Niemann has Daniel murder Lampini and they take over the show and head for Vasaria where the scientist, obsessed with creating life, intends to use Dr. Frankenstein's records for that purpose, as well as to make Daniel normal. In Vasaria Niemann also wants to eliminate his old enemy, the burgomaster (Sig Rumann), but accidentally brings Dracula (John Carradine) to life by removing the stake from his skeleton. He makes a pact with Dracula to guard his coffin by day if Dracula will do his bidding. Dracula murders the burgomaster and kidnaps beautiful Rita (Anne Gwynne) and the police led by Inspector Arnz (Lionel Atwill), give chase. Dracula's coach overturns and he fails to get back to his coffin by dawn and dies. In the village Daniel rescues young gypsy girl Ilonka (Elena Verdugo) from being molested and falls in love with her. At the ruin of Frankenstein's castle, Niemann and Daniel uncover the frozen bodies of werewolf Lawrence Talbot (Lon Chaney) and the Frankenstein monster (Glenn Strange) from ice. Niemann agrees to aid Talbot in ending his curse and they take the monster to Niemann's laboratory. Ilonka falls in love with Talbot and the jealous Daniel tells her Talbot is a werewolf. Niemann kidnaps two of his enemies (Frank Reicher, Michael Mark) and promises to put their brains in the heads of Talbot and the monster. During the full moon Talbot mortally wounds Ilonka but she shoots him with a silver bullet and they die together. Grief stricken, Daniel takes the girl's body to Niemann and then turns on him just as the monster returns to full power under the doctor's electrical equipment. Daniel kills Niemann and is, in turn, murdered by the monster. The villagers chase the monster—who carries Niemann's body—into nearby quicksand where he is engulfed in the quagmire.

Solidly produced by Paul Malvern and with finely paced direction from Erle C. Kenton, HOUSE OF FRANKENSTEIN (originally called DESTINY and CHAMBER OF HORROR) did well enough at the box-office for the filmmakers to produce a followup, HOUSE OF DRACULA, (*supra*).

Released in 8mm as DOOM OF DRACULA.

HOUSE OF FRIGHT (Columbia, 1960) C 88 mins.

Producer, Michael Carreras; director, Terence Fisher; based on the novel *The Strange Case of Dr. Jekyll and Mr. Hyde* by Robert Louis Stevenson; screenplay, Wolf Mankowitz; music/songs, Monty Norman, David Heneker; camera, Jack Asher; editor, Eric Boyd-Perkins.

Paul Massie (Dr. Jekyll/Mr. Hyde); Dawn Addams (Kitty); Christopher Lee (Paul Allen); David Kossoff (Lisuer); Francis De Wolff (Inspector); Norma Marla (Maria); Magda Miller (Sphinx Girl); William Kendall (Clubman); Pauline Shepherd (Girl in Gin Shop); Helen Goss (Nannie); Percy Cartwright (Coroner); Joe Robinson (Corinthia); Arthur Lovegrove (Cabby).

See: DR. JEKYLL AND MR. HYDE (essay).

HYPER SAPIEN (Tri-Star, 1986) C 93 mins.

Producers, Jack Schwartzman, Ariel Levy; director, Peter Hunt; story, Christopher Blue; screenplay, Christopher Adcock, Blue, Marnie Paige; music, Arthur B. Rubinstein; orchestrator, Mark H. Hoder; production designer, Harold Lange; art director, Richard Hudolin; set decorator, Tedd Kuchera; costumes, Kathy Marshall; stunt co-ordinator, Joh Scott; animatronics, Rodger Shaw; sound,

Frank Griffiths; special effects, David Harris; camera, John Coquillon; editor, Robert Benrich.

Sydney Penny (Robyn); Ricky Paull Goldin (Dirt [Robert Edward] McAlpin); Keenan Wynn (Jasper McAlpin); Rosie Marcel (Tavy); Gail Strickland (Senator Myrna King); Dennis Holahen (Uncle Aric); Chuck Shamata (Les); Hersha Parady (Mrs. McAlpin); Patricia Brookson (Cee Gee); Peter Jason (Mr. McAlpin); Jeremy Wilkins (Hyper Sapien Leader); Him Gray (Teel); Marilyn Schreffler (Voice of Kirbi, the Tri-Lat); Gladys Taylor (Lucy); Linda Elder (Lyth); Talia Shire (Dr. Tedra Rosen); Army Archerd (Television Host); David Siversten (Riss); and: Clarice McCord, Trevor Hayden, Maureen Thomas, Greg Solem, Christy Baker.

When their ship lands on the Moon, three aliens leave it and fly to Earth, landing in Wyoming. They are Robyn (Sydney Penny) and three year old Tavy (Rosie Marcel) and their three-eyed, three-legged sloth, Kirbi, who intakes gasoline to speed its growth. The trio comes under the protection of a young rancher's son Dirt (Ricky Paull Goldin) and he takes the aliens to his grandfather's (Keenan Wynn) ranch. Meanwhile Uncle Aric (Dennis Holahen), the commander of the spacecraft and Robyn's uncle, comes looking for them and policeman Les (Chuck Shamata) thinks he is out to assassinate Senator King (Gail Strickland), a friend of the boy's father, who has come to their ranch for a barbecue. At the party the aliens are revealed but they are unharmed and return to their craft.

An obvious imitation of E.T. (1982) (q.v.), HYPER SAPIEN is a dull film aimed at the kiddie market, but one which even moppets ignored. While the Tri-Late Kirbi character is intended to be appealing it is *not.* "Seldom, even in the annals of moppet sci-fi, has there been so much ado about so little." (*Variety*)

I, MONSTER (Cannon, 1973) C 75 mins.

Producers, Max J. Rosenberg, Milton Subtosky; director, Stephen Weeks; based on the novel *The Strange Case of Dr. Jekyll and Mr. Hyde* by Robert Louis Stevenson; screenplay, Subotsky; art director, Tony Curtis; makeup, Harry Frampton, Peter Frampton; music, Carl Davis; camera, Moray Grant; editor, Peter Tanner.

Christopher Lee (Charles Marlowe/Edward Blake); Peter Cushing (Utterson); Mike Raven (Enfield); Richard Hurndall (Dr. Lanyon); George Merritt (Poole); Kenneth J. Warren (Deane); Susan Jameson (Diane); Marjorie Lawrence (Annie); Aimee Delamain (Landlady).

See: DR. JEKYLL AND MR. HYDE (essay).

I WAS A TEENAGE FRANKENSTEIN (American International, 1957) C 74 mins.*

Producer, Herman Cohen; director, Herbert L. Strock; suggested by the novel by Mary Shelley; story/screenplay, Kenneth Langtry; art director, Leslie Thomas; makeup, Philip Scheer; music, Paul Dunlap; camera, Lothrop Worth; editor, Jerry Young.

Whit Bissell (Professor Frankenstein); Phyllis Coates (Margaret); Robert Burton (Dr. Karlton); Gary Conway (Teenager/Teenage Monster); George Lynn (Sergeant Burns); John Cliff (Sergeant McAffee); Marshall Bradford (Dr. Randolph); Claudia Bryar (Arlene's Mother); Angela Blake (Beautiful Girl); Russ Whiteman (Dr. Elwood); Charles Seel (The Jeweler); Paul Keast (Man at Crash); Gretchen Thomas (Woman in Corridor); Joy Stoner (Arlene); Larry Carr (Young Man); Pat Miller (Police Officer).

Following the tremendous box-office reception to I WAS A TEENAGE WEREWOLF (*infra*), producer Herman Cohen turned out this followup directed by Herbert L. Strock. "Body Of A Boy! Mind Of A Monster! Soul Of An Unearthly Thing!" read the poster blurb for I WAS A TEENAGE FRANKENSTEIN which featured the monster's hideous head.

Professor Frankenstein (Whit Bissell) lectures at a California college as the guest of Dr. Karlton (Robert Burton). He wants to create an artificial man like his famous ancestor and has assembled various body parts and enlists Karlton's aid in putting the thing together. Electricity brings the monster (Gary Conway) to life and Frankenstein's secretary Margaret (Phyllis Coates) sees the horrible being, but says nothing. The monster escapes and becomes frightened, breaking into a young girl's room and accidentally killing her. Margaret tells Frankenstein she knows the truth about his experiments and he has his creation murder her and her corpse is tossed into a crocodile pit. When Karlton leaves town, Frankenstein instructs the monster to go to lover's lane and kill a teenager (Gary Conway) and his face is grafted onto the creature's head. When Karlton returns, Frankenstein tells him he plans to take the creature apart, ship him back to his home in England, and then reassemble him. The monster, however, does not like the idea and throws his creator into the crocodile pit. Karlton goes for the law. When the police arrive, the creature falls into an electrical board and dies, his face reverting to the horrible monster Frankenstein created.

The teenage Frankenstein was recreated by Gary Conway in HOW TO MAKE A MONSTER the next year.

*Color sequence.

I WAS A TEENAGE WEREWOLF (American International, 1957) 76 mins.

Producer, Herman Cohen; director, Gene Fowler, Jr.; screenplay, Ralph Thornton; art director, Leslie Thomas; music, Paul Dunlap; camera, Joseph La Shelle; editor, George Gittens.

Michael Landon (Tony Rivers); Yvonne Lime (Arlene); Whit Bissell (Dr. Alfred Brandon); Tony Marshall (Jimmy); Dawn Richard (Theresa); Barney Phillips (Detective Donovan); Ken Miller (Vic); Cindy Robbins (Pearl); Michael Rougas (Frank); Robert Griffin (Police Chief Baker); Joseph Mell (Dr. Hugo Wagner); Malcolm Atterbury (Charles); Eddie Marr (Doyle); Vladimir Sokoloff (Pepi); Louise Lewis (Miss Ferguson); John Launer (Bill); Guy Williams (Chris Stanley); Dorothy Crehan (Mary).

American International Pictures was one of the first Hollywood film companies to realize the movie box-office power of the teenage audience. How better to appeal to that sci-fi/horror film-loving segment of the populace than with a title like I WAS A TEENAGE WEREWOLF? Produced by Herman Cohen, and nicely directed by Gene Fowler, Jr. this atmospheric little film was made in a week's time for $125,000 and went on to gross $2,000,000+ in its first year of domestic release, resulting in an equally successful sequel, I WAS A TEENAGE FRANKENSTEIN (*supra*), the same year. The movie also brought notice to actor Michael Landon who became a top TV star on "Bonanza" and later "Little House on the Prairie" and the fantasy series "Highway to Heaven."*

Tony Rivers (Michael Landon) is a belligerent teenager who worries his girlfriend Arlene (Yvonne Lime) with his fits of anger. At the suggestion of school officials and the police, he agrees to visit Dr. Alfred Brandon (Whit Bissell) for help. The doctor, however, is experimenting with autosuggestion and a drug which will revert a human back to a primitive state. He uses them to experiment on Tony, turning him into a werewolf. Several teenagers are murdered and school janitor Pepi (Vladimir Sokoloff) warns that a man-beast is loose in the community. Tony returns to Brandon for help and when the doctor refuses, he kills him and wrecks the office. Reverting back into a werewolf, Tony stalks the city but is finally shot down by the police. Before dying, he returns to his normal appearance.

The character of a teenage werewolf pops up again in AIP's

*As an in-joke, Landon played an Angel who sometimes reverts to a werewolf in the "I Was a Middle-Aged Werewolf" episode on "Highway to Heaven" (NBC-TV, 10/28/87)

HOW TO MAKE A MONSTER (1958), only here a mad makeup artist (Robert H. Harris) uses an actor (Gary Clarke) playing the part, for his own nefarious purposes.

I WAS A ZOMBIE FOR THE FBI (Ardent Teleproductions, 1982) C 100 mins.

Producers, Marius Penczner, Nancy Donelson; director, Penczner; screenplay, Penczner, John Gillick; camera, Rick Dupree.

James Rasberry (Rex Armstrong); Larry Rasberry (Ace Evans); John Gillick (Bart Brazop); Christine Wellford (Penny Carson); Anthony Isabell (Bret Brazo); and: Lawrence Hall, Rick Crowe, Alan Zellner, Ken Zimmerman, David Mayo, Jeff Bailey, Estelle Helm, Glenda Mace.

Filmed in association with Memphis State University, this tongue-in-cheek genre takeoff is played straight yet is filled with humor. Emmy Award-winning director Marius Penczner, who also made the acclaimed video "TV Dinners," deftly handles the difficult task of producing a send-off *without* making it too cute or boring. The acting is uniformly good and the special effects with the monster at the finale are well-executed. One amusing scene has a policeman reading a tabloid with the headline "UFOs Stole My Wife" while the aliens are taking his car. Set in the South of the late 1960s, the movie enjoyably spoofs sci-fi films, gangsters, law enforcement, the soft drink craze, and just about everything else within its grasp.

A plane carrying the notorious hoodlums, the Brazos brothers (John Gillick, Anthony Isabell), crashes into a UFO and the aliens, who have taken over the local Health Cola Plant which manufactures the popular drink Unicola, decides to use them to control the planet by changing the drink's formula so that anyone who drinks the concoction will be turned into a zombie. Agreeing to the scheme, the gangsters take pretty TV newswoman Penny Carson (Christine Wellford) hostage and demand $1,000,000 in ransom for her and the soft drink formula. Penny's fiancee, FBI agent Rex Armstrong (James Rasberry), saves her and captures the hoodlums. Meanwhile the aliens use the cola plant to make their new zombie-inducing drink. They capture Penny and get the Brazos out of prison, but the brothers try to kill one of the aliens. Later Armstrong and his partner, Ace Evans (Larry Rasberry), are captured by the aliens, as are the gangsters, but the latter aid the FBI in getting free and they kill the aliens' cannibal monster and bring about the space invaders' downfall.

IMMEDIATE DISASTER see STRANGER FROM VENUS.

IN SEARCH OF NOAH'S ARK (Schick Sunn Classic Pictures, 1977) C 95 mins.

Executive producer, Raylan Jensen; producer, Charles E. Sellier, Jr.; director, James L. Conway; based on the book by David Balsiger, Sellier, Jr.; screenplay, Conway, Sellier; technical advisor/historian, David Balsiger; assistant director, David Oyster; art director, Richard Sawyer; camera, George Stapleford; editor, Randy Rennolds.

Vern Adix (Noah); Brad Crandall (Narrator).

Somewhere in the realm between science-fact and science-fiction comes the area of science-maybe, transferred to the cinema as the speculation film. These features proliferated in the 1970s and one of the most successful producers of this kind of movie fare was Sunn Classics Pictures, who assembled such items as: THE MYSTERIOUS MONSTERS (1975), THE AMAZING WORLD OF PSYCHIC PHENOMENA (1976), THE BERMUDA TRIANGLE (1978), BEYOND AND BACK (1978), and IN SEARCH OF HISTORIC JESUS (1980), in addition to IN SEARCH OF NOAH'S ARK (1976), included here as an example of this specie of quasi sci-fi film.

Narrator Brad Crandall focuses on the film's thesis that Noah's

Vern Adix (at head of table) in IN SEARCH OF NOAH'S ARK (1977).

Ark from the great Flood (discussed in the Old Testament) is located in the ice and snow of Turkey's Mount Ararat, as claimed by the Bible. The movie recreates the preparations made by Noah (Vern Adix) for the construction of the vessel and the bringing together of various animals to board the ship, along with his immediate family. Life on the ark during the forty days and nights of rain is examined as is the sending out of the dove by Noah and his repopulating the world following the flood. On a more scientific level, a detailed study of Mount Ararat is given, with sedimentary deposits and salt clusters suggesting there was a flood in the area in ancient times. The film also attempts to prove the existence of the vessel with archaeological studies, surveys and scientific tests in addition to eyewitness accounts dating back to 700 B.C. Most attention is given to timber from the craft brought back by expeditions led by Sir James Bryce and Fernand Navarra, along with aerial photographs which show an ark-like craft buried in Mount Ararat's ice cover. Authorities on the subject are also interviewed and footage from several expeditions to the ark site are included.

THE INCREDIBLE INVASION (Azteca, 1971) C 90 mins.

Producer, Luis Enrique Vergara; directors, Juan Ibanez, Jack Hill; screenplay, Karl Schanzer, Vergara; music, Enrico C. Cabiati; special effects (U.S. sequences), James Tanenbaum; camera, Raul Dominguez, Austin McKinney.

Boris Karloff (Professor John Mayer); Enrique Guzman (Paul); Christina Linder (Laura Mayer); Maura Monti (Isabel); Yerye Beirute (Escaped Convict); and: Tere Valdez, Sergio Kleiner, Mariela Flores, Griselda Meja, Rosangela Balbo, Tito Novarro.

In 1968 Boris Karloff journeyed to Hollywood where he completed his scenes for four feature films in three weeks, for producers, Luis Enrique Vergara and Juan Ibanez. The films were later completed in Mexico but none were issued theatrically in the United States except in Spanish-language cinemas, although two of them appear on TV in dubbed versions. These are THE SNAKE PEOPLE and THE INCREDIBLE INVASION; the other titles being THE FEAR CHAMBER and HOUSE OF EVIL. THE INCREDIBLE INVASION was issued in South America as INVASION SINIESTRA [Sinister Invasion].

Aged Professor John Mayer (Boris Karloff) has developed a machine which can control the destructive powers of radioactive elements and the military wants it, but Mayer thinks it should be saved for the good of mankind. Aliens from outer space also fear the machine and they enter the bodies of Mayer and an escaped sex maniac convict (Yerye Beirute) who murders a young village girl

(Maura Monti). The convict tries to kill Mayer's daughter Laura (Christina Linder), but the scientist expels the influence of the alien who attacked him, and he uses the machine to kill the convict. Aided by his assistant Paul (Enrique Guzman), he eliminates the remaining alien. Wanting no more outer space invasions, Mayer destroys the invention.

THE INCREDIBLE MELTING MAN (American International, 1977) C 86 mins.

Producers, Samuel W. Gelfman, Max J. Rosenberg; director/screenplay, William Sachs; music, Arlon Ober; art director, Michael Levesque; makeup/special effects, Rick Baker; camera, Willy Curtis; editor, James Beshears.

Alex Rebar (Colonel Steve West, the Incredible Melting Man); Burr DeBenning (Dr. Ted Nelson); Myron Healey (General Perry); Michael Alldredge (Sheriff Blake); Ann Sweeny (Judy Nelson); Lisle Wilson (Dr. Loring); Rainbeaux Smith (The Model); Julie Drazen (Carol); Stuart Edmond Rodgers, Chris Whitney (Little Boys); Edwin Max (Harold); Dorothy Love (Helen); Janus Blythe (Nell); Jonathon Demme (Matt).

Having returned to Earth following the first successful space voyage to Saturn, Colonel Steve West (Alex Rebar) becomes ill and learns that he is melting away and the only way to prolong his life is to satisfy his need for human flesh. He escapes from a hospital and devours a young woman and returns home, and does the same to his parents. Air Force General Perry (Myron Healey) orders West captured and two doctors, Ted Nelson (Burr DeBenning) and Loring (Lisle Wilson), try to locate him. When he attacks another young woman, West has his arm severed with a meat cleaver and he goes into hiding, but he begins physically disintegrating. The Air Force dispatches men to find West and they happen upon a trail of human body parts. Nelson and a deputy sheriff corner West, but Nelson is killed and the deputy wounds the astronaut before he is killed by the mutant. With no way to gain nourishment and badly wounded, West melts away.

Reminiscent of the British classic, THE CREEPING UNKNOWN (1956) (see B/V), THE INCREDIBLE MELTING MAN is an inexpensively produced film highlighted by some of Rick Baker's early makeup effects. *Variety* found the feature "often disgusting." The finale of the title creature being swept up into a garbage pail by a janitor is remindful of another AIP "classic" THE CRAWLING HAND (1963) (q.v.) in which the title "thing" ends at a dump being devoured by cats.

Barry Kaufman commented in *Demonique* magazine (#1, 1980),

"The script, written by director William Sachs, is even worse than his uninspired direction. With some awfully contrived sequences, not to mention an abundance of inane dialogue, most of the script seems to be a flashback to some of the worst films of the fifties."

THE INCREDIBLE SHRINKING WOMAN (Universal, 1981) C 88 mins.

Executive producer, Jane Wagner; producer, Hank Moonjean; director, Joel Schumacher; suggested by the story "The Shrinking Man" by Richard Matheson; screenplay, Wagner; production designer, Raymond A. Brandt; set decorator, Jennifer Politox; costumes, Roberta Weiner; music, Suzanne Ciani; assistant director, Katy Emde; sound, John Kean; special camera effects supervisor/camera, Bruce Logan; editors, Jeff Gourson, Anthony Redman.

Lily Tomlin (Pat Kramer/Judith Beasley); Charles Grodin (Vance Kramer); Ned Beatty (Dan Beame); Henry Gibson (Dr. Eugene Nortz); Elizabeth Wilson (Dr. Ruth Ruth); Mark Blankfield (Rob); Maria Smith (Concepcion); Pamela Bellwood (Sandra Dyson); John Glover (Tom Keller); Nicholas Hormann (Logan Carver); James McMullan (Lyle Parks); Shelby Balik (Beth Kramer); Justin Dana (Jeff Kramer); Richard A. Baker (Sidney).

While THE INCREDIBLE SHRINKING MAN (1957) (see B/V) was played straight and has taken on cult status, this feminine counterpart relies too much on the special appeal of comedienne Lily Tomlin, who came to the fore on TV's "Laugh-In" and whose screen career has fluctuated tremendously. For those who appreciate Tomlin and her unsubtle antics, THE INCREDIBLE SHRINKING WOMAN has its moments.

Housewife Pat Kramer (Lily Tomlin) resides in Tasty Meadows with her ad executive husband Vance (Charles Grodin) and children Beth (Shelby Balik) and Jeff (Justin Dana). Because of her endless dependency on chemicals (in foods, cleaners, aerosols) she suddenly starts becoming smaller, much to the chagrin of her husband, his employer (Ned Beatty), and the children. When her bizarre case becomes known, Pat becomes a national hero; but dishonest scientists kidnap her to perfect a serum to make everyone small. But Sidney, a gorilla (Rick Baker), comes to her rescue. The serum works and Pat returns to normal size but then discovers she cannot stop growing!

Heavily focusing on "underplayed" situations involving the suppressed American housewife, this film is purely a Tomlin showcase. While the movie has its amusing sequences, it fails where most sci-fi spoofs fail—it does NOT realize the genre is more fun when taken seriously. In *Horror and Science Fiction Films II* (1982), Donald

Lily Tomlin in THE INCREDIBLE SHRINKING WOMAN (1981).

C. Willis analyzed, "It's part black comedy, part effects stunts, part too-cute parody, part Capra populism, and (most interestingly) part melancholic ode to mother-and-wife-hood." *Variety* complained, "Decision to create a grainy camera look to hide the mattes might have seemed necessary but makes THE INCREDIBLE SHRINKING WOMAN very difficult to watch, even at 88 minutes." That reviewer, however did call the feature " . . . unquestionably funny and often bizarre."

INNERSPACE (Warner Bros., 1987) C 120 mins.

Executive producers, Steven Spielberg, Peter Guber, Jon Peters; co-executive producers, Frank Marshall, Kathleen Kennedy; producer, Michael Finnell; co-producer, Chip Proser; director, Joe Dante; story, Proser; screenplay, Jeffrey Boam, Proser; music, Jerry Goldsmith; production designer, James H. Spencer; art director, William Matthews; set designers, Judy Cammer, Gene Nollman; set decorator, Richard C. Goddard; conceptual designer, Richard Vander Wende; costume designer, Rosanna Norton; special makeup effects, Rob Bottin; assistant director, Pat Kehoe; second unit action director, Glenn Randall, Jr; stunt co-ordinator, Glenn Randall, Jr.; medical adviser, Dr. Jaime Moriguchi; technical adviser, Gentry Lee; supervising sound editor, Mark Mangini; sound, Ken King, Bruce Botnick; optical supervisor, Kenneth Smith; visual effects supervisor, Dennis Mauren; camera, Andrew Laszlo; editor, Kent Beyda.

Dennis Quaid (Lieutenant Tuck Pendleton); Martin Short (Jack Putter); Meg Ryan (Lydia Maxwell); Kevin McCarthy (Victor Scrimshaw); Fiona Lewis (Dr. Margaret Canker); Vernon Wells (Mr. Igoe); Robert Picardo (The Cowboy); Wendy Schaal (Wendy); Harold Sylvester (Peter Blanchard); William Schallert (Dr. Greenbush); Henry Gibson (Mr. Wormwood); John Hora (Ozzie Wexler); Mark L. Taylor (Dr. Niles); Orson Bean (Lydia's Editor); Kevin Hooks (Duane); Kathleen Freeman (Dream Lady); Archie Hahn (Messenger); Dick Miller (Cab Driver); Kenneth Tobey (Man in Restroom); Joe Flaherty, Andrea Martin (Waiting Room Patients); Jason Laskay, Frank Miller (Scrumshaw's Henchmen); Shawn Nelson (Wendell); Chuck Jones, Laura Waterbury, Rance Howard (Supermarket Customers); Kurt Braunreiter, Robert Gray, Brewster Sears (Lab Assault Henchmen); Sydne Squire (Stewardess); John Miranda (Man in Elevator); Jordan Benjamin (Little Kid in Mall); Roberto Ramirez (Chef); Virginia Boyle (Shopping Lady); Herb Mitchell (Camera Store Clerk); Neil Ross (Pod Computer Voice); Charles Aidman (Speaker at Banquet).

Ace pilot Lieutenant Tuck Pendleton (Dennis Quaid) becomes part of a miniaturization experiment in Silicon Valley in which scientists will reduce him in size so he and his craft can enter the human blood stream. First he is to be put into a rabbit, enlarged and then placed in a human. By accident, however, he ends up in a human first, assistant grocery store manager Jack Putter (Martin Short), and he only has a few hours of oxygen supply in which to complete his experiment and use a microchip he is carrying to return to normal size. Evil Victor Scrimshaw (Kevin McCarthy), however, wants tiny Pendleton and the Silicon formula to sell to the highest bidder and he is aided by industrial spy Dr. Margaret Canker (Fiona Lewis), fence Cowboy (Robert Picardo) and hired assassin Mr. Igoe (Vernon Wells). It takes the high strung Putter some time to realize exactly what has happened to him. Eventually he and Pendleton become allies as they try to escape the villains pursuing them. Assisting them is Tuck's girlfriend, newspaper reporter, Lydia Maxwell (Meg Ryan), with whom Jack falls in love.

Reminiscent of an earlier era's classic, FANTASTIC VOYAGE (1966) (see B/V), predictions were high that INNERSPACE would be a box-office smash. Richard Corliss enthused in *Time* magazine,

"This is a film with something—indeed, too funny much—for everybody. A sci-fi thriller in which one brave man is miniaturized to the size of a mite and takes a fantastic voyage into another man's buttock. A buddy picture in which both buddies occupy the same body. . . . Indeed, INNERSPACE plays as if it were the hippest [Dean] Martin-and-[Jerry] Lewis comedy. Tuck is the boozer-crooner-loverboy; Jack is the engaging, zany nerd. Both actors have nifty fun updating these roles. . . ." *Variety* assessed, " . . . an archetypal Steven Spielberg Summer entertainment directed by Joe Dante with his own special brand of fun visual roller-coaster serves up the right blend of comedy, adventure and the fantastic." Kim Newman in the British *Monthly Film Bulletin* explained, "Along the way, the hard science-fiction angle is lost and the film has Tuck's capsule turn up in whatever part of the body is convenient for the plot, and even blows holes in its race-against-time premise. . . . INNERSPACE bears all the tell-tale signs of a play-it-safe attempt to 'go straight' and recapture the commercial high ground. . . ."

But it was Duane Byrge of the *Hollywood Reporter* who proved to be most on mark. ". . . . science-fiction buffs are likely to be disappointed by the generally lackluster special effects and sophisticated moviegoers will feel short-changed by its mechanical, MacGuffinized plot." After six weeks at the domestic box-office, it had grossed a relatively disappointing $25,893,810 and soon disappeared from distribution. It was later decided that the humor-slanted promotional campaign for the film was wrong thinking, and the movie was scheduled for a fresh re-release.

INVADERS FROM MARS (Cannon, 1986) C 99 mins.

Producers, Menahem Golan, Yoram Globus; associate producers, Edward L. Alperson, Jr., Wade H. Williams III; director, Tobe Hooper; based on the screenplay by Richard Blake; screenplay, Dan O'Bannon; Don Jakoby; assistant directors, David Womack, David Upman, Tommy Burns, Carol Bonnefil; second unit director, John Dykstra; production designer, Leslie Dilley; art director, Craig Stearns; set designer, Randy Moore; set decorator Cricket Rowland; invader creatures designer/creator, Stan Winston; music, Christopher Young; music director, Paul Francis Witt; additional synthesizer music, David Storrs; music editor, Jack Tillar; costume designer, Carin Hooper; military technical adviser, Dale Dye; stunt coordinators, Steve Lambert, Eddy Donno; sound, Russell Williams II; supervising sound editor, David Bartlett; special visual effects, Apogee, Dukstra; opticals supervisor, Roger Dorney; animation supervisor, Clint Colver; camera, Daniel Pearl; second unit camera, J. Michael McClary; special effects camera, Richard Rownak; optical camera, Jerry Pooler; editor, Alan Jakubowicz; additional editor, Daniel Lowenthal.

Karen Black (Linda); Hunter Carson (David Gardner); Timothy Bottoms (George Gardner); Laraine Newman (Ellen Gardner); James Karen (General Wilson); Bud Cort (Young NASA Scientist); Louise Fletcher (Mrs. McKeltch); Eric Pierpoint (Sergeant Rinaldi); Christopher Allport (Captain Curtis); Donald Hotton (Old NASA Scientist); Kenneth Kimmins (Officer Kenney); Charlie Dell (Mr. Cross); Jimmy Hunt (Chief); William Bassett (NASA Scientist); Virginia Keehne (Heather); Chris Hebert (Kevin); Mason Nupuf (Doug); William Frankfather (Ed); Joseph Brutsman, Eric Norris (MPs); Debra Berger (Corporal Walker); Eddy Donno (Hollis); Mark Giardino (Johnson); Daryl Bartley, Shonda Whipple, Shawn Campbell, Roy Mansano, Amy Fitzpatrick, Brett Johnson (Classmates); Dale Dye (Squad Leader); Douglas Simpson (Lieutenant); Lenny Low (Communications Officer); Scott Leva, Frederick Menslage, Michael McGrady, Lawrence Poindexter, J. Acheson, Matt Bennett, Aaron Scott Bernard (Marines); Scott Wulff (Young Marine/Drone); Steve Lambert (Demolition Man); Debbie Carrington, Joe Anthony Cox, Matt Bennett, Douglas Simpson, Margarite Fernadez, Salvatore Fondacaro, Lenny Low (Drones).

Director Tobe Hopper came to the cinematic fore with the sickeningly shocking THE TEXAS CHAINSAW MASSACRE (1974) which developed a strong cult following for the director, who was to turn out such good horror fare as TV's SALEM'S LOT (1979) and such failures as LIFEFORCE (1985)(q.v.). Here the director remakes—and slightly reshapes—another cult classic, William Cameron Menzies' 3-D INVADERS FROM MARS (1953) (see B/V). But the result ". . . . was an embarrassing combination of kitsch and boredom." (*Variety*)

Eleven-year-old David Gardner (Hunter Carson) witnesses a spaceship burying itself in the sandpits behind his home, but his parents, George (Timothy Bottoms) and Ellen (Laraine Newman), do not believe him. That day NASA investigator George goes to the sandpit and returns a changed man, with a scar on the back of his neck. When he takes Ellen to the sandpit, she too returns changed—with the same scar. The identical thing happens to the police chief (Jimmy Hunt) and David's teacher (Louise Fletcher). The boy investigates the sandpit and finds caves below it which are the headquarters of Martian invaders who have taken control of many of the locals. He convinces school nurse Linda (Karen Black) of the situation and they alert a scientist (Bud Cort), who wants to communicate with the aliens, and General Wilson (James Karen), who is determined to wipe out the invaders. In the fight that follows, the soldiers invade the caves and David attempts to rescue his parents while Linda is captured by the Martians. However, she and David are saved by the soldiers as Wilson places explosives in the alien ship. When the craft takes off it explodes and the Gardners are released from the Martian control. Suddenly David wakes up from a bad dream and is comforted by his parents. Later he sees a spacecraft land in the sandpit and. . . .

"You can sympathize with the people who think INVADERS FROM MARS is a botch; there's something so anachronistic and out-of-scale about it, the *reductio ad absurdum* of overblown '80s movie making. But they're missing something. If you can tap into Hopper's oddball rhythms and cold sendups, you can enjoy yourself," wrote Michael Wilmington (*Los Angeles Times*). In the British *Monthly Film Bulletin,* Kim Newman decided Hopper could have overcome some of the deficiencies of the original film, but instead " . . . there is basically no more to it than was in the original (mediocre) script, even though the movie is a full half-hour longer."

Overall, this high tech version of INVADERS FROM MARS is a disappointing film which fails to compare with the entertainment value of the original. Of minor interest was the casting of Jimmy Hunt, who played the young boy in the 1953 edition, as the sheriff and the real-life mother-son team of of Karen Black and Hunter Carson in the lead roles. The acting here, however, is NOT appealing (especially Black's overblown performance, Carson's awkwardness, and Bottom's zombie-ish characterization). Since the twist ending is known to those who have seen the much shown original, the remake has little surprise to offer today's audiences. To be noted is that co-star Laraine Newman hosted a syndicated TV series in recent years composed of bad sci-fi and horror films. It is more than remotely possible she might have begun her chore with one of her own failed features—INVADERS FROM MARS.

INVADERS FROM MARS grossed $4,768,372 in its first three weeks at the domestic box-office.

INVASION OF THE BODY SNATCHERS (United Artists, 1978) C 115 mins.

Producer, Robert H. Solo; director, Philip Kaufman; based on the novel by Jack Finney; screenplay, W. D. Richter; production designer, Charles Rosen; music, Denny Zeitlin; makeup effects, Thomas Burman, Edouard Henriques; assistant director, Jim Bloom; sound, Art Rochester; special effects, Dell Rheaume, Russ Hessey; special sound effects, Ben Burlt; camera, Michael Chapman; editor, Douglas Stewart.

Donald Sutherland (Matthew Bennell); Brooke Adams (Elizabeth Driscoll); Leonard Nimoy (Dr. David Kibner); Veronica Cartwright (Nancy Bellicec); Jeff Goldblum (Jack Bellicec); Art Hindle (Geoffrey); Lelia Goldoni (Katherine); Kevin McCarthy (Running Man); Don Siegel (Cab Driver).

"It is pointless and impossible simply to remake a happily remembered old movie. There is an irresistible urge to improve it, expand it, stamp it with the personalities of the remakers. So it is with the new, all-new version of INVASION OF THE BODY SNATCHERS, which was just fine, thank you, as a cheap, neat, slightly loony sci-fi horror picture in 1956." (Richard Schickel, *Time* magazine)

Alien substances like angel hair fall on San Francisco causing the growth of strange pods which develop human form and take over the minds of humans, leaving them as soulless beings who discard their original bodies. Public health investigators Matthew Bennell (Donald Sutherland) and Elizabeth Driscoll (Brooke Adams) notice changes in people, especially the latter's boyfriend Geoffrey (Art Hindle) who develops a harsh personality, the exact opposite of what he had been originally. Nancy (Veronica Cartwright) and Jack (Jeff Goldblum) are friends of Matthew who operate a health spa and they find a strange being developing there and call in Matthew and Elizabeth. This confirms Matthew's theory about the alien pods and he realizes when people go to sleep the aliens take over their minds. He goes to Dr. David Kibner (Leonard Nimoy), a psychotherapist, with the information, but the latter believes all of this is just mass hysteria. Finally Matthew and Elizabeth are captured by Kibner and his minions, who have been taken over by the pods; but they escape. Jack too becomes like the others and Nancy runs from him. Finally it is Elizabeth and Matthew who unite to save themselves. But after exhausting hours of running, Elizabeth sleeps briefly and becomes a pod person. Jack kills her. Later in the street, Nancy encounters Jack but is shocked when she discovers he too has been transformed.

Grossing a surprisingly healthy $11,000,000 in the U.S., this film is as much a homage to the 1956 (see B/V) feature as it is a remake. In fact that film's director, Don Siegel, as well as its star, Kevin McCarthy, make brief appearances in the new edition. Overall, though, the comparison between the two versions is not favorable to the 1978 movie. The new one has none of the zest or aura of mystery about it that the original possessed. What it lacks in feeling, the new feature attempts to compensate with gore effects. Especially nauseating is a scene where one of the pods is displayed growing into a human. Also the flat hero played by Donald Sutherland has none of the likability of Kevin McCarthy in the 1956 film. Richard Schickel

(*Time* magazine) pinpoints another error. " . . . the San Francisco setting is a mistake. It is barely believable that the alien invaders could take root in a small, isolated town, as they did in the original. It is ridiculous to think that they could take over a huge metropolitan area without arousing opposition from more than a handful of people or the interest of the press, which might be counted on to observe with interest phenomena like masses of citizens lined up to collect their pods. The fact is that this film wants to have it both ways: to have a more urbane more 'important' scope than the original, and yet retain some of its inexpensive intimacy as well."

INVASION OF THE STAR CREATURES (American International, 1962) 70 mins.

Producer, Berj Hagopian; director, Bruno Ve Sota; story/screenplay, Jonathan Haze, (uncredited) Dick Miller; art director, Mike McCloskey; electronic music, Jack Cookerly, Elliott Fisher; wardrobe, Dell Adams; makeup, Joseph Kinder; sound, James Hullerton; camera, Basil Bradbury; editor, Lewis J. Guinn.

Robert Ball (Philbrick); Frankie Ray (Penn); Gloria Victor (Dr. Tanga); Dolores Reed (Professor Puna); Mark Ferris (Colonel Rank); Bruno Ve Sota (Hoodlum); and: Slic Slavin, Mark Thompson, Sid Kane, Mike Del Piano, Lenore Bond, Anton Van Stralen, James Almanzar, Allen Dailey, Joseph Martin.

Two mentally subpar G.I.s, Penn (Frankie Ray) and Philbrick (Robert Ball), are with their platoon in the woods when they spot a huge alien creature in a cavern. The soldiers are captured by these Vegemen. In a spacecraft, Penn and Philbrick meet Professor Tanga (Gloria Victor) and Professor Puna (Dolores Reed) from the planet Kallar who are disappointed to extract such limited information from the two unsophisticated recruits by using their ultra-advanced scientific equipment. The two escape the spacecraft and while going through the cave find the Vegemen are grown in pots; they are captured yet again. With the rest of their platoon paralyzed, the boys discover a ray to make the Vegemen disappear and meanwhile romance Tanga and Puna. The alien women fall in love with them and help them combat the Vegemen. With assistance from Colonel Rank (Mark Ferris) and a group of Indians, the boys return to the cave as the spacecraft departs and the two alien women remain with the men they love.

Written by actors Jonathan Haze and Dick Miller (although only Haze receives screen credit), INVASION OF THE STAR CREATURES was made in six days on a $25,000 budget by director Bruno Ve Sota with location shooting at Bronson Caverns in southern California. Originally called MONSTERS FROM NICH-

OLSON MESA (probably because American International president James H. Nicholson would not buy the inane project), the movie is one of those obscure, unbelievably terrible minor efforts which must be seen to be believed. Bill Warren in *Keep Watching the Skies, Volume II* (1986) sums it best, " . . . it's a disaster: boring, unfunny, trite and seemingly endless. It has absolutely nothing in it worth watching." Michael Weldon in *The Psychotronic Encyclopedia of Film* (1983) labeled it, "A stupid science-fiction comedy . . ." On the other hand, the late actor Barry Brown told director Bruno Ve Sota in 1975 (*Magick Theatre* magazine, Number 8, 1987), "It's such anarchic, beautiful comedy. I think if it had starred two of the Marx Brothers in the roles Bob Ball and Frankie Ray played, the film would have been a minor classic."

INVASION SINIESTRA see THE INCREDIBLE INVASION.

INVASION, U.S.A. (Columbia, 1952) 73 mins.

Executive producer, Joseph Justman, producers, Albert Zugsmith, Robert Smith; director, Alfred E. Green; story, Smith, Franz Spencer; screenplay, Smith; music, Albert Glasser; art director, James Sullivan; camera, John L. Russell; supervising editor, W. Donn Hayes.

Gerald Mohr (Vince); Peggie Castle (Carla); Dan O'Herlihy (Mr. Ohman); Robert Bice (George Sylvester); Tom Kennedy (Bartender); Wade Crosby (Congressman); Erik Blythe (Ed Mulvory); Phyllis Coates (Mrs. Mulvory); Aram Katcher (Fifth Columnist Leader); and: Edward G. Robinson, Jr., Noel Neill.

Just how far Hollywood has drifted from the right to the left politically can be judged by a 1950s sci-fi feature like INVASION U.S.A. which deals with an atomic war and an invasion of the country. Here the "gung ho" emphasis is on preparedness, harkening back to pre-World War I and II features, while in recent years the enemy is more often than not the government itself (i.e. CAPRICORN ONE and hangar 19 [qq.v]) in deference to foreign powers. INVASION U.S.A. hits like a sledge hammer in its unsubtle message for the United States to spend money on defense, a subject which continues to be highly controversial to this day. Interpolated with World War II combat footage and Army training films, the picture presents the horrific destruction of Manhattan and its atomic aftermath. The *Hollywood Reporter* called it " . . . a tremendously exciting film . . . packs a big wallop."

In a New York City bar several people discuss relevant topics of the day with television reporter Vince (Gerald Mohr) advocating a universal draft which is laughed at by pretty Carla (Peggie Castle) and businessman George Sylvester (Robert Bice), who refuses to convert his tractor plant for war work. Rancher Ed Mulvory (Erik Blythe) denounces various government policies, while a congressman (Wade Crosby) wants to see a tax increase. When asked his opinion, Mr. Ohman (Dan O'Herlihy) tells them our future depends on our present actions. Suddenly a news flash advises Alaska has been invaded by a foreign power and the group disburses. A spy kills the manufacturer, the congressman dies during the invasion of the nation's capitol and the rancher and his family drown when an atomic bomb is dropped on the Hoover Dam, flooding his land. The nation falls when an atomic bomb devastates Gotham. Back in the bar it all turns out to be a dream instigated by Mr. Ohman and all the people there vow to do more to aid and protect their country.

In the same vein is THE ATOMIC CAFE (1982) which is a compilation of government footage from the 1950s on how to survive a possible nuclear war. Hugh Beaumont and Chet Huntly are among the onscreen narrators.

THE INVISIBLE KILLER (Producers Distributing Corp., 1939) 61 mins.

Associate producer, Sigmund Neufeld; director, Sherman Scott [Sam Newfield]; story, Carter Wayne; adaptor, Joseph O'Donnell; camera, Jack Greenhalgh; editor, Holbrook N. Todd.

Grace Badley (Sue); Roland Drew (Jerry); William Newell (Pat); Alex Callam (Ensler); Frank Coletti (Vanl); Sydney Graler (Lefty); Glen Wilencheck (Sutton); Boyd Irwin (Cunningham); Jeanne Kelly (Gloria).

One of the earliest releases of the newly formed Producers Distributing Corporation, soon to become Producers Releasing Corporation (PRC), was THE INVISIBLE KILLER, which attempted to trade on the popularity of THE INVISIBLE MAN (q.v.) and its theme although the title murderer here was NOT a person, but a chemical substance. The very minor sci-fi ploy has an invention which causes two chemicals to combine when a telephone receiver is lifted, thus eliminating anyone using the phone, or in this case, anyone the villain wants out of the way.

A corrupt gambling syndicate has been running rampant and a number of murders have occurred. Ace reporter Sue (Grace Bradley) vows to smash the ring and bring in the murderer and enlists the help of her policeman beau Jerry (Roland Drew). The two discover the killings are caused by a mysterious chemical and they trap the killer.

Variety printed, "A suspenseful plot ably carried out; though the dialog isn't so hot, goes a long way in saving INVISIBLE KILLER from the graveyard. Still not above the average for independents, the principal drawbacks are obvious economics in production, plain settings, stilted performances on the part of most of the cast, and photography that leaves a bit to be desired."

The director of this feature, Sherman Scott, was actually the prolific Sam Newfield (he also used the name Peter Stewart) and THE INVISIBLE KILLER was officially issued in November, 1939, although its rag-tag distribution did not garner many reviews till early 1940.

THE INVISIBLE MAN (Universal, 1933) 71 mins.

Producer, Carl Laemmle, Jr.; director, James Whale; based on the novel by H. G. Wells; screenplay, R. C. Sherriff; art director, Charles D. Hall; special effects, John P. Fulton; camera, Art Edeson; additional camera/miniatures, John Mescall; editors, Maurice Pivar, Ted Kent.

Claude Rains (Jack Griffin, the Invisible Man); Gloria Stuart (Flora Cranley); William Harrigan (Dr. Kemp); Henry Travers (Dr.

Una O'Connor and Claude Rains in THE INVISIBLE MAN (1933).

Cranley); Una O'Connor (Mrs. Hall); Forrester Harvey (Mr. Hall); Holmes Herbert (Chief of Police); E. E. Clive (Jaffers); Dudley Digges (Chief of Detectives); Harry Stubbs (Inspector Bird); Donald Stuart (Inspector Lane); Merle Tottenham (Milly); Dwight Frye (Reporter); John Carradine (Caller); John Merivale (Boy); Jameson Thomas (Doctor); Walter Brennan (Villager).

THE INVISIBLE MAN (NBC-TV, 5/6/75) C 78 mins.

Executive producer, Harve Bennett; producer, Steven Bochco; director, Robert Michael Lewis; based on the novel by H. G. Wells; teleplay, Bochco; music, Richard Clements; art director, Frank T. Smith; camera, Enzo A. Martinelli; editor, Robert F. Shugrue.

David McCallum (Dr. Daniel Weston); Melinda Fee (Kate Weston); Jackie Cooper (Walter Carlson); Henry Darrow (Dr. Nick Maggio); Arch Johnson (General Turner); Alex Henteloff (Rick Steiner); Ted Gehring (Gate Guard); John McLiam (Blind Man); Paul Kent (Security Chief); and: Milt Kogan, Jon Cedar, Lew Patter.

THE INVISIBLE MAN RETURNS (Universal, 1940) 81 mins.

Producer, Ken Goldsmith; director, Joe May; suggested by the novel *The Invisible Man* by H. G. Wells; story, Siodmak, May; screenplay, Siodmak, Lester Cole, Cecil Belfrage; music, Hans J. Salter, Frank Skinner; music director, Charles Previn; costumes, Vera West; special effects, John P. Fulton; camera, Milton Krasner; editor, Frank Gross.

Sir Cedric Hardwicke (Richard Cobb); Vincent Price (Geoffrey Radcliffe); Nan Grey (Helen Manson); John Sutton (Dr. Frank Griffin); Cecil Kellaway (Inspector Sampson); Alan Napier (Willie Spears); Forrester Harvey (Ben Jenkins); Frances Robinson (Nurse); Ivan Simpson (Cotton); Edward Fielding (Governor); Harry Stubbs (Constable Dukesbury); Mary Field (Woman); Harry Cording (Shopworker); Edmund MacDonald (Mineworker); Matthew Boulton (Policeman); Bruce Lester (Chaplain); Paul England (Detective); Mary Gordon (Cook); Eric Wilton (Fingerprint Man); Leyland Hodgson (Chauffeur); Dave Thursby (Bob the Warden); Jimmy Aubrey (Plainclothesman); Louise Brien (Griffin's Secretary); Ernie Adams (Man); Frank Hagney (Bill the Policeman); Frank O'Connor (Policeman at Colliery); Frank (Policeman Attending Cobb); Ellis Irving, George Hyde, George Kirby, George Lloyd, Dennis Tankard (Miners).

THE INVISIBLE MAN'S REVENGE (Universal, 1944) 78 mins.

Producer/director, Ford Beebe; suggested by the novel *The Invisible Man* by H. G. Wells; screenplay, Bertram Millhauser; art directors, John B. Goodman, Harold H. MacArthur; set decorators, Russell A. Gausman, A. J. Gilmore; assistant director, Fred Frank; music/music director, Hans J. Salter; sound, William Hedgcock; special effects, John Fulton; camera, Milt Krasner; editor, Saul Goodkind.

Jon Hall (Robert Griffin); Alan Curtis (Mark Foster); Evelyn Ankers (Julie Herrick); Leon Errol (Herbert Higgens); John Carradine (Peter Drury); Doris Lloyd (Maud); Ian Wolfe (Jim Feeney); Gray Shadow (Himself); Gale Sondergaard (Lady Irene Herrick); Lester Matthews (Sir Jasper Herrick); Halliwell Hobbs (Cleghorn); Leland Hodgson (Sir Frederick Travers); Billy Bevan (Sergeant); Skelton Knaggs (Al Parry).

H. G. Wells' 1897 novel *The Invisible Man* came to the screen in 1933 following Universal's tremendous box-office success with DRACULA (1931) and FRANKENSTEIN (1931) (q.v.), with James Whale, who directed the latter, helming the project. R. C. Sherriff, whose play *Journey's End* had brought Whale to directorial prominence with the 1930 Tiffany film version of it, adapted Wells' novel to the screen. Thanks to Sherriff's fine adaptation, Whale's flavorful direction, Claude Rains' work in the title role, and John P. Fulton's special effects, THE INVISIBLE MAN proved a commercial bonanza spawning remakes, sequels, and scores of imitations.

On a terribly snowy night a stranger arrives at a remote English pub wanting a room. He is completely garbed and wears dark goggles. Jenny (Una O'Connor), the wife of the innkeeper (Forrester Harvey), shows him a room but when she returns he has taken off his hat and part of his head is "missing." Angry, the man removes all the bandages from his head showing that he is invisible and removing his clothes he causes havoc as Jenny has hysterics. The invisible man goes to the home of Dr. Kemp (William Harrigan) and reveals he is Jack Griffin (Claude Rains), his former medical school friend. Griffin has been working with the Indian drug monocaine which caused him to become invisible. Kemp reveals that the drug may cause insanity, but Griffin refuses to heed the warning. Kemp tells Flora Cranley (Gloria Stuart), Griffin's girlfriend, and her father Dr. Cranley (Henry Travers), about his situation but Griffin goes on a rampage; wrecking a train, robbing a bank, and committing several murders. The police alert everyone to be on their guard for signs of the invisible man and a farmer hears him snoring in his barn and summons the law. They set fire to the building and Griffin is forced out into the cold and the snow where his footprints can be easily tracked. He is shot and as he dies, he returns to his natural self.

For 1933 audiences, the special effects involving the invisible man were new and quite amazing. John P. Fulton accomplished them

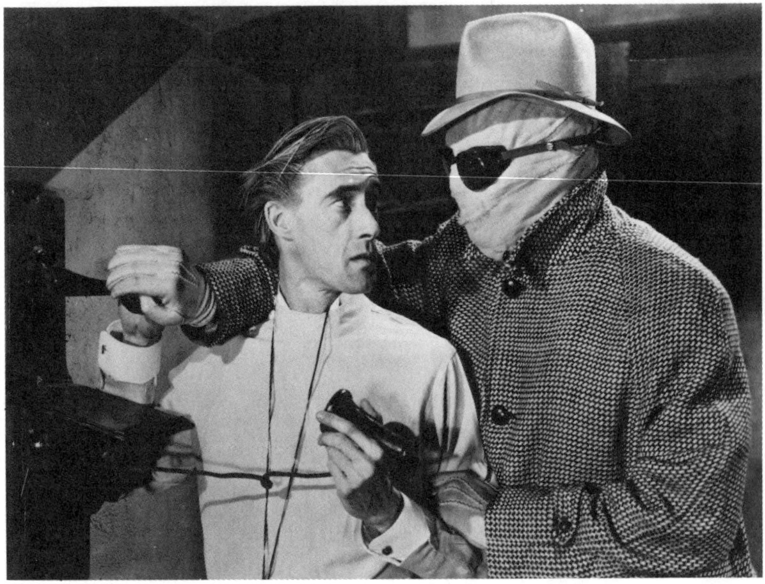

John Carradine and Jon Hall in THE INVISIBLE MAN'S REVENGE (1944).

with the use of piano wires and the traveling matte process in which a double dressed in black velvet, which was almost non reflective, was employed. The use of cinema newcomer Claude Rains (he was the third choice after Boris Karloff and Colin Clive) in the title assignment also greatly enhanced the proceedings as filmgoers could not immediately identify a face with a voice. The actual filming of THE INVISIBLE MAN took eight weeks with another equal period required to complete the special effects.

In regard to the original author's view of the film, James Curtis noted in his book *James Whale* (1982), " . . . H. G. Wells complimented Whale highly on the screen version of his novel, but objected most strenuously to the device of making his scientist a helpless lunatic by way of the drug he took. Whale countered with his basic complaint of much of Wells' work: its lack of simple humanity, as in *Things To Come.* 'After all,' he reasoned, 'in the minds of rational people, only a lunatic would want to make himself invisible in the first place!'"

Universal Pictures used the invisibility techniques in three cliffhangers—THE VANISHING SHADOW (1934) (q.v.), FLASH GORDON (1936) and THE PHANTOM CREEPS (1939) (see B/

V for both) before finally doing a followup film, THE INVISIBLE MAN RETURNS (1940).

Having already made TOWER OF LONDON (1939) and THE HOUSE OF SEVEN GABLES (1940) for the studio, resonant-voiced Vincent Price was chosen for the lead title role. Regarding his performance in THE INVISIBLE MAN RETURNS, Howard Barnes wrote in the *New York Herald Tribune,* "I think he is better in the disembodied sections than in the final sequence." No doubt the actor agreed as Price often joked the Invisible Man was his favorite movie role and one he would repeat in a cameo at the finale of ABBOTT AND COSTELLO MEET FRANKENSTEIN (1948) (q.v.).

About to go to the gallows for the murder of his brother, Geoffrey Radcliffe (Vincent Price) receives a reprieve from Dr. Frank Griffin (John Sutton) who gives him the drug which made his late brother invisible. Although the drug will cause madness it is Geoffrey's only salvation in proving his innocence. He escapes from jail while Griffin works on an antidote. Geoffrey finds out that Willie Spears (Alan Napier) has been given his job by his cousin, Richard Cobb (Cedric Hardwicke), and it was Spears' testimony which convicted him. Willie insists Richard forced him to lie in court but when Geoffrey tries to force a confession from his cousin, he is surprised by Inspector Sampson (Cecil Kellaway) who detects his presence in the cigar smoke. Geoffrey begins showing telltale signs of madness, but in front of Griffin he makes Spears admit he saw Richard murder his brother. The two begin a scuffle which ends up on rails under which mine ore cars travel and the police shoot down Geoffrey as Richard falls into the car below. Before he dies, he confesses to the murder. Returning to the village wearing a scarecrow's outfit, the injured Geoffrey is given a blood transfusion by Frank and the new blood is the antidote needed to make him normal again so he can return to the girl (Nan Grey) he loves.

The same year they conceived THE INVISIBLE MAN RETURNS, writers Joe May (who also directed that feature) and Curt Siodmak turned out a comedy "Invisible" picture derived from the distaff angle, with THE INVISIBLE WOMAN. The rather appealing effort was not a horror film at all but a farce enhanced by the buffoonery of John Barrymore's loony mad scientist and Virginia Bruce as the girl who becomes invisible for social revenge and for general self-centered fun. Her anti-establishment behavior includes getting even with people (her boss, snobbish customers) who have done her wrong.

Half-mad Professor Gibbs (John Barrymore) invents a serum and machine to make people invisible but after his millionaire playboy backer, Richard Russell (John Howard), goes broke he must advertise for people with whom to experiment. Fashion model Kitty Carroll (Virginia Bruce), sick of her nasty boss (Charles Lane) and unappreciative customers, takes the job and promptly becomes invisible. She uses the means to get even with those who treated her badly. To be invisible, Kitty has to be naked and this causes her to take cold and she takes liquor for it and this prolongs her invisibility. By now she and Russell have fallen in love, but gangster Blackie Cole (Oscar Homolka) and his thugs steal Gibbs' machine hoping to make themselves invisible to thwart the law. This fails, however, because the machinery will not work without the serum. Finally the police retrieve the machine and Kitty returns to normal. She and Richard marry. They have a baby and it has inherited Kitty's capacity to become invisible.

Jon Hall played the Invisible Man in the horror/spy film INVISIBLE AGENT (see our volume THE GREAT SPY PICTURES, 1974) in 1942 and returned to the role, although as a different character, for the final installment in the 1940s' Universal series, THE INVISIBLE MAN'S REVENGE. The series was starting to falter and the invisibility angle was wearing thin as when the *New York Times* quipped, " . . . you don't see much when you see an INVISIBLE MAN'S REVENGE."

Returning home to England after several years searching for diamonds in Africa, Robert Griffin (Jon Hall) visits his ex-partners, Lady Irene Herrick (Gale Sondergaard) and Sir Jasper Travers (Leland Hodgson), wanting his share of their fortune. The duo drug him and throw him out and he wanders to the remote home of Dr. Drury (John Carradine), a scientist who has developed an invisibility formula which has worked successfully on his Great Dane dog, Brutus. With nothing to lose, Griffin agrees to be a human guinea pig for Drury and becomes invisible and uses his new power to kill his foes and romance Julie Herrick (Evelyn Ankers), Lady Irene's daughter and his childhood sweetheart. Now wanting to be visible, Griffin is told by Drury that the only antidote is a blood transfusion which will kill the donor. Griffin forces Drury into such a transfusion and the doctor dies. Griffin plans to force romantic rival Mark Foster (Alan Curtis) out of the way by the same method, but in the midst of the transfusion, the police arrive and, when he attempts to kill Mark, Griffin is attacked and is himself killed by Brutus.

Universal would revive the Invisible Man for a brief cameo at the end of ABBOTT AND COSTELLO MEET FRANKENSTEIN (q.v.) in 1948 and then leave him to an even worse fate in 1953 with ABBOTT AND COSTELLO MEET THE INVISIBLE MAN (q.v.).

David McCallum, who had scored so high in popularity on TV

in the 1960s with "The Man From U.N.C.L.E." teleseries starred in a remake of THE INVISIBLE MAN for Universal/NBC-TV in 1975. It was a much-touted pilot for a video series using the H.G. Wells gimmick in a contemporary setting. Scientist Dr. Daniel Weston (David McCallum) is part of a group at the Los Angeles-based KLAE Corporation, which is working to invent a laser beam projection which can make a person invisible. He develops a serum that can make himself invisible. Rather than allow it be used exploitively by the military, he disappears with the secret. As Leonard Maltin judged in *TV Movies and Video Guide* (1987), "Should have disappeared before becoming a series." The disappointing program, which lasted for thirteen installments (9/8/75 to 1/9/76) on NBC-TV dealt with the adventures of McCallum's character (outfitted with a plastic face mask and hands to disguise his invisible status) as he embarked on hazardous assignments for the KLAE Corporation.

After a hiatus of several years, Universal tried yet again, this time updating THE INVISIBLE WOMAN property. A bumbling scientist (Bob Denver) experiments with an invisibility formula only to have it concocted correctly by his pet monkey. The man's newspaper reporter niece (Alexa Hamilton) comes in contact accidentally with the formula and immediately turns invisible. In extricating herself from the situation, the young woman becomes involved with a gangster (Harvey Korman) and his gang who plot to steal a museum treasure. In *Horror and Science Fiction Films III* (1984), Donald C. Willis calls it an "Abysmal throwback to the worst of the old TV-sitcoms. Silly pranks dominate the effects scenes, which prove to be a sterile showcase for some technical gymnastics. . . ." *Variety* reported, "Because of the child target aspect of the pilot, the possibilities that a naked woman running around the city created were downpeddled in the script, perhaps for the better. THE INVISIBLE WOMAN seemed aimed for Saturday morning rather than primetime—competition is too tough at night for simplistic scripting like this to have a ghost of a chance."

After this debacle, H. G. Wells' storyline was allowed to rest in peace—at least for the time being.

INVISIBLE STRANGLER (Seymour Borde & Associates, 1984) C 85 mins.

Executive producer, Fred Jordan; producer, Earle Lyon; associate producer, Robert Fitzgerald; director, John Florea; story, Lyon; screenplay, Arthur C. Pierce; music, Richard Hieronymous, Alan Oldfield; second unit director, Gene Fowler, Jr.; assistant director, Joseph Wonder; sound, William Edmondson; special effects, Roger

George; camera, Alan Stenvoid; second unit camera, Nicholas von Sternberg; editor, Bud S. Isaacs.

Robert Foxworth (Lieutenant Charles Barrett); Stefanie Powers (Candy Barrett); Elke Sommer (Chris); Sue Lyon (Miss de Long); Leslie Parrish (Coleen Hudson); Marianna Hill (Bambi); and: Mark Slade, Frank Ashmore, Alex Dreier, Percy Rodriguez, Jo Anne Meredith, Cesare Danova, John Hart, Roger Sands.

Imprisoned for killing his wife, a man (Roger Sands) uses his powers as a psychic to make himself invisible and then goes after various beautiful women, strangling them to death. Assigned to the case is Los Angeles police lieutenant Charles Barrett (Robert Foxworth) who eventually solves it with the aid of former beauty queen Chris (Elke Sommer), an intended victim.

Filmed initially in 1976 as THE ASTRAL FACTOR and given scant theatrical release under that title in the early 1980s, this feature became known as INVISIBLE STRANGLER for its official release. Its main asset is a bevy of lovely leading ladies, although most of them perform only guest bits, excepting Stefanie Powers as Foxworth's fun-loving wife and Elke Sommer as the beauty queen. The invisibility gimmick makes this a sci-fi entry, but its main operating ploy is the detective motif. *Variety* noted, "Picture becomes silly early on when it turns out that the invisibility adds nothing to sequences which could have been played naturalistically by a wily con staying one step ahead of the police."

The script for this tame sci-fier was by Arthur C. Pierce who penned such genre outings as THE COSMIC MAN (1959), THE HUMAN DUPLICATORS (1964), MUTINY IN OUTER SPACE (1964), and WOMEN OF THE PREHISTORIC PLANET (1965), which he also directed. All are covered in B/V.

THE INVISIBLE WOMAN (Universal, 1940) 72 mins.

Associate producer, Burt Kelly; director, A. Edward Sutherland; suggested by the novel *The Invisible Man* by H. G. Wells; story, Curt Siodmak, Joe May; screenplay, Robert Lees, Fred Rinaldo, Gertrude Purcell; art director, Jack Otterson; assistant director, Joseph McDonough; music director, Charles Previn; special effects, John Fulton; camera, Elwood Bredell; editor, Frank Gross.

Virginia Bruce (Kitty Carroll); John Barrymore (Professor Gibbs); John Howard (Richard Russell); Charlie Ruggles (George); Oscar Homolka (Blackie); Edward Brophy (Bill); Donald MacBride (Foghorn); Margaret Hamilton (Frankie); Anne Nagel (Jean); Kathryn Adams (Peggy); Maria Montez (Marie); Charles Lane (Growley); Mary Gordon (Mrs. Bates); Thurston Hall (Hudson); Eddie Conrad (Hernandez); Kay Linaker, Sara Edwards (Buyers); Kitty O'Neil

(Mrs. Patten); Harry C. Bradley (Want Ad Man); Kernan Cripps (Postman).

See: THE INVISIBLE MAN (essay).

THE INVISIBLE WOMAN (Universal/NBC-TV, 2/13/83) C 100 mins.

Executive producers, Lloyd J. Schwartz, Sherwood Schwartz; producer, Alan J. Levi; associate producer, John Whitman; director, Levi; suggested by the novel *The Invisible Man* by H. G. Wells; teleplay, Lloyd J. Schwartz, Sherwood Schwartz; music, David Frank; song, Lloyd J. Schwartz, Sherwood Schwartz, David Frank; art director, Richard B. Lewis; camera, Dean Cundey; editor, Houseley Stevenson.

Bob Denver (Dr. Dudley Plunkett); Jonathan Banks (Darren); David Doyle (Neil Gilmore); George Gobel (Dr. Farrington); Anne Haney (Mrs. Van Dam); Harvey Korman (Carlisle Edwards); Art La Fleur (Phil); Garrett Morris (Lieutenant Greg Larkin); Ron Pallilo (Spike Mitchell); Richard Sanders (Orville); Mel Stewart (Security Guard); Jacques Tate (Lieutenant Dan Williams); Alexa Hamilton (Sandy Martinson); Scott Nemas (Rodney Sherman); Jake Steinfeld (Attendant); Ken Sansom (Lionel Gilbert); Teri Beckerman (Receptionist); Ronald E. Morgan, Joseph Phelan (Cops); Dan Woren (Gallery Guard); Marsha Warner (Saleslady); Clinton Chase (Officer); David Whitfield (Marvin Carter); Valerie Hall (Miss Tomkins).

See: THE INVISIBLE MAN (essay).

THE ISLAND OF DR. MOREAU (American International, 1978) C 98 mins.

Executive producer, Samuel Z. Arkoff, Sandy Howard; producers, John Temple-Smith, Skip Steloff; director, Don Taylor; based on the novel by H. G. Wells; screenplay, John Herman Shaner, Al Ramrus; music, Laurence Rosenthal; production designer, Philip Jefferies; set decorator, James Berkey; costumes/wardrobe, Richard LaMotte, Emma Porteus, Rita Woods; assistant director, Bob Bender; sound, David Hildyard; camera, Gerry Fisher; second unit camera, Ronnie Taylor; editor, Marion Rothman.

Burt Lancaster (Dr. Moreau); Michael York (Braddock); Nigel Davenport (Montgomery); Barbara Carrera (Maria); Richard Basehart (Sayer of the Law); Nick Cravat (M'Long); The Great John L (Boarman); Bob Ozman (Bullman); Fumio Demura (Hyenaman); Gary Baxley (Lionman); John Gillespie (Tigerman); David Cass (Bearman).

Based on the H. G. Wells novel (1896) and a remake of the classic 1933 Paramount thriller, THE ISLAND OF LOST SOULS

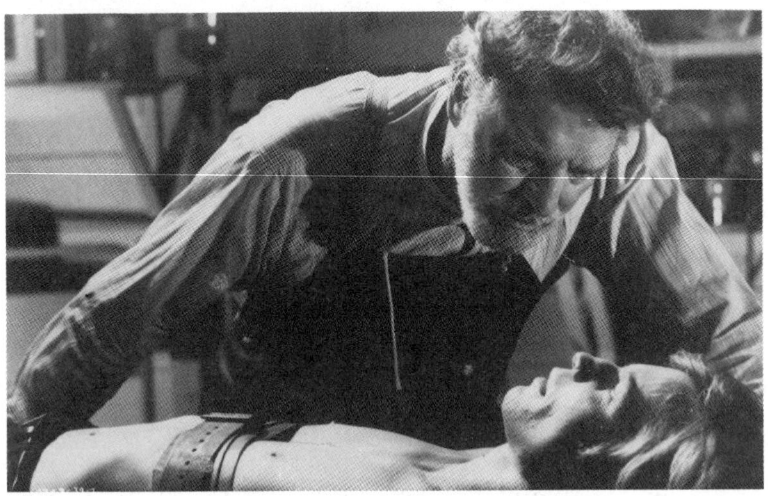

Burt Lancaster and Michael York in THE ISLAND OF DR MOREAU (1978).

(see B/V), THE ISLAND OF DR. MOREAU was a dissatisfying feature film which was lushly photographed, but otherwise was very boring. None of the underlying degeneracy which predominated the 1933 version was evident here. For some unknown reason one of the main plot premises, having the panther girl created from a cat for breeding with a human—was completely abandoned. While the girl was hinted at as being an experimental being, she turned out to be normal—all of which greatly weakened the film, as did Burt Lancaster and Michael York's bland characterizations as the mad scientist and hero.

Sailor Braddock (Michael York) is the sole survivor of a shipwreck and winds up on a remote island lorded over by scientist Dr. Moreau (Burt Lancaster) whom he learns is using surgery to transform animals into men and men into beasts. The isle is populated with his creations, the men-beasts being led by the Sayer of the Law (Richard Basehart). Braddock is attracted to beautiful native girl Maria (Barbara Carrera), the only female on the island. At first he suspects she too may be an experimental animal but he learns she is not and that he is to become one of the doctor's "patients." Before this happens the animals revolt when Moreau breaks the law by killing one of them and they turn on him and use his experiments to kill him while Braddock and Maria escape from the island.

Donald C. Willis rightly complained in *Horror and Science Fiction Films II* (1982), "Rubbery makeup makes the 'manimal' scenes look like carnival time in Costa Rica. Superfluous variations of Cocteau's BEAUTY AND THE BEAST, the Laughton ISLAND OF LOST SOULS and the Lugosi APE MAN."

This film grossed a tepid $4,000,000 at the domestic box-office.

ISLAND OF LIVING HORROR see BRIDES OF BLOOD.

IT STALKED THE OCEAN FLOOR see MONSTER FROM THE OCEAN FLOOR.

IT'S ALIVE! (Azalea/American International TV, 1969) C 80 mins.

Producer, Larry Buchanan; associate producer, Edwin Tobolowsky; director, Buchanan; based on the novella *Being* by Richard Matheson; screenplay, no credit; special effects, Jack Bennett; camera, Robert Alcott.

Tommy Kirk (Wayne Thomas); Shirley Bonne (Lynne Sterns); Billy Thurman (Greevey); Annabelle Macadams [Anne MacAdams] (Bella Pittman); Corveth Ousterhouse (Norman Sterns).

In the mid and late 1960s, American International Television hired Larry Buchanan to remake several of the studio's earlier "B" features to fill out a TV package. Filmed in Dallas, Texas, with minimal budgets and semi-professional casts (except for the use of a "name" for the lead role) these outings have taken on a following due to their general ineptitude. IT'S ALIVE! is the only one of the group based on an outside source, Richard Matheson's novella *Being,* (1954) but it bears little resemblance to its original source.

Near a dinosaur park in a rural area, paleontologist Wayne Thomas (Tommy Kirk) meets visiting married couple Lynne (Shirley Bonne) and Norman Sterns (Corveth Ousterhouse) and the three are captured by farmer Greevey (Billy Thurman) and kept prisoners in a cave. They find the madman has also captured Bella Pittman (Annabelle Macadams) whom he keeps in his house and abuses. Also in the cave is an aquatic monster from prehistoric times and the foursome eventually use the creature which turns on Greevey and kills him as the others escape.

Filmed near the Spider Creek Camp (large life-like models of two dinosaurs are shown early in the film), IT'S ALIVE! is plagued by a long, often unintentionally hilarious flashback sequence where prisoner/housekeeper Macadams recounts to the others how she was captured by Thurman. In *Horror and Science Fiction Films* (1972), Donald C. Willis complained about the director, "By trying several tricks with the camera, Buchanan proves he can't do any of them competently."

IT'S ALIVE (Warner Bros., 1974) C 90 mins.

Executive producer, Peter Sabiston; producer/director/screenplay, Larry Cohen; music, Bernard Herrmann; special makeup, Rick Baker; sound, Alex Vandekar; camera, Fenton Hamilton; editor, Peter Honess.

John Ryan (Frank Davies); Sharon Farrell (Lenore Davies); Andrew Duggan (The Professor); Guy Stockwell (Clayton); James Dixon (Lieutenant Perkins); Michael Ansara (The Captain); Robert Emhardt (The Executive); William Wellman, Jr. (Charlie); Daniel Holzman (Chris).

IT LIVES AGAIN (Warner Bros., 1978) C 91 mins.

Producer/director/screenplay, Larry Cohen; assistant director, Reid Freeman; music, Bernard Herrmann; additional music, Laurie Johnson; sound, Ken Scrivener; camera, Fenton Hamilton; editors, Curt Burch, Louis Fireman, Carol O'Blath.

Frederic Forrest (Eugene Scott); Kathleen Lloyd (Jody Scott); John P. Ryan (Frank Davies); John Marley (Mallory); Andrew Duggan (Dr. Perry); Eddie Constantine (Dr. Forest); James Dixon (Detective Perkins).

Frank (John Ryan) and Lenore Davies (Sharon Farrell) want a second child and she takes a new drug to become fertile. When the baby is born it is a mutated evil being which kills four doctors and nurses in the delivery room. The parents take the baby home and try to protect it from the outside world but it threatens their older son. The creature murders the milkman and kills others. Meanwhile the police investigate. The creature runs off and Frank joins the law in the hunt but feels like his wife; no matter what, the killer is their child and it must be saved. The infant is cornered in a storm sewer and the police snuff out the mutant.

Rick Baker's special effects makeup for the monster is the highlight of this motion picture which hinges between pathos and horror. The film grossed over $7,000,000 at the domestic box-office and developed a reputation for director/producer/writer Larry Cohen. Phil Hardy in *The Film Encyclopedia: Science Fiction* (1984) terms it " . . . a masterful essay in paranoia and dissection of the ties that bind in family life." On the other hand, Donald C. Willis seems more on target in *Horror and Science Fiction Films II* (1982) when he observes, "Unfortunately, the movie leans more toward the dramatic than the comic. It takes itself too sociologically seriously. . . ."

The sequel, IT LIVES AGAIN, appeared in 1978 and opens with Frank Davies (John Ryan) trying to explain to expectant parents (Frederic Forrest, Kathleen Lloyd) what happened to his mutant baby and how such creatures respond to love and affection. It turns out this couple too, along with several others, have used the fertility drug which produced Davies' killer infant. A number of these children are born and embark on a killing spree, with many of them being protected by their parents. However, a policeman (John Marley) whose wife has also given birth to a killer child, wants to destroy them all and finally accomplishes his mission.

IT LIVES AGAIN was more a gory thriller than its predecessor and was less entertaining.

JESSE JAMES MEETS FRANKENSTEIN'S DAUGHTER (Embassy, 1966) C 82 mins.

Producer, Carroll Case; associate producer, Howard W. Koch, Jr.; director, William Beaudine; suggested by the novel *Frankenstein* by Mary Shelley; story/screenplay, Carl K. Hittleman; art director, Paul Sylos; set decorator, Harry Reif; music, Raoul Kraushaar; assistant director, Max Stein; makeup, Ted Coodley; sound, Harold Lewis; sound effects, John Hall; camera, Lothrop Worth; supervising editor, William Austin; editor, Roy Livingston.

John Lupton (Jesse James); Cal Bolder (Hank Tracy/Igor); Narda Onyx (Maria Frankenstein); Steven Geray (Rudolph Frankenstein); Felipe Turich (Manuel); Rosa Turich (Nina) Estelita Rodriguez (Juanita); Jim Davis (Marshal McFee); Raymond Barnes (Lonny); William Fawcett (Jensen the Pharmacist); and: Page Slattery, Nestor Paiva, Dan White, Roger Creed, Fred Stromsoe, Mark Norton.

Outlaws Jesse James (John Lupton) and Hank Tracy (Cal Bolder) are running from a posse, with Hank being wounded. They meet Juanita (Estelita Rodriguez) who takes them to an old mission where Maria Frankenstein (Narda Onyx) resides with her brother Rudolph (Steven Geray). She wants to create an artificial man like that of her grandfather. Maria sends Jesse to a pharmacist (William Fawcett) for medicine. While he is gone she performs an organ transplant on Hank, using an artificial brain once used by her grandfather. She transforms him into monstrous Igor (Cal Bolder), who turns on Jesse and knocks him out when he returns. Maria plans to change Jesse into a monster, but Juanita returns with lawman Marshal McFee (Jim Davis) and in a showdown both Maria and Igor die. Juanita promises to wait for Jesse as he goes off with the lawman.

Directed by William Beaudine and issued on a double bill with BILLY THE KID VS. DRACULA, also directed by Beaudine, this shoestring feature film was near the nadir of the Frankenstein monster's screen career. In *Horror and Science Fiction Films* (1973), Donald C. Willis commented, "The worst western cliches are combined with the worst horror cliches."

JUDAS GOAT see XTRO.

JUNGLE CAPTIVE (Universal, 1945) 64 mins.

Executive producer, Ben Pivar; associate producer, Morgan B. Cox; director, Harold Young; story, Dwight V. Babcock; screenplay, M. Coates Webster, Babcock; art directors, John B. Goodman, Robert Clatworthy; music director, Paul Sawtell; camera, Maury Gertsman; editor, Fred R. Feitshans, Jr.

Otto Kruger (Dr. Stendahl); Amelita Ward (Ann Forrester); Vicky Lane (Paula Dupree, the Ape Woman); Phil Brown (Don Young); Jerome Cowan (Harrigan); Rondo Hatton (Moloch); Eddie Acuff (Bill); Ernie Adams (Jim); Charles Wagenheim (Fred); Eddy Chandler (Motorcycle Cop); Jack Overman (Detective).

Beautiful Acquanetta attained minor screen stardom playing the ape-girl Paula Dupree in CAPTIVE WILD WOMAN (1943) (q.v.) and JUNGLE WOMAN (1944) (*infra*). But she refused to perform the role again and Vicky Lane took over the assignment for this the third and final series segment. While the first two entries were filled with stock footage—mostly from Clyde Beatty's THE BIG CAGE (1932)—this outing was free of such filler. Yet while the initial films had a swift pacing and were enhanced by a tongue-in-cheek quality, JUNGLE CAPTIVE lacked this vitality and proved the least enjoyable of the trio.

The sparse plot finds Dr. Stendahl (Otto Kruger), a biochemist, working in the African jungle with his associate, the deformed Moloch (Rondo Hatton). The doctor had been perfecting a formula to regress people into simians and he has been experimenting on monkeys. When beautiful Paula Dupree (Vicky Lane) becomes his patient, he uses the formula on her and at times she becomes an ape girl. Paula falls in love with Don Young and when jealous over his affections to Ann Forrester (Amelita Ward) she turns into a murderous beast. Eventually Paula kills Stendahl, but dies in the process herself.

Note: Reissue title WILD JUNGLE CAPTIVE (Realart, 1952).

JUNGLE WOMAN (Universal, 1944) 54 mins.

Executive producer, Ben Pivar; associate producer, Will Cowan; director, Reginald LeBorg; story, Henry Sucher; adaptors, Bernard Schubert, Sucher, Edward Dein; dialog director, Emory Horgen; art directors, John B. Goodman, Abraham Grossman; set decorator, Ray Robinson; music director, Paul Sawtell; assistant director, Melville Sayer; sound, Jess Moulin; camera, Jack McKenzie; editor, Ray Snyder.

Evelyn Ankers (Beth Colman); Acquanetta (Paula Dupree); J.

Carrol Naish (Dr. Carl Fletcher); Samuel S. Hinds (Coroner); Lois Collier (Joan Fletcher); Milburn Stone (Fred Mason); Douglass Dumbrille (District Attorney); Richard Davis (Bob Whitney); Nana Bryant (Miss Gray); Pierre Watkin (Dr. Meredith); Christian Rub (George); Alec Craig (Caretaker); Edward M. Hyans, Jr. (Willie); Richard Powers (Joe the Fingerprint Man); Julie London (Girl).

The second of three feature films about Paula Dupree, the unfortunate girl who once having been transformed into a gorilla reverts to that state when sexually aroused. A great deal of stock footage from the first entry, CAPTIVE WILD WOMAN (1943) (q.v.) was used. (In fact, John Carradine of that picture should have received star billing here since there was so much of him to be seen in the spliced-in scenes.)

Ape-girl Paula Dupree (Acquanetta) is brought back to life by deranged scientist Dr. Carl Fletcher (J. Carrol Naish), who is attracted to her when she is in human form. He hopes to cure her of reverting back into a simian state whenever physically excited. Paula, however, still loves animal trainer Fred Mason (Milburn Stone), and hates his girlfriend, Beth Colman (Evelyn Ankers). Again Paula tries to kill Beth and she also turns on and murders Fletcher before "finally" being killed herself.

The character of Paula Dupree would appear a third and final time in JUNGLE CAPTIVE (1944) (*supra*); this time with Vicky Lane in the featured role of the ape-girl.

KAIJU SOSHINGEKI see DESTROY ALL MONSTERS.

THE KILLER SHREWS (McLendon Radio Pictures, 1959) 69 mins.

Executive producer, Gordon McLendon; producer, Ken Curtis; director, Ray Kellogg; story/screenplay, Jay Simms; music, Harry Bluestone; camera, Wilfred Cline; editor, Aaron Steel.

James Best (Thorne Sherman); Ingrid Goude (Ann Craigis); Baruch Lumet (Dr. Milo Craigis); Ken Curtis (Jerry Lacer); Gordon McLendon (Radford Baines); Alfredo DeSoto (Mario); J. H. (Judge) Dupree (Paul Rook).

One of the more engrossing low budget non-Hollywood sci-fi films of the late 1950s is THE KILLER SHREWS, made in Texas by radio station owner Gordon McLendon, who himself has a small role in the film as a scientist. Made for a little over $100,000, this production grossed over $1,000,000 when issued on a double bill with another McLendon entry, THE GIANT GILA MONSTER (q.v.); both directed by Ray Kellogg. Ken Curtis, the producer of THE GIANT GILA MONSTER, here is the co-star. Although tacky in many respects, this production is well developed and paced and the title monsters, when not seen too closely (where they seem like big dogs in fur) are rather frightening. The British *Monthly Film Bulletin* noted, " . . . the action builds up from a shaky start to a suitably horrific climax. . . ."

Boat owner Thorne Sherman (James Best) and Paul Rook (J. H. "Judge" DuPree) take supplies to a remote island where Dr. Milo Craigis (Baruch Lumet) and his daughter, zoologist Ann (Ingrid Goude), and assistants Jerry Lacer (Ken Curtis) and Radford Baines (Gordon McLendon), are working on experiments to make animals smaller via genetic structural changes. They are using tiny, but highly vicious, killer shrews. It develops that some of the shrews have become oversized and that Farrell, who is Ann's fiancee, has allowed some to escape. One of the beasts murders Rook. A storm comes up and the people are forced to stay on the island as the shrews attack their headquarters. A worker (Alfredo DeSoto) is killed by the shrews as is Baines, both dying from the animal's body poisons. Farrell tries to feed Thorne to the shrews because he is jealous of his attentions to Ann, but fails. Farrell takes refuge on the compound's roof while Thorne, Anne and Dr. Craigis weld large metal buckets together and use them as a buttress against the attacking shrews as they head for the boat. Farrell falls from the roof and is devoured by the animals as the trio reach the safety of boat, leaving the mutants to starve to death on the isle as they cannot swim.

KING KONG (Universal, 1976) C 134 mins.

Executive producers, Federico de Laurentiis, Christian Ferry; producer, Dino de Laurentiis; director, John Guillermin; concept by Merian C. Cooper, Edgar Wallace; based on the script by James Creelman, Ruth Rose; screenplay, Lorenzo Semple, Jr.; music, John Barry; choreography, Claude Thompson; production designer, Mario Chiari, Dale Hennesy; art directors, Archie J. Bacon, David A. Constable, Robert Gundlach; set decorator, John Franco, Jr.; costumes/wardrobe, Moss Mabry, Anthea Sylbert, Arny Lipin, Fern Weber; King Kong outfit designer, Rick Baker; assistant directors, David McGiffert, Kurt Neumann; second unit director, William Kronick; stunt co-ordinator, Bill Couch; sound, Harry W. Tetrick, William McCaughey, Jack Solomon, Aaron Rochin, Dan Walln; visual effects, Frank Van Der Veer, Barry Nolan, Harold E. Wellman; camera, Richard Kline; editor, Ralph E. Winters.

Jeff Bridges (Jack Prescott); Charles Grodin (Fred Wilson); Jessica Lange (Dwan); John Randolph (Captain Ross); Rene Auberjonois (Bagley); Julius Harris (Boan); Jack O'Halloran (Perko); Dennis Fimple (Sunfish); Ed Lauter (Carnahan); Jorge Moreno (Garcia); Mario Gallo (Timmons); John Agar (Mayor); Kenny Long (Ape

Masked Man in Dance); Rick Baker (Kong Closeups); Sid Conrad (Petrox Chairman); George Whiteman (Army Helicopter Pilot); Wayne Heffley (Air Force Colonel).

One of the greatest disappointments in the history of motion pictures was Dino de Laurentiis' (and his daughter's) highly touted $24,000,000 remake of KING KONG (1933) (see B/V), itself one of the greatest monster movies of all time. What is so frustrating about the new version is the fact one has to wonder where all the production money went. The film really is no better in quality than the economical Japanese Toho productions of KING KONG VS. GODZILLA (1962) and KING KONG ESCAPES (1967) (see B/V). Although a 40-foot high, six and one-half ton robot was created to appear as Kong in the film, it was used only briefly and unbilled Rick Baker played the character in his well-designed ape suit. There is also NOT much to recommend Kong's island, which not only lacks dinosaurs but any of that prehistoric ambiance. Add to this, a wretched script, and you have some of the faults in 1976's KING

KING KONG (1976).

KONG. Thanks to the producer's hoopla campaign, the film grossed $40,000,000 at the box-office and even garnered an Academy Award for special effects. In retrospect, it has found a place on many viewers Ten Worst Films List!

Fred Wilson (Charles Grodin) of Petrox Oil leads an expedition to a remote island hoping to locate rich oil deposits. The tanker is commanded by Captain Ross (John Randolph) and along the way they rescue Dwan (Jessica Lange) who has escaped from an exploding yacht onto a life raft. Also aboard the tanker, as a stowaway, is zoologist Jack Prescott (Jeff Bridges), who believes the island where they are headed may include "the missing link." Once there, they interrupt a native ceremony and later Dwan is abducted by the natives and a huge ape, King Kong, seizes her and carries her off into the jungle. The crew sets out to rescue Dwan while Kong protects her from a huge snake. Prescott ferrets Dwan away from Kong and they return to the village. Kong follows and breaks through the massive wall which the natives built long ago. However, the beast falls into an immense pit and is drugged. Since the oil deposits on the island cannot be commercially exploited, Wilson decides to take Kong back to civilization and exhibit him, hoping to recoup his expedition costs. On board the ship, Kong goes wild and Wilson plans to kill him, but Dwan calms the beast. Back in New York City, Kong is exhibited at Shea Stadium and the mayor (John Agar) attends the events along with thousands of customers. Kong breaks free from his cage, murders Wilson and goes berserk. Jack and Dwan, now lovers, want to save the beast and return him to his native island. Kong finds Dwan and takes her with him to the top of the World Trade Center. The mayor orders helicopters to fire on it. Kong sets her down and is soon riddled with bullets. He falls to his death on the street below.

When the new KING KONG was exhibited on network television in 1980 a 190-minute version was telecast, adding 56 minutes of footage deleted from the film's initial theatrical release. The new material only added to the tedium.

Even while the remake of KING KONG was in production, producers de Laurentiis talked of a followup, but none occurred until 1986 when he distributed the even worse KING KONG LIVES (*infra*).

KING KONG LIVES (De Laurentiis Entertainment Group, 1986) C 105 mins.

Executive producer, Ronald Shusett; producer, Martha Schumacher; director, John Guillermin; based on the character created by Merian C. Cooper, Edgar Wallace; screenplay, Ronald Shusett, Steven Pressfield; assistant directors, Brian Cooke, Matt Earl Beesley,

Bruce Moriarity; music, John Scott; production designer, Peter Murton; art directors, Fred Carter, Tony Reading, John Wood; costumes, Clifford Capone; creatures, Carlo Rambaldi; stunt coordinator, Bud Davis; special effects makeup, Dean Gates; special effects, Joseph Mercurio; special visual effects, Barry Nolan; sound, David Stephenson; camera, Alec Mills; editor, Malcolm Cooke.

Peter Elliot (King Kong); George Yiasomi (Lady Kong); Brian Kerwin (Hank Mitchell); Linda Hamilton (Amy Franklin); John Ashton (Colonel Nevitt); Peter Michael Goetz (Dr. Ingersoll); Frank Maraden (Dr. Benson Hughes); Alan Sader, Lou Criscuolo (Faculty Doctors); Marc Clement (Crew Chief); Natt Christian, Mac Pirkle (Surgeons); Larry Sprinkle (Journalist); Rod Davis (TV Reporter); Robin Cahall Mazlansky); Don Law (Security Chief); Jack Maloney (Wrangler); Jimmie Ray Weeks (Major Pete); Jeff Benninghofen (Radioman); Jim Grimshaw (Sergeant); Bernard Additon, Michael McLendon (Captains); Jimmy Wiggins (Boyfriend); Mary Swafford (Girlfriend); Michael Forest (Vance); Dandy Stevenson, Lynda Smith (Moms); and: Richard Rhodes, Jayne Linday-Gray, Michael Hunter; Buck Ford, Gary Kaikaka, Duke Ernsberger, Shannon Rowell, Leon Rippy, Wallace Merck, Hershel Sparber.

Following the release of the tepid remake of KING KONG (1976) (*supra*), producer Dino de Laurentiis announced it would be followed by KING KONG IN AFRICA. Mercifully that production failed to materialize. A decade later, however, de Laurentiis and director John Guillerman (who had helmed the 1976 fiasco) reteamed for KING KONG LIVES, which was unleashed for the year end holiday trade. Janet Maslin (*New York Times*) reported that the film " . . . has a dull cast and a plot that's even duller, but the ape himself is in good form. Thanks to Carlo Rambaldi's creature design . . . the apes are lifelike and expressive, generally a lot more so than the people around them." In this outing both Kong and his mate are portrayed by actors garbed in Rambaldi's realistic ape suits.

The plot takes up where the 1976 film ends with Kong (Peter Elliot) supposedly dead after falling from the World Trade Center and being riddled with bullets, bombs, etc. However, Kong is merely in a coma and is kept alive for a decade until an artificial heart can be constructed for him. Blood is donated by Lady Kong (George Yiasomi) who has been captured in Borneo and brought to the States. When Kong recovers he picks up Lady Kong's scent and breaks loose from his confinement and seeks out his benefactress, soon to be his lady love. When the authorities attempt to capture Kong he goes on a rampage, decimating the countryside. Finally the Army shoots down Kong, while Lady Kong gives birth to their offspring.

KING OF THE ZOMBIES (Monogram, 1941) 67 mins.

Producer, Lindsley Parsons; director, Jean Yarbrough; screenplay, Edmund Kelso; art director, Charles Clague; music, Edward Kay; camera, Mack Stengler; editor, Richard Currier.

Dick Purcell (Mac McCarthy); Joan Woodbury (Barbara Windsor); Henry Victor (Dr. Miklos Sangre); John Archer (Bill Summers); Mantan Moreland (Jefferson Davis); Patricia Stacey (Madame Alyce Sangre); Madame Sul-Te-Wan (Tahama); Guy Usher (Admiral Wainwright); Jimmy Davis (Lazarus); Marguerite Whitten (Samantha); Lawrence Criner (Dr. Couille).

Pilot Mac McCarthy (Dick Purcell), along with government agent Bill Summers (John Archer) and the latter's valet Jefferson Davis [Jeff] (Mantan Moreland), crash lands his plane on a remote Caribbean island. There they find the home of reclusive Dr. Miklos Sangre (Henry Victor), who claims to be a European refugee along with his somnambulistic wife, Alyce (Patricia Stacey), and her pretty niece Barbara Windsor (Joan Woodbury). From servants Samantha (Marguerite Whitten) and Tahama (Madame Sul-Te-Wan), Jeff finds out the place is haunted by zombies and later Sangre employs hypnotism to turn Jeff into one of them. Sangre plans to use voodoo to transfer the mind of captured Admiral Wainwright (Guy Usher) into that of his wife to find out what the military man knows about the U.S.'s Panama Canal fortifications. He intends to provide the information to the Nazis, for whom he is an agent. When Mac finds this out, Sangre apparently kills him and turns him into a zombie. Bill, who is on the trail of Wainwright, is captured but escapes. He and the revitalized Jeff interrupt the voodoo ceremony in which Barbara has replaced Alyce, who finally dies before she could be used further. Bill causes the zombies to turn against Sangre and Mac kills the doctor before being brought back to life, while Bill rescues Barbara and Wainwright.

During the World War II years, all kind of plot manipulations were used, especially by the smaller studios, to interpolate anti-Nazi feelings into films and KING OF THE ZOMBIES has to be one of the silliest and most vapid of these. Outside of Henry Victor's crazed scientist and Mantan Moreland's comic asides, the film has little to offer.

Unable to resist leaving *un*well enough alone, Monogram released REVENGE OF THE ZOMBIES (q.v.) two years later.

KINGDOM OF THE SPIDERS (Dimension Pictures, 1977) C 94 mins.

Executive producer, Henry Fownes; producers, Igo Kanter, Jeffrey M. Sneller; director, John "Bud" Cardos; screenplay, Richard Robinson, Alan Caillou; set decorator, Rusty Rosene; assistant director, Larry Kostroff; sound, Bill Kaplan, James Dehr; special effects, Greg Auer; camera, John Morrill; editors, Steve Zaillian, Kanter.

William Shatner (Rack Hansen); Tiffany Bolling (Diane Ashley); Woody Strode (Walter Colby); Lieux Dressler (Emma Washburn); Altovise Davis (Birch Colby); David McLean (Sheriff Smith); Natasha Ryan (Linda Hansen); Marcy Rafferty (Terry Hansen); Joe Ross (Vern Johnson); Adele Malis (Betty Johnson); Roy Engel (Mayor Connors).

On the Arizona desert tarantulas, usually solitary creatures, band together in search of food and begin attacking cattle, then other animals, and soon humans. Veteran Rack Hansen (William Shatner) investigates several mysterious disappearances and finds the spider colonies in the desert. He realizes they are moving toward his community, a small town where his girlfriend Diane Ashley (Tiffany Bolling) resides. An army of the spiders attack the town, killing most of the populace and wrapping them in cocoons for future food supplies. When the phone lines are cut, the town is isolated and help cannot arrive. Rack and Diane take refuge in a store as the spiders wrap a cocoon completely around the town and march off for more food.

Director John "Bud" Cardos began as an actor in Independent-International exploitation items and with Al Adamson co-directed THE FEMALE BUNCH (1971) for Dalia. After KINGDOM OF THE SPIDERS he did such genre efforts as THE DARK (1977) and THE DAY TIME ENDED (1980) (q.v.); but this feature is his best to date. Its frightful nature, horrific sequences and downbeat ending belie the director's exploitation beginnings. (And not to be overlooked is the subtle humor of the script and the well-developed character delineations.) Reviewing the feature upon its video cassette release in 1984, *Fangoria* magazine (February, 1984) observed, "With the exception of a stupid romantic interlude between William Shatner and Tiffany Bolling, the movie is well paced and the tarantula attacks were unsettling enough to make me squirm reflexively."

For the record, the spiders went on their rampage because of man's tampering with their food chain.

KONGA (American International, 1961) C 90 mins.

Producer, Herman Cohen; associate producer, Jim O'Connolly; director, John Lemont; story/screenplay, Aben Kandel, Cohen; art director, Wilfred Arnold; makeup, Jack Craig; music, Gerard Schurmann; music director, Muir Mathieson; wardrobe, Bridget

Sellers; sound, Sidney Rider, Ronald Abbott; sound effects editor, Derek Holding; camera, Desmond Dickinson; editor, Jack Slade.

Michael Gough (Dr. Charles Decker); Margo Johns (Margaret); Jess Conrad (Bob Kenton); Claire Gordon (Sandra Banks); Austin Trevor (Dean Foster); Jack Watson (Superintendent Brown); George Pastell (Professor Tagore); Vanda Godsell (Bob's Mother); Stanley Morgan (Inspector Lawson); Grace Arnold (Miss Barnesdell); Leonard Sachs (Bob's Father); Nicholas Bennett (Daniel); Kim Tracy (Mary); Rupert Osborne (Eric); Waveney Lee (Janet); John Welsh (Commissioner Garland); Sam Sylvano (Konga as a Chimpanzee).

After his successful I WAS A TEENAGE WEREWOLF (1957) and I WAS A TEENAGE FRANKENSTEIN (1957) (qq.v.), producer Herman Cohen went into production in London with I WAS A TEENAGE GORILLA, which became KONGA. (Cohen paid RKO a licensing fee for the use of the name which was so similar to that studio's classic 1933 feature KING KONG [see B/V].) The end results were so lukewarm that the picture is very forgettable.

Scientist Dr. Charles Decker (Michael Gough) returns from Africa with a carnivorous plant which he assumes is a link between animals and plants. Also accompanying him on the trek back to civilization is a chimpanzee named Konga. He tests the serum he develops from the plants on Konga and the animal begins growing. Decker is engaged to his assistant Margaret (Margo Johns), but lusts after pretty co-ed Sandra Banks (Claire Gordon). When Konga is large enough, Decker uses him to kill his enemies, including college dean Foster (Austin Trevor) who scoffed at his theories, rival botanist Professor Tagore (George Pastell) and Sandra's boyfriend Bob Kenton (Jess Conrad). After Margaret overhears Decker profess his love for Sandra, she angrily injects Konga with an overdose of serum and he suddenly grows immensely tall. The oversized animal kills Margaret and abducts Decker, while Sandra is devoured by the plant. Konga tromps through London carrying Decker and in a confrontation, the army shoots him. Konga throws Decker to his death on the pavement before dying himself. As he expires, he returns to his normal size.

Despite its many shortcomings, KONGA did well at the boxoffice and spawned a Monarch Books novelization by Dean Owen, plus a comic book series which was published from 1960-1968.

KRULL (Columbia, 1983) C 117 mins.

Executive producer, Ted Mann; producer, Ron Silverman; associate producer, Geoffrey Helman; director, Peter Yates; screenplay, Stanford Sherman; music, James Horner; production designer, Stephen Grimes; art directors, Tony Reading, Colin Grimes, Norman Dorme, Tony Curtis; set decorator, Herbert Westbrook; costume designer, Anthony Mendleson; assistant director/second unit director, Derek Cracknell; sound, Ivan Sharrock; visual effects supervisor, Derek Meddings; visual effects camera, Paul Wilson; optical effects camera, Robin Browne; camera, Peter Suschitzky; editor, Ray Lovejoy.

Ken Marshall (Prince Colwyn); Lysette Anthony (Lyssa); Freddie Jones (Ynyr); Francesca Annis (Widow of the Web); Alan Armstrong (Torquil); David Battley (Ergo); Bernard Bresslaw (Cyclops); Liam Neeson (Kegan); John Welsh (Seer); Graham McGrath (Titch); Tony Church (Turold); Bernard Archard (Elrig); Belinda Mayne (Vella); Dicken Ashworth (Bardolph); Todd Carty (Oswyn); Robbie Coltrane (Rhun).

In the mists of time, Prince Colwyn (Ken Marshall) must save his beautiful lady love Lyssa (Lysette Anthony), who has been kidnapped by "The Beast," a creature who can take many forms, and his minions. To successfully combat the Beast, Colwyn must find the Glaive, a boomerang-type weapon and he is aided in this quest by a wise old man, Ynyr (Freddie Jones). Colwyn forms a rag-tag band of followers but comes up against an outlaw (Alan Armstrong) and his gang, but they soon join forces to defeat the Beast. The evil creature is headquartered in the Black Fortress, a spaceship which brought him and his Slayer army to Earth. Colwyn has a showdown with the Beast who takes the guise of a Cyclops. The two battle to the finish.

This overly ambitious sci-fi adventure tale interpolates the themes of many successful genre outings, from STAR WARS (1977) to THE THING (1982) (qq.v.). Costing $27,000,000 and grossing less than $9,000,000, it failed to perform in the avalanche of genre films being distributed at the time. *Variety* highlighted the film's faults: "Although inoffensively designed only to please the senses and appeal to one's whimsical sense of adventure, KRULL nevertheless comes off as a blatantly derivative hodgepodge, the recipe for which includes ingredients from nearly every successful film in the fantasy genre. . . . Even though the specifics are different, almost everything about the film seems terribly familiar, and it lacks the freshness and zip which would have been required to make one forget the past in favor of current pleasures."

THE LAND THAT TIME FORGOT (American International, 1975) C 91 mins.

Executive producers, Max J. Rosenberg; Milton Subotsky; producer, John Dark; director, Kevin Connor; based on the novel by Edgar Rice Burroughs; screenplay, James Cawthorn, Michael Moorcock; music, Douglas Gamley; art director, Bert Davey; assistant director, Allan James; sound, George Stephenson; special effects, Derek Meddings; camera, Alan Hume; editor, John Ireland.

Doug McClure (Bowen Tyler); John McEnery (Captain Von Schoenvorts); Susan Penhaligon (Lisa Clayton); Keith Barron (Bradley); Anthony Ainley (Dietz); Godfrey James (Borg); Bobby Farr (Ahm); Decian Mulholland (Olson).

One of Edgar Rice Burroughs' most popular novel series dealt with the underground world of Pellucidar and three of his 1918 novellas about this special world, "The Land That Time Forgot," "The People That Time Forgot" and "Out of Time's Abyss," were published as a novel in 1924 called *The Land That Time Forgot*. This served as the basis for the first of three mid-1970s features, followed by AT THE EARTH'S CORE (1976) and THE PEOPLE THAT TIME FORGOT (1977) (qq.v.).

During World War I, a German submarine sinks a British ship and saves the survivors, including American Bowen Tyler (Doug McClure) and pretty Lisa Clayton (Susan Penhaligon). During a storm the U-boat is knocked off its course and ends up in a strange world in the Arctic where time has stood still and dinosaurs and such still exist. The submarine captain, Von Shoenvorts (John McEnery), decides to team with his captives in surviving in this hostile environment and they are aided by Ahm (Bobby Farr), an intelligent Neanderthal, who teaches them not only to survive but the secret of his god, which aids them in returning home, although Tyler remains behind on the world of Caprona.

Kevin Connor directed this initial Pellucidar outing for the English-based Amicus company, as he was to do with its followups, all of which were released in the U.S. by American International. This film uses the Arctic instead of the Earth's core for its setting while the second entry, AT THE EARTH'S CORE, was true to its literary origin, while the final one in the series, THE PEOPLE THAT TIME FORGOT, is a direct sequel to THE LAND THAT TIME FORGOT. Marc Sigoloff in *The Films of the Seventies* (1984) judged the film, "Silly, but enjoyable, adventure yarn. . . . The special effects are inferior, but in this type of film that is not overly important."

LASERBLAST (Irwin Yablans, 1978) C 85 mins.

Producer, Charles Band; director, Michael Rae; screenplay, Franne Schact, Frank Ray Perilli; wardrobe, Jill Sheridan, Barbara Scott; special effects makeup/props, Steve Neill; alien creatures designer, David Allen; assistant director, Andy Gallerani; sound, Jerry Wolfe; camera, Terry Bowen; editor, Jodie Copelan.

Kim Milford (Billy Duncan); Cheryl Smith (Kathy Farley);

Gianni Russo (Tony Craig); Ron Masak (Sheriff); Dennis Burkley (Peter Ungar); Barry Cutler (Jesse Jeep); Mike Bobenko (Chuck Boran); Eddie Deezen (Froggy); Keenan Wynn (Colonel Farley); Roddy McDowall (Dr. Mellon).

In the California desert a strange battle occurs between two lizard-like aliens and a humanoid fugitive they are chasing. The latter is killed by the two aliens, but his laser gun and pendant remain. Troubled teenage youth Billy Duncan (Kim Milford) finds the items and keeps them. While wearing the pendant he turns into a greenish-colored killer who takes revenge on those who have made fun of him in the past. His girlfriend, Kathy Farley (Cheryl Smith), worries about him and she urges him to see Dr. Mellon (Roddy McDowall) who soon suspects too much and is killed by his patient. Government agent Tony Craig (Gianni Russo) and Colonel Farley (Keenan Wynn) of the Army are assigned to the case and enlist the help of the local lawman (Ron Masak) in tracking down the killer. Meanwhile, the aliens, come looking for the gun and kill Billy when he turns on them.

LASERBLAST is an stimulating, unpretentious little film, in the same vein as I WAS A TEENAGE WEREWOLF (1957) (q.v.). Its main attractions are the alien creatures, created by David Allen, and the fine performance of Cheryl Smith as the heroine. She also highlighted the nightmarish horror film, LEMORA, THE LADY DRACULA (1974), and as Rainbeaux Smith, appeared in many R-rated thrillers.

THE LAST DAYS OF MAN ON EARTH (New World Pictures, 1975) C 81 mins.

Executive producers, Michael Moorcock, Roy Baird, David Puttnam; producers, John Goldstone, Sandy Lieberson; director, Robert Fuest; based on the novel *The Final Programme* by Moorcock; screenplay/production designer, Fuest; music, Paul Beaver, Bernard Krause, Gerry Mulligan; art director, Philip Harrison; camera, Norman Warwick; editor, Barrie Vince.

Jon Finch (Jerry Cornelius); Jenny Runacre (Miss Brunner); Hugh Griffith (Professor Hira); Patrick Magee (Dr. Baxter); Sterling Hayden (Major Wrongway Lindbergh); Harry Andrews (John); Graham Crowden (Dr. Smiles); George Coulouris (Dr. Powys); Basil Henson (Dr. Lucas); Derrick O'Connor (Frank); Gilles Milinaire (Dimitri); Ronald Lacey (Shades); Julie Ege (Miss Ege); Sandy Ratcliff (Jenny); Sarah Douglas (Chaterine); Dolores Del Mar (Fortune Teller).

Also called THE FINAL PROGRAMME in Great Britain, this Robert Fuest film attempts to satirize such films as A CLOCK-

WORK ORANGE (1971) and 2001: A SPACE ODYSSEY (1966) (see B/V for both), but without much success. Cut by eleven minutes for its American release, this elaborately decorated film without substance tried too hard for a cult following and ended up being ignored.

In the near future Professor Hira (Hugh Griffith) informs Jerry Cornelius (Jon Finch) the world will come to an end due to human laxity. Unhappy at this discovery, Jerry joins a group of doctors and genius Miss Bruner (Jenny Runacre) in a project to perfect immortality. They believe the world is destined to change every two thousand years and that a new Messiah will save the planet. Since Jerry and Miss Bruner have the world's two highest IQ's, they are mated, but not before he fails to save his sister and murders his drug using brother (Derrick O'Connor). The result of the sexual encounter is a child who is a murderous apeman.

Lacking in storyline, the filmmakers used sensationalism, such as the sequence where a brain is laid bare.

THE LAST STARFIGHTER (Universal, 1984) C 100 mins.

Producers, Gary Adelson, Edward O. Denault; associate producer, John H. Whitney, Jr.; director, Nick Castle; screenplay, Jonathan Betuel; music, Craig Safan; songs: Safan and Mark Mueller; Safan, Mueller, Melissa Manchester; production designer, Ron Cobb; art director, James D. Bissell; set decorator, Linda Spheeris; set designers, Beverli Egan, Jim Teegarden, Don High; costume designer, Robert Fletcher; assistant director, Brian E. Frankish; design makeup, Terry Smith; technical makeup, Werner Keppler; mechanical effects makeup, Lance Anderson; stunt co-ordinator, Glen Wilder; sound, Jack Solomon; visual effects co-ordinator, Jeffrey A. Okyn; camera, King Baggot; editor, C. Timothy O'Meara.

Lance Guest (Alex Rogan); Robert Preston (Centauri); Dan O'Herlihy (Grig); Catherine Mary Stewart (Maggie); Barbara Bosson (Jane Rogan); Norman Snow (Xur); Chris Hebert (Louis Rogan); Kay E. Kuter (Enduran); Dan Mason (Lord Kril).

Eighteen-year-old Alex Rogan (Lance Guest) lives in a remote trailer park with his divorced mother (Barbara Bosson) and his younger brother Chris (Louis Rogan). Restless Alex is hoping for a better future for himself and a life with girlfriend Maggie (Catherine Mary Stewart). By accident a video game called Starfighter is left at the park instead of its Las Vegas destination, and Alex develops an affinity for it. He becomes a champion at picking off alien invaders and is soon the talk of the area for being the highest scorer. He comes to the attention of rapid-talking Centauri (Robert Preston) who convinces Alex to accompany him on a "car" ride. In actuality

THE LAST STARFIGHTER (1984).

the car is a spacecraft and Centauri is recruiting combatants for the Star League of Planets, a grouping of extraterrestrial civilizations. Centauri admits that the Starfighter video games have been distributed throughout the galaxy to find recruits to operate the Gun Star spaceships in the ongoing battles with the Ko-Dan. Centauri explains further that defector Xur (Norman Snow) has revealed the frontier defense secrets to the Ko-Dan and now the enemy is planning an invasion. Even after meeting with officials of the Star League of Planets, Alex remains suspicious of Centauri and his associates and demands to return home. He does so and finds that the android double left in his place has caused problems and is now destroyed. Centauri comes to Alex's rescue and Alex agrees to return to outer space to fight the Ko-Dan, ignoring Maggie's pleas to remain. In the ensuing space wars with the Ko-Dan, Alex and the lizard-like alien Grig (Dan O'Herlihy) prove heroic and save the galaxy. Centauri, whom Alex thought to be dead, was merely in a trance to heal his wounds, and revives. Alex requests to return to Earth one more time. Once there, he asks Maggie to join him in his new life, and she agrees. As their craft zooms off, Alex's brother Louis begins practicing determinedly on the Starfighter game.

Variety enthused, " . . . director Nick Castle and writer Jonathan Betuel have done something so simple it's almost awe-inspiring. They've taken a very human story and accented it with sci-fi special effects, rather than the other way around. . . . This is not to say the outer-space hardware and digital doo-dahs aren't all on a par with what's become commonplace; they are. But STARFIGHTER employs them judiciously and, better still, has them anchored in a continuing earthly involvement."

Jessica Horsting reported in *Magill's Cinema Annual* (1985), "The marvel of THE LAST STARFIGHTER is simply this: Though it was an effect-laden science-fiction film, virtually none of the cinematic illusions involved extensive model making, blue-screen photography, matte techniques, and optical combinations typical of the genre. Virtually all the effects footage was photo simulation created in the bowels of the Cray X-MZ, the world's most sophisticated computer. . . . The Cray not only created the images in exacting detail but also calculated the correct movement of the image and the everchanging perspectives. . . . Once the data was entered, the computer could create complicated scenes in a fraction of the time necessary to film a similar scene at a fraction of the cost. The results were quite astonishing, with a wide-screen resolution in the video segments that equaled and sometimes surpassed that of the filmed segments."

Those filmgoers astute enough to attend a showing of this warm, lively production had the opportunity to see Robert Preston at his best; playing a space age Professor Harold Hill (of THE MUSIC MAN). With vivacity, wit, and expert timing, he is the consummate con artist, but this time on a mission of interplanetary mercy. It was to be the screen veteran's final film performance.

THE LEECH WOMAN (Universal, 1960) 77 mins.

Producer, Joseph Gershenson; director, Edward Dein; story, Ben Pivar, Francis Rosenwald; screenplay, David Duncan; art directors, Alexander Golitzen, Robert Clatworthy; makeup, Bud Westmore; music, Irving Gertz; assistant director, Joe Kenny; camera, Ellis Carter; editor, Milton Carruth.

Coleen Gray (June Talbot); Grant Williams (Neil Foster); Phillip Terry (Dr. Paul Talbot); Gloria Talbott (Sally); John Van Dreelen (Bertram Garvey); Estelle Hemsley (Old Malla); Kim Hamilton (Young Malla); Arthur Batanides (Jerry); and: Chester Jones.

Made to cash in on the popularity of horror films in the late 1950s and early 1960s, this Universal release is a meandering affair which is, per *Castle of Frankenstein* magazine (Number 24, 1969), "Lurid grade-B nonsense. . . . Okay make-up effects but otherwise mediocre." It also should owe thanks to the eternal youth storyline gimmick of Henry Rider Haggard's *She,* from which it borrowed so liberally.

Dermatologist Dr. Paul Talbot (Phillip Terry) is having an affair with much younger Sally (Gloria Talbott) and has lost interest in his aging wife, June (Coleen Gray). June goes to her lawyer, Neil Foster (Grant Williams), planning a divorce, but Paul suddenly decides to take her to Africa. An old woman, Malla (Estelle Hemsley), has come to him with a story about how her African tribe has developed a youth rejuvenation formula from an exotic orchid and he wants its secrets. He intends to use June for experimentation. Once on the dark continent, Paul, June, and guide Bertram Garvey (John Van Dreelen) are captured by the tribe. Already at the tribal village Malla has become a young woman (Kim Hamilton) after swallowing the potion. Paul dies during the ceremony, June takes the formula and becomes youthful again and she and Garvey, now her lover, escape. Along the way June becomes old and Garvey dies in quicksand; June retakes the formula for a temporary return of her youth. Back home June pretends to be her own niece and finds that Neil, to whom she is now attracted, and Sally are engaged. Jealous, June kills Sally and when Neil arrives, the police follow and find Sally's body. Neil now understands June and her niece are the same person and June suddenly begins to age. As the formula fails, she becomes dust.

THE LEGEND OF PRAGUE see THE GOLEM (essay).

LIFE WITHOUT SOUL (Ocean Film Corp., 1915) 70 mins.

Producer, John L. Dudley; production supervisor, George de Carlton; director, Joseph W. Smiley; based on the novel *Frankenstein* by Mary Shelley; screenplay, Jesse J. Goldberg.

William W. Cohill (Victor Frawley); Percy Darrell Standing (The Brute Man); George DeCarlton (William Frawley); Jack Hopkins (Victor Clerval); Lucy Cotton (Elizabeth Lavenza); Pauline Curley (Claudia Frawley); David McCauley (Servant); Violet DeBiccari (Ellizabeth Lavenza as a Child).

Mary Shelley's classic novel *Frankenstein* (1818) was first brought to the screen by Edison in 1910 with Charles Ogle as the monster. Five years later the Ocean Film Corporation made a five reel silent version of the book called LIFE WITHOUT SOUL, filmed at various locations around the country and aboard an Atlantic Ocean steamer. Percy Darrell Standing played the "Brute Man" as the creation was called, and he did so without any horrific makeup associated later on with the role. At the time of its release—late in 1915—the trade paper *Motion Picture News* commented, "The story is impossible and the difficulties encountered in its production were great, the main being to make a convincing picture of an entirely imaginative story. At times the picture refuses to convince, but its interest is always averagely high because of the theme's unusualness."

Medical student, Dr. Frawley (William W. Cohill), works to create an artificial man and he does so, but his creation, the Brute Man (Percy Darrell Standing) has no soul. The creature, which is not very intelligent, dominates the doctor's life and it turns killer and dispatches his sister (Pauline Curley), his pal Clerval (Jack Hopkins) and finally his new bride, Elizabeth (Lucy Cotton). Frankenstein puts an end to the creation by shooting him and then exhausted by the horrors he has caused, the young doctor dies.

LIFE WITHOUT SOUL is told within the framework of a character reading a book with the action coming to life on the screen; the end finds all the characters as they had been at the beginning. Donald F. Glut in *The Frankenstein Legend* (1973) noted, "This lessened the horror and the impact of the story. Film-makers at the time usually felt that audiences would not accept the depiction of the supernatural or pseudo-science as real and that such stories inevitably had to be revealed as dreams, and tales of madmen, and the like."

LIFEFORCE (Cannon, 1985) C 101 mins.

Producers, Menahem Golan, Yoram Globus; associate producer, Michael J. Kagan; director, Tobe Hooper; based on the novel *Space Vampires* by Colin Wilson; screenplay, Dan O'Bannon, Don Jakoby; second unit director, Derek Cracknell; assistant directors, Cracknell, Richard Hoult, Melvin Lind, Tim Reed, Tony Aherne, Paul Lowin; production designer, John Graysmark; art directors, Alan Tomkins, Bob Cartwright, Tony Reading, Terry Knight; set decorators, Simon Wakefield, Denise Exshaw; music, Henry Mancini; additional music, Michael Kamen, James Guthrie; music editor, Bob Hathaway; costume designer, Carin Hooper; makeup, Dickie Mills, Michael Morris, Sandra Exelby; prosthetic/makeup effects, Nick Maley; sound, George Stephenson, Eric Tomlinson; sound designer, Vernon Messenger; additional sound effects, Jean-Pierre Lelong; sound editor, Nigel Galt; technical advisers, Bernard Alimo, Alexander Beetham, stunt arranger, Peter Diamond; visual effects, Robert Shepherd; optical effects supervisor, Roger Durney; special visual effects, John Dykstra; camera, Alan Hume; second unit camera Jack Lowin; editor, John Grover.

Steve Railsback (Commander Tom Carlsen); Peter Firth (Inspector Caine); Frank Finlay (Fallade); Mathilda May (Space Girl); Patrick Stewart (Dr. Armstrong); Michael Gothard (Bukovsky);

Nicholas Ball (Derebridge); Aubrey Morris (Sir Percy); Nancy Paul (Ellen); John Hallam (Lamson); John Keegan (Guard); Christopher Jagger, Bill Malin (Vampires); Jerome Willis (Pathologist); Derek Benfield (Physician); John Woodnutt (Metallurgist); James Forbes-Robertson (Minister); Peter Porteous (Prime Minister); Katherine Schofield (Prime Minister's Secretary); Owen Holder (Scientist); Jamie Roberts (Rawlings); Russell Sommers (Navigation Officer); Patrick Connor (Fatherly Guard); Sidney Kean, Paul Cooper (Guards); Chris Sullivan (Kelly); Milton Cadman, Ruper Baker (Soldiers); Gary Hildreth (Police Surgeon); Edward Evans (Doctor); Nicholas Donnelly (Police Inspector); Peter Lovestream, Julian Firth (Boys in Park); Carl Rigg, Elizabeth Morton (Radar Technicians); Geoffrey Frederick (Communications Officer); David English, Emma Jacobs, Michael John Paliotti, Brian Carroll (Crewpersons); Richard Oldfield (Mission Leader); Christopher Barr (Trajectory Officer); Burnell Tucker (NASA Man); Tom Booker, Michael Fitzpatrick (NASA Officers); Richard Sharpe (Rescue Ship Crewman); John Golighty (Colonel); William Lindsay (Colonel's Aide); David Beckett (Soldier); Sydney Livingstone (Ned Price); Ken Parry (Sykes); John Edmunds (BBC Commentator); Haydn Wood (Helicopter Pilot); Adrian Hedley (Director of Mime Artists); Corrine Bouggard, Cal McCrystal, Bob Goody, Paul Anthony-Barber, Kristine Landon-Smith (Mime Artists).

Commander Tom Carlsen (Steve Railsback) leads a joint U.S.-British expedition aboard the spaceship *Churchill* to explore Halley's Comet and imbedded in the comet they find a large alien craft. They board the ship and locate mummified aliens and three glass sarcophagi containing three humanoids. They take the humanoids aboard their vessel and set out to return to Earth. The shuttle is charted as orbiting Earth, but there is no communication, so another craft is sent up and finds the crew burned to death and the sarcophagi (containing the humanoids), which they donate to the European Space Research Center in London. At the Center, a beautiful space girl (Mathilda May) and two alien companions emerge from the crystals and kill a guard by draining him of his lifeforce. Meanwhile Carlsen returns to Earth in an escape ship and tells the authorities that the humanoids are really vampires who absorb the lives of others to survive and they can take over other bodies and reanimate those they have killed. The space girl has not harmed Carlsen and he has a telepathic link with her which Scotland Yard Inspector Caine (Peter Firth) uses to track her down. The alien ship unleashes a giant web which absorbs human life, turning the denizens of London into zombie-like vampires. NATO plans to blow up the city with a nuclear bomb as Carlsen and Cadine frantically seek to find the space girl. Carlsen locates her in a cathedral and they have intercourse as he dies. Caine arrives and destroys both vampires.

Based on Colin Wilson's 1976 novel *Space Vampires* (which was the film's working title), LIFEFORCE proved a laughable, financial bust. A silly premise, compounded by overplayed theatrics and inane dialogue (one scene has the naked alien girl on the prowl as someone intones, "She's looking for a man—any man—she wants to steal some energy from him") makes the audience chortle more than shudder. Julian Petley dissected in the British *Monthly Film Bulletin,* "Special effects cannot compensate for the risibility of much of the dialogue, the mugging Steve Railsback and Peter Firth, or the script's unfortunate habit of interjecting lengthy explanations into the unlikeliest and most awkward of places. With the intervention of Inspector Caine, the plot frequently threatens to descend into Agatha Christie territory. . . ." *Variety* judged LIFEFORCE " . . . the unintentional laugh-fest of the season" and added that the filmmakers " . . . may have intended some of this humorously, but not all of it. Explicitness of the effects and broadness of the performances in the service of preposterous dialog push this toward camp and unendurability."

Costing over $20,000,000 to produce, LIFEFORCE grossed only $11,605,000 in eleven weeks at the U.S. box-office.

THE LITTLE SHOP OF HORRORS (Filmgroup, 1961) 70 mins.

Producer/director, Roger Corman; screenplay, Charles B. Griffith; art director, Daniel Haller; music, Fred Katz; assistant director, Richard Dixen; camera, Archie Dalzell; editor, Marshall Neilan, Jr.

Jonathan Haze (Seymour Krelboined); Jackie Joseph (Audrey Fulquard); Mel Welles (Gravis Mushnick); Dick Miller (Burson Fouch); Myrtle Vail (Winifred Krelboined); Leola Wendorff (Siddie Shiva); Jack Nicholson (Wilbur Force); John Shaner (Dr. Phoebus Farb); Meri Welles (Leonara Clyde); Wally Campo (Joe Fink); Jack Warford (Frank Stoolie); Lynn Storey (Mrs. Fishtwanger); Tammy Windsor, Toby Michaels (Teenagers); Dodie Drake (Waitress); Charles B. Griffith (Robber/Drunk Patient/Voice of Audrey, Jr.).

LITTLE SHOP OF HORRORS (Warner Bros., 1986) C 94 mins.

Producer, David Geffen; associate producers, David Orton, Denis Holt; director, Frank Oz; based on the screenplay by Charles Griffith and the play by Howard Ashman; screenplay, Ashman; production designer, Roy Walker; art directors, Stephen Spence, (models) John Fenner; set decorator, Tessa Davies; animatronics co-ordinator, Barbara Griffiths; mechanical design, Neal Scanlan; music, Miles Goodman; music arrangers/adaptors, Robby Merkin, Bob

Gaudio; orchestrator/music supervisor, Merkin; songs, Alan Meken and Howard Ashman; choreography, Pat Garrett; costumes designer, Marit Allen; assistant directors, Dusty Symonds, Gareth Tandy, Nick Heckstall-Smith; special visual effects, Brian Ferren, James N. Shelly, Susan Coursey, Susan Leber, David McDonough, (electronics), Robert C. Francis, Chester T. Hartwell, John C. Huntington III; special camera effects, Robert Rowoholt, John Alagna, Bob Buckles, Sanford Duke, Mitch Wilson; camera, Robert Paynter; second unit camera, Ronnie Maasz, James Devis; editor, John Jympson.

Rick Moranis (Seymour Krelborn); Ellen Greene (Audrey); Vincent Gardenia (Mushnick); Steve Martin (Orin Scrivello, DDS); Tichina Arnold (Crystal); Tisha Campbell (Chiffon); Michelle Weeks (Ronette); James Belushi (Patrick Martin); John Candy (Wink Wilkinson); Christopher Guest (Customer); Bill Murray (Arthur Denton); Stanley Jones (Narrator); Bertice Reading ("Downtown" Old Woman); Ed Wiley, Alan Tilvern, John Scott Martin ("Downtown" Bums); Vincent Wong (Chinese Florist); Mark Wilson, Danny Cunningham, Danny John-Jules, Gary Palmer, Paul Swaby (Doo Wop Street Singers); Miriam Margolyes (Dental Nurse); Abbie Dabner (Boy Patient); Heather Henson (Girl Patient); Peter Whitman (Patient on Ceiling); Michael J. Shannon (TV Reporter); Robert Arden, Stephen Hoye, Bob Sessions (Network Executives); Levi Stubbs (Voice of Audrey II); Bob Sherman (Agent); Doreen Hermitage (*Life* Magazine Lady); Kerry Shale (Her Assistant).

One of the most famous, and perennially popular, sci-fi horror cult films is Roger Corman's two-and-one-half day wonder, THE LITTLE SHOP OF HORRORS, which was lensed in that time period on standing sets (allegedly for $25,000!) with actors from Corman's other pictures each contributing enthusiastically to the proceedings. It resulted in a truly funny and harmless monster movie spoof. At the time of its release *Variety* reported, " . . . the film is a sort of rowdy vegetable that hits the funnybone in about the same way that seeing a man slip on a banana peel does. It's absurd, but different." The *Motion Picture Herald* judged it "horrorifically funny." Through the years, the black-and-white picture has grown in stature; spawning a Broadway musical and its own film version.

Framed in a "Dragnet"-like narrative, the movie is set in Los Angeles' Skid Row where bombastic Gravis Mushnick (Mel Welles) runs a shoddy flower shop, aided by pretty assistant Audrey Fulquard (Jackie Joseph) and none-too-bright delivery boy Seymour Krelboined (Jonathan Haze). Goofy Seymour is about to be fired when flower-eating customer Burson Fouch (Dick Miller) suggests to Mushnick that Seymour's hybrid plant, named Audrey Jr. because

Advertisement for LITTLE SHOP OF HORRORS (1986).

Seymour secretly loves the assistant, might be a draw for his store. Reluctantly Mushnick gives Seymour and Audrey Jr. a week to prove their worth, but perennial mourner/customer Mrs. Shiva (Leola Wendorff) notices the plant looks puny. That night Seymour sits up with Audrey Jr. and accidentally cuts his finger and the plant drinks his blood and becomes stronger. With no more blood to spare, Seymour wanders to the railroad yard the next night and witnesses a man destroyed by a speeding train. He brings the remains back to the flower shop and the plant demands to be fed. Mushnick happens to see this grisly ritual and plans to get rid of

Seymour and the plant, but the next day huge crowds appear to see it, and Mushnick's business prospers. Going to the dentist the following day for a toothache, Seymour accidentally kills sadistic dentist Dr. Farb (John Shaner) and then masquerades as him and pulls all of masochistic patient Wilbur Force's (Jack Nicholson) teeth. Seymour feeds Farb's corpse to Audrey Jr. A society lady (Lynn Storey) wants to give Seymour an award for his healthy plant, while two cops (Wally Campo, Jack Warford) show up searching for Farb. Meanwhile Seymour has proclaimed his love for Audrey and takes her home to meet his mother (Myrtle Vail), a hypochondriac, who feeds them a dinner of health foods and knocks herself out with a tonic which contains almost pure alcohol. Things begin to go sour for Seymour: his Mother does not like Audrey; Mushnick wants to get rid of him and Audrey Jr.; and the police are closing in. Hungry, Audrey Jr. puts a hypnotic spell on Seymour and sends him out for dinner and he returns with a hooker (Meri Welles) he has killed and feeds her to the plant. The next evening the society lady and those connected with the flower shop gather to present the botanical award and to see the blooms blossom on the plant. When they do, they contain the faces of the people fed to the plant. The police and Mushnick chase Seymour who escapes and later returns to the shop. With a knife in hand he jumps into Audrey Jr. and is devoured. Later his mother, Audrey and Mushnick watch in horror as the final bloom opens, revealing Seymour's face.

Danny Peary noted in *Cult Movies* (1981), "LITTLE SHOP is a spoof of both every mad-scientist picture in which blood is needed to keep some experimental creature alive and of every fifties science fiction film in which the emphasis is on giant mutations."

Two decades after the film was released theatrically, Howard Ashman adapted it to the stage as a musical horror comedy and in 1982 it opened Off-Broadway to rave reviews. "Little Shop of Horrors" soon had a London company and was performed widely throughout the U.S. The highlight of the sparkling presentation was Martin Robinson's puppet, Audrey II, which was just as voracious as its movie counterpart. Among the songs by Ashman and Alan Menken were: "Mean Green Mother from Outer Space," "Somewhere That's Green," "Suppertime," "Grow for Me," "Skid Row," and the title tune.

In 1986, director Frank Oz, who has enjoyed a long association with the Muppets, filmed the musical version of LITTLE SHOP OF HORRORS for the Christmas holiday trade. The result for many was a satisfying recreation of the hit musical and, in turn, the original 1960 film. The new film has addled Seymour Krelborn (Rick Moranis) buying the bloodsucking Audrey II which brings business for his Skid Row flower shop boss Mr. Mushnick (Vincent Gardenia) and the love of none-too-bright but very sexy Audrey (Ellen Greene), who had planned to marry sadistic dentist Dr. Orin Scrivello (Steve Martin). Instead, Scrivello dies of dental gas and becomes Audrey II's dinner. Audrey II, meanwhile, is plotting to take over the world, and is busy manipulating Seymour. But he is too enthralled that Audrey is responding favorably to his courtship and that he has become a media favorite due to the well-publicized plant. Having already claimed Mushnick as another victim, Audrey II attempts to pull Audrey into its clutches, but Seymour electrocutes the plant. He and Audrey marry and move to suburbia. Unnoticed by them in their garden a budding sprout from Audrey II is growing.

Rightly hoping that its wide reputation would precede it, and thanks to a cast full of audience-drawing comedians, LITTLE SHOP OF HORRORS grossed $38,699,262 in its first fourteen weeks at the U.S. box-office. Obviously moviegoers agreed with Gene Siskel who commented in his Tribune Media Services' newspaper column, "The songs are joyful, and the plant is a foul-mouthed wonder when it begins to talk."

More conservative in appraising the film when it debuted in England in the spring of 1987, Tom Milne reported for the British *Monthly Film Bulletin*, " . . . clumsy over-emphasis (seemingly endemic to directors raised on TV) mars the film throughout, nowhere more so than in Steve Martin's frenzied over-pitched scenes as the sadistic dentist, where his performance is ruined and his encounter with the masochistic patient . . . reduced to a shambles by direction which mistakes excess for wit." Noting the relationship between this property and the shockingly-in-bad-taste cult favorite, *The Rocky Horror Picture Show* (both the play and film), Milne notes, "The connection is tenuous at the best of times since LITTLE SHOP OF HORRORS is singularly discreet in its blacker moments (Seymour's silhouette seen cutting up the off-screen body), and made even more so by the substitution of a happy ending after adverse preview reaction (originally, Seymour and Audrey were eaten by the triumphant mean green mother from outer space). But it does highlight another problem with the film: the anomaly whereby a big-budget musical, already somewhat incongruously aggrandized from Corman's deliciously apt cheapie conception, attempts to retain the original 60s setting in detail that is roundly denied by the music. A mess, therefore, but not unenjoyable in its Muppety way."

THE LOCH NESS HORROR (Omni-Leisure International, 1983) C 90 mins.

Executive producer, Jane Buchanan; producer/director,Larry

Buchanan; screenplay, Larry Buchanan, Lynn Shubert; music, Richard Theiss; art directors, Tom O'Brian, Jim Burkhart; camera, Robert Ebinger, Jr.; editor, Randy Buchanan.

Sandy Kenyon (Professor George); Mikie McKenzie (Kathleen); Barry Buchanan (Spencer Dean); Kort Falkenberg (Jack Stuart); Preston Hansen (Colonel), Stuart Lancaster (Pruitt); Eric Scott (Benji); Karey-Louis Scott (Fran); and: Don Livingston, Garth Pillsbury, Danny Glover.

In 1940 Scotsman Jack Stuart (Kort Falkenberg) takes a picture of the infamous Loch Ness monster near his estate. More than thirty years later American scientist Spencer Dean (Barry Buchanan) comes to Loch Ness to track the creature on slide scan sonar and he enlists the aid of the crusty Stuart, a local professor (Sandy Kenyon), and Stuart's pretty granddaughter Kathleen (Mikie McKenzie). A hunter (Stuart Lancaster) has two divers also searching for the creature and they retrieve its egg, although one of them is killed. A group of students also descend on Loch Ness to seek out the monster and one (Eric Scott) of them is killed by the creature. A shipwreck is found in the Loch and it turns out to be an old World War II Nazi ship and the story behind it implicates a local hero (Preston Hansen) who had been lax in his duty during an air raid. Eventually explosives set to destroy the airship also kill the creature in its lair, but Spencer and Kathleen save its egg and return it to Loch Ness to hatch.

THE LOCH NESS HORROR was produced, directed, and co-written by Larry Buchanan, the helmsman of such vapid sci-fi productions as THE EYE CREATURES (1965) (see B/V), CURSE OF THE SWAMP CREATURE (1966) (q.v.), and MARS NEEDS WOMEN (1966) (q.v.). While these films have a sleazy look about them, THE LOCH NESS HORROR, made on a $40,000 budget, has a professional production quality which belies its low budget origins. Except for the unconvincing title creature, seen only from the neck up, the movie is well photographed and competently churned out, although too talky.

The only "name" in the cast, at the time, was Eric Scott who played Ben on TV's "The Waltons" series.

LOCK YOUR DOORS see THE APE MAN.

LOOKER (Warner Bros., 1981) C 94 mins.

Producer, Howard Jeffrey; associate producer, John Lugar; director/screenplay, Michael Crichton; music, Barry DeVorzon; production designer, Dean Edward Mitzner; art director, Jack Taylor, Jr.; assistant directors, Scott Easton, John Kretchmer; costumes,

Betsy Cox; stunt co-ordinator, Fred Waugh; commercials writer/producer, Robert Chandler; special effects, Joe Day; camera, Paul Lohmann; editor, Carl Kress.

Albert Finney (Dr. Larry Roberts); James Coburn (John Reston); Susan Dey (Cindy); Leigh-Taylor Young (Jennifer Long); Dorian Harewood (Lieutenant Masters); Tim Rossovich (Moustache Man); Darryl Hickman (Dr. Jim Belfield); Kathryn Witt (Tina); Terri Welles (Lisa); Michael Gainsborough (Senator Harrison); Ashley Cox (Candy); Donna Benz (Ellen); Catherine Parks (Jan); Terry Kiser (Commercial Director); Georgann Johnson, Richard Venture (Cindy's Parents); Anthony Charnota (Masters' Assistant); Terrence McNally (Scanning Room Technician); David Adams (Guard); John Sanderford, Scott Mulhern (Policemen); Jeana Tomasino (Suzy); Barry Jenner (Commercial Producer); and: Arthur Taxier, Richard Milholland, Darrel Maury, Paul Jasmin, Eloise Hardt, Melissa Prophet, Lila Christianson, Lorna Christianson, Gary Combs, Kelly Black, Jerry Douglas, Randi Brooks, Jesse Logan, Joe Medalis, Estelle Omens, Steve Strong, Tawny Moyer, Dick Christie, Katherine DeHetre, Allison Balson, Adam Starr.

Reston Industries is controlled by millionaire John Reston

Albert Finney and Susan Dey in LOOKER (1981).

(James Coburn) who has invented the perfect television commercial which uses beautiful models and computer simulation techniques to give the viewer a subliminal message, selling products and politicians. When a famous Los Angeles plastic surgeon, Dr. Larry Roberts (Albert Finney) is suspected of murdering several of his attractive patients, he finds himself distrustful of the policeman (Dorian Harewood) handling the case and he and a model, Cindy (Susan Dey), work together to discover what has become of his patients and the girl's friends. They trace the dead models to a research institute operated by Jennifer Long (Leigh-Taylor Young) and find out it is a subsidiary of Reston Industries. Infiltrating Reston's operations, the team learn he is using the models for his commercials and then murdering them. Obtaining a light-pulse gun, which puts its target into a trance and makes its user invisible, Roberts hunts Reston, who has the same weapon. The two face-off in a climactic shootout.

The idea of subliminal advertising for political purposes was employed previously in AGENCY (1980) which did not have the advantage of a sci-fi plot or the use of *Playboy* magazine playmates who were not bashful about removing their clothes. *Variety* chided, "With numerous lapses in credibility, [director Michael] Crichton falls back upon motifs better used in his WESTWORLD [see B/V] picture: computer simulations (for robots), tv blurb soundstages (for film backlots) and assorted fancy chases . . . hardware is no substitute for solid storytelling, even in sci-fi."

Analyzing why this production was a box-office dud, Donald C. Willis in *Horror and Science Fiction Films III* (1984) decided, " . . . this movie is apparently not *supposed* to be a campy lark, and rest assured it isn't. In execution, it's a shambles of a mystery, with puzzle, clues, and solution equally silly and offputting."

THE LOST CITY (Regal 1935) twelve chapters.

Producer, Sherman S. Krellberg; director, Harry Revier; screenplay, Perley P. Sheehan, Eddie Graneman, Leon D'Usseau; electrical effects, Kenneth Strickfaden; camera, Roland Price, Eddie Linden; editor, Holbrook Todd.

Kane Richmond (Bruce Gordon); William "Stage" Boyd (Zolok); Claudia Dell (Natcha); Josef Swickard (Dr. Manyus); George F. [Gabby] Hayes (Butterfield); Eddie Fetherstone (Jerry); William Bletcher (Gorzo); Milburn Moranti (Andrews); Margot D'Use (Queen Rama); Jerry Frank (Appolyn); Ralph Lewis (Reynolds); William Millman (Colton); Gino Corrado (Ben Ali); Sam Baker (Hugo).

Chapters: 1) Living Dead Men; 2) Tunnel of Death; 3) Dagger Rock; 4) Doomed; 5) Tiger Prey; 6) Human Beasts; 7) Spider Men;

8) Human Targets; 9) Jungle Vengeance; 10) The Lion Pit; 11) Death Ray; 12) The Mad Scientist.

Electrical engineer Bruce Gordon (Kane Richmond) learns that a series of electrical storms originate from Magnetic Mountain in Central Africa and he leads an expedition there where he meets slave trader Butterfield (George F. Hayes). On the way to the mountain, Bruce falls through a trap door and descends into the Lost City which is controlled by madman Zolok (William "Stage" Boyd), the last of the Ligurian race. He plans to conquer the world with an army of black zombies created by Dr. Manyus (Josef Swickard) who has invented a machine which destroys the will and enlarges body size. Manyus works for Zolok because he fears for his daughter Natcha (Claudia Dell) whom the madman holds prisoner. Bruce's colleagues, Cotton (William Millman) and Reynolds (Ralph Lewis), are also bagged but escape and try to enlist Manyus's aid in creating their own zombie force. Zolok has his hunchback associate Gorzo (William Bletcher) and two giants bring them back. Butterfield hears of the giants and goes to the mountain to raise such an army to control Africa. Along the way he encounters Arab slave trader Ben Ali (Gino Corrado) who also wants the zombies for himself. Ben Ali betrays Butterfield and captures Gorzo and some of the zombies, but they flee. Bruce, Natcha and her father cross the dreaded Path of Skulls and enter the camp of the Spidermen, former pygmies whom the doctor has turned white with one of his formulas. Butterfield encounters slave trader Queen Rama (Margot D'Use) who also wants the professor and he sets out with her natives to capture him. Dr. Manyus later escapes and finds Butterfield and frees him and the latter agrees to help save the others. At the end, everyone is rescued and Zolok, now completely mad, returns to his laboratory in the deserted Lost City. He overloads the electrical equipment and blows up the city.

"Crude, old-fashioned and over-done, THE LOST CITY piles horror upon horror in a manner undreamed of since the days of Pearl White. Its twelve chapters contain enough plot elements and cliffhangers for three times as much film. Members of the large cast, under direction of old-timer Harry Revier, perform in a wild-eyed manner more suited to silent pictures or Italian opera than to a mid-'thirties movie, as one scene after another stretches credulity to the limit. This affront to culture, this paean to *kitsch,* is great entertainment; it keeps the spectator, mouth agape, wondering just what in hell can happen next. There is nary a dull stretch." (George E. Turner and Michael H. Price, *Forgotten Horrors,* 1981).

Kenneth Strickfaden provided the electrical effects for THE

LOST CITY and his expertise greatly buoyed the look of Zolok's futuristic laboratory.

In addition to its twelve chapter release, the film was also distributed in two feature versions; one running 108 minutes and another at 74 minutes. CITY OF LOST MEN is an alternate feature title for this serial. In 1980 a 60-minute version of the film was shown as the premier episode of the PBS-TV series "Matinee at the Bijou."

THE LOST CONTINENT (Lippert, 1951) 83 mins.*

Executive producer, Robert L. Lippert; producer, Sigmund Neufeld; director, Samuel Newfield; story, Carroll Young; screenplay, Richard H. Landau; art director, F. Paul Sylos; music, Paul Dunlap; special effects, Augie Lohman; camera, Jack Greenhalgh; editor, Phil Cahn.

Cesar Romero (Major Joe Nolan); Hillary Brooke (Maria Stevens); Chick Chandler (Lieutenant Danny Wilson); John Hoyt (Michael Rostov); Acquanetta (Native Girl); Sid Melton (Sergeant William Tatlow); Whit Bissell (Stanley Briggs); Hugh Beaumont (Robert Phillips); Murray Alper (M.P.); William Green (Simmons).

When an atomic-powered rocket crashes on an island in the South Pacific, Major Joe Nolan (Cesar Romero) must bid goodbye to his girlfriend Maria (Hillary Brooke) and lead an expedition to the crash site. With him on the flight are scientists Robert Phillips (Hugh Beaumont), Stanley Briggs (Whit Bissell), and Americanized Soviet Michael Rostov (John Hoyt), co-pilot Danny Wilson (Chick Chandler), and Sergeant Willie Tatlow (Sid Melton). Their plane develops engine trouble near the crash location and they make a forced landing. They meet an island girl (Acquanetta) who tells them the crash took place on a remote, high plateau, the home of her people's gods. The men climb the steep mountain and during the climb Briggs falls to his death despite Rostov's efforts to save him. On the plateau everything is lushly green and there is a high radioactivity level. The men are attacked by a dinosaur but manage to elude it and Phillips is almost killed by another giant lizard, but is saved by Rostov. Finally they spot the rocket's remains but cannot get to it because of two nearby dinosaurs. While creating a diversion so the scientist can retrieve a needed device out of the rocket, Willis is mortally wounded. As the remainder of the crew descend the mountain, a tremendous earthquake destroys the lost continent.

Even for its day, LOST CONTINENT was a minor league

*Green tinted sequence.

effort with minimal special effects and the amateurish use of green color tinting in the plateau sequences. Of course the film is remindful of Sir Arthur Conan Doyle's book *The Lost World* (filmed in 1925 and 1960; see B/V), but it is a very pale imitation. *Daily Variety* noted the film " . . . doesn't pack enough entertainment power to hold up in any extended playdates. . . ." Like most of its ilk, the film quickly became TV fare.

In 1968 Hammer Films made its THE LOST CONTINENT but it was NOT a remake of this feature, but a fantasy based on Dennis Wheatley's novel, *Uncharted Seas* (1938). It did contain giant crabs and jellyfish and the land of the title; complete with a race of lost Spanish Conquistadors.

LOST IN THE STRATOSPHERE (Monogram, 1935) 64 mins.

Producer, W. T. Lackey; director, Melville Brown; story, Tristram Tupper; screenplay, Albert DeMond; art director, R. R. Hickson; sound, Ralph Shugart; camera, Ira Morgan; editor, Carl Pierson.

William Cagney (Lieutenant Tom "Soapie" Cooper); June Collyer (Evelyn Worthington); Edward Nugent (Lieutenant Dick "Woody" Wood); Lona Andre (Sophie); Edmund Breese (Colonel Brooks); Frank McGlynn, Sr. (Colonel Worthington); Pauline Garon (Hilda); Matt McHugh (Matthew O'Toole); Hattie McDaniel (Ida Johnson); and: Russ Clark, Jack Mack, June Gittleson.

James Cagney's brother, William, took a stab at starring in minor league films such as this one before going into the production side of filmmaking. LOST IN THE STRATOSPHERE is, in fact, an extremely obscure 1930s sc-fier which saves its then futuristic aspects until the finale, padding the earlier sequences with too much friendly rivalry between Cagney and Eddie Nugent. Stock footage of a large balloon is interpolated into the finale flight scenes.

Roommates Tom Cooper (William Cagney) and Woody Woods (Edward Nugent) fly the mail for the Army and continuously steal each others' girls. Woody falls in love with socialite Evelyn Worthington (June Collyer) who, in turn, meets and becomes infatuated with Tom. Woody breaks off his friendship with Tom but their commander (Edmund Breese) gives them the assignment of going up in a big balloon to study stratospheric and electrical conditions at various altitudes, all for the War Department. The balloon is successfully launched and at 37,000 feet, they are ordered to descend. Instead they are caught in a storm and the gas valves stick, causing the craft to ascend. By radio they are told to parachute out and Evelyn, whose father (Frank McGlynn) developed the project, begs Woody to come down for Tom's sake. Woody orders Tom to bail out, promising to follow, but he stays with the craft. Tom sets down safely and soon learns the balloon has crashed in Canada. Tom and Evelyn fly to Woody who is hospitalized, and he gives them his blessing, saying he wants to return to the stratosphere.

LOST WOMEN see MESA OF LOST WOMEN.

LOST WOMEN OF ZARPA see MESA OF LOST WOMEN.

MAD DOCTOR OF BLOOD ISLAND see BRIDES OF BLOOD.

MAD LOVE (Metro-Goldwyn-Mayer, 1935) 85 mins.

Producer, John W. Considine, Jr.; director, Karl Freund; based on the novel *Les Mains d'Orlac* by Maurice Renard; adaptors, Guy Endore, Freund; screenplay, P. J. Wolfson, John L. Balderston; art director, Cedric Gibbons; music, Dimitri Tiomkin; camera, Chester Lyons, Gregg Toland; editor, Hugh Wynn.

Peter Lorre (Dr. Gogol); Colin Clive (Stephen Orlac); Frances Drake (Yvonne Orlac); Ted Healy (Reagan); Sarah Paden (Marie); Edward Brophy (Rollo); Henry Kolker (Prefect Rosset); Isabel Jewell (Marianne); May Beatty (Francoise); Keye Luke (Dr. Wong); and: Rollo Lloyd, Clarence H. Wilson, Sam Ash, Ian Wolfe, Sara Padden, Billy Gilbert, Charles Trowbridge, Frank Darien, Carl Stockdale, Robert Emmett Keane, Harold Huber, Hooper Atchley, Otto Hoffman.

See: THE HANDS OF ORLAC (essay).

MAD MAX (American International/Filmways, 1979) C 93 mins.

Producer, Byron Kennedy; associate producer, Bill Miller; director, George Miller; story, George Miller, Kennedy; screenplay, George Miller, James McCausland; music, Brian May; art director, Jon Dowding; costumes, Clare Griffin; makeup, Viv Mephan; stunt co-ordinator, Grant Page; sound, Gary Wilkens; special effects, Chris Murray; camera, David Eggby; editors, Tony Paterson, Cliff Hayes.

Mel Gibson (Mad Max); Joanne Samuel (Jessie); Hugh Keays-Byrne (The Toecutter); Steve Bisley (Jim Goose); Roger Ward (Fifi Macaffee); Vince Gil (Nightrider); Tim Burns (Johnny); Geoff Parry (Bubba Zanetti); Paul Johnstone (Cundalini); John Ley (Charlie); Jonathan Hardy (Labatoche); Sheila Florence (May Swaisey); John Farmdale (Grinner); Max Fairchild (Benno); Reg Evans (Station Master); Stephen Clark (Sarse); Howard Eynon (Diabando); Jerry Day (Ziggy); Peter Flemingham (Senior Doctor); Phil Motherwell (Junior Doctor); Mathew Constantine (Toddler); Nic Gazzana (Starbuck); Hunter Gibb (Liar); David Cameron (Underground Mechanic); Robina Chaffey (Singer); Bertrand Cadart (Clunk); David Breacks (Mudguts); Brendan Heath (Sprog); Steve Millcamp (Roop); Lulu Pinkus (Nightrider's Girl); George Novak (Scuttie); Nick Lathouris (Grease Rat); Lisa Aldenhoven (Nurse); Andrew Gilmore (Silvertongue); Neil Thompson (TV Newsreader); Gil Tucker (People's Overseer); Billy Tisdall (Midge); Kim Sullivan (Girl in Chevy).

MAD MAX II (ROAD WARRIOR) (Warner Bros., 1981) C 94 mins.

Producer, Byron Kennedy; director, George Miller; screenplay, Miller, Terry Hayes, Brian Hannant; assistant directors, Hannant, Patrick Clayton; art director, Graham Walker; costumes, Norma Moriceau; makeup, Bob McCarron; stunt co-ordinator, Max Aspin; music/music director, Brian May; special effects, Jeffrey Clifford Kim Priest; camera, Dean Semler; editors, David Stiven, Tim Wellburn, Michael Chirgwin.

Mel Gibson (Max); Bruce Spence (Gyro Captain); Vernon Wells (Wez); Emil Minty (Feral Kid); Mike Preston (Pappagallo); Kjell Nilsson (Humungus); Virginia Hey (Warrior Woman); Syd Heylen (Curmudgeon); Moria Claux (Big Rebecca); David Slingsby (Quiet Man); Arkie Whiteley (Lusty Girl); Steve J. Spears (Mechanic); Max Phipps (Toadie); William Zappa (Farmer); Jimmy Brown (Golden Youth); David Downer (Wounded Man); Tyler Coppin (Defiant Victim); Max Farchild (Broken Victim); Kristoffer Greaves (Mechanic's Assistant); Guy Norris (Mohawk Biker with Bearclaw); Tony Deary (Mohawk Biker); Anne Jones, James McCaedell (Tent Lovers); Kathleen McKay (Young Woman).

A.k.a. THE ROAD WARRIOR.

MAD MAX BEYOND THUNDERDOME (Warner Bros., 1985) C 108 mins.

Producer, George Miller; co-producers, Doug Mitchell, Terry Hayes; associate producers, Steve Amezdroz, Marcus D'Arcy; directors, George Miller, George Ogilvie; screenplay, Hayes, Miller; music, Maurice Jarre; visual design consultant, Ed Verreaux; costumes, Norma Moriceau; production designer, Graham Walker; assistant directors, Steve Andrews, Stuart Freeman, Chris Webb,Ian Kenny, Murray Robertson, Ian Freeman; sound, Roger Savage, Bruce Lamshed; special effects, Mike Wood, Steve Courtley, Brian Cox; camera, Dean Semler; editor, Richard Francis-Bruce.

Mel Gibson (Mad Max); Bruce Spence (Jedediah); Adam Cockburn (Jedediah, Jr.); Tina Turner (Aunty Entity); Frank Thring (The Collector); Angelo Rossitto (The Master); Paul Larsson (The Blaster); Angry Anderson (Ironbar); Robert Grubb (Pigkiller); George

Spartels (Blackfinger); Edwin Hodgeman (Dr. Dealgood); Bob Hornery (Waterseller); Andrew Oh (Ton Ton Tattoo); Helen Buday (Savannah Nix); Mark Spain (Mr. Skyfish); Mark Kounnas (Gekko); Rod Zuanic (Scrooloose); Justine Clarke (Anna Goanna); Shane Tickner (Eddie); Tom Allaylis (Cusha); James Wingrove (Tubba Tintye); Adam Scougall (Finn McCoo); Tom Jennings (Slake); Adam Willits (Mr. Scratch); and: Ollie Hall, Susan Leonard, Ray Turnbull, Lee Rice, Robert Simper, Brian Ellison, Gerard Armstrong, Max Worrall, Virginia Wark, Geeling, Gerry D'Angelo, Travis Latter, Miguel Lopez, Paul Daniel, Tushka Hose, Emily Shocker, Sandie Lillingston, Ben Chesterman, Liam Nikkinen, Dan Chesterman, Christopher Norton, Katherine Cullen, Heilan Robertson, Gabriel Dilworth, Hugh Sands, Rebekah Elmaloglou, Marion Sands, Shari Flood, Kate Tatar, Rachael Graham, Daniel Willis, Sally Morton, William Manning.

Along with his screen performance in GALLIPOLI (1981), Australian actor Mel Gibson became an international star in the title role of the MAD MAX sci-fi films. In this hugely popular trilogy he plays a vigilante out to get even with a post-war mad humanity which killed his wife and child. Along the way he helps a few sane survivors redevelop society. Like most productions focusing on a post-war near future, the MAD MAX films depict a barbarous post apocalyptic world engulfed in filth, fear and anarchy.

Policeman Max (Mel Gibson) leaves the force following the murder of his friend and becomes a vigilante when his wife and child are run down and murdered by a biker gang who terrorizes the countryside looking for scarce and precious gasoline. Mentally unbalanced by the experience—and overwhelmed by the endless violence about him—Max seeks retribution on the marauders responsible for the crime.

A mixture of George Orwell's *1984* and the DEATH WISH movie series, MAD MAX combines the revenge motive, with futuristic machines to produce a grim, actionful feature in which the hero " . . . has not really become one of *them*—he has become just another action-hero, a good man gone better. . . . This film is, at base, an intermittently successful mining of the kinetic excitement of moving cars and cycles." (Donald C. Willis, *Horror and Science Fiction Films III,* 1984). Genre fans will appreciate the scenes where Max jokingly pulls on a Tor Johnson mask (created by Don Post and incorrectly referred to as a Thor Johnson mask) and later nervously handles it in the hospital while waiting to hear the fate of his wife, already knowing his son is dead.

Although modestly budgeted, MAD MAX became Australia's biggest internationally grossing feature, resulting in a higher budget allotment for its sequel, MAD MAX 2, issued in the U.S. as THE ROAD WARRIOR. Taking up where the first film left off, this spirited outing has Max (Mel Gibson) surviving in the outback and coming across a communal group of normal citizens who prevail behind their fortress walls by refining crude oil into gasoline, which is sought by Humungus (Kjell Nilsson) and his band of cutthroats. Max saves the life of a kid (Emil Minty) after the gang gets him and he goes to the walled city and decides to aid its denizens in their war against Humungus. He plans to pit his might against the gang but is run off the road and spared by Gyro (Bruce Spence), a flier who returns him to the city. Max leads a convoy from the city into the desert for a two thousand mile trek to Paraside, on the Queensland Gold Coast. They meet head on with the gang and fight to the bloody finish.

"MAD MAX 2 is a stunning technical achievement which far surpasses the first MAX film in every department. It's also a surefire boxoffice winner—bigger, bolder, and infinitely more spectacular and powerful than the original," wrote *Variety.* In the U.S. alone the film grossed over $11,000,000.

The third and most elaborately staged series offering, MAD MAX BEYOND THUNDERDOME, opens with Max (Mel Gibson) wandering the desert and being robbed of his truck by flying road agent Jedediah (Bruce Spence) and his son (Adam Cockburn). He takes after the thief and reaches the desert comunity of Bartertown, where all and everything are for sale, and he is captured by the Collector (Frank Thring) who brings Max to his boss, ruler Aunty Entity (Tina Turner). She promises to return Max's possessions if he will aid her in battling the king of underground, the dwarf-giant The Master (Angelo Rossitto). The two meet in mortal combat in the Thunderdome and Max is nearly killed before he finds out the Master is sensitive to high-pitched sound. But when he finds out the dwarf under the helmet is child-like with scientific ability, he does not kill him. For his failure to eliminate The Master, Max is abandoned to die in the desert where he is found by Savannah (Helen Buday), one of a group of children left in the desert by a captain whom they believe will return and who now think Max is that man. The group set out into the desert to find paradise and Max follows, hoping to stop them and they arrive in Bartertown, where The Master is now Aunty Entity's prisoner. The band rescues The Master and they escape into the desert with Aunty and her men in pursuit. They meet Jedediah who agrees to assist them. Max, to give the others time to board the plane and escape, rams his vehicle into the oncoming guards and destroys them and is again stranded in the desert as the others fly off to Sydney.

Costing around $13,000,000, MAD MAX BEYOND THUNDERDOME again proved the popularity of the film series, grossing $36,230,219 in its first seven weeks at the U.S. box-office. It was not up to the second feature, however, as noted by *Variety.* "If THUNDERDOME's takings fall a little short of the second MAX saga, reason could be that in opting to expand on the characters and strive for more originality in the narrative, the production team has sacrificed some of the pace, tension and rip-roaring action which were at the heart of the genre's appeal." Richard Combs opined in the British *Monthly Film Bulletin,* "If ever there was a film that proved there is only a finite number of plots to be had, this is it; and although MAD MAX BEYOND THUNDERDOME is long on effects and set-pieces, it is short on the smaller incidents that make the difference in any story."

Analyzing the power of this series, Sally Hibbin observes in *Magill's Cinema Annual* (1986), "The credibility and success of the Mad Max films stem from their remarkably constructed mythology, which includes a completely fantastic world with its own internal logic and dynamics. The filmmakers realize this world both in their narrative and in their visuals, providing a coherent and compelling vision of a possible future. . . . Everything in the Mad Max world has a punk, makeshift feel to it. Everyday objects are there but used for completely different purposes. Costumes are made of chicken wire, dog muzzles, and other leftovers from the pre-Holocaust period. . . . Central to this mythology is the character of Max himself. In each of the three films, Max can be likened to classic heroes of fiction. In the first film, he is essentially an avenger in the traditional mold, . . . [I]t is evident that Max effectively has nowhere else to go. As a character, he has turned full circle—from idealism through despair and back again. Once hope has returned to the world, the nihilistic vision of the Mad Max films no longer has a reason to continue."

THE MAD MONSTER (Producers Releasing Corp, 1942) 77 mins.

Producer, Sigmund Neufeld; director, Sam Newfield; screenplay, Fred Myton; art director, Fred Preble; music, David Chudnow; special effects, Gene Stone; camera, Jack Greenhalgh; editor, Holbrook N. Todd.

Johnny Downs (Tom Gregory); George Zucco (Dr. Lorenzo Cameron); Anne Nagel (Lenora Cameron); Sarah Padden (Grandmother); Glenn Strange (Pedro); Gordon Demain (Professor Fitzgerald); Mae Busch (Susan); Reginald Barlow (Professor Warwick); Robert Strange (Professor Blaine); Henry Hall (Country Doctor); Edward Cassidy (Father); Eddie Holden (Harper); John Elliott

(Professor Hatfield); Charles "Slim" Whitaker (Policeman); Gil Patric (Lieutenant Detective).

"He created a beast—for vengeance! A monster comes to life behind the barred door of the crazed scientist's laboratory . . . and seeks human prey!—The year's most terrifying shocker!" read the advertising blurbs for this low-budget PRC outing which was made in five days by producer Sigmund Neufeld and his director brother, Sam Newfield. Donald F. Glut in *Classic Movie Monsters* (1978) judged it, " . . . a ludicrous effort. . . . [it] is so outrageously naive and unintentionally humorous that it is a delight to watch."

Loony scientist Dr. Lorenzo Cameron (George Zucco) has been experimenting with a formula he has developed from the blood of wolves. He needs a guinea pig and injects the formula into his dimwitted but likable handyman Pedro (Glenn Strange), turning him into a huge wolflike man with fangs. The doctor controls Pedro with a whip and keeps him caged, sending him out only to kill those who have ridiculed his theories. Cameron's daughter (Anne Nagel) and her beau (Johnny Downs) begin to suspect something and he

Glenn Strange in THE MAD MONSTER (1942).

turns on them, ordering Pedro to silence them. However, the monster instead murders him before being shot himself.

THE MAD MONSTER provided veteran actor (and also singer/songwriter) Glenn Strange with his first screen monster role, but hardly his last. He was to portray Frankenstein's famed creation three times oncamera, in HOUSE OF FRANKENSTEIN (1944), HOUSE OF DRACULA (1945), and ABBOTT AND COSTELLO MEET FRANKENSTEIN (1948) (qq.v.), as well as Atlas in MASTER MINDS (1949).

THE MADMEN OF MANDORAS (Crown International, 1963) 74 mins.

Producer, Carl Edwards; director, David Bradley; story, Steve Bennett; screenplay, Richard Miles, Bennett; art director, Frank Sylos; makeup, Maurice Seiderman; sound, Gordon Williams, Don Rogers; camera, Stanley Cortez; editor, Leon Selditz.

Walter Stocker (Phil Daly); Audrey Caire (Kathy Daly); Carlos Rivas (Carmine); John Holland (John Coleman); Dani Lynn (Suzanne Coleman); Marshall Reed (Frank Dvorak); Nestor Paiva (Police Chief Alaniz); Scott Peters (David Garrick); Pedro Regas (Padua); Keith Dahle (Tom Sharon); Bill Freed (Mr. H); and; Chuck Beston, Hap Holmwood, Dick McHale.

A noted American scientist, John Coleman (John Holland), disappears following a conference in which he discloses the existence of a deadly nerve gas. His whereabouts are unknown by his assistant (Marshall Reed) and his son-in-law Phil Daly (Walter Stocker) but they learn that the scientist's daughter Suzanne (Dani Lynn) has also disappeared. Phil and his wife Kathy (Audrey Caire) are told by a mysterious stranger that Coleman and Suzanne are in danger but the man is shot. They find an address for a hotel on the Caribbean island of Mandoras and there discover the population living in fear. The police chief (Nestor Paiva) takes them to the hotel where they are held prisoners. A young man, Carmine (Carlos Rivas), advises them the island is under the control of a Nazi group who have developed Nerve Gas G and are out to destroy Coleman's antidote for the deadly weapon. Later Kathy is kidnapped as is the president of the island and Phil finds them as captives in a bunker beneath the presidential palace. There Adolf Hitler's brain is being kept alive and he is behind the plot to take over the world with the new deadly gas. Phil helps the captors to escape as the Nazis meet on the beach to distribute the gas to various parts of the world. The police arrive and in the fight a hand grenade destroys the car carrying Hitler's head. The mad scheme is over.

Allegedly pieced together from footage filmed at various times in different locales, MADMEN OF MANDORAS (shown on TV as THEY SAVED HITLER'S BRAIN) is as dreadful as it sounds. Its only redeeming factors are Stanley Cortez' fine cinematography for some of the footage and the wax model of Hitler's head, which allegedly cost $3,000 to make, but was melted down for the fiery climax. The feature has taken on a cult status on TV due to its gross ineptness and is often screened as part of "worst film" series. John McCarthy summed it up in *Video Screams* (1983), "Bad, bad, bad. But funny."

THE MAGICIAN (Metro-Goldwyn-Mayer, 1926) 71 mins.

Director, Rex Ingram; based on the novel by W. Somerset Maugham; adaptor, Ingram; camera, John F. Seitz; editor, Grant Whytock.

Alice Terry (Margaret Dauncey); Paul Wegener (Oliver Haddo); Ivan Petrovich (Dr. Arthur Burdon); Firmin Gemier (Dr. Porhoet); Gladys Hamer (Susie Boud).

Master magician Oliver Haddo (Paul Wegener) is a student of the occult and after long years of search finds a formula for the creation of life in an old volume in a Paris library. Meanwhile beautiful Margaret Dauncey (Alice Terry), the niece of noted Dr. Porhoet (Firmin Gemier) is injured while modeling for a sculpture, and famous American scientist Dr. Arthur Burdon (Ivan Petrovich) performs a delicate operation on her spine. Haddo is one of those who witnesses the surgery. While she recovers Margaret and Burdon fall in love but Haddo places her under his hypnotic spell and takes her to Monte Carlo with Burdon in pursuit. In the Sorcerer's Tower, Haddo plans to use her virgin blood in his secret formula but Burdon and Dr. Porhoet stop him and Haddo tumbles in a furnace and dies. Margaret is freed of his evil spell.

Adapted from W. Somerset Maugham's 1908 novel, THE MAGICIAN was filmed in France by director Rex Ingram with his wife Alice Terry starring and the famous German actor, Paul Weneger (who gained fame as THE GOLEM, q.v.) as the villain. Despite its grotesque trappings, the movie was NOT overly popular as reflected by *Photoplay* magazine, "Rex Ingram messes around with some more weird characters and with some weirder emotions." Carlos Clarens reported in *An Illustrated History of the Horror Film* (1967), "The high point of the film was a nightmarish sequence in which the hypnotized heroine (Alice Terry) sees herself in the midst of an orgiastic rite presided over by Pan himself, a prancing, naked satyr played by Stowitts, the American dancer at the Follies Bergere." William K. Everson noted in *Classics of the Horror Film* (1974), "Although both author Somerset Maugham and prestige director

Rex Ingram might resent the honor, THE MAGICIAN is one of the few authentic silent examples of the 'Mad Doctor' genre of horror thrillers."

THE MAGICIAN, thought lost to the ages, was rediscovered in the early 1970s.

LES MAINS D'ORLAC see THE HANDS OF ORLAC (essay).

MAN BEAST (Favorite Films, 1955) 67 mins.

Producer, Jerry Warren; associate producer, Ralph Brooke; director, Warren; screenplay, Arthur Cassidy; second unit director, Brooke; music director, Josef Zimanich; art director, Ralph Tweer; camera, Victor Fisher; editor, James R. Sweeney.

Rock Madison (Lon Raynon/The Yeti); Virginia Maynor (Connie Hayward); Tom Maruzzi (Steve Cameron); Lloyd Nelson (Trevor Hudson); George Wells Lewis (Dr. Erickson); George Skaff (Varga); Jack Haffner (Kheon); Wong Sing (Trader).

MAN BEAST beat THE ABOMINABLE SNOWMAN (1957) (q.v.) into theatres by one year, but it was preceded by THE SNOW CREATURE (q.v.) issued two years before. All three features deal with the Abominable Snowman, or Yeti, of the Himalayas. This outing, however, is definitely the most minor of the trio and its only notoriety is that it was the debut production of Jerry Warren, best remembered for carving up Mexican horror films and adding footage of Hollywood players to bolster box-office appeal in the United States. MAN BEAST contains less stock footage than most of Warren's releases; the stock stuff mainly comprising mountain climbing footage which Warren purchased from the Allied Artists film library. The on-location shooting was done at a ski resort around Bishop, California, and the Yeti suit was reworked from the one used in WHITE PONGO (1945) (q.v.). While *Variety* weighed the feature as "just fair entertainment-wise", the movie did have the advantage of being distributed in some locales on a double bill with the hugely popular GODZILLA (see B/V).

When her brother disappears in the Himalayas looking for the Yeti, or Abominable Snowman, Connie Hayward (Virginia Maynor) and Trevor Hudson (Lloyd Nelson) put together an expedition to find him. Their guide Steve Cameron (Tom Maruzzi) takes them to the camp of Dr. Erickson (George Wells Lewis) who believes the Yeti may be a missing link between mankind and sub-humans. When they reach her brother's site, it is deserted except for his guide Varga (George Skaff). When the group is attacked by the Yeti, Vargo tells them he is descended from their race and that the Yeti kidnap women to breed with them to improve their stock. Varga, however, is in cahoots with the Snowmen and through his actions all are killed save for Connie and Steve, who have fallen in love. Varga falls to his death trying to kill the pair and Connie and Steve escape.

For the record, top-billed Rock Madison, who only has a small part in the film, also plays the Yeti.

THE MAN IN HALF MOON STREET (Paramount, 1944) 92 mins.

Producer, Walter MacEwen; director, Ralph M. Murphy; based on the play by Barre Lyndon; adaptor, Garrett Fort; screenplay, Charles Kenyon; art directors, Hans Dreier, Walter Tyler; music, Miklos Rozsa; makeup, Wally Westmore; camera, Henry Sharp; editor, Tom Neff.

Nils Asther (Julian Karell); Helen Walker (Eve Brandon); Reinhold Schunzel (Dr. Kurt Van Bruecken); Paul Cavanagh (Dr. Henry Latimer); Edmond Breon (Sir Humphrey Brandon); Marion Lowry (Allen Guthrie); Matthew Boulton (Inspector Garth); Brandon Hurst (Simpson—Julian's Butler); Aminta Dyna (Lady Minerva Aldergate); Arthur Mulliner (Sir John Aldergate); Edward Fielding (Colonel Ashley); Reginald Sheffield (Mr. Taper the Art Critic); Eustace Wyatt (Inspector Lawson); Forrester Harvey (Harris the Cabby); Konstantin Shayne (Dr. Vishanoff).

Barre Lyndon's play "The Man in Half-Moon Street" (1939) was the basis for two feature films; one made by Paramount in 1944 and the other, THE MAN WHO COULD CHEAT DEATH, a color remake by Hammer Films (with U.S. release by Paramount) in 1959. Both productions follow the same plotline, with some variances. Overall both are engaging thrillers concerning the use of gland transplants to gain immortality.

In the 1944 edition, Julian Karell (Nils Asther) is a scientist who appears to be in his mid-30s and he romances beautiful Eve Brandon (Helen Walker) who is unaware of his terrible secret. Julian is actually 104 years old and retains his youth via gland transplants. When he fails to obtain the needed glands—even by murder—he quickly deteriorates into old age and literally dies by falling apart.

In the 1959 version, Dr. Georges Bonner (Anton Diffring) is a sculptor loved by model Margo Philippe (Delphi Lawrence), but he is attracted to Janine Dubois (Hazel Court), the fiancee of Dr. Pierre Gerrard (Christopher Lee). Gerard does not like Bonner and is jealous of him. Elderly Dr. Ludwig Weiss (Arnold Marie) arrives to operate on Bonner since this is the only way he can remain youthful as he is really over 100 years old. Weisz, however, is too elderly for the gland transplant and convinces Gerard, who greatly respects him, to perform the surgery. When he finds out that Bonner has

Nils Asther and Helen Walker in THE MAN IN HALF MOON STREET (1944).

murdered for the glands for the operation and that he plans to make Janine immortal too, Gerard refuses to cooperate. Weisz presses him to do it and he does. Janine finds a terribly scarred Margo and realizes what Bonner has done to her. She rejects Bonner's advances and he suddenly turns old and realizes Gerrard has double-crossed him. In revenge he plans to kill Janine but Margo sets him on fire and the two die in the flames, as Gerrard rescues Janine.

Gerald D. MacDonald wrote of the remake in *Library Journal* (July, 1959), "Few horror films have been presented with such Technicolored elegance and high production values. Not all of the elements of the plot are completely explained when the film comes to an end. But during the time it is unfolded it induces 'a willing suspension of disbelief.'"

THE MAN IN THE WHITE SUIT (GFD, 1951) 97 mins.

Producer, Michael Balcon; director, Alexander Mackendrick; based on the play by Roger MacDougall; screenplay, MacDougall, John Dighton, Mackendrick; music, Benjamin Frankel; camera, Douglas Slocombe; editor, Bernard Gribble.

Alec Guinness (Sidney Stratton); Joan Greenwood (Daphne Birnley); Cecil Parker (Alan Birnley); Michael Gough (Michael Corland); Ernest Thesiger (Sir John Kierlaw); Howard Marion Crawford (Granford); Henry Mollison (Hoskins); Vida Hope (Bertha); Patric Doonan (Frank); Duncan Lamont (Harry); Harold Goodwin (Wilkins); Colin Gordon (Bill); Joan Harben (Miss Johnson); Arthur Howard (Roberts); Rody Hughes (Green); Stuart Latham (Harrison); Miles Malleson (The Tailor); Mandy Miller (Gladdie); Brian Worth (King); Billy Russell (Watchman).

Long considered a classic of British screen comedy, THE MAN IN THE WHITE SUIT is an adroit social satire with its plotline firmly embedded in the science fiction motif. In *British Sound Films* (1984), David Quinlan judged it "[A] gloriously inventive social comedy." Interestingly this thoroughly British feature was directed by American Alexander Mackendrick.

Humble chemist Sidney Stratton (Alec Guinness) hopes to produce a fabric that will NEVER become dirty or wear out. He is fired from one job because of his experiments and his girlfriend Daphne Birnley (Joan Greenwood) persuades her manufacturer father (Cecil Parker) to give him a position. He continues his testing

Alec Guinness in THE MAN IN THE WHITE SUIT (1951).

and creates a white suit of indestructible artificial cloth. The result is great exhilaration as the fabric will provide clothing for all and will NEVER have to be replaced. Factory workers, however, realize they will soon lose their jobs, and grasping businessmen, led by Sir John Kierlaw (Ernest Thesiger), want to keep the formula under wraps to prevent the collapse of their financial empires. Sidney, however, believing that what he wants to do is best for mankind, persists and Daphne deserts him. With a mob after him, Sidney tries to hide but cannot do so and when finally cornered the suit simply falls apart as it is torn from him. Now the danger is over for the workers and the bosses and Sidney realizes the flaw in his formula and he sets out out to perfect it.

John Baxter wrote in *Science Fiction in the Cinema* (1970), "As science fiction, THE MAN IN THE WHITE SUIT has more claim to eminence than most other films concerning technological marvels . . . the excellent script, mainly by director Alexander Mackendrick, marshals a wide variety of situations to attack the less logical features of British life . . . its universality of subject and expression qualify it as the best type of science fiction."

THE MAN OF STONE see THE GOLEM (essay).

THE MAN THEY COULD NOT HANG (Columbia, 1939) 72 mins.

Executive producer, Irving Briskin; producer, Wallace Macdonald; director, Nick Grinde; story, Leslie T. White, George W. Sayre; screenplay, Karl Brown; music director, Morris W. Stoloff; camera, Benjamin Kline; editor, William Lyon.

Boris Karloff (Dr. Henryk Savaard); Lorna Gray [Adrian Booth] (Janet Savaard); Robert Wilcox (Scoop Foley); Roger Pryor (District Attorney Drake); Don Beddoe (Lieutenant Shane); Ann Doran (Betty Crawford); Joseph de Stephani (Dr. Stoddard); Charles Trowbridge (Judge Bowman); Byron Foulger (Lang); Dick Curtis (Kearney); James Craig (Watkins); John Tyrrell (Sutton).

Scientist Dr. Henryk Savaard (Boris Karloff) devises a mechanical heart to revive the dead and to test it he kills a volunteer student. His assistant Betty Crawford (Ann Doran) turns him over to the law. They refuse to believe his claims and he is arrested and tried and convicted of murder and hanged. Another assistant, Lang (Byron Foulger), takes his body and brings him back to life with his invention. Wanting revenge, Savaard sets out to kill those responsible for his conviction. He murders six of the jurors and brings the rest to his home which he has rigged with traps. Several of them die but the doctor's daughter Janet (Lorna Gray) tries to stop him. She ends up being accidentally electrocuted. As he restores her to life, the police arrive and kill Savaard. Janet destroys his machine.

THE MAN THEY COULD NOT HANG was the first of five sci-fi-horror films Boris Karloff headlined for Columbia between 1939 and 1942, followed by: THE MAN WITH NINE LIVES (1940), BEFORE I HANG (1940) (q.v.), THE DEVIL COMMANDS (1941) (q.v.), and THE BOOGIE MAN WILL GET YOU (1942). *Variety* printed, "Plot is inconsistent with the deep interest of Karloff in promoting life by his discovery to deliberately turn murderer in the end. The unexpected and implausible revenge doesn't jell . . ."

This film was purportedly inspired by actual experiments conducted by Dr. Robert Cornish who restored life to dead dogs.

THE MAN WHO COULD CHEAT DEATH (Paramount, 1959) C 83 mins.

Executive producer, Anthony Hinds; producer, Michael Carreras; director, Terence Fisher; based on the play *The Man in Half Moon Street* by Barre Lyndon; screenplay, Jimmy Sangster; production designer, Bernard Robinson; makeup, Roy Ashton; music, Richard Bennett; camera, Jack Asher; editor, James Needs.

Anton Diffring (Dr. Georges Bonnet); Hazel Court (Janine Dubois); Christopher Lee (Dr. Pierre Gerrard); Arnold Marle (Dr. Ludwig Weiss); Delphi Lawrence (Margo Philippe); Francis de Wolff (Inspector Legris); Gerda Larsen (Street Girl).

See: THE MAN IN HALF MOON STREET.

THE MAN WHO SAW TOMORROW (Warner Bros., 1981) C 85 mins.

Executive producer, David L. Wolper; producers, Robert Guenette, Lee Kramer, Paul Drame; director, Guenette; screenplay, Guenette, Alan Hopgood; art director, Mike Minor; set decorator, Carole Cole, Robert Perkins; costumes, Pat Tonnema, Clair Griffin; music, William Loose, Jack Tillar; sound, Gary Cunningham, Kenneth Isley; camera, Tom Ackerman, Erik Daarstad, David Haskins; editors, Peter Wood, Scott McLennan.

Orson Welles (Narrator); Voice of Philip L. Clarke.

The prophecies of Michel de Nostradamus have long enthralled readers and today, more than four hundred years after he lived, there are scores of books available about the seer and his predictions. This Warner Bros. documentary takes a look at the life and works of the prophet, with serious narration by Orson Welles augmented by all kinds of film, ranging from the Zapruder footage of John F. Kennedy's assassination to a clip from WHEN WORLDS COLLIDE (1951) (see B/V) to depict the end of the world.

The major interest herein lies in the supposed correct predictions made by Nostradamus concerning the past (his proponents claim he was ninety percent accurate); such as the French Revolution, the rise and fall of Napoleon Bonaparte, the Civil War, Hitler and World War II, the killings of John and Robert Kennedy and the Ayatollah Khomeini coup in Iran. Even more provocative are the seer's claims for the future, including a terrible earthquake in the spring of 1988, an atomic holocaust in New York City in 1999, a long war, and a thousand years of peace before the world comes to an end in 3797.

"Visually TOMORROW is a hodge-podge of clips from old feature films, newsreels, talking-head interviews, nature footage, and hokey dramatized 'scenes' without audible dialog. And special effects." (*Variety*)

THE MAN WITH THE SYNTHETIC BRAIN see BLOOD OF GHASTLY HORROR.

MANHUNT OF MYSTERY ISLAND (Republic, 1945) fifteen chapters.

Associate producer, Ronald Davidson; directors, Spencer Bennet, Wallace A. Grissell, Yakima Canutt; screenplay, Albert DeMond, Basil Dickey, Jesse Duffy, Alan James, Grant Nelson, Joseph Poland; music, Richard Cherwin; special effects, Howard Lydecker, Theodore Lydecker; camera, Bud Thackery; editors, Cliff Bell, Harold R. Minter.

Richard Bailey (Lance Reardon); Linda Stirling (Claire Forrest); Roy Barcroft (Mephisto); Kenne Duncan (Brand); Forrest Taylor (Professor Forrest); Forbes Murray (Hargraves); Jack Ingram (Armstrong); Harry Strang (Braley); Edward Cassidy (Melton); Frank Alten (Raymond); Lane Chandler (Reed); Russ Vincent (Ruga); Dale Van Sickel (Barker); Tom Steele (Lyons); Duke Green (Harvey).

Chapters: 1) Secret Weapon; 2) Satan's Web; 3) The Murder Machine; 4) The Lethal Chamber; 5) Mephisto's Mantrap; 6) Ocean Tomb; 7) The Death Drop; 8) Bombs Away; 9) The Fatal Flood; 10) The Sable Shroud; 11) Satan's Shadow; 12) Cauldron of Cremation; 13) Bridge to Eternity; 14) Power Dive to Doom; 15) Fatal Transformation.

Professor Forrest (Forrest Taylor) has invented a radi-atomic power transmitter to supply power to various parts of the world to aid in traffic control and he needs radium for its use. He disappears while searching for radium fields and his daughter Claire (Linda

Stirling) and detective Lance Reardon (Richard Bailey) learn he is being held prisoner on remote Mystery Island in the Pacific Ocean. Claire and Lance arrive and think her father's captor is one of the four men who own the isle: Hargraves (Forbes Murray), Armstrong (Jack Ingram), Melton (Edward Cassidy) or Braley (Harry Strang), all descendants of Captain Mephisto who ruled the small dominion two hundred years before. They also discover that one of the quartet has invented a transformation chair which permits him to become the actual Mephisto (Ray Barcroft) by changing his molecular blood structure. Mephisto and henchman Brand (Kenne Duncan) track Claire and Lance at all times and attempt to do them in. Along the way Melton and Armstrong are killed. Finally Claire and Lance set a trap by leaving Hargraves and Braley alone in Mephisto's mansion. Mephisto however, captures Lance and plans to put him in the transformation chair, turn him into Mephisto and leave him for the police. Claire, though, arrives and kills Mephisto who reverts back to his original self, as one of the owners. Claire and Lance leave with the rescued Professor Forrest.

With the futuristic radi-atomic power transmitter, the transformation chair, and a radium detector, MANHUNT OF MYSTERY ISLAND is laced with sci-fi apparatus. It is full of cliffhanger finales such as a cave tunnel flood and a collapsing suspension bridge. But the serial has one drawback, as noted by Jim Harmon and Donald F. Glut in *The Great Movie Serials* (1972), "The scenes in which Captain Mephisto changed into the shadowed personage of whomever it was that wanted the other three out of the way—and the reverse scenes—became monotonous when used at least once per chapter. Stretched over a length of fifteen episodes, the overuse of those particular shots exceeded the boring to approach the unbearable. But the direction of three capable men—Spencer Bennett, Wallace A. Grissell, and ex-stuntman Yakima Canutt—made up for it in action."

In 1966, a 100-minute feature version was issued to TV culled from the serial and titled CAPTAIN MEPHISTO AND THE TRANSFORMATION MACHINE.

MARS NEEDS WOMEN (Azalea/American International TV, 1966) C 80 mins.

Producer, Larry Buchanan; associate producer, Edwin Tobolowsky; director/screenplay, Buchanan; makeup, Annabelle Wienick; camera, Robert C. Jessup; editor, Buchanan.

Tommy Kirk (DOP); Yvonne Craig (Marjorie); Byron Lord (Page); Anthony Houston, Warren Hammack, Cal Duggan, Larry Tanner (Martians); and: Bill Thurman, Pat Delaney, Donna Lindberg,

Sherry Roberts, Bubbles Cash, Roger Ready, Neil Fletcher, George Edgley, Dick Simpson, Barnett Shaw, Chet Davis, Ron Scott, Don Campbell, Gordon Buloe, Claude Earls, Bob Lorenz, David Englund, Ann Palmer, Pat Cranshaw, Sally Casey, Sylvia Rundell, Terry Davis.

A message from space reaches the Earth and it reads "Mars Needs Women." Martian DOP (Tommy Kirk) arrives on Earth with the mission of returning with five females required for genetic experiments. He tells Earthlings their planet will be destroyed unless the women return with him to help repopulate that dying planet. Scientist Marjorie (Yvonne Craig), also a go-go dancer, agrees to help and the problem of repopulating Mars is solved.

MARS NEEDS WOMEN, a loose remake of PAJAMA PARTY (1964), was hatched by producer/director Larry Buchanan for his Dallas, Texas-based Azalea Pictures which churned out TV movies for American International on miniscule budgets. This effort includes liberal doses of stock footage, something NOT common with Azalea productions, plus a tacked-on soundtrack, a common Azalea practice. The result is one of the very worst of the series Buchanan created for AIP.

Brief sequences from this movie appear in Paramount's bad film tribute, IT CAME FROM HOLLYWOOD (1982), making it the only feature included in this compilation which did not have theatrical release.

THE MASK OF FU MANCHU (Metro-Goldwyn-Mayer, 1932) 72 mins.

Producer, (uncredited) Irving Thalberg; directors, Charles Brabin, King Vidor; based on the novel by Sax Rohmer; adaptor, Rohmer; screenplay, Irene Kuhn, Edgar Allan Woolf, John Willard; art director, Cedric Gibbons; costumes, Adrian; special effects, Kenneth Strickfaden; camera, Gaetano (Tony) Gaudio, Ben Lewis; editor, Ben Lewis.

Boris Karloff (Dr. Fu Manchu); Lewis Stone (Nayland Smith); Karen Morley (Sheila Barton); Myrna Loy (Fah Lo See); Jean Hersholt (Professor Von Berg); Lawrence Grant (Sir Lionel Barton); David Torrence (McLeod); Charles Starrett (Terrence Granville); and: Herbert Bunton, Gertrude Michael, Ferdinand Gottschalk, C. Montague Shaw, Willie Fung.

Evil Oriental ruler Dr. Fu Manchu (Boris Karloff) hates the white race and plans to exterminate it with the mask and sword of Genghis Khan as his rallying point. An expedition to the Gobi Desert, financed by the British Musuem, hopes to locate these ceremonial relics and keep them from the tyrant. Scotland Yard

Myrna Loy, Charles Starrett and Boris Karloff in THE MASK OF FU MANCHU (1932).

Inspector Nayland Smith (Lewis Stone) accompanies the expedition which includes Professor Von Berg (Jean Hersholt), Sir Lionel Barton (Lawrence Grant), and his daughter (Karen Morley) and her boyfriend, Terrence Granville (Charles Starrett). Fu Manchu and his minions torment the members of the expedition and when the mask and sword are discovered by them, he kidnaps the party and takes them to his palace. All are sentenced to die by torture and in the crocodile pit except Terry who is to be used as a love slave by Fu Manchu's beautiful, but mentally twisted daughter, Fah Lo See (Myrna Loy). Just as Fu Manchu is gathering his minions to set out to destroy all whites, Smith and Von Berg escape their bonds and they turn the madman's death ray on him. As he dies, his people disperse. It is decided to bury the mask and sword of Genghis Khan at the bottom of the sea.

Based on Sax Rohmer's popular novels about Fu Manchu and the Yellow Peril, this big budget, glossy MGM production was "A blood-and-thunder thriller of nightmare dimensions." (*Film Weekly*) The film provided Boris Karloff with a meaty role as the wicked villain and the plot employs an underplayed ambiance of perverted sex (especially concerning the alluring daughter) and miscegenation. The film also features an intriguing combination of ancient powers (the mask and sword) and futuristic apparatus in Manchu's laboratory, especially his death ray. Dennis Gifford notes in his book, *Karloff, The Man, The Monster, The Movies* (1973), " . . . the unpleasant parade of ingenious torture devices, which both he [Karloff]) and Myrna Loy, as his sexy daughter, relish, must have sat uneasily upon the conscience of self-styled family entertainer Louis B. Mayer."

MASK OF THE GOLEM see THE GOLEM (essay).

MASTERS OF THE UNIVERSE (Cannon, 1987) C 106 mins.

Executive producer, Edward R. Pressman; producers, Menahem Golan, Yoram Globus; co-producer, Elliot Schick; director, Gary Goddard; screenplay, David Odell; music, Bill Conti; production designer, production designer co-ordinator, Rachel Rosenthal; William Stout; art director, Robert Howland; set designers, Daniel Gluck, Michael Johnson; set decorator, Kathe Kloppe; costume designer, Julie Weiss; makeup, Todd McIntosh; stunt co-ordinator, Walter Scott; stunt choreography, Loren Janes; supervising sound editors, John Larson, Robert A. Rutledge; special effects, Richard Edlund; camera, Hanania Baer; editor, Anne V. Coates.

Dolph Lundgren (He-Man); Frank Langella (Skeletor); Meg Foster (Evil-Lyn); Billy Barty (Gwildor); Courteney Cox (Julie Winston) James Tolkan (Detective Lubic); Christina Pickles (Sorceress of Castle Greyskull)); Robert Duncan McNeil (Kevin); John Cypher (Man-At-Arms); Chelsea Field (Teela); Tony Carroll (Beastman); Pons Maar (Saurod); Anthony DeLongis (Blade); Robert Towers (Karg); Barry Livingston (Charlie); Jessica Nelson (Monica); Gwynne Gilford (Mrs. Winston); Walter Scott (Mr. Winston); Walt P. Robles (Carl the Janitor); Cindy Eyman (Gloria).

On the planet Eternia, The Sorceress of Castle Greyskull (Christina Pickles), whose powers come from the planet's moons and who uses this power to control the forces of light which work for good, is kidnapped by the evil Skeletor (Frank Langella), who wants to absorb her powers to control the universe. The sorceress' protector, the superhuman He-Man (Dolph Lundgren), vows to free her from the energy field in which she has been imprisoned. A cosmic key is needed to save the Sorceress but when He-Man and allies Man-At-Arms (Jon Cypher) and Teela (Chelsea Field) are accidentally sent to Earth, the key is lost, and found by Julie (Courteney Cox) and her boyfriend (Robert Duncan McNeil). Both He-Man and Skeletor, and the latter's underlings, try to retrieve the cosmic key. At Skeletor's castle, the final showdown occurs.

MASTERS OF THE UNIVERSE is a live-action feature based on the popular television cartoon program, "He-Man," which in turn has its origins in the seemingly endless series of Mattel toys (which also includes He-Man's sister, She-Ra—see THE SECRET OF THE SWORD, 1985, q.v.). Regarding MASTERS OF THE UNIVERSE, *Variety* reported, "All elements are of epic proportions in this Conan-Star War hybrid ripoff. . . . the result is a colossal bore. But the tedium will be lost on 5-9 year old 'Masters' fans, who will flock to see this pic anyway."

The film grossed $17,024,393 in its first seven weeks at the U.S. box-office.

THE MAZE (Allied Artists, 1953) 80 mins.

Executive producer, Walter Mirisch; producer, Richard Heermance; director, William Cameron Menzies; based on the novel by Maurice Sandoz; screenplay, Dan Ullman; production designer, Menzies; music, Marlin Skiles; camera, Harry Neumann; editor, John Fuller.

Richard Carlson (Gerald McTeam); Veronica Hurst (Kitty Murray); Katherine Emery (Mrs. Murray); Michael Pate (William); John Dodsworth (Dr. Bert Dilling); Hillary Brooke (Peggy Lord); Stanley Fraser (Robert); Lillian Bond (Mrs. Dilling); Gwen McGiveney (Simon); Robin Hughes (Richard Roblar).

Scotsman Gerald McTeam (Richard Carlson) is engaged to beautiful Kitty Murray (Veronica Hurst), but he is called to his ancestral castle home following the death of his uncle, thus postponing his wedding. When he does not return, Kitty and her aunt, Mrs. Murray (Katherine Emery), go to the castle but find they are not welcome. Since Gerald looks much older and very worried they insist on staying but find they are locked in their room at night. The servants, William (Michael Pate) and Roger (Stanley Fraser), are not friendly and at night Kitty and her aunt witness mysterious lights and movements in the maze surrounding the castle. One night Mrs. Murray finds a remote room strangely arranged with low bookshelves and no furniture, and something large scampers from the room, causing her to faint. Later that night Kitty and her aunt manage to leave their room to investigate the activities in the maze and Mrs. Murray again sees the creature which goes upstairs and leaps from a window, falling to its death on the pavement below. Gerald confesses that the creature was his uncle, Sir Philip McTeam, who had lived for two hundred years with the mind of a human but the body of a frog because he did not develop beyond the amphibian stage as an embryo. With the secret and the matter concluded, Gerald and Kitty are free to marry.

Originally issued in 3-D, THE MAZE is an engrossing minor sci-fi film, relying more on pathos than thrills. The "monster" is a genetic freak and one which brings forth audience empathy, not repulsion.

MESA OF LOST WOMEN (Howco, 1953) 70 mins.

Producers, G. William Perkins, Melvin Gale; directors, Herbert Tevos, Ron Ormond; screenplay, Tevos; music, Hoyt Curtin; camera, Earl Struss, Gilbert Warrenton; editors, Hugh Winn, Ray Lockert.

Jackie Coogan (Dr. Arana); Richard Travis (Dan Mulcahey); Allan Nixon (Doc Tucker); Lyle Talbot (Narrator); Mary Hill (Doreen); Robert Knapp (Grant Phillips); Tandra Quinn (Tarantella); Harmon Stevens (Masterson); Samuel Wu (Wu); George Barrows (George); and: Chris-Pin Martin, John Martin, Angelo Rossitto, Fred Kelsey, Katherine Victor.

Lunatic scientist Dr. Arana (Jackie Coogan) works in Mexico's remote Zarpa Mesa experimenting on a growth hormone from insects which he has injected into humans, creating dwarfs and spider women. When he decides to create a super race with women having the ferocity of spiders, his associate Masterson (Harmon Stevens) refuses to help and Arana drives him mad and tosses him into the desert. Masterson ends up in an asylum and later escapes. He makes pilot Don Mulcahey (Richard Travis) and Doreen (Mary Hill) fly him back to Zarpa Mesa. There they are attacked by the dwarfs and spider women and are captured and taken to Arana. Masterson concocts a bomb, orders Doc and Doreen to leave, and then explodes the device, killing all the inhabitants, save for one spider woman who escapes.

Filmed in 1952, this mini production had theatrical release dates from that year through 1956 and was also entitled LOST WOMEN and LOST WOMEN OF ZARPA. The British *Monthly Film Bulletin* noted, "The attempts at horror are more ludicrous than thrilling." This movie is considered one of the worst sci-fi motion pictures ever produced.

A MESSAGE FROM MARS (United Kingdom Films, 1913) 4,000'.

Producer, Nicholson Ormsby-Scott; director, J. Wallett Waller; based on the play by Richard Ganthoney; screenplay, Waller.

Charles Hawtrey (Horace Parker); E. Holman Clark (Ramiel); Crissie Bell (Minnie); Frank Hector (Arthur Dicey); Hubert Willis (Tramp); Kate Tyndale (Aunt Martha); Evelyn Beaumont (Bella);

Eileen Temple (Mrs. Clarence); R. Crompton (God of Mars); B. Stanmore (Wounded Man); Tonie Reith (His Wife).

A MESSAGE FROM MARS (Metro, 1921) 5,187'.

Director, Maxwell Karger; based on the play by Richard Ganthoney; screenplay, Artuhur J. Zellner, Arthur Maude; camera, Arthur Martinelli.

Bert Lytell (Horace Parker); Raye Dean (Minnie Talbot), Maude Milton (Martha Parker); Alphonz Ethier (The Messenger); Gordon Ash (Arthur Dicey); Leonard Mudie (Fred Jones); Mary Louise Beaton (Mrs. Jones); Frank Currier (Sir Edwards); George Spink (The Butler).

Martian Ramiel (E. Holman Clark) uses a crystal ball to spy on the Earth and he observes the greedy actions of industrialist Horace Parker (Charles Hawtrey). The Martian is reprimanded by his superiors for such activities and must make amends by going to Earth and reforming the human race. At a Punch and Judy show he is met with open hostility and denounced, but eventually his message of salvation is heeded and he reforms Parker.

This four-reeler was made in Great Britain and was based on Richard Ganthony's 1899 stage play; the plot may have been filmed in either Australia or New Zealand in 1909 but this cannot be confirmed. In *The Film Encyclopedia: Science Fiction* (1984), Phil Hardy provides, "Basically a religious fairy-tale that seems to have adapted *A Christmas Carol* to a somewhat more up-to-date and even outlandish setting, the Science Fiction elements that could have been introduced via the Martian fantasy are almost totally lacking."

In 1921 Metro Pictures remade the vehicle and in it self-centered Horace Parker (Bert Lytell) agrees to finance a machine which will communicate with Mars. The stipulation is he must be given full credit for its invention. Refusing to attend a party with his fiancée Minnie Talbot (Raye Dean), he remains home and falls asleep studying the plans for the device. He is visited by a messenger (Alphonz Ethier) from Mars who has been sent to reform the Earth's most selfish man. He shows Horace the suffering around him and takes him to the home of a soldier whom he once refused to help. Horace awakens to find the soldier's home on fire, and he rescues the man's family. He invites those less fortunate than himself to his home, thus rewinning Minnie's love. *Photoplay* magazine chided that the film " . . . can hardly be said to challenge the interest of the adult mind."

METEOR (American International, 1979) C 103 mins.

Executive producers, Sandy Howard, Gabriel Katzka; producers, Arnold Orgolini, Theodore Parvin; director, Ronald Neame; story, Edmund H. North; screenplay, Stanley Mann, North; production designer, Edward Carfagno; art director, David Constable; set decorator, Barbara Krieger; music, Laurence Rosenthal; assistant director, Daniel J. McCauley; sound, Jack Solonon; special effects, Glen Robinson, Robert Steaples; camera, Paul Lohmann; editor, Carl Kress.

Sean Connery (Dr. Paul Bradley); Natalie Wood (Tatiana); Karl Malden (Sherwood); Brian Keith (Dubov); Martin Landau (Adlon); Trevor Howard (Sir Michale Hughes); Richard Dysart (Secretary of Defense); Henry Fonda (The President); Joseph Campanella (Easton); Roger Robinson (Hunter); Bo Brundin (Maheim); James Richardson (Alan); Katherine DeHetre (Jan); Michael Zaslow (Mason); John McKinney (Watson); John Findlater (Tom Easton); Paul Tulley (Bill Frager); Allen Williams (Michael McKendrick); Gregory Gay (Russian Premier); Zitto Kazann (Hawk-Faced Party Member); Bibi Besch (Mrs. Bradley); Clyde Kusatsu (Yamashiro); Burke Byrnes (Coast Guard Officer).

A Japanese astronomer discovers a new comet which a California associate proves is heading toward Earth. NASA is alerted and Dr. Paul Bradley (Sean Connery) theorizes the comet could collide with an asteroid in the belt between Mars and Jupiter and that the crash would send debris hurtling toward the Earth. The government sends the spacecraft Explorer 10, on its way to Mars for mapping and exploration, to study the impending crash, but the astronauts stay behind and their ship is destroyed. With huge chunks of rock coursing towards Earth, the super powers agree to work together by aiming their missiles in space at the oncoming meteors to destroy them. Soviet scientist Dubov (Brian Keith), aided by translator Tatiana (Natalie Wood), join blustery Bradley in this project. Meanwhile rock fragments begin striking around the planet, and one causes a huge tidal wave which pounds Tokyo and another strikes the Alps causing massive avalanches. When it is announced a meteor may fall on the East Coast, the U.S. President (Henry Fonda) is evacuated to the Midwest and when missiles miss their target, a massive meteor devastates New York City. Finally the U.S. and Soviet missiles work in tandem and detonate the last big meteor threatening the planet.

METEOR is a disaster picture that turned out a financial disaster. Grossing a modest $6,000,000 at the American box-office, the expensively-produced film was and is a big disappointment. Its complicated plot demands plenty of special effects but they are not overly impressive and the storyline drags badly. The characters at best are wooden figures and after the extensive re-editing (before the film's initial release), most of the players have nothing to do but stand around.

METEOR MONSTER see TEENAGE MONSTER.

THE MIGHTY GORGA (American General Pictures/Western International, 1969) C 83 mins.

Producers, Robert V. O'Neil, David L. Hewitt; director, David L. Hewitt; screenplay Jean Hewitt, David L. Hewitt; music, Charles Walden; sound, Mike Beardsley; camera/editor, Gary Graver.

Anthony Eisley (Mark Remington); Megan Timothy (April Adams); Kent Taylor (Bwana Jack Adams); Scott Brady (Morgan); Lee Parrish (George); Bruce Kemp (Witch Doctor); Sheldon Lee (Kabula); Gary Graver (Zoo Keeper); Graydon Clark (Mark's Brother); Gary Kent (Tracker).

Near bankruptcy, circus owner Mark Remington (Anthony Eisley) treks to Africa to obtain exotic animals to buoy his business. Once there he plans to join forces with big game hunter Bwana Jack Adams (Kent Taylor), but finds him missing and his animal compound run by the man's daughter (Megan Timothy). She is being harassed by another hunter, Morgan (Scott Brady), who wants the property for himself. After Morgan burns her animal stockade, the girl goes with Mark into the jungle in search of her father and they are trailed by Morgan. On a remote plateau they locate Bwana Jack, now a prisoner of a tribe who worship a 50-foot gorilla. The three uncover a treasure guarded by a dragon and do battle with a dinosaur before escaping from the plateau. They are cornered by Morgan, however, who demands a priceless necklace they have taken with them. The gorilla arrives and kills him as the others return to civilization.

A tattered imitation of KING KONG (1933) (see B/V), THE MIGHTY GORGA is an unintentional laugh fest due to its production deficiencies, mauled lines, and tacky monsters. Wretched from start to finish.

MINDWARP: AN INFINITY OF TERROR see GALAXY OF TERROR.

MISSION GALACTICA: THE CYCLON ATTACK see BATTLESTAR GALACTICA.

THE MODERN DR. JEKYLL see DR. JEKYLL AND MR. HYDE (essay).

THE MOLE PEOPLE (Universal, 1956) 78 mins.

Producer, William Alland; director, Virgil Vogel; screenplay, Laszlo Gorog; art directors, Alexander Golitzen, Robert E. Smith; music director, Joseph Gershenson; special camera effects, Clifford Stine; camera, Ellis Carter; editor, Irving Birnbaum.

John Agar (Dr. Roger Bentley); Cynthia Patrick (Adad); Hugh Beaumont (Dr. Jud Bellamin); Alan Napier (Elinu); Nestor Paiva (Professor Etienne Lafarge); Phil Chambers (Dr. Paul Stuart); Rodd Redwing (Nazer); Robin Hughes (Officer); Arthur Gilmour (Sharu); Yvonne de Lavallade (Dancer); James Logan (Officer); Kay Kuter, John Dodsworth, Marc Hamilton, Pat Whyte (Guards); Joseph Abdullah, Billy Miller (Arabs); Eddie Parker, Jue Rubino (Molemen).

On a scientific expedition to the Asiatic mountain ranges, Dr. Roger Bentley (John Agar), Dr. Jud Bellamin (Hugh Beaumont), Dr. Paul Stuart (Phil Chambers), and Professor Etienne Lafarge (Nestor Paiva), find a mysterious shaft which has claimed the life of one of their party. They climb down the opening only to have it close on them by a rock slide. The group explore their underground prison and come upon the survivors of the lost Sumerian race, who

John Agar, Cynthia Patrick, and Hugh Beaumont in THE MOLE PEOPLE (1956).

inhabit a city dropped below ground level five thousand years before by an earthquake. The Sumerians are ruled by the evil high priest Elinu (Alan Napier), leader of a faction who cannot tolerate light and who sacrifice virgins to the eye of Isthar, which proves to be a shaft which brings in the light of the sun. The Sumerians use the prehistoric Mole People as their slaves and treat them savagely. Elinu wants to kill the explorers but they are saved when the light from a flashlight overcomes the dim-visioned Elinu and his followers. Adad (Cynthia Patrick), who has normal vision, agrees to aid the men in escaping, while the Mole People murder Lafarge. Later, as the revolt against their masters begins, the Mole People aid the explorers. As Roger, Jud and Adad make their way to the surface, an earthquake rocks the city and destroys it. On the surface, the girl is pinned by falling debris and dies as she sees the sun for the only time in her life.

THE MOLE PEOPLE is a catchy sci-fier which is decently executed, despite the interior of the Sumerian city being put together on the cheap. The claustrophobic effects of the underworld are well conveyed and while the script has its deficiencies, it is a pleasing, if farfetched thriller.

THE MONSTER (Metro-Goldwyn, 1925) 63 mins.

Director, Roland West; based on the play by Crane Wilbur; screenplay, Willard Mack, Albert Kenyon; titles, C. Gardner Sullivan; camera, Hal Mohr; editor, A. Carle Palm.

Lon Chaney (Dr. Ziska); Gertrude Olmsted (Betty Watson); Hallam Cooley (Watson's Head Clerk); Johnny Arthur (The Under Clerk); Charles A. Sellon (The Constable); Walter James (Caliban); Knute Erickson (Daffy Dan); George Austin (Rigo); Edward McWade (Luke Watson); Ethel Wales (Mrs. Watson).

THE MONSTER is one of the few extant Lon Chaney silent films and one in which he plays the typical mad scientist, although the screen stereotype would not become standard till the coming of talkies. Filmed at the Hal Roach Studio but issued by Metro-Goldwyn, the movie is "A real thriller with lots of mystery" (*Photoplay* magazine). It was adapted from Crane Wilbur's 1922 play of the same title.

Deranged scientist Dr. Ziska (Lon Chaney) experiments with reviving the dead at his remote sanitarium. He abducts passing motorists and uses them in his work, confining them in a dungeon, and trying to transfer souls between men and women. Businessman Luke Watson (Robert McWade) is kidnapped by the doctor and his clerk (Johnny Arthur) who has just obtained a mail order detective license, attempts to find him. He goes to the sanitarium but Ziska captures him for an experiment. Also held hostage by the madman is

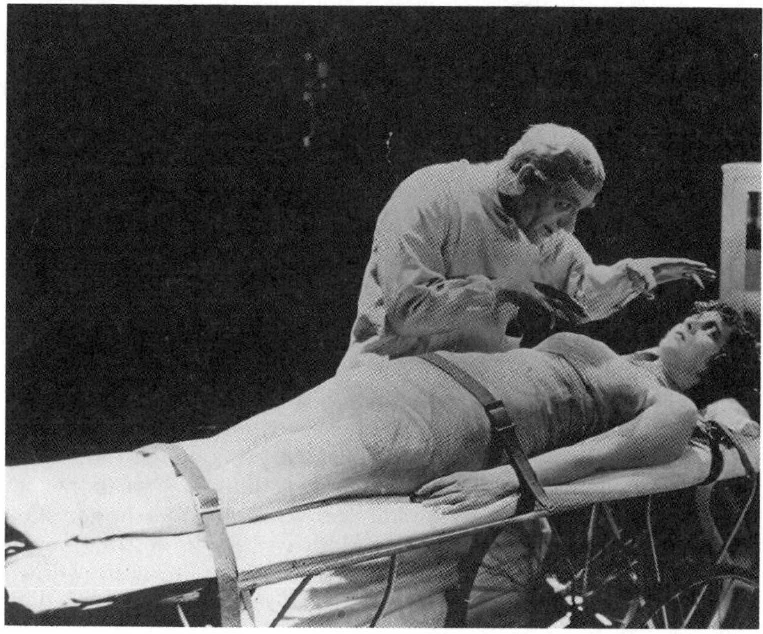

Lon Chaney and Gertrude Olmstead in THE MONSTER (1925).

Watson's pretty daughter, Betty (Gertrude Olmstead), and his senior clerk, Hal (Hallan Coley). Johnny escapes and goes for the police and they return in time to save Betty from being operated on by Ziska, who is captured.

Scott MacQueen, in his essay on director Roland West, wrote in *Between Action And Cut* (1985), "West's stylistic trademarks are fully developed in THE MONSTER, though he approaches the subject as theatre rather than film. Typically, the story is set almost entirely at night, which allows West and the excellent cameraman Hal Mohr to indulge in some sophisticated lighting set-ups and shadow play. Spotlights and dimmer lights emphasize and reveal events within West's carefully posed tableaux."

THE MONSTER AND THE APE (Columbia, 1945) fifteen chapters.

Producer, Rudolph C. Flothow; director, Howard Bretherton; screenplay, Sherman Lowe, Royal K. Cole; assistant director, Leonard J. Shapiro; music, Lee Zahler; camera, L. W. O'Connell; editors, Dwight Caldwell, Earl Turner.

Robert Lowery (Ken Morgan); George Macready (Professor

Ernst); Ralph Morgan (Professor Arnold); Carole Mathews (Babe Arnold); Willie Best (Flash); Jack Ingram (Nordik); Anthony Warde (Flint); Ted Mapes (Butley); Eddie Parker (Blake); Stanley Price (Mead); Ray Corrigan (Thor the Ape).

Chapters: 1) The Mechanical Terror; 2) The Edge of Doom; 3) Flames of Fate; 4) The Fatal Search; 5) Rocks of Doom; 6) A Friend in Disguise; 7) A Scream in the Night; 8) Death in the Dark; 9) The Secret Tunnel; 10) Forty Thousand Volts; 11) The Mad Professor; 12) Shadows of Destiny; 13) The Gorilla at Large; 14) His Last Flight; 15) Justice Triumphs.

Professor Ernst (George Macready) is actually an enemy spy who plots to steal a robot called Metalogen Man which Professor Arnold (Ralph Morgan) of the Bainbridge Research Foundation has constructed for Ken Morgan (Robert Lowery), the representative of a large business firm. With the aid of his henchmen and a trained ape named Thor (Ray Corrigan), Ernst plans to abscond with the robot for his own nation, as the electronic man houses a weapon with deadly rays. When Thor tries to kill Ken, Arnold shoots the ape. Ken and girlfriend Babe Arnold (Carole Mathews), the professor's daughter, destroy Ernst's henchmen in a plane crash. In a showdown between Ernst, Ken and Arnold, the spy falls to his death from a high cliff.

At best, this 15-episode Columbia serial is schlock entertainment. Hero Robert Lowery is justly stalwart, but the promised confrontation between the two monsters is puny at best.

In 1966 the serial was reissued, intact, to television.

MONSTER FROM THE OCEAN FLOOR (Lippert, 1954) 64 mins.

Producer, Roger Corman; director, Wyott Ordung; screenplay, William Danch; production designer, Ben Hayne; music, Andre Brumer; camera, Floyd Crosby; editor, Ed Samson.

Anne Kimball (Julie Blair); Stuart Wade (Steve Dunning); Dick Pinner (Dr. Baldwin); Jack Hayes (Joe); Wyott Ordung (Pablo); Inez Palange (Tula); and: David Garcia.

Wyott Ordung, who wrote the infamous ROBOT MONSTER (1953) (q.v.), directed this sci-fier, the first genre outing for producer Roger Corman. Filmed at under $20,000, the feature is a flimsy production whose title character is a paltry thing who does battle with a toy submarine. As *Castle of Frankenstein* magazine (Number 19, 1972) declared, "slow, dull grade-B underwater s-f . . . not even recommended for most fanatical Cormaniacs."

On a Mexican vacation, illustrator Julie Blair (Anne Kimball) observes what appears to be a sea monster. Local marine biologist,

Steve Dunning (Stuart Wade), who works from his small submarine, dismisses her story, but she manages to tear off some of the creature's flesh and Steve determines it is part of a giant amoeba. Julie devises a way to capture the creature but in her underwater confrontation with it, the monster grabs her with one of its tentacles. Steve comes to the rescue and kills the creature by charging his submarine through its only eye.

According to the film's advertising poster, and some of the dialogue, the monster was created by the use of atomic energy.

A.k.a. IT STALKED THE OCEAN FLOOR.

THE MONSTER MAKER (Producers Releasing Corp., 1944) 64 mins.

Producer, Sigmund Neufeld; director, Sam Newfield; story, Lawrence Williams; screenplay, Pierre Gendron, Martin Mooney; art director, Paul Palmentola; set decorator, Elias H. Reif; assistant director, Mel DeLay; music, Albert Glasser; music supervisor, Paul Chudnow; sound, Ferol Redd; camera, Robert Cline; editor, Holbrook N. Todd.

J. Carrol Naish (Dr. Igor Markoff); Ralph Morgan (Lawrence); Tala Birell (Maxine); Wanda McKay (Patricia Lawrence); Terry Frost (Blake); Glenn Strange (Giant); Alexander Pollard (Butler); Sam Flint (Dr. Adams); Ace the Dog (Himself).

Deranged scientist Dr. Igor Markoff (J. Carrol Naish) lusts after beautiful Patricia Lawrence (Wanda McKay), who is engaged to Blake (Terry Frost). Tiring of the doctor's unwanted attentions, Patricia tells her concert pianist father Lawrence (Ralph Morgan) who then asks the doctor to leave his daughter alone. Angry, Markov knocks out Lawrence with a blow on the head and with the aid of his assistant (Glenn Strange) injects him with a formula which causes acromegaly, leading to deformity of the face and hands. As weeks go by, Lawrence becomes increasingly weaker and his face becomes bloated and hideous. Nearly insane, he goes to Markov, whom he has read has experimented with the disease, and the doctor wants to barter for Patricia. He makes Lawrence a prisoner and tells Patricia her father needs help. When she arrives, Markov molests her, but she is saved by Markov's mistress Maxine (Tala Birell), whom the doctor has tried to dispose of with his giant gorilla. Markov is killed when he attempts to abduct Patricia. Meanwhile Maxine develops an antidote for the doctor's serum and Lawrence is cured and resumes his career.

THE MONSTER MAKER is a wonderfully fun 1940s' poverty row thriller from PRC in which J. Carrol Naish (in a role Bela Lugosi would have relished) plays the epitome of the mad scientist: evil, murderous and lustful. In fact the corrupt character of Markov is really the insane person who killed the original mad doctor and stole his identity. Among the highlights of this film are: a giant gorilla running loose but kept at bay by a German shepherd dog; Lawrence's transformation from a normal man into a ghoulish monster; Markov's endless desire to seduce Patricia; etc.

THE MONSTER MEETS THE GORILLA see BELA LUGOSI MEETS A BROOKLYN GORILLA.

THE MONSTER OF FATE see THE GOLEM (essay).

MONSTER ON THE CAMPUS (Universal, 1958) 77 mins.

Producer, Joseph Gershenson; director, Jack Arnold; screenplay, David Duncan; art director, Alexander Golitzen; set decorators, Russell A. Gausman, Julia Heron; makeup, Bud Westmore; music, Gershenson; special camera effects, Clifford Stine; camera, Russell Metty; editor, Ted J. Kent.

Arthur Franz (Dr. Donald Blake); Joanna Moore (Madeline Howard); Judson Pratt (Mike Stevens); Nancy Walters (Sylvia Lockwood); Troy Donahue (Jimmy Flanders); Phil Harvey (Sergeant Powell); Helen Westcott (Molly Riordan); Alexander Lockwood (Gilbert Howard); Whit Bissell (Dr. Oliver Cole); Ross Elliott (Sergeant Eddie Daniels); Richard Cutting (Forest Ranger); Eddie Parker (Monster Double).

At a California university, Dr. Donald Blake (Arthur Franz) obtains a preserved Coelacanth, a giant fish thought extinct for millions of years, for scientific research. A dog makes its way into his laboratory and laps up water mixed with blood from the fish and the canine turns into a wolf briefly. Blake accidentally cuts his skin on the teeth of the fish and blacks out; later an ape-like man murders a young nurse. Blake continues to experiment on the fish but blood from it spills into his pipe and when he smokes it, he becomes the apeman and murders a guard. Fearing the truth, Blake goes to his mountain retreat where he again takes in the blood of the fish and he turns into the ape creature and murders a forest ranger (Richard Cutting) and almost harms his fiancée, Madeline Howard (Joanna Moore). Realizing what he must do, Blake, upon the arrival of the police, takes the serum he made from the fish's blood, again becomes the ape creature and is killed by the lawmen. Before he dies, Blake reverts to human form.

The plot premise of the prehistoric fish is fascinating since a Coelacanth, thought extinct for over seventy million years, was found just before World War II and a whole school of them turned up near Madagascar after the war. Arthur Franz handles the title role in good form, although in the monster sequences he is doubled by Eddie Parker who had done so before on behalf of Bela Lugosi in FRANKENSTEIN MEETS THE WOLFMAN (1943) (q.v.) and BRIDE OF THE MONSTER (1955) (see B/V) among many others.

THE MONSTER THAT CHALLENGED THE WORLD (United Artists, 1957) 85 mins.

Producer, Arthur Gardner, Jules V. Levy; director, Arnold Laven; story, David Duncan; screenplay, Pat Fiedler; art director, James Vance; music, Heinz Roemheld; camera, Lester White; underwater camera, Scotty Welborn; editor, John Faure.

Tim Holt (Lieutenant Commander John Twillinger); Audrey Dalton (Gail MacKenzie); Hans Conreid (Dr. Jess Rogers); Harlan Warde (Lieutenant Bob Clemens); Casey Adams [Max Showalter] (Tad Johns); Mimi Gibson (Sandy MacKenzie); Gordon Jones (Josh Peters); Marjorie Stapp (Connie Blake); Dennis McCarthy (George Blake); Barbara Darrow (Jody Sims); Bob Beneveds (Mort Beatty); Michael Dugan (Clarke); Mack Williams (Captain Masters); Eileen Harley (Sally); Jody McCrea (Seaman Fred Johnson); William Swan (Seaman Howard Sanders); Charles Tannen (Wyatt); Byron Kane (Coroner); Hal Taggert (Mr. Davis); Gil Frye (Deputy Scott); Dan Gachman (Deputy Brewer); Milton Parsons (Mr. Dobbs); Ralph Moody (Old Gatekeeper).

Atomic explosions result in the emergence of prehistoric sea snail eggs and they hatch with huge mollusk-type creatures attacking Navy ships. Lieutenant Commander John Twillenger (Tim Holt) is assigned to the case and is aided by Dr. Jess Rogers (Hans Conreid). The creatures attack a Naval base and drain the liquids from the bodies of those they kill. Twillenger locates their lair and uses explosives to destroy the creatures. One survivor is caught in a canal lock and crushed to death; but Rogers has kept an egg in his laboratory and an accident causes it to hatch. The thing attacks John's girl friend, Gail MacKenzie (Audrey Dalton), and her little daughter Sandy (Mimi Gibson). However, he manages to rescue them and destroy the monster with scalding hot water and machine gun blasts.

Made in sixteen days on a $200,000 budget, MONSTER THAT CHALLENGED THE WORLD is considered one of the more neglected genre sleepers of the 1950s. Western star of the 1940s, Tim Holt, easily handles the lead assignment (although he suffered a broken arm from the film's action sequences) and the title monsters are particularly revolting and scary: black, large and slimy creatures with bulging eyes.

MONSTERS FROM NICHOLSON MESA see INVASION OF THE STAR CREATURES.

MONSTERS OF THE NIGHT see THE NAVY VS. THE NIGHT MONSTERS.

MONSTRO DE LA MONTA HEUCA see THE BEAST OF HOLLOW MOUNTAIN.

MRS. DEATH see LA SENORA MUERTE.

MURDER BY TELEVISION (Imperial Distributing Company, 1935) 60 mins.

Presenter, William M. Pizor; associate producer, Edward M. Spitz; director, Clifford Sanforth; screen idea, Clarence Hennecke, Carl Coolidge; screenplay, Joseph O'Donnell; art director, Lewis Rachmil; TV technician, Milton M. Stern; technical supervisor, Henry Spitz; music, Oliver Wallace; art director, Louis Rachmil; camera, James Brown, Arthur Reed; editor, Lester Wilder.

Bela Lugosi (Arthur Perry/Edwin Perry); June Collyer (June Houghland); Huntley Gordon (Dr. H. M. Scofield); George Meeker (Richard Grayson); Henry Mowbray (Police Chief Nelson); Charles Hill Mailes (Professor Houghland); Charles K. French (John Jordan); Claire McDowell (Mrs. Houghland); Hattie McDaniel (Maid); Allan Jung (Ah Ling); Henry Hall (Hammond); William "Billy" Sullivan (Reardon the Watchman); Larry Francis (Policeman); William Tooker (Assistant).

Professor Houghland (Charles Hill Mailes) invents a perfect television device and sets up a demonstration at his home for several experts. The initial test is quite successful, but at the beginning of the second one, the professor drops dead. Police Chief Nelson (Henry Mowbray) arrives and finds several suspects, including: Houghland's associate Arthur Perry (Bela Lugosi); businessman Jordan (Charles K. French), who sought to bribe Perry for the plans; Richard Grayson (George Meeker), who has promised his company would get the TV device; and Dr. H. M. Scofield (Huntley Gordon) who made a mysterious call before the murder. Also at the house is the dead man's daughter June (June Collyer). It is soon discovered the device's plans have been stolen along with the tube which hold its secrets. House servant Ah Ling (Allan Jung) blames Perry for the crime and kills him. Perry, however, soon reappears, but it proves to be his honest brother (Lugosi) who has come to investigate the matter. He reveals it was the doctor who committed the crime by the

Bela Lugosi in MURDER BY TELEVISION (1935).

use of his own invention which developed a death ray which killed the professor.

Cranked out on poverty row, MURDER BY TELEVISION uses the plot motif of television at a time when the device was still considered science fiction. Otherwise the movie is dull going with its too predictable plot, and not even Bela Lugosi in dual roles can save it from being far below average.

The film had a brief initial release as THE HOUGHLAND MURDER CASE.

MURDER BY THE CLOCK (Paramount, 1931) 74 mins.

Director, Edward Sloman; based on the book by Rufus King and the play by Charles Behan; screenplay, Henry Myers; camera, Karl Struss.

William "Stage" Boyd (Lieutenant Valcour); Lilyan Tashman (Laura Endicott); Irving Pichel (Phillip Endicott); Regis Toomey (Officer Cassidy); Sally O'Neill (Jane); Blanche Frederici (Mrs. Julia Endicott); Walter McGrail (Herbert Endicott); Lester Vail (Thomas Hollander); Martha Mattox (Miss Roberts); Frank Sheridan (Chief of Police); Frederick Sullivan (Medical Examiner); Willard Robertson (Police Captain); Charles D. Brown (O'Brien); Harry Burgess (Coroner); Guy Oliver (Watchman); John Rogers (Valet); Lenita Lane (Nurse).

Members of the Endicott family begin dying in their mysterious old house presided over by Philip Endicott (Irving Pichel), pretty Laura Endicott (Lilyan Tashman) and nephew Thomas Hollander (Lester Vail). The police, led by Lieutenant Valcour (William "Stage" Boyd) and Officer Cassidy (Regis Toomey) are called to investigate, but this does not stop the killings. The nephew is murdered but is brought back to life by a mysterious drug, yet he is soon disposed of again. Finally Valcour discerns that slightly insane Laura is luring the men to their deaths and by tracing fingerprints found on the victims he uncovers that insane Philip Endicott is the culprit.

The *New York Times* commented, "With its murder and double murders, its misunderstandings and the assault of the detectives, the picture presents, if anything, a little too much of the theory of sudden death and destruction. No sooner has one gentleman crumpled to the floor than another starts on the road that has no ending. There are so many that at times it becomes a little confusing and amateur detectives in the audience clutch their seats with despair of the police on the screen."

The very slight sci-fi angle in this old-house-murder-mystery-thriller is the use of the baffling drug which revives the dead, although not for long as in the case of Lester Vail's character who turns up as a victim twice!

THE MUTATIONS (Columbia, 1974) C 91 mins.

Executive producer, J. Ronald Getty; producer, Robert D. Weinbach; director, Jack Cardiff; screenplay, Weinbach, Edward Mann; music, Basil Kirchin; art director, Herbert Smith; assistant director, Brian Dunbar; sound, Ted Karnon, Brian Ford; camera, Paul Beesen; editors, Russell Weelnough, David Beesley.

Donald Pleasence (Dr. Nolter); Tom Baker (Lynch); Brad Harris (Brian); Julie Ege (Hedi Nolter); Michael Dunn (Burns); Scott Antony (Tony); Jill Haworth (Lauren); Olga Anthony (Bridget); Lisa Collings (Prostitute).

British scientist Dr. Nolter (Donald Pleasence) experiments with cross breeding between plants and animals, which he believes is the only hope for the survival of civilization. He is assisted by the deformed Lynch (Tom Baker). His experiments go afoul, however, and result in mutations like a lizard woman and a frog boy. These rejects are given over to Burns (Michael Dunn), the evil dwarf owner of a traveling freak show. When his daughter's (Julie Ege) boyfriend (Brad Harris) gets too interested in what is going on, the doctor turns him into a mobile Venus fly trap. The artificial plant-humans turn on the biochemist and it is the prospective son-in-law who drains him of life.

THE MUTATIONS is "Not exactly the sort of cinematic fare that helps popularize science with the masses." (Ed Naha, *The Science Fictionary,* 1980). Phil Hardy complained in *The Film Encyclopedia: Science Fiction* (1984), "In comparison to Tod Browning's FREAKS, which treated its characters with compassion, MUTATIONS, in the manner of TERROR OF TINY TOWN (1938), a western with a cast of midgets, invites us to leer at Pleasence's misshapen creations and his deformed assistants."

Donald Pleasence, for all his hammy, leery-eyed performances, has established himself firmly as a staple of the horror/sci-fi/fantasy genre in films like: 1984 (1955) (see B/V), THE FLESH AND THE FIENDS, CIRCUS OF HORRORS and THE HANDS OF ORLAC (q.v.) (all 1960), FANTASTIC VOYAGE (1966) (see B/V), THX 1138 (1969) (see B/V), TALES THAT WITNESS MADNESS, FROM BEYOND THE GRAVE, DR. JEKYLL AND MR. HYDE (q.v.) and THE DEVIL WITHIN HER (all 1973), ESCAPE TO WITCH MOUNTAIN (1975) (q.v.), LAND OF THE MINOTAUR, THE UNCANNY, OH, GOD! (all 1977), DRACULA and night creature (both 1979), THE MONSTER CLUB and ESCAPE FROM NEW YORK (q.v.) (both 1981), just to name a few.

MY SCIENCE PROJECT (Buena Vista, 1985) C 94 mins.

Producer, Jonathan Taplin; associate producer, E. Darrell Hallenbeck; director/screenplay, Jonathan Betuel; music, Peter Bernstein; orchestrators, David Spear, Joel Rosenbaum, Alf Claussen, Brian Mann; music editor, Curtis Roush; production designer, David L. Snyder; art director, John B. Mansbridge; set decorator, Jerry Wunderlich; assistant director, Jerry Sobul; sound, Jim Webb; supervising sound editor, Colin C. Mouat; special sound effects, Alan Howarth; animation design supervisor, John Van Vliet; visual effects supervisor, John Scheele; special optical effects supervisor, Gregory Van Der Veer, William Kilduff; effects designer, Peter Lloyd; special mechanical effects supervisor, Michael Lantieri; camera, David M. Walsh; miniature camera, Peter Anderson, King Baggot, Richard Mosier; camera effects, Philip Meador; editor, C. Timothy O'Meara.

John Stockwell (Michael Harlan); Danielle Von Zerneck (Ellie Sawyer); Fisher Stevens (Vince Latello); Raphael Sbarge (Sherman); Richard Masur (Detective Nulty); Barry Corbin (Lew Harlan); Ann Wedgeworth (Dolores); Dennis Hopper (Bob Roberts); Candace Silvers (Irene); Beau Dremann (Matusky); Pat Simmons (Crystal); John Vidor, Vincent Barbour, Jaime Alba (Jocks); Robert Beer

(President Dwight D. Eisenhower); John Carter (General); Cameron Young (General's Aide); Noel Conlon (Secret Serviceman); Jackson Bostwick (Sentry); Robert DoQui (Desk Sergeant); Elven Havard (Fireman); Linda Houy (Librarian); Robin Allyn (Ellie's Friend); Michael Berryman, (Mutant); Chuck Hemingway (Coy); Pamela Springsteen (Hall Monitor); Matt Hoelscher (Preppy); Jack O'Leary, Scott Bailey Spangler (Sentries at Air Force Guardhouse); Clare Peck (Policewoman); Joel Harrison (Wino); Ann Culotta (Trucker's Wife); Hank Galia (Neanderthal Man); Frank Welker (Alien Voices).

In 1957 a flying saucer crash lands in the Midwest and President Dwight D. Eisenhower (Robert Beer) orders the craft dismantled and the story silenced. Nearly three decades later, two teenagers, Mike Harlan (John Stockwell) and Ellie Sawyer (Danielle Von Zerneck), go to the deserted air field where the ship had been taken and find an energy-absorbing machine from the alien craft. Mike, who has been ordered by his science teacher, Bob Roberts (Dennis Hopper), to immediately turn in his science project, uses this device to pass the course. With pal Vinnie Latello (Fisher Stevens), Mike tests the machine and finds it can materialize images and objects from the past and future and when they show it to Bob he connects it to a electricity supply and a whirlwind is created which causes the teacher to disappear. With dynamite stolen from his dad's hardware store, Mike, Vinnie and Ellie cut off the power, but are questioned by a policeman (Richard Masur) about Roberts' disappearance. Another student, science whiz Sherman (Raphael Sbarge), finds the device and reconnects it to a power source, causing a whirlwind which engulfs the entire school in a time trap, which imprisons Ellie. Mike, Vinnie and Sherman try to save the girl and find themselves both in the past and future. They disarm a group of Vietcong and use their weapons to combat a huge dinosaur. They rescue Ellie and disconnect the machine. Roberts returns with bright prospects for the future.

Another in a long line of the sci-fi/teenage ilk, MY SCIENCE PROJECT is one of the more innocent, and easier to take, genre efforts. The characters are pleasant, their situations absorbing, and the special effects (particularly the dinosaur) acceptable. Still the movie failed to make any noticeable impact in the sci-fi glutted market of the mid-1980s and abroad it was issued only on video cassette.

THE MYSTERY OF LOST RANCH (Vitagraph, 1925) 5 reels.

Directors, Harry S. Webb, Tom Gibson; story, Barr Cross; continuity, George Hull.

Pete Morrison (Jim Preston); Beth Darlington (Alice Blair); Percy Challenger (Professor Blair); Duke R. Lee (Dan Carstars); Barney Furey (Don Bannister); Bud Osborne (Jed Curtis).

Pete Morrison had a long and interesting career as a Western movie star, beginning in 1908 as a juvenile lead after rodeo work. A fine horseman who did his own stunts, Morrison was a compact, agile man who made a long series of silents for Universal and even headlined film productions made in Central and South America. When sound arrived he was reduced to supporting roles before retiring in the mid-1930s. THE MYSTERY OF LOST RANCH is an unusual, if low grade, feature Morrison starred in for producer Harry S. Webb in the twilight days of Vitagraph Pictures. In the 1920s it was rare indeed to incorporate a sci-fi (let alone a spy) motif to flesh out a Western film's storyline.

A scientist named Blair (Percy Challenge) develops a death ray, but he disappears and two other scientists hire cowboy Jim Preston (Pete Morrison) to locate him. Peter finds Blair living in a remote valley near the Grand Canyon with his daughter (Beth Darlington) and that he is testing the new ray on the area's wildlife. Pete learns the two men who hired him are really foreign spies out to steal Blair's death ray and Peter joins forces with the scientist in combatting these agents. Pete falls in love with the girl and she aids her father and Pete in defeating the spies.

THE NAVY VS. THE NIGHT MONSTERS (Realart, 1966) C 87 mins.

Producer, George Edwards; associate producer, Madelyn Broder; director, Michael A. Hoey; based on the novel *Monster from the Earth's End* by Murray Leinster; screenplay, Hoey; art director, Paul Sylos; music, Gordon Zahler; assistant director, Dick Dixon; make-up, Harry Thomas; sound, Clarence Peterson; special effects, Edwin Tillman; camera, Stanley Cortez; editor, George White.

Mamie Van Doren (Lieutenant Nora Hall); Anthony Eisley (Lieutenant Charles Brown); Pamela Mason (Maria); Billy Gray (Petty Officer Fred Twining); Bobby Van (Ensign Rutherford Chandler); Walter Sande (Dr. Arthur Beecham); Phillip Terry (Spalding); and: Edward Faukner, Russ Bender.

In the mid-1960s Jack Broder revived briefly his Realart Pictures which in the early 1950s had produced a few low budget films in addition to reissuing the classic Universal features of the 1940s and 1950s. THE NAVY VS. THE NIGHT MONSTERS was a throwback to the type of sci-fi junk which had entertained moviegoers a decade earlier. Even the cast (Mamie Van Doren, Anthony Eisley, Pamela Mason, Billy Gray, Bobby Van, Phillip

Terry, et al) gave the movie the look of being a reissue rather than a new feature. The poster blurb exclaimed, "A Nightmare Comes Alive . . . Terrifying Acid Bleeding Monsters Multiply By The Millions . . . Ready To Cremate The Human Race!" *Variety* termed it an "Okay exploitation picture."

On a remote Naval base in the South Pacific, Lieutenant Charles Brown (Anthony Eisley) is the temporary commmanding officer. A plane crash lands and he and his rescue team, including nurse Nora Hall (Mamie Van Doren) and Arthur Beecham (Walter Sande), a biologist, find the science team passengers dead and the pilot in a state of shock. The cargo is prehistoric vegetation found preserved in ice at the Antarctic. Hoping to save the vegetation, Beecham plants the six foot high trees near the island's hot springs and soon several people disappear. Brown and his colleagues discover the trees, which are mobile and spew acid, are devouring the inhabitants. When the prehistoric trees converge on the Naval base, Brown employs home made bombs to destroy them.

Filmed as THE NIGHT CRAWLERS, the movie was issued in England as MONSTERS OF THE NIGHT.

THE NEANDERTHAL MAN (United Artists, 1953) 77 mins.

Producer, Aubrey Wisberg, Jack Pollexfen; director, E. A. DuPont; screenplay, Wisberg, Pollexfen; art director, Walter Koestler; music, Albert Glasser; special effects, Jack Rabin; camera, Stanley Cortez; editor, Fred Feitshans.

Robert Shayne (Dr. Cliff Groves); Doris Merrick (Ruth Marshall); Richard Crane (Dr. Ross Harkness); Joyce Terry (Jan the Maid); Robert Long (Jim Oakes); Dick Rich (Sheriff Andrews); Jean Quinn (Celia).

Scientist Dr. Cliff Groves (Roger Shayne) is working on a formula which brings forth man's primitive instincts and at the same time reverts him back to the higher intellect the doctor believes belonged to the Neanderthals. Groves develops a serum and tries it on his house cat, turning it into a sabre-toothed tiger which escapes. When he uses the formula on his mute house maid (Joyce Terry), she changes into a simian creature before returning to normal. Finally Groves injects the formula into himself and becomes a Neanderthal man. However, instead of possessing high intelligence, he has the urge to kill. He turns on his colleague Dr. Ross Harkness (Richard Crane) and abducts his girlfriend, Ruth Marshall (Doris Merrick), before being killed by the sabre-toothed tiger.

THE NEANDERTHAL MAN was the third sci-fi film done by

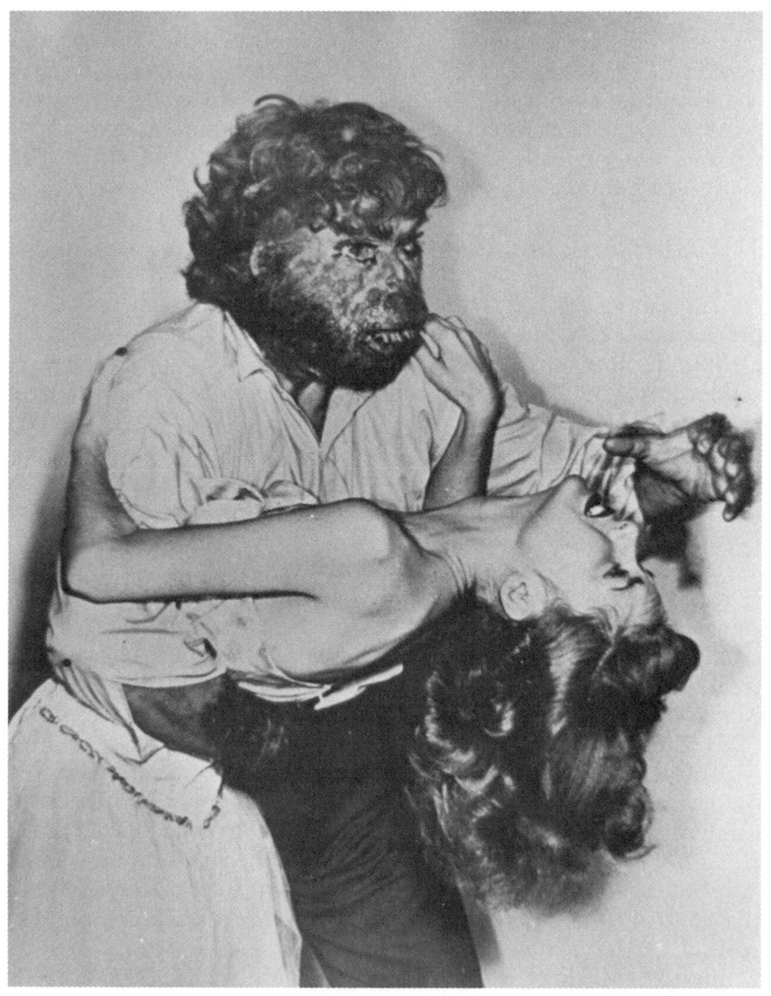

Robert Shayne and Beverly Garland in THE NEANDERTHAL MAN (1953).

the production team of Aubrey Wisberg and Jack Polexfen, following THE MAN FROM PLANET X (1951) (see B/V) and CAPTIVE WOMEN (1952) (q.v.). For this outing they hired the once-renowned German director E. A. Dupont who made the famous silent feature VARIETY (1925). Dupont's later screen work, however, tended to be leaden and this feature is no exception. Bill Warren noted in *Keep Watching the Skies!* (1982), "It was unquestionably a cheap and rapidly made film, and Dupont seems to have brought none of the inventiveness to it that some other directors who worked under equally shaky conditions applied to their films. The picture [is] unimaginative, dull and ponderous. . . ."

THE NEPTUNE FACTOR (Twentieth Century-Fox, 1973) C 98 mins.

Executive producers, David M. Perlmutter, Harold Greenberg; producer, Sanford Howard; director, Daniel Petrie; screenplay, Jack DeWitt; production designers, Dennis Lynton Clark, Jack McAdam; set decorator, Ed Watkins; assistant director, Frank Ernst; underwater director, Paul Stader; music, Lalo Schifrin, William McCauley; special effects, Films Opticals of Canada, Lee Howard; sound, Kenneth Heley-Ray, Joe Grimaldi, Bill O'Neill, Des Dollery; camera, Harry Makin; underwater camera, Lamar Boren, Paul Herberman; editor, Stan Cole.

Ben Gazzara (Commodore Adrian Blake); Yvette Mimieux (Dr. Leah Jansen); Walter Pidgeon (Dr. Andrews); Ernest Borgnine (Mack MacKay); Chris Wiggins (Captain Williams); Donnelly Rhodes (Bob Cousins); Ed McGibbon (Shepherd); Michael J. Reynolds (Hamilton); David Yorston (Stephens); Stuart Gillard (Bradley); Mark Walker (Moulton); Kenneth Pogue (Thomas); Frank Perry (Submarine Captain).

Ocean Lab II is an experimental underwater test station located on the edge of a deep trench and hooked to its supply ship *Triton* by cables. A seaquake breaks the cables and the craft disappears into the trench. When no trace of the craft is found, the ship's captain (Chris Wiggins) sends for the Neptune, a deep diving submersible, under the control of Commodore Adrian Blake (Ben Gazzara). He and several of the *Triton's* crew, including Dr. Leah Jansen (Yvette Mimieux), Mack MacKay (Ernest Borgnine) and Bob Cousins (Donnelly Rhodes), descend in the craft to locate the lost test station and its crew. They dive quite deep and find the entrance to a cave and photograph it, and then return to the surface because of failing life support systems. Although Blake is opposed to diving in unknown waters, he goes along with the others and they dive again, going through the underwater grotto trailing a metallic sound. They

Advertisement for THE NEPTUNE FACTOR (1973).

discover a new undersea kingdom populated by huge plants and sea animals. They find evidence they are near their quest and continue their voyage to its successful finale.

Termed an undersea version of MAROONED (1969) (see B/V), this feature also titled CONQUEST OF THE DEEP and THE NEPTUNE FACTOR—AN UNDERSEA ODYSSEY. It was distributed to TV as THE NEPTUNE DISASTER. By any name it was a "Dreary s-f adventure" (Donald C. Willis, *Horror and Science Fiction Films II* [1982]). In *The Psychotronic Encyclopedia of Film* (1983), Michael Weldon weighed the film, "Laughable all-star underwater mess with an obvious model sub and normal-sized eels and fish used to represent horrible giant sea monsters."

NIEBO ZOWIET see BATTLE BEYOND THE SUN.

THE NIGHT CRAWLERS see THE NAVY VS. THE NIGHT MONSTERS.

NIGHT FRIGHT (Independent, 1974) C 75 mins.

Producer, Wallace P. Clyce, Jr.; director, James A. Sullivan; story/screenplay, Russ Marker; music, Christopher Trussel; art director, Bill Mitchel; special effects, Jack Bennett; camera, Robert C. Jessop; editor, Arthur Sullivan.

John Agar (Sheriff Clint Crawford); Bill Thurman (Deputy Ben Whitfield); Carol Gilley (Joan Scott); Roger Ready (Professor Alan Clayton); Ralph Bates, Jr. (Chris); Dorothy Davis (Judy); and: Darlene West, Gary McLain, Frank Jolly, Billy Holly, Byron Lord.

A flying object (never shown on screen) falls near the remote Satan's Hollow and soon after a pair of teenagers are mysteriously mauled and murdered. Sheriff Clint Crawford (John Agar) investigates but is hampered by the presence of federal investigators who will not allow him near the crash site. His deputy (Bill Thurman) finds a large, mysterious footprint and the sheriff takes a cast of it to a local professor (Roger Ready) who cannot identify it. Although local teenagers are ordered to stay clear of the area, they go there anyway for a party and one of them is murdered and a girl is chased by a large, hairy creature which has also killed the deputy. The girl's sister (Carol Gilley), the fiancee of the sheriff, arrives and they try to get away from the thing. The Sheriff leads it on a chase and later returns to town with two teens (Ralph Bates, Jr.; Dorothy Davis) who have been driving in the area. The professor tells the sheriff the creature is a mutant from a spaceship which has returned to Earth with experimental animals used to study the effects of radiation in space. The sheriff sets up a decoy to capture the monster and in a wooded area he employs a dummy of his fiancee and fills it with explosives. When the creature attacks, it is destroyed.

In *Horror and Science Fiction Films II* (1982), Donald C. Willis labels this feature "Truly tacky." The movie is low grade with long, draggy scenes of teenagers rocking and rolling, and a monster which is none too frightening. Despite its professional look, the film has remained obscure in theatrical/tv/or video cassette distribution.

NIGHT OF THE GHOULS (Atomic Productions, 1959) 60 mins.

Executive producer, Major J. C. Foxworthy; producer, Edward

D. Wood, Jr.; associate producers, Margaret Usher, Paul Marco, Tom Mason, Tony Cardoza, Walt Brannon, Gordon Chesson; director/ screenplay, Wood, Jr.; music, Gordon Zahler; art director, Kathleen O'Hara Everett; assistant director, Ronnie Ashcroft; makeup, Harry Thomas; costumes, Mickey Meyers; camera, William C. Thompson; editor, Donald A. Davis.

Kenne Duncan (Dr. Acula); Tor Johnson (Lobo); Criswell (Narrator); Duke Moore (Lieutenant Dan Bradford); Valda Hansen (Sheila/The White Ghost); John Carpenter (Captain Robbins); Paul Marco (Patrolman Kelton); Don Nagel (Patrolman Crandel); Bud Osborne (Mr. Darmoor); Jeannie Stevens (The Black Ghost); Margaret Mason (Martha); Clay Stone (Young Man); Marcelle Hemphill (Mrs. Foster); Tony Cardoza (Tony); Carl Johnson (Ghoul); Harvey B. Dunne (Henry); Edward D. Wood, Jr., Conrad Brooks (Fighting Juveniles); Conrad Brooks (Drunk).

Also called REVENGE OF THE DEAD, this picture did not see distribution until 1984 when it was issued on video cassette by The Nostalgia Merchant. Produced, directed, and written by Edward D. Wood, Jr. as a sequel to his earlier Bela Lugosi starrer BRIDE OF THE MONSTER (1955) (see B/V), the film was never released theatrically (although Allied Artists expressed interest in it in the early 1960s) due to unpaid film laboratory bills. With the movie finally shown, it was further documentation of the filmmaker responsible for GLEN OR GLENDA? (1953), JAIL BAIT (1954), PLAN 9 FROM OUTER SPACE (1958) (see B/V), and THE SINISTER URGE (1961).

The police receive reports of strange sightings of ghosts at remote Willows Lake where a mad scientist once created monsters with atomic energy (a reference to BRIDE OF THE MONSTER) and Lieutenant Dan Bradford (Duke Moore) and Patrolman Kelton (Paul Marco) are assigned to investigate. The place has been taken over by Karl, known as Dr. Acula (Kenne Duncan), a fake swami, who works with the scarred giant Lobo (Tor Johnson), a survivor of the late mad scientist's experiments, and the beautiful White Ghost (Valda Hansen). Dr. Acula claims to be able to raise the dead and is being paid by a man (Bud Osborne) who has hired him to bring his wife back to life. Bradford pretends to want a seance to contact a departed loved one, but he uses the ruse as an excuse to search the house. When he is found out, Bradford is captured by Lobo, as is Kelton. Two more policemen, Captain Robbins (John Carpenter) and Officer Crandel (Don Nagel) arrive and save their comrades. Lobo is shot. Realizing the outcome is near, Dr. Acula and The White Ghost try to escape but find themselves cornered by ghouls whom the fake swami has accidentally resurrected by his incantations. The revived corpses carry Dr. Acula off with them while The White Ghost escapes into the swamp only to be lured into the underworld by The Black Ghost (Jeannie Stevens), another ghoul. The four policemen find the house at Willows Lake populated only by skeletons.

Hosted and narrated by famed TV seer Criswell (who did the same task for PLAN 9 FROM OUTER SPACE and later starred in the Wood-scripted pornographic/horror entry, ORGY OF THE DEAD, 1966), the movie was not a disappointment to those who waited a quarter of a century to view Wood's much discussed but unseen creation. As *Variety* pointed out, "The late filmmaker Edward D. Wood Jr. displays his usual minimal approach, utilizing barely-dressed sets [typically a blank wall with a lonely looking picture hanging on it], poor acting tending towards swishiness in the supporting cast and an assortment of silly sound effects and cheapo insert shots which lamely try to inject humor into a dull script."

Several of the roles are continuations from previous Wood features. Tor Johnson returns as Lobo from BRIDE OF THE MONSTER while Paul Marco is again Patrolman Kelton as he had been in BRIDE OF THE MONSTER and PLAN 9 FROM OUTER SPACE. John Carpenter, a one-time "B" Western star and producer, plays Captain Robbins, a part performed by Harvey B. Dunne in BRIDE OF THE MONSTER (Dunne is also in this feature) and Criswell, as noted, again narrates here as he did in PLAN 9.

For trash movie lovers, assistant director Ronnie Ashcroft also directed the equally mind-boggling THE ASTOUNDING SHE MONSTER (1958) (see B/V), while Harry Thomas, who worked on several Wood films, did the horrific makeup for Lobo; the film was photographed by Wood's usual cameraman, William C. Thompson, and the musical score was by Gordon Zahler, who also did the score for PLAN 9 and Wood's TV show THE FINAL CURTAIN (1957), written originally for Bela Lugosi, but which eventually starred Dickie Moore.

THE NIGHTS OF PRAGUE see THE GOLEM (essay).

1984 (Atlantic, 1984) C 117 mins.

Executive producer, Marvin J. Rosenblum; producer, Simon Perry; co-producers, Al Clark, Robert Devereux; associate producer, John Davies; director, Michael Radford; based on the novel by George Orwell; screenplay, Radford; production designer, Allan Cameron; music, Dominic Muldowney, Eurythmics; assistant director, Chris Rose; costumes, Emma Porteuous; art directors, Martin

Herbert, Grant Hicks; sound, Bruce White; camera, Roger Deakins; editor, Tom Priestley.

John Hurt (Winston Smith); Richard Burton (O'Brien); Suzanna Hamilton (Julia); Cyril Cusack (Carrington); Gregor Fisher (Parsons); James Walker (Syme); Andrew Wilde (Tillotson); David Trevena (Tillotson's Friend); David Cann (Martin); Anthony Benson (Jones); Peter Frye (Rutherford); Roger Lloyd Pack (Waiter); Rubert Baderman (Winston as a Boy); Corinna Seddon (Winston's Mother); Martha Parsey (Winston's Sisters); Merelina Kendall (Mrs. Parsons); P. J. Nicholas (William Parsons); Lynne Radford (Susan Parsons); Pip Donaghy (Inner Party Speaker); Shirley Stelfox (Whore); Janey Key (Instructress); Hugh Walters (Artsem Lecturer); Phyllis Logan (Telescreen Announcer); Pam Gems (The Washerwoman); Joscik Barbarossa (Aaronson); John Boswall (Goldstein); Bob Flag (Big Brother).

In 1984 director Michael Bradford turned out this second screen adaptation of George Orwell's prophetic novel (written in 1948) about a future world controlled entirely by the omnipotent state; no doubt to commemorate the year of the novel's title. Whether the viewer feels society has gone beyond *1984,* or will never reach there, Orwell's condemnation of the submission of human will is worth heeding in a world where all manners of tyrants continue to exist and prosper.

The new version follows the novel closely as did the less elaborate but fine 1956 release (see B/V). Thinkspeak writer Winston Smith (John Hurt) privately rebels against the government of and by Big Brother, and its intentional endless foreign wars which keep the masses inflamed and in poverty. He meets pretty Julia (Suzanna Hamilton). They break the law by becoming lovers and they enlist the aid of a government official (Richard Burton) whom they believe is sympathetic to their cause. Too late they find out they have been betrayed and both are mentally tortured to the point where they denounce one another and are left as shells, thankful only to Big Brother that their torment is over.

When released on video cassette, TV/radio critic Jeffrey Lyons noted in *Video Review* magazine, "I noticed, initially, how the movie seems to have more life [on video cassette at home] than it did in the theatre. The drab, gray look of the monolithic world Orwell envisioned . . . seems even more frightening; the dank, depressing late-'40s look at the future world, an emotionless totalitarian state where feelings are forbidden and independent thoughts are crimes seems far more fascinating on video than on the big screen. Indeed, Big Brother was in my home, watching me. Fascinating. But only initially. . . . For soon after one's eye gets accustomed to the dinginess of that world, it's up to the actors to carry the story. And again, for a time, they do. . . . *1984* is only half a loaf; atmosphere and interesting music by the Eurythmics are all right, but we're soon wanting more. Orwell dealt in ironies, in frightening possibilities which have turned out to be not so far-fetched. But not much of that is conveyed in *1984.* Just atmosphere, atmosphere, atmosphere."

For the record, Richard Burton gave his final film appearance in *1984,* in the role performed in the original movie by Michael Rennie.

NORTH STAR (Warner Bros. TV/ABC-TV. 8/16/86) C 85 mins.

Executive producers, Clyde Phillips, Daniel Grodnik; producer, Howard Lakin; associate producer, John W. Rogers; director, Peter Levin; teleplay, Lakin; assistant directors, Anthony Brand, Mitchell Book; set decorator, Edward Joseph McDonald; makeup, Robert Norin; costume supervisor, Joie Hutchinson; music, Brad Fiedel; special effects, David Stipes, Richard Bennett; sound editor, James Troutman; camera, Michael D. Margulies; editors, Skip Schoolnik, Jack Fegan.

Greg Evigan (Major Jack North); Deborah Wakeham (Dr. Alison Taylor); Mitchell Ryan (Colonel Evan Marshall); Mason Adams (Dr. Karl Janss); David Hayward (Bill Harlow); Robin Curtis (Janie Harlow); Richard Garrison (Sonny Landham); Steven Williams (Security Guard); Ken Foree (Astronaut).

Shown as a part of a sci-fi double feature on ABC-TV with CONDOR (q.v.), this telefilm tells of astronaut Major Jack North (Greg Evigan) who develops an I.Q. of one thousand following a spacewalk in which he is hit by a powerful solar ray. Back on Earth he is committed to an Army hospital for tests and upon release learns that he has extraordinary powers whenever touched by sunlight. Back in the hospital, he meets brilliant scientist Dr. Alison Taylor (Deborah Wakeham) to whom he is attracted, but she has a husband lost in the South American jungles. When North's astronaut partner (David Hayward) is murdered, he uses his unique powers to track the killer, since he learns he is next on the list. Helping him is a professor (Mason Adams) as North finds the killer is someone close to him.

The *Hollywood Reporter* judged, "A bag of second-rate special effects (lots of glitter around North's pupils) cannot carry this hokum, and NORTHSTAR burns out before igniting viewers' imaginations." *Variety* reported, "The dialog throughout is amusingly expository, and the characters, weighed down by both the script and the acting, seldom hit home. As a series concept, this doesn't look like it could have ever flown—the super-powers are at once too complicated and too unexplained to serve as the basis for a strong series."

1000 YEARS FROM NOW see CAPTIVE WOMEN.

L'OR see GOLD.

ORGY OF BLOOD see BRIDES OF BLOOD.

ORGY OF THE BLOOD PARASITES see THEY CAME FROM WITHIN.

ORLACS HANDE see THE HANDS OF ORLAC (essay).

ORLAK, THE HELL OF FRANKENSTEIN (Columbia, 1960) 103 mins.

Producer/director, Rafael Baledon; suggested by the novel *Frankenstein* by Mary Shelley; screenplay, Alfredo Ruanova, Carlos Enrique Taboada; music, Fondo Jorge Perez; camera, Fernando Colin.

Joacquin Cordero (Jaime/Orlak); Andres Soler (Dr. Frankenstein); Rosa de Castilla (Estela); Irma Dorantes (Elvira), and: Pedro D'Aquillon, Armando Calva, David Reynosa, Carlos Nieto, Carlos Ancira.

Producer/director Rafael Baledon shot this feature in Mexico City as a four-part television program and then stitched it together and issued it theatrically as ORLAK, EL INFIERNO DE FRANKENSTEIN [Orlak, The Hell of Frankenstein]. It played in the U.S. only in Spanish-language theatres and has yet to surface on American TV. The film's most stimulating aspect is its appearance since its dark contours beautifully capture the feel of the theme of horror, although the plot itself is only executed in a workman-like, unpretentious manner.

Dr. Frankenstein (Andres Soler) is freed from prison by former convict Jaime (Joaquin Cordero) and they take refuge in the mad doctor's castle. There he houses his creation, an artificial man, Orlak (Joaquin Cordero), who has a metal body with a metal box for a head which the doctor controls by remote units. The creature can talk, lives on human blood and fears fire. Frankenstein operates on Orlak and gives him a face made of rubber with electrodes on its neck. The mad scientist uses Orlak to murder those responsible for sending him to prison as well as his unfaithful girlfriend, singer Estela (Rosa de Castilla). Orlak, however, takes a fancy to his creator's new love,

Elvira (Irma Dorantes), the daughter of the judge who sentenced Frankenstein to prison, and he abducts her. Frankenstein follows and corners the monster who ventures near the fire and melts.

L'ORRIBLE SEGRETO DEL DR. HICHCOCK see THE HORRIBLE DR. HICHCOCK.

OUTLAND (Ladd Co./Warner Bros., 1981) C 109 mins.

Executive producer, Stanley O'Toole; producer, Richard Roth; associate producer, Charles Orme; director/screenplay, Peter Hyams; music, Jerry Goldsmith; choreography, Anthony Van Laast; assistant directors, David Tringham, Bob Wright; art director, Malcolm Middleton; costumes, John Mollo; camera, Stephen Goldbatt; editor, Stuart Baird.

Sean Connery (O'Niel); Peter Boyle (Sheppard); Frances Sternhagen (Dr. Lazarus); James B. Sikking (Montone); Kika Markham (Carol); Clarke Peters (Ballard); Steven Berkoff (Sagan); John Ratzenberger (Tarlow); Nicholas Barnes (Paul O'Niel); Manning Redwood (Lowell); Pat Starr (Mrs. Spector); Hal Galili (Nelson); Angus MacInnes (Hughes); Stuart Milligan (Walters); Eugene Lipinski (Cane); Norman Chancer (Slater); Ron Travis (Fanning); Anni Domingo (Morton); Bill Bailey (Hill); Chris Williams (Caldwell); Marc Boyle (Spota); Richard Hammat (Yario); James Berwick (Rudd); Gary Olsen (Worker); Isabelle Lucas (Nurse); Sharon Duce (Prostitute); P. H. Moriarty, Doug Robinson (Men); Angelique Rockas (Maintenance Woman); Judith Alderson, Rayner Bourton (Prostitutes in Leisure Club); Julia Depyer, Nina Francoise, Brendon Hughes, Philip Johnston, Norri Morgan (Dancers in Leisure Club).

When this elaborate sci-fier first appeared critics likened its plot to that of the classic Western HIGH NOON (1952). *Variety* summarized, "While there are several mile-wide plot holes and one key under-developed main character, the film emerges as a tight, intriguing old-fashioned drama that gives audiences a hero worth rooting for." Donald C. Willis opined in *Horror and Science Fiction Films II* (1982), "As a reworking of HIGH NOON, OUTLAND is less provocative and amusing than RIO BRAVO; as if it's almost non-existent (the space setting merely provides an excuse for a few nice effects and stunt); as an actor vehicle (for Connery and Sternhagen) it passes—both have bright moments. The 'suspense' is hardly killing." Most seemed to agree that what the movie needed was a fire-spouting villain, something not provided by Peter Boyle's cold, calculating Sheppard.

On Jupiter's moon, Io, mine workers are dying mysteriously and federal district Marshal O'Niel (Sean Connery) investigates.

The trip costs him his wife and son who are tired of his endless treks around the solar system. On Io he witnesses a psychotic miner commit suicide by going out into the planet's hostile atmosphere without a space suit. O'Niel enlists the help of flippant psychologist Dr. Lazarus (Frances Sternhagen) who assists him in unraveling the mystery behind the deaths. However, he receives little aid from Sheppard (Peter Boyle), the general manager of the Con-Am mining company. O'Niel uncovers that Sheppard is giving the miners drugs to increase their productivity but the huge dosages causes them to go insane. In a shootout confrontation, O'Niel outwits Sheppard and brings about his downfall.

In their essay for *Magill's Cinema Annual* (1982), Frances M. Malpezzi and William M. Clements pointed out "OUTLAND, however, is much more than a mere futuristic reworking of a classic Western film. Peter Hyams has infused the film with a moral universe which resembles that of hard-boiled detective film and fiction. . . . The ability of the detective. . . . to maintain his nobility and sense of honor in the immoral world in which he exists is the hallmark of the hard-boiled detective genre. O'Niel is much like the typical protagonists of these films, and OUTLAND evinces as much influence from them as from HIGH NOON."

PANICO EN EL TRANSIBERIANO see HORROR EXPRESS.

PANTHER GIRL OF THE CONGO (Republic, 1955) twelve chapters.

Associate producer/director, Franklin Adreon; screenplay, Ronald Davidson; music, R. Dale Butts; special effects, Howard Lydecker, Theodore Lydecker; camera, Bud Thackery; editor, Cliff Bell.

Phyllis Coates (Jean Evans); Myron Healey (Larry Sanders); Arthur Space (Dr. Morgan); John Day (Cass); Mike Ragan (Rand); Morris Buchanan (Tembu); Roy Glenn, Sr. (Chief Danka); Archie Savage (Ituri); Ramsay Hill (Commissioner Stanton); Naaman Brown (Orto); Dan Ferniel (Ebu); James Logan (Harris).

Chapters: 1) The Claw Monster; 2) Jungle Ambush; 3) The Killer Beast; 4) Sands of Doom; 5) Test of Terror; 6) High Peril; 7) Timber Trap; 8) Crater of Flame; 9) River of Death; 10) Blasted Evidence; 11) Double Danger; 12) House of Doom.

Famous chemist Dr. Morgan (Arthur Space) develops a formula from hormones which turns crawfish into huge claw monsters and with his henchmen Cass (John Day) and Rand (Mike Ragan) he uses the creatures to frighten natives away from his African district because he has discovered a diamond mine in the jungle. When

Myron Healey in the serial PANTHER GIRL OF THE CONGO (1955).

Panther Girl Jean Evans (Phyllis Coates) and big game hunter Larry Sanders (Myron Healey) begin taking pictures of the wild life in the area, Morgan becomes concerned because they see and photograph one of the claw monsters and he fears this will bring in the authorities. Morgan and his minions try to stop Jean and Larry in several ways, but *always* fail. Jean and Larry show the pictures of the claw monsters to District Commissioner Stanton (Ramsay Hill) and he agrees to bring in the police. When they arrive, Larry and Jean lead them to an abandoned gold mine where they repulse a band of natives. Later in a shootout Cass and Rand are killed. Locating a bottle of special acid, Jean and Larry realize Morgan is behind the activities and at his bungalow they find a crated claw monster. Morgan threatens them with a bottle of deadly gas, but in an ensuing fight, the bottle breaks. Jean and Larry escape as Morgan dies from the fumes.

"Horror Stalks The Jungle! The Most Exciting Serial Ever Filmed!" claimed the poster for this 12-chapter cliffhanger, Republic's penultimate serial. While Phyllis Coates was an alluring heroine and Myron Healey a stalwart hero, the film was a tired effort despite the inclusion of a mad scientist and his claw monsters. Phyllis Coates wore the same costume Frances Gifford did in JUNGLE GIRL (1941) to match stock footage from that earlier serial.

In 1966 a 100-minute feature version of the serial was released to TV as THE CLAW MONSTERS.

PARASITE (Embassy, 1982) C 85 mins.

Executive producer, Irwin Yablans; producer/director, Charles Band; screenplay, Alan Adler, Michael Shoob, Frank Levering; music, Richard Band; art director, Pamela Warner; stunt co-ordinator, Harry Wowchuk; assistant director, Peter Manoogian; 3-D consultant, Randall Larson; special makeup effects, Stan Winston, James Kagel, Lance Anderson; camera, Mae Ahlberg; editor, Brad Arensman.

Robert Glaudini (Dr. Paul Dean); Demi Moore (Patricia); Luca Bercovici (Ricus); James Davidson (Merchant); Al Fann (Collins); Vivian Blaine (Miss Dailey); Tom Villard (Zeke); Cherie Currie (Dana).

Issued to take advantage of the revival of the 3-D craze, PARASITE proved to be a pitiful sci-fi film whose optical effects were nullified by the clumsy 3-D glasses needed to view it. *Variety* judged, " . . . PARASITE is lethargic between its terror scenes making it a test of patience for all but the fanatical followers of horror cheapies."

In 1992, following a nuclear war, scientist Dr. Paul Dean (Robert Glaudini) has developed parasites for government use. He studies one species while another grows in his stomach and he hopes to neutralize the parasite before it brings about his death and begins a reproduction process which could destroy the world. Dean has set up headquarters in a remote western community but when one of the parasites escapes and begins killing the inhabitants, businessman Merchant (James Davidson) goes after Dean, although they must unite to stop an invading gang. The fast-growing, rampaging parasite is destroyed by high pitch sounds while Dean and the other parasite he carries are killed in a fire.

Perhaps the most disgusting scene in this minor film occurs when the creature devours floozie Miss Daley, played by 1940s musical comedy star Vivian Blaine, who is sadly wasted in this tripe.

THE PEOPLE THAT TIME FORGOT (American International, 1977) C 90 mins.

Presenter, Samuel Z. Arkoff; executive producer, Max J. Rosenberg; producer, John Dark; director, Kevin Connor; based on the novel by Edgar Rice Burroughs; screenplay, Patrick Tilley; music, John Scott; production designer, Maurice Carter; art directors, Bery Davey, Fernando Gonzales; assistant director, Byron

Coates; costumes, Brenda Dabbs; special effects, John Richardson, Ian Wingrove; sound, George Stephenson; camera, Alan Hume; editors, John Ireland, Barry Peters.

Patrick Wayne (Ben McBride); Doug McClure (Bowen Tyler); Sarah Douglas (Lady Charlotte [Charly]); Dana Gillespie (Ajor); Thorley Walters (Norfolk); Shane Rimmer (Hogan); Tony Britton (Captain Lawton); John Hallam (Chang-Sha); David Prowse (Executioner); Milton Reid (Sabbala); Kiran Shah (Bolum); Richard Parmentier (Lieutenant Whitby); Jimmy Ray (Lieutenant Graham); Tony McHale (Telegraphist).

Following the good box-office returns from THE LAND THAT TIME FORGOT (1976) and AT THE EARTH'S CORE (1975) (qq.v.), Amicus-American International released the third film in their Edgar Rice Burroughs Pellucidar series, based on the author's 1918 novella. Unfortunately this feature, which is a direct sequel to the initial outing, is vapid and brought the series to a halt.

In 1916 American Bowen Tyler (Doug McClure) is left in the prehistoric Arctic land of Caprona and three years later his pal, flyer Major Ben McBride (Patrick Wayne), flies over the area in an attempt to locate and rescue Tyler. With him is comely photographer Charly (Sarah Douglas) and the two discover and land in the lost world there. They are confronted by dinosaurs and cave men and finding Tyler, the trio fight the inhabitants of the evil City of Skulls before returning home.

Since its plotline is so anemic, THE PEOPLE THAT TIME FORGOT has to rely especially on special effects, thrills and a fast pace to keep it entertaining, and it succeeds only in the initial creative area.

Among the film's better moments are Milton Reid's inhuman caveman Sabbala, cavegirl Ajor (Dana Gillespie), and the nosey flying dinosaur who keeps pecking at McBride's plane which he finds is inedible.

THE PHANTOM (Actondramas/Artclass, 1931) 60 mins.

Director, Alan James; screenplay, Alvin J. Neitz [Alan James]; assistant director, Jerry Callahn; camera, Lauron Draper; editor, Ethel Davey.

Guinn Williams (Dick Mallory); Aileen Ray (Ruth Hampton); Niles Welch (Sam Crandall); Tom O'Brien (Pat Collins); Sheldon Lewis (The Thing); Wilfred Lawson (John Hampton); Violet Knight (Lucy); William Gould (Dr. Weldon); Bobby Dunn (Shorty); William Jackie (Oscar); Horace Murphy (Police Chief Murphy).

An airplane rescues a condemned murderer, The Phantom, after he climbs over the prison wall and jumps on a passing train. The

Phantom intends to get even with District Attorney John Hampton (Wilfred Lawson) for trying to send him to the electric chair and promises to be at Hampton's home that evening for his revenge. Newspaper editor Sam Crandall (Niles Welch) is in love with Hampton's daughter, society writer Ruth (Aileen Ray), but she loves Dick Mallory (Guinn Williams) and Crandall hires Mallory as a novice reporter to cover the story, hoping the Phantom will put him out of the way. At the house a number of mysterious events occur, instigated by a caped, masked figure. Ruth is abducted, but Dick trails and finds she has been taken to an asylum where the Phantom conducts his experiments. To gain revenge he plans to put Ruth's brain in an ape, but Dick foils the scheme and the law arrives. Ruth is saved.

Thanks to home video, this obscure early talkie old-haunted-house mystery thriller has surfaced, complete with such genre requisites as: a hooded fiend, a dense policeman, a nervous butler, and an hysterical maid. It has to be one of the most incongruously cast films of all time. Having Guinn "Big Boy" Williams as the romantic lead, an ace newspaper reporter, is mind-boggling; while aging, plump, and shrill-voiced former serial queen Aileen Ray is the "virginal" heroine. For its sci-fi slant, there is the deranged scientist's rather cramped laboratory, complete with bubbling chemicals, the operating table for the brain transfer operation, and. . . .

PHANTOM FROM SPACE (United Artists, 1953) 72 mins.

Producer/director, W. Lee Wilder; story, Myles Wilder; screenplay, Bill Raynor, Myles Wilder; music, William Lava; special effects, Alex Welden, Howard Anderson; camera, William Clothier; editor, George Gale.

Ted Cooper (Lieutenant Hazen); Rudolph Anders (Dr. Wyatt); Noreen Nash (Barbara Randall); James Seay (Major Andrews); Harry Landers (Lieutenant Bower); Jack Daly (Wakeman); Dick Sands (Phantom); and: Lela Nelson, Michael Mark, Jim Bannon.

Following the huge success of THE THING (see B/V) in 1951, motion pictures about space invaders began to proliferate and one of the earliest of these is W. Lee Wilder's PHANTOM FROM SPACE, an engrossing "B" sc-fi entry which is well paced and enjoys offbeat locales. The title character is an innocuous fellow which Wilder (brother of director Billy) wisely either keeps invisible or in a space suit. When seen he is nothing more than a tall, pale human with a bald, elongated head.

A mysterious object is spotted over the California skies and is detected on radar. Lieutenant Hazen (Ted Cooper), of the Federal Communications Commission, is assigned to look into the matter,

Harry Landers, Ted Cooper, and Noreen Nash in PHANTOM FROM SPACE (1953).

and so are the Los Angeles police, headed by Lieutenant Bowers (Harry Landers), when a strange-suited man disturbs picnickers and is later blamed for two homicides. The creature is traced to an oil refinery by scientist Dr. Wyatt (Rudolph Anders) and Barbara Randall (Noreen Nash). The phantom removes his suit and becomes invisible. The suit is analyzed and is determined to be of alien origin. Major Andrews (James Seay) of the Army joins in the hunt and it becomes clear that the alien is dying without the life support system of his suit. Barbara communicates limitedly with the being. When an ultraviolet light is aimed at him, he becomes visible, but falls from a high ladder and dies. His spacesuit turns to dust.

THE PHANTOM FROM 10,000 LEAGUES (American Releasing Corp., 1956) 81 mins.

Producers, Jack Milner, Dan Milner; director, Dan Milner; story, Dorys Lukather; screenplay, Lou Rusoff; music, Ronald Stein; camera, Bryden Baker; editors, Jack Milner, Dan Milner.

Kent Taylor (Dr. Ted Stevens [Ted Baxter]); Cathy Downs (Lois King); Michael Whalen (Professor King); Helene Stanton

(Wanda); Philip Pine (George); Rodney Bell (Bill Grant); Pierce Lyden (Andy); Vivi Janiss (Ethel); Michael Garth (Sheriff).

Noted oceanographer Dr. Ted Stevens (Kent Taylor) and Bill Grant (Rodney Bell), a special investigator for the Defense Department, find a dead fisherman on the beach and theorize he died from radiation poisoning. Stevens uses the alias of Ted Baxter and informs Grant he wants to visit Pacific College of Oceanography's Professor King (Michael Whalen) about the matter. He tries to locate the professor, but the man's daughter, Lois (Cathy Downs), cannot find him and Ted later sees the professor checking the fisherman's boat with a geiger counter. King knows Stevens' identity and tells him so and later Ted swims in the ocean and spots a monster-like creature guarding an underwater weapon. It turns out it was King who developed the weapon and the mutant guarding it and that his assistant (Philip Pine) is working for a foreign agent (Helene Stanton) for the sale of both to another government. Two murders are committed and the sheriff (Michael Garth) proves the assistant is the culprit. Ted confronts King about the monster and the weapon and after a tanker is destroyed as it crosses over the ray gun weapon, King burns his papers and takes a bomb underwater to destroy the atomic ray light and the monster. The creature, however, tries to stop King and in a fight between them, the bomb explodes destroying the weapon and killing both King and his creation. Ted comforts Lois with the fact her father made his own decision to destroy his evil creation.

THE PHANTOM FROM 10,000 LEAGUES was made independently by Dan and Jack Milner and sold to the fledgling American Releasing Corporation (soon to become American International Pictures) as a dual bill item to join DAY THE WORLD ENDED (see B/V). "Sheer Horror as a living nightmare stalks the ocean floor!" read the poster for this low-level sci-fier; the monster is hardly more than a greyish blob. At least veteran actor Kent Taylor gives a very credible performance in the lead role.

THE PINK CHIQUITAS (Shapiro Entertainment, 1986) C 86 mins.

Executive producer, Syd Cappe; producer, Nicholas Stiliadis; associate producers, George Flak, Carl Zittrer; director/screenplay, Anthony Currie; music, Paul J. Zaza; art director, Danny Addario; camera, Nicholas Stiliadis; editor, Stephen F. Withrow.

Frank Stallone (Tony Mareda, Jr.); John Hemphill (Mayon Ernie); Do Lake (Barney); Bruce Pirrie (Clip Bacardi); Elizabeth Edwards (Marianne); Claudia Udy (Nurse); McKinley Robinson (Trudy Jones); Cindy Valentine (Sheila); Gerald Issac (Dwight Wright); Eartha Kitt (Meteorite's Voice).

Starring Frank Stallone (Sylvester's brother) as a flashy detective and the voice of Eartha Kitt as a sexy meteorite, this Canadian-produced feature tries to spoof the sci-fi genre and jabs at both gangster and detective films. The film's main asset is not taking itself seriously and " . . . writer-director Anthony Currie has fun with a lot of plot elements and allows the cast to exploit the cardboard parameters of their absurd characters." (*Variety*)

Following the funeral of his well known sleuth father, detective Tony Mareda, Jr. (Frank Stallone) meets a pretty hitchhiker and agrees to take her to Beansville where they stop at a drive-in showing ZOMBIE BEACH PARTY III. Also at the drive-in is television weatherman Clip Bacardi (Bruce Pirrie) and his librarian date Marianne (Elizabeth Edwards) who intend to oppose the town's corrupt mayor Ernie (John Hemphill) in the next election. As the two discuss the possibilities of life in outer space a pink meteor appears and the moviegoers leave the drive-in in search of the fallen star. When a group of girls find the meteor it turns them into nymphomaniacs called pink chiquitas. They plan to dominate the world and enslave all men. After they take Mareda, the mayor tries to hush up the incident. Mareda subdues the pink chiquitas and drains them of their powers by pushing the meteor into a river.

PIRANHA (New World, 1978) C 92 mins.

Executive producers, Roger Corman, Jeff Schechtman; producer, Jon Davison; co-producer, Chako Van Leeuwen; director, Joe Dante; story, Richard Robinson, John Sayles; screenplay, Sayles; music, Pino Donaggio; art directors, Bill Mellin, Kerry Mellin; camera, Jamie Anderson; editors, Mark Goldblatt, Dante.

Bradford Dillman (Paul Grogan); Heather Menzies (Maggie McKeon); Kevin McCarthy (Dr. Robert Joak); Keenan Wynn (Jack); Dick Miller (Buck Gardner); Barbara Steele (Dr. Mengers); Belinda Balaski (Betsy); Melody Thomas (Laura); Bruce Gordon (Colonel Waxman); Barry Brown (Trooper); Paul Bartel (Dumont); Shannon Collins (Suzie); Shawn Nelson (Whitney); Richard Deacon (Earl); Janie Squire (Barbara); Roger Richman (David); Bill Smillie (Jailer); Guich Kooch (Pitchman); Jack Pauleson (Man in Canoe); Eric Henshaw (Father in Canoe); Robert Vinson (Soldier); Virginia Dunnam (Girl); and: Hill Farnsworth, Bruce Barbour, Robyn Ray, Mike Sullivan, Jack Cardwell, Roger Creed, Nick Palmisano, Bobby Sargent.

Dr. Robert Joak (Kevin McCarthy) worked on a secret government project during the Vietnam War in which he developed a strain of piranha which were planned for use in North Vietnam waterways, but the project came to naught. The school of mutants remained in

Keenan Wynn in PIRANHA (1978).

their experimental tank in Hoak's remote mountain laboratory. Insurance investigator Maggie McKeon (Heather Menzies) is sent by her boss (Richard Deacon) to track two missing hitchhikers and she enlists the aid of hermit Paul Grogan (Bradford Dillman). The two find Hoak's lab and accidentally release the piranhas into the mountain streams. Hoak advises them the fish can withstand the cold and will migrate south. This means they will be heading to a summer resort where Grogan's daughter is vacationing. He and Maggie fail to convince the resort owner, Buck Gardner (Dick Miller), of the danger. An authority on the fish, Dr. Mengers (Barbara Steele), is called in but the fish attack the campers and although Grogan saves his child, many of the guests are killed or badly hurt. Grogan stops the predators by polluting the water with poison.

While on the surface PIRANHA is a gore thriller about killer fish, it is far more subtle and satirical. It pokes fun at the sci-fi genre as well as the big budget exploitation items such as JAWS (1975). It is also loaded with a cast of veteran genre performers (Kevin McCarthy, Barbara Steele, Dick Miller, Keenan Wynn), numerous shock effects, enough gore for the 1970s film buffs, and even a cute little monster in the opening lab sequences.

In 1981, James Cameron (as Ovidio Assonitis) produced/directed PIRANHA II: THE SPAWNING, a thriller about a Caribbean resort club being attacked by murderous flying fish, mutated by a government project. It had none of the wit or charm of the 1978 Joe Dante feature!

PLANET OF HORROR see GALAXY OF TERROR.

PRADZSKE NOCI see THE GOLEM (essay).

PRAGUE NIGHTS see THE GOLEM (essay).

PREDATOR (Twentieth Century-Fox, 1987) C 107 mins.

Executive producers, Laurence P. Pereira, Jim Thomas; producers, Lawrence Gordon, Joel Silver, John Davis; associate producers, Beau E. L. Marks, John Vallone; director, John McTiernan; screenplay, Jim Thomas, John Thomas; production designer, Vallone; art directors, Frank Richwood, Jorge Saenz; music, Alan Silvestri; camera, Donald McAlpine; editors, John F. Link, Mark Helfrich.

Arnold Schwarzenegger (Dutch); Carl Weathers (Dillon); Elpidia Carrillo (Anna); Bill Duke (Mac); Jesse Ventura (Blain); Sonny Landham (Billy); Richard Chaves (Poncho); R.G. Armstrong (General Phillips); Shane Black (Hawkins).

Following the mega box-office success of THE TERMINATOR (1984) (q.v.) in which Arnold Schwarzenegger portrayed an android hit man from the future, the star headlined PREDATOR, which has him as a mercenary at odds with an alien killer. "PREDATOR is a slightly above-average actioner that tries to compensate for tissue-thin plot with ever more-grisly death sequences and impressive special effects. Telegraphed story line slows pace though, as audience spends most of film waiting for the inevitable ultimate confrontation." (*Daily Variety*).

When a U.S. senator's plane is gunned down in a South American trouble spot, mercenary Dutch (Arnold Schwarzenegger) and his rescue team are called in by the government to find the politician. Once there Dutch meets an old comrade, Dillon (Carl Weathers), now a CIA operative. The team decimate a guerilla band, but find no trace of the senator and head out of the jungle only to be prey for a mysterious attacker. At first it is thought more guerillas are to blame, but as the men die one by one, and by means of futuristic weapons, it becomes clear they are the victims of an alien attacker and that what crashed was a UFO. Only Dutch survives and he meets the alien in a showdown.

Newspaper/television critic Gene Siskel opined in his Tribune Media Services column, "There's nothing wrong with the movie; it delivers exactly what Arnold's audience wants, but I'm not part of that crowd. I'm tired of jungle fights and creatures with weird fangs." Admittedly, one of the weaker links in the adventure tale occurs when the space creature leaves the trees and lumbers around the jungle swamp, losing much of its mystique.

Despite the critical slams, PREDATOR grossed $56,471,713 in its first fifteen weeks at the U.S. box-office.

PROJECT MOONBASE (Lippert, 1953) 63 mins.

Producer, Jack Seaman; director, Richard Talmadge; screenplay, Robert A. Heinlein, Seaman; production designer, Jerome Pycha, Jr.; music, Herschel Burke Gilbert; special effects, Jacques Fresco; camera, Willard Thompson; editor, Roland Gross.

Donna Martell (Colonel Breiteis); Hayden Rorke (General Greene); Ross Ford (Major Moore); Larry Johns (Dr. Wernher); Herb Jacobs (Dr. Roundtree); Barbara Morrison (Molly Prattles); Ernestine Barrier (Madame President); James Craven (Commodore Carlson); John Hedloe (Adjutant); Peter Adams (Captain Carmody); Robert Karnes (Sam); John Straub (Chaplain); Charles Keane (Spacom Operator); John Tomecko (Blockhouse Operator); Robert Paltz (Bellboy).

Noted science fiction author Robert A. Heinlein and producer Jack Seaman wrote the script for this space opera which apparently was conceived as two pilots for a TV series which did not sell and was then sewn together into a feature and issued theatrically. The futuristic action might have been gripping to early 1950s audiences, but is trite by today's standards. Only the then-futuristic idea of a woman president and a female chief astronaut have any prophetic merit.

In 1970 the United States has a large space station in orbit, but the moon has not been colonized. Colonel Breiteis (Donna Martell) leads a three person expedition, with Major Moore (Ross Ford) and scientist Dr. Wernher (Larry Johns), to orbit the moon to find a suitable place for landing and exploration. Once in flight they find Wernher is a Soviet spy trying to sabotage the U.S. space program and during a fight with Moore, the ship goes out of control and crash lands on the moon. The trio establish a base, but the spy is killed when he falls putting up a TV antenna, while a rescue mission is on the way. By now Britels and Moore are in love and by television the president (Ernestine Barrier) of the United States performs their wedding ceremony, making them the first couple to be wed on the moon (No doubt to be followed by a "honey"moon.)

PROPHECY (Paramount, 1979) C 102 mins.

Producer, Robert L. Rosen; associate producer, Alan Levine; director, John Frankenheimer; screenplay, David Seltzer; production designer, William Craig Smith; set director, George Gaines; costumes, Ray Summers; makeup, Thomas R. Burman; assistant directors, Andy Stone, Robert Cohen, Paul Tucker; music, Leonard Rosenman; special effects, Robert Dawson; camera, Harry Stradling, Jr.; editor, Tom Rolf.

Talia Shire (Maggie Vern); Robert Foxworth (Robert Vern); Armand Assante (John Hawks); Richard Dysart (Isely); Victoria Racimo (Ramona); George Chutesi (M'Rai); Tom McFadden (Pilot); Evans Evans (Cellist); Burke Byrnes (Father); Mia Bendixsen (Girl); Johnny Timko (Boy); Everett L. Creach (Kelso); Charles H. Gray (Sheriff); and: Lyvingston Holms, Graham Jarvis, James H. Burk, Bob Terhune, Lon Katzman, Steve Shemayme, John A. Shemayme, Jaye Durkus, Renato Moore, Mel Waters, Roosevelt Smith, Eric Mansker.

When a series of killings by wild animals plague an Indian reservation in Maine, environmentalist Robert Vern (Robert Foxworth) and his wife Maggie (Talia Shire) investigate, aided by Indians John Hawks (Armand Assante) and Ramona (Victoria Racimo). Nearby is a large lumber company which has been dumping waste into the streams. It turns out the waste contains Methyl mercury, which ingested by the fish, can cause mutations in the offspring of the fish and the people who eat them. They do not realize this until after Maggie eats some of the fish and becomes pregnant. Exploring the area they find a mutated bear cub in a river and save it only to find its mother, who has become a murderous twenty foot giant, is on their trail. The bear pursues them to a remote cabin, but they finally kill the beast. Leaving the area, Maggie must decide whether or not to have an abortion and nearby another mutated bear stalks the forest.

PROPHECY is an uneasy mixture of environmentalist propaganda and shock effects. Certainly the huge, mutated bear is one of the most monstrous creatures to ever populate a film and when it is oncamera the action does not falter. Unfortunately the ugly beast is not often in sight, until near the finale, and it is mostly talk and more talk about saving humans, wildlife, air, and water. According to Phil Hardy in *The Film Encyclopedia: Science Fiction* (1984), " . . . [the film] is probably best remembered as yet another of director [John] Frankenheimer's disastrous attempts to rehabilitate himself in Hollywood in the seventies by playing the genre game."

Although highlighted by Harry Stradling, Jr.'s cinematography

and Robert Dawson's special effects, the film failed to excite at the box-office.

PSYCHO A-GO-GO see BLOOD OF GHASTLY HORROR.

Q (THE WINGED SERPENT) (United Film Distributors, 1982) C 100 mins.

Presenter, Samuel Z. Arkoff; executive producers, Don Sandburg, Richard DiBona; producer, Larry Cohen; music, Robert Ragland; special camera effects, Randy Cook, David Allen, Peter Kuran; camera, Armando Crespi; editor, Armand Lebowitz.

Michael Moriarty (Jimmy Quinn); David Carradine (Detective Shepard) Candy Clark (Joan); Richard Roundtree (Sergeant Powell); Malachi McCourt (Police Commissioner).

Samuel Z. Arkoff, along with James H. Nicholson, was one of the founders of American International Pictures which changed the habits of the moviegoing public, switching emphasis from the adult to the teenage audience with cheap horror films, low budget sci-fi entries, its more expensively-mounted Edgar Allan Poe features, and beach movies. By the mid-1970s Arkoff sold his interest in the company but remained associated with it until 1982 when he presented Larry Cohen's fantasy release, THE WINGED SERPENT, better known as Q. Despite being a visually appealing production, Q proved to be a hard sell and in many ways a 1980s equivalent to the old PRC chiller, THE FLYING SERPENT (1946), starring George Zucco.

Gotham police are baffled by a series of mysterious murders in highrise apartments and the apparent ritual killings, by flaying, of several people. At the same time junkie Jimmy Quinn (Michael Moriarty), a mob getaway auto driver, is forced by the gang to partake in a robbery and he ends up with the stolen diamonds. With nowhere to turn, he goes to the Chrysler building to see his attorney but his office is closed and he heads to the top of the building where he finds a large egg. Meanwhile a large feathered bird is sighted above the city and it is the one which has been attacking highrise dwellers. Police Detective Shepard (David Carradine) believes the connection between the bird and the ritual killings and Quinn realizes he can demand anything he wants because he knows the sanctuary of the bird. The bird is mortally wounded in a shootout with the law and its egg destroyed. But still another egg has been left to hatch.

Q refers to the Aztec god Quetzalcoatl, who has been reincarnated in this film. *Variety* rated the movie "a delightful science-

fiction winner" while, on the other hand, Donald C. Willis in *Horror and Science Fiction Films III* (1984) believes having the lead role be a loser hurt the feature, "[Director Larry] Cohen very much wants us to like this poor-slob-redeemed character; but we like the bird." He added, the movie " . . . is closer to appalling than enthralling."

QUINTET (Twentieth Century-Fox, 1979) C 100 mins.

Executive producer, Tommy Thompson; producer, Robert Altman; associate producer, Allan Nicholls; director, Altman; story, Altman, Lionel Chetwynd, Patricia Resnick; screenplay, Frank Barhydt, Altman, Resnick; music, Tom Pierson; production designer, Leon Ericksen; art director, Wolf Kroeger; assistant directors, Thompson, Charles Braive; costumes, Scott Bushnell; camera, Jean Boffety; editor, Dennis M. Hill.

Paul Newman (Essex); Vittorio Gassman (Saint Christopher); Fernando Rey (Grigor); Bibi Andersson (Ambrosia); Brigitte Fossey (Vivia); Nina Van Pallandt (Deuca); David Langton (Goldstar); Tom Hill (Francha); Monique Mercure (Redstone's Mate); Craig Richard Nelson (Redstone); Maruska Stankova (Jaspera); Anne Geraty (Ae-

Paul Newman in QUINTET (1979).

on); Michael Maillot (Obelus); Max Fleck (Wood Supplier); Francoise Berd (Charity House Woman).

"If you've seen other recent [Robert] Altman films you know why this one disappeared so fast," wrote Michael Weldon in *The Psychotronic Encyclopedia of Film* (1983), and he was on target about this self-absorbed, overlong, snobbish and boring look at the future. The script is nearly incomprehensible and several of the players appear to have difficulty with the English language—not just foreign actors—thus making the picture almost unintelligible at times. With captivating cinematography by Jean Boffety, the film is visually engaging, but at two hours in length it stultifies the rest of the senses.

In the near future, after a nuclear war, another Ice Age has crippled the Earth and most of the population dies and is devoured by the starving animal life. A few survivors exist in sheltered cities and into one of these Essex (Paul Newman) and his wife Viva (Brigitte Fossey) seek refuge only to have the woman murdered by a bomb which has been purposely planted. Essex wants vengeance and he finds the culprit is one of three Quintet players: St. Christopher (Vittorio Gassman), Ambrosia (Bibi Andersson) and Deuca (Nina Van Pallandt). With Grigor (Fernando Rey) as the referee, these players amuse themselves with their deadly game which leads to murder. Essex is determined to become the fourth player to carry out his revenge.

DIE RACHE DES HOMUNKULUS see HOMUNCULUS.

RADAN see RODAN.

RADIO-MANIA (Teleview Corp./W. W. Hodkinson Corp., 1923) 5,100'.

Presenter, Herman Holland; director Roy William Neill; screenplay, Lewis Allen Browne; titles, Joseph W. Farnham; assistant director, Charles Van Arsdale; camera, George Folsey.

Grant Mitchell (Arthur Wyman); Margaret Irving (Mary Langdon); Gertrude Hillman (Mrs. Langdon); W. H. Burton (Mr. Sterling); Isabelle Vernon (Landlady); J. D. Walsh (Buz Buz); J. Burke (Gin Gin); Peggy Smith (Pux Pux); Betty Borders (Tuz Tuz); Alice Effinger, Peggy Williams (Martian Flappers).

Also shown as THE MAN FROM MARS and MARS CALLING, this inventive sci-fi picture from the silent era was shot in a crude 3-D version (a process called Teleview) for its scenes of Mars, depicting Martians with outsized heads and brains, mounted on small bodies. *Variety* defined the Teleview gimmick as " . . . a device which resembles the old-fashioned stereoscope. . . . It is explained that the glass used . . . is ordinary window glass, the effect being obtained by a revolving shutter arrangement created by a small motor concealed in the equipment. . . . The 'Teleview' pictures are taken with a camera with two lenses. When viewed by the naked eye they are blurred and vague. Through the machine they are remarkably clear but seem restricted to small projection space."

Inventor Arthur Wyman (Grant Mitchell) wins money as a prize for an article he has written on Albert Einstein. He uses the funds to invent a radio with which he can communicate with Mars. He is successful and the Martians tell him how to turn coal into diamonds and clay into gold. He awakes to discover it was all a dream and is very depressed until encouraged by girlfriend Mary Langdon (Margaret Irving) he invents a soundless alarm clock.

RADIOACTIVE DREAMS (ITM, 1984) C 95 mins.

Producers, Thomas F. Karnowski, Moctescuma Espanza; director/screenplay, Albert F. Pyun; music, Pete Robinson; camera, Charles Minskil; editor, Dennis O'Connor.

John Stockwell (Young Philip); Michael Dudikoff (Marlowe); and: Lisa Blout, Michele Little, Don Murray, George Kennedy.

In the year 2010, fifteen years after Earth has been devastated by nuclear annihilation, two young men, Marlowe (Michael Dudikoff) and Young Philip (John Stockwell), emerge from their abandoned mine shaft home to make their way in the world. The young men were left in the mine as boys by their gangster fathers the day the world ended, with enough food to exist. For education, they had detective books and magazines from which they formed their view of life. Thinking themselves detectives, which they refer to as "dicks," the duo set out to locate the person who holds control of the launch of the last nuclear missile and they arrive at a place called Video City which is populated by such yesteryear stereotypes as: hippies, bikers, punk rockers, and disco dancers.

With the glut of science fiction movies released in the late 1970s and well into the 1980s, it was inevitable that lackluster genre takeoffs like RADIOACTIVE DREAMS would appear and interpolate other film story formats, in this case the private eye characters. Made in 1984, the feature received minor release and even less notice. The reasons for this were duly noted by Henry Sheehan in *The Hollywood Reporter* who wrote the " . . . production is a misfired attempt to craft a youth comedy version of apocalyptic sci-fi. Unfortunately, the humor is witless, the action is clumsy, and the vision of the future is hopelessly derivative and constricted."

RAGE (Tiber International/Arco Film, 1986) C 91 mins.

Producer, Paoio Ferrara; director, Anthony Richmond [Tonino Ricci]; screenplay, Jaime Comas Gil, Eugenie Benito; music, Stelvie Cipriani; assistant director, Giancario Bastianoni; stunt co-ordinator, Roland Zamperla; set designer, Javier Fernandez; camera, Luciano Vittori; editor, Vincanzo Tomassi.

Conrad Nichols (Rage); Stelie Candelli (Young Woman); Werner Pochat (The Soldier); Taida Urruzola (Weapons Expert); Chris Huerta (Slash).

Following World War III, Rage (Conrad Nichols) is given orders to lead a mission to find Alpha Base, which emits a continuous radio signal and holds technical data and uranium reserves required by the nuclear survivors. Along with Rage on the expedition is an old soldier friend (Werner Pochat) and a young woman (Stelie Candelli) along with a weapons expert (Taida Urruzola). They travel to warlord Slash (Chris Huerta) for a map to Alpha Base, but the scar-faced leader sends his minions after them. The group thwarts them in a battle aboard a locomotive. The expedition finds Alpha Base but it is deserted and has no uranium reserves. They bring back a copy of the Bible and it helps them to restart civilization.

Using costumes and vehicles from older war movies, RAGE is a poorly dubbed, mediocre entry from Europe, an Italian-Spanish co-production, which took years to reach the U.S. Boasting such incongruities as a heroine who goes on a dangerous mission wearing next-to-nothing and an obviously fake scar on the villain's face, the film follows all the expected plot ploys necessary for such fare, including a culminating lengthy, and boring battle sequence. *Variety* judged the import a "cheap mishmash".

RAVAGERS (Columbia, 1979) C 91 mins.

Executive producer, Saul David; producer, John W. Hyde; director, Richard Compton; based on the novel *Path to Savagery* by Robert Edmond Alter; screenplay, Donald S. Sanford; production designer, Ronald E. Hobbs; costumes, Ron Talsky; assistant director, Pat Kehoe; music, Fred Karlin; sound, Garry Cunningham; camera, Vincent Saizis; editor, Maury Winetrobe.

Richard Harris (Falk); Ann Turkel (Faina); Art Carney (Sergeant); Ernest Borgnine (Rann); Anthony James (Leader); Woody Strode (Brown); Alana Hamilton (Miriam); Seymour Cassel (Blindman).

Ravagers are a gang of murderous thugs who terrorize the population following World War III. They rape and murder Miriam (Alana Hamilton), the wife of Falk (Richard Harris), and he vows revenge. He kills the Ravagers responsible for his spouse's demise, but finds himself being hunted by their comrades. He is forced to abandon his New York city home and takes sanctuary with absent-minded Sergeant (Art Carney), who has set out to rebuild civilization on an old aircraft carrier, and is aided by Faina (Ann Turkel) and Rann (Ernest Borgnine). The vicious Ravagers follow Falk and there is the showdown between the two factions.

RAVAGERS is only another excuse for a pessimistic view of tomorrow, combining the revenge theme of the DEATH WISH movie series (starring Charles Bronson) with science fiction. The result is a violent, downbeat and uninteresting melodrama. Phil Hardy decided in *The Film Encyclopedia: Science Fiction* (1984), "Directed in the vulgar style of [Richard] Compton's Southern-vigilante films (MACON COUNTY [1974], and RETURN TO MACON COUNTY [1975]) and limply scripted by [Donald] Sanford, the film updates the vigilante theme to no purpose and wastes its strong cast."

RETURN FROM WITCH MOUNTAIN (Buena Vista, 1978) C 93 mins.

Producers, Ron Miller, Jerome Courtland; director, John Hough; based on characters created by Alexander Key; screenplay, Malcolm Marmorstein; music, Lalo Schifrin; art directors, John B. Mansbridge,

Anthony James, Christopher Lee, Ike Eisenmann, and Bette Davis in RETURN FROM WITCH MOUNTAIN (1978).

Jack Senter; set decorator, Frank R. McKelvy; costumes, Chuck Keehne, Emily Sundby; assistant director, Michael Dmytryk; sound, Herb Taylor, Ron Ronconi; special effects, Eustace Lycett, Art Cruickshank, Danny Lee; camera, Frank Phillips; editor, Bob Bring.

Bette Davis (Letha); Christopher Lee (Victor); Kim Richards (Tia); Ike Eisenmann (Tony); Denver Pyle (Uncle Bene); Jack Soo (Mr. Yokomoto); Anthony James (Sickle); Dick Bakalyan (Eddie); Ward Costello (Mr. Clearcole); Christian Juttner (Dazzler); Poindexter (Crusher); Brad Savage (Muscles); Jeffrey Jacquet (Rocky);

See: ESCAPE TO WITCH MOUNTAIN.

THE RETURN OF CAPTAIN INVINCIBLE (Seven Keys Film Distributors, 1983) C 90 mins.

Producer, Andrew Gaty; associate producer, Brian Burgess; director, Philippe Mora; screenplay, Steve de Souza, Gaty; production designer, David Copping; art director, Owen Patterson; music, William Motzing; sound, Ken Hammond; camera, Mike Molloy; editor, John Scott.

Alan Arkin (Captain Invincible); Christopher Lee (Mr. Midnight); Kate Fitzpatrick (Patty Patria); Bill Hunter (Tupper/Coach); Graham Kennedy (Australian Prime Minister); Michael Pate (U. S. President); Hayes Gordon (Kirby); Max Phipps (Admiral); Noel Ferrier (General).

Superhero Captain Invincible (Alan Arkin) is drummed out of the United States during the 1950s' red-baiting era (he wore a red cape!) and he ends up in the Australian outback a hopeless drunk. Three decades later the President (Michael Pate) of the United States, who revered him as his boyhood hero, asks him to return home to recover a stolen hypno-ray, a top secret weapon. The ray has been taken by Mr. Midnight (Christopher Lee), a madman who intends to purify New York City by having ethnic groups relocated to the sea coast and then using the ray to break the land away so they will float out to sea. At first Captain Invincible is not up to the task, but with the help and encouragement from law officer Patty Patria (Kate Fitzpatrick), he regains his powers and starts flying again. He thwarts the sinister Mr. Midnight.

This satire on SUPERMAN (1978) (q.v.) and its ilk was made in Australia, but received faint notice stateside. *Variety* opined, "A terrific premise for escapist fantasy, which is muddled in its execution. Result is an uneven, inconsistent film which is inspired, nearly brilliant in parts, but which fails to jell as a whole. As a musical comedy it is light on laughs; as an adventure it has moments of edge-of-the-seat excitement, but loses momentum when it most needs it: in the final 15 minutes."

It should be noted that some of the film's music was composed by Richard Hartley and Richard O'Brien, who did the same for THE ROCKY HORROR SHOW (1975) (q.v.).

RETURN OF DR. X (Warner Bros., 1939) 62 mins.

Producer, Bryan Foy; director, Vincent Sherman; based on the short story "The Doctor's Secret" by William J. Makin; screenplay, Lee Katz; art director, Esdras Hartley; costumes, Milo Anderson; makeup, Perc Westmore; music, Bernhard Kaun; technical advisor, Dr. Leo Schulman; camera, Sid Hickox; editor, Thomas Pratt.

Wayne Morris (Walter Barnett); Rosemary Lane (Joan Vance); Humphrey Bogart (Marshall Quesne); Dennis Morgan (Michael Rhodes); John Litel (Dr. Francis Flegg); Lya Lys (Angela Merrova); Huntz Hall (Pinky); Charles Wilson (Detective Ray Kincaid); Vera Lewis (Miss Sweetman); Howard Hickman (Chairman); Olin Howland (Undertaker); Arthur Aylesworth (Guide); Jack Mower (Detective Sergeant Moran); Creighton Hale (Hotel Manager); John Ridgely (Rodgers); Joe Crehan (Editor); Glenn Langan, William Hopper (Internes); and: Ian Wolfe, Virginia Brissac, George Reeves, John Harmon, Ed Chandler, Howard Hickman.

The success of DR. X (q.v.) in 1932 caused Warner Bros. to evolve another horror film using the same audience-grabbing title.

Several murders occur in which the victims are found bloodless and newspaper reporter Walter Barnett (Wayne Morris) and medical interne Michael Rhodes (Dennis Morgan) investigate. The trail leads to Dr. Francis Flegg (John Litel). An actress (Lya Lys) with Type One blood is murdered and soon all the patients in the local hospital with that type blood disappear. Rhodes and Barnett return to Flegg's and find him mortally wounded, but before dying he confesses his attacker was Xavier who is really Marshall Quesne (Humphrey Bogart), a murderer who had been executed and brought back to life by Flegg's experiments. Quesne has committed all the killings because he requires the rare blood type to live. When Rhodes' girlfriend, nurse Joan Vance (Rosemary Lane), reveals she has Type One blood they use her as bait to capture Quesne. The murderer abducts her but the rescue team arrives with the law and Quesne is shot. He dies for the second time.

Humphrey Bogart was NONE too fond of his role in this film as Richard Gehman quoted him in *Bogart* (1965). "This was one of the pictures that made me march into Jack Warner and ask for more money again. You can't believe what this one was like. I had a part that somebody like Bela Lugosi or Boris Karloff should have played. I was this doctor, brought back to life, and the only thing that nourished this poor bastard was blood. If it'd been Jack Warner's blood, or Harry's, or Pop's, maybe I wouldn't have minded as much. The trouble was, they were drinking mine and I was making this stinking movie."

For the record, this is *not* a sequel to DR. X.

RETURN OF THE APE MAN (Monogram, 1944) 60 mins.

Producers, Sam Katzman, Jack Dietz; associate producer, Barney Sarecky; director, Philip Rosen; screenplay, Robert Charles; art director, David Milton; music, Edward Kay; assistant director, Art Hammond, Richard L'Estrange; sound, Glen Glenn; camera, Marcel Le Picard; editor, Carl Pierson.

Bela Lugosi (Professor Dexter); John Carradine (Professor Gilmore); Frank Moran (Ape Man); Judith Gibson (Anne); Michael Ames (Steve Rogers); Mary Currier (Mrs. Hilda Gilmore) Ed Chandler (Sergeant); Mike Donovan (Policeman); George Eldridge (Patrolman); Horace Carpenter (Watchman); Ernie Adams (Bum); and: Frank Leigh.

RETURN OF THE APE MAN was Bela Lugosi's final Monogram feature; having starred in nine entries for the studio between 1941 and 1944. In many ways it is one of the best of the group, at least from a humorous point of view as it appears to be almost a parody which takes itself quite seriously. Some of its dialogue is priceless. In one scene Lugosi's character says to the half-human title creature, "Did you kill somebody again?" The creature responds, "I killed Hilda." Lugosi then asks him why he committed the crime and the ape man says, "I didn't mean to."

Scientists Dexter (Bela Lugosi) and Gilmore (John Carradine) revive a dead drunk and keep him alive on ice for four months. They travel to the Arctic where after seven months they find a prehistoric man (Frank Moran) imbedded in ice and they bring him home. Gilmore suggests turning him over to science, but Dexter revives the creature who proves to be murderous. Dexter intends to give the ape man half of a human brain so he can communicate with him, but Gilmore refuses to go along. Dexter turns the tables on him and kills Gilmore and uses his brain for the experiment. The brute escapes and kills Gilmore's wife Hilda (Mary Currier) and when the police arrives, Dexter attempts to hide the monster who kills him and disappears. It abducts Gilmore's niece (Judith Gibson) and takes her to the laboratory where it accidentally sets the place afire and is consumed in the blaze.

Not only is RETURN OF THE APE MAN (not a direct sequel to THE APE MAN [q.v.]) saddled with a screwy script and dialogue, it is also lacking in adequate production values. A cellophane-like substance was used for ice in the lab sequence and Don Miller noted wryly in *B Movies* (1973), "It failed to explain how the relic of another age happened to be wearing plainly evident long drawers." Also the film's advertising prominently featured George Zucco but the distinguished British actor is nowhere to be seen in the picture. As originally planned, former boxer Frank Moran was to play the title creature in the early scenes and after the creature's refinement through the brain operation, George Zucco was to take over the characterization. Illness, however, prevented Zucco's appearance in the production and Moran sustained the part throughout. The film's advertising, however, had been completed and no effort was made to correct Zucco's billing in a *non*-appearance.

In *The Films of Bela Lugosi* (1980), Richard Bojarski wrote, "The script, after a promising start, meandered into formula situations, rescued only by the menacing unpredictability of the creature, ably acted by Frank Moran, who was immune to bullets, but not fire."

THE RETURN OF THE GOLEM see THE GOLEM (essay).

RETURN OF THE JEDI (Twentieth Century-Fox, 1983) C 133 mins.

Executive producer, George Lucas; producer, Howard Kazanjian; co-producers, Robert Watts, Jim Bloom; director, Richard Marquand; story, Lucas; screenplay, Lawrence Kasdan, Lucas; production designer, Norman Reynolds; art directors, Fred Hole, James Schroppe; set decorator, Joe Johnston; costumes, Aggie Guerard Rodgers, Nilo Rodis-Jamero; makeup/creature design, Phil Tippett, Stuart Freeborn; music, John Williams; choreography, Gillian Gregory; conceptual artist, Ralph McQuarrie; assistant directors, David Tomblin, Roy Button, Michael Steele; visual effects supervisors, Richard Edlund, Dennis Muren, Ken Ralston; visual effects art director, Joe Johnston; optical camera supervisor, Bruce Nicholson; matte painting supervisor, Michael Pangrazio; model shop supervisors, Lorne Peterson, Steve Gawley; animation supervisor, James Keefer; stop motion animator, Tom St. Amand; special effects supervisors, Roy Arbogast, Kit West; sound, Tony Dawe, Randy Thom; sound designer, Ben Burtt; camera, Alan Hume; editors, Sean Barton, Marcia Lucas, Dwayne Dunham; visual effects editor, Arthur Repola.

Mark Hamill (Luke Skywalker); Harrison Ford (Hans Solo); Carrie Fisher (Princess Leia Organa); Billy Dee Williams (Lando Calrissian); Anthony Daniels (C-3PO); Sebastian Shaw (Anakin Skywalker); Ian McDiarmid (Emperor); Frank Oz (Yoda); David Prowse (Darth Vader); James Earl Jones (Voice of Darth Vader);

Alec Guinness (Ben [Obi-Wan] Kenobi); Kenny Baker (R2-D2); Michael Pennington (Moff Jerjerrod); Kenneth Colley (Admiral Piett); Michael Carter (Bib Fortuna); Denis Lawson (Wedge); Tim Rose (Admiral Ackbar); Dermot Crowley (General Madine); Caroline Blakiston (Mon Mothman); Warwick Davis (Wicket); Kenny Baker (Paploo); Jeremy Bulloch (Boba Fett); Femi Taylor (Oola); Michele Gruska (Sy Snootles); Claire Davenport (Fat Dancer); Jack Purvis (Teebo); Mike Edmonds (Logray); Jane Busby (Chief Chirpa); Nicki Reader (Nicki); Malcolm Dixon, Mike Cottrell (Ewok Warriors); Adam Bareham, Jonathan Oliver (Stardestroyer Controllers); Pip Miller, Tom Mannion (Stardestroyer Captains); Toby Philpott, David Barclay, Mike Edmonds (Jabba Puppeteers); Michael McCormick, Deep Roy, Simon Williamson, Hugh Spirit, Swim Lee, Michael Quinn, Richard Robinson (Puppeteers).

Preceded by STAR WARS (1977) and THE EMPIRE STRIKES BACK (1980) (qq.v.), RETURN OF THE JEDI (announced as REVENGE OF THE JEDI) was the final segment in the George Lucas trilogy, although episodes involving other characters and events are promised. This feature also spawned two EWOK (q.v.) TV movies. Costing $32,500,000 and grossing domestically $165,500,000, RETURN OF THE JEDI closed out the "Luke Skywalker" series by neatly tieing together all the plot elements from the first two films while increasing the special effects spectacle. Apart from the effects, however, the movie suffers from the same weakness of THE EMPIRE STRIKES BACK: an indifferent plot which, this time, is saddled by mostly indifferent performances.

Luke Skywalker (Mark Hamill), now fully mature and trained as a Jedi Knight, rescues pal Han Solo (Harrison Ford) from his state of frozen animation in carbonite and Han rejoins Wookie co-pilot Chewbacca (Peter Mayhew) and renews his increasingly growing romance with Princess Leia Organa (Carrie Fisher). On the planet Tatooine they do battle with the evil Jabba the Hutt, who has captured Leia. Once she is freed, the group has a bigger task—fighting The Emperor (Ian MacDiarmid) and his cohort Darth Vader (Dave Prowse; voice of James Earl Jones) and their new invincible *Death Star II,* a spacecraft/weapon which has a defensive screen around it centered on the planet Endor. The Rebels head to Endor and enlist the aid of the inhabitants, small fuzzy creatures called Ewoks, and there they marshall their forces to attack the death ship. Luke makes his way onboard the Empire craft and faces Darth Vader, whom he knows is his father. He also learns that Leia is his twin sister and in the showdown between the two, Vader renounces the forces of the dark and dies. Meanwhile with the Ewoks, the rebels cut the power for the defense screen and their ships attack and destroy the Empire vessel. The Empire is defeated; Han and Leia become lovers, and Luke alone, a fulfilled Jedi Knight. Adding to the optimistic tone is the ghostly reunion of Yoda, Ben Kenobi, and Darth Vader, the latter no longer a threatening evil force.

Variety reported to its readers, "There is good news, bad news and no news about RETURN OF THE JEDI. The good news is that George Lucas & Co. have perfected the technical magic to a point where almost anything and everything—no matter how bizarre—is believable. The bad news is the human dramatic dimensions have been sorely sacrificed. The no news is the picture will take in millions regardless of the pluses and minuses." The reviewer pinpointed the main weakness of the feature by saying it " . . . suffers a lot in comparison to the initial STAR WARS, when all was fresh. One of the apparent problems is neither the writers or the principal performers are putting in the same effort."

THE RETURN OF THE LIVING DEAD (Orion, 1985) C 91 mins.

Executive producers, John Daly, Derek Gibson; producer, Tom Fox; associate producer, Sam Crespoi-Horowitz; director, Dan O'Bannon; story, Rudy Ricci, John Russo, Russell Streiner; screenplay, O'Bannon; music, Matt Clifford; production designer, William Stout; art director, Robert Howland; assistant director, David M. Robertson; camera, Jules Brenner; editor, Robert Gordon.

Clu Gulager (Burt); James Karen (Frank); Don Calfa (Ernie); Thom Matthews (Freddy); Beverly Randolph (Tina); John Philbin (Chuck); Jewel Shepard (Casey); Miguel Nunez (Spider); Brian Peck (Scuz); Linnea Quigley (Trash); Mark Venturini (Suicide); Jonathan Terry (Colonel Glover); Cathleen Cordell (His Wife); Drew Dreighan, James Dalesandro (Paramedics); John Durbin, David Bond (Radio Corps); Bob Libman (Tac Squad Captain); John Stuart West, Michael Crabtree, Ed Krieger (Riot Cops); and: Robert Craighead, Paul Cloud (Cops); Leigh Drake (Dispatcher); and: Derrick Brice, Terrence M. Houlihan, Allan Trautman, Robert Bennett, Jerome Daniels Coleman, Cherry Davis.

George A. Romero's NIGHT OF THE LIVING DEAD (1968) (see B/V) has acquired a vast cult following despite its amateurish production values and performances. Its scripter, John Russo, is given co-author credit for the storyline of this tongue-in-cheek look at the subject and early on in THE RETURN OF THE LIVING DEAD some of its characters state that the 1968 scenario did not divulge the full story of the living dead attacking humans at a remote Pennsylvania farm house. The film then goes its own path with an updated version of the narrative set in Louisville; populated

Clu Gulager, James Karen, and Thom Matthews in RETURN OF THE LIVING DEAD (1985).

with a set of brain-eating, vocal and somewhat humorous zombies. The most alluring of them is Trash (Linnea Quigley), a punk rocker devoured by horny old zombies in a graveyard, who returns as one of them wearing only leg warmers and a fright face.

Two medical bumblers accidentally release chemicals stored in metal cylinders the Army sent to Louisville's Uneeda Medical Supply Warehouse after the zombie plague near Pittsburgh in the late 1960s. The chemical seeps into the ground at a nearby graveyard causing the resurrection of dozens of corpses who must feed on the brains of the living, turning them into zombies. In the cemetery that night are a gang of partying punk rockers. When the dead arise, they join forces with mortician Ernie (Don Calfa) and the owner (Clu Gulager) of the warehouse and his assistant (Thom Matthews), along with a physician (James Karen), in combatting the zombies. The army is dispatched and the city of Louisville is destroyed in a nuclear blast, eliminating the zombies and the chemical which spawned them.

Like most features of its ilk, THE RETURN OF THE LIVING DEAD contains excessive gore, but its humorous approach at its subject helps to make it more palatable. David Hinckley (New York *Daily News*) noted the film has "flaws" but added, " . . . there are worse ways to kill 91 minutes." *Variety* weighed it a " . . . sporadically hilarious frequently draggy takeoff. . . ."

THE REVENGE OF FRANKENSTEIN (Columbia, 1958) C 91 mins.

Executive producer, Michael Carreras; producer, Anthony Hinds; director, Terence Fisher; suggested by the novel *Frankenstein* by Mary Shelley; screenplay, Jimmy Sangster; additional dialogue, Hurford Janes; art director, Bernard Robinson; makeup, Phil Leakey; music, Leonard Salzedo; music director, Muir Mathieson; camera, Jack Asher; editors, James Needs, Alfred Cox.

Peter Cushing (Dr. Victor Stein [Victor Frankenstein]); Francis Matthews (Dr. Hans Kleve); Eunice Gayson (Margaret); Michael Gwynn (Karl); John Welsh (Bergman); Lionel Jeffries (Fritz); Oscar Quitak (Karl Werner the Dwarf); Richard Wordsworth (Up Patient); Charles Lloyd Pack (President); John Stuart (Inspector); Michael Ripper (Kurt); George Woodridge (Janitor); Margery Cresley (Countess Barsynsha); Anne Walmisley (Vera); Richard Wordsworth (Patient); Ian Whittaker (Boy); Avirl Leslcle (Girl).

The success of CURSE OF FRANKENSTEIN (1957) (q.v.) convinced London's Hammer Films to continue its series and it brought forth THE REVENGE OF FRANKENSTEIN the next year. This sturdy effort was considered shocking at the time of release since Baron Frankenstein was shown in his actual medical work with brains, eyes, etc. being displayed in full view as he assembled them into his new creation. Following this episode, however, the series went downhill.

Baron Victor Frankenstein (Peter Cushing) is doomed to execution, along with a dwarf guard, Karl Werner (Oscar Quitak). At the moment of truth, the guard pushes a priest under the guillotine and saves Frankenstein who has promised him a new—and perfect—body. Setting up practice in a charity hospital in Carlsbruck as Dr. Stein, the scientist secretly constructs a new body from amputations performed on his various patients. Recognized by Dr. Hans Kleve (Francis Matthews), the Baron shows him his new creation which lacks only a brain. (His previous brain transplant with a monkey failed when the creature became a cannibal.) Keeping his promise to Karl, Frankenstein installs his brain in the new body. The new Karl (Michael Gwynn) burns his old body but is badly beaten by a sadistic janitor (George Woodbridge), causing brain damage. Karl becomes his former self and craves human flesh. The monster invades a party attended by Stein and Kleve and reveals his creator before being killed. The hospital patients turn on Frankenstein and beat him to death. Before dying he gives Kleve instructions on how to transplant his brain into a fresh body he has created. Not long afterwards, a Dr. Frank (Peter Cushing) takes up practice in London.

REVENGE OF THE DEAD see THE GOLEM (essay).

REVENGE OF THE STEPFORD WIVES (NBC-TV, 10/12/80) C 100 mins.

Executive producer, Edgar J. Scherick; producers, Robert A. Papazian, Scott Rudin; director, Robert Fuest; based on characters created by Ira Levin; teleplay, David Wiltse; music, Laurence Rosenthal; art director, Tom H. John; camera, Ric Waite; editor, Jerrold L. Ludwig.

Sharon Gless (Kay Foster); Julie Kavner (Megan Brady); Audra Lindley (Barbara Parkinson); Don Johnson (Andy Brady); Mason Adams (Wally) Arthur Hill (Dale "Diz"; Corbett); Ellen Weston (Kitten); Thomas Hill (Dr. Edgar Trent); Gay Rowan (Angelina); Jim McKrell (Bruce Manson); Lee Benard (Sally Tashis); Edward Bell (Gary Tarshis); Sheldon Feldner (Norman Kahn); Howard Witt (Police Chief); Peter Maloney (Henry the Druggist); Stephanie Blackmore (Druggist's Wife); Melissa Newan (Muffin Sheridan).

See: THE STEPFORD WIVES.

REVENGE OF THE ZOMBIES (Monogram, 1943) 61 mins.

Producer, Lindsley Parsons; director, Steve Sekely; screenplay, Edmund Kelson, Van Norcross; art director, David Milton; music director, Edward Kay; camera, Mack Stengler; editor, Richard Currier.

John Carradine (Dr. Max Heinrich von Altermann); Robert Lowery (Larry Adams); Gale Storm (Jennifer Rand); Bob Steele (Sheriff); Veda Ann Borg (Lila von Altermann); Mantan Moreland (Jeff); Mauritz Hugo (Scott Warrington); Barry MaCollum (Dr. Keating); Madame Sul-Te-Wan (Beulah); James Basmettc (Lazarus); Sybil Lewis (Rosella); Robert Cherry (Pete).

Val Lewton's beautifully eerie I WALKED WITH A ZOMBIE (1943) was successful commercially and Monogram Pictures, the same year, churned out REVENGE OF THE ZOMBIES, which, like its earlier KING OF THE ZOMBIES (1941) (q.v.) revolved around a mad scientist creating the title creatures to do the bidding of the Third Reich. The result was ". . . . so cut and dried it wouldn't scare you unless one of the living dead bolted the screen and walked down into the theatre." (New York *Daily News*).

In the Louisiana bayous, deranged scientist and Nazi Dr. Max Heinrich von Altermann (John Carradine) is striving to create an army of bullet proof zombies for his Homeland's use; the army composed of the local black population. The doctor sacrifices his wife

Lila (Veda Ann Borg) for the cause and she becomes a zombie, but he cannot control her mind. Because of her disappearance, Jennifer Rand (Gale Storm) and Larry Adams (Robert Lowery), along with the latter's chauffeur Jeff (Mantan Moreland) arrive at the remote mansion with investigator Scott Warrington (Mauritz Hugo). When several other people are reported missing, the sheriff (Bob Steele) also shows up to delve into the situation. As von Altermann plots to make Jennifer his unwilling bride, Lila assumes control of the zombie army and they kill the madman before they too perish.

Don Miller in *B Movies* (1973) recorded that the film " . . . didn't have much out of the ordinary . . . but director Steve Sekely had been trained in the Danubia studios of Budapest, where you did what you could and above all, made it artistic. Sekely must have taken aside cameraman Mack Stengler and held an earnest conference, for the composition of some of the scenes in Carradine's laboratory are quite resourceful, giving the film a more expensive appearance than actually was the case. The fact that for all their artistry some of the shots didn't quite match in the cutting is a relatively minor, if sore, point."

British release title: THE CORPSE VANISHES.

REVOLT OF THE ROBOTS see AELITA.

THE ROAD WARRIOR see MAD MAX II.

ROBOCOP (Orion, 1987) C 103 mins.

Executive producer, Jon Davison; producer, Arne Schmidt; associate producers, Stephen Lim, Phil Tippett; director, Paul Verhoeven; screenplay, Edward Neumeier, Michael Miner; music, Basil Poledouris; production designer, William Sandell; art director, Gayle Simon; set decorator, Robert Gould; set designer, James Tocci; Robocop designer/creator, Rob Bottin; ED-209 designers/creators, Craig Davies, Peter Ronzani; matte painting, Rocco Gioffre; costumes, Erica Edell Phillips; assistant director, Michele A. Panelli, second unit director, Mark Goldblatt; sound, Robert Wald; special effects, Dale Martin; special camera effects, Peter Kuran, Visual Concept Engineering; special sound effects editing, Stephen Flick, John Pospisil, camera, Jost Vacano; editor, Frank J. Urioste.

Peter Weller (Murphy the Robocop); Nancy Allen (Lewis); Ronny Cox (Jones); Kurtwood Smith (Clarence); Miguel Ferrer (Morton); Robert DoQui (Sergeant Reed); Daniel O'Herlihy (Old Man); and: Ray Wise, Felton Perry, Paul McCrane, Jesse Goins, Del Zamora, Calvin Jung.

ROBOCOP (a robot policeman) proved to be a box-office

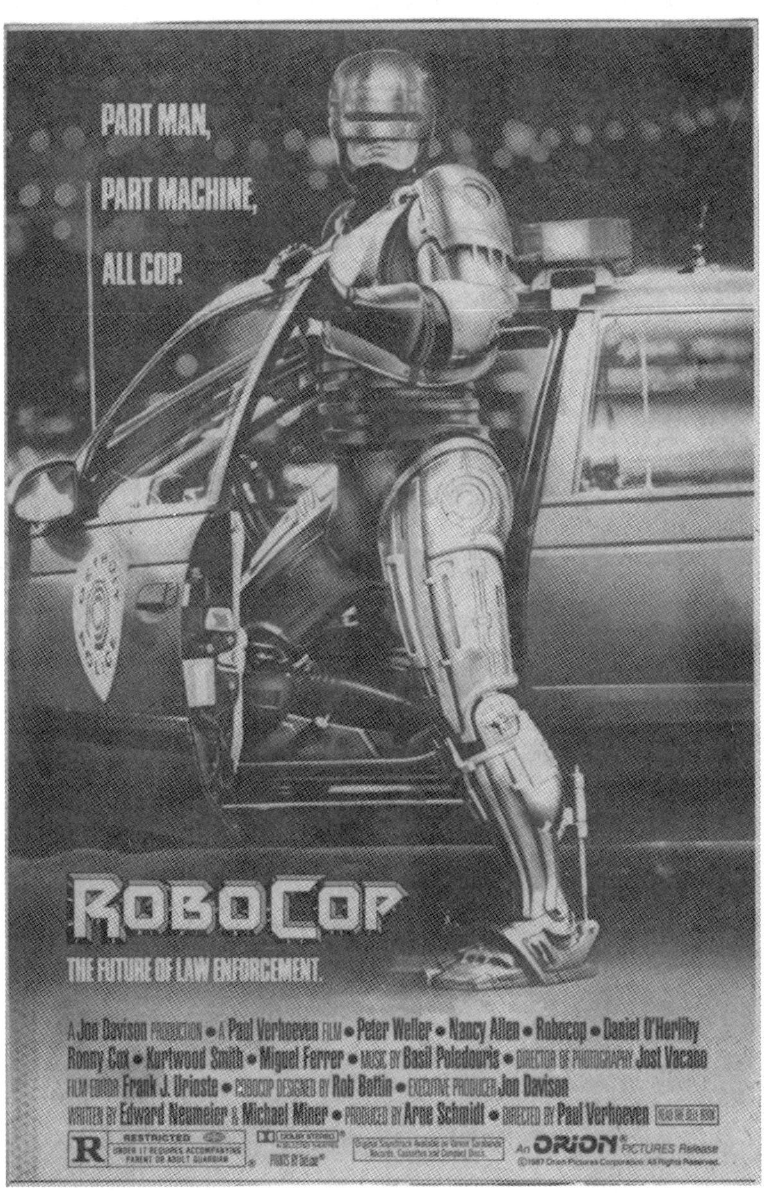

Advertisement for ROBOCOP (1987).

sensation in the summer of 1987, grossing $53,356,612 in its first seventeen weeks of domestic release. Its success launched an impressive merchandising campaign including a comic book from Marvel Comics, a Robocop doll, a computer game, the film's novelization, posters, T-shirts, etc. Jack Mathews justly noted in his background article on the feature film in the *Los Angeles Times,* "Orion appears to have hit the home run that all studios try for and seldom achieve. It has created a brand new hero, with a clear track for further exploitation. You don't even have to ask whether a sequel is being considered."

In 1991 Detroit is a hotbed of crime controlled by a gang of sadistic thugs and the police have become so ineffective that law enforcement has come under the domain of corporate manager Jones (Ronny Cox) and his corrupt inventor/henchman Morton (Miguel Ferrer) who has developed robots to combat the criminal elements. One of them is a computer/android who requires the brain of a human to function. This is supplied when Officer Murphy (Peter Weller) is mutilated by a gang of drug dealers and his brain is implanted in the robot who is also given the cop's face. Although his memory is basically gone, Robocop has fleeting remembrances of his loving family and the thugs who murdered him. With partner Lewis (Nancy Allen) he sets out to rid the city of its low life, while the young woman attempts to bring out the human side of her super robot partner.

Rated R (originally X) for its excessive carnage, ROBOCOP met with mixed critical reaction. Gene Siskel in his Tribune Media Services movie review column stated, "The fine Dutch director Paul Verhoeven tells what could have been another high-tech assault picture with fresh visuals and a refreshing sense of humor, especially about big business." Duane Byrge assessed in *The Hollywood Reporter,* "While those whose tastes don't include the spectacle of large machines noisily blasting each other are not likely to be enticed by ROBOCOP, this shocked look at the urban future should engage and crank up action fans." Like most films of its ilk, ROBOCOP takes a dim view of humanity in the future, as noted by *Daily Variety,* "It's a bleak world they inhabit, one where there's a thin line between lawfulness and lawlessness. Nearly everyone depicted here, anyway, exhibits a certain out-for-number-one mentality, be he cop or crook."

Manufactured on a tight budget of $13,500,000, ROBOCOP's sequel is projected to cost ten to twenty-five percent higher. As if to appease the critics, ROBOCOP II is targeted to be more satirical and not as violent as the first feature.

For the 1988 Oscars, Stephen Flick and John Pospisil were

voted a special sound effects editing Academy Award for their work on ROBOCOP.

ROBOT HOLOCAUST (Tycin Entertainment, 1986) C 79 mins.

Producer, Cynthia DePaula; director/screenplay, Tim Kincaid; production designer, Medusa; art director, Marina Zurkow, Ruth Lounsbury; costume designer, Celeste Hines; assistant director, Rebecca Rothbaum; robot masks, Ralph Cordero; robot suits, Valarie McNeill; sound, Mike Cribben; special makeup effects, Tom Lauten; robot creature effects designer, Ed French; special visual effects, Jeremie Frank; camera, Arthur D. Marks; editor, Barry Zetlin.

Norris Culf (Neo); Nadine Hart (Deeja); Rick Gianasi (Torque); Michael Downend (Jorn); Angelika Jager (Valeria): and: George Gray, Nicholas Reiner, Michael Azzolina, John Blaylock, Amy Brentano.

The planet New Terra has been destroyed virtually by a revolt of robots against the humans and the atmosphere poisoned with radiation. Neo (Norris Culf) and Deeja (Nadine Hart) lead a group of human rebels on a long journey to the Power Station, where the planet's artificial atmosphere is controlled by the Dark One and his assistant Valeria (Angelika Jager). A captive at the station is Jorn (Michael Downend), a scientist who has developed an implant device which permits humans to breathe in the radioactive atmosphere, and he is being tortured by Valeria who demands the secret of the device which Jorn has already put in his daughter, Deeja. The Dark One, Valerie, and their forces are overwhelmed and the rebels regain control of their destiny.

Variety, screening a copy of the home video cassette release print, termed this New York City-filmed feature "an okay science-fiction adventure" but added it "lacks the production values and large-scale setpieces required of a theatrical action pic, but is a suitable entry for homevideo fans."

ROBOT MONSTER (Astor, 1953) 63 mins.

Executive producer, Al Zimbalist; producer/director, Phil Tucker; screenplay, Wyott Ordung; music, Elmer Bernstein; special effects, Jack Rabin, David Commons; camera, Jack Greenhalgh; editor, Bruce Shoengarth.

George Nader (Roy); Claudia Barrett (Alice); Selena Royle (Mother); Gregory Moffett (Johnny); John Mylong (Professor); Pamela Paulson (Carla); George Barrows (Ro-Man).

One of the most endearing and enduring bottom-of-the-barrel junk sci-fiers is Phil Tucker's notorious ROBOT MONSTER, shot in 3-D for under $20,000 at southern California's Bronson Canyon.

The title creature is a giant gorilla wearing a space helmet and he lives in a cave with a TV screen and a bubble machine. Also called MONSTER FROM MARS and MONSTER FROM THE MOON, the film literally has no assets except competent cinematography by veteran Jack Greenhalgh and Elmer Bernstein's (debut) film score.

On a family outing in the desert, a young boy, Johnny (Gregory Moffett) falls asleep and when he awakes he finds that the world has been destroyed by alien invader Ro-Man (George Barrows) and that only his family has survived the holocaust. They include his father, The Professor (John Mylong); his mother, Martha (Selena Royle); his older sister, Alice (Claudia Barrett), and her boyfriend, Roy (George Nader); as well as his younger sister, Carla (Pamela Paulson). They take shelter in an area protected by a special serum concocted by the Professor. Ro-Man, under orders from his superior, The Great One, is determined to kill them and spends much of his time decimating the Earth and repopulating it with dinosaurs. Ro-Man kills little Alice and later does the same to Roy, who has married Alice. Ro-Man, however, lusts after Alice and intends to save her from extermination. This angers The Great One and he turns a death ray on the Earth destroying it along with Ro-Man. Johnny wakes up from a deep sleep to find it was all a dream. As the family goes home, Ro-Man emerges from his cave.

The *Los Angeles Times* was kind when it evaluated ROBOT MONSTER as a "crazy, mixed-up movie" while the *Hollywood Citizen-News* thought it "ancient and hackneyed . . . incredible. . . ." and *The Hollywood Reporter* termed it "loaded with inconsistencies." The movie was also filled with stock shots from ONE MILLION B.C. (1940) (see B/V) as well as military documentary footage. *Fangoria* magazine (May, 1983) noted, "When it comes to sheer, unadulterated obliqueness. . . . few movies can compare to ROBOT MONSTER. . . . The meandering plot-line and the out-of-whack dialogue both have to be witnessed first-hand to be believed."

THE ROBOT VS. THE AZTEC MUMMY (AIP-TV, 1966) 61 mins.

Producer, William C. Stell; director, Rafael Portillo; story, Stell, Alfred Salazar; art director, J. Torres Torija; music, Antonio Diaz Conde; camera, Enrique Wallace; editors, Jorge Bustos, Jose Li-Ho.

Ramon Gay (Dr. Krupp "The Bat"); Rosita Arenas (Flora); Crox Alvarado (Edward); Luis Aceves Castenada (Dr. Pinkley); Jorge Mondragon (Bruno); and: Emma Roldan.

A sequel to LA MOMIA (1957), this Mexican-made production was released south-of-the-border as MOMIA CONTRA EL

ROBOT HUMANO [The Mummy Vs. the Human Robot]. It was distributed in the U.S. directly to TV by K. Gordon Murray Productions in a hilariously dubbed version which makes the feature a delightful reverse classic. Running a little over one hour, the movie is mainly composed of flashback footage from LA MOMIA supplemented with new scenes about a mad scientist and his human robot invention. This creation was made by the doctor from various corpses and covered with sheet metal with light bulbs for ears. The contraption, which can destroy anything it touches, is not only howlingly funny to view, but it moves at the speed of an inch worm and in the finale confrontation with the Mummy, the robot is mashed into a pile of junk in a matter of seconds.

From the stock footage from LA MOMIA, the viewer learns a crazed scientist called The Bat (Ramon Gay) is after a gold breastplate from an ancient Aztec tomb protected by the living mummy Popoca. An expedition opens the tomb and obtains the breastplate, but later returns it to the tomb. The Bat, who wants the precious artifact to finance the building of a thousand human robots to conquer the world, plans to steal the treasure, which also includes an Aztec princess' bracelet. The Mummy, however, has other ideas and in a showdown with the Bat and his one human robot, the Mummy destroys the robot by tearing it to pieces and then killing The Bat.

Adding to the pleasures of THE ROBOT VS. THE AZTEC MUMMY is the fact the Mummy is so flimsy it appears as if it would disintegrate if caught in the rain. The madman also has an inept assistant named Bruno, who gets his face burned with acid, and who meets a bad end at the hands of the slow-moving Mummy. Add to this "Aztec choreography," a pit of snakes, the scientist's junkyard looking laboratory, ineptly staged fight sequences, atrocious dubbing, inane narration, and plot ploys which have the Mummy pull back at the sight of a cross and be driven away by flashlights and you have an hour of pure hilarity.

THE ROCKY HORROR PICTURE SHOW (Twentieth Century-Fox, 1975) C 100 mins.

Executive producer, Lou Adler; producer, Michael White; associate producer, John Goldstone; director, Jim Sharman; based on the stage musical by Richard O'Brien; screenplay, Sharman, O'Brien; songs, O'Brien; art director, Terry Ackland Snow; assistant director, Mike Gowans; sound, Ron Barron; special effects, Wally Veevers; camera, Peter Suschitzky; editor, Graeme Clifford.

Tim Curry (Dr. Frank N. Furter); Susan Sarandon (Janet Weiss); Barry Bostwick (Brad Majors); Richard O'Brien (Riff Raff); Jonathan Adams (Dr. Everett Scott); Nell Campbell (Columbia); Peter

Hinwood (Rocky); Meatloaf (Eddie); Patricia Quinn (Magenta); Charles Gray (Narrator); Jeremy Newson (Ralph Hapschatt); Hilary Labow (Betty Munroe); Frank Lester (Wedding Dad); Mark Johnson (Wedding Guest); Koo Stark, Petra Leah, Gina Barrie (Bridesmaids); John Marquand (Father).

A failure at the box-office when first released, this satirical sci-fi horror film (based on a 1973 British stage musical) has since become the most popular cult movie of all time. In the late 1970s impromptu shows were put on with the film in its selected showings and it started the "Midnight Movie" craze of the late 1970s and early 1980s. The film is one which you either love or hate; there is no middle ground. Many people go to see the audience more than the film as Danny Peary noted in *Cult Movies* (1981), " . . . I believe that your enjoyment is totally dependent on how funny, creative, and unified the ROCKY HORROR fanatics are on the night you attend the show."

THE ROCKY HORROR PICTURE SHOW is narrated by a criminologist (Charles Gray). After attending a wedding, cleancut Brad Majors (Barry Bostwick) and Janet Weiss (Susan Sarandon) plan to marry but get lost in the rain somewhere in Ohio. They end up at a remote castle where they meet a weird butler, Riff Raff (Richard O'Brien) and maid Magenta (Patricia Quinn). Stripped to their underclothes they are paraded before the convention of visitors from the planet Transsexual. The castle's owner, the bizarre Dr. Frank-N-Furter (Tim Curry), appears and gives life to his creation, the handsome Rocky Horror (Peter Hindwood) who hates his creator but later seduces both Janet and Brad. Brad's high school science teacher, Dr. Everett Scott (Jonathan Adams), arrives looking for his motorcyclist nephew Eddie (Meatloaf), whom the doctor has murdered. It turns out Dr. Frank-N-Furter has served Eddie for dinner to his guests and then turns Brad, Janet, the teacher and Groupie Columbia (Nell Campbell) into statues and promises to reward the maid and butler for their loyalty. Later Frank-N-Furter joins Brad, Janet and wheelchair-ridden Scott in a dance with Rocky before the alien guests. As the doctor plans to return to his home planet, the maid and butler kill him with a laser gun and Rocky picks up his body and climbs up the RKO tower while the maid is killed. The butler transports the castle back to the galaxy of Transylvania to be lost in time and space as Brad, Janet and Scott escape back to reality.

"It is fairly easy to identify the sources of the film's appeal," states Howard H. Prouty in *Magill's Survey of Cinema, Series II*, volume V (1981). "As is apparent from the opening song—'Science Fiction Double Feature,' the lyrics mouthed by a gigantic pair of lips—THE ROCKY HORROR PICTURE SHOW is both a tribute to and an affectionate send-up of science-fiction/horror films—not the sophisticated technological marvels of the 1970s, but the more basic mad scientist/rampaging creature potboilers of the 1930s, 1940s, and (especially) 1950s. . . . Psychologists have observed that the most sympathetic characters in these films are often not the ostensible heroes, but the 'monsters'—hounded by 'civilization' (usually shown at its paranoid worst) and invariably losing out to the combined forces of Good and Science. THE ROCKY HORROR PICTURE SHOW infuses this sentiment with a kinky sexuality and a youth-oriented antiestablishmentism, and turns the generic formula upside down."

RODAN (Distributors Corp. of America, 1957) C 79 mins.

Producer, Tomoyuki Tanaka; director, Inoshiro Honda; story, Takashi Kuronuma; screenplay, Takeshi Kimmura, Takeo Murata; art director, Tatsuo Kita; music, Tadashi Uamauchi; special effects, Eiji Tsuburaya; camera, Isamu Ashida.

Kenji Sawara (Shigero); Yumi Shirakawa (Kyo); Akihiko Hirata (Dr. Kashiwagi); Akko Kobori (Nishimura); Yasuko Nakata (Young Woman); Monosuke Yamada (Ohsaki); Yoshimubi Tojima (Izeki); and: Kiyoharu Ohnaka.

As a followup to the highly successful GODZILLA (1956) (see B/V), Toho Pictures of Japan and director Inoshiro Honda and special effects wizard Eiji Tsuburaya concocted RADAN, issued in the U.S. by Distributors Corporation of America (DCA) as RODAN.

Due to atomic testing, an earthquake opens a vast area connected to a mine shaft and there giant larvae hatch and devour several miners. Two huge eggs hatch into prehistoric baby birds who eat the larvae and quickly grow into giant flying reptiles. Shigero (Kenji Sawara) witnesses all this and develops a mental block. One of the flying reptiles, Rodan, causes a great deal of destruction and attacks and levels Sasebo City. Rodan is soon joined by the second monster and the duo threaten to devastate Japan. The creatures are traced to a cave on Mount Aso and the army sets up installations there. A volcano breaks loose and one of the monsters is destroyed in the lava and as the other comes to rescue it, the flying reptile is overwhelmed by the artillery.

The Hollywood Reporter felt "the special effects are unusually realistic and convincing" and these effects are certainly the film's strong suit. Plotwise the movie is little more than a series of mass destructions by the monsters, but they are persuasively depicted and quite entertaining. Donald F. Glut noted in *Classic Movie Monsters* (1978), "Audiences were again treated to the wizardry of Eiji

Advertisement for RODAN (1957).

Tsuburaya, who equaled the masterful work he did on GOJIRA [GODZILLA]. For added effect Tsuburaya showed cars, shards of rooftops and other debris flying into the air by the gales created by the Rodans' wings. The pterodactyl-like monsters did not even have to touch a building to reduce it to rubble."

Rodan would reappear in GHIDRAH, THE THREE-HEADED MONSTER (1965), MONSTER ZERO (1965) (see both in B/V) and DESTROY ALL MONSTERS (1968) (q.v.).

ROLLER BLADE (New World, 1986) C 97 mins.

Producer, Donald G. Jackson; associate producer, Ron Amick; director, Jackson; story, Jackson; screenplay, Jackson, Randall Frakes; music, Robert Garrett; assistant director/stunt co-ordinator, Clifford Davidson; set designer, Jackson, Amick; special visual effects, Tony Tremblay, Amick; camera, Jackson; editor, Amick.

Suzanne Solari (Sister Sharon Cross); Jeff Hutchinson (Marshall Goodman); Shaun Michelle (Hunter/Sister Fortune); Katina Garner (Mother Speed); Sam Mann (Waco); Robby Taylor (The Deputy/Dr. Saticoy); Chris Douglas-Olen Ray (Chris Goodman); and: Michelle Bauer, Barbara Peckinpaugh, Lisa Marie.

Following the Third World War, the city of Los Angeles is in a state of chaos with the evil Dr. Saticoy (Robby Taylor) and his minions at odds with Mother Speed (Katina Garner), a wheelchair-ridden woman who has a magic crystal which can heal and resurrect the dead. Saticoy wants the crystal and has his cohort Hunter (Shaun Michelle) join Mother's gang, using the name Sister Fortune. The young woman, however, sees through Saticoy's evil and joins forces with Sister Sharon (Suzanne Solari) and a policeman (Marshall Goodman) to bring Saticoy's diabolical reign of terror to an end.

Donald G. Jackson produced and directed this "amateurish junker released directly to the homevideo market" (*Variety*) as well as having penned the original story and co-authored its screenplay. The movie seems like it was shot sans sound with voices later dubbed in, giving it an even more slipshod appearance. *Variety* complained, "Special effects (some of which appear to be executed by video techniques) are poor and there is no evidence of a futuristic society in the west coast and familiar looking freaks." A plot ploy has practically the entire cast moving around on roller skates.

To pep up the proceedings, the movie includes nudity provided by several actresses. To date, a promised sequel, HOLY THUNDER, has not surfaced.

SANTO CONTRA EL DOCTOR MUERTE [Santo Against Dr. Death] (Cinematografica Pelimex, S.A., 1974) C 96 mins.

Director, Rafael Romero Marchent; screenplay, Marchent, Jose Luis Navarro Basso; music, Gregorio Garcia Segura; sets, Jaime P. Cubero; camera, Godofredo Pacheco.

Santo (Himself); Antonio Pica (Dr. Death); Carlos Romero Marchent (Interpol Agent); and: Helga Line, George Rigand, Mirta Miller, Isabel Hidalgo, Frank Brana, Lorenzo Robeldo.

Interpol commissions celebrated wrestler and crime fighter Santo (Himself) to go to Madrid to investigate a series of stolen paintings. His adversary is Dr. Death (Antonio Pica), who is known as Doctor Man, a noted restorer of famous paintings. He is the head of a ring which damages priceless pictures and restores them for sizeable fees. For the formula necessary to reclaim the pictures, Dr. Death uses a virus which he injects into his former models producing a tumor. When the girls die, the doctor employs the fluids from the cancer to achieve a perfect copy of the painting which he is restoring. The physician informs the museum director in Mexico City, where the paintings have originated, their copy is a fake and he keeps the original for himself. Using his contacts in Madrid, Santo uncovers the doctor's devious activities, brings him to justice, and recovers the priceless pictures.

Wearing a silver head mask, wrestler Santo has been the hero of Spanish and Mexican films since the 1960s, mostly in the realm of science fiction and horror pictures, of which there have been at least a score. Over the years Santo has been the adversary of such supernatural and super-science foes as: Dracula, Frankenstein's monster, the Wolfman, the Mummy, zombies, various vampires, and mad scientists such as Dr. Death in this mediocre feature in the long-running series. Occasionally Santo has also teamed with another wrestler, The Blue Demon, in battling minions of evil.

When Santo's early features were acquired for TV by American International, his character was called "Samson" in the dubbed prints to avoid conflict with Leslie Charteris' renown detective "The Saint," since Santo in Spanish means "saint."

SATURN 3 (Associated Film Distribution, 1980) C 88 mins.

Presenter, Lord Lew Grade, Elliott Kastner; executive producer, Martin Starger; producer/director, Stanley Donen; story, John Barry; screenplay, Martin Barry; production designer, Stuart Craig; art director, Norman Dorme; music, Elmer Bernstein; orchestrator, Christopher Palmer; special effects, Colin Chilvers, Roy Spencer, Terry Schubert, Jeff Luff; camera, Billy Williams; editor, Richard Marden.

Farrah Fawcett (Alex); Kirk Douglas (Adam); Harvey Keitel (Benson); Douglas Lambert (Captain James); Ed Bishop (Harding); Christopher Muncke (Crewman).

On Triton, a moon of Saturn, an experimental space station exists in which nutritional experiments are being conducted to feed an overpopulated Earth. Conducting the tests are Adam (Kirk Douglas) and his assistant Alex (Farrah Fawcett), a young woman who was born in space and who has never seen Earth, a place Adam believes has become totally decadent. Arriving on Triton is Major James (Harvey Keitel) who has come with Hector, a robot in the new Demigod Series, who is to aid with the station's experiments. Unknown to Adam and Alex, James is really Benson, an escaped murderer, who has killed the real Major James and assumed his identity. The robot is his own evil creation and he brings it to life to take over the station, kill Adam and have Alex for himself. Realizing their plight, Adam and Alex oppose Benson as best they can but the robot kidnaps Alex and falls in love with her since its thought patterns are similar to its creator. Realizing the sinister aspect of his monster, Benson tries to immobilize the robot but it kills him and assimilates his body and brain. Adam is injured in a fight with the robot but he and Alex manage to set a trap for the robot which brings

Farrah Fawcett, Harvey Keitel, and Kirk Douglas in SATURN 3 (1980).

about its destruction. To make the plan succeed, Adam gives up his life. Left alone, Alex plans to journey to Earth.

Stanley Donen, more noted for his musicals and sophisticated comedies, directed SATURN 3 from John Barry's story, and production-wise it is strong, aided by Elmer Bernstein's resourceful score. Sadly, though, the feature is another failed attempt to establish Farrah Fawcett as movie box-office. Her character has no depth and Harvey Keitel's (stereotyped) psychopath and his horrific creation Hector are too downbeat to sustain viewer interest. Shock effects are minimal, although the special effects and set designs are appealing. Grossing $5,000,000 at the U.S. box-office, SATURN 3 burned out as a disappointing space opera.

SCANNERS (Avco Embassy, 1981) C 102 mins.

Executive producers, Victor Solnicki, Pierre David; producer, Claude Heroux; director/screenplay, David Cronenberg; music, Howard Shore; art director, Carol Spier; costumes, Delphine White; assistant director, Jim Kaufman; sound, Don Cohen; camera, Mark Irwin; editor, Ron Sanders.

Stephen Lack (Vale); Jennifer O'Neill (Kim); Patrick Mcgoohan (Dr. Ruth); Lawrence Dane (Keller) Charles Shamata (Gaudi);

Adam Ludwig (Crostic); Michael Ironside (Revok); Victor Desy (Dr. Gatineau); Mayor Moore (Trevellyan); Robert Silverman (Pierce).

People have developed the power to seep into other peoples' nervous systems and destroy them. These invaders are Scanners and one group, led by Revok (Michael Ironside), is using the power for loathsome purposes. Dr. Ruth (Patrick Mcgoohan) of the ComSec Research Program asks another Scanner, Vale (Stephen Lack), to infiltrate the group and bring Revok and his henchmen to justice. After much detective work, and several deaths, Vale finds that ComSec is connected with the drug supplier Biochemical Amalgamated which has developed Ephemerol. This drug is given to pregnant women resulting in their offspring becoming Scanners and he uncovers the fact that he and Revok are brothers who were the first Scanners developed from the drug. The siblings embark on a mental battle for supremacy.

Followers of director/writer David Cronenberg revel in this violent sci-fi feature, famous for its exploding head sequence in the first reel. Plotwise, the film is a mixed bag as annotated by *Variety* " . . . lack of any rooting interest vitiates any possible suspense and highly elegant visual style works against much shock value. Ending is also a bit puzzling."

Phil Hardy wrote in *The Film Encyclopedia: Science Fiction* (1984), "Outstripping such second cousins as CARRIE (1976), PATRICK (1978) and THE FURY (1978) [q.v.] with its effects and effectiveness, SCANNERS also signalled the virtual end of the telekinetic thriller cycle by pushing it to its limit, as if Science Fiction *per se* were turning violently on its upstart mutant offspring, and seeing it off."

SCANNERS grossed $6,200,000 at the domestic box-office.

SCARED TO DEATH (Lone Star Pictures International, 1982) C 95 mins.

Executive producer, William Malone; producers, Rand Marlis, Gil Shelton; director/screenplay, Malone; music, Tom Chase; Ardell Hake; monster effects/designer, Malone, Robert Short; camera, Patrick Prince; editor, Warren Chadwick.

John Stinson (Ted Lonergan); Diana Davidson (Jennifer Stanton); Jonathan David Moses (Lou Capell); Toni Jannotta (Sherry Carpenter); Kermit Eller (Syngenor); and: Walter Edmiston, Pamela Bowman.

Los Angeles is plagued with a series of grizzly murders where the victims—usually young women—die from a loss of spinal fluids. Unable to solve the case, the police assign detective Ted Lonergan (John Stinson) to the case and he is abetted by Jennifer Stanton (Diana Davidson). The detective finds out that the maniac killer is actually a Syngenor, a creature which resulted from a DNA experiment which went off kilter. The monster had escaped from the Los Angeles laboratory where it was created and took refuge in the city's sewers, coming up to attack victims and extract their spinal fluids with its long tongue. The police corner the creature and bring about its demise.

This low-budget item, made in 1980, was filmed as THE ABERDEEN EXPERIMENT and received minor theatrical distribution, having been lost in the shuffle of sci-fi and horror films which saturated the market at the time. *Variety* commented, "Filmmaker William Malone's self-designed creature is effective when glimpsed briefly, but looks like a man in a rubber suit when shown too fully in the final reels. Besides the careful ALIEN imitation regarding the monster's appearance and attacks, pic's climax for dealing with the beast is taken from THE FLY." The trade paper added, " . . . little interest is created during the sluggish non-horror scenes."

It should be noted this film has *nothing* to do with the 1947 Cinecolor murder mystery thriller, SCARED TO DEATH, starring Bela Lugosi, or a contemporary picture called SCARED TO DEATH, which is also known as THERE WAS ONCE A CHILD.

SCREAM AND SCREAM AGAIN (American International, 1970) C 94 mins.

Executive producer, Louis M. Heyward; producers, Max J. Rosenberg, Milton Subotsky; director, Gordon Hessler; based on the novel by Peter Saxon; screenplay, Christopher Wicking; art director, Don Mingaye; music, David Whittaker; assistant director, Ariel Levy; camera, John Coquillon; editor, Peter Elliot.

Vincent Price (Dr. Browning); Christopher Lee (Prime Minister Fremont); Peter Cushing (Benedek); Judy Huxtable (Sylvia); Alfred Marks (Detective Superintendent Bellaver); Michael Gothard (Keith); Anthony Newlands (Ludwig); Marshall Jones (Konratz); Peter Sallis (Schweitz); David Lodge (Detective Inspector Strickland); Uta Levka (Jane); Christopher Matthews (Dr. David Sorel); Judi Bloom (Helen Bradford); Clifford Earl (Detective Sergeant Jimmy Joyce); Kenneth Benda (Professor Kingsmill).

London is plagued with a series of apparently unrelated but gory homicides. Detective Superintendent Bellaver (Alfred Marks) is in charge of the investigation and an autopsy by Dr. David Sorel (Christopher Matthews) reveals that two of the victims—young women—were drained of their blood. Helen Bradford (Judi Bloom), an undercover policewoman, agrees to be a decoy to catch the killer and he turns out to be Keith (Michael Gothard) who is so strong he

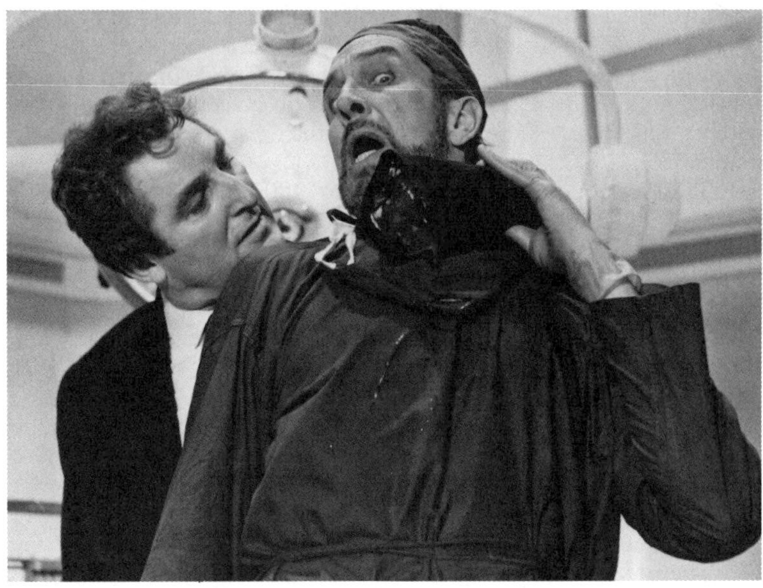

Marshall Jones and Vincent Price in SCREAM AND SCREAM AGAIN (1970).

escapes his handcuffs but leaves his hand behind. He later commits suicide by throwing himself into an acid vat in the laboratory of kindly scientist Dr. Browning (Vincent Price). Bellaver is told by Prime Minister Fremont (Christopher Lee) to close the case as he had been requested to do so by Konratz (Marshall Jones), a foreign agent, who is solidifying his power in his Eastern European homeland by eliminating his enemies. When Bellaver does not heed Fremont's directive, Konratz has him killed. Sorel and Helen suspect Browning is involved in the crimes and go to his home and both are captured. They learn the doctor is attempting to make a race of supermen from the body parts of his victims, but Konratz arrives before Browning operates on Helen. In a struggle Konratz tumbles into the acid vat and Fremont arrives only to murder Browning. He tells Sorel and Helen that Browning once worked for Konratz but double-crossed him. They learn the Prime Minster, like Konratz and Browning, is one of the super race.

This mixed-up, hard-to-follow, violent and gory sci-fi horror thriller was merely an excuse to team Vincent Price, Christopher Lee, and Peter Cushing for box-office allure, although the latter two only have minor assignments. London's *Kine Weekly* reported, "This farrago of horrific nonsense is a bit too complicated and mysterious to make a big impression. . . ." The critic for the London *Daily Mirror* complained, "The only real horrific events I found in this film were some ear-shattering sessions of pop music."

THE SECRET OF THE SWORD (Miracle, 1985) C 91 mins.

Executive producer, Lou Scheimer; producer, Arthur H. Nadel; directors, Ed Friedman, Lou Kachivas, Marsh Lamore, Bill Reed, Gwen Wetzler; screenplay, Larry Ditillo, Bob Forward; graphic designer, Connie Schurr; chief animator, Doris Plough; background design supervisors, Lorenzo Martinez, John Howley; background designers, Tim Callahan, Dan St. Pierre, Armando Norte, Thomas Shannon; storyboard supervisor, Bob Arkwright; music, Shuki Levy, Haim Saban, Erika Lane; music directors, Levy, Saban; song, Erika Scheimer, Levy, Saban; educational/psychological consultant, Donald F. Roberts; special effects head, Shurl Lupin; camera, F. T. Ziegler; editors, Joe Gall, Rick Gehr, Robert Crawford.

Voices of: John Erwin (Adam/He-Man); Melendy Britt (Adora/She-Ra); Alan Oppenheimer (Bo); George DiCenzo (Transformer Robot Hordak); Erik Gunden (Cowl); and: Linda Gary, Erika Scheimer.

Years before on the planet of Eternia, the evil Horde leader, Transformer Robot Hordak (George DiCenzo) steals the infant Adora, daughter of the rulers of the planet, and raises her to be leader of his troops, although his invasion of Eternia fails. At Castle Greyskull, the Sorceress beckons Prince Adams (John Erwin), who has the power to become the invincible He-Man, and sends him to Etheria to locate his long-lost sister and aid the planet's people in their struggle with the invading horde. There he joins the freedom fighters but is opposed by Adora, whom he convinces of the Horde's evil. She attempts to turn on the Horde but is put under a spell by the evil Shadow Weaver. Hordak captures He-Man and plans to drain him of his energy and use it to take the planet, but Adora is visited by the Sorceress who tells her the truth about her past and gives her a magic sword which transforms her into the superwoman She-Ra (Melendy Britt). She rescues her brother and they return to Eternia where the girl is reunited with her parents. Hordak follows and joins forces with his old foe Skeletor, once a Horde captain whom he abandoned on the planet when he was defeated there, and they plan to recognize Eternia. Skeletor, though, turns on Hordak and captures Adora for himself. But she transforms into She-Ra and defeats him and decides to return to Etheria to bring about the downfall of Hordak and the Evil Horde.

An offshoot of the popular "He-Man" TV series and the Mattel line of toys of the same name, "She-Ra" became equally popular with little girls who were enchanted with Mattel's vast array of dolls and other playthings. As for this animated feature, it did not meet with critical acclaim as reflected by the British *Monthly Film Bulletin,* "The animation is crude, one-dimensional and lacking in detail, and looks shockingly primitive alongside the Disney features of fifty years ago—which were also, of course, much more specific and positive about their moral lessons." *Variety* agreed, "The animated movements are surprisingly tv-jerky for a full-length feature and the narrative line is encumbered by an equally staccato effect."

The film launched the syndicated "She-Ra" TV series which was introduced by this feature, telecast in five parts as "The Sword of She-Ra."

LA SENORA MUERTE [Mrs. Death] (Columbia, 1968) C 90 mins.

Executive producer, Jorge Garcia Besne; producer, Luis Enrique Vergara; director, Jaime Salvador; screenplay, Ramon Obon, Jr.; art directors, Octavio Ocampo, Jose Mendez.

Regina Torne (Marlene); John Carradine (Fadel); Elsa Cardenas; Victor Junco (Policeman); Miguel Angel Alvarez (Angel); and: Isela Vega, Carlos Ancira, Mario Orea, Alicia Ravel, Patricia Ferrer, Carlos Ortigosa.

In the late 1960s veteran character star John Carradine traveled south-of-the-border to appear in a quartet of Mexican horror films: as Count Dracula in LAS VAMPIRAS (1967), Satan in AUTOPSIA DE UN FANTASMA (1967), the Jekyll/Hyde reworking known as PACTO DIABOLICO (1968), and this sic-fi entry in which he starred as an insane scientist. Unfortunately none of these motion pictures have ever played in the U.S. except in Spanish-language theaters, thus depriving the star's many fans of seeing him in four of his more obscure screen characterizations.

Pretty Marlene (Regina Torne) is suffering from facial cancer and her fiancé Andres (Miguel Angel Alvarez) takes her to famous scientist Fadel (John Carradine) in search of a cure. The mad doctor uses the blood of a recently murdered young woman to restore Marlene's lovely face but the treatment is only temporary. Since Marlene was the one who accidentally killed the girl, Fadel blackmails her into murdering other victims to provide him with the female hormone fluids required for his experiments. A policeman is ordered to investigate the rash of murders. Marlene turns on Fadel and both die in a laboratory explosion.

Combining science fiction, horror and sexploitation, LA SENORA MUERTE is an interesting example of the more mature type of Mexican thriller feature, far above such items as ROBOT VS.

Regina Torne in LA SENORA MUERTE (1968).

THE AZTEC MUMMY (1959) (q.v.), but not nearly as entertaining. Here the main interests are John Carradine in another of his weird scientist roles and the scene where Marlene becomes lost in a wax museum and runs up against life-like wax figures of various creatures, including Frankenstein's monster.

SERGEANT DEADHEAD (American International, 1965) C 69 mins.

Producers, James H. Nicholson, Samuel Z. Arkoff; co-producer, Anthony Carras; director, Norman Taurog; screenplay, Louis M. Heyward; music, Les Baxter; songs, Guy Hemric and Jerry Styner; art director, Howard Campbell; assistant director, Claude Binyon, Jr.; camera, Floyd Crosby; editors, Ronald Sinclair, Fred Feitshams, Eve Newman.

Frankie Avalon (Sergeant O. K. Deadhead/Private Donovan); Deborah Walley (Colonel Lucy Turner); Cesar Romero (Admiral Stoneham); Fred Clark (General Rufus Fogg); Gale Gordon (Captain Weiskopf); Harvey Lembeck (Private McEvoy); John Ashley (Private Filroy); Buster Keaton (Private Blinken); Reginald Gardiner (Lieutenant Commander Talbott); Eve Arden (Lieutenant Kinsey); Pat Buttram (The President); Donna Loren (Susan); Romo Vincent

(Tuba Player); Ted Windsor (Sergeant Keefer); Norman Grabowski, Mike Nader (Air Police); Ed Faulkner (Radioman); Bobbi Shaw (Gilda); Patti Chandler (Patti); Salli Sachse (Sue Ellen); Luree Holmes (Luree); Sue Hampton (Ivy); Jo Collins (Gail); Bob Harvey (Bellhop); Jerry Brutsche (Newsman); Andy Romano, John Macchia (Marine MPs); Mary Hughes, Astrid DeBrea, Jean Ingram, Peggy Ward, Stephanie Nader, Lycanne Ladue, Janice Levinson, Alberta Nelson (WAFS); Sallie Dornan (Secretary).

Also titled SERGEANT DEADHEAD THE ASTRONUT!, this comedy told of girl-shy and accident prone Sergeant O.K. Deadhead (Frankie Avalon) being sent to the guardhouse after accidentally exploding a miniature rocket during a WAF drill and exacting the ire of the WAF commander, Lieutenant Kinsey (Eve Arden). His being jailed, however, eases the mind of commanding officer General Rufus Fogg (Fred Clark), since his missile base is scheduled to launch a secret rocket into space containing a chimpanzee which will be used to test personality changes in space and Fogg does not want Deadhead to gum up the operation. Just as Fogg is assuring his visiting superiors, Admiral Stoneham (Cesar Romero), Captain Weiskopf (Gale Gordon), and British Lieutenant Commander Talbott (Reginald Gardiner), that all is going well with the launch, he finds out Deadhead has escaped from incarceration. He does not know, however, that pals Private Kilroy (John Ashley) and Private McEvoy (Harvey Lembeck), have urged Deadhead to take sanctuary in the missile. During the flight, Deadhead has a personality change, and becomes an aggressive woman chaser, and plans to go ahead with his planned wedding to WAF Corporal Lucy Turner (Deborah Walley). To avoid embarrassing publicity, Fogg has Deadhead kidnapped when he lands and in his place is his look-alike, Private Donovan (Frankie Avalon), who will marry Lucy. Deadhead again escapes from the guardhouse, reverts to his old self and arrives in time to wed Lucy himself.

"It's The Funniest Foul Up Of the Space Age!" bragged the poster for this mild comedy whose main asset was its cast of veteran players, including: Cesar Romero, Eve Arden, Gale Gordon, Reginald Gardiner, Pat Buttram, and Buster Keaton.

LA SFIDA DE KING KONG see WHITE PONGO.

SHADOW OF CHINATOWN (Victory, 1936) fifteen chapters.

Producer, Sam Katzman; director, Robert F. Hill; story, Rock Hawkey [Robert Hill]; screenplay, William Buchanan, Isadore Bernstein, Basil Dickey; sets, Fred Preble; camera, Bill Hyer; editor, Charles Henkel.

Bela Lugosi (Victor Poten); Joan Barclay (Joan Whiting); Herman Brix [Bruce Bennett] (Martin Andrews); Luana Walters (Sonya Rokoff); Maurice Liu (Willy Fu); Charles King (Grogan); William Buchanan (Healy); Forrest Taylor (Police Captain Walters); James B. Leong (Wong); Henry F. Tung (Dr. Wu); Paul Fung (Tom Chu); George Chan (Old Luee); John Elliott (Captain); Moy Ming (Wong's Brother); Jack Cowell (White Chinese); and: Roger Williams, Lester Dorr, Henry Hall.

Chapters: 1) The Arms of the God; 2) The Crushing Walls; 3) 13 Ferguson Alley; 4) Death on the Wire; 5) The Sinister Ray; 6) The Sword Thrower; 7) The Noose; 8) Midnight; 9) The Last Warning; 10) The Bomb; 11) Thundering Doom; 12) Invisible Gas; 13) The Brink of Disaster; 14) The Fatal Trap 15) The Avenging Powers.

Sam Katzman launched the first of his many cliffhangers with this serial headlining Bela Lugosi. The poster blurb announced, "Thrills and Chills and Shivering Shocks as a Crazed Scientist Terrorizes the Underworld!" Besides Lugosi as the wicked Victor Potel and Luana Walters as the sexy villainess Sonya Rokoff, the drawn out and vapid chapterplay had little to offer. Like many serials, the film injected science fiction to bolster the plot. Here sci-fi involves a futuristic television that lets the villains spy on the good guys and gals at will, a mechanical "God," a death ray, and an undetectable poison gas.

European promoters want all West Coast Chinatowns closed to tourists and hire beautiful Eurasian Sonya Rokoff (Luana Walters) to accomplish the job and she enlists the aid of Victor Poten (Bela Lugosi), a mad man who hates both the white and yellow races. Newspaperwoman Joan Whiting (Joan Barclay) fastens onto the story and is aided by writer Martin Andrews (Herman Brix [Bruce Bennett]). Through his tele-audient device Poten finds out about their involvement and tries to get them out of the way, but fails. He uses assorted plot machinations from Andrews' novels to carry out his closing of Chinatown and Police Captain Walters (Forrest Taylor) thus suspects Martin of the crimes. On a ship to Los Angeles, Poten plans to have his henchman Grogan (Charles King) kill Martin but fails and then tries to kill Grogan for his failure. The man lives and falls in love with Sonya and attempts to eliminate Poten but winds up being murdered by him. By now Sonya has rebelled against Poten and he kidnaps her but she escapes and joins Martin and Joan in fighting her former ally. At Martin's house, Poten rigs a chandelier to kill Martin but Sonya gets in the way and dies. Poten falls into a nearby bay and apparently drowns but is later arrested at a Chinese merchants dinner and jailed.

SHADOW OF CHINATOWN, also called THE YELLOW PHANTOM, was also issued in a 65-minute feature version.

THE SHADOW OF THE EAGLE (Mascot, 1932) twelve chapters.

Producer, Nat Levine; directors, Ford Beebe, B. Reeves Eason; story, Beebe, Colbert Clark; camera, Ben Kline, Victor Scheurich; stunt supervisor, Yakima Canutt; supervising editor, Wyndham Gittens; editor, Ray Snyder.

John Wayne (Craig McCoy); Dorothy Gulliver (Jean Gregory); Walter Miller (Danby); Kenneth Harlan (Ward); Richard Tucker (Evans); Pat O'Malley (Ames); Yakima Canutt (Boyle); Edmund Burns (Clark); Roy D'Arcy (Gardner); Billy West (Clown); Edward Hearn (Nathan Gregory); Lloyd Whitlock (Green); Little Billy (Midget); Ivan Linow (Strong Man); James Bradbury, Jr. (Ventriloquist); Ernie Adams (Helly); Bud Osborne (Moore); Monte Montague (Policeman).

Chapters: 1) The Carnival Mystery; 2) Pinholes; 3) The Eagle Strikes; 4) Man of a Million Voices; 5) The Telephone Cipher; 6) Code of the Carnival; 7) Eagle or Vulture?; 8) On the Spot; 9) The Thieves Fall Out; 10) The Man Who Knew; 11) The Eagle's Wings; 12) The Shadow Unmasked.

A mysterious pilot called The Eagle has been using skywriting to threaten an aircraft company and the chief suspect is Nathan Gregory (Edward Hearn) whose anti-aircraft ray gun invention was allegedly stolen by the firm. Also a suspect is Craig McCoy (John Wayne), a stunt pilot at the carnival owned by Gregory, who loves Gregory's daughter Jean (Dorothy Gulliver). Craig retrieves the plans but Gregory is missing and Craig goes to the corporation's board of directors meeting to inform them his boss is not guilty of threatening them. At the crucial moment, the lights go out, and company executive Clark (Edmund Burns) is murdered. Gregory returns to his carnival but when accused of the homicide he gets away and Craig and Jean later find that he is held prisoner in an asylum. Jean is also captured by The Eagle but she obtains a gun and summons help. Craig reaches the asylum and despite danger to Jean, manages to unmask The Eagle, who is killed trying to escape.

THE SHADOW OF THE EAGLE was the first of a trio of serials John Wayne performed in for Mascot Pictures. It was followed by THE HURRICANE EXPRESS (1932) and THE THREE MUSKETEERS (1933). Yakima Canutt was the stunt supervisor on the film, as well as playing the role of henchman Boyle, and this was the first of many projects on which Wayne and Canutt worked together. Shot in twenty-one days, the serial is fast-paced but shoddy in production values: the aerial cloud writing, for example, is cartoon animation. Ford Beebe, in his serial directorial debut, helmed the project with B. Reeves Eason; thus creating the system of having serial directors alternate working days for faster work schedules.

SHANKS (Paramount, 1974) C 93 mins.

Executive producer, William Castle; producer, Steven North; director, Castle; screenplay, Ranald Graham; production designer, Boris Leven; set decorator, John Austin; assistant director, Sheldon Schrager; music, Alex North; sound, David Ronne; camera, Joseph Biroc; editor, David Berlatsky.

Marcel Marceau (Malcolm Shanks/Old Walker); Tsilla Chelton (Mrs. Barton); Philippe Clay (Mr. Barton); Cindy Eilbacher (Celia); Larry Bishop, Don Calfa, Giff Manard, Mondo, Phil Adams (Motorcycle Gang); Helena Kallianiotes (Biker's Old Lady); Read Morgan (Cop); Lara Wing (Little Girl); William Castle (Grocer).

Producer/director William Castle closed out his long film career with SHANKS, which he produced and directed as well as making a cameo appearance as the grocer. Castle, best remembered for the gimmicks he employed to promote horror films like MACABRE (1958), THE TINGLER (1959), THE HOUSE ON HAUNTED HILL (1959), and HOMICIDAL (1960), had a career which ran from the sublime to the near ridiculous. Among his best remembered works are THE WHISTLER (1944), WHEN STRANGERS MARRY (1944), THE NIGHT WALKER (1967), and as producer of ROSEMARY'S BABY (1967). Although not an unentertaining feature, SHANKS is hardly his best creative effort nor was it a good finale to his motion picture career.

Elderly scientist Walker (Marcel Marceau) develops a means to keep people alive after death by electrically rewiring their bodies, making them puppets. He is the benefactor of deaf-mute puppeteer Malcolm Shanks (Marcel Marceau) and the old man shares with Shanks his secret before he passes away. Shanks continues Walker's work by taking revenge on his nasty in-laws (Philippe Clay, Tsilla Chelton) and making them puppets. A lovely young woman, Celia (Cindy Eilbacher), is attracted to Shanks and they fall in love. Their bliss is interrupted by the arrival of vicious bikers who beat, rape, and murder Celia. In revenge, Shanks turns his army of puppets on them and the bikers are eliminated. Shanks restores Celia as a puppet.

French mime Marcel Marceau, along with other top pantomimists, shared top billing in this offbeat tale which boasts very little dialogue.

THE SHAPE OF THINGS TO COME (Film Ventures, 1979) C 95 mins.

Executive producer, Harry Alan Towers; producer, William Davidson; director, George McCowan; based on the novel by H. G. Wells; screenplay, Martin Lager; music, Paul Hoffert; special effects, Wally Gentleman; camera, Reginald Morris.

Jack Palance (Omnus); Carol Lynley (Niki); John Ireland (Senator Smedley); Barry Morse (Dr. John Caball); Nicholas Campbell (Jason Caball); Eddie Benton (Kim Smedley); Greg Swanson (Voice of Sparks); Marc Parr (Sparks the Robot); William Hutt (Voice of Lomax); Bill Lake (Astronaut); Arods Bess (Merrick); Lynn Green (Lunar Technician); Albert Humphries (Robot Technician); Michael Klinbell, Wili Liberman, Rod McEwan, Jonathan Hartman, Angelo Pedari (Robots); Danny Gage, Jo-Anne Lang, Terry Martin, Lutz Brodie, Terry Spratt, Linda Carter, Bill Jay (Members of Niki's Army).

Following World War III, pacifists establish a new colony, New Washington, on the Moon. There they are shielded from radiation sickness coming from Earth by a drug called Radio Q2, made from the substance Delat Three. A robot (Jack Palance) named Omnus, from a distant planet, steals the substance, along with pretty Niki (Carol Lynley), and demands the inhabitants of the moon base surrender or he will destroy the Earth. The base's leader, Senator Smedley (John Ireland), plans to capitulate, but is thwarted by Jason Cabell (Nicholas Campbell), his father, Dr. John Caball (Barry Morse); Smedley (Eddie Benton), a robot technician; and Sparks, a robot. The quartet head for Omnus' planet to regain the substance and rescue Niki from the renegade robot.

Also called H.G. WELLS' THE SHAPE OF THINGS TO COME, this uninspired Canadian-made sci-fi film has nothing do with the Wells novel or the marvelous 1936 adaptation (see B/V) of that famous book. Never issued in the U.S., except on TV, it was shown theatrically in Canada and Europe and proved to be an abortive genre effort.

THE SHE CREATURE (American International, 1956) 77 mins.

Executive producer, Samuel Z. Arkoff; producer, Alex Gordon; director, Edward L. Cahn; story, Jerry Zigmond; screenplay, Lou Rusoff; art director, Don Ament; monster created by, Paul Blaisdell; music, Ronald Stein; camera, Frederick E. West; editor, Ronald Sinclair.

Chester Morris (Dr. Carlo Lombardi); Marla English (Andrea); Tom Conway (Timothy Chappel); Cathy Downs (Dorothy Chappel); Lance Fuller (Ted Erickson); Ron Randell (Lieutenant Ed James);

Frieda Inescort (Mrs. Chappel); Frank Jenks (Police Sergeant); El Brendel (Olaf); Paul Dubov (Johnny); Bill Hudson (Bob); Flo Bert (Maria); Jeanne Evans (Mrs. Brown); Kenneth MacDonald (Professor Anderson); Paul Blaisdell (Creature); Jeanne Evans (Mrs. Brown); Jack Mulhall, Stuart Holmes, Franklyn Farnum, Edmund Cobb, Luana Walters, Edward Earle, Creighton Hale (Guests).

Hypnotist Dr. Carlo Lombardi (Chester Morris) employs his beautiful lover Andrea (Marla English) as his assistant in a supposedly sham act. To gain publicity he predicts several murders which do occur and Lieutenant Ed James (Ron Randell) and his associate (Frank Jenks) investigate. Millionaire businessman Timothy Chappel (Tom Conway) and his wife (Frieda Inescort) are interested in Lombardi's act and agree to bankroll a national campaign for him involving books and media appearances. The Chappels' daughter, Dorothy (Cathy Downs) loves researcher Dr. Ted Erickson (Lance Fuller) who is skeptical of Lombardi. When Andrea falls for Ted, the extremely jealous Lombardi plots revenge. It seems he has used hypnosis to revert the young woman back in time to millions of years ago when she was a giant sea creature. He is able to bring this monster through a time warp and cause it to commit the murders he

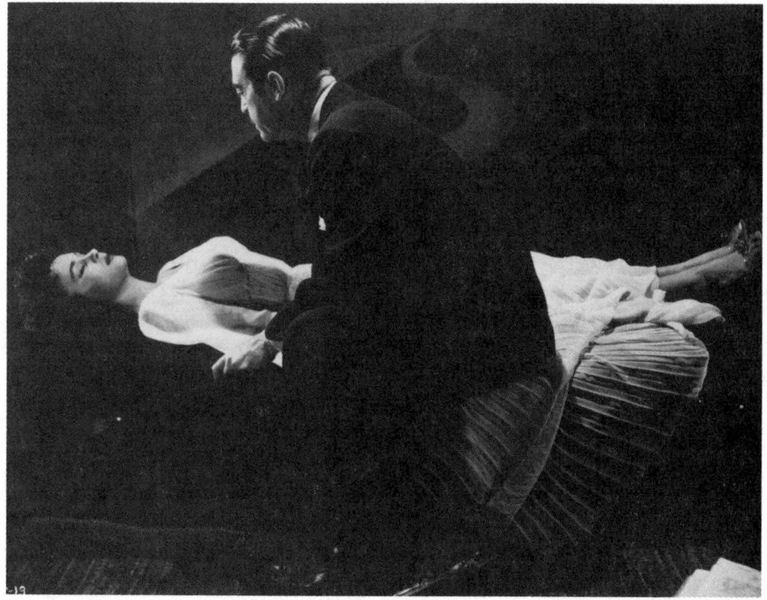

Marla English and Chester Morris in THE SHE CREATURE (1956).

predicts and he orders the creature to snuff out Ted. Andrea's subconscious will not permit her prehistoric alter-ego to kill the man she loves. The monster goes on a rampage in the Chappel beachfront home, killing Timothy and Lieutenant James and mortally wounding Lombardi who releases Andrea from his hypnotic spell before dying.

Loosely based on the 1950s Bridey Murphy case, this combination horror/sci-fi thriller was filmed at Malibu's Paradise Cove for slightly over $100,000 by producer Alex Gordon who populated it with a delightful cast of veteran players (i.e. Jack Mulhall, El Brendel and his wife Flo Bert, Luana Walters, Edward Earle, Franklyn Farnum, Kenneth MacDonald, Stuart Holmes, Paul Dubov, Edmund Cobb). Its more than able direction was handled by experienced Edward L. Cahn who reteamed with Gordon for a followup, VOODOO WOMAN (q.v.), the next year. An entertaining little item, which was issued on a double bill with IT CONQUERED THE WORLD (see B/V), THE SHE CREATURE's costume was devised and enacted by Paul Blaisdell. The monster outfit was a large scaly suit, with bulging breasts, and a head with tentacles and long teeth; a most terrifying, if bulky, predator. Blaisdell wore the suit again for a guest bit in THE GHOST OF DRAGSTRIP HOLLOW (1959); and THE SHE CREATURE was remade into one of the all-time worst movies, CREATURE OF DESTRUCTION (1967), with veteran radio actor Les Tremayne as the hypnotist.

SHE MONSTER OF THE NIGHT see FRANKENSTEIN'S DAUGHTER.

SHIVERS see THEY CAME FROM WITHIN.

SHOCK WAVES (Joseph Brenner, 1977) C 84 mins.

Producer, Reuben Trane; director, Ken Wiederhorn; screenplay, John Harrison, Wiederhorn; music, Richard Einhorn; makeup, Alan Ormsby; camera, Trane; editor, Norman Gay.

Peter Cushing (SS Commander Scar); Brooke Adams (Rose); John Carradine (Captain Ben); Fred Buch (Chuck); Jack Davidson (Norman); Luke Halprin (Keith); D. J. Sidney (Beverly); Don Stout (Dobbs); Jay Maeder (Death Corps Member).

Also called DEATH CORPS and made on a modest budget in Florida in 1975, SHOCK WAVES turned out to be an interesting minor sci-fi thriller which did well at the box-office due to the name draw factor of stars Peter Cushing and John Carradine. "Once They Were Almost Human! Beneath the Living . . . Beyond the Dead . . . From the Depths of Hell's Ocean . . . The Deep End of Horror!," read the poster blurb for this Joseph Brenner release about Nazi zombies.

Captain Ben (John Carradine) runs a Caribbean boat charter service and on a cruise his boat is overturned after being hit by a mysterious ship. Several survivors, including Rose (Brooke Adams) and Keith (Luke Halpin), are washed ashore to a remote island. Exploring the isle they find a large house presided over by Scar (Peter Cushing). They learn he is a former Nazi scientist who helped the SS develop a corps of invincible zombies who take their nourishments from humans but live underwater. When the war ended, Scar took refuge on the island and keeps watch over the sunken vessel and its crew. The zombies rise up to prey on the shipwrecked survivors.

Reviewing the film's video cassette release on Prism, *Fangoria* magazine (June, 1985) noted, " . . . SHOCK WAVES is low on gore content and high on old-fashioned, low-budget chills." Regarding the zombies, the reviewer penned, " . . . they are one of the best monster gangs to come down the pike in a long time."

SHORT CIRCUIT (Tri-Star, 1986) C 99 mins.

Executive producers, Mark Damon, John Hyde; producers, David Foster, Lawrence Turman; supervising producer, Gregg Champion; co-producer, Dennis Jones; associate producers, Gary Foster, Dana Satler; director, John Badham; screenplay, S. S. Wilson, Brent Maddock; art director, Dianne Wager; set decorator, Garret Lewis; assistant directors, Jerry Ziesmer, Bryan Denegal; music, David Shire; robots, Syd Mead, Eric Allard; sound, Willie D. Burton; special electrical effects, Bob Jason, Larry Keys, Walter Nichols; robot voices synthesizer, Frank Serafine; visual consultant, Philip Harrison; camera, Nick McLean; editor, Frank Morriss.

Ally Sheedy (Stephanie Speck); Steve Guttenberg (Dr. Newton Crosby); Fisher Stevens (Ben Jabituya); Austin Pendleton (Howard Marner); G. W. Bailey (Skroeder); Brian McNamara (Frank); Tim Blaney (Number Five's Voice); Marvin McIntyre (Duke); John Garber (Otis); Penny Santon (Mrs. Cepeda); Vernon Weddle (General Washburne); Barbara Tarbuck (Senator Mills); Tom Lawrence (Marner's Aide); Fred Slyter (Norman); Billy Ray Sharkey (Zack); Robert Krantz, Jan Speck (Reporters); Marguerite Happy (Barmaid); Howard Krick (Farmer); Marjorie Huehes (Farmer's Wife); Herb Smith (Gate Guard); and: Jack Thompson, Walter Scott, Mark Reckley, Lisa McLean, Karl Wickman.

Sheltered computer genius Dr. Newton Crosby (Steve Guttenberg) works for the Defense Department at the Nova Military complex and there develops a series of robots called DOD, the ultimate weapon. On the day the DOD is introduced to the military establishment, a bolt of lightning hits DOD Number 5 and it starts to malfunction and escapes from the complex and begins spouting peace talk. By chance No. 5 comes under the protection of animal-loving Stephanie Speck (Ally Sheedy) who tries to stop the military from returning the robot to the weapons complex or worse yet, rewiring its circuitry. She and Newton, who have fallen in love, escape with No. 5 to live in peace on a Montana farm.

SHORT CIRCUIT depends on characterization and the robot for its appeal as it lacks the other ingredients requisite for contemporary box-office success: sex and violence. For fans of Steve Guttenberg, his self-contained, slightly looney scientist has its charm, although on the human side it is Ally Sheedy as the warm individualist who breathes life and conviction into the proceedings with her devotion for the lovable robot.

SHORT CIRCUIT grossed $40,456,961 in its first fourteen weeks of domestic release. In 1988 a sequel SHORT CIRCUIT II was produced and directed by Kenneth Johnson, starring Michael McKean and Cynthia Gibb, with No. 5 the Robot back, along with Fisher Stevens as the sidekick from the original picture.

SING SING NIGHTS (Monogram, 1934) 60 mins.

Producer, Paul Malvern; director, Lewis D. Collins; based on the novel by Harry Stephen Keeler; screenplay, Marion North, Charles Logue; technical director, E. R. Hickson; sound, J. A. Stransky; camera, Archie Stout; editor, Carl Pierson.

Conway Tearle (Floyd Cooper); Mary Doran (Anne McCaigh); Hardie Albright (Howard Trude); Boots Mallory (Ellen Croft); Ferdinand Gottschalk (Professor Varney): Berton Churchill (Governor Duane); Jameson Thomas (Robert McCaigh); Henry Kolker (Kurt Nordon); Richard Tucker (Attorney General); Lotus Long (Li Sung); Mary Doran (Ann McKye); George Baxter (Sergei Krenwicz); and: Edward Keane, Lew Kelly.

Although its title makes it appear to be a gangster film, and several of its scenes take place behind bars, SING SING NIGHTS is a murder mystery with a tinge of sci-fi in that its plot revolves around a scientific device which records truth through pulse beats even though the brain may be concealing the actual facts. While now obsolete, such an apparatus was futuristic when this "B" programmer was released. Taken from Harry Stephen Keller's 1928 novel, this feature is an intriguing one with a number of scenes changes in its complicated plot and good work by its cast.

New York Press war correspondent Floyd Cooper (Conway

Tearle) is found murdered in his posh Manhattan apartment and three men—newspaper reporter Howard Trude (Hardie Albright), Manchurian Sergei Krenitz (George Baxter) and Englishman Robert McCaigh (Jameson Thomas)—all confess to the crime. Although only one is guilty the trio are convicted and on the eve of their executions the governor (Berton Churchill) sends scientist Professor Varney (Ferdinand Gottschalk) to Sing Sing with his futuristic lie detector device to determine who is the true killer. All three agree to the experiment and each tells how he met Cooper and how the man double-crossed them and took their women: coffee plantation manager McCaigh's wife (Mary Doran), Krenitz's Chinese mistress (Lotus Long), and Drew's fiancee (Boots Mallory), and how he was a munitions runner using his fame as a war correspondent and author as a front. The machine proves one of the three stories is bogus and the two innocent men are set free.

SINISTER INVASION see THE INCREDIBLE INVASION.

SKY BANDITS (Monogram, 1940) 56 mins.

Producer, Phil Goldstone; director, Ralph Staub; based on the novel *Renfrew Rides the Sky* by Laurie York Erskine; screenplay, Edward Halperin; songs, Johnny Lange and Lew Porter; camera, Eddie Linden.

James Newill (Sergeant Renfrew); Louise Stanley (Madeleine Lewis); Dewey Robinson (Uncle Dinwiddie); William Pawley (Morgan); Jim Farley (Inspector Warren); Dave O'Brien (Constable Kelly); Ted Adams (Gary); Dwight Frye (Spivey); Joseph Stefani (Professor Lewis); Jack Clifford (Whispering Smith); Karl Hackett (Hawthorne); Bob Terry (Hutchinson); Kenne Duncan (Brownie); Eddie Fetherstone (Buzz Murphy); Snub Pollard (Cabin Owner).

The last of eight theatrical "Renfrew of the Royal Mounted" features, SKY BANDITS was the sixth to be issued by Monogram; the first two coming from the Grand National exchange. Its science fiction aspects gives the film zest as does its north woods setting, but overall it is a draggy production with forced comedy centering around hero Renfrew's faulty memory and the antics of Jack Clifford as a deaf hotel keeper. The film contains one classic line. A scientist opines, "Humanity might best be served if science keeps out of warfare."

Morgan (William Pawley) and his hijackers have hired a renowned scientist, Professor Lewis (Joseph Stefani), to perfect a ray invented by Spivey (Dwight Frye). They have told Lewis he is doing secret government work but actually they use the ray to knock planes out of the sky and steal their cargo. The gang uses a ham radio operator (Dewey Robinson) who masquerades as a children's radio show host but who, in reality, gives the gang codes about the flights which he acquires by bugging the local airport. When a cargo plane is brought down by the ray and two flyers killed, Mountie Renfrew (James Newill) gets on the case as Lewis' daughter Madeleine (Louise Stanley) arrives to find her dad. Morgan plots to kill Lewis and his daughter once they serve his purpose but the jealous Spivey tells Lewis the truth and the man is afraid for his daughter's safety. In searching for the missing plane, Renfrew comes across Morgan's cabin and becomes suspicious; he later goes back to investigate but the gang attacks him and he escapes. When he returns with partner Kelly (Dave O'Brien) and Inspector Warren (Jim Farley) they find the gang gone. Renfrew traps the culprits, the professor is exonerated, and Renfrew romances Madeleine.

Johnny Lange and Lew Porter wrote a trio of songs for star James Newill but "Allez-Op," "You're the Kind of a Girl for Me" and "Lady in the Clouds" were mundane at best.

THE SNOW CREATURE (United Artists, 1954) 80 mins.

Producer/director, W. Lee Wilder; screenplay, Myles Wilder; art director, Frank Sylos; music, Manuel Compinsky; special effects, Lee Zavitz; camera, Floyd D. Crosby; editor, Jodie Copelan.

Paul Langton (Frank Parrish); Leslie Denison (Peter Wells); Taru Shimada (Subra); Rollin Morlyana (Leva); Robert Kine (Inspector Karma); Robert Hinton (Airline Manager); Darlene Fields (Joyce Parrish); George Douglas (Corey, Jr.); Robert Bice (Fleet); Rudolph Anders (Dr. Dupont); Bill Phipps (Lieutenant Dunbar): Jack Daly (Edwards); Rusty Westcott (Warehouse Guard).

On an expedition to the Himalayan Mountains, Frank Parrish (Paul Langton) refuses to accept the natives' stories about the Yeti, or Abominable Snowman. When his guide (Teru Shimada) claims his wife was abducted by a Yeti, Parrish does not believe him so the man sets out to find them but fails. The guide, however, locates another Yeti and with the aid of Parrish and other members of the expedition captures the creature and returns it to the United States. In Los Angeles, the custom agents refuse to let Parrish bring in the giant creature and it breaks out of its wooden cage and terrorizes the city, killing several citizens. The law tracks the snowman to the city sewers where it is killed.

Producer/director W. Lee Wilder finished his 1950s horror/sci-fi trilogy, which included PHANTOM FROM SPACE (1953) (q.v.) and KILLERS FROM SPACE (1954) (see B/V) with this feature, the first film made about the Abominable Snowman. *Variety* termed it "bush league science fiction" but overall it is an entertain-

THE SNOW CREATURE (1954).

ing, if mild project. Its chief highlight is keeping the title creature largely in shadows and little seen, thus not negating its shock value.

Unlike the later THE ABOMINABLE SNOWMAN OF THE HIMALAYAS (1957) (q.v.) or even the crude MANBEAST (1956) (q.v.), THE SNOW CREATURE makes no attempt to speculate on the origin of the Yeti—here it simply exists.

SOLARBABIES (Metro-Goldwyn-Mayer, 1986) C 94 mins.

Producers, Irene Walzer, Jack Frost Sanders; director, Alan Johnson; screenplay, Walon Green, Douglas Anthony Metrov; production designer, Anthony Pratt; art director, Don Dossett; set decorator, Graham Sumner; costumes, Bob Ringwood; music, Maurice Jarre; assistant director, Juan Carlos L. Rodero; sound, Jim Willis; visual effects, Richard Edlund; camera, Peter MacDonald; editor, Conrad Buff.

Richard Jordan (Grock); Jami Gertz (Terra); Jason Patric (Jason); Lukas Haas (Daniel); James Le Gros (Metron); Claude Brooks (Rabbit); Peter DeLuise (Tug); Petre Kowanko (Gavial); Adrian Pasdar (Darkstar); Sarah Douglas (Shandray); Charles Durning (The Warden).

In the bleak future, the Protectorate rules the Earth in a police state and those in power have access to much desired water, since a lot of the planet has turned into an arid wasteland. Near an outlying orphanage, a mysterious sphere called Bodhi lands and a group of youngsters, called the Solarbabies, find it after participating in an unauthorized rollerskate-ball game, with a group of peers who are more submissive to the authorities, including the warden (Charles Durning) of the establishment. The Solarbabies realize the importance of the sphere which attempts to guide them to rebel against the authoritarian rulers but the evil Darkstar (Adrian Pasdar) steals Bodhi and the Solarbabies pursue him. Police chief Grock (Richard Jordan) orders his men on their trail and the chase takes them to Tiretown, where they are confronted by a junkyard gang. The Bodhi battles a huge robot and wins, freeing the planet from its stagnant rule and opening the gates for a better future.

Created by Mel Brooks' Brooksfilms, SOLARBABIES was no more successful than Brooks' out-and-out sci-fi spoof SPACEBALLS (1987) (q.v.). Although this film was apparently done straight, it has moments which appear to be failed attempted satire. It should be noted that Brooks had nothing to do with the actual production of the feature which is highlighted by finely executed special effects.

"This futuristic teenage morality tale pitting good against evil plods along unconvincingly as it swiftly becomes more laughable than plausible. Stillborn concept barely makes the slightest pretension of originality while conjuring key aspects of some of the biggest hits of the past few years. It's a a dud." (*Daily Variety*). Bill Desowitz informed in *The Hollywood Reporter* that " . . . the film is not fresh enough or imaginative enough to cross over and capture substantial box-office revenues. . . . The overall mood seems better suited for Saturday morning fare or the Disney Sunday Movie."

SOLARIS (Sovexport, 1972) C 165 mins.

Director, Andrei Tarkovsky; based on the book by Stanislas Lemm; screenplay, Tarkovsky; music, Edward Artemyer; art director, Mikhail Romadin; camera, Vadim Jusov.

Natalia Bondarchuk (Hari); Youri Yarvet (Snaut); Donatas Banionys (Chris Kelvin); Anatoli Solinstsin (Sartorius); Vladislav Dvorjetzki (Burton): Nikolaï Grinko (Father); Sos Sarkissian (Gibarian).

Chris Kelvin (Donatas Banionys), a psychologist, is sent to a distant planet called Solaris to determine what happened to eighty-five astronauts sent there on an expedition. When he arrives he finds only three alive on the space station which orbits the planet, with the leader having committed suicide. The remaining crew members will not talk and Chris is surprisingly confronted with his dead wife, Hari (Natalia Bondarchuk) who had killed herself years ago. Hari is not a specter, however, but real and they rekindle their love as Chris realizes the seas on the planet below have powers to bring back the past, eventually with tragic results.

This Soviet film is a psychological melodrama set in the realm of the future with space travel as a background. More than two-and-one-half hours long, it becomes very trying at times, especially to audiences accustomed to STARS WARS-type action. In *The Film Encyclopedia: Science Fiction* (1984), Phil Hardy termed the film "The classic Soviet Science Fiction counterpart to 2001—A SPACE ODYSSEY (1968) [see B/V]. Like the American film, it offers . . . [a] kind of confused humanist philosophy. . . . It is interesting to note that both 2001 and SOLARIS offer intellectual banalities cloaked in cinematic splendour. . . ." Donald C. Willis decided in *Horror and Science Fiction Films II* (1982), "SOLARIS is a sf-comedy-drama about squaring one's life morally, about being and not being where one ought (morally) to be. Quite wryly, it acknowledges that total moral reconciliation of one's life, and of the people in one's life, is impossible—there's always a corner of it that won't stay tucked. The passing of time insures that every act or state of moral reconciliation is temporary, of *speeding up* this process, this moral cycle. Life on Solaris is an aggravation of life on Earth."

SOMEWHERE IN TIME (Universal, 1980) C 103 mins.

Producer, Stephen Deutsch; associate producer, Steven Bickel; director, Jeannot Szwarc; based on the novel *Bid Time Return* by Richard Matheson; screenplay, Matheson; music, John Barry; production designer, Seymour Klate; set decorator, Mary Ann Biddle; assistant director, Burt Bluestein; sound, Charles I. King III, Robert Heman, Earl M. Madery, Rex A. Sinkard; camera, Isadore Mankofsky; editor, Jeff Gourson.

Christopher Reeve (Richard Collier); Jane Seymour (Elise McKenna); Christopher Plummer (W. F. Robinson); Teresa Wright (Laura Roberts); Bill Erwin (Arthur); George Voskovec (Dr. Gerald Finney); Susan French (Older Elise); John Alvin (Arthur's Father); Eddie Gale (Genevieve); Sean Hayden (Young Arthur); Richard Matheson (Astonished Man).

Following his success in the title role of the remake of SUPERMAN (1978) (q.v.), Christopher Reeve followed that blockbuster film with a starring role in the time travel feature, SOMEWHERE

Jane Seymour and Christopher Reeve in SOMEWHERE IN TIME (1980).

IN TIME. Here, however, a scientifically constructed time machine is not used, but instead, Reeve travels through time cerebrally. "Beyond fantasy. Beyond obsession. Beyond time itself. . . . he will find her" read the poster ad for this romantic sci-fi fantasy.

Modern, and very successful, playwright Richard Collier (Christopher Reeve) falls in love with the image of actress Elise McKenna (Jane Seymour) which he has found in a 1912 photograph. Using his mental processes he travels through time back to her era where she is about to become the toast of the American stage. The two meet at the Grand Hotel at Michigan's Mackinac Island and begin a passionate love affair, much to the chagrin of her possessive manager, W. F. Robinson (Christopher Plummer). The two lovers, however, must figure out how to rectify their love in view of the fact they are from, literally, two different times.

Richard Matheson adapted the well-photographed film from his novel *Bid Time Return* (1975) while Jeannot Szwarc, fresh from his JAWS 2 (1978) success, directed; the music background (adored by many moviegoers) was mostly by Rachmaninoff. Vincent Canby, in the *New York Times* stated he wanted to "nominate it for the '1980 Hanover Square' award that each year goes to the big-budget screen romance with the highest giggle content. . . . [it] does for time travel what the Hindenberg did for the dirigibles. . . ."

THE SON OF DR. JEKYLL (Columbia, 1951) 74 mins.

Director, Seymour Friedman; suggested by the novel *The Strange Case of Dr. Jekyll and Mr. Hyde* by Robert Louis Stevenson; screenplay, Mortimer Braus, Jack Pollexfen; music, Paul Sawtell; camera, Henry Freulich; editor, Gene Havlick.

Louis Hayward (Edward Jekyll); Jody Lawrence (Lynn); Alexander Knox (Dr. Curtis Lanyon); Lester Matthews (John Utterson); Gavin Muir (Richard Daniels); Paul Cavanagh (Inspector Stoddard); Rhys Williams (Michaels); Doris Lloyd (Lottie Sarelle); Claire Carleton (Hazel Sarelle); Patrick O'Moore (Joe Sarelle); James Logan, Leslie Denison (Constables); Robin Camp (Willie Bennett).

See: DR. JEKYLL AND MR. HYDE (essay).

SON OF FRANKENSTEIN (Universal, 1939) 95 mins.

Producer/director, Rowland V. Lee; suggested by the novel by Mary Shelley; screenplay, Willis Cooper; art director, Jack Otterson, Richard Riedel; makeup, Jack Pierce; music, Frank Skinner; music director, Charles Previn; camera, George Robinson; editor, Ted J. Kent.

Basil Rathbone (Baron Wolf von Frankenstein); Boris Karloff (The Monster); Bela Lugosi (Ygor): Lionel Atwill (Krogh); Josephine

Hutchinson (Elsa von Frankenstein); Donnie Dunagen (Peter von Frankenstein); Emma Dunn (Amelia); Edgar Norton (Benson); Perry Ivins (Fritz); Lawrence Grant (Burgomaster); Lionel Belmore (Lang); Michael Mark (Ewald Neumuller); Caroline Cook (Mrs. Neumuller); Gustav von Seyffertitz, Lorimer Johnson, Tom Ricketts (Burghers).

Baron Wolf von Frankenstein (Basil Rathbone) returns to his family's castle with his wife Elsa (Josephine Hutchinson) and small son Peter (Donnie Dunagan). There is still resentment in the village for the horrors created by Frankenstein's father and in examining the elder Frankenstein's laboratory he meets Ygor (Bela Lugosi), a broken-necked criminal who was hanged yet lived. Ygor reveals the Monster (Boris Karloff) still lives but has no strength. Aided by Benson (Edgar Norton), his butler, Frankenstein reactivates his father's electrical equipment but the creature is not revived. Later Peter tells his father of making friends with a giant and Frankenstein understands the monster is strong again. Jurors who sent Ygor to the gallows are being killed and Inspector Krogh (Lionel Atwill) suspects Frankenstein of the crimes but the Baron knows the monster is doing the killings at Ygor's beckoning. Frankenstein confronts Ygor

Boris Karloff and Bela Lugosi in SON OF FRANKENSTEIN (1939).

who tries to dispatch him and he shoots the criminal. In anger the monster abducts Peter but does not kill him. When Krogh and his men arrive, the monster tears off Krogh's artificial arm as he holds the boy underfoot. Wolf swings from a chain and rams the monster off a ledge into a burning sulphur pit below where it is consumed.

Donald F. Glut in *The Frankenstein Legend* (1973) termed it " . . . the most elaborate, expensive, lengthy Frankenstein movie . . . made by Universal. SON OF FRANKENSTEIN was the most superbly mounted film in the series and may even have been filmed (through not released) in color. Gone are the stark blacks and whites of the typical Universal black and white film. The images are in variations of rich grays reminiscent of a color film printed on black and white stock. Many of the sets are simple and uncluttered as were those of many early color films."

SON OF FRANKENSTEIN is best remembered for the performances of Bela Lugosi as the broken-necked rogue Ygor and Lionel Atwill as the one-armed police inspector. Ygor provided Lugosi with a hearty characterization (one he repeated in THE GHOST OF FRANKENSTEIN [1942, q.v.]) and he easily stole the film from Karloff's laconic Monster. Atwill, too, is vivid, especially in the scene where he informs Baron Frankenstein how, as a child, the monster had snatched off his arm. It is ironic that later in the film when the two meet again, the monster rips off his artificial limb to use as a weapon. The film is also notable for Frank Skinner's music score and for its gaunt sets.

Overall, though, it is the least stirring of the first three FRANKENSTEIN series films; relying too much on visual aesthetics rather than gripping and graphic dramatics.

SON OF INGAGI (Sack Amusement, 1940) 66 mins.

Producer/director, Richard C. Kahn; screenplay, Spencer Williams, Jr.; songs, The Four Toppers and Spencer Williams; sound, Cliff Ruberg; camera, Roland Price, Herman Schopp; editor, Dan Milner.

Zack Williams (N'Gina, the Ape Man); Laura Bowman (Dr. Helen Jackson); Alfred Grant (Robert Lindsay); Daisy Bufford (Eleanor Lindsay); Arthur Ray (Zeno Jackson); Spencer Williams, Jr. (Detective Nelson); Earl J. Morris (Bradshaw); Jesse Graves (Chief of Detectives); The Four Toppers (Singers).

A reclusive scientist (Laura Bowman) wills her money and old mansion to the recently married daughter (Daisy Bufford) of the man she once loved. The scientist had brought a giant apeman (Zack Williams) back from Africa and after it drinks a formula she has made, it goes mad and kills her. The apeman then kills a lawyer (Earl

J. Morris) who was attempting to find $20,000 in gold the woman hid in the mansion. Zeno Jackson (Arthur Ray), the scientist's ex-convict brother, locates the precious ore but the apeman murders him and in turn is dealt a death wound by the dying man. A detective (Spencer Williams, Jr.) finds the gold and gives it to the girl and her new husband (Alfred Grant).

"Terror Reigns When the Giant of the Jungles Breaks Loose" read the ads for this all-Negro production which attempted to associate itself with the notorious pseudo-documentary INGAGI (1939), which allegedly told of native women mating with African gorillas. This outing, though, was a comedy mystery and a fairly good one for its genre. It should be noted that Spencer Williams, Jr., who wrote the script and songs and co-starred as the detective, later became the beloved Andrew H. Brown on TV's "Amos 'n Andy" series.

SON OF INGAGI offers a female scientist—for a change—plus the already standard sci-fi plot ingredients of a secret formula and a giant killer ape.

SON OF KONG, (RKO, 1933) 70 mins.

Executive producer, Marian C. Cooper; associate producer, Archie Marshek; director, Ernest B. Schoedsack; based on characters created by Edgar Wallace; screenplay, Ruth Rose; art directors, Van Nest Polglase, Al Herman; models, Marcel Delgado; music, Max Steiner; special effects, Willis O'Brien; camera, Edward Linden, Vernon Walker, J. O. Taylor; editor, Ted Chessman.

Robert Armstrong (Carl Denham); Helen Mack (Hilda Peterson): Frank Reicher (Captain Englehorn); John Marston (Helstrom); Clarence Wilson (Peterson); Victor Wong (Charlie the Cook); Lee Kohlmar (Mickey); Ed Brady (Red); Noble Johnson (Chief); Katharine Ward (Mrs. Hudson); Gertrude Sutton (Servant Girl); Steve Clemento (Witch King); Gertrude Short (Reporter); James L. Leong (Trader); Frank O'Connor (Process Server).

Following the huge success of KING KONG (see B/V) in 1933, RKO, saved from bankruptcy by the giant simian, rushed a sequel, SON OF KONG into production under the fake title JAMBOREE. Costing about $250,000, less than half the original's financing, SON OF KONG was a pale attempt to recapture the aura of the initial production, although on its own it has a special charm and is worth viewing. Almost tongue-in-cheek, SON OF KONG suffers from the lack of animation sequences which Willis O'Brien had deftly constructed for the original. Kiko, the title character, is a cute and amusing fellow and his run-ins with the assorted denizens of Skull Island are well accomplished, yet not overly involved. A

Styracosaurus, cut from the original KING KONG, makes a short but welcome appearance as does a sea serpent who conveniently finishes off the villain of this piece. Contemplated, but not filmed for SON OF KONG because of expense, was to be a spectacular sequence in which all the island's dinosaurs run amuck as the terrain is wrenched by a tremendous earthquake.

Following the financial disaster of the giant ape, Kong, wrecking New York City, documentary filmmaker Carl Denham (Robert Armstrong) slips out of Gotham, and away from his creditors, aboard Captain Engelhorn's (Frank Reicher) boat and the two take up freight hauling in the remote South Seas islands. On Dakang, Denham spots pretty Hilda Peterson (Helen Mack) working in her father's (Clarence Wilson) second-rate side show. Peterson is killed later in a fray with Helstrom (John Marston), the man who originally sold Denham the map to Skull Island. Hilda is discovered as a stowaway in the ship and in order to escape the area, Helstrom concocts a story about buried treasure on Skull Island. The party goes there but meets with a cool reception from the native chief (Noble Johnson) and finding an opening in the rocks they land on the island where Denham and HIlda find a baby Kong and rescue him from quicksand. They also turn up a real treasure but are terrorized by the primeval animals on the isle. Baby Kong protects them. Helstrom attempts to steal the treasure and their boat but a sea serpent kills him as the island is hit by a devastating earthquake and begins to sink. Englehorn and the others man their boat and little Kong holds Denham and Hilda above the water until they are rescued and then he dies with the island. Denham and Hilda plan to return to America.

S.O.S. COAST GUARD (Republic, 1937) twelve chapters.

Associate producer, Sol C. Siegel; directors, William Witney, Alan James; story, Morgan Cox, Ronald Davidson; screenplay, Barry Shipman, Franklyn Adreon; music, Raoul Krauschaar; camera, William Nobles; editors, Helene Turner, Edward Todd.

Ralph Byrd (Terry Kent); Bela Lugosi (Professor Boroff); Maxine Doyle (Jean Norman); Herbert Rawlinson (Commander Boyle); Richard Alexander (Thorg); Lee Ford (Snapper McGee); John Piccori (Rackerby); Lawrence Grant (Rabinisi); Thomas Carr (Jim Kent); Carleton Young (Dodds); Allen Connor (Dick Norman); George Chesebro (Degado); Randy Weeks (Wies).

Chapters: 1) Disaster at Sea; 2) Barrage of Death; 3) The Gas Chamber; 4) The Fatal Shaft; 5) The Mystery Ship; 6) Deadly Cargo; 7) Undersea Terror; 8) The Crash; 9) Wolves at Bay; 10) The Acid Trail; 11) The Sea Battle; 12) The Deadly Circle.

Republic Pictures' seventh serial, S.O.S. COASTGUARD, co-starred Bela Lugosi and Ralph Byrd, and was filmed in four weeks on location near Santa Barbara. Directed swiftly by William Witney and Alan James, the cliffhanger proved to be a popular matinee item and its sci-fi plot is hinged on the villain's invention of a disintegrating gas. Edward Connor in his article "The First Eight Serials of Republics" in *Screen Facts* magazine (No. 7, 1964), commented, "Scenes showing the effects of the disintegrating gas were well done, using a distortion lens or—where a mountain was involved—melting the emulsion on the film. Two elements needed for the gas bore the colorful names 'arnatite' and 'zanzoid'."

Mad inventor Professor Boroff (Bela Lugosi) has invented a gas which will disintegrate any matter. Foreign agents from the European country of Morovania want the gas for its war effort and after Boroff kills Jim Kent (Thomas Carr), his brother, Coast Guard Commander Terry Kent (Ralph Byrd), vows revenge. Aiding him is his girlfriend, Jean Norman (Maxine Doyle), and his superior officer, Commander Boyle (Herbert Rawlinson). In league with Boroff are: Rickerby (John Piccori), Rabinisi (Lawrence Grant), Dodds (Carleton Young), and the giant Thorg (Richard Alexander), who does Boroff's dirty work. Boroff kidnaps Jean and tries to force her to tell him Terry's plans, but when cornered by the Coast Guard Boroff shoots Thorg to make his getaway and the giant strangles him.

In *The Great Movie Serials* (1972) Jim Harmon and Donald F. Glut noted, "In this Republic serial, Lugosi has somewhat stiffer competition than usual. As the Coast guard officer hero, perennial screen Dick Tracy, Ralph Byrd, offers more qualities of presence and resourcefulness than the somewhat wooden figures Lugosi was usually pitted against." Footage from S.O.S. COAST GUARD reappeared in two other Republic cliffhangers, HAWK OF THE WILDERNESS (1938) and DICK TRACY VS. CRIME, INC. (1941). A sixty-nine minute feature version of the serial was issued theatrically in 1942.

SPACE MONSTER (American International TV, 1965) C 80 mins.

Producer, Burt Topper; director/screenplay, Leonard Katzman; music, Marlin Skiles; camera, Robert Tobey.

James L. Brown (Hank); Francine York (Lisa); Russ Bender (John Andros); Baynes Barron (Paul).

Four astronauts, Hank (James L. Brown), John (Russ Bender), Paul (Baynes Barron), and Lola (Francine York)—the first woman in space—board a spacecraft and trouble forces them to land on an uncharted planet. Once there the ship plunges into the ocean and they fight such obstacles as underwater mountain ranges, giant crabs and a sea monster, the latter killing opportunistic scientist Paul. They also find an alien spaceship and meet its inhabitant, a man-like creature with a visible brain. Lolan's experiments prove the planet can be inhabited and they name it for Paul. Freeing themselves, the astronauts return home to report their contact with alien life.

Made as FIRST WOMAN IN SPACE, FLIGHT BEYOND THE SUN and VOYAGE BEYOND THE SUN, this sub-par affair apparently was never released theatrically but went directly to television via American International TV. It is a slipshod outing with cramped sets, mediocre special effects and a spaceman who looks as if he has been on the receiving end of too many Keystone pie fights.

This film was written and directed by Leonard Katzman, the man behind the success of CBS-TV's "Dallas." On that program, this film's star, James Brown (also of TV's "Rin-Tin-Tin" fame) has the recurring role of Captain McSween.

SPACE RAIDERS (New World, 1983) C 82 mins.

Producer, Roger Corman; director/screenplay, Howard R. Cohen; music, James Horner; songs, Murphy Dunne; assistant director, Gordon Boos; stunt co-ordinator, Rick Barker; second unit director, Mary Ann Fisher; special effects makeup, Mike Jones; sound, Mark Ulano; special effects supervisor, Tom Campbell; camera, Alec Hirschfield; editors, Anthony Randel, R. J. Kizer.

Vince Edwards (Hawk); David Mendenhall (Peter); Patsy Pease (Amanda); Thom Christopher (Flightplan); Lucva Bercovici (Ace); Drew Snyder (Aldebarian); Dick Miller (Used Spacecraft Salesman); and: Ray Stewart, George Dickerson.

Producer Roger Corman is an experienced hand at molding feature films from bits and pieces of other movies and SPACE RAIDERS is a prime example of his ingenuity. Unfortunately the results are hardly pleasing as *Variety* noted, "With SPACE RAIDERS, producer Roger Corman hits the lowest ebb of his career, fashioning a nonsensical, uninteresting Outer Space picture out of leftovers from an earlier film." This prior production is BATTLE BEYOND THE STARS (1980) (q.v.) and this rehash not only uses that film's musical score but also its miniatures and much of its outer space scenes.

Spaceman Hawk (Vince Edwards) opposes a powerful alien organization called the "Company." He and his crew commandeer one of the aliens' spaceships and onboard is stowaway Peter (David Mendenhall), a young boy, and his pet bug. The crew and Hawk plan to steal four more alien space vessels and return David to his home planet, but the Company's huge robot ship pursues them resulting in a space battle in which the alien craft is demolished.

Outside of the reused, but exceedingly well done, special effects, SPACE RAIDERS has little to offer outside a bit of offbeat humor (e.g. a hideous alien hooker, Dick Miller as a fast-talking used spaceship huckster, and an alien reading a magazine written in his own language).

SPACEBALLS (Metro-Goldwyn-Mayer/United Artists, 1987) C 96 mins.

Producer, Mel Brooks; co-producer, Ezra Swerdlow; director, Brooks; screenplay, Brooks, Thomas Meehan, Ronny Graham; music, John Morris; orchestrator, Jack Hayes; music editor, Eugene Marks; song: Jeff Prescette, Clyde Lieberman, Brooks; production designer, Terence Marsh; art directors, Harold Michelson, Diane Wager; set designers, Pete Kelly, Richard McKenzie, Jacques Valin; set decorator, John Franco, Jr.; costumes, Peter Donfeld; alien monsters, Industrial Light & Magic; visual effects supervisor, Donfeld; assistant directors, Dan Kolstrud, Mitchell Bock, Carl D. Bonnefil; sound designers, Randy Thom, Gary Rydstrom; supervising sound editor, Michael John Baxteman; sound editors, Glad Pickering, Ronald Sinclair, George Simpson; sound, Jeff Wesler, Don Coufal, Jim Steube; vocal effects supervisor, Norman B. Schwartz; sound effects editors, Ken Fischer, Ernie Fosselius, Ronald Jacobs, Sandino Bailo-Laped; special visual effects, Apogee, Inc.; camera, Nick McLean; editors, Conrad Buff IV, Nicholas C. Smith.

Mel Brooks (President Skroob/Yogurt); John Candy (Barf); Rick Moranis (Dark Helmet); Bill Pullman (Lone Starr); Daphne Zuniga (Princess Vespa); Dick Van Patten (King Roland); George Wyner (Colonel Sandurz); Michael Winslow (Radar Technician); Joan Rivers (Voice of Dot Matrix); Lorene Yarnell (Dot Matrix); John Hurt (Himself); Jm. J. Bullock (Aristocrat); Leslie Bevis (commanderette Ircon); Jim Jackman (Major Asshole); Michael Pniewski (Laser Gunner); Sandy Helberg (Dr. Schlotkin); Stephen Tobolowsky (Captain of the Guard); Jeff MacGregor (Snotty); Henry Kaiser (Magnetic Beam Operator); Denise Gallop (Charlene); Dian Gallup (Marlene); Gail Barle, Dey Young (Waitresses); Rhonda Shear (Woman in Diner); Robert Prescott (Sand Cruiser Driver); Jack Riley (TV Newsman); Tom Dreesen (Megamaid Guard); Rudy DeLuca (Vinnie); Tony Griffin, Rick Ducommun (Prison Guards); Ken Olfson (Head Usher); Wayne Wilson (Trucker in Cap); Ira Miller (Short Order Cook); Earl Finn (Guard with Captain); Tommy Serdlow (Troop Leader); Deanna Booher (Bearded Lady); Johnny

Silver (Caddy); Brenda Strong (Nurse); Dom Deluise (Voice of Pizza the Hutt).

Producer/writer/director Mel Brooks (America's comedy auteur) has none-too-graciously broadly spoofed most movie genres in the past two decades, including the horror/sci-fi field with YOUNG FRANKENSTEIN (1974) (q.v.). SPACEBALLS, however, is a direct takeoff on sci-fi films, specifically STAR WARS (1977) (q.v.) and its ilk. The result, with Brooks playing two roles, is largely unfunny with only a few audience-grabbing sight gags; but nothing in the all-too-obvious production warrants its overbloated $25,000,000 budget. Perhaps Brooks should have examined the past and understood better that science fiction films are difficult to spoof since in many ways they are tongue-in-cheek even when serious. Above all, they rarely have little to do with reality.

The leader (Mel Brooks) of one planet is attempting to steal the atmosphere of Druidia, while a princess (Daphne Zuniga) runs away from her wedding with a young, drugged-out aristocrat (Jm. J. Bullock). The princess takes along her robot adviser Dot Matrix (voice of Joan Rivers) in her spacemobile only to be kidnapped by the evil Dark Helmet (Rick Moranis) as the forces of good set out to rescue her.

The *Hollywood Reporter* printed, "Space films are Mel Brooks' latest target in this STAR WARS parody that might be appropriately titled SCHTICK WARS. You don't have to be Jewish to be turned off by this movie but it sure helps to understand the jokes. . . . While the story is way out there, the dialogue is mired in the Borscht Belt—tired gags and routines keep SPACEBALLS manically earthbound." (One of Brooks' "jokes" is to parody the STAR WARS' catchphrase, which he translates into "May the schwartz be with you!") *Los Angeles Weekly* complained, "Forgetting for the moment that it's already ten years too late for a STAR WARS satire, what's disheartening about SPACEBALLS is how much of it falls totally flat. . . . When Brooks cooks, he's the king of satire and audacity, and certain parts, like the strange time-war sequence involving the cassette of SPACEBALLS, are extremely clever. But they're few and very far between." Tom Milne (British *Monthly Film Bulletin*) added, "The pity of it is that, either half-obscured beneath the thick debris of waste matter or half-buried by Brooks' seeming inability to pace his gags properly, there are some genuine inspirations."

SPACEBALLS grossed $36,725,144 in its first ten weeks of domestic release.

SPACECAMP (Twentieth Century-Fox, 1986) C 108 mins.

Executive producer, Leonard Goldberg; producers, Patrick

Bailey, Walter Coblenz; associate producer, David Salven; director, Harry Winer; story, Bailey, Larry B. Williams; screenplay, W. W. Wickett, Casey T. Mitchell; music, John Williams; music editor, Kenneth Wannberg; songs: Mark Knopfler; Jerry Williams; Joseph Williams and Paul Gordon; Joseph Williams and Amy La Television; Joseph Williams and Gordon; assistant directors, James B. Simons, Tena Psyche Yatroussis; animator supervisor, Jeff Burks; production designer, Richard MacDonald; art directors, Richard J. Lawrence, Leon Harris; set decorator, Richard C. Goddard; costumes designer, Patricia Norris; makeup, Zoltan Elek, Katalin Elek; sound, David MacMillan, Armin Steiner; special sound effects, Ed Bannon, Bruce Glover; special vocal effects, Frank Welker; special consultant, Joel Cohen; special visual effects supervisor, Barry Nolan; flying wire consultant, Bob Harman; special effects co-ordinator, Chuck Gaspar; camera, William Fraker; second unit camera, Robert Jessup, Jack Cooperman; optical camera supervisor, David Williams; blue screen camera, Tom Anderson; editor, John W. Wheeler, Timothy Board.

Kate Capshaw (Andie Bergstrom); Lea Thompson (Kathryn); Kelly Preston (Tish); Larry B. Scott (Rudy); Leaf Phoenix (Max); Tate Donovan (Kevin); Tom Skerritt (Zach Bergstrom); Barry Primus (Brennan); Terry O'Quinn (Launch Director); Mitchell Anderson (Banning); T. Scott Coffey (Gardener); Daryl Roach, Terry White, Peter Scranton (NASA People); Hollye Rebecca Suggs (Young Andie); Susan Becton, Kevin Gage (Counselors); Ron Harris (Tom the Technician); Kathy Hanson (Girl); D. Ben Casey (Rudy's Father); Scott Holcomb (Hideo Takamini); Saundra McGuire (Rudy's Mother); Bill Phillips (Kathryn's Father); Jon Steigman (Bully in Dorm); Adrian Wells (Rudy's Brother).

Issued only a few months following the Challenger Space Shuttle disaster early in 1986, SPACECAMP's story of a group of youngsters and their leader being accidentally launched into space had topical value. However, this was negated by the production itself which was one-third science lecture, one-third a study of the quirks of the kids involved, and one-third their space adventures. *Variety* carped, "Most of the film, in fact, has a processed, programmed feel about it with exposition and editing shrugging along with no apparent rhythm or reason, although some scenes manage a modicum of suspense . . . but wonders of space are more of a backdrop to the slight human story. . . . Instead of a view of Earth through young and unspoiled eyes, we get a trite teen comedy set in space." The *Hollywood Reporter* registered, "Its box office seems grounded to boys who go for anything with the word 'space' in the title. Derivative and fitted out with some of the better parts of STAR

WARS, E.T. and CLOSE ENCOUNTERS, SPACE CAMP has many of the right parts but none of the magic. If the script isn't there it's hard to get a movie off the ground, and SPACE CAMP'S turgid, expository storyline is about as dynamic as a federally funded educational booklet."

Five youngsters come to the NASA Space Camp in Huntsville, Alabama, to learn about becoming astronauts: Kathryn (Lea Thompson), a go-getter in love with Kevin (Tate Donovan) who is training to be the group commander; a brilliant yuppie-type girl Tish (Kelly Preston), Rudy (Larry B. Scott), a young black who wants to put a fast food eatery in space; and computer genius Max (Leaf Phoenix), who develops an affinity for the project's robot. The group's avuncular leader, Andie (Kate Capshaw), leads them through the mechanics necessary to "become" astronauts, but the robot takes the process too seriously and it causes the gang and their leader to actually be launched into space where they must put their learning into operation to survive and return home.

SPACEFLIGHT IC-1 (Twentieth Century-Fox, 1965) 65 mins.

Producers, Robert L. Lippert, Jack Parsons; director, Bernard Knowles; story/screenplay, Harry Spalding; art director, Harry White; music, Elisabeth Lutyens; music director, Phil Martell; assistant director, Gordon Gilbert; wardrobe, Jean Fairlie; makeup, Harold Fletcher; sound, Jock May; sound editor, Clive Smith; camera, Geoffrey Faithfull; supervising editor, Robert Winter; assistant editor, Colin Miller.

Bill Williams (Captain Mead Ralston); Kathleen Breck (Kate Saunders); John Cairney (Steven "Doc" Thomas); Donald Churchill (Carl Walcott); Jeremy Longhurst (John Saunders); Linda Marlowe (Helen Thomas); Margo Mayne (Joyce Walcott); Norma West (Jan Ralston); Tony Doonan (Griffith); James Terry (Captain Burnett); John Lee (Dr. Garth); Chuck Julian (Webster); Max Kirby (Clown); Mark Lester (Don); Stuart Middleton (Michael); Anthony Honour (Robert).

In the year 2015 the Earth is stifled by overpopulation and nuclear weapons and Space Ship IC-1, under the command of Captain Mead Ralston (Bill Williams), is sent into outer space to locate a planet with conditions like those on Earth for relocating the population. Four married couples—all doctors, scientists and engineers—make up the crew and they are also supposed to have children, but only Jan Ralston (Norma West) is able to do so. Dr. Helen Thomas (Linda Marlowe) becomes sick and the Captain exiles her to her cabin and refuses her request to have another child. As a result she commits suicide and her husband, Dr. Steven Thomas

SPACEFLIGHT IC-1

Astronauts hurtle through outer space to save the world—or destroy themselves

STARRING

BILL WILLIAMS • John Cairney

Linda Marlowe • Kathleen Breck • Donald Churchill

PRODUCED BY ROBERT L. LIPPERT and JACK PARSONS

DIRECTED BY BERNARD KNOWLES • WRITTEN BY HARRY SPALDING

A LIPPERT FILMS LTD. PRODUCTION

RELEASED BY 20th CENTURY-FOX

(John Cairney), and the other crew members mutiny. Captain Ralston threatens to detonate the ship with a master key he controls and they back down. He insists Dr. Thomas be executed but first one of the replacement crew members, kept in suspended animation, must be revived. The man, Griffith (Tony Doonan), comes to life but he goes mad and kills Ralston just as he is about to destroy the ship. Griffith dies from temperature change as the dead Ralston and the master key are ejected into space and the ship continues its journey.

A soap opera in outer space, SPACEFLIGHT IC-1 lacks the production values requisite to carry out its dark vision. A depressing, pessimistic, sci-fi entry, the movie had only Bill Williams for box-office appeal and it was distributed on the lower half of double bills. British-made, the movie was hampered by lackluster scripting and directing. In *Science Fiction Movies* (1976), Philip Strick observed, "No destination is specified for the occupants of SPACE FLIGHT IC-1, exploring space with colonization in view but they'll be lucky if they get here; authoritarianism, friction and mutiny among an undistinguished cast indicate that another couple of generations should find them in the 'mindless savage' category, fighting and feuding among the stainless steel corridors."

SPACEHUNTER: ADVENTURES IN THE FORBIDDEN ZONE (Columbia, 1983) C 90 mins.

Executive producer, Ivan Reitman; producers, Don Carmody, John Dunning, Andre Link; director, Lamont Johnson; story, Stewart Harding, Jean LaFleur; screenplay, Edith Rey, David Preston, Dan Goldberg, Len Blum; 3-D consultant, Ernest McNabb; music, Elmer Bernstein; production designer, Jackson DeGovia; art director, Michael Minor; special makeup effects, Thomas R. Burman; assistant director, Tony Lucibello; stunt co-ordinator, Walter Scott; sound, Richard Lightstone; special effects co-ordinator, Dale Martin; special effects supervisors, Gene Warren, Jr., Peter Kleinow; model shop supervisors, Dennis Schultz; matte paintings, Matte Effects; effects animator, Ernest D. Farino; special optical effects, Image 3; optical camera, Phil Huff, Mike Warren; camera, Frank Tidy; editor, Scott Conrad.

Peter Strauss (Wolff); Molly Ringwald (Niki); Ernie Hudson (Washington); Andrea Marcovicci (Chalmers); Michael Ironside (Overdog McNabb); Beeson Carroll (Grandma Patterson); Deborah Pratt (Meagan); Aleisa Shirley (Reena); Cali Timmins (Nova); Paul Boretski (Jarrett); Patrick Rowe (Duster); Reggie Bennett (Barracuda Leader).

On the planet Terra Eleven in the 21st century, Earthman Wolff

Molly Ringwald in SPACEHUNTER: ADVENTURES IN THE FORBIDDEN ZONE (1983).

(Peter Strauss) is the captain of a salvage ship. With him are young tomboy orphan Niki (Molly Ringwald) and Washington (Ernie Hudson), his former training school mate who is now a sector commander. Three young girls are shipwrecked on the planet, which is called "the garbage heap of the universe" and Wolff learns they have been kidnapped by Overdog (Michael Ironside), who leads a group of mutants who exist by draining the energy from those they capture. Wolff and his comrades try to retrieve the girls and are forced to attack Overdog and his helpers who are sequestered behind a huge, impregnable fortress.

Another entry in the 3-D revival craze, this sci-fi picture depended far more on visual effects than plot. Costing over $12,000,000, the feature is " . . . a muddled action film, lacking the story values which could attract a wide audience. . . ." (*Variety*) The reviewer added, "Aside from fine stuntwork in an early battle with misfits aboard a vast sail-rigged galleon running on railroad tracks and the impressive depth effects in the final reel battles at Overdog's Iron sculpture-plus-neon fortress, SPACEHUNTER is a dull trek picture." Donald C. Willis observed in *Horror and Science Fiction*

Films III (1984), "Story-wise, a pretty tired crossing of STAR WARS and PAPER MOON. . . . Overdog himself seems to be operated by crane, like a motion-picture camera. He's the latest in movie man-machine hybrids, a human wrecking-crane."

The 3-D consultant on this film was Ernest McNabb, who developed the twin-camera system used on the feature, and the full name of the piece's villain is Overdog McNabb—coincidence? At any rate, the motion picture grossed over $8,000,000 at the domestic box-office.

SPACESHIP see THE CREATURE WASN'T NICE.

SPACEWAYS (Lippert, 1953) 76 mins.

Producer, Michael Carreras; director Terence Fisher; based on the radio play by Charles Eric Maine; screenplay, Paul Tabori, Richard Landau; art director, J. Elder Wills; music, Ivor Slaney; assistant director, Jimmy Sangster; camera, Reginald Wyer; editor, Maurice Rootes.

Howard Duff (Stephen Mitchell); Eva Bartok (Lisa Frank); Alan Wheatley (Smith); Philip Leaver (Dr. Keppler); Michael Medwin (Toby Andrews); Andrew Osborn (Philip Crenshaw); Cecile Chevreau (Vanessa Mitchell); Anthony Ireland (General Hays); Hugh Moxey (Colonel Daniels); David Horne (Minister); Jean Webster-Brough (Mrs. Daniels); Leo Phillips (Sergeant Peterson); Marianne Stone (Mrs. Rogers).

American scientist Steve Mitchell (Howard Duff) is assigned to work on a British rocket project which will be used eventually to place a satellite in space. He uncovers that his wife Vanessa (Cecile Chevreau) is having an affair with his colleague, Crenshaw (Andrew Osborn), who is suspected of being a spy for a foreign power. About the time the rocket is launched, Vanessa and Crenshaw disappear and military man Smith (Alan Wheatley) suspects that Mitchell placed them in the rocket. To prove his innocence, Steve volunteers to go in another rocket and examine the first one, accompanied by Lisa Frank (Eva Bartok), a colleague who is in love with him. Just as they are launched, Smith locates Crenshaw, who has murdered Vanessa for refusing to continue their affair. In space Steve and Lisa discover the truth about the fate of Vanessa and Crenshaw, but as they return to Earth they begin having troubles with the rocket. For a time it appears they are doomed to destruction. Finally they correct the problem and head home safely.

According to Allen Eyles, Robert Adkinson and Nicholas Fry in *The House of Horror* (1973), SPACEWAYS was " . . . the first British picture to cash in on the Hollywood space cycle that had included

ROCKETSHIP X-M and DESTINATION MOON" (see both in B/V). Based on a radio program, the film is far more talk than action but for its time it was futuristic enough and the scenes toward the finale with the rocket in peril and the hero and heroine seemingly doomed have suspense. Overall, though, SPACEWAYS looks just like what it is—a studio-bound space opera.

SPECTER OF DR. HICHCOCK see THE HORRIBLE DR. HICHCOCK.

THE SPECTER see THE HORRIBLE DR. HICHCOCK.

THE SPIDER see EARTH VS. THE SPIDER.

STAR TREK: THE MOTION PICTURE (Paramount, 1979) C 132 mins.

Producer, Gene Roddenberry; associate producer, Jon Povill; director, Robert Wise; based on the teleseries by Roddenberry; screen story, Alan Dean Foster; screenplay, Harold Livingston; music, Jerry Goldsmith; production designer, Harold Michelson; art directors, Michelson, Leon Harris; set decorator, Linda De Scenna; makeup, Freed Phillips; costume designer, Robert Fletcher; special visual effects, Douglas Trumbull, John Dykstra; camera, Richard H. Kline; editor, Todd Ramsay.

William Shatner (Captain James T. Kirk); Leonard Nimoy (Mr. Spock); DeForest Kelley (Dr. Leonard "Bones" McCoy); James Doohan (Montgomery Scott [Scotty]); George Takei (Sulu); Majel Barrett (Dr. Chapel); Walter Koenig (Chekov); Nichelle Nichols (Uhura); Persis Khambatta (Ilia); Stephen Collins (Decker); Mark Lenard (Klingon Captain); Billy Van Zandt (Alien Boy); Grace Lee Whitney (Janice Rand); David Gautreaux (Commander Branch); Howard Itzkowitz (Lieutenant Commander Sonak); Marcy Lafferty (Chief DiFalco); Terrence O'Connor (Chief Ross); Michael Rougas (Lieutenant Cleary); Roger Aaron Brown (Epislon Technician); Gary Faga (Airlock Technician); Jeri McBride (Technician); Michele Ameen Billy (Lieutenant).

STAR TREK II: THE WRATH OF KHAN (Paramount, 1982) C 113 mins.

Executive producer, Harve Bennett; producer, Robert Sallin; director, Nicholas Meyer; based on the teleseries created by Gene Roddenberry; screen story, Bennett, Jack B. Sowards; screenplay, Sowards; production designer, Joseph R. Jennings; art director, Michael Minor; set decorator, Charles M. Graffeo; music, James

Horner; "Star Trek" theme by Alexander Courage; stunt co-ordinator, Bill Couch; sound, Jim Alexander; special sound effects, Alan Howarth; special visual effects, Industrial Light & Magic; special visual effects supervisors, Ken Ralston, Jim Veilleux; special effects supervisor, Bob Dawson; special sound effects, Alan Howarth; camera, Gayne Rescher; editor, William P. Dornisch.

William Shatner (Admiral James T. Kirk); Leonard Nimoy (Mr. Spock); DeForest Kelley (Dr. Leonard "Bones" McCoy); James Doohan (Chief Engineer Montgomery Scott [Scotty]); Walter Koenig (Chekov); George Takei (Sulu); Nichelle Nichols (Commander Uhura); Bibi Besch (Dr. Carol Marcus); Merritt Butrick (David); Paul Winfield (Terrell); Kirstie Alley (Saavik); Ricardo Montalban (Khan); Judson Scott (Joachim); Ike Eisenmann (Peter); and: John Vargas, John Winston, Paul Kent, Nicholas Guest, Russell Takaki, Kevin Sullivan, Joel Marstan, Terera E. Victor, Dainne Harper, David Ruprecht, Marcy Vosburgh.

STAR TREK III: THE SEARCH FOR SPOCK (Paramount, 1983) C 105 mins.

Executive producer, Gary Nardino; producer, Harve Bennett; director, Leonard Nimoy; based on the teleseries created by Gene Roddenberry; screenplay, Bennett; music, James Horner; "Star Trek" theme by Alexander Courage; art director, John E. Chilberg II; set designers, Cameron Birnie, Blake Russell; set decorator, Tom Pedigo; executive consultant, Roddenberry; assistant director, John Hockridge; costume designer, Robert Fletcher; special makeup appliances, The Burman studio; special (physical) effects supervisor, Bob Dawson; special sound effects, Alan Howarth, Frank Serafine; sound, Gene S. Cantamessa; special visual effects supervisor, Kenneth Ralston at Industrial Light & Magic; optical camera supervisor, Kenneth F. Smith; special effects art directors, Nilo Rodis, David Carson; supervising modelmaker, Steve Gawley; creature supervisor, David Sosalla; matte painting supervisor, Michael Pangrazio; animation supervisor, Charles Mullen; miniature pyrotechnics/fire effects, Ted Moehnke; camera, Charles Correll; editor, Robert F. Shugrue; special effects editors, Bill Kimberlin, Jay Ignaszewski.

William Shatner (Commander James T. Kirk); Leonard Nimoy (Mr. Spock); DeForest Kelley (Dr. Leonard "Bones" McCoy); James Doohan (Chief Engineer Montgomery Scott [Scotty]); George Takei (Sulu); Walter Koenig (Chekov); Nichelle Nichols (Uhura); Mark Lenard (Sarek); Merritt Butrick (David); Dame Judith Anderson (High Priestess); Robin Curtis (Saavik); Christopher Lloyd (Kurge); James B. Sikking (Captain Styles); Allan Miller (Alien at Bar); Robert Hooks (Commander Morrow); Scott McGinnis (Lieutenant); Cathie Shirriff (Valkris); Stephen Liska (Klingon Torg); John Larroquette (Klingon Maltz); Carl Steven (Spock at Nine); Vadia Potenza (Spock at Thirteen); Stephen Manley (Spock at Seventeen); Joe W. Davis (Spock at Twenty-Five). Dave Cadiente (Klingon Sergeant); Bob Cummings, Branscombe Richmond (Gunners); Philip Richard Allen (Captain Esteban); Jeanne Mori (Helmsman on USS *Grissom*); Mario Marcelino (Communications aboard USS *Grissom*); Alan Shanklin (Alien); Sharon Thomas (Waitress); Conroy Gedeon (Civilian Agent); James B. Sikking (Captain Styles, USS *Excelsior*); Miguel Ferrer (1st Officer, USS *Excelsior*); Mark Lenard (Sarek); Katherine Blum (Vulcan Child); Gary Faga, Douglas Alan Shanklin (Prison Guards); Grace Lee Whitney (Woman in Cafeteria); Frank Welker (Spock Screams); Teresa E. Victor (USS *Enterprise* Computer); Harve Bennett (Flight Recorder); Judi Durand (Space Dock Controller); Frank Force (Elevator Voice); John Meier (Stunts for William Shatner); Al Jones (Stunts for Christopher Lloyd).

STAR TREK IV: THE VOYAGE HOME (Paramount, 1986) C 119 mins.

Executive producer, Ralph Winter; producer, Harve Bennett; co-producer, Industrial Light & Magic; associate producers, Brooke Breton, Kirk Thatcher; director, Leonard Nimoy; based on the teleseries created by Gene Roddenberry; story, Nimoy, Bennett; screenplay, Steve Meerson, Peter Krikes, Bennett, Nicholas Meyer; production designer, Jack T. Collis; executive consultant, Roddenberry; stunt co-ordinator, R. A. Rondell; visual consultant, Ralph McQuarrie; art directors, Joe Aubel, Pete Smith, Nilo Rodis; set designers, Dan Gluck, James Bayliss, Richard Berger; set decorator, John Dwyer; music, Leonard Rosenman; additional music, Rosenman and the Yellowjackets; orchestrator, Ralph Ferraro; supervising music editor, Else Blangsted; songs: Alexander Courage, Craig Huxley; Kirk Thatcher and Mark Mangini; costume designer, Robert Fletcher; makeup, Wes Dawn, Jeff Dawn, James L. McCoy; sound, Gene S. Cantamessa; sound effects editors, David Stone, Michael J. Benavente, Warren Hamilton, Stephen Flick; sound effects, Mark Mangini; special sound effects, John Popisil, Alan Howarth, George Budd; video supervisor, Hal Landaker; visual effects supervisor, Ken Ralston; visual effects, Industrial Light & Magic; animation supervisor, Ellen Lichtwardt; camera, Don Peterman; visual effects camera, Don Dow; matte camera, Craig Barron; Randy Johnson; underwater camera, Jack Cooperman, Peter Romano; editors, Peter E. Berger, Mike Gleason.

William Shatner (Admiral James T. Kirk); Leonard Nimoy (Mr. Spock); DeForest Kelley (Dr. Leonard "Bones" McCoy); James

Doohan (Engineering Officer Montgomery Scott [Scotty]); George Takei (Sulu); Walter Keonig (Chekov); Nichelle Nichols (Lieutenant Uhura); Jane Wyatt (Amanda); Catherine Hicks (Dr. Gillian Taylor); Mark Lenard (Sarek); Robin Curtis (Lieutenant Saavik); Robert Ellenstein (Federation Council President); John Schuck (Klingon Ambassador); *Starfleet Personnel:* Brock Peters (Admiral Cartwright); Michael Snyder (Starfleet Communications Officer); Michael Berryman (Starfleet Display Officer); Mike Brislane (Saratoga Science Officer); Grace Lee Whitney (Commander Rand); Jane Wiedlin (Alien Communications Officer); Vijay Amritraj (Starship Captain); Majel Barrett (Commander Chapel); Nick Ramus (Saratoga Helmsman); Thaddeus Golas, Martin Pistone (Controllers); *In Old San Francisco:* Scott DeVenney (Bob Briggs); Viola Stimpson (Lady on Tour); Phil Rubenstein, John Miranda (Garbagemen); Joe Knowland (Antique Store Owner); Bob Sarlatte (Waiter); Everett Lee (Cafe Owner); Richard Harder (Joe); Alex Henteloff (Nichols); Tony Edwards (Pilot); Eve Smith (Elderly Patient); Tom Mustin, Greg Karas (Interns); Raymond Singer (Young Doctor); David Ellenstein, Judy Levitt (Doctors); Teresa E. Victor (Usher); James Menges (Jogger); Kirk Thatcher (Punk on Bus); Naval Personnel: Jeff Lester (FBI Agent); Joe Lando (Shore Patrolman); Newell Tarrant (CDO); Mike Timoney, Jeffrey Martin (Electronic Technicians); 1st Sergeant Joseph Naradzay (Marine Sergeant); 1st Lieutenant Donald W. Zautcke (Marine Lieutenant).

The cult status which has remained with the "Star Trek" (NBC-TV, 1966-69) TV series finally resulted in a feature film, after many delays, in 1979 and the movie proved successful enough to spawn three sequels to date. Overall, though, the features have been satisfying to only rabid Trekkies and less appetizing to the average moviegoer, even sci-fi fans. In fact, the initial entry of the quartet was rather poor; the series hit a high mark with the second entry, almost sank to the level of the first with the third installment, and came back to a higher water mark in the fourth film using underplayed comedy. Still the STAR TREK films have been big box-office with the debut motion picture grossing $56,000,000 and its followup coming in at $40,000,000.

STAR TREK—THE MOTION PICTURE is set in the 23rd century with the starship *Enterprise* in drydock above San Francisco being fitted with ultra-modern weaponry. The Federation asks the ship's former captain, James T. Kirk (William Shatner), to take over from Commander Will Decker (Stephen Collins) and lead his old crew members, including Dr. Leonard "Bones" McCoy (DeForest Kelley), Scotty (James Doohan), Sulu (George Takei), Uhura (Nichelle Nichols) and Chekov (Walter Koenig), on a mission to find out what mysterious force is destroying enemy Klingon ships in their territory. The mysterious object is moving toward Earth and devouring everything in its path. Decker is jealous of Kirk's command but when the latter almost loses the ship in a time warp, he comes to Kirk's rescue and the two reach an understanding. As the *Enterprise* travels to the center of the disturbance they pick up another passenger, Mr. Spock (Leonard Nimoy), who has his own reasons for wanting to find out about the invader which is called V'ger. They near the thing and its forces enter the ship and kill Ilia (Persis Khambatta), a Deltan, who springs back to life. Kirk and Spock conclude the thing is a long forgotten space probe which has taken on a mentality of its own and is returning to its home base, Earth. The crew work to destroy the marauding satellite which is on a collision course with Earth.

Even to the most rabid Star Trek enthusiast, this first theatrical outing was a disappointment, mainly due to its faulty plot and lengthy running time (132 minutes!). Outside of some of the famous character interaction, for which the video series was noted, the motion picture failed to capture the flavor of the small screen adventures. When shown on network TV and issued on video cassette, eleven minutes was added to the film's running time.

STAR TREK II: THE WRATH OF KHAN had its origins in an episode of the TV series called "Space Seed" and that segment's guest star, Ricardo Montalban, repeated his characterization of Khan in this feature, the best STAR TREK feature film to date. *Variety* correctly reviewed it as " . . . a very satisfying space adventure, closer in spirit and format to the popular tv series than its big-budget (and not well-liked) STAR TREK: THE MOTION PICTURE predecessor. Bound to captivate, 'Trek' fans with premiere special effects to attract other space pic enthusiasts. . . ."

Starship explorers Terrell (Paul Winfield) and Chekov (Walter Koenig) accidentally land on a planet where the wicked Khan (Ricardo Montalban) was marooned by Captain Kirk (William Shatner) fifteen years prior. In the ensuing years, Khan's wife has died and he vows revenge on Kirk. He places brain control devices in the spacemen and takes their ship and he and his few followers leave their planet. Meanwhile Kirk, who has been assigned a desk job with the Federation, goes along with friends Spock (Leonard Nimoy) and Dr. McCoy (DeForest Kelley), in commanding the *Enterprise* to rescue Terrell and Chekov. They head for the Regulus space station where Kirk's former paramour, Dr. Carol Marcus (Bibi Besch) and her son David (Merritt Butrick), are working on the super secret Genesis Effects which will bring life to arid planets. Khan finds out about Genesis and plans to use it to trap Kirk, who learns David is really his son. Kirk, Carol and David become stranded on a planet where the Genesis Effect is to be ignited, with Khan having trapped them there, although he and his ship lose a battle with the *Enterprise.* Mr. Spock calculates a way to save them and gives his life to do so while the new planet bursts into bloom.

STAR TREK III: THE SEARCH FOR SPOCK is a direct sequel to the second film. Captain Kirk (William Shatner) has defeated the evil Khan, but is depressed over the death of his long-time friend, Mr. Spock (Leonard Nimoy). He also learns his pal Dr. McCoy (De Forest Kelley) is going mad but a visit from Spock's father, Sarek (Mark Lenard), informs him that Spock's essence is being harbored in McCoy's body and to save him they must resurrect Spock. Kirk, McCoy and the old *Enterprise* crew "borrow" the ship from headquarters and defy the quarantine on the Genesis Effects planet and go there hopefully to find Spock, whose body was ejected to the planet in a small capsule. There they find a young boy, who is the revived Spock without memory, but the planet is growing much too quickly and is about to destroy itself as the wicked Klingons, who have also learned about the Genesis project and want its secrets for themselves, trap Kirk and some of the crew on the dying planet. At the last minute they escape (after Kirk's son has sacrificed his life) and defeat the Klingons as the planet destroys itself. Kirk and the crew take the boy Spock back to his home planet where he undergoes a secret ceremony in which a high priestess (Judith Anderson) returns Spock to his old self.

DeForest Kelley, Walter Koenig, William Shatner, James Doohan, and George Takei in STAR TREK III: THE SEARCH FOR SPOCK (1984).

Although the special effects for the dying Genesis planet are interesting as are the villainous Klingons, STAR TREK III is almost on a par with the undernourished initial outing. It is a morose, darkly unilluminated film with none of the fun usually associated with the series' characters. Even more disturbing is the fact the multi-tiered climax of the film—the defeat of the Klingons, the escape from the planet and its destruction—does *not* come at the film's finale. Instead the audience is subjected to the tedious ceremony of Spock's resurrection in an incredibly incomprehensible sequence. As for the direction of the "epic" by co-star Leonard Nimoy (which received tremendous media coverage), it was adequate at best.

STAR TREK IV: THE VOYAGE HOME finds Kirk (William Shatner), the newly-resurrected Spock (Leonard Nimoy) and the rest of the *Enterprise* crew returning home on a captured Klingon tub following the loss of their own ship in the destruction of the Genesis planet. Kirk will face court proceedings for commandeering the *Enterprise* in the first place but strange signals from Earth interrupt their trek. They learn the planet is near destruction due to the vaporization of its oceans by outer space signals in a language which turns out to be the song of the long-exterminated humpback whale. Without actual whales to answer the alien call, the planet will blow up, so Kirk and the crew take their craft through a time warp to the San Francisco of the 20th century to find two whales and bring them back through time and save their world. Landing, Kirk and Spock set out in search of the whales and enlist the aid of a biologist (Catherine Hicks) while Dr. McCoy (DeForest Kelley) and Scotty (James Doohan) find materials to build a tank to hold the mammals, as Sulu (George Takei) learns to understand the workings of a helicopter needed to transport the materials for their unique mission. Meanwhile Uhura (Nichelle Nichols) and Chekov (Walter Koenig) obtain dilithium crystals for their ship to return to the 23rd century. The tasks are accomplished and the crew shoots through time and returns home. The Earth is saved.

Directed and co-written by Leonard Nimoy, STAR TREK IV is an improvement over number three, with its reliance on humor—mainly based on quips at the not fully recovered Spock and the cultural clashes between the 20th and 23rd centuries. *Daily Variety* approved, "Latest Excursion is warmer, wittier, more socially relevant and truer to its tv origins than prior odysseys, which will satisfy the legions of trekkies while conquering a galaxy of new admirers with its more commercial treatment." Michael Wilmington opined in the *Los Angeles Times,* "Breathe there any non-Trekkies with hide so tough they won't find something to enjoy in this rollicking, allegorical, super-space opera? Well, perhaps. But they're likely to be outnumbered and outflanked. . . . It has an irresistibly sure touch, an easy command of its audience. It hits the right buttons, strikes the right chords plays with our expectations with the right blend of savvy, guile and imagination. It's reminiscent of an old trouper—a Chevalier, Hope or Crosby in their later years. Short of wind, it captures us with a wink or a word, a nudge on our mutual memory banks."

STAR TREK IV: THE VOYAGE HOME grossed $109,567,069 in its first 22 weeks of domestic distribution, proving the property still has lots of box-office vitality and insuring the emergence of STAR TREK V. In the meantime, a brand new syndicated "Star Trek: The Next Generation" television series appeared, complete with new cast and surroundings and was sufficiently impressive to earn good ratings. And through all of this, the original "Star Trek" TV episodes continue to be aired.

STAR WARS (Twentieth Century-Fox, 1977) C 121 mins.

Producer, Gary Kurtz; director/screenplay, George Lucas; music, John Williams; production designer, John Barry; art directors, Norman Reynolds, Leslie Dilley; set decorator, Roger Christian; costumes/wardrobe, John Mollo, Ron Beck; stunt co-ordinator, Peter Diamond; sound, Don McDougal, Bob Minkler, Ray West, Mike Minkler, Les Fesholtz, Richard Portman, Derek Ball, Stephen Katz; special visual effects supervisor, John Dykstra; special production/mechanical effects supervisor, John Stears; special dialogue/sound effects, Ben Burtt; sound editors, Sam Shaw, Robert R. Rutledge, Gordon Davidson, Gene Corso; composite optical camera, Robert Blalack; optical camera, Paul Roth; animation/rotoscope designer, Adam Beckett; stop motion animators, Jn Berg, Phil Tippet; camera, Gilbert Taylor; second unit camera, Carroll Ballard, Rick Clemente, Robert Dalva, Tak Fujimoto; editors Paul Hirsch, Marcia Lucas, Richard Chew.

Mark Hamill (Luke Skywalker); Harrison Ford (Han Solo); Carrie Fisher (Princess Leia Organa); Peter Cushing (Grand Moff Tarkin); Alec Guinness (Ben Kenobi); Anthony Daniels (C-3PO); Kenny Baker (R2-D2); Peter Mayhew (Chewbacca); David Prowse (Lord Darth Vader); James Earl Jones (Voice of Lord Darth Vader); Phil Brown (Uncle Owen Lars); Shelagh Fraser (Aunt Beru Lars); Jack Purvis (Chief Jawa); Alex McCrindle, Eddie Byrne (Rebel Generals); Don Henderson, Richard LeParmentier, Leslie Schofield (Imperial Military Chiefs); Drewe Henley, Dennis Lawson, Garrick Hagon, Jack Klaff, William Hootkins, Angus McInnis, Jeremy Sinden, Graham Ashley (Rebels).

Avoiding gore and aiming for the general market, the space

fantasy STAR WARS turned out to be a feature film with huge mass appeal due to its serial-like plot, John Dykstra's miniatures and special effects and John Stears' production and mechanical effects. Almost remindful of the FLASH GORDON (see B/V) cliffhangers starring Buster Crabbe, STAR WARS revitalized the science fiction film genre and until E.T. (q.v.) came along five years later, it was the biggest grossing film of all-time, with a domestic box-office take of \$193,500,000. Two blockbuster sequels followed: THE EMPIRE STRIKES BACK (1980) and THE RETURN OF THE JEDI (1983) (qq.v.) and together this trio of motion pictures have a domestic box-office income exceeding \$500,000,000.

"A long time ago, in a galaxy far, far away" Princess Leia Organa (Carrie Fisher) leads the forces of the Rebellion against the Imperial Outland Empire ruled by the evil Grand Moff Tarkin (Peter Cushing), who is assisted by the imposing Darth Vader (Dave Prowse; voice of James Earl Jones), the dark Lord of Sith. Leia possesses the constructural plans for the *Death Star,* Tarkin's gigantic spaceship/weapon which is capable of destroying whole planets. He has done such to Leia's home planet and plans to torture the princess to

Peter Mayhew, Mark Hamill, Alec Guinness, and Harrison Ford in STAR WARS (1977).

retrieve the plans. She puts the plans, and a plea for help, in robot R2D2 (Kenny Baker) who with fellow robot C-3P0 (Anthony Daniels) is placed in a space pod and expelled from the Death Star. They land on a nearby planet and are found by Luke Skywalker (Mark Hamill) who discovers the princess' message and falls in love with her image. He seeks out a neighbor, Obi-Wan "Ben" Kenobi (Alec Guinness), who is mentioned in the message, and learns from him that his late father, like Kenobi, had been a Jedi knight who had fought the Imperial Outland forces. Returning home, Luke finds his farm home in ruins and his aunt and uncle, with whom he lived, murdered. With Kenobi and the robots, Luke goes to a nearby town to get transportation to rescue the princess and hires fly-by-night freight cargo captain Han Solo (Harrison Ford) and his associate, Chewbacca (Peter Mayhew), a huge Wookie co-pilot. On the flight to the *Death Star,* Kenobi teaches Luke the secrets and powers of the Jedi knights. On the star ship they manage to rescue Leia and escape to Solo's vessel but Kenobi stays behind to do battle with Darth Vader, his old pupil who took up the dark side of "The Force." In a fight with laser swords Kenobi is cut in half and then disappears. Tarkin and his ship follow the invaders who land on a nearby planet and mobilize the small force there and an all-out attack is launched with Solo battling Darth Vader. Meanwhile Luke boards a small craft and following the plans Leia had taken, flies into the *Death Star* and deposits explosives which destroys the craft, killing Tarkin. Knocked out of control by Solo's ship, Darth Vader heads into deep space. On a closeby planet, Luke and Solo are given medals by Leia for the valiant efforts on behalf of the rebellion.

Ed Naha wrote in *The Science Fictionary* (1980), "The movie that gave new meaning to the word 'profits,' STAR WARS revitalized the sagging sf film industry and made millionaires out of half the Los Angeles phone directory. Lavish effects, nonstop action, and a plot that would cause no mental strain on the part of a collie all combined to make this film the biggest moneymaker [before E.T.] in the history of sf cinema." It is interesting to note the producers of this feature had no notion of the impact it was to make and often had to resort to shoestring activities to get it completed. For example, David Prowse's scenes as Darth Vader were shot without a soundtrack which was to be dubbed in later. Without money enough to return to England for the requisite dubbing, they hired James Earl Jones for the part in Hollywood, thus giving the character different actors for appearance and voice.

STAR WARS, with its remarkable technical wizardry, resulted in a host of imitators, with TV's "Battlestar Gallactica" being a good example. It also spawned several takeoffs, the best being the twelve minute short HARDWARE WARS (1978) in which kitchen appliances do battle in outer space. There was also a thirteen-week "Star Wars" radio series in which Mark Hamill reprised his Luke Skywalker role. The film also generated a huge, and successful, merchandizing campaign involving items such as books, comic books, toys, clothes, records, etc.

Nominated for ten Oscars, STAR WARS earned six Academy Awards for its effects and for John Williams' musical score.

STARCRASH (New World, 1979) C 92 mins.

Producers, Nat Wachsberger, Patrick Wachsberger; director, Lewis Coates [Luigi Cozzi]; screenplay, Coates [Cozzi], Nat Wachsberger; music, John Barry; production designer, Aurelia Curnolla; electronic special effects supervisor, Ron Hays; special effects directors, Armando Valcuda, Germano Natali; Dolby sound consultant, Don Digiroiamo; camera, Paul Beeson, Roberto D'Ettore; editor, Sergio Montanari.

Marjoe Gortner (Akton); Caroline Munro (Stella Star); Christopher Plummer (The Emperor); David Hasselhoff (Simon L.); Robert Tessier (Thor); Joe Spinelli (Count Zarth Arn); Nadia Cassini (Queen of the Amazon); Judd Hamilton (Elle); Hamilton Camp (Voice of Elle).

The Emperor of the Universe (Christopher Plummer) is at war with the wicked Count Zarth Arn (Joe Spinelli) and he assigns secret agent Stella Starr (Caroline Munro) to ferret out Arn's hideout and destroy it. For her mission she takes along her robot comrade Elle (Judd Hamilton) and a warrior alien, Akton (Marjoe Gortner). Along the way they find the Emperor's lost son, Simon L. (David Hasselhoff), and he joins their crusade. Arn confronts the group with sundry obstacles, including: insect robots, Red Monsters and his warriors. They find his fortress hideout but Arn escapes and sets off a missile which will hit directly at the Emperor's capital. To avert this, Stella brings a floating city into the missile's path and saves the Empire and brings about the villain's downfall.

"Operating on the principle of the Christmas tree, STARCRASH is decorated brightly, with stars and planets of all colors (or at least red, yellow, blue, and white), spaceships of all sizes (inc. one dubbed Murray Leinstar), ray guns and rifles, robots, monsters, and Ms. Munro (the latter as Stella Star) the choicest ornament of all . Some of the decorations seem to have been added a bit hastily, but with tree-trimming (as with movies), it's the festive spirit that counts. Fun fluff." (Donald C. Willis, *Horror and Science Fiction Films II,* 1982)

Also called THE ADVENTURES OF STELLA STAR, the film's main asset (no pun intended) is the very scantily clad Caroline

Munro in the lead role. This lovely has also decorated such fantasy outings as DRACULA A.D. 1972 (1972), THE GOLDEN VOYAGE OF SINBAD (1973), AT THE EARTH'S CORE (1976) (q.v.) and THE SPY WHO LOVED ME (1977).

STARMAN (Columbia, 1984) C 115 mins.

Executive producer, Michael Douglas; producer, Larry J. Franco; co-producer, Barry Bernardi; director, John Carpenter; screenplay, Bruce A. Evans, Raynold Gideon; music, Jack Nitzsche; production designer, Daniel Lomino; set decorator, Robert Benton; set designer, William Joseph Durrell, Jr.; Starman transformations, Dick Smith, Stan Winston, Rick Baker; visual consultant/second unit director, Joe Alves; assistant director, Larry Franco; stunt coordinator, Terry Leonard; sound, Tommy Causey; special visual effects supervisor, Bruce Nicholson; supervising modelmaker, Ease Owyeung; matte painting supervisor, Michael Pangrazio; animation supervisor, Charles Mullen; head effects animator, Bruce Walters; camera, Donald M. Morban; editor, Marion Rothman; visual effects editor, Michael Gleason.

Jeff Bridges (Starman); Karen Allen (Jenny Hayden); Charles Martin Smith (Mark Shermin); Richard Jaeckel (George Fox); Robert Phalen (Major Bell); Tony Edwards (Sergeant Lemon); John Walter Davis (Brad Heinmuller); Ted White (Deer Hunter); Dirk Blocker, M. C. Gainey (Cops); Sean Faro (Hot Rodder); Buck Flower (Cook); Russ Benning (Scientist); Ralph Coshan (Marine Lieutenant); David Wells (Fox's Assistant); Anthony Grumbach (NSA Officer); Jim Deeth (S-61 Pilot); Alex Daniels (Gas Station Attendant); Carol Rosenthal (Gas Customer); Mickey Jones (Trucker); Lu Leonard (Roadhouse Waitress); Charlie Hughes (Bus Driver); Byron Walls (Police Sergeant); Betty Bunch (Truck Stop Waitress); Victor McLemore (Roadblock Lieutenant); Steven Brennan (Roadblock Sergeant); Pat Lee (Bracero Wife); Judith Kim (Girl Barker); Ronald Colby (Cafe Waiter); Robert Stein (State Trooper); Kenny Call (Donnie Bob); Jeff Ramsey, Jerry Gatlin (Hunters); David Daniell, Randy Tutton (Lettermen).

Army missiles shoot down a UFO in upstate Wisconsin and the alien inside enters the lakeside home of Jenny Hayden (Karen Allen) a young widow whose husband Scott has died recently. The alien, a ball of light, finds a lock of Scott's hair Jenny has saved in a scrapbook and clones himself into an exact replica (Jeff Bridges) of the late husband. At first the young woman is very frightened but she begins to understand the alien's plight and eventually falls in love with him and agrees to aid him in his quest to reach a rendezvous with another ship before he dies from the Earth's hostile atmos-

Jeff Bridges and Karen Allen in STARMAN (1984).

phere. They embark on a cross-country journey, first by auto then by truck and railroad, as they are chased by a State Department bureaucrat (Richard Jaeckel) who wants the alien for examination purposes and by a scientist (Charles Martin Smith) who hopes to communicate with him. Eventually the duo reach their destination and the mother ship arrives and thwarts the government as the alien returns home.

With pleasing performances by Jeff Bridges and Karen Allen in the lead assignments, and good support from Richard Jaeckel and Charles Martin Smith, the film benefits more from solid acting than sound logic. An examination of its plot reveals a conglomeration of such other genre outings as THE MAN WHO FELL TO EARTH (1976) (see B/V), CLOSE ENCOUNTERS OF THE THIRD KIND (1977) (q.v.) and E.T. (1982) (q.v.), but without the special assets of any of them. The relationship between the alien and the heroine is the film's strong suit, something not overly appealing to an age of gadget and special effects sci-fi movie buffs.

Variety grumbled, " . . . story has frequent holes and lapses of plausibility which they (the writers) try to patch over with exposition after the fact. Pic is like a jigsaw puzzle with missing pieces that director John Carpenter is never totally successful in weaving together in a full-blooded and human film, as E.T. was able to." Chris

Potter wrote in *Video Times* magazine (July, 1985), "Sadly, it's also what we've come to expect from John Carpenter, who always seems on the verge of doing something great yet never has the imaginative pizzazz to quite pull it off."

On September 19, 1986, on ABC-TV, a teleseries version of STARMAN debuted with Robert Hays in the title role, C. B. Barnes as his teenage son, and Michael Cavanaugh as the government official relentlessly hounding Hays. It had fitful Nielsen popularity ratings and was cancelled, despite a heavily-publicized write-in campaign by viewing fans, ending on September 4, 1987. The series chose to turn the premise into a futuristic version of "The Fugitive" teleseries with every week Starman and his son only one step ahead of his governmental adversary.

STARSHIP INVASIONS (Warner Bros., 1977) C 89 mins.

Executive producers, Earl A. Glick, Norman Glick; producers, Norman Glick, Ed Hunt, Ken Cord; director/screenplay, Hunt; music, Gil Meel; art director, Karen Bromley; assistant director, Gary Flanagan; sound, Tony Van Den Akker; special effects, Warren Keillor; camera, Mark Irwin; editors, Millie Moore, Ruth Hope.

Robert Vaughn (Professor Allan Duncan); Christopher Lee (Captain Rameses); Daniel Lion (Anaxi); Tiiu Leek (Phi); Helen Shaver (Betty Duncan); Henry Ramer (Malcolm); Victoria Johnson (Gezeth); Doreen Lipson (Dorothy); Sherry Ross (Sagnac).

With his planet threatened by an unstable solar system, evil Captain Rameses (Christopher Lee) brings his Legion of the Winged Serpent to Earth and sets up headquarters under the Atlantic Ocean in the Alien Galactic Center, which is unknown to humans. He supervises experiments to determine if the planet is fit for habitation. Aliens from other worlds arrive at the site and warn Rameses not to break treaties barring contact with humans while the increase in UFO sightings and the disappearance of many people incite the military to fire on the craft. This causes Rameses to use an orbiting craft employing radio waves to make people commit mass suicide. UFO expert, Professor Duncan (Robert Vaughn), is visited by two aliens, Anaxi (Daniel Pilon) and Phi (Tiiu Leek), who are opposed to Rameses and they ask his help in defeating the invader. Together they thwart Rameses and bring about his demise.

This crude sci-fier, filmed in Canada as ALIEN ENCOUNTERS, had only the marquee value of Robert Vaughn and Christopher Lee to pull it through and as a result it received few theatrical playdates. (Some sources claim the film was issued directly to TV, but this is incorrect.) *Cinefantastique* magazine (Vol. 6, No. 3, 1977) commented its " . . . level of sophistication . . . should be embarrassing to Lee and Vaughn."

Perhaps the most absurd scene in STARSHIP INVASIONS occurs when a beautiful alien girl disrobes and makes sexual advances towards a middle-aged portly farmer who has just been kidnapped by the UFO occupants.

THE STEPFORD CHILDREN (NBC-TV, 3/15/87) C 100 mins.

Executive producers, Edgar J. Scherick, Gary Hoffman; producer, Paul Pompian; director, Alan J. Levi; based on characters created by Ira Levin; teleplay, Bill Bleich; music, Joseph Conlan; production designer, Greg Gonseca; sound, Dennis Carr; camera, Steve Shaw; editor, Michael Berman.

Barbara Eden (Laura Harding); Don Murray (Steven Harding); Tammy Lauren (Mary Harding); Pat Corley (Sheriff Weston); Ken Swofford (Frank Gregson); Richard Anderson (Lawrence Dalton); Sharon Spelman (Sandy Gregson); James Staley (Swimming Instructor); Raye Birk (George Larson); Debbie Baker (Lois Gregson); Dick Butkus (Tom Wilcox); James Coco (Mr. Jamison); Randall

Advertisement for THE STEPFORD CHILDREN (1987).

Batnikoff (David Harding); John Cameron Mitchell (Kenny); Judy Baldwin (Stepford Wife); Pirie Jones (Stepford Husband); Michael Murray (Hank Wilcox); John Hostetter (Mr. Moreland).

See: THE STEPFORD WIVES.

THE STEPFORD WIVES (Columbia, 1975) C 114 mins.

Executive producer, Gustave M. Berne; producer, Edgar J. Scherick; director, Byran Forbes; based on the novel by Ira Levin; screenplay, William Goldman; music, Michael Small; production designer, Gene Callahan; set decorator, Robert Drumheller; assistant director, Peter Scuppa; sound, Dick Vorisck, James Sabal; camera, Owen Roizman; editor, Timothy Gee.

Katharine Ross (Joanna Eberhart); Paula Prentiss (Bobby); Peter Masterson (Walter Eberhart); Nanette Newman (Carol); Patrick O'Neal (Dale Coba); Carol Rosson (Dr. Fancher); William Prince (Artist); Paula Trueman (Welcome Wagon Lady); Remak Ramsay (Atkinson); John Aprea (Policeman).

Businessman Walter Eberhart (Peter Masterson) and his wife Joanna (Katharine Ross) move to the suburban community of Stepford, Connecticut. Joanna does not like the place and finds the town's women very passive except for lively Bobby (Paula Prentiss). Both women begin to suspect something is very amiss in the town and Bobby suddenly becomes like the others—very subservient and complacent. Further investigation shows Joanna that Dale Coba (Patrick O'Neal), the head of the local men's club, is behind a plot in which all the town's wives are transformed into android slaves.

Based on Ira Levin's best-selling novel (1972) and grossing $4,000,000 at the box-office, THE STEPFORD WIVES was a "Fairly embarrassing excursion into slice-of-life sf" (Ed Naha, *The Science Fictionary,* 1980). The actual transformation of the women into perfect zombies is never detailed, but this domestic-oriented sci-fi item was sufficiently intriguing to spawn two TV movies.

REVENGE OF THE STEPFORD WIVES, telecast on NBC-TV on October 12, 1980, is set a decade after the film on which it was based. Now the men of Stepford, Connecticut, are neutralizing women into programmed, perfect companions with drugs. A television reporter (Sharon Gless) arrives in town, notices the women are all *too* passive, and discovers the town's terrible secret. She is assisted by Megan Brady (Julie Kavner), a free spirit freshly moved to Stepford, who is not yet fully indoctrinated into the domestic household slave regimen. Michael Weldon in *The Psychotronic Encyclopedia of Film* (1983) labeled it, "A totally useless 'sequel' to a pretty useless feature."

THE STEPFORD CHILDREN came along on NBC-TV on

March 15, 1987, and it related of Steven Harding (Don Murray) relocating his second wife, lawyer Laura (Barbara Eden), and teenagers (Tammy Lauren, Randall Batinkoff), in his hometown of Stepford. Both Laura and the children soon suspect something is wrong in the community because of its over wholesome ambiance and passive denizens. Following a dramatic change in the behavior of the son's girlfriend (Debbie Barker) they unfold the truth about how rebellious citizens are altered by the local men's club into passive automans. *The Hollywood Reporter* queried, "Why can't TV let dead ideas stay buried?"

STRANGE INVADERS (Orion, 1983) C 94 mins.

Producer, Walter Coblanz; associate producers, Richard Moore, Joel Cohan; director, Michael Laughlin; screenplay, William Condor; production/costume designer, Susanna Moore; art director, Emad Helmy; set decorator, Gus Meunier; music, John Addison; assistant director, David Shepherd; sound, Peter Shewchuk; special visual effects, Private Stock Effects Inc., Chuck Comisky, Ken Jones, Larry Benson; visual effects designers, John Muto, Robert Skotak; camera, Louis Horvath; editor, John W. Wheeler.

Paul LeMat (Charles Bigelow); Nancy Allen (Betty Walker); Diana Scarwid (Margaret); Michael Lerner (Willie Collins); Louise Fletcher (Mrs. Benjamin); Wallace Shawn (Earl); Fiona Lewis (Waitress/Avon Lady); Kenneth Tobey (Arthur Newman); June Lockhart (Mrs. Bigelow); Charles Lane (Professor Hollister); Lulu Sylbert (Elizabeth Bigelow).

Highly intelligent aliens from a distant star system come to Earth and take over the bodies of several people in a 1958 midwestern town. The people they possess disappear in blue spheres. Years later a little girl (Lulu Sylbert) realizes that Margaret (Diana Scarwid) is not really her mother and runs away from home and her father, Christopher Bigelow (Paul LeMat) who is separated from his wife, goes in search of her and is assisted by Betty Walker (Nancy Allen), a tabloid reporter. The alien living in Margaret's body decides to stay on Earth and goes to New York City and the other aliens head to the city to get her and the child. On Margaret's trail, Christopher and Betty piece the mystery together after talking to a scientist (Louise Fletcher) and a victim (Michael Lerner) of an alien attack. The duo return to the midwest town for a showdown with the visitors and the blue spheres return as the aliens abandon the planet.

Although its plot is reminiscent of INVASION OF THE BODY SNATCHERS (1956) (see B/V) and (1978) (q.v.), STRANGE INVADERS is more of a spoof than a straight sci-fi thriller, although it does include several shocker sequences. Its greatest asset is the teaming of Paul LeMat and Nancy Allen in the lead characterizations. Its biggest problem " . . . is its perceptible shift in tone, from light satire to straight-away horror" (*Variety*).

STRANGER FROM VENUS (Eros, 1954) 75 mins.

Producers, Burt Balaban, Gene Martel; director, Balaban; story, Desmond Leslie; screenplay, Hans Jacoby; music, Eric Spear; camera, Kenneth Talbot; editor, Peter Hunt.

Patricia Neal (Susan North); Helmut Dantine (The Stranger); Derek Bond (Arthur Walker); Cyril Luckham (Dr. Meinard); Marigold Russell (Gretchen); Arthur Young (The Scientist).

Issued in the U.S. only to TV by Princess Films as STRANGER FROM VENUS, this British feature was released in that country as IMMEDIATE DISASTER. A minor effort at best, it attempted to emulate THE DAY THE EARTH STOOD STILL (1951) (see B/V), even to using that film's female star, Patricia Neal, in a starring assignment. Cheaply made and not very credible, this set-bound talkie piece seemed old-fashioned even when first released.

American Susan North (Patricia Neal) is driving along a deserted English road when her car mysteriously stops and a Stranger (Helmut Dantine) approaches. Later at a nearby inn the Stranger, who has fallen in love with Susan, tells those present that he is from Venus and has come to warn Earthlings against continued atomic testing. Susan's fiancé, Arthur Walker (Derek Bond), arrives and is immediately jealous of her affection for the alien. Arthur notifies the military and they set a trap for the alien but the Stranger warns them that parts of the planet will be destroyed if the ship is harmed. Arthur backs down but it is too late for the Stranger because he has stayed too long on the planet and dies from exposure to the atmosphere.

Bill Warren commented in *Keep Watching the Skies!* (1982), "IMMEDIATE DISASTER is a well-intentioned film; it is trying to promote peace and understanding by means of a symbolic alien visitor. But the capabilities of American director Burt Balaban were not up to the most modest demands of the script; the picture is excruciatingly lifeless."

A.k.a.: THE VENUSIAN.

SUPERGIRL (Tri-Star, 1984) C 114 mins.

Executive producer, Ilya Salkind; producer, Timothy Burrill; director, Jeannot Szwarc; based on the comic strip character; screenplay, David Odell; production designer, Richard Macdonald; art director, Terry Ackland-Snow; set decorator, Peter Young; stunt co-ordinator, Alf Joint; costumes, Emma Porteus; music, Jerry Goldsmith; sound, Derek Ball, Robin Gregory; special visual effects, Derek Meddings; optical visual effects, Roy Field; travelling matte consultant, Dennis Bartlett; special effects supervisor, John Evans; flying effects specialist, Bob Harman; video co-ordinator, Chris Warren; process background camera, Ronald Goodman; visual effects camera, Paul Wilson; camera, Alan Hume; editor, Malcolm Cooke.

Faye Dunaway (Selena); Helen Slater (Supergirl/Linda Lee); Peter O'Toole (Zaltar); Mia Farrow (Alura); Brenda Vaccaro (Bianca); Peter Cook (Nigel); Simon Ward (Zor-El); Marc McClure (Jimmy Olsen); Hart Bochner (Ethan); Maureen Teefy (Lucy Lane); David Healy (Mr. Danvers); Sandra Dickinson (Pretty Young Lady); Robyn Mandell (Myra); Jenifer Landor (Muffy); Diana Ricardo (Mrs. Murray); Nancy Lippold (Billy-Jo); Sonya Leite (Betsy); Virginia Greig (Jodie); Nancy Wood (Nancy); Linsey Beauchamp (Ali); Michelle Taylor (Amy); Virginia Greig (Jodie); Julia Lewis (Gloria); Matt Frewer, Bill McAllister (Truck Drivers); Sally Cranfield (Argonian Teacher); Martin Serene (Eddie); Keith Edwards, Bradley Lavelle (Lucy's Friends); Carole Charnow (Cashier); Shezwae Powell (Waitress); Glory Annen (Midvale Protestor); Sandra Martin (Selenas Astral Image); and: Sandra Dickinson, Martha Parsey, Kelly Hunter, Christian Fletcher, Karen Hale, Jane Sumner, Bailie Walsh, Gay Baynes, Fred Lee Owen, Edwin Van Wyk, Orla Pederson, Russell Sommers, Dulcie Huston, David Graham.

SUPERGIRL was an exploitive attempt to mold super heroes in the feminine gender, a big screen counterpart to TV and comics' "Wonder Woman." This Tri-Star release was an expensively-mounted, all star effort assembled to repeat the box-office bonanza of the Christopher Reeve SUPERMAN (see infra) series, but with only modest results. The concept of Supergirl, despite a hefty merchandising campaign to coincide with the film, failed to attract public attention.

On the planet Argo, the life-giving Omegahedron Stone is stolen by wicked Selena (Faye Dunaway) and taken to Earth by the sorceress. With the blessing of her parents, Alura (Mia Farrow) and Sor-El (Simon Ward), young Kara (Helen Slater) is dispatched to Earth to retrieve the precious life force. Kara, cousin of Superman who is on a mission to another galaxy, ends up near an exclusive girl's school and becomes student Linda Lee (Helen Slater) and her roommate is Lucy Lane (Maureen Teefy), younger sister of *Daily Planet* reporter Lois Lane. Aided by her mentor, Zaltar (Peter O'Toole), Kara goes after the stone but Selena and her associates, Blanca (Brenda Vaccaro) and Nigel (Peter Cook) oppose her at every turn. Jealousy flares when school groundskeeper Ethan (Hart Bochner) is sought after by the lustful Selena, but the young man falls in love with Linda. Kara/Linda and Selena confront one another at the latter's mountain castle and Selena brings forth a monster to fight for her. The evil ones are thwarted and the stone returned to Argo.

Variety confided, "David Odell's screenplay is filled with witty lines and enjoyable characters, but Jeannot Szwarc's direction is rather flat, partly compensated by some of the performances." The *LA Weekly* was more direct, "SUPERGIRL is a superdog, with fine actors uttering nonsensical dialogue under nincompoop direction."

SUPERMAN (Warner Bros., 1978) C 143 mins.

Presenters, Alexander Salkind, Ilya Salkind; executive producer, Ilya Salkind; director, Richard Donner; based on comic strip characters created by Jerry Siegel, Joe Shuster; screenplay, Mario Puzo, David Newman, Leslie Newman, Robert Benton; additional script material, Norman Enfield; music, John Williams; assistant directors, Vincent Winter, Michael Dryhurst, Allan James, Gareth Tandy; production designer, John Barry; costumes, Yvonne Blake; creative supervisor/director of special effects, Colin Chilvers; creative supervisor/director of optical visual effects, Roy Field; creative supervisor/director of mattes and composites, Les Bowie; creative director of process camera, Denys Coop; model sets director/creator, Derek Meddings; camera, Geoffrey Unsworth; editor, Stuart Band.

Marlon Brando (Jor-El); Gene Hackman (Lex Luthor); Christopher Reeve (Superman/Clark Kent); Ned Beatty (Otis); Jackie Cooper (Perry White); Glenn Ford (Pa Kent); Trevor Howard (First Elder); Margot Kidder (Lois Lane); Jack O'Halloran (Non); Valerie Perrine (Eve Teschmacher); Maria Schell (Vond-Ah); Terence Stamp (General Zod); Phyllis Thaxter (Ma Kent); Susannah York (Lara); Jeff East (Young Clark Kent); Marc McClure (Jimmy Olsen); Sarah Douglas (Ursa); Harry Andrews (Second Elder); Aaron Smolinksi (Baby Superman); Diane Sherry (Laura Lang); John Stuart (Elder); Jeff Atcheson (Coach); Jill Ingham (Perry White's Secretary); Bill Bailey (State Senator); Rex Reed (Himself); Weston Gavin (Mugger); Roy Stevens (Warden); Larry Hagman (Army Colonel); Kirk Alyn, Noel Neill (Couple on Train); Chief Tug Smith (Indian Chief); George Harris II (Officer Mooney); and: Vass Anderson, John Hollis, James Garbuti, Michael Gover, David Neal, William Russell, Penelope Lee, Alan Cullen, Lee Quigley, Brad Flock, David Petron, Billy J. Mitchell, Robert Henderson, Larry Lamb, James Brockington, John Cassady, John F. Parker, Antony Scott, Ray Evans, Sue Shifrin, Miquel Brown, Vincent Marzello, Benjamin Feitelson, Lise Hilboldt, Leueen Willoughby, Pieter Stuyck,

Stephen Kahan, Paul Avery, Rex Everhardt, Lawrence Trimble, Phil Brown, Colin Etherington, Mark Wynter.

SUPERMAN II (Warner Bros., 1980) C 127 mins.

Executive producer, Ilya Salkind; producer, Pierre Spengler; director, Richard Lester; based on comic strip characters created by Jerry Siegel, Joe Shuster; story, Mario Puzo; screenplay, Puzo, David Newman, Leslie Newman; creative consultant, Tom Mankiewicz; production designers, John Barry, Peter Murton; art director, Maurice Fowler; costumes, Yvonne Blake, Susan Yelland; music, Ken Thorne, from original material composed by John Williams; second unit directors, David Tomblin, Robert Lynn; assistant director, Dusty Symonds; makeup, Stuart Freeborn; supervisor of optical/visual effects, Roy Field; additional flying sequences/director of miniature effects, Derek Meddings; flying unit special effects director, Zoran Perisic; flying unit director of camera, Denys Coop; director of miniature camera, Paul Wilson; flying effects, Bob Harman; astronautical consultant, Harry Lange; special effects, Colin Chilvers; camera, Geoffrey Unsworth, Bob Paynter; Wesscam camera, Ronald Goodman; editor, John Victor-Smith; optical/special effects editor, Peter Watson.

Gene Hackman (Lex Luthor); Christopher Reeve (Superman/Clark Kent); Ned Beatty (Otis); Jackie Cooper (Perry White); Sarah Douglas (Ursa); Margot Kidder (Lois Lane); Jack O'Halloran (Non); Valerie Perrine (Eve Teschmacher); Susannah York (Lara); Clifton James (Sheriff); E. G. Marshall (President); Marc McClure (Jimmy Olsen); Terence Stamp (General Zod); Leueen Willoughby (Leueen); Robin Pappas (Alice); Roger Kemp (Spokesman); Roger Brierley, Anthony Milner, Richard Griffith (Terrorists); Melissa Wiltsie (Nun); Alain DeHay (Gendarme); Marc Boyle (C.R.S. Man); Alan Stuart (Cab Driver); John Ratzenberger, Shane Rimmer (Controllers); John Morton (Nate); Jim Dowdell (Boris); Angus McInnes (Warden); Antony Sher (Bellboy); Elva May Hoover (Mother); Hadley Kay (Jason); Todd Woodcroft (Father); John Hollis (Krypton Elder); Gordon Rollings (Fisherman); Peter Whitman (Deputy); Bill Bailey (J. J.); Dinny Powell (Boog); Hal Galili (Man at Bar); Marcus D'Amico (Willie); Richard Parmentier (Reporter); Don Fellows (General); Michael J. Shannon (President's Aide); Tony Sibbald (Presidential Imposter); Tommy Dugan (Diner Owner); Pamela Mandel (Waitress); Pepper Martin (Rocky); Eugene Lipinski (Newsvendor); Cleon Spencer, Carl Parris (Kids).

SUPERMAN III (Warner Bros., 1983) C 123 mins.

Executive producer, Ilya Salkind; producer, Pierre Spengler;

associate producer, Robert Simmonds; director, Richard Lester; based on comic strip characters created by Jerry Siegel, Joe Shuster; screenplay, David Newman, Leslie Newman; music, Ken Thorne, from original material composed by John Williams; songs, Giorgio Moorder; assistant directors, David Lane, Dusty Symonds; production designer, Peter Murton; art directors, Brian Ackland-Snow, Charles Bishop, Terry Ackland-Snow; set decorator, Peter Young; costumes, Vangie Harrison; director of special effects/miniatures, Collin Chilvers; flying/second unit director, David Lane; stunt coordinator, Paul Weston; makeup, Paul Engelen, Stuart Freeborn; supervisor of optical/visual effects, Roy Field; model unit camera, Harry Oakes, model unit art director, Charles Bishop; process camera, John Harris; Zoptic front projection supervisor, David Wynn Jones; traveling matte supervisor, Dennis Bartlett; aerial Wesscam camera, Ronald Goodman; background camera, Bob Bailin; optical/matte camera, Peter Harman, Martin Body, camera, Robert Paynter; editor, John Victor Smith.

Christopher Reeve (Superman/Clark Kent); Richard Pryor (Gus Gorman); Jackie Cooper (Perry White); Margot Kidder (Lois Lane); Annette O'Toole (Lana Lang); Marc McClure (Jimmy Olsen); Annie Ross (Vera Webster); Pamela Stephenson (Lorelei Ambrosia); Robert Vaughn (Ross Webster); Gavan O'Herlihy (Brad); Graham Stark (Blind Man); Henry Woolf (Penguin Man); Gordon Rollings (Man in Cap); Peter Wear (Bank Robber); Justin Case (Mime); Bob Todd (Dignified Gent); Terry Camilleri (Delivery Man); Stefan Kalipha (Data School Instructor); Helen Horton (Miss Henderson); Lou Hirsch (Fred); Bill Reinbold (Wages Man); Shane Rimmer (State Policeman); Al Matthews (Fire Chief); Barry Dennen (Dr. McClean); Enid Saunders (Minnie Bannister); Kevin Harrison Cork (D. J.); Robert G. Henderson (Mr. Simpson); Paul Kaetheler (Ricky); R. J. Bell (Mr. Stokis); Pamela Mandell (Mrs. Stokis); Peter Whitman (Man at Cash Point); Ronnie Brody (Husband); Sandra Dickinson (Wife); Philip Gilbert (Newsreader); Pat Starr (White Coated Scientist); Gordon Signer (Mayor); John Bluthal (Pisa Vendor); George Chisholm (Street Sweeper); David Fielder (Olympic Runner); Robert Beatty (Tanker Captain); Chris Malcolm, Larry Lamb (Miners).

SUPERMAN IV: THE QUEST FOR PEACE (Cannon, 1987) C 85 mins.

Producers, Menahem Golan, Yoram Globus; associate producers, Michael Kaga, Graham Easton; director, Sidney J. Furie, based on the comic strip by Jerry Siegel, Joe Shuster; story, Christopher Reeve, Lawrence Konner, Mark Rosenthal; screenplay, Konner,

Rosenthal; production designer, John Graysmark; art director, Leslie Tomkins; costume supervisor, Colin Wilson; makeup supervisor, Stuart Freeborn; assistant directors, Gino Marotta, Paul Lowin; second unit directors, Harrison Ellenshaw, David Lane, Reeve; flying/second unit director, Michael Higgins; stunt co-ordinator, Alf Joint; music, John Williams; music adaptor/director, Alexander Courage; additional music, Paul Fishman; sound, Danny Daniel, Peter Kramper; sound editors, Stan Fiferman, Terry Poulton, Tony Message, Jack T. Knight; visual effects supervisor, Ellenshaw; special effects editor, Graham Farrow; TV/computer & electronic effects, Ira Curtis Coleman; camera, Ernest Day; second unit camera, Godfrey Godar; visual effects camera, Brandy Hill; model camera, Harry Oakes; matte camera, Peter Hammond; computer cameras, Ronnie Wass; editor, John Shirley.

Christopher Reeve (Superman/Clark Kent); Gene Hackman (Lex Luthor); Margot Kidder (Lois Lane); Mariel Hemingway (Lacy Warfield); Jackie Cooper (Perry White); Mark Pillow (Nuclear Man); Mark McClure (Jimmy Olsen); Jon Cryer (Lenny); Sam Wanamaker (David Warfield); Clive Mantle (Other Nuclear Man); Damian McLawhorn (Jeremy); William Hootkins (Harry Howler); Jim Broadbent (Jean-Pierre Dubois); Stanley Lebor (General Romoff); Don Fellows (Levon Hornsby); Robert Beatty (U.S. President); Bradley Lavelle (Tall Marshal—Chain Gang); Mac McDonald (Marshal); Czeslaw Grocholski, Steve Plytas, John Hollis (Russian Generals); William Armstrong, Elizabeth Richardson (Farmers at Ohio Farmhouse); Bob Sherman (Senator—Pentagon); Eiji Kusuhara (U.N. Guard); Yuri Borienko (Russian General—Red Square); Dorota Zienska, Jiri Stanislav (Cosmonauts); Ron Travis (Convict); Indira Joshi (U.N. Secretary General); Douglas W. Iles (Chief of Staff); Ted Maynard (Army Chief); Raymond Marlowe (Navy Chief); John Cagan (Technician); Malcolm Bullivant (Swedish U.N. Guard); David Garth, Esmond Knight (Elders); Dennis Creaghan (Bill Compton); Bookie Daniels (Woman at Metro Club); Guinevere John, Peter Penry-Jones (Tourists at Great Wall of China); Barbara Rosenblat (Clark Kent's Neighbor); Witold Scheybal (Russian Premier); Bernard Spear (New York Cabbie); Michael Sundin (Clone at Metro Club); Rex Robinson (Subway Engineer); Kerry Shale (MBC Newscaster); and: Susannah York (Voice of Superman's Mother).

Already popular from newspaper comic strips, radio, movie serials (see B/V) with Kirk Alyn and the TV series starring George Reeves, the character of "The Man of Steel," Superman returned to the screen in 1978 in this big budget production which garnered an Academy Award for special effects and over $80,000,000 at the box-

Christopher Reeve and Margot Kidder in SUPERMAN (1978).

office, resulting in three sequels; the quartet of features starring Christopher Reeve in the title role.

On the distant planet Krypton, Jor-El (Marlon Brando) warns its leaders that their planet is doomed but they refuse to listen so he and his wife (Susannah York) place their small son in a spacecraft which heads to Earth as Krypton is destroyed. On Earth, the boy is found by a farmer (Glenn Ford) and his wife (Phyllis Thaxter) who adopt him and call him Clark Kent. As he grows, Clark (Jeff East) shows superhuman power and skill and after his adopted father dies he goes to the Arctic and constructs a fortress of Solitude where he communicates with his dead father and learns the truth of his existence. A grown man, Clark (Christopher Reeve) relocates in Metropolis and is hired by newspaper editor Perry White (Jackie Cooper) as a reporter for the *Daily Planet* and works with Lois Lane (Margot Kidder) and Jimmy Olsen (Marc McClure). At this time he also becomes Superman and thwarts evil in the city, including the various schemes of subterranean dweller Lex Luthor (Gene Hackman), his mistress Eve Teschacher (Valerie Perrine) and dim-witted associate Otis (Ned Beatty). Lex has purchased land in California and plans to bomb along the San Andreas Fault to bring about a new coastline which he will own. Superman stops him and continues his romance with Lois Lane.

As *Variety* enthused, "Magnify James Bond's extraordinary physical powers while curbing his sex drive and you have the essence of SUPERMAN, a wonderful, chuckling, preposterously exciting fantasy. . . ."

Two years later, the sequel SUPERMAN II arrived and it grossed over $65,000,000 at the U.S. box-office. This film, which utilized much footage filmed at the time of the original, finds Superman (Christopher Reeve), alias reporter Clark Kent, renouncing his special powers for the love of Lois Lane (Margot Kidder). Trouble develops, however, when Krypton native General Zod (Terence Stamp) and his cohorts, who were thrown off the planet for treason long before its destruction, arrive on Earth and ally themselves with master criminal Lex Luthor (Gene Hackman) in a bid to take over the world. They use their sinister powers to keep the U.S. president (E.G. Marshall) in line, but Superman eventually realizes what he must do. He returns to his Arctic retreat where his powers return and he stops Zod and his comrades and puts an end—for the time being—to Luthor's evil activities. Lois accepts Superman for what he is and realizes she must share him with the world.

In assessing the virtues of this followup, Grant Davidson wrote in *Magill's Cinema Annual* (1982), "SUPERMAN II did not suffer the constraints of having to conform to a legend well-known to every American over the age of six. . . . the sequel was thus free to create a new legend in virtually any direction that it desired. . . . Whereas the original had concentrated on the character of Superman, its successor attempted to delineate more fully the character of Clark Kent . . . , depicting a fairly believable image of a man caught in an identity crisis." Davidson goes on to laud the film's special effects and to note, "Its spectacular battle scenes will probably never be topped for sheer brilliance and execution. The only technically weak scene is one in which the 'man of steel' rescues a boy from the torrents of Niagara Falls. It is obviously a superimposition of one film upon another and not a good one at that, but that is the only flaw in a rather sophisticated package." Phil Hardy in *The Film Encyclopedia: Science Fiction* (1984) observed the political satire in SUPERMAN II: "[Director Richard] Lester pushes the parallels between Superman minus his powers and an emasculated America—and this at the time of the Iranian hostage affair—into the realm of comic-strip absurdity."

SUPERMAN III followed in 1983 and showed that the series was loosing its grip on audience interest. Thanks to the teaming of Christopher Reeve and comedian Richard Pryor, the feature pulled in $36,400,000 at the American box-office, but it was a weak, unsatisfactory offering. Part of the problem was the shrinking of the Lois Lane (Margot Kidder) role to a mere cameo; ditto Perry White (Jackie Cooper) and Jimmy Olsen (Marc McClure), and the use of Robert Vaughn as a very anemic villain.

In SUPERMAN III, Lois Lane (Margot Kidder) is off on assignment as Clark Kent (Christopher Reeve) returns home for a class reunion where he meets former schoolmate Lana Lang (Annette O'Toole) to whom he is attracted. Meanwhile Gus Gorman (Richard Pryor) is an out-of-work cook who becomes a computer programmer by accident at a corporation run by crooked Ross Webster (Robert Vaughn). First Gus learns to program an embezzlement operation and then Webster sends him to Kent's hometown to program a weather satellite to decimate the Columbian coffee crop, thus making Webster a fortune on the coffee beans he already owns. Superman stops Gus from destroying the local chemical plant and in doing so saves Lana's young son (Gavan O'Herlihy). To get even, Gus formulates Kryptonite, the one substance to which Superman is allergic and the compound he develops causes Superman to have a split personality: one good and one evil. Superman overcomes the effects of the compound, thwarts evil Webster's machinations and puts a stop to Gus' shenanigans.

Variety reported, " . . . SUPERMAN III emerges as a surprisingly soft-cored disappointment. Putting its emphasis on broad comedy at the expense of ingenious plotting and technical wizardry, the film does have distinct commercial promise which will be largely hinged on Richard Pryor's comic lure and the built-in SUPERMAN audience. But there's virtually none of the mythic or comic sensibility that marked its predecessors. . . ."

Just when everyone despaired (or rejoiced) that there would be no further installments of SUPERMAN, Christopher Reeve agreed to return to the lead assignment, IF he could assist with the scenario.

SUPERMAN IV: THE QUEST FOR PEACE arrived in the summer of 1987 with new producer and director (Sidney J. Furie) and on-location shooting in London. While the series regulars returned for this fourth installment, the feature was short on running time (due to last minute editing), action, plot, special effects, and appeal. As critic Gene Siskel put it, "It's as if all the scenes are half-written to save money."

Superman (Christopher Reeve) takes lady friend Lois Lane (Margot Kidder) on a flying trip around the world and while this is happening arch rival Lex Luthor (Gene Hackman) with the help of his nephew Lenny (Jon Cryer) escapes from prison and begins nuclear arms negotiations with Russian, French, and American groups to "make the world fit for war profiteers to live in," but to do this he must get Superman out of the way. Meanwhile grasping tycoon David Warfield (Sam Wanamaker) purchases the *Daily Planet* newspaper as a toy for his daughter Lacy (Mariel Hemingway). Superman, in the guise of Clark Kent, and Lois return to work and find the newspaper has been turned into a muckraking tabloid, much to the chagrin of editor Perry White (Jackie Cooper) and bumbling novice reporter Jimmy Olsen (Marc McClure) and Lois becomes jealous when Lacy makes eyes at Clark. When Superman learns what Luthor is up to, he promises the United Nations he will destroy all the world's nuclear weapons and to combat him Luthor and Lenny construct a superbeing, Nuclear Man, who is intent on destroying the "Man of Steel." The two meet in combat in various part of the world as Nuclear Man attempts to destroy the Statue of Liberty, causes a volcanic eruption of Mount Etna, demolishes the Great Wall of China, etc. Superman finds his opponent's main weakness and destroys him, once again smashing Luthor's evil schemes.

Michael Wilmington chided in the *Los Angeles Times,* "Sequels to big-budget popular hits usually end up super-schlock, hollow and inflated. But this one isn't even super-schlock; it's shallow and deflated. The effects have a comparatively cheap shop veneer; some of the outer-space battles look as if they were staged before dioramas in a planetarium—and the cinematography doesn't have that gloriously superficial Hollywood sheen. This is a special effects extravaganza with skimped-looking extravagance." The British *Monthly Film Bulletin's* Anne Billson wrote, "In an attempt to cover for their lack of invention, the writers have plugged the gaps by doubling up on almost every plot element: Superman makes two separate peace-mongering speeches to the United Nations, has two romantic interludes with Lois Lane, two tediously protracted bouts of fisticuffs with Nuclear Man, and two different girlfriends—Lois and Lacy—resulting in much tiresome slipping in and out of costume on a double date." *Daily Variety* summed it up best, "From the evidence here it seems clear that even Superman needs a rest once in awhile, and that time has arrived."

In its first five weeks at the domestic box-office, SUPERMAN IV earned a comparatively paltry $15,597,925 and disappeared from sight until its low-keyed video cassette release in January 1988.

SWAMP THING (Embassy, 1982) C 90 mins.

Executive producer, Al Ruban; producers, Benjamin Melniker, Michael E. Uslan; director, Wes Craven; based on DC Comics characters; screenplay, Craven; music, Harry Manfredini; assistant directors, Todd Corman, Tony Cecere; costumes, Patricia Bolomet, Bennett Choate, Paul A. Simmons; stunt co-ordinator, Ted Duncan; art directors, David Nichols, Robb Wilson King; special make-up effects, William Munns; camera, Robin Goodwin; editor, Richard Bracken.

Louis Jourdan (Arcane); Adrienne Barbeau (Alice Cable); Ray Wise (Dr. Alec Holland); David Hess (Ferret); Nicholas Worth (Bruno); Dick Durock (Swamp Thing); Don Knight (Ritter); Al Ruban (Charlie); Ben Bates (Arcane Monster); Nanette Brown (Dr. Linda Holland); Reggie Batts (Jude); Mimi Meyer (Secretary); Karen Price (Messenger); Bill Erickson (Young Agent); Dov Gottesfeld (Commando); Tommy Madden (Little Bruno).

In a remote Louisiana bayou, Professor Alec Holland (Ray Wise) works on a secret government project which will make plants more aggressive in hostile climates and to do this he develops a vegetable cell with an animal nucleus. Government agent Alice Cable (Adrienne Barbeau) investigates Holland's activities and she is aided by local denizen, Charlie (Al Ruban), a young black boy. Wealthy, but wicked, Arcane (Louis Jourdan) wants Holland's formula for his own ends and sends his henchmen (David Hess, Nicholas Worth) to get it. Holland tries to stop the thugs and in the struggle his formula is poured on him, setting him on fire. He runs into the swamp and changes into a huge, hulking green monster, The Swamp Thing (Dick Durock), who has the power to bring people back to life. Alice tries to help the Swamp Thing and also combat Arcane. She is killed doing so, but the Swamp Thing brings her back to life, as he does for Charlie also. Arcane arrives on the scene and the formula turns him into a reptile type creature who does battle with the Swamp Thing and loses. The Swamp Thing goes deep into the bayou hoping to experiment on his returning to normal.

SWAMP THING, based on the D.C. Comics' character, entailed a huge merchandising campaign to promote the film, with everything from books and records to toys and games. Unfortunately the film did not catch the public's fancy, nor did the merchandise.

"Tepid, occasionally agreeable comic-book-inspired feature is part-adventure, part-sf, part-monster-movie, part-romance, part-comedy, and part-ultra-jiggle show (courtesy of Adrienne Barbeau)—all adding up to . . . ? The most curious aspect of the movie is that it seems to take place all in a day or so—which means that the monster has hardly been a monster 24 hours before he begins waxing tragic." (Donald C. Willis, *Horror and Science Fiction Films III,* 1984).

In 1989 a sequel went into production.

TEENAGE MONSTER (Howco International, 1957) 65 mins.

Producer/director, Jacques Marquette; screenplay, Ray Buffum, Marquette; makeup, Jack Pierce; music, Walter Green; camera, Taylor Byars; editor, Irving Schoenberg.

Anne Gwynne (Ruth Cannon); Gloria Castillo (Kathy North); Stuart Wade (Sheriff); Gilbert "Gil" Perkins (Charles Cannon); Stephen Parker (Charles Cannon as a Boy); Charles Courtney (Marv Howell); Norman Leavitt (Deputy); Jim McCullough (Jim Cannon); Gaybe Morradian (Fred Fox); and: Arthur Berkeley, Frank Davis.

In 1957 American International Pictures hit the box-office jackpot with I WAS A TEENAGE WEREWOLF, followed by I WAS A TEENAGE FRANKENSTEIN (qq.v.). Late in the year Howco International joined the financial bandwagon with TEENAGE MONSTER, produced and directed by Jacques Marquette, who also co-scripted the film. In the 1980s Marquette was the cinematographer for the "Hardcastle and McCormick" action teleseries. This inferior low budget entry was issued on a double with THE BRAIN FROM PLANET AROUS (see B/V) and got dismal reviews. *Variety* panned it as "a silly bit of nonsense" while the Los Angeles Times complained about "sleazy production, absurd casting. . . ."

Set in the old West in a remote area, a young boy (Stephen Parker) is bathed in the light of a meteorite. As he grows up he becomes a horrible looking, hairy creature with an imbecilic mind. The young man Charles Cannon (Gilbert Perkins) is shielded from the outside world by his loving mother Ruth (Anne Gwynne) but he kidnaps a young girl (Gloria Castillo) and takes her to the mountains. The sheriff (Stuart Wade) and a posse follow and gun down Charles and rescue the girl.

The prime interest of this slim exploitation item is the star billing given to Anne Gwynne, who returned to the screen after an absence of several years to play the mother in this feature. In the past she was in such genre efforts as BLACK FRIDAY (1940), FLASH GORDON CONQUERS THE UNIVERSE (1940) (see B/V), WEIRD WOMAN (1944), THE HOUSE OF FRANKENSTEIN (1944) (q.v.), and DICK TRACY MEETS GRUESOME (1947).

The film was shot in a week's time on a $57,000 budget and its most convincing aspect was Jack Pierce's monster makeup. It was a werewolf-type creation remindful of his work on "The Wolfman" films at Universal in the 1940s; only the newer edition had longer and shaggier hair.

TV title: METEOR MONSTER.

THE TERMINATOR (Orion, 1984) C 106 mins.

Executive producers, John Daly, Derek Gibson; producer, Gale Anne Hurd; director, James Cameron; [suggested by a story by Harnan Ellison]; screenplay, Cameron, Hurd; assistant directors, Betsy Magruder, Thomas Irvine, Robert Roda; art director, George Costello; costumes, Hilary Wright; special effects, Stan Winston; camera, Adam Greenberg; editor, Mark Goldblatt.

Arnold Schwarzenegger (Terminator); Michael Biehn (Kyle Reese); Linda Hamilton (Sarah Connor); Paul Winfield (Traxler); Lance Henriksen (Vukovich); Rick Rossovich (Matt); Bess Motta (Ginger); Earl Boen (Silberman); Dick Miller (Pawn Shop Clerk); Shawn Schepps (Nancy); Bruce M. Kerner (Desk Sergeant); Franco Columbu (Future Terminator); Bill Paxton (Punk Leader); Brad Reardon, Brian Thompson (Punks); William Wisher, Jr., Ken Fritz, Tom Oberhaus (Policemen); Ed Dogans (Cop in Alley); Joe Farago (TV Anchorman); Hettie Lynne Hurtes (Anchorwoman); Tony Mirelez (Station Attendant); Philip Gordon, Anthony R. Trujillo (Mexican Boys); Stan Yale (Derelict); Norman Friedman (Cleaning Man); Barbara Powers (Ticket Taker); Wayne Stone (Tanker Driver); David Pierce (Tanker Partner).

Enterprising muscle man Arnold Schwarzenegger caused a commercial sensation in the title role of THE TERMINATOR, the part placing him in the same league as Charles Bronson and Chuck Norris in the celluloid action department. Actually the star plays a villainous role, although he was scheduled originally to portray the hero, done here by Michael Biehn. (It was decided that Schwarzenegger's outstanding body build better fitted the part of the cyborg, Terminator.) The elaborate, well-paced film was a tremendous financial success and set Schwarzenegger on the path of more such high action features, but now always as the hero.

Set in 2020 following the last war, Terminator (Arnold Schwarzenegger) is a part-human, part-machine android employed by the superintelligent machines who have taken over the world from the human race. They assign him to return to the Los Angeles of the 1980s to terminate Sarah Connor (Linda Hamilton), a young woman about to give birth to a boy who, in the future, is destined to save the human race from the mechanisms. Via a time warp contraption, Terminator rushes back through the decades to carry out his assignment but he is followed by Kyle Reese (Michael Biehn), a human survivor of the holocaust and the reign of the machines. He plans to stop Terminator and save both the woman and her child-to-be.

Variety judged this film ". . . . a blazing, cinematic comic book, full of virtuoso moviemaking, terrific momentum, solid performances from the three leads, and a compelling story that weds a post-nuclear future to present-day Los Angeles." Director James Cameron's contribution to this film is particularly fine; this was his second feature film, his first being another genre outing, PIRANHA II—THE SPAWNING (1981).

THE TERMINATOR proved to be a runaway box-office success, grossing over $40,000,000 in domestic release. Next, director James Cameron helmed ALIENS (1986) (q.v.) which was even more successful.

As a result of a screen credit dispute after the release of THE TERMINATOR, writer Harlan Ellison was given special acknowledgement in trade paper ads and in the video cassette release version for helping to provide the basis of the film, tracing back to an episode he had written for "The Outer Limits" teleseries decades before.

TERROR IS A MAN see BRIDES OF BLOOD.

TERROR OF FRANKENSTEIN see VICTOR FRANKENSTEIN.

TERROR ON BLOOD ISLAND see BRIDES OF BLOOD.

TERROR VISION (Empire Pictures, 1986) C 83 mins.

Executive producer Charles Band; producer, Albert Band; associate producer, Debra Dion; director/screenplay, Ted Nicolaou; production designer, Giovanni Natalucci; set decorator, Gayle Sion; pyrotechnics, Armando Grilli; music, Richard Band; electronics orchestrator, Christopher Stone; music supervisors, Don Perry, Richard Band; music editor, TJV Productions; costume designer, Kathie Clark; makeup, Alessandro Jacoponi; special effects makeup, John Carl Buechler; sound, Mario Bramonti; supervising sound editor, John Kwiatkowski; special sound effects, John Paul Fasal; monster vocal effects, Frank Welker; camera, Romano Albani; editor, Tom Meshelski.

Diane Franklin (Suzy Putterman); Gerrit Graham (Stanley Putterman); Mary Woronov (Raquel Putterman); Chad Allen (Sherman Putterman); Jonathan Gries (O.D.); Jennifer Richards (Medusa); Alejandro Rey (Spiro); Bert Remsen (Grandpa); Randi Brooks (Cherry); Sonny Carl Davis (Norton); Ian Patrick Williams (Nutty); William Paulson (Pluthar); John Leamer (Chauffeur).

With the continued popularity of sci-fi films in the 1970 and 1980s and the emergence of cult following for schlock examples of

The Do-It-Yourself 100
picks up things from everywhere.
TERRORVISION
Empire Pictures Presents a CHARLES BAND Production "TERRORVISION"
Starring DIANE FRANKLIN GERRIT GRAHAM MARY WORONOV CHAD ALLEN JONATHAN GRIES JENNIFER RICHARDS
ALEJANDRO REY as SPIRO and BERT REMSEN as GRAMPA Director of Photography ROMANO ALBANI
Music Composed by RICHARD BAND Music Supervised by DON PERRY
TV Monster and Special Effects Makeup Designed and Fabricated by JOHN BUECHLER AND MECHANICAL AND MAKEUP IMAGERIES, INC.
Art Director GIOVANNI NATALUCCI Executive in Charge of Production ROBERTO BESSI Associate Producer DEBRA DION
Executive Producer CHARLES BAND Produced by ALBERT BAND Written and Directed by TED NICOLAOU
© 1986 ALTAR PRODUCTIONS, INC. ALL RIGHTS RESERVED © 1986 EMPIRE ENTERTAINMENT

the genre from the 1950s and 1960s, movie producers turned increasingly to lampooning the latter types of films and TERROR VISION is such a product. One aspect of the feature has a TV horror hostess called Medusa (Jennifer Richards) whose "Medusa's Midnight Horror Show" features such camp outings as ROBOT MONSTER (1953) (q.v.) and EARTH VS. THE FLYING SAUCERS (1956) (see B/V). TERROR VISION, however, attempts too hard to be a hilariously funny bad film but lacks the naive charm of the type of movie it tries so hard to emulate.

Far out in space on the planet Pluton, Pluthar (William Paulson), transmits his pet hungry beast into space and he lands in Miami and ends up in the Putterman home via a recently installed satellite dish. While Stanley Putterman (Gerrit Graham) and his wife Raquel (Mary Woronov) are entertaining Spiro (Alejandro Rey) and Cherry (Randi Brooks) the hungry beast materializes out of the family TV as son Sherman Putterman (Chad Allen) and his Grandpa (Bert Remsen) are watching a horror movie and the creature devours Grandpa. No one believes Sherman when he tells them what happened because the monster can turn its tongues into the head of those it has eaten. It then eats everyone else in the house plus the TV repairman (Sonny Carl Davis). When daughter Suzy Putterman (Diane Franklin) returns home with her heavy-metal musician man O.D. (Jonathan Gries) they find the creature in a good mood and make friends with it. Seeing the possibilities of exploiting the hungry beast they call TV horror hostess Medusa (Jennifer Richards) and invite her to see the creature so perhaps she will feature it on her TV show. Meanwhile Pluthar appears and promises to return his pet's victims to life but Medusa destroys his protective helmet and the monster devours the humans and takes on the guise of Medusa.

When released in its home video cassette version, TERROR VISION was edited to 72 minutes.

LE TESTAMENT DU DR. CORDELIER see DR. JEKYLL AND MR. HYDE (essay).

THE TESTAMENT OF DR. CORDELIER see DR. JEKYLL AND MR. HYDE (essay).

THEY CAME FROM BEYOND SPACE (Embassy, 1967) C 85 mins.

Producers, Max J. Rosenberg, Milton Subotsky; director, Freddie Francis; based on the story "The Gods Hate Kansas" by Joseph Millard; screenplay, Subotsky; art directors, Don Mingaye, Scott

Slimon; production designer, Bill Constable; music, James Stevens; music director, Philip Martell; assistant director, Ray Corbett; wardrobe, Eileen Welch; makeup, Bunty Philipps; models/models camera, Bowie Films; sound, George Smith, George Stephenson; camera, Norman Warwick; editor, Peter Musgrave.

Robert Hutton (Dr. Curtis Temple); Jennifer Jayne (Lee Mason); Zia Mohyeddin (Farge); Bernard Kay (Richard Arden); Michael Gough (Monj); Geoffrey Wallace (Allan Mullane); Maurice Good (Stilwell); Luanshiya Greer (Girl Attendant); John Harvey (Bill Trethowan); Diana King (Mrs. Trethowan); Paul Bacon (Rogers); Christopher Banks (Doctor on Street); Dermot Cathie (Peterson); Norman Claridge (Dr. Andrews); James Donnelly (Guard); Frank Forsyth (Blake); Leonard Grahame (McCabe); Michael Hawkins (Williams); Jack Lambert (Doctor in Office); Robin Parkins (Maitland); Edward Rees (Bank Manager); Katy Wild (Girl in Street); Kenneth Kendall (TV Commentator).

Freddie Francis has directed intriguing sci-fi films such as DAY OF THE TRIFFIDS (1962) (see B/V), THE EVIL OF FRANKENSTEIN (1964) (q.v.), THE DEADLY BEES (1967) (see B/V), TROG (1970) (q.v.), and THE CREEPING FLESH (1972), but THEY CAME FROM BEYOND SPACE is one of his lesser efforts. *Variety* called it a "Routine sci-fi tale, not up to Freddie Francis' usual level, but adequate bottom-half support. . . ." The film was based on Joseph Millard's *Startling Stories* (November, 1941) tale, "The Gods Hate Kansas."

When meteorites fall on a farm, government agent Lee Mason (Jennifer Jayne) and scientist Allan Mullane (Geoffrey Wallace) investigate and a mysterious ray turns them into robots. Lee's superior, Dr. Curtis Temple (Robert Hutton), and government agent Richard Arden (Bernard Kay) arrive at the scene and are knocked out by a ray gun carried by Lee. When he comes to, Temple realizes that an alien has taken over Lee's body and a plague spreads through the area which cannot be contained. Temple uses a ray gun to free Lee of the alien and through her learns what is really transpiring. Temple, Lee and Mullane fly to the Moon where they locate the aliens. They are intelligences without bodies who are using the plague victims to help repair their crashed spaceship. When the earthlings revolt, Temple persuades the alien leader Monj (Michael Gough) that force is not necessary and he and his comrades will aid him in the task of rebuilding his craft.

Although made in Great Britain the film was not issued there until the fall of 1968, a year after its U.S. distribution.

THEY CAME FROM WITHIN (American International, 1976) C 88 mins.

Executive producers, John Dunning, Andre Link, Alfred Pariser; producer, Ivan Reitman; director/screenplay, David Cronenberg; music supervisor, Reitman; makeup/special effects, Joe Blasco; camera, Robert Saad; editor, Patrick Dodd.

Paul Hampton (Roger St. Luc); Joe Silver (Rollo Linsky); Lynn Lowry (Forsythe); Alan Migicovsky (Nicholas Tudor); Susan Petrie (Janine Tudor); Barbara Steele (Betts); Ronald Mlodzik (Merrick).

Scientists working on a project to correct bodily imbalances develop a small parasite which is both deadly and an aphrodisiac. The small creatures get loose near Montreal and cause havoc. First they attack people openly, then one emerges from a drain into Betts' (Barbara Steele) bathwater and into her body. Later she transmits the creature to Forsythe (Lynn Lowry) when they kiss. Other residents of their apartment complex are attacked, including Nicholas Tudor (Alan Migicovsky), who, at first cannot tolerate the invasion but who soon begins to enjoy the creatures. His wife Janine (Susan Petrie) sees one of the parasites come out of her husband's mouth and calls Dr. Linsky (Joe Silver) who is savagely attacked by them when he examines Nicholas. Dr. St. Luc (Paul Hampton) tries to control the monsters but they get the best of him and entering the city proper set out to take over all humanity.

"T-E-R-R-O-R Beyond the Power of Priest Or Science To Exorcise!" read the poster for this film which also showed a comely young lady bathing in a tub as "something" causes her to have a look of terrible fright. THEY CAME FROM WITHIN, made in Canada in 1974 as ORGY OF THE BLOOD PARASITES, was director/writer David Cronenberg's first feature and the one which began his growing cult status. When issued in Canada it was called THE PARASITE MURDERS and in Britain it went by the title SHIVERS.

In *For One Week Only* (1983), Richard Meyers noted, "What . . . could have become a sex comedy was transformed into pure horror by Cronenberg's concentration on how the parasites spread rather than what fun they cause." Regarding the gore in the picture, Meyer interpreted, "The effects were created by special effects make-up artist Joe Blasco, who was once Lawrence Welk's make-up man. It was he who devised a system of balloon like bladders beneath fake skin to create the lesbian neck and Tudor torso images. This was the same technique that the dean of American make-up men, Dean Smith, would use in ALTERED STATES; Rob Bottin would use in THE HOWLING; and Rick Baker would use in AN AMERICAN WEREWOLF IN LONDON."

THEY SAVED HITLER'S BRAIN see MADMEN OF MANDORAS.

THE THING (Universal, 1982) C 108 mins.

Executive producer, Wilbur Stark; producers, David Foster, Lawrence Turman; co-producer, Stuart Cohen; associate producer, Larry Franco; director, John Carpenter; based on the story "Who Goes There?" by John W. Campbell, Jr.; screenplay, Bill Lancaster; music, Ennio Morricone; production designer, John J. Lloyd; art director, Henry Larrecq; set decorators, John Dwyer, Graeme Murray; special makeup effects creator/designer, Rob Bottin; assistant director, Larry Franco; sound, Thomas Causey; special camera effects, Albert Whitlock; special effects, Roy Arbogast; camera, Dean Cundey; editor, Todd Ramsay.

Kurt Russell (MacReady); A. Wilford Brimley (Blair); T.K. Carter (Nauls); David Clennon (Palmer); Keith David (Childs); Richard Dysart (Dr. Copper); Charles Hallahan (Norris); Peter Maloney (Bennings); Richard Masur (Clark); Donald Moffat (Garry); Joel Polis (Fuchs); Thomas Waites (Windows); Norbert Weisser (Norwegian); Larry Franco (Norwegian Passenger with Rifle); Nate Irwin (Helicopter Pilot); William Zeman (Pilot); and: Anthony Cecere, Kent Hays, Larry Holt, Melvin Jones, Eric Manaker, Denver Mattson, Clint Rowe, Ken Strain, Rock Walker, Jerry Wills.

At a remote Antarctic outpost, U.S. soldiers stop a Norwegian from killing a large dog but the man dies warning them about the creature. Later the animal turns into a monstrous thing which tries to devour other animals at the outpost. Looking for the answer to the riddle, the Americans, led by MacReady (Kurt Russell) and Blair (A. Wilford Brimley), go to the Norwegian camp only to find it empty. Nearby, however, they locate an uncovered space craft which they theorize may have been buried there for one hundred thousand years. Back at the camp, the men realize an alien from the craft has escaped and it has the power to devour and transform its shape into any living thing. Further they hypothesize one of them has been taken over by the alien and they play a cat-and-mouse game attempting to ferret out the creature and either destroy or contain it. Finally only two of the men are left alive and neither can be sure the other has not been inhabited by the alien.

Director John Carpenter's elaborate remake of the 1951 sci-fi classic THE THING FROM OUTER SPACE (see B/V) grossed "only" $10,000,000 at the box-office and was deemed a commercial failure. Carpenter adhered faithfully to the film's literary original, John W. Campbell, Jr.'s short story "Who Goes There?," but in doing so created a bland, femaleless *film noir* highlighted by Rob

Bottin's special makeup effects which " . . . are perhaps the most extraordinary ever seen onscreen—if they weren't so repellent, they would truly be wonders to behold. . . ." (*Variety*)

In fact, THE THING's biggest weakness is its almost endless display of flying blood and guts which becomes so revolting it detracts from what little storyline suspense the film can muster. While THE THING promised to be a classic remake of a genre gem, it turned out to be a pedestrian, depressing and totally disappointing feature which sadly uses special effects technology to make its viewers ill rather than aesthetically satisfied.

THE THREE STOOGES IN ORBIT (Columbia, 1962) 87 mins.

Producer, Norman Maurer; director, Edward Bernds; story, Maurer; screenplay, Elwood Ullman; art director, Don Ament; set decorator, Richard Mansfield; music, Paul Dunlap; assistant directors, Eddie Sacta; costumes, Ted Tetrick, Pat Page; makeup, Frank McCoy; sound supervisor, Charles J. Rice; sound, William Bernds; camera, William F. Whitley; editor, Edwin Bryant.

Moe Howard (Moe); Larry Fine (Larry); Joe De Rita (Curly Joe); Carol Christensen (Carol); Edson Stroll (Captain Tom Andrews); Emil Sitka (Professor Danforth); George Neise (Ogg); Rayford Barnes (Zogg); Norman Leavitt (Williams); Nestor Paiva (Chairman); Peter Dawson (General Bixby); Peter Brocco (Dr. Appleby); Don Lamond (Colonel Smithers); Thomas Glynn (George Galveston); Maurice Manson (Mr. Lansing); Jean Charney (WAF Sergeant); Duane Ament (Personnel Clerk); Bill Dyer (Colonel Lane); Roy Engel (Welby); Jane Wald (Bathing Girl); Cheerio Meredith (Tooth Paste Old Maid).

TV stars The Three Stooges, Moe (Moe Howard), Larry (Larry Fine) and Curly Joe (Joe De Rita), rent a room from Professor Danforth (Emil Sitka) in his old castle. The professor is developing a weapon, a tank/submarine/helicopter, for the military and Martians Ogg (George Neise) and Zogg (Rayford Barnes) are after it. Danforth's daughter Carol (Carol Christensen) arrives to witness a demonstration of the weapon for Captain Tom Andrews (Edson Stroll) of the Air Force but the Stooges make a fiasco of the event. The Martians steal the invention but the Stooges cling to it and cause it to crash land at their TV studio where they are offered a new contract as Carol and Tom plan to wed. The Martians are destroyed and their sinister plan foiled.

One of a series of hastily-constructed features The Three Stooges headlined for Columbia following the team's rediscovery by TV audiences, THE THREE STOOGES IN ORBIT is an enjoyable minor effort in which the "boys" continue their usual slam-bang antics as they battle invading Martians. Stock footage of flying saucers from EARTH VS. THE FLYING SAUCERS (1956) (see B/V) was used and the makeup for the Martians (to give credit where it is due) was truly original and a bit horrifying; not the usual for a low budget feature. *Variety* acknowledged the movie had " . . . wild Stooge approach [which] manages to extract the last ounce of visual fun from creaky ideas. . . ."

TIME AFTER TIME (Warner Bros./Orion, 1979) C 112 mins.

Producer, Herb Jaffe; director, Nicholas Meyer; story, Kearl Alexander, Steve Hayes; screenplay, Meyer; music, Miklos Rozsa; production designer, Edward C. Carfagno; set decorator, Barbara Knieger; stunt co-ordinator, Everett Creach; assistant director, Michael Daves; sound, Jerry Jost; special effects, Larry Fuentes, Jim Blount; camera, Paul Lohmann; editor, Donn Cambern.

Malcolm McDowell (H. G. Wells); David Warner (Dr. John Lesley Stevenson); Mary Steenburgen (Amy Robbins); Charles Cioffi (Lieutenant Mitchell); Andonia Katsaros (Mrs. Turner); Patti D'Arbanville (Shirley); Geraldine Baron (Carol); Kent Williams (Assistant); James Garrett (Edwards); Keith McConnel (Harding); Leo Lewis (Richardson); Byron Webster (McKay); Karin Mary Shea (Jenny); Laurie Main (Inspector Gregson); Joseph Maher (Adams); Michael Evans (Sergeant); Ray Reinhardt (Jeweler); Stu Klitsner (Clergyman); Larry J. Blake (Guard); Rita Conde (Maid); Read Morgan (Booking Policeman); Shelley Hack (Docent); and: Jim Haynie, John Colton, James Cranna, Bill Breadley, Hilda Haynes,

H. G. Wells' novel *The Time Machine* (1895) is a true literary science fiction classic and it was attractively adapted to the screen in Britain in 1960 (see B/V) and again in a vapid TV version in 1978 (q.v.). TIME AFTER TIME uses the theme of time and travel but in the engaging context of having Wells himself as the chief protagonist. The result is an appealing sci-fi/romance/thriller which transports the staid Victorian hero into the wild and violent culture of the 1970s as he pursues murderer Jack the Ripper through time and finds his true love.

One evening writer/inventor H. G. Wells (Malcolm McDowell) invites a group of friends and colleagues to his home to listen to his theories on time travel and for a demonstration of a contraption he has invented to circumvent time. One of the guests is Dr. John Lesley Stevenson (David Warner), who is actually the fiendish killer Jack the Ripper. The Ripper has committed a gruesome homicide and is traced to Wells' house by the police and as they close in on him, the doctor escapes into the future in Wells' invention. Waiting for the machine to return, Wells follows Stevenson to the year 1979, which he expects to be imbued with a utopian society. The machine stops in San Francisco which Wells finds to be almost anarchistic with society involved in fast living, drugs, and violence. He encounters pretty bank teller Amy Robbins (Mary Steenburgen) and she befriends him and they soon become lovers. He tells her about his special quest for the Ripper and she agrees to help him and they enlist the aid of skeptical police Lieutenant Mitchell (Charles Cioffi). Wells confronts Stevenson who tells him he is in his element with the seedy life he has found, complete with plenty of ready-made victims. By using the time machine, Wells and Amy find out she will be the Ripper's upcoming victim and they set out to thwart his machinations. They corner him in the museum where the machine is located and Wells removes a handle just as the Ripper thrusts himself into the future, causing him to be lost in time forever. Wells and Mary return together in the time machine back to the Victorian era.

Balanced with a mixture of imaginative and charming touches—as well as heavy dollops of violence—TIME AFTER TIME benefits greatly from the rich film score by veteran Miklos Rozsa.

TIME BANDITS (Handmade Films, 1981) C 110 mins.

Executive producers, Denis O'Brien, George Harrison; producer, Terry Gilliam; associate producer, Neville C. Thompson; director, Gilliam; screenplay, Michael Palin, Gilliam; art director, Norman Garwood; production designer, Milly Burns; music, Mike Moran; song, George Harrison; camera, Peter Biziou; editor, Julian Doyle.

John Cleese (Robin Hood); Sean Connery (King Agamemnon); Shelley Duvall (Pansy); Katherine Helmond (Mrs. Ogre); Ian Holm (Napoleon Bonaparte); Michael Palin (Vincent); Ralph Richardson (Supreme Being); Peter Vaughan (Ogre); David Warner (Evil Genius); David Rappaport (Randall); Kenny Baker (Fidgit); Jack Purvis (Wally); Mike Edmonds (Og); Malcolm Dixon (Strutter); Tiny Ross (Vermin); Craig Warnock (Kevin); David Baker (Kevin's Father); Sheila Fearn (Kevin's Mother); Jim Broadbent (Compere); John Young (Reginald); Myrtle Devenish (Beryl); Brian Bowes (Stunt Knight/Hussar); Leon Lissek (Refugee); Terence Bayler (Lucien); Preston Lockwood (Neguy); Charles McKeown (Theater Manager); David Leland (Puppeteer); John Hughman (Great Rumbozo); Derrick O'Connor (Robber Leader); Peter Jonfield (Arm Wrestler); Derek Deadman (Robert); Jerold Wells (Benson); Roger Frost (Cartwright); Martin Carroll (Baxi Brazilla III); Marcus Powell (Horse Flesh); Winston Dennis (Bull-Headed Warrior); Del Baker (Greek Fighting Warrior); Juliette James (Greek Queen); Ian Muir

(Giant); Mark Holmes (Troll Father); Andrew MacLachlan (Fireman); Chris Grant (Voice of TV Announcer); Tony Jay (Voice of Supreme Being); Edwin Finn (Supreme Being's Face); Neil McCarthy, Declan Mulholland (Robbers); Frances De La Tour (Salvation Army Major).

The Supreme Being (Ralph Richardson) is disappointed with various portions of human history and decides to rectify the situation. He sends a young British youth, Kevin (Craig Warnock), and six dwarfs (David Rappaport, Kenny Baker, Jack Purvis, Mike Edmonds, Malcolm Dixon, Tiny Ross), back through time to make corrections and they meet such historical characters as Robin Hood (John Cleese), King Agamemnon (Sean Connery), and Napoleon Bonaparte (Ian Holm). They do battle with an ogre (Peter Vaughan) and speed into the future for a showdown with the Evil Genius (David Warner).

A mixture of fantasy and comedy, aimed at both juvenile and adult audiences, TIME BANDITS was successful at none of its enterprises. It was not overly funny (in fact it was labored during long stretches) or horrifying, nor did it appeal to the age groups to

Craig Warnock and Sean Connery in TIME BANDITS (1981).

which it was aimed. *Variety* contended, "When you can count the laughs in a comedy on the fingers of one hand, it isn't so funny. TIME BANDITS is a kind of potted history of many myths and the eternal clash between good and evil as told in the inimitable idiom of Monty Python."

THE TIME MACHINE (Schick Sunn Classics/NBC-TV, 11/5/78) C 100 mins.

Executive producers, Charles E. Sellier, Jr. James L. Conway; producer, James Simmons; director, Henning Schellerup; based on the novel by H. G. Wells; teleplay, Wallace Bennett; music, John Cacavas; art director, Paul Staheli; camera, Stephen W. Gray; supervising editor, James D. Wells; editor, Trevor Jolley.

John Beck (Neil Perry); Priscilla Barnes (Weena); Andrew Duggan (Bean Worthington); Rosemary DeCamp (Agnes); Jack Kruschen (John Bedford); Whit Bissell (Ralph Branly); John Hansen (Ariel); R. G. Armstrong (General Harris); John Doucette (Sheriff Finley); Parley Baer (Henry Haverson); and: John Zaremba, Bill Zuckert, Hyde Clayton, Craig Clyde, Debbie Dutson, Buck Flower, Tom Kelly, Julie Parris, Michael Ruud, Kerry Summers.

Schick Sunn Classics Pictures, the outfit which produced such speculation theatrical features as IN SEARCH OF NOAH's ARK (1976) (q.v.), made this unimpressive remake of the classic H. G. Wells novel for its series of "Classic Illustrated" telefilms on NBC-TV. Anemic at best, and padded with obvious stock footage, the film is pale indeed when compared to the near-classic 1960 (see B/V) version; in fact, it is more comparable to THE TIME TRAVELERS (1964) (see B/V).

Updated to the 1970s (to avoid budget costs in recreating the Victorian era from the novel), scientist Neil Perry (John Beck) invents a machine in which he can travel through time. He launches himself to the distant future where he finds the world populated by the passive Elois and the underground, cannibalistic Morlocks. He falls in love with Weena (Priscilla Barnes), an Elois woman, and leads her people to fight and overcome the Morlocks.

Actor Whit Bissell appears in both the 1960 and 1978 version of the H.G. Wells tale, *but* in different roles.

TIME RIDER (Jensen-Farley Pictures, 1983) C 83 mins.

Executive producer, Michael Nesmith; producer, Harry Gittes; director, William Dear; screenplay, Dear, Nesmith; art director, Linda Pearl; music, Nesmith; camera, Larry Pizer; editors, Suzanne Pettit, Kira Secrist, R. J. Kizer.

Fred Ward (Lyle Swann); Belinda Bauer (Clair); Peter Coyote

(Reese); Ed Lauter (Padre); Richard Masur (Claude); Tracey Walter (Carl); L. Q. Jones (Potter); Chris Mulkey (Daniels); Macon McCalman (Dr. Sam); Jonathan Banks (Jesse); Laurie O'Brien (Terry); William Dear (Technician).

Cyclist Lyle Swann (Fred Ward) is riding cross country when he accidentally rides through an experimental time machine device placed in the desert and he is transported back in time to the West of the 1880s. He winds up in a small town overrun by outlaw Reese (Peter Coyote) and his henchmen (Richard Masur, Carl Dorsett), and when he is found out, Reese attempts to gain control of Swann's motor bike. Swann is aided by pretty gun-toting Clair (Belinda Bauer) and the local priest (Ed Lauter) and in a showdown fight with the gang at the site of his time warp transport, he is returned to his own time.

Although TIME RIDER has an engrossing premise, the film's ability to hold the viewer's interest soon pales after the rider is transported to the Old West. Then too, Ed Lauter appears uncomfortably cast as a padre. Only Belinda Bauer's sex appeal does much to save the film until its exciting finale. *Variety* correctly labeled the feature's assets, "Considering the picture is pap that any concentrated attention will make shambles of, it's nonetheless a plesasant enjoyable 83 minutes. . . ."

A few years later, in 1987, in the CBS-TV series OUTLAWS, the plot premise was reversed. A group of Western bad men are transported ahead in time to contemporary America and hire out as adventurers.

TIME STALKERS (CBS-TV, 3/10/87) C 100 mins.

Executive producers, Charles Fries, Ted Raynor; producers, John Newland, Richard Maynard; director, Michael Schultz; based on the story "The Tintype" by Ray Brown; teleplay, Brian Clemens; music, Craig Safan; production designer, Shay Austin; art director, Richard Bryan Douglas; camera, Harry Mathias; editor, Conrad Gonzales.

William Devane (Scott McKenzie); Lauren Hutton (Georgia Crawford); Klaus Kinski; John Ratzenberger; Forrest Tucker (Cody); Tracey Walter, James Avery, R. D. Call, John Considine, Daniel Pintauro, Gail Young.

The wife and son of college professor Scott McKenzie (William Devane) are incinerated in an auto crash after being hit by a speeding vehicle chased by the police. An enthusiast of the Old West, McKenzie obtains an old trunk in an auction and in it is a tintype which pictures a gunman with three men he has killed. McKenzie notices the gunman has a .357 magnum handgun, a weapon not

History will change
if they can stop a murderer
who's got all the time
in the world to hide.
William Devane
Klaus Kinski
Lauren Hutton
TIMESTALKERS
WORLD PREMIERE · CBS TUESDAY NIGHT MOVIES
TELEPLAY BY BRIAN CLEMENS STORY BY RAY BROWN AND BRIAN CLEMENS DIRECTED BY MICHAEL SCHULTZ
9PM KCBS-TV 2

invented until a century after the picture was taken. He consults his friend Cody (Forrest Tucker), a Western authority, on the anachronism but pretty Georgia Crawford (Lauren Hutton) arrives and asks McKenzie's help. She is from the year 2586 and is on a mission to capture a killer (Klaus Kinski), the gunslinger in the tintype. The professor agrees to assist the young woman and they skip through time, killing a villain and reviving another person before eliminating the killer in a vehicle chase which results in MacKenzie altering time.

"History will change if they can stop a murderer who's got all the time in the world to hide" read the ads for this world premiere TV movie which mingles time travel, the Old West, and contemporary crime. In *TV Guide* Judith Crist commented that the telefilm ". . . . is one of the most original and interesting science-fictioners to arrive on-screen. . . . it's high-style entertainment with flashbacks and flashforwards keeping the intercentury action racing." In *The Hollywood Reporter* Miles Beller termed it "an energetic sci-fier" while *Daily Variety* acknowledged, "Cartoon telefilm has the courage to be innovative; give it that much!"

Forrest Tucker made his final film appearance in the strong role of Western historian Cody while Klaus Kinski made a rare stateside appearance as the time traveling hit man.

TIME WALKER (New World, 1982) C 83 mins.

Executive producer, Robert Shafter; producers, Dimitri Villard, Jason Williams; director, Tom Kennedy; screenplay, Karen Levitt, Tom Friedmann; music, Richard Band; stunt co-ordinator, Harry Wowchuk; second unit director, Skip Schoolnik; transformation scene, New World Effects; sound, Mark Uland; camera, Robbie Greenberg.

Ben Murphy (Professor Doug McCadden); Nina Azelrod (Susy Fuller); Kevin Brophy (Peter); James Karen (Wendell Rossmore); Robert Random (Parker); Austin Stoker (Dr. Ken Melrose); Clint Young (Willoughby); Shari Belafonte-Harper (Linda); Antoinette Bower (Dr. Hayworth); Jason Williams (Jeff); and; Melissa Prophet, Sam Chew, Jr., Gerard Prendergast, Jack Olson.

The 3,000-year-old mummy of Tutankhamen is brought to the California Institute of Sciences and is accidentally given a huge overdose of X-rays and this releases an alien whose touch has killed the Pharaoh and whom the Egyptians had buried in their ruler's body. Buried with the mummy are the crystals the alien needs to reactivate the transmitter which will return him to his own dimension. A student steals the crystals thinking they are jewels and the revived mummy goes in search of them, the student having given the gems to co-eds he has been romancing. Meanwhile Professor Doug

McCadden (Ben Murphy), who brought the mummy to the Institute, figures out what has happened and attempts to stop the alien as the aged space visitor leaves a trail of corpses due to the touch of the green fungus which surrounds this floating visitor. As the mummy gathers the final crystal it is cornered by McCadden who is transported into another dimension by the alien.

Although cheaply and crudely executed, TIME WALKER is at times a scary film, with the alien mummy a frightful persona. If only the human performers had as much panache as the title character!

TIME WARP see THE DAY TIME ENDED.

THE TITAN FIND see CREATURE.

TORTURE SHIP (Producers Distributing Corp., 1939) 56 mins.

Associate producer, Sig Neufeld; director, Victor Halperin; suggested by the story "A Thousand Deaths" by Jack London; screenplay, George Sayre; camera, Jack Greenhalgh; editor, Holbrook N. Todd.

Lyle Talbot (Lieutenant Bob Bennett); Irving Pichel (Dr. Herbert Stander); Jacqueline Wells [Julie Bishop] (Joan Martel); Sheila Bromley (Mary Slavish); Anthony Averill (Dirk); Eddie Holden (Ole Olson); Russell Hopton (Harry); Wheeler Oakman (Ritter); Leander de Cordova (Ezra); Dmitri Alexis (Murano); Skelton Knaggs (Jesse); Adla Kuznetzoff (Krantz); Stanley Blystone (Briggs); Julian Mailison (Paul); William Chapman (Bill); Fred Walton (Fred).

Producers Distributing Corporation, soon to become Producers Releasing Corporation (PRC), inaugurated its film schedule with TORTURE SHIP, a gangster melodrama with touches of science fiction. Allegedly based on Jack London's story "A Thousand Deaths," it was a "Quickie action thriller that misses fire all the way on its possibilities. . . ." (*Variety*). The trade paper added, "Yarn has so many unreasonable and unexplainable points that it will annoy even the most juveminded. Production is fair, not revealing the film's cheapie nature. It's rather slow in getting started, however. . . . ."

A number of gangsters and convicted criminals are pirated aboard a ship owned by Dr. Herbert Stander (Irving Pichel). These include falsely convicted Bob Bennett (Lyle Talbot), a former Navy lieutenant, and Joan Martel (Jacqueline Wells); along with Mary Slavish (Sheila Bromley), Dirk (Anthony Averill), Harry (Russell Hopton) and Ritter (Wheeler Oakman). What they do not know is that the doctor believes all criminality is controlled by glands and he has been experimenting on the subject but has been banned by his profession so he has set up practice on the boat and plans to use the criminals as guinea pigs. Bennett takes over as captain of the vessel and Slavish, following an operation performed by Stander, admits that Joan was a dupe in a swindle she perpetrated. The gangsters revolt against the doctor and he is killed and Bob and Joan manage to keep them under control until they can bring the yacht into port.

In *B Movies* (1973) Don Miller declared TORTURE SHIP " . . . was nothing but a seedy crook melodrama, more than a trifle foolish in its overacting and limp direction by Victor Halperin, negating any possibility of making something out of the tale. . . ."

TRACK OF THE MOON BEAST (Cinema Shares, 1977) C 90 mins.

Director, Dick Ashe; screenplay, William Finder, Charles Sinclair; music, Henry O. Glass, Bob Orpin; monster designer, Rick Baker; monster makeup, Joe Blasco; camera, E. S. Wood.

Chase Cordell (Paul Carlson); Donna Leigh Drake (Kathy Nolan); Gregorio Sala (Professor Johnny Longbow); Francine Kessler (Janet Price); Joe Blasco (The Monster); and: Patrick Wright, Craufurd McCallum, Fred McCaffrey, Timothy Wayne Brown, Alan Swain, Tim Butler, Jeanne Swain.

While carrying out his duties in the desert southwest, mineralogist Paul Carlson (Chase Cordell) is hit by particles from a Moon meteor and during the cycle of the full moon he turns into a giant lizard. A professor (Gregorio Sala) and a young woman (Donna Leigh Drake) try to help him but when a cure fails the lizard man is killed.

Shot in 1972 this low budget, but effectively made thriller was done on location in the southwest, providing scenic value in addition to its innate chills. The lizard monster is particularly effective, the suit engineered by Rick Baker who was to become a top flight designer of screen monsters.

TRANS-ATLANTIC TUNNEL (Gaumont-British, 1935) 90 mins.

Producer, Michael Balcon; director, Maurice Elvey; based on the novel *Der Tunnel* by Bernhard Kellerman; screenplay, Curt Siodmak; dialogue, Clemence Dane, L. du Garde Peach; camera, Gunther Krampf; editor, Charles Frend.

Richard Dix (McAllen); Leslie Banks (Robbie); Madge Evans (Ruth McAllen); Helen Vinson (Varlia); C. Aubrey Smith (Lloyd); Basil Sydney (Mostya); Henry Oscar (Grellier); Hilda Trevelyan (Mary); Cyril Raymond (Harriman); Jimmy Hanley (Geoffrey—Grown-up); Walter Huston (U.S. President); George Arliss (Prime Minister of England).

This stimulating British-American co-production included a cast from both sides of the Atlantic in a story adapted to the screen by Curt Siodmak from Bernhard Kellermann's novel *Der Tunnel* (1913) which Curtis Bernhardt had filmed in Germany in 1933 for Bavaria-Film with Paul Hartmann; a French language version starred Jean Gabin. That feature dealt with the construction of a tunnel under the Atlantic Ocean between Europe and America. Philip Strick reported in *Science Fiction Movies* (1976), "To judge from the stills, the floodings, eruptions and disasters that haunt the project were stunningly portrayed. . . . The original Bernhardt film, although cluttered with stirring expressions of support for the new Germany, is probably the archetype [version]. . . ."

The 1935 motion picture was produced by Gaumount British Pictures under the direction of Maurice Elvey (whose 1929 feature HIGH TREASON also dealt with a vast tunnel construction) and told how problems developed for American engineer McAllen (Richard Dix) and his wife Ruth (Madge Evans) during the construction of a tunnel under the Atlantic between England and America, due to the machinations of a rival, Robbie (Leslie Banks). Once the problems are overcome, however, the project is completed and dedicated by the American President (Walter Huston) and the British Prime Minister (George Arliss), both promising a stronger bond between the two nations.

In contrast to DER TUNNEL, which was a nationalist tract for Germany, TRANS-ATLANTIC TUNNEL, also called THE TUNNEL, attempted to cement better relations between the two English-speaking nations in preference to Germany. Phil Hardy observed in *The Film Encyclopedia: Science Fiction* (1984), " . . . despite its spectacular modernist decor and superb special effects (such as a 50-foot 'radium drill' boring through the ocean bed), most of which were achieved through model work, and numerous conversations about the tunnel as an instrument of world peace, the grandeur of the project . . . is lost. In its place is an elaborate romantic drama."

THE TRANSFORMERS—THE MOVIE (De Laurentiis Entertainment Group, 1986) C 86 mins.

Executive producers, Margaret Loesch, Lee Gunther; supervising producer, Jay Bacal; producer, Tom Griffin; co-producer/director, Nelson Shin; based on the Hasbro toy "The Transformers"; story consultant, Flint Dille; screenplay, Ron Friedman; music, Vince DiCola; animation, Toei Animation Co., Ltd; supervising animation director, Kozo Morishita; sound, R. William A. Thiederman, W. Howard Wilmarth, Peter S. Reale; special effects, Masayuki Kawachi, Shoji Sato; editor, David Hankins.

Voices of: Orson Welles (Planet Unicorn); Robert Stack (Ultra Magnus); Leonard Nimoy (Megatron); Eric Idle (Wreck Gar); Judd Nelson (Hot Rod, Rodimus Prime); Lionel Stander (Kup).

Like many sci-fi oriented children's cartoon TV series, THE TRANSFORMERS also made it to the big screen in this feature-length production which utilized name performers' voices for box-office lure for the adult trade. The result, however, is low-grade TV animation blown up for theatres with its only asset being just another promotional activity for the popular Hasbro toys. Otherwise the animated feature is bogged down with a lame plot, a noisy heavy metal rock score, and the waste of its voice-over cast. Its only asset is the soon-tiring effects of the characters transforming into assorted other objects, but this is something TV fans could witness any day on the small screen for nothing.

In the year 2005, the wicked Planet Unicorn (Orson Welles) orders captive Megatron (Leonard Nimoy) to lead his minions of Decepticons in conquering the universe and he is opposed by Ultra Magnus (Robert Stack) and The Transformers who can turn into such things as fast cars, jet planes, and powerful dinosaurs. The Transformers (also called Autobots) also want to take back their planet Cybertron. The forces of good defeat the Decepticons and destroy the evil planet.

Variety was correct in its prognosis, "THE TRANSFORMERS, in which Orson Welles plays a planet, is pure headache material. Target audience of cartoon watchers will also probably find the film unintelligible, noisy and unoriginal. Boxoffice prospects are dismal." (The film grossed only $4,837,143 in its first two weeks of domestic release.)

TROG (Warner Bros., 1970) C 93 mins.

Producer, Herman Cohen; director, Freddie Francis; story, Peter Bryan, John Gilling; screenplay, Aben Kandel; music, John Scott; art director, Geoffrey Tozer; assistant director, Douglas Hermes; camera, Desmond Dickinson; editor, Oswald Hafenrichter.

Joan Crawford (Dr. Brockton); Michael Gough (Sam Murdock); Bernard Kay (Inspector Greenham); Kim Braden (Anne); David Griffin (Malcolm); John Hamill (Cliff); Thorley Walters (The Magistrate); Jack May (Dr. Selbourne); Geoffrey Case (Bill); Robert Hutton (Dr. Richard Warren); Simon Lack (Colonel Vickers); David Warbeck (Alan Davis); Chloe Franks (Little Girl); Maurice Good (Reporter).

While working in a remote area of England, anthropologist Dr. Brockton (Joan Crawford) finds a Troglodyte, living in an underground cave. She believes the creature, called Trog for short, is the missing link and she takes him to her laboratory and attempts to raise him like a child. Thanks to her kindness, Trog responds favorably but often reverts to his hostile nature. Dr. Brockton is aided in her research on Trog by Dr. Richard Warren (Robert Hutton) but another scientist, Dr. Sam Murdock (Michael Gough), is jealous of her discovery. When he fails to turns the locals against the doctor, Murdock releases Trog from his confines and the creature kills a dog and several villagers and kidnaps a small girl (Chloe Franks) who he takes to his cave lair. Dr. Brockton follows and convinces Trog to set the girl free. Then against her will, the police set off explosives which seals off the cave, burying Trog inside.

TROG was Joan Crawford's final theatrical feature film and it was produced in England by her close friend, Herman Cohen, for whom she had starred in the successful British horror thriller BERSERK (1968). TROG received unanimously poor reviews and is often deprecated by sci-fi film writers but in reality it is a modestly entertaining minor feature highlighted by Joan Crawford's sincere and touching performance as the anthropologist. The makeup for TROG, however, is not overly convincing and the film would have been better served if the title creature were less in view. The movie was filmed on the English Moors in cold weather and the budget, according to Bob Thomas in *Joan Crawford: A Biography* (1978), did not allow for portable dressrooms on location. Therefore between takes, "Joan huddled in a car parked on the English moor and did not complain."

TRON (Buena Vista, 1982) C 96 mins.

Executive producer; Ron Miller; producer Donald Kushner; director/screenplay, Steven Lisberger; music, Wendy Carlos; songs, Journey; production designer, Dean Edward Mitzneer; art director, John Mansbridge, Al Roelofs; set decorator, Roger Shook; assistant director, Lorin B. Saloh; electronic world conceptual artists, Syd Mead, Jean Giraud, Peter Lloyd; electronic conceptual design, Giraud, Richard Taylor; mechanical special effects, R. J. Spetter; visual effects concepts, Lisberger; visual effects supervisors, Taylor, Harrison Ellenshaw; effects technical supervisor, John Scheele; background design, Peter Lloyd; background composite supervisor, Marta Russell; effects animation supervisor, Lee Dyer; airbrush supervisor, Greg Battes; effects ink/paint supervisor, Auril Pebley; animation compositing camera supervisor, Jim Pickel; computer effects supervisor, Taylor; computer image choreography, Bill Kroyer, Jerry W. Rees, Magi Synthavision; technology concepts, Phillip Mittleman; technical supervisor, Larry Elin Popielinski; object digitizing, Art Durinski; computer production co-ordinator, Lynn

Wilkinson; computer images design supervisor, Kenny Mirman; computer systems supervisor, Judson Hosebush; sound effects designer/synthesis, Frank Serafine; sound department supervisor, Bob Hathaway; supervising sound editor, Gordon Ecker, Jr.; camera, Bruce Logan; editor, Jeff Gourson.

Jeff Bridges (Kevin Flynn/Clu); Bruce Boxleitner (Alan Bradley/Tron); David Warner (Ed Dillinger/Sark); Cindy Morgan (Lora/York); Barnard Hughes (Dr. Walter Gibbs/Dumont); Dan Shor (Ram); Peter Jurasik (Crom); Tony Stano (Peter/Sark's Lieutenant).

Computers and the computer game craze of the late 1970s and the early 1980s led to the combination of computerization and live action in this sci-fi thriller which is delicious to behold but empty from the point of view of storyline. It should be noted, as revealed in the film's credits, the in-depth computerization utilized for the film resulted in the use of more crafts people for the visual effects unit and computer generated images unit than for the rest of the cast and credits combined.

Kevin Flynn (Jeff Bridges) is a computer games designer whose very fine programs have been filched by Ed Dillinger (David Warner) who has risen to the top of the field with his Master Control Program (MCP) as a result. David wants to prove that Dillinger stole his work and he enlists the aid of friend Alan Bradley (Bruce Boxleitner) who is working on the "Tron" program which is keeping surveillance on MCP and its increasing power. When Dillinger discovers Flynn's mission, MCP transforms him into a computer-stored program, thus catapulting him into the world of computers. There he finds that MCP has developed humanoid computer programs which are forced into various physical combat by Sark (David Warner), Dillinger's self-created henchman in this new world. Kevin, who is very knowledgeable about computer games, finds allies in Tron (Bruce Boxleitner), York (Cindy Morgan), and Ram (Dan Shor), and the quartet set out to halt the conspiracy of Dillinger and his MCP.

While the special effects illuminated the production, they cause their own set of problems within the routine storyline. "Of the six million dollars devoted to effects (one-third of the entire budget), as much as thirty percent was spent on research and development. The viewer is treated to some of the most imaginative images ever devised on celluloid—unfortunately, at the expense of plot—but even the fifty-three minutes of computer and artist-generated excitement wears thin after awhile." (Les Paul Robley, *Magill's Cinema Annual,* 1983)

DER TUNNEL see TRANS-ATLANTIC TUNNEL.

Cindy Morgan, Bruce Boxleitner, and Jeff Bridges in TRON (1982).

THE TWILIGHT PEOPLE (Dimension, 1972) C 84 mins.

Executive producers, Roger Corman, David Cohen; producers, John Ashley, Eddie Romero; director, Romero; screenplay, Jerome Small, Romero; production designer, Roberto A. Formoso; music, Ariston Avelino, Tito Arevalo; set decorator/optical special effects, Richard Abelardo; camera, Fredy Conde; editor, Ben Barcelon.

John Ashley (Matt Farrell); Pat Woodell (Neva Gordon); Charles Macaulay (Dr. Gordon); Eddie Garcia (Pereira); Jan Merlin (Steinman); Pam Grier (Ayesa, the Panther Woman); Ken Metcalfe (Antelope Man); Tony Gosalves (Bat Man); Mona Moreno (Wolf Woman); Kim Ramos (Ape Man).

Following the success of his "Blood Island" series of sci-fi/horror films made in the Philippines with director Eddie Romero, American actor/producer John Ashley (who later did TV's popular "The A-Team") made an offshoot of the series with THE TWILIGHT PEOPLE, a repulsive thriller reminiscent of H. G. Wells' novel *Island of Dr. Moreau* (1896) which was filmed under that title as well as THE ISLAND OF LOST SOULS (1933) (see B/V). While hardly a cinematic classic, the film does have a colorful, and somewhat sympathetic, menagerie of human/animal horrors who forget their primeval difference and use teamwork to thwart a mad scientist.

Big game hunter Matt Farrell (John Ashley) comes to a remote tropical island where he is kidnapped by Dr. Gordon's (Charles Macaulay) thugs. The doctor plans to use him for breeding purposes in experiments he has been conducting with his assistant, daughter Neva (Pat Woodell), in creating a master race. What he has conjured up is a dungeon full of half-humans, half-animal creature who spend most of their time fighting among themselves. Gordon wants to use Farrell to breed with the female creatures to create a stronger species. Naturally Farrell is opposed to the idea and convinces Neva of the horrors her father is perpetrating. They set the menagerie free and trek through the jungle to escape Gordon and his henchmen. Along the way the creatures adapt to the terrain and to one other. When Gordon is killed and the creatures set free, Matt and Neva depart for a life together.

The poster for this feature reads "Animal Desire . . . Human Lust . . . Evolved From Evil . . . Test Tube Terrors, Half Beast, All Monster" and pictured is a thinly clad, comely lass, in a cellar full of half-human beasts about to pounce on her. *Fangoria* magazine (March, 1984) assessed the Cultvideo release of this thriller, "To try to pinpoint all that's wrong with this movie would be senseless, if not completely exhausting. Suffice it to say that, for some reason, as bad as TWILIGHT PEOPLE is, I found this particularly garish brand of trash to be oddly—*very* oddly—engaging."

THE TWO FACES OF DR. JEKYLL see DR. JEKYLL AND MR. HYDE (essay).

THE TWO FACES OF DR. JEKYLL see HOUSE OF FRIGHT.

TWO TICKETS TO TERROR see BLOOD OF GHASTLY HORROR.

2010: THE YEAR WE MADE CONTACT (Metro-Goldwn-Mayer/ United Artists, 1984) C 116 mins.

Producer, Peter Hyams; associate producers, Neil A. Machlis, Jonathan A. Zimbert; director, Hyams; based on the novel *2010: Odyssey Two* by Arthur C. Clarke; screenplay, Hyams; music, David Shire; production designer, Albert Brenner; set decorator, Rick Simpson; makeup supervisor, Michael Westmore; costume designer, Patricia Norris; stunt co-ordinator, M. James Arnett; visual displays/graphics, Video-Image; video effects supervisor, Greg McMurray; special visual effects supervisor, Richard Edlund; visual futurist, Syd Mead; visual effects art director, George Jenson; sound designer, Dale Strumpell; supervising sound editor, Richard L. Anderson; matte department supervisor, Neil Krepela; mechanical effects supervisor, Thaine Morris; model shop supervisor, Mark Stetson; optical supervisor, Mark Vargo; animation supervisors, Terry Windell, Garry Waller; stop-motion animator, Randall William Cook; miniature mechanical effects, Bob Johnston; special effects supervisor, Henry Millar; special effects, David Blitstein, Andy Evans; camera, Hyams; visual effects camera, Dave Stewart; editor, James Mitchell;

Roy Scheider (Dr. Heywood Floyd); John Lithgow (Walter Curnow); Helen Mirren (Tanya Kirbuk); Bob Balaban (Dr. R. Chandra); Keir Dullea (Dave Bowman); Douglas Rain (HAL 900—Voice); Madolyn Smith (Caroline Floyd); Dana Elcard (Dimitri Moisevitch); Taliesin Jaffe (Christopher Floyd); James McEachin (Victor Milson); Mary Jo Deschanel (Betty Fernandez); Elya Baskin (Maxim Brailovsky); Savely Kramarov (Vladimir Rudenko); Oleg Rudnik (Vasali Orlov); Natasha Shneider (Irina Yakununa); Vladimir Skomarovsky (Yuri Svetlanov); Victor Steinbach (Nikolai Ternovsky); Jan Triska (Alexander Kovalev); Larry Carroll (Anchorman); Herta Ware (Jessie Bowman); Cheryl Carter (Nurse); Ron Recasner (Hospital Neurosurgeon); Robert Lesser (Dr. Hirsch); Olga Mallsnerd (SAL 9000); Delana Michaels, Gene McGarr (Commercial Announcers); and: Arthur C. Clarke.

Stanley Kubrick and Arthur C. Clarke's highly regarded 2001: A SPACE ODYSSEY (1966) (see B/V) set the tone for the cerebral motion picture space epic. This over-literal followup, based on Clarke's 1981 book, attempts to carry on the storyline of the initial film and to answer several of the enigmas posed by it. Production-wise the feature, which altered Clarke's plot concept to some degree (e.g. in Clarke's book there are three space ships heading to Jupiter: one from the U.S., one from the Soviet Union, and another from the People's Republic of China) is every bit as good as the original but in conception and plot there is much to be desired, leaving the viewer with more questions than it answers.

Nine years before, American astronaut David Bowman (Keir Dullea) disappeared after the American spaceship *Discovery* went into orbit around Jupiter. In 2010 the Soviets send their spacecraft *Leonov* to gain any information stored in the still orbiting U.S. ship and three Americans go along: the initiator of the original mission, Dr. Heywood Floyd (Roy Scheider); engineering specialist Walter Curnow (John Lithgow); and Dr. R. Chandra (Bob Balaban), who originally programmed HAL, *Discovery's* multi-tasked computer. They are under the command of the ship's humorless captain, Russian Tanya Kirbuk (Helen Mirren). As the mission nears Jupiter, the captain informs Floyd that strange signals are coming from the planet's moon Europa and a probe sent there explodes. The Russian craft rendezvous with the U.S. ship and it is reactivated and Chandra reawakens HAL and attempts to learn why it malfunctioned originally. A black monolith is orbiting near the ship and a probe to it also explodes. On Earth, the conflict between the two super powers reaches a point of near war and at the same time, Bowman's girlfriend (Mary Jo Deschanel) and mother (Herta Ware) have visions of him and he assures them that "something wonderful" is about to happen to the world. On the U.S. ship, Bowman also appears to Floyd and informs him it will be dangerous for the mission to stay near Jupiter for more than two days. The two spacecraft have split due to the tensions on Earth but Floyd persuades Tanya to reunite the craft so their combined thrusts can launch them out of Jupiter's orbit. She agrees with the plan when the black monolith disappears quite suddenly. HAL must accept the mission which will result in the destruction of the *Discovery* to save the *Leonov.* The computer does as programmed just as Jupiter explodes and a new sun is created. In his final message, HAL warns the Earth that the solar system should be used for peaceful purposes. Tension ends on Earth as a black monolith stands in the primeval world of Europa which has awakened to life thanks to the solar system's new sun.

Variety reported of this long-anticipated sequel, "Sixteen years after the original, one sampling of this sequel will be sufficiently exciting for the older audience and more importantly, probably too tame for the younger crowd who think science-fiction started with STAR WARS. . . . [T]he HAL mystery is the most satisfying substance of the film and handled the best. Unfortunately, it lies against a hodge-podge of bits and pieces about the monolith, world peace, the mystical presence of astronaut David Bowman . . . all surrounded by technically respectable but otherwise uninspired celestial acrobatics." The British *Monthly Film Bulletin* complained, "The first observation to be made about 2010 is that, all claims to the contrary, it provides no answers to the questions raised by 2001. . . . What we've really wanted to know for seventeen years is the purpose of that mesmerizing trip through the Star Gate, who constructed the monoliths, who provided the astronaut with his elegant suite of rooms, and what the Star Child would think to do next. By the end of 2010, we are little the wiser."

In 1987 Arthur C. Clarke's *2061: Odyssey Three* was published. In an author's note he admitted that the *Challenger* space tragedy of 1986 had altered his concept for his latest book continuation which was to have utilized information gained from the Galileo Mission (to have been launched from the Challenger and which was to have visited all the major satellites). Instead of waiting several more years for the delayed mission to produce new information, he decided to release his newest installment, which continues the adventures of Heywood Floyd, who once again encounters Dave Bowman, HAL and this time an alien race intending to use Earth and humanity for evolutionary purposes.

THE TWONKY (United Artists, 1953) 72 mins.

Producer/director, Arch Oboler; based on the short story by Lewis Padgett [Henry Kuttner]; screenplay, Oboler; music, Mack Meakin; camera, Joseph Biroc; editor, Betty Steinberg.

Hans Conreid (Kerry West); Billy Lynn (Coach Trout); Gloria Blondell (Eloise); Janet Warren (Caroline West); Ed Max (Ed); Al Jarvis (Mailman); Norman Field (Doctor); Trilby Conreid (Baby); William Phipps (Student); Steve Roberts (Government Agent); Florence Ravenel (Nurse).

Philosophy professor Kerry West (Hans Conreid), who hates television, is given a set by his wife Caroline (Janet Warren) to keep him company while she is away on her many trips. Much to his chagrin, the TV set has been taken over by an alien robot and the creature, which walks and does household chores, sets out to improve Kerry's life, much against his will. When a neighbor (Gloria Blondell) notices something awry in the West household a government agent (Steve Roberts) is called in. The Twonky attempts to restricts Kerry's speech on individual behavior. It is the last straw. He destroys the set.

Arch Oboler was famous for his radio program "Lights Out" and he made several lively sci-fi movies like FIVE (1951) and THE BUBBLE (1967) (see B/V for both), but THE TWONKY is the nadir of his screen career. Adapted from Henry Kuttner's (Lewis Padgett) short story, "The Twonky," producer/director/writer Oboler changed the format of the tale from having the alien take over a radio to a TV set, amplifying Oboler's dislike for the video medium. What results, however, is an unfunny and "unbelievably bad" (*Variety*) movie which could not be saved by star Hans Conreid's exasperating performance as the typical man harried by a TV set.

UFORIA (Universal, 1985) C 100 mins.

Executive producers, Melvin Simon, Barry Krost; producer, Gordon Wolf; co-producer, Susan Spinks; associate producer, Jeanne Field; director/screenplay, John Binder; assistant directors, Anthony Brand, Irwin Marcus; production designer, William Malley; costumes, Betsy Heimann, Thomas Ed Sunly; sound, Kirk Francis; camera, David Myers; editor, Dennis M. Hill.

Cindy Williams (Arlene); Harry Dean Stanton (Brother Bud); Fred Ward (Sheldon); Beverly Hope Atkinson (Naomi); Harry Carey, Jr. (George Martin); Diane Diefendorf (Delores); Robert Gray (Emile); Ted Harris (Gregory); Darrell Larson (Toby); Peggy McKay (Celia Martin); Hank Worden (Colonel); Alan Beckwith (Brother Roy); and: Andrew Winner, Pamela Lamont, Herman Lee Montgomery, Joel Unger; Esther Sutherland, Erik Stern, Robert A. Weisler, Ashley Robb, Jennifer Robb, Marji Martin, Julie Wakefield, Karen Stern, Kedric Wolfe, Nick Edwards, Sally Russell, Dwayne Smith, Gary Rowles, Terry Young, Oma Drake.

Made in 1981 and originally called HOLD ONTO YOUR DREAMS, this offbeat slender film seems to have its origins in the writings of Erich Von Daniken (see CHARIOTS OF THE GODS? in B/V) which dealt with aliens having brought religion and culture to Earth in the long ago past. This theory has many followers and UFORIA exploits this thought in a serio-comic vein while getting ingratiating performances from stars Cindy Williams, Fred Ward, and Harry Dean Stanton. Unfortunately the film proved to be a hard sell for Universal, despite Cindy "Laverne and Shirley" Williams for marquee value, and it did not receive much release until the mid-1980s when it finally acquired minor cult status.

A small desert town is invaded by a swift and smooth talking faith healer evangelist (Harry Dean Stanton) who preaches to his disciples from his portable tent. He has an influence on a pretty grocery store clerk (Cindy Williams) who is conducting an affair with a drifter (Fred Ward) who wants to become a country and western singing star. The preacher, however, is quite surprised to find the young woman believes both in flying saucers and that aliens brought religion to Earth. Through her research she is convinced she is the new Noah who will lead followers into the heaven of a spacecraft. The preacher is quick to exploit the young woman's beliefs as he encourages the drifter to take stolen autos across the border and to split the profits. Eventually the drifter learns through his love for the young woman his need to make a better life for himself.

Kevin Thomas, in the *Los Angeles Times* called the film " . . . a sweet little-off-the-beaten track movie with a whimsical flying saucer angle—and a finish that has the misfortune to be all too much like that of CLOSE ENCOUNTERS (and now, alas COCOON?)."

THE UNKNOWN TERROR (Twentieth Century-Fox, 1957) 77 mins.

Producer, Robert Stabler; director, Charles Marquis Warren; screenplay, Kenneth Higgins; art director, James W. Sullivan; music, Raoul Kraushaar; camera, Joseph Biroc; editor, Fred W. Berger.

John Howard (Dan Mathews); Mala Powers (Gina Mathews); Paul Richards (Pete Morgan); May Wynn (Concha); Gerald Milton (Dr. Ramsey); Duane Gray (Lino); Charles Gray (Jim Wheatley); Charles Postal (Butler); Patrick O'Moore (Dr. Willoughby); William Hamel (Trainer); Richard Gilden (Raul Rom); Martin Garralaga (Old Indian); Sir Lancelot (Himself).

Tossed out on a double bill with the horror film BACK FROM THE DEAD, THE UNKNOWN TERROR is a science fiction item accomplished in a workmanlike fashion by director Charles Marquis Warren but falls short in the area it needs to succeed in most—special effects. The monsters in this film appear to be draped in soap suds which doubles for fungus. It is not convincing and today's audiences find the suds-covered creatures funny. Otherwise the feature is a passable entry issued in the days when TV had revived interest in monster movies and this one was one of scores of pictures made to take quick advantage of this box-office cycle.

When her brother disappears into the South American jungles, Gina Mathews (Mala Powers) persuades her husband Dan (John Howard) to go with her in search of her sibling and they are accompanied by their friend Pete Morgan (Paul Richards), who is physically disabled. They trek through the dense jungle until they reach the cave of Death where a scientist Dr. Ramsey (Gerald Milton) and his native wife Concha (May Wynn) save the locals from

Paul Richards, John Howard, and Mala Powers in THE UNKNOWN TERROR (1957).

tribal sacrifices only to turn them into monsters by infecting them with the growing fungus coming from the cave. Gina enters the cave in search of her brother who has become a victim of the experiment, and Ramsey plans to infect her but Dan dynamites the cave, with the doctor and the monsters inside, thus saving his wife.

UNKNOWN WORLD (Lippert, 1951) 74 mins.

Producers, J. R. Rabin, I. A. Block; director, Terrell [Terry] O. Morse; screenplay, Millard Kaufman; music, Ernest Gold; mechanical special effects, Willis Cook; special effects, Rabin, Block; camera, Allen G. Siegler, Henry Freulich; editor, Morse.

Victor Kilian (Dr. Jeremiah Morley); Bruce Kellogg (Wright Thompson); Otto Waldis (Dr. Max A. Bauer); Jim Bannon (Andy Ostengaard); Tom Handley (Dr. James Paxton); Dick Cogan (George Coleman); Marilyn Nash (Joan Lindsey); George Baxter (Presiding Officer).

UNKNOWN WORLD is one of those sci-fi motion pictures from the early 1950s which seemed to believe that its futuristic plot was sufficient to carry it to box-office success without worrying about the fact it was almost endless and that it provided little of the action and fantasy it promised. Only the film's Cyclotram, a machine used for boring through the earth, is of any interest and it is not often seen except for its interiors. No doubt with tongue-in-cheek, but still squarely on the mark, Donald C. Willis described the film in *Horror and Science Fiction Films* (1973), "Six scientists drill to the center of the earth in a specially designed vehicle: Film is just one long bore."

Fearing nuclear disaster, a group of people form a society to save themselves and plan to build a Cyclotram, a machine to pierce into the Earth's core to find a haven in case of nuclear fallout. Leading the organization is Dr. Jeremiah Morley (Victor Kilian) and other members include Joan Lindsey (Marilyn Nash), Dr. Max Bauer (Otto Waldis, Dr. James Paxton (Tom Handley), and Dr. George Coleman (Dick Cogan). When they are unable to get financing for the project, they accept millionaire Wright Thompson (Bruce Kellogg) who will pay for the machine's construction. After it is built all the society members, plus engineer Andy Ostengaard (Jim Bannon), begin the expedition at a mountain in the Aleutian Islands. Their descent takes them 1,500' below the land's crust, and along the way Paxton and Coleman die from poisonous gas. They stop at a huge cavern, which has a large lake and clouds, but no vegetation. Although the group hopes this will be their paradise they find it to be a barren land and Andy is killed in an accident. When a volcano erupts and a storm threatens them, Joan, Bauer and Wright return to the Cyclotram, but Morley refuses to give up his dream and drowns in a tidal wave. The machine goes down another 1,000' and then returns to the Earth's surface, emerging in the ocean near a tropical isle.

UNTAMED WOMEN (United Artists, 1952) 70 mins.

Producer, Richard Kay; director, W. Merle Connell; screenplay, George W. Sayre; art director, Paul Sprunck; sets, James R. Connell; music, Raoul Kraushar; special effects, Sprunck, Alfred Schmid; camera, Glen Gano; editor, William Connell.

Mikel Conrad (Steve); Doris Merrick (Sandra); Richard Monahan (Benny); Mark Lowell (Ed); Morgan Jones (Andy); Midge Ware (Myra); Judy Brubaker (Valdra); Carol Brewster (Tannus); Autumn Rice (Cleo); Lyle Talbot (Colonel Loring); Montgomery Pittman (Professor Warren); Miriam Kaylor (Nurse Edmunds).

When in need of stock footage of dinosaurs, get it from ONE MILLION B.C. (see B/V) seems to have been the credo of low budget filmmakers in the 1950s through the 1970s. UNTAMED

WOMEN is a good example of this ploy for the film's slim plot appears to be an excuse to air yet again the old footage from the Hal Roach production. It did not seem to help much. *Variety* disapproved, " . . . the story is ludicrous, the acting amateurish, and the production values meagre. . . ."

Bomber pilot Steve (Mikel Conrad) is found floating on a raft in the Pacific Ocean and is brought to a military doctor, Colonel Loring (Lyle Talbot), who injects him with a truth serum. Steve relates how his plane was shot down during World War II and how he and three crew members, Andy (Morgan Jones), Benny (Richard Monohan), and Ed (Mark Lowell) are stranded on a remote island where the population is entirely female. The leader of the women, Sandra (Doris Merrick), as well as the others, fear them because they had been molested previously by bearded men from the sea. To prove their innocence, the flyers are forced to go to a valley inhabited by dinosaurs and other prehistoric beasts. When they survive the ordeal, the women accept them. Steve and Sandra fall in love and she gives him a medallion which was handed down from the tribe's Druid ancestors. The savages who had once attacked the women return and a battle ensues. However, a volcano erupts and everyone and everything on the island is killed but Steve who escapes as the isle sinks into the ocean. To prove his tale, Steve shows the doctor his medallion.

V (Warner Bros. TV/NBC-TV, 5/1-2/83) C 205 mins.

Executive producer, Kenneth Johnson; producer, Chuck Bowman; associate producer, Patrick Boyriven; director/teleplay, Johnson; music, Joe Harnell; art director, Gary Lee; production designer, Charles R. Davis; costume designer, Brienne Glytoor; camera, John McPherson; editors, Alan Marks, Jack Schoengarth, Paul Dixon, Robert Richard.

Marc Singer (Mike Donovan); Faye Grant (Dr. Juliet Parrish); Jane Badler (Diana); Michael Durrell (Robert Maxwell); Peter Nelson (Brian); David Packer (Daniel Bernstein); Neva Patterson (Eleanor); Josh Brooks (Tommy Peterson); Blair Tefkin (Robin Maxwell); Michael Wright (Elias Taylor); Bonnie Bartlett (Mrs. Bernstein); Leonard Cimino (Abraham Bernstein); Richard Herd (John); Evan Kim (Tony); Richard Lawson (Dr. Ben Taylor); George Morfogen (Stanley Bernstein); Andrew Prine (Steven); Hansford Rowe (Plant Supervisor); Jenny Sullivan (Kristine Walsh); Penelope Windust (Kathleen Maxwell); Rafael Campos (Sancho); Frank Ashmore (Martin); Caleb Taylor (Jason Bernard); Diane Civita (Harmony); Viveka Davis (Barbara); Eric Johnston (Sean Donovan); Michael Alldredge (Quentin); Camila Ashland (Ruby); Michael

Bond (Denny); Robert Englund (Willie); Jenny Neymann (Marge Donovan); Stack Pierce (Black Alien Captain); Myron Healey (Professor); and: Curt Lowens, William Russell, Michael Swan, Stephanie Falkner, Ron Hajak, Dick Harwood, David Hooks, Bonnie Johns, Joanna Kerns, Mike Monahan, Jennifer Perito, Nathan Roberts, Robert Vandenberg, Momo Yashima.

Shown in two parts, this elaborate TV movie was produced/directed/written by Kenneth Johnson and it told of lizard-like aliens invading the Earth in the guise of humans. Technically well made, the telefeature was a drawn-out soap opera which *Variety* labeled, "Elemental, sentimental and undistinguished. V should be adored by the diehard incredulous." The production used shock effects such as an alien eating a rodent or a pretty young girl having sex and becoming impregnated by one of the alien lizards. But overall, except for the space hardware, the movie was bland. It did, however, result in an NBC-TV series of the same title, which had a short run (10/26/84 to 3/22/85).

Fifty flying saucers, each carrying several thousand aliens, appear over the major cities of the world. Earthlings are informed the aliens, who appear to be human, are from the Canis Major constellation and need the planet's wastes to make chemicals required by their endangered sphere. People on Earth try to accept the aliens but a TV news cameraman (Marc Singer) and his assistant (Evan Kim) photograph an alien in its true reptile form and opposition breaks out against the invaders as they attempt to subdue the human race. With the aid of informers and black marketeers, the aliens are partially successful and one alien (Peter Nelson) impregnates a young girl (Blair Tefkin) who loves him, and scientists hope their offspring might lead to discoveries on how to combat the aliens. Meanwhile an alien commander (Jane Badler) continues the subjugation of the humans who, in small cores, try to rid the planet of the enemy.

Donald C. Willis summed it up in *Horror and Science Fiction Films III* (1984), "An unbearably glib fusion of schlock and social comment, V (for 'Victory,' a la Z) is HOLOCAUST as based on a joke from 'The Twilight Zone'—to wit, the 'To Serve Man' alien-cookbook story."

VALLEY OF GWANGI (Warner Bros.-Seven Arts, 1969) C 95 mins.

Producer, Charles H. Schneer; associate producer, Ray Harryhausen; director, Jim O'Connolly; screenplay, William E. Bast; additional material, Julian More; art director, Gil Parrondo; music/music director, Jerome Moross; assistant director, Pedro Vidal; wardrobe designer, John Furness; sound, Malcolm Stewart; visual effects, Harryhausen; camera, Erwin Hillier; editor, Henry Richardson.

James Franciscus (Tuck Kirby); Gila Golan (T. J. Breckenridge); Richard Carlson (Champ Connors); Laurence Naismith (Professor Horace Bromley); Freda Jackson (Tia Zorina); Gustavo Rojo (Carlos dos Orsos); Dennis Kilbane (Rowdy); Mario de Barros (Bean); Curtis Arden (Lope); Jose Burgos (Dwarf).

Around 1900 an American Wild West show is set up in a rural Mexican town and a strange animal they had been exhibiting has escaped and the owners, Tuck Kirby (James Franciscus) and Champ Connors (Richard Carlson), and their crew go to a remote valley to locate it and there they find a prehistoric world populated by dinosaurs. They decide to capture a large allosaurus the locals call Gwangi, and use him as an exhibit. They lasso and tie up the lizard and return him to town in a large cart and cage him, but a superstitious Gypsy, Tia Zorina (Freda Jackson), frees the beast which runs rampant in the town. Eventually the creature is cornered in a church which is set afire, bringing about the demise of Gwangi.

This mixture of Western and science fiction was first conceived in the 1940s by animator Willis O'Brien as GWANGI and elements of it later turned up in MIGHTY JOE YOUNG (1949) (see B/V) and THE BEAST OF HOLLOW MOUNTAIN (1956) (q.v.). The animation for this feature was executed by Ray Harryhausen, O'Brien's one-time assistant, and the results are excellent. In addition to Gwangi, the film contains several other dinosaurs and all of them are beautifully animated and very realistic. Unfortunately the arid terrain of the film gives it a vapid look, despite the superior cinematography, and the film's slow opening narrative hampers it as well. The movie's chief asset is the title creature itself. Gwangi is an appealing monster and one does not like his ultimate fate, since he was forcefully removed from his habitat. His destruction is inevitable but unfortunate since he was hardly the cause of the havoc he had caused. If left alone, Gwangi would not have bothered the populace—but left alone, there would have been no film plot!

VALLEY OF GWANGI was not successful when released theatrically, but TV and video showings have remedied that situation. When the motion picture was issued, Bill Warren noted its best asset in an essay in *Photon* magazine (Number 18, 1969), "In several scenes in town, notably inside his cage and within the cathedral, Gwangi is incredibly realistic. Harryhausen told me he tried to give Gwangi a personality 'insofar as an allosaurus can have a personality.'"

THE VANISHING SHADOW (Universal, 1934) twelve chapters.

Director, Louis Friedlander [Lew Landers]; story, Ella O'Neill;

screenplay, Het Manheim, Basil Dickey, George Morgan; art director Thomas F. O'Neill; camera, Richard Fryer; editors, Edward Todd, Alvin Todd, Friedlander [Landers].

Onslow Stevens (Stanley Stanfield); Ada Ince (Gloria Barnett); Walter Miller (Ward Barnett); James Durkin (Carl Van Dorn); William Desmond (MacDonald); Richard Cramer (Dorgan); Sidney Bracey (Denny); Edmund Cobb (Kent); James Durkin (Carl Van Dorn); and: Beulah Hutton, Monte Montague.

Chapters: 1) Accused of Murder; 2) The Destroying Ray; 3) The Avalanche; 4) Trapped; 5) Hurled from the Sky; 6) Chain Lightning; 7) The Tragic Crash; 8) The Shadow of Death; 9) Blazing Bulkheads; 10) The Iron Death; 11) The Juggernaut; 12) Retribution.

Universal had great success with THE INVISIBLE MAN (q.v.) in 1933 and the next year invisibility was applied as a plot ploy for THE VANISHING SHADOW which also contained such sci-fi realism items as a futuristic laboratory, a death ray, and a huge robot. In this case invisibility was attained not from a drug, as in the 1933 feature, but by wearing a "belt of invisibility."

When his father dies from the results of a smear campaign, scientist Stanley Stanfield (Onslow Stevens) vows revenge against the man responsible, the corrupt Ward Barnett (Walter Miller), despite the fact Stanley loves Barnett's daughter, Gloria (Ada Ince). Barnett, however, wants Stanley out of the way and has him framed for the murder of a gangster. With the aid of inventor Carl Van Dorn (James Durkin), Stanley uses a belt which makes him invisible, along with a death ray and a robot, to beat his foes. Stanley proves Barnett's guilt and the police shoot the latter as he tries to escape, allowing Stanley and Gloria to wed.

This twelve chapter cliffhanger was directed by Louis Friedlander, who as Lew Landers, became a very prolific director of "B" movies and his horror/sci-fi genre outings included: THE RAVEN (1935), THE BOOGIE MAN WILL GET YOU (1942) (see B/V), THE MAN WHO RETURNED TO LIFE (1942), RETURN OF THE VAMPIRE (1943), JUNGLE MANHUNT (1951), RUN FOR THE HILLS (1953), and TERRIFIED (1963).

THE VENUSIAN see STRANGER FROM VENUS.

VICTOR FRANKENSTEIN (Films Around the World, 1977) C 92 mins.

Presenter, Irving Shapiro; associate producer, Tony Donald; director, Calvin Floyd; based on the novel *Frankenstein* by Mary Shelley; screenplay, Yvonne Floyd, Calvin Floyd; art director, Ralf Laksson; makeup, Kerstin Elg; costumes, Kersti Gustafsson; music,

Gerard Victory; camera, Tony Forsberg, John Wilcox; editor, Susanna Linnman.

Leon Vitali (Victor Frankenstein); Per Oscarsson (The Monster); Stacey Dorning (Elisabeth); Mathias Henricsson (Ship Captain); Jan Ohlsson (William Frankenstein); Nicholas Clay (Henry); Archie O'Sullivan (Professor Waldhem).

Found by a ship captain (Mathias Henricsson) stranded in the ice in a quest to find the North Pole, Victor Frankenstein (Leon Vitali) tells the man his horror story. Living near Geneva, Switzerland, Victor leaves his fiancee Elisabeth (Stacey Dorning) to study with Professor Waldhem (Archie O'Sullivan) at a faraway university in Engelstadt. After two years he earns his degree and begins experiments in an attempt to create a man. He succeeds but is repulsed by his creation and goes back to Geneva. The creature (Per Oscarsson) follows and murders Victor's younger brother William (Jan Ohlsson). Victor hunts for the killer and finds his creation who tells him how he has been rejected by society because of his ugliness. He forces Frankenstein to create a mate for him but the doctor fails to finish the experiment and in revenge the creature murders Victor's best friend Henry (Nicholas Clay) and then kills Elisabeth on her wedding night. When the police refuse to believe Frankenstein's account about his creation he sets out to find him and the chase leads to the Arctic. The creature boards the ship but Victor dies of heart failure before their final confrontation and his creation wanders off to die in the Arctic wastes.

A Swedish-Irish co-production, with filming in both countries, VICTOR FRANKENSTEIN is a faithful rendering of Mary Shelley's novel highlighted by superb cinematography by Tony Forsberg in Sweden and John Wilcox in Ireland. Unfortunately Leon Vitali is not overly appealing in the title assignment and although Per Oscarsson brings a good deal of pathos to the role of the creature he is not particularly repulsive in appearance, thus negating society's reaction to him. While the motion picture may be true to its literary source it points up the basic uninteresting aspects of the original in deference to the thrills provided by its cinema hybrids, such as the Universal and Hammer series.

A.k.a.: TERROR OF FRANKENSTEIN.

VIDEODROME (Universal, 1983) C 88 mins.

Executive producers, Pierre David, Victor Solnicki; producer, Claude Heroux; associate producer, Laurence Nessls; director/screenplay, David Cronenberg; production designer, Carol Spier; art director, Nick Kosonic; music, Howard Shore; special makeup effects, Rick Baker; camera, Mark Irwin; editor, Ronald Sanders.

James Woods (Max Renn); Sonja Smits (Bianca O'Blivion); Deborah Harry (Nicki Brand); Peter Dvorsky (Harlan); Les Carlson (Barry Convex); Jack Creley (Professor Brian O'Blivion); Lynne Borman (Masha); Julie Khaner (Briley); Reiner Schwarz (Moses); David Bolt (Rafe); Larry Cadeau (Rena King); Sam Malkin (Bum).

The emergence of television by satellite and cable TV in the mid-1970s changed the complexion of home entertainment. This horror/sci-fi effort made in Canada by cult director David Cronenberg examines the underbelly of this phenomenon in a feature full of shock effects which solidified Cronenberg's auteur reputation among his followers.

Max Renn (James Woods) runs a sleazy, erotic-oriented cable television outfit in Toronto and he continuously looks for new programs and he finds one called Videodrome, which appears to be from the Orient. He tries to track down the origins of the show but is warned by a supplier to leave it alone because the graphic violence in the films is real and not staged. Renn persists, however, and finds the station he wants is actually in Pittsburgh and is run by Brian O'Blivion (Jack Creley) whom he learns uses his mental powers to control the program's viewers. Renn's lover, Nicki Brand (Deborah Harry), becomes addicted to the cruelty on Videodrome and this brings about her demise. Renn uncovers that O'Blivion is really dead and that his daughter Bianca (Sonja Smits) hides this fact by using his old videos to make it seem he is still living. Wearing a special helmet, Renn is taken through the horrible world of Videodrome, one from which he can no longer escape.

Variety recorded, "Horror specialist David Cronenberg has come up with his most densely plotted and talky film in VIDEODROME. However, neither factor gets in the way of the picture's visceral charms, which are considerable. . . . Picture is a real find for horror buffs looking for new thrills and may attract a videophile audience with its high-tech prophesizing."

VILLAGE OF THE GIANTS (Embassy, 1965) C 80 mins.

Producer/director, Bert I. Gordon; based on the novel *The Food of the Gods* by H. G. Wells; story, Bert I. Gordon; screenplay, Alan Caillou; art director, Franz Bachelin; set decorator, Robert R. Benton; music/music director, Jack Nitzsche; songs: Ron Elliott, Frank C. Slay and Frederick A. Picariello; Nitzsche and Russ Titelman; choreography, Toni Basil; assistant director, James Rosenberger; makeup, Wally Westmore; costumes, Leah Rhodes, Frank Richardson; visual effects, Bert I. Gordon, Flora Gordon; process camera, Farciot Edouart; camera, Paul C. Vogel; editor, John Bushelman.

Tommy Kirk (Mike); John Crawford (Horsey); Beau Bridges (Fred); Ronny Howard (Genius); Joy Harmon (Merrie); Bob Random (Rick); Tisha Sterling (Jean); Charla Doherty (Nancy); Tim Rooney (Pete); Kevin O'Neal (Harry); Gail Gilmore (Elsa); Toni Basil (Red); Hank Jones (Chuck); Jim Begg (Fatso); Vicki London (Georgette); Joseph Turkel (Sheriff); The Beau Brummels, Freddy Cannon, Mike Clifford (Singers).

When their car becomes stuck in an avalanche of mud, eight teenagers return home and Mike (Tommy Kirk) and Nancy (Charla Doherty) go to her house where her younger brother, Genius (Ronny Howard), has cooked up goo which enlarges everything. Seeing it work on ducks, the teenagers eat the concoction and grow into giants. They take over the town and force the adults to live by the strict rules they had once placed on their now-giant offspring. The youths also take the sheriff's (Joseph Turkel) daughter (Joy Harmon) hostage but Genius devises a vapor antidote and the teenagers are returned to normal size.

This inane sci-fi/rock 'n roll comedy was Bert I. Gordon's first screen adaptation of H. G. Wells' classic 1904 novel *The Food of the Gods*. Filmed in "Perceptovision," the film is as awful as it sounds, compounded by almost endless "music" contributed by current pop teenage idols like Freddy Cannon, The Beau Brummels and Mike Clifford. The highlight of the production to many is the film's poster art which depicts a teenage boy climbing up a giant girl's bosom!

When Embassy Home Entertainment issued VILLAGE OF THE GIANTS on video cassette, *Fangoria* magazine (October, 1985) zeroed in on producer/director/story writer Bert I. Gordon's penchant for special effects. "The special effects engineered by . . . Gordon are actually not as bad as some of his earlier efforts (perhaps because he was assisted here by process-shot pioneer Farciot Edouart), but they still sure look goofy at times."

Gordon must have liked this Wells' work because he produced it again, this time in a straight rendition, but with no better results as 1976's FOOD OF THE GODS (q.v.).

VOODOO MAN (Monogram, 1944) 62 mins.

Producers, Sam Katzman, Jack Dietz; associate producer, Barney Sarecky; director, William Beaudine; screenplay, Robert Charles; set designer, David Milton; music director, Edward Kay; camera, Marcel Le Picard; editor Carl Pierson.

Bela Lugosi (Dr. Richard Marlowe); John Carradine (Job); George Zucco (Nicolas); Michael Ames [Tod Andrews] (Ralph Dawson); Wanda McKay (Betty Benton); Ellen Hall (Mrs. Marlowe); Louise Currie (Sally Saunders); Henry Hall (Sheriff); Dan

White (Deputy); Pat McKee (Grego); Terry Walker (Alice); Ethelreda Leopold, Claire James, Dorothy Bailer (Zombies); Mary Currier (Mrs. Benton); Mici Gotz (Marie the Housekeeper).

Dr. Richard Marlowe (Bela Lugosi) lives in a remote area where he attempts to work out formulas to bring back life to his wife Evelyn (Ellen Hall), who has been mentally, but not physically, dead for over twenty years. Now he is working with voodoo priest Nicholas (George Zucco) who is trying to transfer souls from young women he and assistant Job (John Carradine) abduct along the road by their gas station. Sally Saunders (Louise Currie) is to be a bridesmaid at friend Betty Benton's (Wanda McKay) wedding and she stops at the station as does the prospective groom, Hollywood script writer Ralph Dawson (Michael Ames). Sally is kidnapped by Nicholas and Job and used in a soul transference ceremony but it fails and due to Job's stupidity she is allowed to go free (the young women they capture are kept alive, albeit soulless, in glass cases) and she goes to Betty's home where Marlowe is called in to attend her. Realizing Betty would be a good subject for the experiment, he has her kidnapped but during the ceremony, in which Evelyn does come to life, Ralph arrives with the law and saves Betty while Marlowe is shot and he and his wife both die.

Similar to THE CORPSE VANISHES (1942) (q.v.), this fun Bela Lugosi thriller has the incongruous casting of suave George Zucco as a gas station attendant and John Carradine as a moron. *The Hollywood Reporter* concluded, "The story is no more absurd than the majority of its predecessors, occasionally poking sly fun at the whole scheme of horror pictures." Regarding Bela Lugosi's emoting in the film, Richard Bojarski decided in *The Films of Bela Lugosi* (1980), "The character of Dr. Marlowe gave Lugosi an opportunity to play a desperate individual whose obsession in bringing his wife back to normalcy draws our sympathy, despite his experiments leaving behind shells of human lives. In spite of the cliched script, Lugosi alternated between menace and compassion with his usual sincerity."

VOODOO WOMAN (American International, 1957) 77 mins.

Producer, Alex Gordon; director, Edward L. Cahn; screenplay, Russell Bender, V. I. Vass; art director, Bart Carre; assistant director, Art Hammond; music, Darrell Calker; song, Calker and John Blackburn; sound Glen Glenn; camera, Frederick E. West; editor, Ronald Sinclair.

Marla English (Marilyn Blanchard); Tom Conway (Dr. Roland Gerard); Touch [Michael] Connors (Ted Bronson); Lance Fuller (Rick [Harry]); Mary Ellen Kay (Susan Gerard); Paul Durov (Marcel); Martin Wilkins (Chaka); Norman Willis (Harry West); Otis

Greene (Bobo); Emmett E. Smith (Gandor); Paul Blaisdell (Monster); Giselle D'Arc (Singer); Jean Davis (Native Girl).

Deep in the jungles of a remote island, where the natives practice voodoo, expatriate scientist Dr. Roland Gerard (Tom Conway) lives with his wife Susan (Mary Ellen Kay). Unknown to her he is experimenting with a native girl (Jean Davis) and he turns her into a giant, murderous creature. He plans to take her back to civilization to show his colleagues who had previously denounced his work. At a small seaport, Marilyn Blanchard (Marla English) arrives with her weak-willed lover Rick (Lance Fuller) and with the aid of guide Ted Bronson (Touch [Michael] Connors), intending to steal the natives' golden voodoo idols. The monster wrecks the native village but reverted back to the form of a woman she is found in the jungle by Rick who brings about her accidental death. When the rampaging primitives attack the outsiders, Dr. Gerard saves them and convinces Marilyn to become his new subject, explaining it will make her a priestess. She agrees and murders Rick when the natives demand a sacrifice. Marilyn becomes a monster and turns on Gerard who hands his wife and Bronson over to the natives for sacrifice. The creature returns to the village and kills Gerard and the natives run away. Changing back to her "real" self, Marilyn attempts to steal the golden idols but dies by falling into a cauldron. Ted and Susan escape and return home.

Filmed on a $60,000 budget, VODOO WOMAN was producer Alex Gordon and director Edward L. Cahn's celluloid followup to their earlier THE SHE CREATURE (1956) (q.v.) and as in that feature Paul Blaisdell created and portrayed the monster. It appears he used the same monster suit but with a new, fearsome looking head for the role of the Voodoo Woman. While not as good as THE SHE CREATURE, VOODOO WOMAN is an appealing sci-fi/monster "B" production highlighted by lovelies Marla English and Mary Ellen Kay, newcomer Touch (later to become famous as Michael or Mike) Connors, and veteran Tom Conway as the mad scientist. Conway, completely different here from the suave "Falcon" detective who brought him screen stardom in the 1940s, conveys a cold evil quality to the role of the madman who used women for experiments which converts them into hideous monsters.

WARHOL'S FRANKENSTEIN see FLESH FOR FRANKENSTEIN.

THE WASP WOMAN (Allied Artists, 1960) 73 mins.

Producer/director, Roger Corman; story, Kinta Zertuche;

screenplay, Leo Gordon; art director, Daniel Haller; music, Fred Katz; camera, Harry Newman; editor, Carlo Lodato.

Susan Cabot (Janice Starlin); Fred [Anthony] Eisley (Bill Lane); Barbara [Barboura] Morris (Mary Dennison); Michael Marks (Eric Zinthrop); William Roerick (Arthur Cooper); Frank Gerstle (Hellman); Bruno Ve Sota (Nightwatchman).

Producer/director Roger Corman made THE WASP WOMAN for his own company, Filmgroup, and on a budget of $50,000. He based it on a magazine article he had read about using bee jelly as a cosmetic rejuvenation formula, only he changed it to wasps, thus having the title creature a giant, wingless female wasp.

Janice Starlin (Susan Cabot) is the president of a huge cosmetics firm whose profits are declining because she is getting older and can no longer be employed for its advertising. One of the company's honey suppliers, Eric Zinthrop (Michael Marks), has been readying a rejuvenation formula derived from queen wasps' jelly and Janice is impressed with its possibilities. He uses the formula on a cat and it reverts into a kitten and later Janice uses the compound he recommended only for external use and it makes her much younger, to the surprise of co-workers Bill Lane (Fred [Anthony] Eisley) and Arthur Cooper (William Roerick) and secretary Mary Dennison (Barbara Morris). When the cat, now reverted to old age, attacks Zinthrop he kills it but goes into shock and ends up in a hospital. Janice starts turning older and returns to the lab for more of the wasp formula, only to transform into a huge wasp who kills the snooping Cooper. The next night she murders a nightwatchman (Bruno Ve Sota). After a visit from Janice, Zinthrop, now out of his coma, tells Mary his fear of his boss and that she may try to murder Bill. Mary goes to the lab and Bill arrives and he and Zinthrop follow her and there they find Janice, now a giant wasp, has captured Mary and intends to devour her. Zinthrop tosses a bottle of acid at the wasp woman and Bill pushes her out of her office building window. As she falls to her death Zinthrop succumbs.

THE WATCHER IN THE WOODS (Buena Vista, 1980) C 100 mins.

Producer, Ron Miller; co-producer, Tom Leetch; director, John Hough; based on the novel *A Watcher in the Woods* by Florence Engel Randall; screenplay, Brian Clemens, Harry Spalding, Rosemary Anne Sisson; music/music director, Stanley Myers; production designer, Elliott Scott; art director, Alan Cassie; set decorator, Ian Whittaker; assistant director, Richard Hoult; sound editor, Jim Shields; special effects, John Richardson; camera, Alan Hume; editor, Geoffrey Foot.

Bette Davis (Mrs. Aylswood); Carroll Baker (Helen Curtis); David McCallum (Paul Curtis); Lynn-Holly Johnson (Jan Curtis); Kyle Richards (Ellie Curtis); Ian Bannen (John Keller); Richard Pasco (Tom Colley); Frances Cuka (Mary Fleming); Benedict Taylor (Mike Fleming); Eleanor Summerfield (Mrs. Thayer); Georgina Hale (Young Mrs. Aylswood); Katherine Levy (Karen Aylswood).

This motion picture was Disney Studio's attempt to break into the adult film market with a well-constructed, sci-fi tale which would appeal also to the family trade. Plagued with production problems from the start, the feature emerged in 1980 in a 100-minute version whose abrupt ending proved so unsatisfying that the feature was withdrawn quickly. An elaborate special effects finale was fashioned and tacked on the end of the film but it too was off kilter, so director Vincent McEveety was assigned to redo the finish and after further re-editing the feature emerged again in 1981, now running a little over 80 minutes. The final result is a pleasant mystery/sci-fi offering which has more gloss than story and for Bette Davis fans it is disappointing since her top-billed role is hardly a meaty one.

An American family headed by Paul Curtis (David McCallum)

Bette Davis and Kyle Richards in THE WATCHER IN THE WOODS (1980).

and his wife Helen (Carroll Baker), along with children Jan (Lynn-Holly Johnson) and Ellie (Kyle Richards), rent a remote home in England from a mysterious older woman, Mrs. Aylswood (Bette Davis), who resides nearby. The girls explore the area and find that mysterious things have been going on for three decades, ever since Mrs. Aylswood's daughter vanished. The locals insist that witchcraft or black magic is involved. Jan especially is bothered by the peculiar goings-on and sets out to solve the mystery. She learns that by some accident aliens took the lost girl and one of them remained in her place and through Jan the re-transference can be made. With Mrs. Aylswood, Jan agrees to the experiment and at the right time the aliens return, take their own and return Karen Aylswood (Katherine Levy), who has not aged.

The special effects sequence of the interchange of the alien for the teenage girl is well-executed, even spectacular, but not overly engrossing. *Fangoria* magazine (April, 1984) summed it up best when reviewing the film when Disney issued it to the home video cassette marketplace, "The picture is competently made and fairly entertaining, but the story is old news and, despite its more mature target audience, the movie looks like just another Disney kiddie-oriented fantasy."

THE WATTS MONSTER see DR. BLACK, MR. HYDE.

THE WEREWOLF (Columbia, 1956) 78 mins.

Producer, Sam Katzman; director, Fred F. Sears; story/screenplay, Robert E. Kent, James B. Gordon; art director, Paul Palmentola; music director, Mischa Bakaleinikoff; camera, Edwin Linden; editor, Harold White.

Steven Ritch (Duncan March, the Werewolf); Don Mecgowan (Deputy Sheriff Jack Haines); Joyce Holden (Amy Standish); Eleanore Tanin (Helen Marsh); Kim Charney (Chris Marsh); Harry Lauter (Clovey); Larry J. Blake (Dirgus); Ken Christy (Dr. James Gilchrist); James Gavin (Fanning); S. John Launer (Dr. Emery Forrest); George M. Lynn (Dr. Morgan Chambers); George Cisar (Hoxie); Don C. Harvey (Deputy).

Two scientists, Dr. Emery Forrest (S. John Launer) and Dr. Morgan Chambers (George M. Lynn), work on an antidote for atomic radiation and concoct a serum derived from wolves. They require someone to experiment on and come across car crash victim Duncan March (Steven Ritch) and they use the serum on him. He later escapes and a series of wolf killings occur in a remote area. The two experimentalists are convinced March is the murderer. They corner March in a cave but he becomes a werewolf and kills them and disappears into the mountains. By now the law, led by Deputy Sheriff Jack Haines (Don Megowan), is hunting the werewolf, and they even have March's wife (Eleanore Tanin) and son (Kim Charney) try to coax him down and when this fails a posse is formed to trap the killer. March, in wolf form, is injured after being caught in a trap and as he nears a bridge construction site he is shot and killed by the posse.

THE WEREWOLF is an entertaining sci-fi/horror film, due mainly to its mountainous location shooting, good pacing by director Fred F. Sears and star Steven Ritch's interpretation of the menace, a man who is the victim of science gone afoul and helpless in correcting the situation.

THE WHITE GORILLA (Special Attractions, 1947) 62 mins.

Producer, Adrian Weiss; director, Harry L. Fraser; screenplay, Monro Talbot; art director, Thomas Connoly; music, Lee Zahler; sound, Glen Glenn; camera, Bob Cline.

Ray "Crash" Corrigan (Steve Collins/Narrator/White Gorilla); Lorraine Miller (Ruth Stacey); George Lewis (Hutton); Francis Ford (Stacey); Charles King (Morgan); Budd Buster (Carter).

An expedition goes deep into the jungle in search of the Lost City and its hidden treasure and they encounter danger from the environs and natives along with a huge white gorilla which hates humans and carries off a young woman (Lorraine Miller) who is part of the expedition. A black gorilla comes to her rescue and defeats the white beast as the explorers find the hidden city and its one-eyed god statue which protects the treasure.

THE WHITE GORILLA is one of the most incredulous film excursions ever pasted together. It actually relates two stories: the expedition looking for the lost city which is footage from the 1927 Weiss Brothers-Artclass ten chapter serial PERILS OF THE JUNGLE starring Eugenia Gilbert and Frank Merrill; and the conflict between the white and black gorilla (the white one portrayed by Western film star Ray "Crash" Corrigan). The latter's plotline has the white gorilla being exiled by its fellow primates for being the wrong color! With the use of a narrator the film tells its two stories although none of it makes much sense but the feature proves to be funnier played seriously than most screen comedies. Straight-faced the hero tells how to find the Lost City: "Turn left at the elephant trail. You can't miss it."

The Weiss Brothers had used the famous Selig zoo wild animals when producing the above-mentioned chapterplay PERILS OF THE JUNGLE in the 1920s, thus the re-use of this footage does have an authentic look to it. But the new material shot in the

Hollywood suburbs of the mid-1940s is tacky indeed, on par with most of the ill-conceived gorilla suit costumes used in the picture. Donald C. Willis in *Horror and Science Fiction Films II* (1982) observed, "The effect of this generational graft lies somewhere between camp and modernism. The 'epic' gorilla battles are curiously dainty."

The same year this film was issued Ray Corrigan again played a white gorilla in WHITE PONGO (*infra*).

WHITE PONGO (Producers Releasing Corp., 1945) 74 mins.

Producer, Sigmund Neufeld; director, Sam Newfield; story/screenplay, Raymond L. Schrock; art director, Edward C. Jewell; music director, Leo Erdody; assistant director, Bill Connor; sound, John Carter; camera, Jack Greenhalgh; editor, Holbrook N. Todd.

Richard Fraser (Bishop); Maris Wrixon (Pamela); Lionel Royce (Van Doorn); Al Eben (Kroegert); Gordon Richards (Sir Harry); Michael Dyne (Carswell); George Lloyd (Baxter); Larry Steers (Dr. Kent); Milton Kibbee (Gunderson); Egon Brecher (Old Doctor); Joel Fluellen (Mumbo Jumbo); Ray "Crash" Corrigan (White/Black Gorilla).

During the 1940s cowboy film hero Ray "Crash" Corrigan supplemented his income by donning an ape suit and portraying giant simians in various low-grade feature like NABONGA (1944), THE WHITE GORILLA (1945) (*supra*), UNKNOWN ISLAND (1948) and this PRC release. In WHITE PONGO Corrigan actually plays two apes: his usual dark gorilla plus the title character, a white gorilla thought to be the missing link. Besides boasting two gorillas, the film also sports a number of alternate titles, including BLOND GORILLA and CONGO PONGO while in England it was retitled ADVENTURE UNLIMITED and in Italy it became LA SFIDA DE KING KONG [The Challenge of King Kong].

An undercover investigator (Richard Fraser) believes a safari guide (Gordon Richards) is guilty of murder and he joins the group, which includes a pretty young woman (Maris Wrixon), to gain evidence against the man. The expedition is led by a scientist (Lionel Royce) who is searching for the missing link but once they are deep in the jungle the guide strands them as he searches for gold. A giant white ape (Ray "Crash" Corrigan) attacks the group and kidnaps the girl. The scientist believes the ape is the missing link as the creature kills the guide and the policeman saves the girl.

Even a quick look at WHITE PONGO reveals that every expense was spared in filming this jungle "epic" by the brother team of producer Sigmund Neufeld and director Sam Newfield, the same duo who churned out scores of cheap Westerns for PRC during the 1940s.

WILD IN THE STREETS (American International, 1968) C 97 mins.

Executive producer, Burt Topper; producers, James H. Nicholson, Samuel Z.Arkoff; associate producer, William J. Immerman; director, Barry Shear; based on the story "The Day It All Happened, Baby" by Robert Thom; screenplay, Thom; art director, Paul Sylos; set decorator, Harry Reif; music, Les Baxter; songs, Barry Mann and Cynthia Weil; assistant directors, Chuck Colean, Lew Borzage; costume supervisor, Richard Bruno; makeup, Fred Williams; sound, Al Overton; camera, Richard Moore; editors, Fred Feitshans, Eve Newman.

Shelley Winters (Mrs. Flatow); Christopher Jones (Max Frost [Max Flatow]); Diane Varsi (Sally LeRoy); Ed Begley (Senator Allbright); Hal Holbrook (John Fergus); Millie Perkins (Mary Fergus); Richard Pryor (Stanley X); Bert Freed (Max Jacob Flatow, Sr.); Kevin Coughlin (Billy Cage); Larry Bishop (Abraham); May Ishihara (Fuji Ellie); Michael Margotta (Jimmy Fergus); Don Wyndham (Joseph Fergus); Kellie Flanagan (Young Mary Fergus); Salli Sachse (Hippie Mother); Paul Frees (Narrator); Walter Winchell, Melvin Belli, Kenneth Banghart, Louis Lomax, Dick Clark, Jack Latham, Pamela Mason, Allan J. Moll, Army Archerd, Gene Shacove (Themselves).

Destroying his family's auto with a bomb he has fashioned, teenager Max Flatow (Christopher Jones) takes the money he has saved peddling LSD and sets out on his own and within a few years he has become Max Frost, the most popular entertainer in the country and a millionaire with an entourage and a girlfriend, Sally LeRoy (Diane Varsi), a former child star. One day his mother (Shelley Winters) sees him on TV and arranges a family reunion but when she accidentally runs over a child with her car her son rejects her for good. A corrupt liberal California congressman, John Fergus (Hal Holbrook), decides to run for President and to appeal to the youth vote he has Max appear at his rallies. Once there Max demands that the voting age be lowered to fourteen and mass demonstrations cause many states to do so. Max backs Sally's election to Congress and drugging lawmakers with LSD they pass a bill eliminating voting age requirements. Max campaigns and is elected President and his first act in office is to send everyone over thirty-five to retirement homes where they are kept sedated. When Max kills a crawfish belonging to two seven-year-olds, they vow to get rid of everyone over ten years of age.

Grossing some $5,500,000 at the U.S. box-office, WILD IN

THE STREETS was one of the most successful of the 1960s' youth protest films; it packed a mighty satirical punch, almost as prophetic of the future as 1984 (q.v.). *Variety* judged it a " . . . well-made futuristic political drama-comedy. Exploitable, but not just an exploitation pic." Although not a big budget item, the film " . . . assumes a look several times its budget through extensive and diverse set-ups, admirably researched and utilized newsreel footage and the presence of a sizable recruitment of authenticating media personalities." (*The Hollywood Reporter*)

Originally the film was to conclude with Shelley Winters in a forced retirement camp singing "The Battle Hymn of the Republic," but studio executives wisely insisted another scene with the small children plotting to overthrow the youths be inserted; it generated a far better finale impact than did the draft ending.

WILD JUNGLE CAPTIVE see JUNGLE CAPTIVE.

THE WINGED SERPENT see Q.

THE WIZARD (Fox, 1927) 61 mins.

Presenter, William Fox; director, Richard Rosson; based on the novel *Balaoo* by Gaston Leroux; screenplay, Harry O. Hoyt, Andrew Bennison; titles, Malcolm Stuart Boyles; assistant director, Park Frame; camera, Frank Good.

Edmund Lowe (Stanley Gordon); Leila Hyams (Anne Webster); Gustav von Seyffertitz (Dr. Paul Coriolos); E. H. Calvert (Edwin Palmer); Barry Norton (Reginald Van Lear); Oscar Smith (Sam); Perle Marshall (Detective Murphy); Norman Trevor (Judge Webster); George Kotsonaros (The Ape); Maude Turner Gordon (Mrs. Van Lear).

Based on Gaston Leroux's 1912 novel, *Balaoo,* this old house, clutching-hand thriller combined horror and sci-fi elements into "One of Monsieur Leroux's thrilling mystery yarns enacted by Edmund Lowe and other capable performers" (*Photoplay* magazine). The feature, now claimed lost, was highlighted by Frank Good's shadowy cinematography and was especially memorable for George Kotsonaros' performance as the human gorilla and Gustav von Seyffertitz as the spidery mad scientist.

Madman Dr. Paul Coriolos (Gustav von Seyffertitz) wants revenge for the execution of his son and he targets those he believes were responsible. He develops an ape man creature (George Kotsonaros) to do his bidding in killing those he wants out of the way. Newspaperman Stanley Gordon (Edmund Lowe) investigates and finds that two of the intended victims are Judge Webster

(Norman Trevor) and his daughter Anne (Leila Hyams), who is loved by Stanley. He saves the two and puts a stop to the evil Coriolos, whose murderous creature turns on him.

The film was reworked in the sound era as DR. RENAULT'S SECRET (q.v.) in 1942, this time with the ape man (J. Carrol Naish) having been evolved by an insane scientist (George Zucco) from a lower primate.

WIZARD OF MARS (American General Pictures, 1965) C 81 mins.

Producer/David L. Hewitt; associate producer, Gary R. Heacock; director, Hewitt; story, Hewitt, Armando Busick; screenplay, Hewitt; art director, Busick; makeup, Jean Lister; technical advisor, Forrest J. Ackerman; special effects, Hewitt; camera, Austin McKinney; editor, Jim Graeff.

John Carradine (Wizard of Mars); Roger Gentry (Commander Steve); Vic McGee (Doc); Jerry Rannow (Charlie the Co-Pilot); Eve Bernhardt (Dorothy the Navigator).

Four astronauts, Steve (Roger Gentry), Charlie (Jerry Rannow), Doc (Vic McGee) and Dorothy (Eve Bernhardt), are forced to crash land on Mars. They trek across the barren red planet to find the main stage of their rocket so they can return to Earth. They use inflatable rafts and go down a river and are attacked by monsters and they find an ancient city and talk to a composite Martian (John Carradine), who aids them in returning home before their oxygen supply expires.

David L. Hewitt produced, directed, wrote, and did the special effects for this trite sci-fier, whose "technical consultant" was monster magazine editor Forrest J. Ackerman. This film is bottom rung all the way and played only on the bottom half of drive-in and grind house showings (usually with other Hewitt clinkers, DR. TERROR'S GALLERY OF HORROR (1966) and JOURNEY TO THE CENTER OF TIME (1966) [see B/V]). Visually the film has little to offer outside desert locales substituting for Mars, a mundane netherworld and the attacking river monsters, which look like something one might use to unstop a sink. The level of acting by the astronauts is pre-high school play time. Most disappointing of all is top-billed John Carradine's very brief appearance as the Martian. Viewed only as an enlarged head, he is on screen for only a few minutes towards the end of the feature.

XTRO (New Line Cinema, 1983) C 80 mins.

Executive producer, Robert Shaye; producer Mark Forstater; associate producer, James M. Crawford; director, Harry Bromley

Roger Gentry and Jerry Rannow in WIZARD OF MARS (1965).

Davenport; based on original screenplay by Parry, Davenport; screenplay, Robert Smith, Iain Cusassie; additional dialogue, Jo Ann Kaplan; music, Davenport; synthesizer effects, Shelton Leigh Palmer; assistant director, Jake Wright; art director, Andrew Mollo; sound, John Midgley; special makeup effects, Robin Grantham, John Webber; creature effects, Francis Coates; special effects, Tom Harris; camera, John Metcalfe; additional camera, John Simmons; editor, Nick Gaster.

Philip Sayer (Sam Phillips); Bernice Stegers (Rachel Phillips); Danny Brainin (Joe Daniels); Simon Nash (Tony Phillips); Maryam D'Abo (Analise); David Cardy (Michael); Anna Wing (Miss Goodman); Peter Mandell (Clown).

Sam Phillips (Philip Sayer) is playing with his young son Tony (Simon Nash) when he is whisked away by an alien craft. Three years later he returns in the guise of a large beetle-like creature who rapes a young woman and the next day she gives birth to the full-sized Sam. He returns to his wife Rachel (Bernice Stegers) and son but finds she has a boyfriend, Joe Daniels (Danny Brainin), who lives with them. Sam has super-mental powers and he bites his son on the shoulder, leaving spores in the wound which give the boy powers to animate his toys. Tony sucks the stomach of pretty family friend, Analise (Maryam D'Abo), impregnating her with alien eggs. The young woman soon becomes wrapped in a cocoon as the eggs incubate while Sam and Tony leave in a UFO. One of Tony's animated toys, a clown, tends to the girl and her alien offspring.

The entire purpose of XTRO, like some other sci-fi films of the period (i.e. the remake of THE THING, 1982, q.v.) appears to be to use film's new special effects technology for weird and sickening visuals. XTRO is packed with them, such as the gyrating human grasshopper, the woman giving birth to a full-sized man, the boil-sized wound on the boy's shoulder, the lad's tooth work on the comely young lady's tummy, and her giving birth to alien larvae, not to mention the boy's bathing in alien blood.

The major weakness of this film (originally called JUDAS GOAT) is its story, as reported by *Variety,* "XTRO . . . is an imitative, chintzy British monster picture. Well-timed for release and obviously exploitable for horror film audiences, film is too silly and underdeveloped in story values to expand beyond the diehard fans."

THE YELLOW PHANTOM see SHADOW OF CHINATOWN.

YOUNG FRANKENSTEIN (Twentieth Century-Fox, 1974) 108 mins.

Producer, Michael Gruskoff; director, Mel Brooks; based on characters created by Mary Shelley in the novel *Frankenstein;* screenplay, Gene Wilder, Brooks; music, John Morris; production designer, Dale Hennesy; set decorator, Bob De Vestel; assistant director, Marvin Miller; sound, Richard Portman, Gene Cantamessa; special effects, Kenneth Strickfaden; camera, Gerald Hirschfeld; editor, John Howard.

Gene Wilder (Dr. Frederick Frankenstein); Peter Boyle (Monster); Marty Feldman (Igor); Madeline Kahn (Elizabeth); Cloris Leachman (Frau Blucher); Teri Garr (Inga); Kenneth Mars (Inspector Kemp); Richard Haydn (Herr Falkstein); Liam Dunn (Mr. Hilltop); Gene Hackman (Blind Man); Danny Goldman (Medical Student); Leon Askin (Herr Waldman); Oscar Beregi (Sadistic Jailer); Lou Cutell (Frightened Villager); Arthur Malet (Village Elder); Richard Roth (Kemp's Aide); Monte Landis, Rusty Blitz (Gravediggers); Anne Beesley (Little Girl); Terrence Pushman, Ian Abercrombie, Randolph Dobbs (Villagers); and: John Dennis, Michael Fox, Patrick O'Hara, John Madison, Rich Norman, Rolfe Sedan, Norbert Schiller, Lidia Kristen, Anatol Winogradoff.

Mel Brooks has kidded practically every film genre in a series of mostly successful feature films and YOUNG FRANKENSTEIN was his takeoff on the Universal horror/sci-fi films of the 1930s and the result is one of his most satisfying motion pictures. It grossed nearly $40,000,000 at the box-office. Ed Naha in *The Science Fictionary* (1980) termed it, "A simply wonderful parody of those classic Universal films of yesteryear, lovingly constructed and supremely executed." Phil Hardy opined in *The Film Encyclopedia: Science Fiction* (1984), ". . . YOUNG FRANKENSTEIN is a far more restrained offering less surreal and far more unified in tone, a pastiche rather than a parody."

American scientist Dr. Frederick Frankenstein (Gene Wilder) returns to his German homeland and goes to the castle of his grandfather where Frau Blucher (Cloris Leachman), the housekeeper, bitterly longs for the good old days. With the aid of Igor (Marty

Marty Feldman in YOUNG FRANKENSTEIN (1974).

Feldman), a hunchback and village girl Inga (Teri Garr), he puts together a monster (Peter Boyle), like the one created by his grandfather. Due to Igor's bungling, the monster is given an inferior brain and the giant creature runs away from the castle and takes residence with a blind hermit (Gene Hackman) who tries unsuccessfully to civilize him. The doctor finally captures his creation and alters his brain and turns him into a song-and-dance man but the two fail to impress his colleagues at a scientific convention. Dejected, the monster kidnaps Frankenstein's fiancee, Elizabeth (Madeline Kahn), once the consort of Igor, who becomes enraptured by the monster's sexual prowess; she marries him. Frankenstein weds Inga.

One of the best assets of YOUNG FRANKENSTEIN—filmed in black and white—is its recreation of the James Whale "Frankenstein" series setting. This was accomplished in part by special effects expert Kenneth Strickfaden, who came out of semi-retirement (he had contributed the machines used in DRACULA VS. FRANKENSTEIN, 1971, q.v.) to supply the gadgetry which provides the movie with such a realistic look. Also very amusing is Marty Feldman's performance as the nutty, bug-eyed hunchback, Igor, whose hump keeps moving!

ZONE TROOPERS (Empire Pictures, 1986) C 88 mins.

Executive producer, Charles Band; producer, Paul De Mio; associate producer, Debra Dion; director, Danny Bilson; screenplay, Bilson, De Meo; music, Richard Band; costumes, Jill Ohanneson; assistant director, David Boyd; sound, Mario Bramonti; special effects, John Buechler; camera, Mac Ahlberg; editor, Ted Nicolaou.

Tim Thomerson (The Sarge); Timothy Van Patten (Joey); Art La Fleur (Corporal Mittens); Biff Manard (Dolan); William Paulson (The Alien).

In Italy in 1944, an Allied platoon finds itself surrounded by the Germans. The platoon is led by Iron Sarge (Tim Thomerson) and includes young Joey (Timothy Van Patten), Corporal Mittens (Art La Fleur), and a brash journalist, Dolan (Biff Manard). As the men push forward they come upon a craft operated by a strange man (William Paulson) and Joey believes the strangers are aliens. It is realized eventually the strangers are from outer space and the soldiers attempt to keep them from falling into enemy hands although it is the aliens who bring about the Nazis' destruction and insure the safety of the G. I. platoon.

Only a few films, like SHOCK WAVES (1977) (q.v.), and REVOLT OF THE ZOMBIES (1936) have tried to unite the war film genre with horror and sci-fi and ZONE TROOPERS does so, but with very mixed results. *Variety* noted, "Surprisingly, ZONE

TROOPERS is a competent, moderately amusing war saga with the aliens just along for the ride. Obviously shooting for the sci-fi effects crowd, pic is likely to be more pleasing to World War II buffs since it is basically the same old story with many of the pleasing cliches and characters intact. Arrival of aliens is actually the least entertaining part of the pic and, with little for them to do, the film comes to a virtual standstill."

Shot on location in Italy, the film is visually appealing as are John Buechler's special effects.

SCIENCE FICTION ON RADIO AND TV

A Supplement to the data in the Base Volume, including additions and corrections (noted by italics).

RADIO

THE AVENGERS, 1945; with James Monks.

BEYOND MIDNIGHT (from South Africa).

THE BLACK MASK, syndicated.

THE CREAKING DOOR (from South Africa)

DREADFUL JOHN AT MIDNIGHT, CBS.

EERIE STORIES.

THE ELEVENTH HOUR (from South Africa)

EXPLORING TOMORROW, *1957*.

FRANKENSTEIN, syndicated, 1931; with George Edwards.

THE HAUNTING DOOR, NBC.

THE HERMIT'S CAVE, syndicated, 1940-43; with Mel Johnson.

MURDER AT MIDNIGHT, syndicated, 1946; Mutual, 1950; with host Raymond Morgan.

NELSON OLMSTEAD, NBC, 1946; with Nelson Olmstead.

OUT OF THE NIGHT, Grace Gibson syndication.

SPACE PATROL, (add to cast) Lyn Osborn.

STAR WARS, syndicated, 1981; with Mark Hamill, David Ackroyd, Stephen Elliott, Brock Peters, Ann Sacs, Perry King.

STRANGEST OF ALL, syndicated, 1963; with Frank Edwards.

TALES OF THE SUPERNATURAL, Grace Gibson syndication.

THEATRE 10:30.

TOM CORBETT, SPACE CADET, *ABC, 1952*.

WEIRD CIRCLE, *1946*.

X MINUS ONE, NBC, *4/22/55* to 1/9/58 (formerly DIMENSION X, 1950-55).

TELEVISION

Compiled by Vincent Terrace

AIRWOLF, CBS-TV, 1/22/84 to 7/23/86; with Jan-Michael Vincent, Ernest Borgnine, Jean Bruce Scott, Alex Cord.

AIRWOLF '87, USA-TV, 1/23/87 (premiere); with Barry Van Dyke, Michele Scarabelli, Geraint Lynn Davies.

ALF, NBC-TV, 9/22/86 (premiere); with Max Wright, Anne Schedeen, Andrea Elson, Brian Gregory, Paul Fusco (voice of ALF).

ALF (cartoon) NBC-TV, 9/26/87 (premiere); with the voices of Paul Fusco, Prunella Gillis, Len Carlson, Greg Morton.

THE AMAZING SPIDER-MAN, CBS-TV, 4/5/78 to 7/6/79; with Nicholas Hammond, Robert F. Simon, Michael Pataki, Ellen Bry, Chip Fields.

AMAZING STORIES, NBC-TV, 9/29/85 to 5/15/87; guests include Penny Peyser, Drew Barrymore, Dom DeLuise, John Lithgow, Christina Applegate, Loni Anderson, Hayley Mills.

AMERICA 2100 (pilot), ABC-TV, 7/24/79; with Karen Valentine, Sid Caesar, Mark King, Jon Cutler.

ARK II, CBS-TV, 9/11/76 to 8/25/79; with Terry Lester, Jean Marie Hon, Jose Flores.

THE ASTRONAUTS (pilot), CBS-TV, 8/11/82; with Granville Van Dusen, Brianne Leary, McLean Stevenson.

THE BIONIC SIX (cartoon), syndicated 4/86; with the voices of Carol Bilger, Bobbi Block, Norman Bernard, Alan Oppenheimer, Neil Ross.

BLACKSTAR (cartoon), CBS-TV, 9/12/81 to 2/4/84; with the voices of George DiCenzo, Linda Gary, Alan Oppenheimer.

BLAKE'S 7, syndicated 1980; with Gareth Thomas, Glynis Barber, Sally Knyvette, Paul Darrow, Josette Simon.

BRAVESTARR (cartoon), syndicated 9/87; with the voices of Susan Blu, Peter Cullen, Pat Farley, Linda Gary, Alan Oppenheimer.

BRIDE OF BOOGEDY (pilot), ABC-TV, 4/12/87; with Richard

Masur, Mimi Kennedy, Tammy Lauren, Howard Witt, Eugene Levy. [This was a sequel to MR. BOOGEDY, *infra.*]

BUCK ROGERS IN THE 25TH CENTURY, NBC-TV, 9/27/79 to 8/20/81; with Gil Gerard, Erin Gray, Tim O'Connor, Pamela Hensley, Michael Ansara.

CAPTAIN POWER AND THE SOLDIERS OF THE FUTURE, syndicated 9/87; with Tim Dunigan, Sven Thorsen, Jessica Steen, Maurice Dean Wint.

CENTAURIONS-POWERXTREME (cartoon), syndicated 4/86; with the voices of Pat Farley, Neil Ross, Vince Edwards, Diane Pershing, Jennifer Darling.

CHALLENGE OF THE GOBOTS (cartoon), syndicated 5/85; with the voices of Rene Auberjonois, Candy Brown, Peter Cullen, Sparky Marcus, Lou Richards.

DEFENDERS OF THE EARTH (cartoon), syndicated 4/86; with the voices of William Callaway, Buster Jones, Sarah Partridge, Diane Pershing.

DINOSAUCERS (cartoon), syndicated 9/87, with the voices of Len Carlson, Rob Cowan, Marvin Goldbar, Leslie Toth, Gordon Masters.

DROIDS: THE ADVENTURES OF R2D2 AND CP30 (cartoon), ABC-TV, 9/7/85 to 9/7/86, with the voices of Anthony Daniels, Don Francks, Graeme Campbell.

EARTHLINGS (pilot), ABC-TV, 7/5/84; with Mike Connors, Dan Hedaya, Robin Dearden, Ilene Graff, James Cromwell.

EWOKS (cartoon), ABC-TV, 9/7/85 to 9/5/87; with the voices of Gree Summer Francks, Jim Keenshaw.

THE FANTASTIC FOUR (cartoon), NBC-TV, 9/9/78 to 9/1/79; with the voices of Mike Road, Ginny Tyler, Ted Cassidy, Frank Welker.

THE FANTASTIC JOURNEY, NBC-TV, 2/3/77 to 4/21/77; with Jared Martin, Roddy McDowall, Carl Franklin, Katie Saylor.

FLASH GORDON (cartoon), NBC-TV, 9/8/79 to 12/1/79; with the voices of Robert Ridgely, Diane Pershing, Alan Oppenheimer, Melendy Britt, Allan Melvin.

FUZZBUCKET (pilot), ABC-TV, 5/18/86, with Chris Hebert, Joe Regalbuto, Wendy Phillips, Hal Smith.

GALAXY HIGH SCHOOL (cartoon), CBS-TV, 9/13/86 (premiere); with the voices of Susan Blu, Pat Carroll, Nancy Cartwright, Gino Conforti, Jennifer Darling, Henry Gibson, Howard Morris.

GHOSTBREAKER (pilot), NBC-TV, 9/8/67; with Kerwin Matthews, Diana Van Der Vlis, Norman Fell, Margaret Hamilton.

GHOSTBUSTERS (cartoon), syndicated 9/86; with the voices of Peter Cullen, Alan Oppenheimer, Susan Blu, Linda Gary, Erika Scheimer.

THE GIANT HEEP (cartoon special), ABC-TV, 6/7/86; with the voices of Anthony Daniels, Long John Bradley, Lellany Brown.

GOLTHAR AND THE GOLDEN LANCE (cartoon), syndicated 9/85; with the voices of Bob Arbogast, Corey Burton, Jennifer Darling, George DiCenzo, Chuck McCann.

HAUNTED HOLLYWOOD, syndicated 9/86; with host John Carradine.

HE-MAN AND THE MASTERS OF THE UNIVERSE (cartoon); syndicated 5/83; with the voices of George DiCenzo, Linda Gary, John Erwin, Alan Oppenheimer.

THE INCREDIBLE HULK, CBS-TV, 3/10/78 to 5/19/82; with Bill Bixby, Lou Ferrigno, Jack Colvin.

THE INHUMANOIDS (cartoon); syndicated 12/86; with the voices of Michael Bell, Dick Gautier, Neil Ross, Richard Sanders, Susan Silo.

JASON OF STAR COMMAND, CBS-TV, 9/15/79 to 8/29/81; with Craig Littler, John Russell, James Doohan, Susan O'Hanlon.

THE LITTLE PRINCE (cartoon); syndicated 9/84; with the voices of Katy Leigh, Julie McWhirter, Hal Smith.

LOGAN'S RUN, CBS-TV, 9/16/77 to 1/16/78; with Gregory Harrison, Heather Menzies, Randolph Powell, Donald Moffat.

MANIMAL, NBC-TV, 9/30/83 to 12/31/83; with Simon MacCorkindale, Melody Anderson, Michael D. Roberts, Reni Santoni.

THE MISFITS OF SCIENCE, NBC-TV, 10/4/85 to 2/21/86; with Dean Paul Martin, Kevin Peter Hall, Mark Thomas Miller, Courteney Cox, Max Wright.

MR. BOOGEDY (pilot); ABC-TV, 4/20/86; with Richard Masur, Mimi Kennedy, Benjamin Gregory, John Astin, Howard Witt.

THE MONSTER SQUAD, NBC-TV, 9/1/76 to 9/2/77; with Fred Grandy, Henry Polic II, Michael Lane, Paul Smith.

MORK AND MINDY, ABC-TV, 9/14/78 to 8/5/82; with Robin Williams, Pam Dawber, Conrad Janis, Elizabeth Kerr, Tom Poston.

THE NEW ADVENTURES OF WONDER WOMAN, CBS-TV, 9/23/77 to 9/11/79; with Lynda Carter, Lyle Waggoner, Normann Burton.

THE NEW JETSONS (cartoon); syndicated 9/85; with the voices of Rene Auberjonois, Michael Bell, George DiCenzo, Susan Blu, Mel Blanc, Foster Brooks.

NUMBER 13 DEMON STREET, syndicated 1962; with Lon Chaney, Jr., Karen Kadler.

OTHERWORLD, CBS-TV, 1/26/85 to 3/16/85; with Sam Groom, Gretchen Corbett, Jonna Lee, Tony O'Dell.

OUT OF THIS WORLD, syndicated 9/87; with Donna Pescow, Maureen Flannigan, Doug McClure.

OUT OF TIME (special), NBC-TV, 1/29/85; with Amy Locane, R. D. Robb, Adam Baldwin.

OUT OF THE BLUE (pilot), CBS-TV, 8/12/68; with Shirley Jones, John McMartin, Marvin Kaplan, Carl Ballantine.

PHOTON, syndicated 9/86; with Christopher Lockwood, Loretta Haywood, Graham Ravey, Eros Rivers.

THE RAY BRADBURY THEATRE (pilot), HBO CABLE, 2/22/86;USA Cable 10/1/87 (premiere); with Ray Bradbury (host), Drew Barrymore, Jeff Goldblum, Peter O'Toole.

THE REAL GHOSTBUSTERS (cartoon), ABC-TV, 9/13/86 (premiere); with the voices of Arsenio Hall, Lorenzo Music, Laura Summer, Frank Welker.

REALLY WEIRD TALES, HBO CABLE, 10/4/86 to 10/15/86; with host Joe Flaherty.

SABER RIDER AND THE STAR SHERIFFS (cartoon), syndicated 9/87; with the voices of Townsend Coleman, Peter Cullen, Michael Bell, Diane Pershing.

SCARY TALES (pilot), syndicated 10/86; with Justine Bateman, Marc McClure, Michael Tulin in episode "Night Elevator."

SECTAURS-WARRIORS OF SYMBION, (cartoon), syndicated

3/86; with the voices of Peter Renaday, Peter Cullen, Laurie Faso, Frank Welker, B. J. Ward.

SHE-RA: PRINCESS OF POWER (cartoon); syndicated 9/85; with the voices of Linda Gary, George DiCenzo, Alan Oppenheimer.

SPACE ACADEMY, CBS-TV, 9/10/77 to 9/8/79; with Jonathan Harris, Pamelyn Ferdin, Ric Carrott, Maggie Cooper, Ty Henderson.

SPACE FORCE (pilot), NBC-TV, 4/28/78; with Fred Willard, Jimmy Boyd, Hilly Hicks, Maureen Mooney, Richard Paul.

SPACE STARS (cartoon), NBC-TV, 9/12/81 to 9/11/82; with the voices of Gary Owens, Alexandra Stoddart, Frank Welker, Darryl Hickman, Mike Road.

SPIDER-MAN AND HIS AMAZING FRIENDS (cartoon), NBC-TV, 6/12/81 to 9/11/82; with the voices of Anne Lockhart, George DiCenzo, Alan Dinehart, Keye Luke, Sally Julian.

SPIDER-WOMAN (cartoon), ABC-TV, 9/22/79 to 3/1/80; with the voices of Joan Van Ark, Bruce Miller, Bryon Scott.

SPIRAL ZONE (cartoon); syndicated 9/87; with the voices of Michael Bell, Kelly Day, Alex Ditts, Shawn McMannus, Frank Welker.

STAR COM: THE U.S. SPACE FORCE (cartoon), syndicated 9/87; with the voices of Philip Akin, Elva Mai Hoover, Susan Roman, Greg Swanson, Doug Stratton.

STAR MAIDENS, syndicated 9/77; with Judy Geeson, Liz Harrow, Dawn Addams.

STARMAN, ABC-TV, 9/19/86 to 9/11/87 with Robert Hays, C. B. Barnes, Michael Cavanaugh.

STARSTRUCK (pilot), CBS-TV, 6/9/79; with Beeson Carroll, Tainia Myren, Megan King, Guy Raymond, Elvia Allman.

STAR TREK: THE NEXT GENERATION, syndicated 10/87; with Patrick Stewart, Jonathan Frakes, LeVar Burton, Denise Crosby, Cheryl McFadden.

TALES FROM THE DARKSIDE, syndicated 9/84; with guests including Justine Bateman, Phyllis Diller, Theresa Saldana, Margaret O'Brien.

TALES OF THE UNEXPECTED (a.k.a. ROALD DAHL'S TALES OF THE UNEXPECTED), syndicated 9/79 to 9/82; with hosts Roald Dahl, John Houseman.

TERRAHAWKS (cartoon), syndicated 12/84; with the voices of Dennis Bryer, Jerry Hitcher, Ann Ridler.

THEATRE MACABRE; syndicated 1970; with host Christopher Lee.

THE THIRTEEN GHOSTS OF SCOOBY-DOO (cartoon), ABC-TV, 9/14/85 to 2/22/86; with the voices of Vincent Price, Casey Kasem, Heather North, Lennie Weinrib.

THE 13TH GATE (pilot), NBC-TV, 7/20/65; with David Opatoshu, Joyce Taylor, Jeremy Slate.

THUNDERBIRDS: 2086 (cartoon), syndicated 9/85; with the voices of Robert McFadden, Earl Hammond, Lynne Lipton.

TIGER SHARKS (cartoon), syndicated 9/87; with the voices of Seth Green, Bob McFadden, Camille Bonora, Larry Kenney, Maggie Jakobson.

TRANSFORMERS (cartoon), syndicated 9/84; with the voices of Richard Bell, Peter Cullen, Casey Kasem, Don Messick, Scatman Crothers.

TRIPODS, PBS syndication, 9/85; with John Shackley, Henry Parker, Carl Sell.

TURBO TEEN (cartoon), CBS-TV, 9/8/84 to 8/31/85; with the voices of T. K. Carter, Pamela Hayden, Frank Welker, Clive Revill.

THE TWILIGHT ZONE, CBS-TV, 9/29/85 (premiere); with narrator/host, Charles Aidman.

THE UNEXPLAINED (pilot), NBC-TV, 7/10/86; with Peter Votrian, Barry Froner, Leo Gordon, Whit Bissell.

THE UNKNOWN (pilot), ABC-TV, 5/4/64, with David McCallum, Scott Marlowe, Vera Miles, Barbara Bain.

V, NBC-TV, 10/26/84 to 3/22/85; with Marc Singer, Faye Grant, Jane Badler, June Chadwick, Blair Tefkin, Michael Ironside, Lane Smith.

VOLTRON-DEFENDER OF THE UNIVERSE (cartoon), syndicated 1984; with the voices of Jack Angel, Michael Bell, Peter Cullen, Neil Ross, B. J. Ward.

VOYAGERS!, NBC-TV, 10/3/82 to 8/7/83; with Jon-Erik Hexum, Meeno Peluce.

THE WORLD BEYOND (pilot), CBS-TV, 1/27/78; with Granville Van Dusen, JoBeth Williams, Barnard Hughes.

WORLD OF DARKNESS (pilot), CBS-TV, 4/17/77; with Granville Van Dusen, Tovah Feldshuh, Beatrice Straight.

ABOUT THE AUTHORS

JAMES ROBERT PARISH, Los Angeles-based direct marketing consultant and free-lance writer, was born in Cambridge, Massachusetts. He attended the University of Pennsylvania and graduated Phi Beta Kappa with a degree in English. A graduate of the University of Pennsylvania Law School, he is a member of the New York Bar. As president of Entertainment Copyright Research Co., Inc. he headed a major researching facility for the film and television industries. Later he was a film reviewer-interviewer for *Motion Picture Daily* and *Variety*. He is the author of over 70 volumes, including: *The Fox Girls*, *Good Dames*, *The Slapstick Queens*, *The RKO Gals*, *The Tough Guys*, *The Jeanette MacDonald Story*, *The Elvis Presley Scrapbook*, and *The Hollywood Beauties*. Among those he has co-written are *The MGM Stock Company*, *The Debonairs*, *Liza!*, *Hollywood Character Actors*, *The Hollywood Reliables*, *The Funsters*, *The Best of MGM*, and his ongoing series, *Actors' Television Credits*. With Michael R. Pitts, he has co-written such tomes as *Hollywood on Hollywood*, *The Great Western Pictures* (base volume and supplement) *The Great Gangster Pictures* (base volume and supplement), *The Great Spy Pictures* (base volume and supplement), and *The Great Science Fiction Pictures* (base volume and supplement).

MICHAEL R. PITTS is an Indiana-based free-lance writer who has authored or co-authored a number of entertainment-oriented books, including *Kate Smith: A Bio-Bibliography*, *Western Movies*, *Horror Film Stars* and *Hollywood and American History*. For Scarecrow Press he has published such works as *Famous Movie Detectives*, *Hollywood on Record* and two editions of *Radio Soundtracks: A Reference Guide*. With James Robert Parish he has written *The Great .... Pictures* series and other volumes. Mr. Pitts has been published in many periodicals both in the U.S. and abroad and he writes record review columns for *The Big Reel* and *Classic Images* magazines. He has also written record album liner notes. He resides with his wife Carolyn and daughter Angela.